A TOUR THROUGH THE WHOLE ISLAND OF GREAT BRITAIN

Daniel Defoe was a Londoner, born in 1660 at St Giles, Cripplegate, the son of James Foe, a tallow-chandler. He changed his name to Defoe from *c.* 1695. He was educated for the Presbyterian Ministry at Morton's academy for Dissenters at Newington Green. But in 1682 he abandoned this plan and became a hosiery merchant in Cornhill. After serving briefly as a soldier in the Duke of Monmouth's rebellion, he became well established as a merchant and travelled widely in England, as well as on the Continent. Between 1697 and 1701 he served as a secret agent for William III in England and Scotland, and between 1703 and 1714 for Harley and other ministers. During the latter period he also, single-handed, produced the *Review*, a pro-government newspaper. A prolific and versatile writer he produced some 500 books on a wide variety of topics including politics, geography, crime, religion, economics, marriage, psychology and superstition. He delighted in role-playing and disguise, a skill he used to great effect as a secret agent, and in his writing he often adopted a pseudonym or another personality for rhetorical impact. His first extant political tract (against James II) was published in 1688, and in 1701 appeared his satirical poem, *The True-Born Englishman*, which was a bestseller. Two years later he was arrested for *The Shortest Way with Dissenters*, an ironical satire on High Church extremism, committed to Newgate and pilloried. He turned to fiction relatively late in life and in 1719 published his great imaginative work, *Robinson Crusoe* (also published by Penguin). This was followed in 1722 by *Moll Flanders* (Penguin) and *A Journal of the Plague Year* (Penguin), and in 1724 his last novel, *Roxana* (Penguin), appeared. His other works include *A Tour Through the Whole Island of Great Britain*, a guide-book in three volumes (1724–6; abridged Penguin edition, 1971), *The Complete English Tradesman* (1726), *Augusta Triumphans* (1728), *A Plan of the English Commerce* (1728) and *The Complete English Gentleman*, not published until 1890. He died on 24 April 1731. Defoe had a great influence on the development of the English novel and many consider him to be the first true novelist.

•

Pat Rogers was educated at Cambridge, where he took a double first in English and was a Fellow of Sidney Sussex College. He has lectured at King's College, London, and between 1973 and 1976 was Professor of English at the University College of North Wales. Since 1977 he has been Professor of English at the University of Bristol. He is the author of *Grub Street* (1972), *The Augustan Vision* (1974), *Henry Fielding* (1979) and *Robinson Crusoe* (1979), and has edited *Defoe: The Critical Heritage*, *Contexts of English Literature: The Eighteenth Century* and *Jonathan Swift: The Complete Poems* (Penguin).

DANIEL DEFOE

A Tour through the Whole Island of Great Britain

Abridged and edited
with an introduction and notes
by Pat Rogers

PENGUIN BOOKS

PENGUIN BOOKS

Published by the Penguin Group
27 Wrights Lane, London W8 5TZ, England
Viking Penguin Inc., 40 West 23rd Street, New York, New York 10010, USA
Penguin Books Australia Ltd, Ringwood, Victoria, Australia
Penguin Books Canada Ltd, 2801 John Street, Markham, Ontario, Canada L3R 1B4
Penguin Books (NZ) Ltd, 182–190 Wairau Road, Auckland 10, New Zealand

Penguin Books Ltd, Registered Offices: Harmondsworth, Middlesex, England

First published 1724–6
Published in the Penguin English Library 1971
Reprinted in Penguin Classics 1986
10

Printed and bound in Great Britain by
Antony Rowe Ltd, Chippenham, Wiltshire

Set in Linotype Juliana

for Polly

CONTENTS

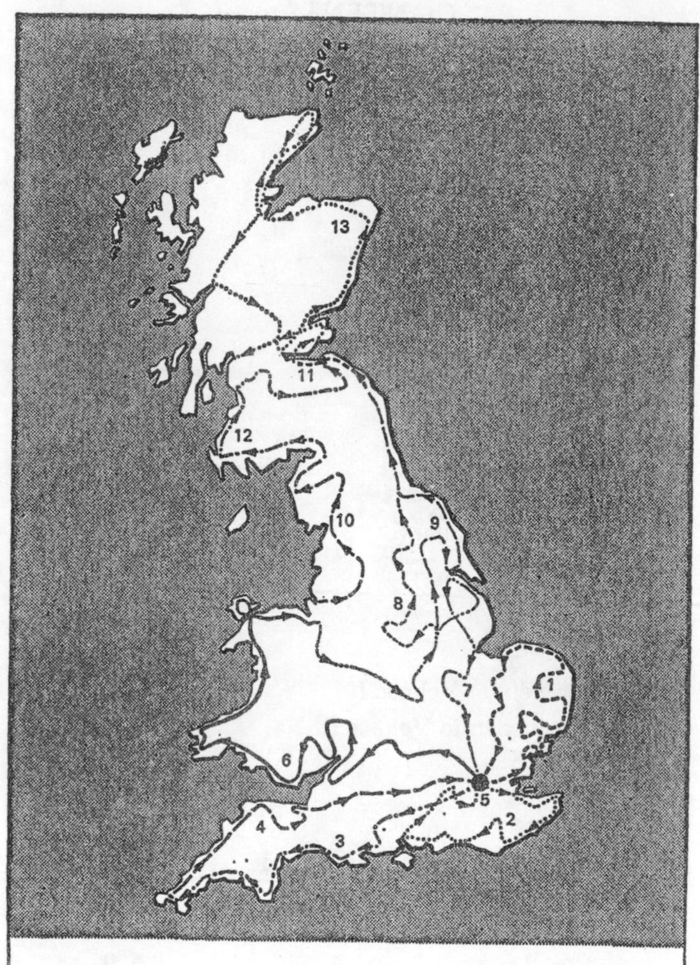

Map showing the supposed route of the various tours

INTRODUCTION

1

IN his lifetime Defoe was a mystery man. And three hundred years after his birth freaks of circumstance still play around his career. It is almost a comic irony that the first major English novels should have been written by a middle-aged journalist. The great tradition of fiction in our language was instituted by a Puritan with an eye to the main chance; its first representative guise is not the novel as dramatic poem, but the rogue's tale and *chronique scandaleuse*. Less comforting, for those who have any esteem or any hopes for literary history, is the thought that Defoe has gone down to posterity as the Great Reporter. He is still widely regarded as a literalist, an observer, a semi-creative talent. Now the first thing to be said about this is that Defoe was no more a positivist than was John Bunyan. He wrote prophecies and occult visions. He was responsible for the best-known ghost story of the century, *The Apparition of Mrs Veal* (1706), and a most successful *History of Apparitions* (1727). He compiled a *Political History of the Devil* and a *System of Magick* (both 1726). He was well versed in angelology and parapsychology. Quite apart from this, we should recall that Defoe was the author of a *History of the Pirates* (1724–8), as well as *Letters by a Turkish Spy* (1718) and innumerable criminal biographies. He composed a *New Voyage Round the World* (1724) and a journey to the moon called *The Consolidator* (1705): in fact, we have as much reason to believe that Defoe was a pioneer lunar explorer as that he circumnavigated the globe. And so one could go on. The truth is that Defoe possessed a wild inventive streak, a demonic imaginative power all his own. He was not just a reporter – he was the Great Fabricator.

There is a sadder irony here. Granted this situation, one

would have expected Defoe's *Tour* to have been widely appreciated as the quintessential, literalist, reportorial centre-piece of his career. Actually the work has become famous partly on false pretences. It has been extensively used by social and economic historians, yet at the same time it has been treated as an accidental offshoot from Defoe's major literary endeavours. Again this is untrue, and a reductive untruth at that. The *Tour* embodies all Defoe's accumulated skills as chronicler, polemicist and creative writer. It is, in short, a deeply imaginative book.

Nevertheless, on a surface level the *Tour* is the liveliest introduction which exists to Britain in the early eighteenth century. 'When a survey is demanded of Queen Anne's England and its everyday life, our thoughts turn to Daniel Defoe, riding solitary and observant through the countryside.' These are the words of G. M. Trevelyan, opening a section called 'Defoe's England' he set at the head of the third part of his *English Social History*. Defoe, continues Trevelyan,

> first perfected the art of the reporter.... So then, the account that this man gives of the England of Anne's reign is for the historian a treasure indeed. For Defoe was one of the first who saw the old world through a sharp pair of modern eyes. His report... occupies the central point of our thought and vision.

Another distinguished historian, Dorothy George, also gives the title 'Defoe's England' to a survey confessedly based on the *Tour*. 'Far the best authority for early eighteenth-century England is Defoe,' she writes. 'His famous *Tour through the whole Island of Great Britain* shows us the country as it appeared to a skilled observer with a marvellous eye for significant detail, who was also a man of business as well as a consummate journalist.' More recently Professor Peter Mathias has called Defoe 'the keenest observer of economic growth of his time in his *Tour of the Whole Island*'. Whole sections of books such as Mantoux's *Industrial Revolution in the Eighteenth Century*, Cole and Postgate's *The Common People* and other works are quarried directly from the pages of Defoe. Economic historians such as Christopher Hill, T. S. Ashton, Sir John Clapham, the Hammonds and E. Lipson have cited the *Tour* extensively as a primary source of information. The leading modern authority on inland navigation bases his map covering this period wholly on what Defoe reports. All this makes an eloquent testimony to the utility of the *Tour*: it has been given the status of an honorary blue book, and one almost expects to find it listed among official reports together with the journals of parliament and *Statutes of the Realm*. A further irony here, that Defoe – whose undertakings were always very private enterprises – should be given this quasi-official standing.

Not of course that he is reliable in every detail. He is always liable to confuse the generations of a particular family; he quite often gets names wrong; and his estimates of population are rarely better than informed guesses. Occasionally he is very badly out: he computes the figure for Manchester at 50,000 when it was perhaps 10,000, and for London at a million and a half, which is a good fifty per cent too high. More generally, it could be argued that Defoe's picture in some respects is a partial one. He is visibly stronger on distribution and commerce than on industrial manufacture, perhaps because he himself had been in the wholesale business. The heroes of his book are provincial merchants and City financiers, rather than captains of industry such as Abraham Darby or the ironmaster Ambrose Crowley. Moreover, the constant emphasis Defoe puts on the role of London in the national economy, valuable as it is, grows somewhat repetitive: it may not be without a certain metropolitan chauvinism. Defoe possibly exaggerates for his own rhetorical ends the triumphs of the cit turned gentleman – men like Josiah Child, Robert Clayton 'and hundreds more; whose beginnings were small ... and who have exceeded even the greatest part of the nobility of England in wealth, at their death, and all of their own getting'. Equally, he lays a heavy insistence on the falls brought about by the South Sea disasters of 1720. This suits his general purpose, in underlining the mutability of things; but it is arguable that Defoe makes too much of a few exceptional cases, such as the forfeited estates of the directors of the South Sea Company.

But these are marginal objections. Defoe remains an indispensable source for all students of England immediately before the industrial revolution. Thanks to his framework of 'tours' (whether or not these were actually undertaken as they are described), he is able to give a superb account of travel and communications at a moment of growing economic pressures. His famous appendix on turnpike roads provides a comprehensive and detailed review of the subject: but most of all a timely one, since many of the acts which Defoe mentions were only just passing through parliament in the year he was writing (1725). His unembarrassed curiosity about such matters gives his work a special amplitude of instance. We might well adapt Bagehot's phrase for Dickens, and say that Defoe writes his *Tour* 'like a special correspondent for posterity'. Again, Defoe is splendidly effective in picking up the exact social nuance – the difference between Tunbridge Wells and Epsom, Bury St Edmunds and Bath as pleasure resorts, say. He is keenly alive to that characteristic process of the age by which money gained in trade was turned into landed property, the great symbol of power and social prestige. He is good on the decline of many market towns, and observant about the effect on a town's hinterland when it enters a period of sharp prosperity or decline. And if he lacks Arthur Young's knowledge of agricultural methods, he has much more to tell us when the wheat leaves the fields and barns and reaches the corn-factor's store or the market.

When the *Tour* came out its author was already well into his sixties. He had been a professional writer for a quarter of a century, but it was only in the previous five years that he had reaped a full creative harvest. Between 1719 and 1724 there had appeared in extraordinary profusion the works of Defoe's imaginative maturity – *Robinson Crusoe*, with two rather low-pressure sequels; then the strangely neglected *Memoirs of a Cavalier*, among his most powerful evocations of the troubled century into which he was born. After this the deluge: *Captain Singleton, Moll Flanders*, A *Journal of the Plague Year*, and *Colonel Jacque*. Lastly, four months before the opening volume of the *Tour*, there was published *The Fortunate Mistress*, otherwise known as *Roxana*. Defoe, in short, was at the peak of his artistic achievement when he produced the *Tour*. Yet, if he was a late developer, the roots of that achievement are planted deep in his earlier experience.

Daniel Foe was born in London around the time of the Restoration. Within three years the Act of Uniformity had been passed through the zeal and political assurance of Lord Clarendon, who was Charles II's Lord Chancellor as he was later James II's father-in-law. James Foe, a City tallow-chandler, took his puritanical faith into the Presbyterian church. The young Daniel was brought up in an atmosphere of religion and moderate prosperity, an induction to the values of the Protestant ethic which was never to lose its influence upon him. By the early 1670s he was at school near Dorking under an Independent minister named Fisher, who had been ejected in 1662. About 1674 the student moved on to the famous academy for dissenters at Newington Green, then an outlying village to the north-east of London. Its master was Charles Morton, for whom Defoe retained in later years the warmest respect and admiration. The natural progression might have been into the dissenting ministry, but for some reason Daniel Foe did not take this step. By 1683 he was established as a hose-factor – that is a wholesaler, something different from (and deemed superior to) the retail trade of 'hosier', which is what his journalistic opponents liked to twit him with in years to come. It is not altogether clear how Defoe got the capital to set himself up so young; his wife brought him a substantial dowry on their marriage in 1684, but this was scarcely enough by itself. At all events, he was travelling widely as a merchant for a number of years. A brief interruption was provided by the Western rising in 1685, when Defoe fought on behalf of the Duke of Monmouth's unsuccessful attempt to oust James II. Three years later Defoe was happy to greet William III's army after a more fortunate rebellion.

Up to this point in his career the businessman had done well. In the last decade of the century things began to go wrong: Defoe speculated in that notoriously venturesome field, marine insurance, and in general seems to have diversified his interests more than was prudent. His first bankruptcy ensued in 1692. As with his later failure, in 1706, there may have been a measure of ill luck attending the circumstances. But a string of Chancery suits against Defoe proves that he was not always very regular in his commercial habits. There is a contradiction in his character: he was capable of showing both foresight and intemperance. His literary resources display the same mixture: at times, the most elaborate rhetorical mask – at others, the most naked self-exposure. In any case, he managed to salvage something from his first failure. By 1695 he held two minor public offices, one connected with the royal lottery, and had tacked the aristocratic particle 'De' to his name.

It was not until 1701 that he became famous with his plain-spoken verse satire, *The True-Born Englishman*, an attack on xenophobic attitudes and especially the myth of a pure 'English' strain. The following year saw another hugely popular satire, this time in prose. Unfortunately *The Shortest Way with the Dissenters* laid on the irony too thickly, and its absurd parody of extremist ideas backfired on Defoe. He was sent to Newgate prison and pilloried, the latter fate occasioning another successful work, the *Hymn to the Pillory*. Eventually Defoe was rescued from his distress, mainly because two leading ministers, Godolphin and Harley, recognized his possible worth as a government agent. For the next few years he worked as a kind of private psephologist for Harley, and also as a special representative in Scotland during the Union negotiations. At the same time he was conducting his newspaper, *The Review*, which he kept going almost single-handed until 1713. When Harley came to power in 1710, Defoe continued to bring out a stream of pamphlets;

and when the ministry tottered and finally fell he found himself back in gaol. After an abortive trial in the King's Bench, Defoe managed to make his peace with the new ministry in 1715 and he began to work on its behalf. Defoe being Defoe, his practices were so indirect as to incur renewed suspicion as to his loyalty. It is not the least surprising aspect of his belated success in the novel form that he should have begun this career in such disturbing conditions. Widely active in journalism (much of it surreptitious), threatened by prosecution, set about by family troubles, and subpoenaed by the very ministry he claimed to be serving, he scarcely enjoyed the happiest circumstances for creative writing.

This then was the situation in which he embarked on the series of novels that preserves his name today, and which directly preceded the *Tour*. His later years, predictably, show a falling cadence. He produced several more books of great interest, including *The Complete English Tradesman* and various criminal lives. But if his output was undiminished, his creative vigour was perhaps abated. He had been advised to take the waters as early as 1712, had suffered a bad illness three years later, and was in uncertain health thereafter. When almost seventy he was obliged to flee from yet another creditor (the debt having been incurred half a lifetime before), and he was still living in seclusion away from his family when his final illness, a 'lethargy', came on him. He died in obscure lodgings in April 1731.

A good deal of Defoe's direct experience went into the making of the *Tour*. A more speculative issue is when he actually conceived the book; and equally so, what special fieldwork he undertook. The evidence is too complicated to review here. It is enough to say that there are abundant signs that Defoe did continue his travels into the 1720s and probably carried out fresh research for the purposes of the book, mainly in 1722 when there was a lull in his publications. One of his biographers has asserted that the *Tour* is based on Defoe's travels as a merchant around 1685–90; whilst the eminent historian G. M. Trevelyan thought that the relevant experience was acquired in the reign of Anne during the service for Harley. Defoe assuredly used memories he had retained from both periods. But internal evidence suggests that he also had much up-to-date information to hand, especially with the earlier 'circuits'. Full demonstration of this point has had to be reserved for another place; but in summary we can be reasonably confident that Defoe composed most of the first volume around the end of 1722 and the beginning of 1723, appendices and corrections dating from the winter of 1723–4. The bulk of Volume II dates from the late summer of 1724, with additions the following spring. Volume III is harder to fix accurately, but seems mostly the work of late 1725.

2

The *Tour* was first published in three volumes appearing at intervals of just over a year, in 1724–6. The third volume was dated 1727 but actually published in August 1726. It was not until 1738 that the work came out as a genuine entity – seven years after Defoe's death. This second edition introduced a number of alterations in an attempt to bring the text up to date, and this was to be the pattern of future editions. The editor remarked that the book had been 'for some time past very scarce', one of many indications that the *Tour* remained an excellent commercial proposition throughout its publishing history. In 1742 came a further rescension. For this the novelist and printer Samuel Richardson, author of *Clarissa*, was chiefly responsible, and indeed he may even have had a hand in the 1738 version. (Richardson's firm printed both the second and third editions.) Another departure in 1742 was the extension to four volumes, and this example too was followed in subsequent issues of the work. The need for more space was occasioned partly by the inclusion of some skimpy remarks on the Channel Islands, the Hebrides and other offshore islands omitted by Defoe. But the opportunity was also taken to include an abstract of the seats of the gentry, arranged by county, and a list of the British peerage along with the schedule of parliamentary constituencies. In other words, Defoe's 'journeys' have been overlaid by the banal function of an official handbook: the *Tour* was forced to be Whitaker as well as Baedeker. Throughout the middle years of the century the work continued to appear, roughly twice a decade. By 1779 the ninth edition was reached, the last full version of the *Tour* to appear for 150 years. Inevitably as time went on the concoction of Defoe and editorial water grew more and more diluted, but the main plan of the book was preserved.

Some idea of the *Tour's* popularity can be gained by comparing trade figures. In 1772 one ninety-sixth share in the rights cost the bookseller Lowndes £1.11.6: two years before, he had bought for one guinea an eighth share in four works that included *Moll Flanders* and *Roxana* – and they were probably makeweights to a life of Prince Eugene which was the real selling line. Defoe the great novelist, oddly enough, is an invention of the nineteenth and twentieth centuries. By contrast the *Tour* might claim both literary fame and commercial success. A nice judge of both attributes, William Strahan, was to put out the 1778 edition. He was among the shrewdest operators the English book trade has ever seen. The friend of Benjamin Franklin, an M.P., holder of lucrative official patents as King's Printer and Law Printer, Strahan had reached the head of his profession by 1775.* In that year he printed Dr Johnson's *Journey to the Western Islands*, thus augmenting a list which included the great *Dictionary*, *Rasselas*, Hume's *History*, *Tristram Shandy* and novels by Richardson and Smollett. But Strahan was publisher as well as printer. His list for 1776 included *The Wealth of Nations* and Gibbon's *Decline and Fall* – perhaps the most distinguished seasonal output on record. Remunerative works of genius are not all that common; yet

* It is not known whether George Strahan, the bookseller who issued the original *Tours* was a relative of William, but he may well have been.

Strahan had found another in 1778, hacked and distorted as the *Tour* was by this time.

In order to understand the success enjoyed, initially by Defoe's own text, more lastingly by the formula he devised, we must give some thought to the development of travel literature in England. Without delving into the prehistory of the subject, we can see the genre emerging with the great Tudor topographers, Leland, Harrison and Camden. The scholarly cleric Leland made the journeys on which his *Itinerary* was based during the 1530s: but he died in 1552, with his planned *Britannia* unwritten. It was not until 1710–12 that the Oxford antiquary Thomas Hearne, famous alike for his learning, crustiness and High Toryism, published the *Itinerary*. Its content remained skeletal – a sort of frozen work in progress, with clipped itemised entries and no running narrative. But the fullness and accuracy of Leland's survey give it a permanent interest, especially as a graphic record of an England still largely medieval in landscape, the visual testimony to a feudal and military past. William Harrison's *Description of Britain* (1577), written as an appendix to Holinshed's chronicle, is more analytical than Leland, less close to the detailed geography of the country. It supplied none the less a vivid picture of the nation, its customs, manners and occupations, with a hint of the realism of portraiture found in Elizabethan satire and city comedy. Then came Camden, whose *Britannia* (the first of many editions, 1586) displays formidable antiquarian zeal and a lucid, connected manner of writing. Just as the structure of Defoe's 'tour' – the imaginative vehicle of a number of 'circuits' – expresses his primary literary intention, so the organization of *Britannia* reveals Camden's attitude to his material and to his rhetorical task. Significantly, the work is set out according to the distribution of the British tribes. Counties are a further subdivision: an afterthought of administrative history.

At the start of the seventeeth century various tributaries can be seen to flow from this main stream of topographic inquiry. Poets as different as Drayton, with his fanciful, anecdotal and mythopoeic *Poly-olbion* (1612–22), and John Taylor, a kind of ur-McGonigall who produced doggerel accounts of his trips by land and water, can be related to a growing craze for travel books. A flood of county histories, of which Dugdale's Warwickshire is unrepresentative only in its exceptional quality, illustrate another side of this vogue. And as the century went on, the trend continued unabated. 'A new discovery of England was in progress,' Mr Christopher Morris has said of the Restoration era.

Treatises were written on Stonehenge and poems on 'the Wonders of the Peak'. A new edition of Camden's *Britannia* [1695], brought up to date by Bishop Gibson, seems to have lain on the parlour tables of most well-to-do people.... A devoted band of antiquaries and topographers were grubbing up the English past. Ogilby's wonderful road-book had appeared in 1675 and there were also surveys, comparable with modern directories and gazetteers, such as . . . Chamberlayne's *Angliae Notitia* [from 1669]. Statisticians like Gregory King and Sir William Petty were trying to estimate the population. The English were becoming highly immodest about their own political discoveries, their own great men or 'worthies', their own architecture and landscape and, above all, their own prosperity.

Now this mood of self-discovery has very precise literary analogues. The form apt to a country emerging into a consciousness of its own power and nationhood has traditionally been the epic. And indeed great poets projected a definitive English epic more than once at this time. If the task never became quite the shirt of Nessus that the Great American Novel was to prove until the provident canonization of *Moby Dick*, then that was purely because these poets sublimated their heroic ambitions elsewhere – Milton in *Paradise Lost*, Dryden in satire and elevated tragic writing, Pope in his Homer and ultimately in *The Dunciad*. The *Brutiads* and *Boadiceas* we do possess will induce no regret that patriotic self-awareness fled from the high literary forms.

Against all decorum, it reappeared most feelingly in the tame foothills of Parnassus allotted to the travel-book.

Coming nearer Defoe's own time, the best-known journeys today are those of Celia Fiennes, made just before the turn of the century. Defoe was already an experienced traveller by this date, and in any case he cannot have been influenced by the *Journeys*, since they remained in manuscript until 1888. Miss Fiennes compels admiration as a person, as she uncomplainingly rides along the ill-made road, charting an erratic course between noxious inns and the comfortable homes of her endless relatives. (On one level her progress is like a conducted tour round *Familiae Minorum Gentium.*) But as a writer she lacks Defoe's awareness of a larger reality; her England is all microcosm, no macrocosm, and she reveals little sense of history. Her *Journeys* are perhaps best read as the charming notebook of a picturesque traveller born before her time. To be sure, her standards of beauty, of comfort, of emotional intensity, are not those which will be current when the picturesque moment arrives, almost a century later. But her headlong impressionistic style converts even the most housewifely sentiments into the accents of sensibility.

In the vein of travels *per se*, nothing else of this quality anticipated Defoe's *Tour*. The book which may have set him to work would be adequate at best as an effective cause, certainly not as a sufficient inspiration for Defoe so to enhance the status of travel literature. *A Journey through England. In Familiar Letters* (1714–23: the title of the third volume is modified to suit the Scottish tour described) is the work of John Macky. A Scot, with a biography even more chequered than Defoe's own, Macky assuredly knew his way around Britain and the Continent. But his journey is shapeless, its itinerary wholly arbitrary and imaginatively unconvincing. The writer hedgehops from one town to the next, alighting now and then to 'do' a country seat. We have no real sense of *place*, none of the buoyancy and movement Defoe achieves. In fact, the work is little more than an annotated road-book, with villages dismissed from view and the vistas of daylight and champaign Defoe grants us wholly obliterated. One moment we are in the Isle of Man, the next Cornwall. These are the classic signs of a guide-book pure and simple: the entries would be just as useful if the putative topographical framework were demolished, and the text presented as an alphabetical sequence of localities.

Defoe was certainly aware of Macky's book, and alludes to it sneeringly on several occasions. However, a greater spur to his creative energies was provided by more imposing figures than Macky. As we have seen, Edmund Gibson translated and supplemented Camden's *Britannia* in 1695; a further edition came out in 1722, just when Defoe was beginning on the *Tour*. Two years before, John Strype had issued his splendid new version of Stow's *Survey of London*. Several major antiquarian works were reprinted about this time, including books by Dugdale and Elias Ashmole. John Stevens's *History of Abbeys [and] Monasteries* was published in February 1722; Nathan Bailey's *Antiquities of London and Westminster* in September of the same year. Perhaps more important than any of these was an attempt to outflank Camden in the collaborative *Magna Britannia* (1720–31), of which three volumes had appeared by 1724. There were several schemes along these lines (the famous publisher Jacob Tonson had been planning a 'Britannia' around 1718), and we misinterpret Defoe's intentions unless we realize that his book was meant partly as a rival to Camden, and not just to Macky.

After the death of Defoe the passion for travel increased, and with it the demand for information met by successive reissues of the *Tour*. In the seventeenth century most of the travellers had been, if not scholars, at least amateur antiquarians, virtuosi, collectors. The typical figures were men like Pepys, John Evelyn or Ralph Thoresby, whose respectability was mixed with a certain independence or nonconformity. As the Georgian period went by, a clear separation grew up between serious archaeological investigation and the new phenomenon which we might call genteel tourism. The round of country houses and gardens became an established part of life for well-bred ladies and gentlemen: one did not need to be a connoisseur to take a general interest in architectural 'improvements', to which the Hanoverians were so addicted. There was even something resembling a tourist industry; it was said in the 1750s that 'it is well for the county of Norfolk that three or four noblemen have done so much to their places, else very few strangers would visit a country that has so few natural beauties to attract them'. But the visitors were not exactly trippers in a modern sense; they were consciously cultivating the art of travel, *ars peregrinandi*, as part of the civilized life.

It is in this context that the many literary travellers of the eighteenth century should be assessed. Disregarding John Wesley, whose ceaseless journeys up and down the country had a very different basis, it is notable that it was the provincials who had come up to London, and thenceforth adopted metropolitan standards, who devised the most effective literary vehicle for their travels. It is Smollett in *Humphry Clinker*, Sterne in the *Sentimental Journey* and Johnson in his *Journey to the Western Isles* who are able to use physical travel as an emblem of mental and moral discovery. By contrast Pope – a great devotee of jaunts – and in turn Horace Walpole, an obsessive visitor of other people's residences, and Gray, one of the first to enthuse over the Lake District, were unable to make direct use of their interest. Much the same applies to Cowper, who travelled rarely but with keen delight. The point is that all these men were in one way or another committed to an anti-metropolitan standpoint. Yet their rusticity had an air of play-acting (think of Strawberry Hill, Pope's grotto or his tower at Stanton Harcourt), and something of calculation about it. They were never able to forge an idiom through which to express their undoubted interest in travelling the English countryside.

The journey has been a ubiquitous *motif* in literature from Homer onwards. Yet it might be said that only in the eighteenth century does travel become the basic psychic fact – the overriding image in the new novel form. It is a commonplace that Fielding and Smollett rely heavily on elements of picaresque (even if we define that term more stringently than is the present fashion); it is well known that the itinerant Quixote figure crops up everywhere in fiction of the age. Not only Yorick but Tristram too can be followed on his journeys. As to Defoe himself, all his heroes and heroines move about a great deal from place to place. Moll Flanders, Colonel Jack and the Cavalier actually do so in specified parts of Britain; and whilst it may be true, as Professor Monk has written, that in these books 'there is no landscape ... geography abounds, but one can find not a single observed *mise en scène*', that has to do with Defoe's descriptive method – the way he presents situations at a local level – rather than with the overall trajectory of the novel. The 'travel' framework remains, even though Defoe neglects to take snapshots as he goes – he did not encounter the twentieth-century belief that you haven't been anywhere at all unless you have the pictures to prove it. Finally, at a deeper level, it could be argued that even the apparently statuesque closet-dramas of Richardson depend on a notion of movement. People may not move very much – at least Clarissa is relatively static, and this is a cause and an emblem of her tragedy. Her sexual and familial dependence is fitly represented by her bodily arrest. But if people are comparatively stationary, words aren't. It is letters which zoom across the country in *Clarissa*, and it is letters which define the nature of the book in far more than a pedantically formal sense. The message is the medium. Correspondence operates as the literal authorial method in the novel; but it also enacts the processes of contact and relationship between the characters. In Richardson's world, if you can't write to someone, you don't exist for them. If you can't set down a sensation in epistolatory form, then you haven't experienced it. Richardson is supposed to deal with a fiercely private, inward world. The truth is that his imagination is peopled by characters whose identity is created wholly within the public sphere of the letter. His method is further from interior monologue than ordinary third-person narrative would be. In short, the dynamism of his books is set up by the psychic space covered by letters, the inner momentum corresponding to the externalized movement along the open road in *Tom Jones*.

When we reach the middle of the century, travel has become quicker and more comfortable altogether. In 1700 the roads had been scarcely less dirty, dangerous and unreliable than they were in the Middle Ages. The gradual spread of the turnpike trusts was accompanied by a new approach to road-making, with first Metcalf and later Telford and Macadam revolutionizing the methods in use. This in turn stimulated innovations in the design of conveyances; by 1784 the first royal mail-coach covered the journey from London to Bath in the unprecendented time of sixteen hours. Fifty years earlier Dover was still a two-days' journey from the capital, with an overnight stop at Canterbury. Exeter took six days to reach, Edinburgh twice that (with a slight speeding-up in the summer months). Until well on in the century there was no direct service to Birmingham; passengers left the Chester road at Castle Bromwich, seven miles away. The deficiency was not as serious as it might appear, in that the town basically consisted of a single street, with no street-lighting, no assembly room and for long no bookseller's shop. At the same period Glasgow was still, in Trevelyan's phrase, a pretty little country town, unimaginably remote from southern England. As this situation slowly changed, and travel grew a less venturesome business, the literature of topography naturally modified its character also. The formal guidebook came into being, till no less a writer than Wordsworth is found contributing to a genre now regarded as somewhat anonymous. His *Topographical Description* of the Lakes first appeared in 1810, appended to a volume of 'select views'.

In this heyday of tourism two particular trends make themselves felt. There is first of all the picturesque tour, undertaken as a kind of aesthetic adventure by persons of sensibility. Of this phase of taste, Martin Price has written, 'The picturesque in general recommends the rough or rugged, the crumbling form, the complex or difficult harmony. It seeks a tension between the disorderly and irrelevant and the perfected form.' Moreover, says Price, 'its favourite scenes are those in which form ... is at the point of dissolution. It turns to the sketch, which precedes formal perfection, and the ruin, which succeeds it.' What is notable is that so many of the picturesque theorists should also have been inveterate tourists – a certain restlessness of temperament contributing to both predilections alike. The most famous of these travellers is of course Rev. William Gilpin. He has usually been treated as a figure of fun, not altogether justly. The unguarded remark made at Tintern Abbey, 'A mallet judiciously used (but who durst use it?) might be of service in fracturing some of [the gable-ends, which] hurt the eye with their regularity', seems less eccentric in the context of Gilpin's whole body of thought. It might also be recalled that so serious an antiquary as William Stukeley, who had early made himself an expert on the archaeology of Roman Britain and whose *Itineranium Curiosum* (1724) was heavily quarried by succeeding editors of the *Tour*, did not scruple to take away pottery and pieces of mosaic from the sites he described so enthusiastically.

Secondly, there are the 'farmer's tours' made by Arthur Young in the 1760s and 1770s. Young's chief interest was ostensibly agrarian improvement, and he affects a blunt no-nonsense manner, as though the sophistications of authorship were worthy only of contempt. In fact Young was an accomplished writer, who used his battery of honorific terms (*improvement, enclosure, fertile, cultivated*, and so on) with an economy both deft and sure. He responded with warm immediacy to any pleasing landscape, and though Cobbett would have found suspect his passion for what was new (fresh plantations, hedges, ditches), Young describes the agricultural revolution of his times with intelligence as well as a great deal of *brio*. Occasionally we detect the glazed eye of the fanatic, but Young has too much common sense ever to be shrill.

One can hardly say as much of William Cobbett's *Rural Rides*. Cobbett undertook his travels as a kind of fact-finding mission; he had already booked space in his own newspaper, the *Political Register*, and at times the journey itself comes to seem like a by-product of this campaign. Like a Royal Commission, Cobbett gave himself terms of reference which made the nature of his conclusions a foregone conclusion. Bluff, opinionated, iterative, he seldom sticks to the visible scene for long. Cobbett's England, Mr John Derry rightly points out, is a subjective entity. He describes the countryside and the weather, but his real interests are ideas and beliefs. He sets before us a *paysage moralisé*, with a villainous 'system' of exploitation eating up English rural life. In this manichean world, notions of pristine rude health are constantly opposed to those of effete and corrupt modernity. Cobbett sprays italics and capitals across the page to lend this dialectic an even more urgent emphasis. He displays along with ordinary nostalgia for the pre-industrial era what might be termed a displaced yearning – a nostalgia of situation rather than time. Somehow the things Cobbett valued were never quite before him. As a result there is in *Rural Rides*, for all the wealth of detailed description and close observation, a quality of impatient polemicism: the vigour derives from what Cobbett doesn't see, rather than what he does.

The full range of English topographic writing over three centuries – its diverse aims, effects, methods – can hardly be illustrated in this short space. But some of the main trends between 1530 and 1830 should emerge from a rapid collation of some passages, chosen at random from major contributors to the genre. Leland, for instance, when he comes to Northampton, potters about conscientiously:

> The toune ... stondith on the north side of Avon ryver, on the brow of a meane hill, and risith stille [continuously] from the

south to the north. Al the old building of the toune was of stone, the new is of tymbre.

There be yn the waulle of Northampton 4. gates, namid by este, west, north and south. The Este gate is the fairest of them all.

There is a faire suburb withoute the South gate: and another, but lesse, withoute the Weste gate, yn the wich is a very pratie house ex lapide polite quadrato, it longith to Mr — . . .

This dogged accumulation of fact mirrors the experience of a foot traveller, with time to see everything and no particular criteria of selection. Camden's *Britannia*, on the other hand, has much of the pomp, the Latinate sense of consequence and the slow-wheeling amplitude of an Elizabethan royal 'progress'. When Camden makes his visitation of Northampton, you feel it would be as hard to stop him in his tracks as a line of state coaches on some grand ceremonial occasion. He sends forward etymological outriders:

Beneath these places, the Aufona, or Nen, glides forward with a gentle small stream, and is soon after increased by a little river from the north where, at their very meeting, the town, called, from the river, Northafandon . . . is so seated, that on the west side it is watered with this little river, and on the south side with the other: which I was of late too easily induced to believe the ancient Bannaventa; but I erred in my conjecture, and my confession must atone for it. As for the name, it may seem to have had it from the situation upon the north side of the Aufona. . . . On the west side it had an old castle, to which the very antiquity of it added a beauty; it was built by Simon da Sancto Licio, commonly called Senliz, the first earl of Northampton of that name: who joined likewise to it a beautiful church dedicated to St Andrew, for his own burying place; and as it is reported, rebuilt the tower . . .

Bishop Gibson's translation nicely conveys this ponderous impetus.

Celia Fiennes is much more interested in getting from place to place, and also much closer to the physicalities of travelling:

From Warwick we went towards Daventry all along part of the Vale of the Red Horse which was very heavy way and could not reach thither being 14 mile; about 11 mile we came to a place called Nether Shugar a sad village, we could have no entertainment; just by it on the top of a steep hill is Shuggbery Hall a seate of Sir Charles Shuggberys, who seeing our distress, being just night and the horses weary with the heavy way, he very curteously tooke compassion on us and treated us very handsomly that night, a good supper serv'd in plaite and very good wine, and good beds; my Lady Shuggbery was the Lord Leigh's Daughter and that day dineing there her Coach drove by us when in distress enquireing for her lodging, which caused Sir Charles to come out and meete us, shewed a generous hospitable spirit to strangers, and with a great deale of good humour my Lady entertained us; the house stands within a good parke...

And so on for another fourteen lines. This straggling style, with its elliptical syntax and chatty miscellany of information, is precisely fitted to Celia Fiennes's mode of tourism. She is the traveller following her own nose, with no ambition to cover any particular region, and wholly unembarrassed about leaving her planned route in the cause of comfort.

No single passage can reflect all of Cobbett's moods, from vehemence to cutting irony and pensive melancholia. But take this fairly representative passage, which follows a description of the decline at Weyhill sheep fair – Cobbett having visited the fair as a boy almost fifty years earlier:

From this dismal scene, a scene formerly so joyous, we set off back to Uphusband pretty early, were overtaken by the rain, and got a pretty good soaking. The land along here is very good. This whole country has a chalk bottom; but, in the valley on the right of the hill over which you go from Andover to Weyhill, the chalk lies far from the top, and the soil has few flints in it. It is very much like the land about Malden and Maidstone. Met with a farmer who said he must be ruined, unless another '*good war*' should come! This is no uncommon notion. They saw high prices *with* war, and they thought the war was the *cause*.

Here is much of Cobbett in little. The language is clear and direct; the style moves readily to exclamation and emphatic contrast. Cobbett has a good fund of comparative knowledge, at any rate as regards southern England. He is aware of geology but basically his concerns are human; his anecdotes are recounted not to illumine life's little ironies but to forward a running argument. There is just enough literal circumstance ('a pretty good soaking', 'on the right of the hill') to convince us that Cobbett really has been in Hampshire. That much established, the narrative can shift to its real locale of social criticism ('this dismal scene', and so on).

All these varied approaches have their own merit. Yet it seems to me that Defoe achieved the most satisfactory mode of literary tourism. That is, he hit on the best blend of objective fact and personal commentary; the neatest amalgam of gazetteer and traveller's tale; the densest mixture of history and prophecy, myth and reportage, observation and impression, formal coverage and informal anecdote. Defoe had perhaps travelled the country over a longer period than any of the writers just considered. With the exception of Camden, he had easily the best-stocked mind. His background as businessman, soldier, economic writer and spy was as wide as Cobbett's own. He was as responsive to 'improvement' as Arthur Young, yet as conscious of an English heritage as ever William Harrison was. He had the shrewd practicality of Celia Fiennes and the same capacity to muse over the ruins of time as Leland. Above all, he had the most deeply creative spirit among this group. He was the only one to evolve a literary vehicle (the 'tour' or 'circuit') that could straddle the literal and the imaginative. His idiom combines the expressive resources of epic or the novel with the factual fidelity of journalism; his *Tour* shows us the real England but also (in Celia Fiennes's words, oddly) 'an Idea of England'.

3

As we have seen, the information which the *Tour* incorporates is based on a lifetime of sharp-eyed observation, as businessman, government spy and journalist. The striking thing about the book, however, is the way in which it is irradiated by a poet's vision, even though it is a singular kind of poetry – sometimes literal-minded, often crotchety, modulating from puritanical intensity to well-bred irony, by turns brutally stark and gaily allusive. Defoe brought one very special quality to his undertaking. He has a marvellously acute sense of *process*. And this comes out not merely in his joyous celebration of 'the great social transition he saw proceeding around him', as G. D. H. Cole implies. He does assuredly write of the emerging order in graphic and warmly appreciative language. But he is alive also to the loss and decay of what has gone before. For every image of growth, 'rising' towns or 'flourishing' country, there is a counter-image of exhaustion – barren land or broken remains. Continually Defoe sets against his picture of health and plenty an idiom of devastation. His *Tour* is pervaded by a sense of the fragility of human contrivances, very close to that of Pope in the *Epistle to Burlington*, that most central Augustan utterance. To take one example among many, the town of Dunwich in Suffolk:

> This town is a testimony of the decay of public things, things of the most durable nature.... The ruins of Carthage, or the great city of Jerusalem, or of ancient Rome, are not at all wonderful to me; the ruins of Nineveh, which are so entirely sunk, as that 'tis doubtful where the city stood; the ruins of Babylon, or the great Persepolis, and many capital cities, which time and the change of monarchies have overthrown; these, I say, are not at all wonderful, because being the capitals of great and flourishing kingdoms, where those kingdoms were overthrown, the capital cities necessarily fell with them. But for a private town, a sea-port, and a town of commerce, to decay, as it were of itself (for we never read of Dunwich being plundered, or ruined, by any disaster . . .); this I must confess, seems owing to nothing but to the fate of things, by which we see that towns, kings, countries, families, and persons, have all their elevation, their medium, their declination, and even their destruction in the womb of time, and the course of nature.

This is not just a purple passage, stuffed out with hollow rhetoric. Throughout the book we get the same keen sensitivity to the depredations of time, almost as it occurs in an Elizabethan sonnet. Repeatedly Defoe uses phrases such as 'the injury of time', 'time the great devourer', or 'ruins eaten up by time'. It is this which gives energy and tension to what would otherwise be a perfunctory survey of 'the improving temper of the present age'. Alternatively, one could describe this quality as Virgilian. Indeed, there is a direct link between a famous passage in the first *Georgic* and Defoe's comments on the battle-field of Towton. Virgil has this:

> *scilicet et tempus veniet, cum finibus illis*
> *agricolo incurvo terram molitus aratro*
> *exesa inveniet scabra robigine pila,*
> *aut gravibus rastris galeas pulsabit inanis,*
> *grandiaque effossis mirabitur ossa sepulcris.*

(Yes, and there will come a time in that country when the farmer, labouring upon the earth with his curved plough, will find spears eaten up by rust and mildew, or with his heavy rake will knock into empty helmets, and he will be amazed at the huge bones in the graves he has upturned.)

And now Defoe:

> Tradition guided the country people, and they us, to the very spot; but we had only the story in speculation; for there remains no marks, no monument, no remembrance of the action, only that the ploughmen say, that sometimes they plough up arrow-heads and spear-heads, and broken javelins, and helmets, and the like; for we could only give a short sigh to the memory of the dead, and move forward.

This elegiac note is remarkably common in a work widely supposed to be an uncritical response to a brave new economic world.

Again, the *Tour* is beautifully organized. Unlike Macky, Defoe gives point and direction to his book. There are a number of ways in which he does this (e.g. by stressing the small 'compass' of a tour – a word equally applicable to the confines of the narrative and to the limits of its geographic scope). But above all Defoe's tour is more intelligently conceived than Macky's harumscarum journey. Initially Defoe keeps to the strict 'circuit', with London as the start-and-finish line. Letters 1 and 2 are complete in themselves. Letter 5 is a perambulation of the capital. Other trips occupy two letters; thus, 3 and 4 describe a 'progress' to Land's End, out and return. Similarly 6 and 7, with Anglesey the hinge of the journey. When Defoe reached his final volume, he obviously could not retain this scheme. A tour of northern Scotland could hardly have its base camp in London – which was a good fortnight's travelling distant, as late as Culloden. Accordingly Defoe hit on a sensible compromise. Letters 8-10 all describe a route taken northwards from the Midlands, starting from the point reached in earlier trips, i.e. the Trent or the Mersey. Scotland is simply parcelled up into three convenient units: 11, the Border to the Forth, with Edinburgh; 12, the Border to the Clyde, with Glasgow; and 13, the remainder of Scotland, covered in an anti-clockwise circuit as seen on the map. Perhaps the *Tour* loses a little in symmetry of design as a result of these shifts in the third volume. Yet it retains a shapeliness that is far beyond Celia Fiennes or Cobbett, not to mention John Macky. This spatial diagram, crude as it must be, gives some approximation of the layout, viewed chiefly from a London vantage-point.

out	1	return
out	2	return
out	3	
	4	return
[London and	5	Westminster]
out	6	
	7	return
Trent –	8	– Tees
Trent –	9	– Border
Mersey –	10	– Border*
Border –	11	– Forth/Clyde valley (E)
Border –	12	– Forth/Clyde valley (W)
Forth/Clyde valley (E)	13	– Forth/Clyde valley (W)

* Defoe seems to have changed his plans here. In Volume III, the Scottish sections are headed not, as one would expect, Letters 4–6 but 3–5. It would appear that Defoe originally meant to cover the North of England in two letters but was forced to take three.

This complex interlocking pattern is beautifully adapted to Defoe's aim of comprehensive but intelligible coverage. He has ordered his material so that the formal contours of the book mirror social, economic and geographic reality. Literary expression and topography are wedded in the *Tour's* grand design.

This then is not just a guide-book. Yet it *is* a guide-book, the liveliest ever written. Poised half-way between the meandering Tudor antiquaries and the limp functionality of Baedeker a century later, the work still makes fascinating reading. Its appeal owes something to the intrinsic qualities of the material, the fund of anecdote and legend it contains, the curiously explicit details of commercial life which Defoe ferreted out. He was fortunate, too, in the historical moment at which the *Tour* came into being. In particular, Defoe's own knowledge of Scotland, acquired at first hand as the Union was forged, gives special point to what is virtually an account of the Scottish people on the eve of colonization. But, most of all, the book lives because of that intriguing, elusive, engaging personality behind it. A good deal of the writer's own experience went into the *Tour*, and yet it is far from a direct transcript. There is shrewd observation of contemporary Britain in its pages, and yet its true inner momentum derives from an astonishingly clear sense of history. The book is couched in the form of a series of journeys, and yet it is not (like Celia Fiennes's or Cobbett's travels) based on an identifiable once-for-all progress through the country. Defoe compounded several trips of his own, undertaken over many years, and interlarded his own memories with crafty borrowing from published sources. What he gives us is not a tour, straight, but the experiential equivalent of such a tour. For this task he needed all his literary art: all those funded resources which he had developed, as a great reporter certainly, but as a great creator too. The English epic found its Augustan expression not in some strutting *Brutiad* but in the modest-looking tour through Britain of Daniel Defoe.

In another work published during 1724, *The Great Law of*

Subordination Consider'd, Defoe outlined the circumstances in which he had originally set out to travel about the country:

> As ... I made myself Master of the History, and *ancient State* of *England,* I resolv'd in the next Place, to make my self Master of its *Present State* also; and to this Purpose, I travell'd in three or four several Tours, over the whole Island, critically observing, and carefully informing myself of every thing worth observing in all the Towns and Countries through which I pass'd.
>
> I took with me an *ancient Gentleman* of my Acquaintance, who I found was thorowly acquainted with almost every Part of *England,* and who was to me as a walking Library, or a moveable Map of the Countries and Towns through which we pass'd; and we never fail'd to enquire of the most proper Persons in every Place where we came, what was to be seen? what Rarities of Nature, Antiquities, ancient Buildings were in the respective Parts? or, in short, every thing worth the Observation of Travellers.

Defoe certainly achieved his aim of rendering 'the present state' of England. Here is a cantata to the praise of the British: their commerce, their industry, their history, their cities and villages, their country seats and market towns. Yet it is also in places a requiem for vanished splendours. Out of this picture of *grandeur et décadence* there emerges not just a mirror of Britain, as the older writers put it, but a vision of nationhood.

PAT ROGERS

A SUMMARY OF DEFOE'S CAREER

1660?	Defoe born in London, almost certainly in the parish of St Giles, Cripplegate.	
1665	The Plague: Defoe possibly taken to the country as an evacuee.	
1666	The Great Fire of London.	*Tour*, p. 296
c. 1668	Defoe visits Harwich and Ipswich.	*Tour*, pp. 66–7
c. 1670	Takes the waters at Bath.	*Tour*, p. 361
c. 1670	Defoe goes to study at Rev. James Fisher's school at Dorking.	*Tour*, p. 161
c. 1674–1679	A student at Morton's dissenting academy at Stoke Newington.	
c. 1682	Decides against entering the ministry, but probably active as a lay-preacher.	
c. 1683	Becomes a hose-factor in Cornhill, and embarks on ambitious mercantile career.	
1684	Marries Mary Tuffley.	
1685	Fights in the army of the Duke of Monmouth defeated at Sedgemoor.	*Tour*, p. 254
1688	Rides to Henley to meet the army of William III on its way to London: in the midst of his earliest series of journeys.	*Tour*, p. 275
1690	Travels with the King to Chester and makes a business trip to Liverpool.	*Tour*, p. 540
1692	First bankruptcy, for about £17,000, caused through losses in marine insurance.	
1695	Official post connected with the Glass Duty.	
1696	Manager of the royal lottery.	
c. 1698	Visits Scotland for the King.	

1701	First important work, *The True-Born Englishman*; meets Robert Harley.	
1702	*The Shortest Way with the Dissenters* causes a storm; Defoe becomes a fugitive.	
1703	Defoe arrested, convicted for sedition; escapes but recaptured and stands in the pillory. First collection of his works.	
1704	Defoe begins weekly paper, *The Review*, published till 1713. Begins to travel in the service of Harley, and later of Lord Treasurer Godolphin.	
1706	Bankrupt again, owing to failure of his brick factory at Tilbury.	
1706–1710	In Scotland on behalf of Godolphin and Harley, resident there for long periods.	*Tour*, p. 593
1709	Proposes a plan to settle Palatinate refugees.	*Tour*, p. 202
1712	Visits Derbyshire to take the waters.	*Tour*, pp. 462, 468
1713	Arrested at least twice for political and other reasons. Imprisoned in Queen's Bench gaol but released.	
1715	Tried for libel but the case dropped.	
1717	Begins to write for Mist's *Weekly Journal*.	
1719	First part of *Robinson Crusoe*. Active in journalism.	
1720	In trouble with the authorities again but escapes punishment. *Memoirs of a Cavalier. Captain Singleton.*	
1722	*Moll Flanders. A Journal of the Plague Year. Colonel Jacque.*	
1724	*The Fortunate Mistress* [*Roxana*]. *A History of the Pirates*, vol. i. Vol. i of the *Tour* published, 21 May.	
1725	Pamphlets concerning Jack Sheppard, Jonathan Wild and other criminals. *Complete English Tradesman.* Vol. ii of the *Tour* published, 8 June.	

1726 Vol. iii of the *Tour* published, 9 August.

1728 Lawsuit with the assignee of an old creditor; finally forced to go into hiding.

1731 Died whilst still a fugitive, 24 April. Buried in Bunhill Fields.

A NOTE ON THE TEXT

ABRIDGEMENT does not have to be desecration, even where a major writer is concerned. I have sought to do as little violence upon the person of the *Tour* as possible, and have retained the shape and rhythm of Defoe's prose wherever I can. The present text is based on the first edition (1724–6). Emendations have been made according to strict rules:

(1) Spelling is modernized, *except* in the case of proper nouns and in that of words which have lost their earlier morphological state. Thus, Muzzle-Hill, not Muswell Hill; murther, and not murder.

(2) Typography is normalized to follow standard modern practice. Initial capitals are replaced by lower-case letters and italics by roman type. Where Defoe uses italics for rhetorical emphasis I have preserved this usage. Contractions are expanded, and *ſ* replaced by s.

(3) Punctuation is left intact, except that a number of heavy stops – generally colons – are replaced by a full period, as they would be today. Intermediary capitals within the sentence, at the start of a clause, are brought down to lower case. Otherwise I have taken the view that Defoe's pointing habits (unlike his orthography) are of more than antiquarian interest, since they offer a guide to the contour and direction of his sentences.

(4) The errata to the first edition have been silently incorporated, and one or two other misprints set right.

(5) Excisions have been made as follows. (*a*) Wherever possible, discrete blocks of the text, such as complete paragraphs, have been left out as a whole. (*b*) Where this cannot be achieved, cuts have been made to coincide with integral units of syntax. This means omitting either a full sentence, a separable clause following a colon, a parenthesis, or some other member of this kind. (*c*) In a limited number of cases it has been necessary to combine two sentences, or portions of them, to form a single statement. Where this has been done, I have had careful regard to the original cadences and have not distorted the shape or sense of what Defoe

wrote. The order of the original has been left undisturbed and every word in this edition was present in the text of 1724–6.

(6) Paragraphs have been combined in a number of cases. Elsewhere, as recorded in the notes, material presented by Defoe in tabular form has been set as ordinary prose.

SUGGESTIONS FOR FURTHER READING

THE best connected and most judicious biography is James Sutherland, *Defoe* (2nd edn 1950). A mine of information, though strongly partisan and rather cumbrous in organization, is J. R. Moore, *Daniel Defoe Citizen of the Modern World* (Chicago, 1959). Moore has also compiled the standard bibliography, *A Checklist of the Writings of Daniel Defoe* (Bloomington, 1960), an invaluable aid despite the fact that some of Moore's attributions have not been accepted by other scholars. There is a good edition of the *Letters* by G. H. Healey (Oxford, 1955). An important reprint is the text of Defoe's newspaper *The Review*, ed. A. W. Secord (New York, 1938), which contains many glimpses into Defoe's working life as it bears on the composition of the *Tour*. There are now many secondary works on aspects of Defoe's career, but none of them takes much account of the *Tour*.

Brief essays on the *Tour* have been published by G. D. H. Cole, reprinted in his *Persons and Periods* (Pelican edn 1945), and by Edmund Blunden, in *Votive Tablets* (1931). The most pleasant introduction to travelling in this period is Esther Moir, *The Discovery of Britain: The English Travellers 1540–1840* (1964). See also Joan Parkes, *Travel in England in the Seventeenth Century* (1925). The edition of *The Journeys of Celia Fiennes* by Christopher Morris (1947) has a useful introduction and judicious, though not comprehensive, notes. There are innumerable works of social history to complement Defoe's findings from a modern standpoint, but mention may be made of one outstanding study, Dorothy George's *London Life in the Eighteenth Century* (Peregrine edn 1965).

Facsimile of the title-page of the first edition of Volume I (1724)

A

TOUR

Thro' the whole ISLAND of

GREAT BRITAIN,

Divided into

Circuits *or* Journies.

GIVING

A Particular and Diverting ACCOUNT of Whatever is CURIOUS and worth OBSERVATION, *Viz.*

I. A DESCRIPTION of the Principal Cities and Towns, their Situation, Magnitude, Government, and Commerce.

II. The Customs, Manners, Speech, as also the Exercises, Diversions, and Employment of the People.

III. The Produce and Improvement of the Lands, the Trade, and Manufactures.

IV. The Sea Ports and Fortifications, the Course of Rivers, and the Inland Navigation.

V. The Publick Edifices, Seats, and Palaces of the NOBILITY and GENTRY.

With Useful OBSERVATIONS *upon the Whole.*

Particularly fitted for the Reading of such as desire to Travel over the ISLAND.

By a GENTLEMAN.

LONDON:

Printed, and Sold by G. STRAHAN, in *Cornhill.*
W. MEARS, at the *Lamb* without *Temple-Bar.*
R. FRANCKLIN, under *Tom*'s Coffee-house, *Covent-Garden*,
S. CHAPMAN, at the *Angel* in *Pall-Mall.*
R. STAGG, in *Westminster-Hall*, and
J. GRAVES, in St. *James*'s-*Street*. MDCCXXIV.

PREFACE TO THE FIRST VOLUME

IF this work is not both pleasant and profitable to the reader, the author most freely and openly declares the fault must be in his performance, and it cannot be any deficiency in the subject. As the work it self is a description of the most flourishing and opulent country in the world, so there is a flowing variety of materials; all the particulars are fruitful of instructing and diverting objects.

If novelty pleases, here is the present state of the country described, the improvement, as well in culture, as in commerce, the increase of people, and employment for them. Also here you have an account of the increase of buildings, as well in great cities and towns, as in the new seats and dwellings of the nobility and gentry; also the increase of wealth, in many eminent particulars. If antiquity takes with you, though the looking back into remote things is studiously avoided, yet it is not wholly omitted, nor any useful observations neglected; the learned writers on the subject of antiquity in Great Britain have so well discharged themselves, that we can never over-value their labours, yet there are daily farther discoveries made, which give future ages, room, perhaps not to mend, yet at least to add to what has been already done.

In travelling through England, a luxuriance of objects presents it self to our view. Where-ever we come, and which way soever we look, we see something new, something significant, something well worth the traveller's stay, and the writer's care; nor is any check to our design, or obstruction to its acceptance in the world, to say the like has been done already, or to panegyric upon the labours and value of those authors who have gone before, in this work. A complete account of Great Britain will be the work of many years, I might say ages, and may employ many hands. Whoever has travelled Great Britain before us, and whatever they have written, though they may have had a harvest, yet they have always, either by necessity, ignorance or negligence passed over so much, that others may come and glean after them by large handfuls.

Nor could it be otherwise, had the diligence and capacities of all who have gone before been greater than they are; for the face of things so often alters, and the situation of affairs in this great British Empire gives such new turns, even to nature it self, that there is matter of new observation every day presented to the traveller's eye.

The fate of things gives a new face to things, produces changes in low life, and innumerable incidents; plants and supplants families, raises and sinks towns, removes manufactures, and trades; great towns decay, and small towns rise; new towns, new palaces, new seats are built every day; great rivers and good harbours dry up, and grow useless; again, new ports are opened, brooks are made rivers, small rivers navigable, ports and harbours are made where none were before, and the like. Several towns, which antiquity speaks of as considerable, are now lost and swallowed up by the sea, as Dunwich in Suffolk for one; and others, which antiquity knew nothing of, are now grown considerable. In a word, new matter offers to new observation, and they who write next, may perhaps find as much room for enlarging upon us, as we do upon those that have gone before.

The author says, that indeed he might have given his pen a loose here, to have complained how much the conduct of the people diminishes the reputation of the island, on many modern occasions, and so we could have made his historical account a satire upon the country, as well as upon the people; but they are ill friends to England, who strive to write a history of her nudities, and expose, much less recommend her wicked part to posterity; he has rather endeavoured to do her justice in those things which recommend her, and humbly to move a reformation of those, which he thinks do not. A description of the country is the business here, not descanting upon the errors of the people; and yet, without boasting, we may venture to say, we are at least upon a level with the best of our neighbours, perhaps above them in morals, whatever we are in their pride; but let that stand as it does, till times mend.

The observations here made, as they principally regard the present state of things, so, as near as can be, they are adapted to the present taste of the times. The situation of things is given not as they have been, but as they are; the improvements in the soil, the product of the earth, the labour of the poor, the improvement in manufactures, in merchandises, in navigation, all respects the present time, not the time past. In every county something of the people is said, as well as of the place, of their customs, speech, employments, the product of their labour, and the manner of their living, the circumstances as well as situation of the towns, their trade and government; of the rarities of art, or nature; the rivers, of the inland, and river navigation; also of the lakes and medicinal springs, not forgetting the general dependance of the whole country upon the city of London, as well for the consumption of its produce as the circulation of its trade.

The preparations for this work have been suitable to the author's earnest concern for its usefulness; seventeen very large circuits, or journeys have been taken through divers parts separately, and three general tours over almost the whole English part of the island; in all which the author has not been wanting to treasure up just remarks upon particular places and things, so that he is very little in debt to other men's labours, and gives but very few accounts of things, but what he has been an eye-witness of himself.

Besides these several journeys in England, he has also lived some time in Scotland, and has travelled critically over great part of it; he has viewed the north part of England, and the south part of Scotland five several times over; all which is hinted here, to let the readers know what reason they will have to be satisfied with the authority of the relation, and that the accounts here given are not the produce of a cursory view, or raised upon the borrowed lights of other observers.

It must be acknowledged, that some foreigners, who have pretended to travel into England, and to give account of things when they come home, have treated us after a very indifferent manner. As they viewed us with envy, so they have made their account rather equal to what they wished we should be, than to what we are; and wrote as if they were afraid the country they wrote to should be in love with us, and come away to live among us: in short, speaking of England, they have, like the Israelitish spies, carried abroad a very ill report of the land. It is worth no man's while to examine and confute foreign authors, whose errors are their ignorance.

But after all that has been said by others, or can be said here, no description of Great Britain can be, what we call a finished account, as no clothes can be made to fit a growing child; no picture carry the likeness of a living face; the size of one, and the countenance of the other always altering with time: so no account of a kingdom thus daily altering its countenance, can be perfect.

Even while the sheets are in the press, new beauties appear in several places, and almost to every part we are obliged to add appendixes, and supplemental accounts of fine houses, new undertakings, buildings, &c. and thus posterity will be continually adding; every age will find an increase of glory. And may it do so, till Great Britain as much exceeds the finest country in Europe, as that country now fancies they exceed her.

A TOUR IN CIRCUITS, THROUGH THE ISLAND OF GREAT BRITAIN

Letter 1

Containing a description of the Sea-Coasts of the Counties of Essex, Suffolk, Norfolk, etc., as also of part of Cambridge-shire

I BEGAN my travels, where I purpose to end them, viz. at the city of London, and therefore my account of the city itself will come last, that is to say, at the latter end of my southern progress; and as in the course of this journey I shall have many occasions to call it a circuit, if not a circle, so I chose to give it the title of circuits, in the plural, because I do not pretend to have travelled it all in one journey, but in many, and some of them many times over; the better to inform my self of every thing I could find worth taking notice of.

I hope it will appear that I am not the less, but the more capable of giving a full account of things, by how much the more deliberation I have taken in the view of them, and by how much the oftener I have had opportunity to see them.

I set out, the 3d of April, 1722,[1] going first eastward, and took what I think, I may very honestly call a circuit in the very letter of it; for I went down by the coast of the Thames through the marshes or hundreds, on the south-side of the county of Essex, till I came to Malden, Colchester, and Harwich, thence continuing on the coast of Suffolk to Yarmouth; thence round by the edge of the sea, on the north and west-side of Norfolk, to Lynn, Wisbich, and the Wash; thence back again on the north-side of Suffolk and Essex, to the west, ending it in Middlesex, near the place where I began it, reserving the middle or centre of the several counties to some little excursions, which I made by themselves.

Passing Bow-Bridge, where the county of Essex begins, the

first observation I made was, that all the villages which may be called the neighbourhood of the city of London are increased in buildings to a strange degree, within the compass of about 20 or 30 years past at the most.

The village of Stratford, the first in this county from London, is not only increased, but, I believe, more than doubled in that time; every vacancy filled up with new houses, and two little towns or hamlets, as they may be called, on the forest side of the town, entirely new, one facing the road to Woodford, and Epping, and the other facing the road to Illford. And as for the hither part, it is almost joined to Bow, in spite of rivers, canals, marshy-grounds, &c. Nor is this increase of building the case only, in this and all the other villages round London; but the increase of the value and rent of the houses formerly standing, has, in that compass of years above-mentioned, advanced to a very great degree, and I may venture to say at least a fifth part; some think a third part, above what they were before.

This is indeed most visible, speaking of Stratford in Essex; but it is the same thing in proportion in other villages adjacent, especially on the forest-side; as at Low-Layton, Laytonstone, Walthamstow, Woodford, Wansted, and the towns of West-Ham, Plaistow, Upton, &c. In all which places, or near them, (as the inhabitants say) above a thousand new foundations have been erected, besides old houses repaired, all since the Revolution. And this is not to be forgotten too, that this increase is, generally speaking, of handsome large houses, from 20*l.* a year to 60*l.*, very few under 20*l.* a year; being chiefly for the habitations of the richest citizens, such as either are able to keep two houses, one in the country, and one in the city; or for such citizens as being rich, and having left off trade, live altogether in these neighbouring villages, for the pleasure and health of the latter part of their days. The truth of this may at least appear, in that they tell me there are no less than two hundred coaches kept by the inhabitants within the circumference of these few villages named above, besides such as are kept by accidental lodgers.

This increase causes those villages to be much pleasanter and more sociable than formerly, for now people go to them, not for retirement into the country, but for good company; of which, that I may speak to the ladies as well as other authors do, there are in these villages, nay, in all, three or four excepted, excellent conversation, and a great deal of it, and that without the mixture of assemblées, gaming houses, and public foundations of vice and debauchery; and particularly I find none of those incentives kept up on this side the country.

Mr Camden, and his learned continuator, Bishop Gibson,[2] have ransacked this country for its antiquities, and have left little unsearched; and, as it is not my present design to say much of what has been said already, I shall touch very lightly where two such excellent antiquaries have gone before me; except it be to add what may have been since discovered, which as to these parts is only this; that there seems to be lately found out, in the bottom of the marshes, (generally called Hackney-Marsh, and beginning near about the place now called the Wyck), between Old-Ford and the said Wyck, the remains of a great stone causeway, which, as it is supposed, was the highway, or great road from London into Essex, and the same, which goes now over the great bridge between Bow and Stratford. That the great road[3] lay this way; and that it was one of those famous highways made by the Romans, there is undoubted proof, by the several marks of Roman work, and by Roman coins, and other antiquities found there.

From hence the great road passed up to Layton-stone, a place by some known, now as much, by the sign of the Green-Man, formerly a lodge upon the edge of the forest; and crossing by Wansted House, went over the same river which we now pass at Ilford; and passing that part of the great forest which we now call Henault Forest, came into that which is now the great road, a little on this side the Whalebone, a place on the road so called, because a rib-bone of a great whale, which was taken in the river of Thames the same year that

Oliver Cromwel died, 1658, was fixed there for a monument of that monstrous creature, it being at first about eight-and-twenty foot long.

According to my first intention of effectually viewing the sea-coast of these three counties, I went from Stratford to Barking, a large market-town, but chiefly inhabited by fishermen, whose smacks ride in the Thames, at the mouth of their river, from whence their fish is sent up to London to the market at Billingsgate, by small boats. One thing I cannot omit in the mention of these Barking fisher-smacks, viz. that one of those fishermen, a very substantial and experienced man, convinced me, that all the pretences to bringing fish alive to London market from the North Seas, and other remote places on the coast of Great Britain, by the new-built sloops called fish-pools,[4] have not been able to do any thing, but what their fishing-smacks are able on the same occasion to perform. These fishing-smacks are very useful vessels to the public upon many occasions; as particularly, in time of war they are used as press-smacks, running to all the northern and western coasts to pick up seamen to man the navy, when any expedition is at hand that requires a sudden equipment. At other times, being excellent sailors, they are tenders to particular men of war; and on an expedition they have been made use of as machines, for the blowing up fortified ports and havens; as at Calais, St Maloes,[5] and other places.

This parish of Barking is very large; and by the improvement of lands taken in, out of the Thames, and out of the river which runs by the town, the tithes, as the townsmen assured me, are worth above 600l. per annum, including small tithes. A little beyond the town, on the road to Dagenham, stood a great house, ancient, and now almost fallen down, where tradition says the Gunpowder Treason Plot[6] was at first contrived, and that all the first consultations about it were held there.

This side of the county is rather rich in land, than in inhabitants, occasioned chiefly by the unhealthiness of the air; for these low marsh grounds, which, with all the south-side of the county, have been saved out of the River Thames, and out of the sea, where the river is wide enough to be called so, begin here. From hence eastward, growing wider and wider, till we come beyond Tilbury, when the flat country lies six, seven, or eight miles broad, and is justly said to be both unhealthy, and unpleasant. However the lands are rich, and, as is observable, it is very good farming in the marshes, because the landlords let good penny-worths, for it being a place where every body cannot live, those that venture it, will have encouragement, and indeed it is but reasonable they should.

Several little observations I made in this part of the county of Essex.

1. We saw passing from Barking to Dagenham, the famous breach, made by an inundation of the Thames, which was so great, as that it laid near 5000 acres of land under water, but which after near ten years lying under water, and being several times blown up has been at last effectually stopped by the application of Captain Perry;[7] the gentleman, who for several years had been employed, in the Czar of Muscovy's works, at Veronitza, on the River Don.

2. It was observable that great part of the lands in these levels, especially those on this side East Tilbury, are held by the farmers, cow-keepers, and grazing butchers who live in and near London, and that they are generally stocked (all the winter half year) with large fat sheep, (viz.) Lincolnshire and Leicestershire wethers, which they buy in Smithfield in September and October, when the Lincolnshire and Leicestershire graziers sell off their stock, and are kept here till Christmas, or Candlemas, or thereabouts, and though they are not made at all fatter here, than they were when bought in, yet the farmer, or butcher finds very good advantage in it, by the difference of the price of mutton between Michaelmas, when 'tis cheapest, and Candlemas when 'tis dearest; this is what the butchers value themselves upon, then they tell us at the market, that it is right marsh-mutton.

3. In the bottom of these marshes, and close to the edge of the rivers stands the strong fortress of Tilbury, called Tilbury Fort, which may justly be looked upon, as the key of the river of Thames, and consequently the key of the city of London. It is a regular fortification, the design of it, was a pentagon, but the water bastion as it would have been called, was never built. The esplanade of the fort is very large, and the bastions, the largest of any in England, the foundation is laid so deep, and piles under that, driven down two on end of one another, so far, till they were assured they were below the channel of the river, and that the piles, which were shod with iron, entered into the solid chalk rock adjoining to, or reaching from the chalk-hills on the other side. These bastions settled considerably at first, but they are now firm as the rocks of chalk which they came from, and the filling up one of these bastions, as I have been told by good hands, cost the Government 6000*l.*

The works to the land side are complete; the bastions are faced with brick. There is a double ditch, or moat, the innermost part of which is 180 foot broad, there is a good counterscarp, and a covered way marked out, with ravelins, and tenailles. On the land side there are also two small redoubts of brick, but of very little strength, for the chief strength of this fort on the land side consists in this, that they are able to lay the whole level under water, and so to make it impossible for an enemy to make any approaches to the fort that way. On the side next the river, there is a very strong curtain, with a noble gate called the water-gate in the middle, and that ditch is pallisadoed. Before this curtain above and below the said vacancy, is a platform in the place of a counterscarp, on which are planted 106 pieces of cannon, generally all of them carrying from 24 to 46 pound ball; a battery, so terrible, as well imports the consequence of that place. Besides which, there are smaller pieces planted between, and the bastions and curtain also are planted with guns, so that they must be bold fellows who will venture in the biggest ships the world has heard of, to pass such a battery, if the men appointed to serve the guns, do their duty like stout fellows, as becomes them.

The present government of this important place is under the prudent administration of the Right Honourable the Lord Newbrugh.[8]

From hence, there is nothing for many miles together remarkable, but a continued level of unhealthy marshes, called, the Three Hundreds, till we come before Leigh, and to the mouth of the River Chelmer, and Black-water. These rivers united make a large firth, or inlet of the sea, which by Mr Camden is called *Idumanum Fluvium*; but by our fishermen and seamen, who use it as a port, 'tis called Malden-Water. In this inlet of the sea is Osey or Osyth Island, commonly called Oosy Island, so well known by our London men of pleasure, for the infinite number of wild-fowl, that is to say, duck, mallard, teal and widgeon, of which there are such vast flights, that they tell us the island, namely the creek, seems covered with them, at certain times of the year, and they go from London on purpose for the pleasure of shooting; and indeed often come home very well loaden with game. But it must be remembered too, that those gentlemen who are such lovers of the sport, and go so far for it, often return with an Essex ague on their backs, which they find a heavier load than the fowls they have shot.

'Tis on this shore, and near this creek, that the greatest quantity of fresh fish is caught, which supplies not this country only, but London markets also. All along, to the mouth of Colchester Water, the shore is full of shoals and sands, with some deep channels between; all of which are so full of fish, that not only the Barking fishing-smacks come hither to fish, but the whole shore is full of small fisher-boats in very great numbers, belonging to the villages and towns on the coast, who come in every tide with what they take; and selling the smaller fish in the country, send the best and largest away upon horses, which go night and day to London market.

N.B. I am the more particular in my remark on this place, because in the course of my travels the reader will meet with the like in almost every place of note through the whole island, where it will be seen how this whole kingdom, as well as the people, as the land, and even the sea, in every part of it, are employed to furnish something, and I may add, the best of every thing, to supply the city of London with provisions; I mean by provisions, corn, flesh, fish, butter, cheese, salt, fuel, timber, &c. and cloths also; with every thing necessary for building, and furniture for their own use, or for trades; of all which in their order.

On this shore also are taken the best and nicest, though not the largest oysters in England; the fishermen take them at the mouth of, that they call, Colchester Water, and about the sand they call the Spits, and carry them up to Wyvenhoo, where they are laid in beds or pits on the shore to feed, as they call it; and then being barrelled up, and carried to Colchester, which is but three miles off, they are sent to London by land, and are, from thence, called Colchester oysters.

The chief sort of other fish which they carry from this part of the shore to London, are soles, which they take sometimes exceeding large, and yield a very good price at London market. Also sometimes middling turbet, with whitings, codling, and large flounders; the small fish as above, they sell in the country. In the several creeks and openings on this shore, there are also other islands, but of no particular note, except Mersey, which lies in the middle of the two openings, between Malden Water and Colchester Water; being of the most difficult access, so that 'tis thought a thousand men well provided, might keep possession of it against a great force, whether by land or sea. The Government formerly built a fort on the south-east point of it: and generally in case of Dutch war, there is a strong body of troops kept there to defend it.

I have one remark more, before I leave this damp part of the world, and which I cannot omit on the women's account;

namely, that I took notice of a strange decay of the sex here; insomuch, that all along this county it was very frequent to meet with men that had had from five to six, to fourteen or fifteen wives; nay, and some more; and I was informed that in the marshes on the other side the river over-against Candy Island, there was a farmer, who was then living with the five and twentieth wife, and that his son who was but about 35 years old, had already had about fourteen; indeed this part of the story, I only had by report, though from good hands too; but the other is well known, and easy to be inquired in to, about Fobbing, Curringham, Thundersly, Benfleet, Prittlewell, Wakering, Great Stambridge, Cricksea, Burnham, Dengy, and other towns of the like situation. The reason, as a merry fellow told me, who said he had had about a dozen and a half of wives, (though I found afterwards he fibbed a little) was this; that they being bred in the marshes themselves, and seasoned to the place, did pretty well with it; but that they always went up into the hilly country, or to speak their own language into the uplands for a wife: that when they took the young lasses out of the wholesome and fresh air, they were healthy, fresh and clear, and well; but when they came out of their native air into the marshes among the fogs and damps,[9] there they presently changed their complexion, got an ague or two, and seldom held it above half a year, or a year at most; and then, said he, we go to the uplands again, and fetch another; so that marrying of wives was reckoned a kind of good farm to them. It is true, the fellow told this in a kind of drollery, and mirth; but the fact, for all that, is certainly true; and that they have abundance of wives by that very means. As first you seldom meet with very ancient people among the poor, as in other places we do, so, take it one with another, not one half of the inhabitants are natives of the place; but such as from other countries, or in other parts of this county settle here for the advantage of good farms; for which I appeal to any impartial enquiry, having myself examined into it critically in several places.

From the marshes, and low grounds, being not able to travel without many windings, and indentures, by reason of the creeks, and waters, I came up to the town of Malden, a noted market town situate at the conflux or joining of two principal rivers in this county, the Chelm or Chelmer, and the Blackwater, and where they enter into the sea. When I have said this, I think I have done Malden justice, and said all of it that there is to be said, unless I should run into the old story of its antiquity, and tell you it was a Roman colony in the time of Vespasian, and that it was called Camolodonum. How the Britons under Queen Boadicia,[10] in revenge for the Romans' ill usage of her, for indeed they used her majesty ill; they stripped her naked, and whipped her publicly through their streets for some affront she had given them : as for that story, it is so fully related by Mr Camden,[11] at the beginning of his *Britannia*, that I need only refer the reader to it, and go on with my journey.

I made it my road to pass through Witham, a pleasant well situated market-town, in which, and in its neighbourhood, there are as many gentlemen of good fortunes, and families, as I believe can be met with in so narrow a compass in any of the three counties, of which I make this circuit. Nearer Chelmsford, hard by Boreham, lives the Lord Viscount Barrington,[12] who though not born to the title, or estate, or name which he now possesses, had the honour to be twice made heir to the estates of gentlemen, not at all related to him, at least one of them, as is very much to his honour mentioned in his patent of creation. His name was Shute, his uncle a linen draper in London, and served sheriff of the said city, in very troublesome times. He changed the name of Shute, for that of Barrington, by an Act of Parliament, obtained for that purpose, and had the dignity of a baron of the kingdom of Ireland conferred on him by the favour of King GEORGE. His lordship is a Dissenter, and seems to love retirement. He was a Member of Parliament for the town of Berwick upon Tweed.

It is observable, that in this part of the country, there are several very considerable estates purchased, and now enjoyed by citizens of London, merchants and tradesmen, as Mr Western [13] an iron merchant, near Kelvedon, Mr Cresnor, a wholesale grocer, who was, a little before he died, named for sheriff at Earls Coln, Mr Olemus, a merchant at Braintree, Mr Westcomb, near Malden, Sir Thomas Webster at Copthall, near Waltham, and several others. I mention this, to observe how the present increase of wealth in the city of London, spreads it self into the country, and plants families and fortunes, who in another age will equal the families of the ancient gentry, who perhaps were bought out.

The product of all this part of the country is corn, as that of the marshy feeding grounds mentioned above, is grass, where their chief business is breeding of calves, which I need not say are the best and fattest, and the largest veal in England, if not in the world; and as an instance, I eat [14] part of a veal or calf, fed by the late Sir Josiah Child [15] at Wansted, the loin of which weighed above 30*l.* and the flesh exceeding white and fat.

The story of Kill Dane, which is told of the town of Kelvedon, three miles from Witham, namely, that this is the place where the massacre of the Danes was begun by the women, and that therefore it was called Kill Dane. I say of it, as we generally say of improbable news, it wants confirmation. The true name of the town is Kelvedon, and has been so for many hundred years.

COLCHESTER is an ancient Corporation; the town is large, very populous; the streets fair and beautiful; and though it may not be said to be finely built, yet there are abundance of very good and well-built houses in it. It still mourns, in the ruins of a civil war; during which, or rather after the heat of the war was over, it suffered a severe siege; which, the garrison making a resolute defence, was turned into a blockade, in which the garrison and inhabitants also, suffered the utmost extremity of hunger, and were at last obliged to surrender at discretion, when their two chief officers, Sir Charles Lucas,[16] and Sir George Lisle, were shot to death under the castle-wall. The inhabitants had a tradition, that no grass would grow upon the spot where the blood of those two gallant gentlemen was spilt; and they showed the place bare of grass for many years, but whether for this reason, I will not affirm; the story is now dropped, and the grass, I suppose, grows there as in other places.

However, the battered walls, the breaches in the turrets, and the ruined churches still remain, except that the church of St Mary's (where they had the royal fort) is rebuilt; but the steeple, which was two thirds battered down, because the besieged had a large culverine upon it, that did much execution, remains still in that condition. The lines of contravallation, with the forts built by the besiegers, and which surrounded the whole town, remained very visible in many places; but the chief of them are demolished.

The River Coln, which passes through this town, compasses it on the north and east-sides, and served in those times for a complete defence on those sides. The river is navigable within three miles of the town for ships of large burthen; a little lower it may receive even a royal navy. And up to that part called the Hithe, close to the houses, it is navigable for hoys and small barks. This Hithe is a long street, passing from west to east, on the south-side of the town; at the west-end of it, there is a small intermission of the buildings, but not much; and towards the river it is very populous; (it may be called the Wapping of Colchester).

The town may be said chiefly to subsist by the trade of making bays, which is known over most of the trading parts of Europe, by the name of Colchester bays, though indeed the whole county, large as it is, may be said to be employed, and in part maintained, by the spinning of wool for the bay trade of Colchester, and its adjacent towns.[17]

The town of Colchester has been supposed to contain about 40000 people, including the out-villages which are within its liberty. One sad testimony of the town being so populous is, that they buried upwards of 5259 people in the Plague Year, 1665. But the town was severely visited indeed, even more in proportion than any of its neighbours, or than the city of London.

The government of the town is by a mayor, high steward, a recorder, or his deputy, eleven aldermen, a chamberlain, a town-clerk, assistants, and eighteen common-council-men. Their high-steward (this year, 1722) is Sir Isaac Rebow,[18] a gentleman of a good family and known character, who has generally, for above 30 years, been one of their representatives in Parliament. He has had the honour, several times, to lodge and entertain the late King William, of glorious memory, in his returning from Holland, by way of Harwich to London. Their recorder is Earl Cowper,[19] who has been twice Lord High-Chancellor of England: but his lordship not residing in those parts, has put in his deputy, who dwells in the town. There are in Colchester eight churches, besides those which are damaged, and five meeting-houses, whereof two for Quakers; besides a Dutch church and a French church.

Public edifices are,

1. Bay-Hall, an ancient society kept up for ascertaining the manufactures of bays. This corporation is governed by a particular set of men who are called Governors of the Dutch Bay Hall. And in the same building is the Dutch church.

2. The Guild hall of the town, called by them the Moot Hall; to which is annexed the town gaol.

3. The Work-house, being lately enlarged, and to which belongs a corporation, or a body of the inhabitants, consisting of sixty persons incorporated by Act of Parliament anno 1698, for taking care of the poor. They are in number eight and forty; to whom are added the mayor and aldermen for the time being, who are always guardians by the same charter: these make the number of sixty, as above.

4. The castle of Colchester is now become only a monument showing the antiquity of the place, it being built as the walls of the town also are, with Roman bricks; and the

Roman coins dug up here, and ploughed up in the fields adjoining, confirm it. The inhabitants boast much, that Helena, the mother of Constantine the Great,[20] first Christian Emperor of the Romans, was born there; and it may be so for aught we know; I only observe what Mr Camden[21] says of the castle of Colchester, viz. 'In the middle of this city stands a castle ready to fall with age.' Though this castle has stood an hundred and twenty years from the time Mr Camden wrote that account, and it is not fallen yet; nor will another hundred and twenty years, I believe, make it look one jot the older.

There are two CHARITY SCHOOLS set up here, and carried on by a generous subscription, with very good success.

From Colchester, I took another step down to the coast, the land running out a great way into the sea, south, and S.E. makes that promontory of land called the Nase, and well known to sea-men, using the northern trade. Here one sees a sea open as an ocean, without any opposite shore, though it be no more than the mouth of the Thames. This point called the Nase, and the N.E. point of Kent, near Margate, called the North Foreland, making (what they call) the mouth of the river, and the port of London, though it be here above 60 miles over.

At Walton, under the Nase, they find on the shore, copperas-stone in great quantities; and there are several large works called Copperas Houses, where they make it with great expense. The sea gains so much upon the land here, by the continual winds at S.W. that within the memory of some of the inhabitants there, they have lost above 30 acres of land in one place.

From hence we go back into the country about four miles, because of the creeks which lie between; and then turning east again, come to Harwich, on the utmost eastern point of this large country. Harwich is a town so well known, and so perfectly described by many writers, I need say little of it. 'Tis strong by situation, and may be made more so by art. But 'tis many years since the government of England have had any occasion to fortify towns to the landward; 'tis enough that the harbour or road, which is one of the best and securest in England, is covered at the entrance by a strong fort, and a battery of guns to the seaward, just as at Tilbury, and which sufficiently defend the mouth of the river. And there is a particular felicity in this fortification, viz. that though the entrance or opening of the river into the sea, is very wide, especially at high-water, at least two miles, if not three over; yet the channel, which is deep, and in which the ships must keep and come to the harbour, is narrow, and lies only on the side of the fort; so that all the ships which come in, or go out, must come close under the guns of the fort.

The harbour is of a vast extent; for, as two rivers empty themselves here, viz, Stour from Mainingtree, and the Orwel from Ipswich, the channels of both are large and deep, and safe for all weathers; so where they join they make a large bay or road, able to receive the biggest ships, and the greatest number that ever the world saw together; I mean, ships of war. In the old Dutch War, great use has been made of this harbour; and I have known that there has been 100 sail of men of war and their attendants, and between three and four hundred sail of collier ships, all in this harbour at a time, and yet none of them crowding, or riding in danger of one another. Harwich is known for being the port where the packet-boats between England and Holland, go out and come in. The inhabitants are far from being famed for good usage to strangers, but on the contrary, are blamed for being extravagant in their reckonings, in the public houses, which has not a little encouraged the setting up of sloops, which they now call passage-boats, to Holland, to go directly from the river of Thames. This, though it may be something the longer passage, yet as they are said to be more obliging to passengers, and more reasonable in the expense, and as some say also the vessels are better sea-boats, has been the reason why so many passengers do not go or come by the way of Harwich, as formerly were wont to do.

The account of a petrifying quality in the earth here, though some will have it to be in the water of a spring hard by, is very strange. They boast that their town is walled, and their streets paved with clay, and yet, that one is as strong, and the other as clean as those that are built or paved with stone. The fact is indeed true, for there is a sort of clay in the cliff, between the town and the beacon-hill adjoining, which when it falls down into the sea, where it is beaten with the waves and the weather, turns gradually into stone: but the chief reason assigned, is from the water of a certain spring or well, which rising in the said cliff, runs down into the sea among those pieces of clay, and petrifies them as it runs, and the force of the sea often stirring, and perhaps, turning the lumps of clay, when storms of wind may give force enough to the water, causes them to harden every where alike; otherwise those which were not quite sunk in the water of the spring, would be petrified but in part. These stones are gathered up to pave the streets, and build the houses, and are indeed very hard. The same spring is said to turn wood into iron. But this I take to be no more or less than the quality, which as I mentioned of the shore at the Ness, is found to be in much of the stone, all along this shore, (viz.) of the copperas kind; and 'tis certain, that the copperas stone (so called) is found in all that cliff, and even where the water of this spring has run; and I presume, that those who call the hardened pieces of wood, which they take out of this well by the name of iron, never tried the quality of it with the fire or hammer; if they had, perhaps they would have given some other account of it. On the promontory of land, which they call Beacon-Hill, and which lies beyond, or behind the town, towards the sea, there is a light-house, to give the ships directions in their sailing by, as well as their coming into the harbour in the night.

Harwich is a town of hurry and business, not much of gaiety and pleasure; yet the inhabitants seem warm in their nests, and some of them are very wealthy. There are not many (if any) gentlemen or families of note, either in the town, or very near it. They send two members to Parliament; the present are, Sir Peter Parker, and Humphrey Parsons, Esq.[22]

And now being at the extremity of the county of Essex, of which I have given you some view, as to that side next the sea only; I shall break off this part of my letter, by telling you, that I will take the towns which lie more towards the centre of the county. On the road from London to Colchester, before I came into it at Witham, lie four good market-towns at equal distance from one another; namely, Rumford, noted for two markets, (viz.) one for calves and hogs, the other for corn and other provisions; most, if not all, bought up for London market. At the farther end of the town, in the middle of a stately park, stood Guldy Hall, vulgarly Giddy Hall, an ancient seat of one Coke, sometime Lord-Mayor of London, but forfeited, on some occasion, to the Crown. It is since pulled down to the ground, and there now stands a noble stately fabric or mansion-house, built upon the spot by Sir John Eyles,[23] a wealthy merchant of London, and chosen sub-governor of the South-Sea Company, immediately after the ruin of the former sub-governor and directors, whose overthrow makes the history of these times famous.

Brent-Wood and Ingarstone, and even Chelmsford itself, have very little to be said of them, but that they are large thorough-fare towns, full of good inns, and chiefly maintained by the excessive multitude of carriers and passengers, which are constantly passing this way to London, with droves of cattle, provisions, and manufactures for London. The last of these towns is indeed the county-town, where the county jail is kept, and where the assizes are very often held.

Four market-towns fill up the rest of this part of the country; Dunmow, Braintre, Thaxted, and Coggshall; all noted for the manufacture of bays, as above, and for very little else, except I shall make the ladies laugh, at the famous old story of the Flitch of Bacon at Dunmow, which is this:

One Robert Fitz-Walter,[24] a powerful baron in this county, in the time of Hen. III, on some merry occasion, which is not preserved in the rest of the story, instituted a custom in the priory here; that whatever married man did not repent of his being married, or quarrel, or differ and dispute with his wife, within a year and a day after his marriage, and would swear to the truth of it, kneeling upon two hard pointed stones in the church-yard, which stones he caused to be set up in the priory church-yard, for that purpose. The prior and convent, and as many of the town as would, to be present: such person should have a flitch of bacon. I do not remember to have read, that any one ever came to demand it; nor do the people of the place pretend to say, of their own knowledge, that they remember any that did so; a long time ago several did demand it, as they say, but they know not who; neither is there any record of it; nor do they tell us, if it were now to be demanded, who is obliged to deliver the flitch of bacon, the priory being dissolved and gone.

The forest of Epping and Henalt, spreads a great part of this country still. Formerly, ('tis thought) these two forests took up all the west and south part of the county. Probably this forest of Epping has been a wild forest ever since this island was inhabited, and may show us, in some parts of it, where enclosures and tillage has not broken in upon it, what the face of this island was before the Romans' time; that is to say, before their landing in Britain.

The constitution of this forest is best seen, I mean, as to the antiquity of it, by the merry grant of it from Edward the Confessor, before the Norman Conquest to Randolph Peperking, one of his favourites, who was after called Peverell, and whose name remains still in several villages in this county; as particularly that of Hatfield Peverell, in the road from Chelmsford to Witham, which is supposed to be originally a park, which they called a field in those days; and Hartfield may be as much as to say a park for deer; for the stags were in those days called harts; so that this was neither more or less than Randolph Peperking's Hartfield; that is to say, Ralph Peverell's deer-park.[25] But I return to King Edward's merry way, as I call it, of granting this forest to this Ralph Peperking, which I find in the ancient records,[26] in the very words it was passed in, as follows. Take my explanations with it, for the sake of those that are not used to the ancient English.

The Grant in Old English	*The Explanation in Modern English*
Iche EDWARD Koning,	I EDWARD the King,
Have given of my forrest the kepen of the Hundred of Chelmer and Dancing,	Have made Ranger of my forest of Chelmsford Hundred, and Deering Hundred,
To RANDOLPH PEPERKING, And to his kindling,	Ralph Peverell, for him and his heirs for ever;
With heorte and hind, doe and bocke,	With both the red and fallow deer,
Hare and fox, cat and brock,	Hare and fox, otter and badger;
Wild fowle with his flock;	Wild fowl of all sorts,
Patrich, pheasant hen, and pheasant cock,	Partridges and pheasants,
With green and wild stub and stock,	Timber and underwood, roots and tops:
To kepen and to yemen with all her might,	With power to preserve the forest,
Both by day, and eke by night;	And watch it against deer stealers and others:
And hounds for to hold, Good and swift, and bold:	With a right to keep hounds of all sorts,
Four greyhound, and six raches,	Four grey-hounds, and six terriers,
For hare and fox, and wild cattes,	Harriers and fox-hounds, and other hounds.
And therefore Iche made him my book;	And to this end I have registered this my Grant, in the Crown rolls or books;
Witness the Bishop of Wolston, And book ylrede many on,	To which the bishop has set his hand as a witness for any one to read;
And Sweyne of Essex, our brother,	Also signed by the king's brother (or, as some think, the Chancellor Sweyn, then Earl or Count of Essex)
And taken him many other	He might call such other witnesses to sign as he thought fit.
And our steward Howelin, That by-sought me for him.	Also the king's high steward was a witness, at whose request this Grant was obtained of the king.

I shall next proceed to the county of Suffolk, as my first design directed me to do.

From HARWICH therefore, having a mind to view the harbour, I sent my horses round by Maningtree, where there is a timber bridge over the Stour, called Cataway Bridge, and took a boat up the River Orwell, for Ipswich. A traveller will hardly understand me, especially a seaman, when I speak of the River Stour and the River Orwell at Harwich, for they know them by no other names than those of Maningtre-Water, and Ipswich-Water; so while I am on salt water, I must speak as those who use the sea may understand me, and when I am up in the country among the in-land towns again, I shall call them out of their names no more.

It is twelve miles from Harwich up the water to Ipswich. In former times, that is to say, since the writer of this remembers the place very well, and particularly just before the late Dutch Wars, Ipswich was a town of very good business; particularly it was the greatest town in England for large colliers or coal-ships, employed between New Castle and London. They built also there so prodigious strong, that it was an ordinary thing for an Ipswich collier, if no disaster happened to him, to reign (as seamen call it) forty or fifty years, and more. In the town of Ipswich the masters of these ships generally dwelt, and there were, as they then told me, above a hundred sail of them, belonging to the town at one time, the least of which carried fifteen-score, as they compute it, that is, 300 chaldron of coals; this was about the year 1668 (when I first knew the place). This made the town be at that time so populous, for those masters, as they had good ships at sea, so they had large families, who lived plentifully, and in very good houses in the town, and several streets were chiefly inhabited by such.

The loss or decay of this trade, accounts for the present pretended decay of the town of Ipswich. The ships wore out, the masters died off, the trade took a new turn; Dutch flyboats taken in the war, thrust themselves into the coal-trade for the interest of the captors, such as the Yarmouth and London merchants, and others; and the Ipswich men dropped gradually out of it, being discouraged by those Dutch flyboats. These Dutch vessels which cost nothing but the caption, were bought cheap, carried great burthens, and the Ipswich building fell off for want of price, and so the trade decayed, and the town with it; I believe this will be owned for the true beginning of their decay, if I must allow it to be called a decay.

But to return to my passage up the river. In the winter time those great collier-ships, abovementioned, are always laid up, as they call it. That is to say, the coal trade abates at London, the citizens are generally furnished, their stores taken in, and the demand is over; so that the great ships, the northern seas and coast being also dangerous, the nights long, and the voyage hazardous, go to sea no more, but lie by, the ships are unrigged, the sails, &c. carried ashore, the top-masts struck, and they ride moored in the river, under the advantages and security of sound ground, and a high woody shore, where they lie as safe as in a wet dock. And it was a very agreeable sight to see, perhaps two hundred sail of ships, of all sizes lie in that posture every winter: all this while, which was usually from Michaelmas to Lady Day, the masters lived calm and secure with their families in Ipswich; and enjoying plentifully, what in the summer they got laboriously at sea, and this made the town of Ipswich very populous in the winter.

The sight of these ships thus laid up in the river, as I have said, was very agreeable to me in my passage from Harwich, about five and thirty years before the present journey; and it was in its proportion equally melancholy to hear, that there were now scarce 40 sail of good colliers that belonged to the whole town.

In a creek in this river called Lavington-Creek we saw at low water, such shoals, or hills rather, of mussels that great boats might have loaded with them, and no miss have been made of them. Near this creek Sir Samuel Barnardiston [27] had a very fine seat, as also a decoy for wild ducks, and a very noble estate.

Ipswich is seated, at the distance of 12 miles from Harwich, upon the edge of the river, which taking a short turn to the west, the town forms, there, a kind of semi-circle, or half moon upon the bank of the river. It is very remarkable, that though ships of 500 tons may upon a spring tide come up very near this town, and many ships of that burthen have been built there; yet the river is not navigable any farther than the town itself, or but very little; no not for the smallest boats, nor does the tide, which rises sometimes 13 or 14 foot, and gives them 24 foot water very near the town, flow much farther up the river than the town, or not so much as to make it worth speaking of.

He took little notice of the town, or at least of that part of Ipswich, who published in his wild observations[28] on it, that ships of 200 ton are built there. I affirm, that I have seen a ship of 400 ton launched at the building-yard, close to the town; and I appeal to the Ipswich colliers (those few that remain) belonging to this town, if several of them carrying seventeen score of coals, which must be upward of 400 ton, have not formerly been built here; but superficial observers, must be superficial writers, if they write at all; and to this day, at John's Ness, within a mile and half of the town it self, ships of any burthen may be built and launched even at neap tides. I am much mistaken too, if since the Revolution, some very good ships have not been built at this town, and particularly the *Melford* or *Milford*-galley, a ship of 40 guns; as the *Greyhound* frigate, a man of war of 36 to 40 guns, was at John's Ness.

But the neighbourhood of London, which sucks the vitals of trade in this island to itself, is the chief reason of any decay of business in this place; and I shall in the course of these observations, hint at it, where many good sea-ports and large towns, though farther off than Ipswich, and as well fitted for commerce, are yet swallowed up by the immense indraft of trade to the city of London; and more decayed beyond all comparison, than Ipswich is supposed to be. And if it be otherwise at this time, with some other towns, which are lately increased in trade and navigation, wealth, and people, while their neighbours decay, it is because they have some particular trade or accident to trade, which is a kind of nostrum to them, inseparable to the place, and which fixes there by the nature of the thing; as the herring-fishery to Yarmouth; the coal trade to New-Castle; the Leeds clothing-trade; the export of butter and lead, and the great corn trade for Holland, is to Hull; the Virginia and West-India trade at Liverpool, the Irish trade at Bristol, and the like. Thus the war has brought a flux of business and people, and consequently of wealth, to several places, as well as to Portsmouth, Chatham, Plymouth, Falmouth, and others; and were any wars like those, to continue 20 years with the Dutch, or any nation whose fleets lay that way, as the Dutch do, it would be the like perhaps at Ipswich in a few years, and at other places on the same coast.

But at this present time an occasion offers to speak in favour of this port; namely, the Greenland fishery,[29] lately proposed to be carried on by the South-Sea Company. On which account I may freely advance this, without any compliment to the town of Ipswich, no place in Britain, is equally qualified like Ipswich. Whether we respect the cheapness of building and fitting out their ships and shallops; also furnishing, victualling, and providing them with all kind of stores; convenience for laying up the ships after the voyage; room for erecting their magazines, ware-houses, rope-walks, cooperage, &c. on the easiest terms; and especially for the noisome cookery, which attends the boiling their blubber, which may be on this river, (as it ought to be) remote from any places of resort; then their nearness to the market for the oil when 'tis made, and, which above all, ought to be the chief thing considered in that trade, the easiness of their putting out to sea when they begin their voyage, in which the same wind that carries them from the mouth of the haven, is fair to the very seas of Greenland.

I could say much more to this point, if it were needful, and in few words could easily prove, that Ipswich must have the preference of all the port towns of Britain, for being the best centre of the Greenland trade. But whether we shall ever arrive at so happy a time, as to recover so useful a trade to our country, which our ancestors had the honour to be the first undertakers of, and which has been lost only through the indolence of others, and the increasing vigilance of our neighbours, that is not my business here to dispute. What I have said, is only to let the world see, what improvement this town and port is capable of; I cannot think, but that Providence, which made nothing in vain, cannot have reserved so useful, so convenient a port to lie vacant in the world, but that the time will some time or other come (especially considering the improving temper of the present age) when some peculiar beneficial business may be found out, to make the port of Ipswich as useful to the world, and the town as flourishing, as nature has made it proper and capable to be.

As for the town, it is true, it is but thinly inhabited, in comparison of the extent of it; but to say, there are hardly any people to be seen there, is far from being true in fact; and whoever thinks fit to look into the churches and meeting-houses on a Sunday, or other public days, will find there are very great numbers of people there.

It happened to be my lot to be once at this town, at the time when a very fine new ship, which was built there, for some merchants of London, was to be launched; and if I may give my guess at the numbers of people which appeared on the shore, in the houses, and on the river, I believe I am much within compass, if I say there were 20,000 people to see it; but this is only a guess. But a view of the town is one of the surest rules for a gross estimate. It is true, here is no settled manufacture: the French refugees, when they first came over to England, began a little to take to this place; and some merchants attempted to set up a linen manufacture in their favour; but it has not met with so much success as was expected, and at present I find very little of it. The poor people are however employed, as they are all over these counties, in spinning wool for other towns where manufactures are settled.

The country round Ipswich, as are all the counties so near the coast, is applied chiefly to corn, of which a very great quantity is continually shipped off for London; and sometimes they load corn here for Holland, especially if the market abroad is encouraging. They have 12 parish-churches in this town, with three or four meetings; but there are not so many Quakers here as at Colchester, and no Anabaptists, or Antipoedo Baptists, that I could hear of, at least there is no meeting-house of that denomination. There is one meeting-house for the Presbyterians, one for the Independents, and one for the Quakers: the first is as large and as fine a building of that kind as most on this side of England, and the inside the best finished of any I have seen, London not excepted; that for the Independents is a handsome new-built building, but not so gay or so large as the other.

There is a great deal of very good company in this town; and though there are not so many of the gentry here as at Bury, yet there are more here than in any other town in the county; and I observed particularly, that the company you meet with here, are generally persons well informed of the world, and who have something very solid and entertaining in their society. This may happen, perhaps, by their frequent conversing with those who have been abroad, and by their having a remnant of gentlemen and masters of ships among them, who have seen more of the world than the people of an inland town are likely to have seen. I take this town to be one of the most agreeable places in England, for families who have lived well, but may have suffered in our late calamities of stocks and bubbles, to retreat to, where they may live within their own compass; and several things indeed recommend it to such;

1. Good houses, at very easy rents.
2. An airy, clean, and well governed town.

3. Very agreeable and improving company almost of every kind.

4. A wonderful plenty of all manner of provisions, whether flesh or fish, and very good of the kind.

5. Those provisions very cheap; so that a family may live cheaper here, than in any town in England of its bigness, within such a small distance from London.

6. Easy passage to London, either by land or water, the coach going through in a day.

The large spire steeple,[30] which formerly stood upon that they call the Tower-Church, was blown down by a great storm of wind many years ago, and in its fall did much damage to the church. The government of this town is by two bailiffs, as at Yarmouth: and two justices. There has been lately a very great struggle between the two parties for the choice of these two magistrates, which had this amicable conclusion, namely, that they chose one of either side; so that neither party having the victory, 'tis to be hoped it may be a means to allay the heats and un-neighbourly feuds, which such things breed in towns so large as this is.

There are some things very curious to be seen here, however some superficial writers have been ignorant of them. Dr Beeston,[31] an eminent physician, began, a few years ago, a physic garden adjoining to his house in this town; and as he is particularly curious, and as I was told exquisitely skilled in botanic knowledge, so he has been not only very diligent, but successful too, in making a collection of rare and exotic plants, such as are scarce to be equalled in England.

From Ipswich I took a turn into the country to Hadley, principally to satisfy my curiosity, and see the place where that famous martyr, and pattern of charity and religious zeal in Queen Mary's time, Dr Rowland Taylor,[32] was put to death; the inhabitants, who have a wonderful veneration for his memory, show the very place where the stake which he was bound to, was set up, and they have put a stone upon it, which no body will remove; but it is a more lasting monument to him that he lives in the hearts of the people. I say more lasting than a tomb of marble would be, for the memory of that good man will certainly never be out of the poor people's minds, as long as this island shall retain the Protestant religion among them; how long that may be, as things are going, and if the detestable conspiracy of the Papists now on foot, should succeed, I will not pretend to say.

A little to the left is Sudbury, which stands upon the River Stour. I know nothing for which this town is remarkable, except for being very populous and very poor. They have a great manufacture of says and perpetuana's; and multitudes of poor people are employed in working them; but the number of the poor is almost ready to eat up the rich. However this town sends two members to Parliament, though it is under no form of government particularly to itself, other than as a village, the head magistrate whereof is a constable. Near adjoining to it, is a village called Long-Melfort, and a very long one it is, from which I suppose it had that addition to its name; it is full of very good houses, and, as they told me, is richer, and has more wealthy masters of the manufacture in it than in Sudbury itself.

From this part of the country I returned north-west by Lenham, to visit St Edmund's Bury, a town of which other writers have talked very largely, and perhaps a little too much. It is a town famed for its pleasant situation and wholesome air, the Montpelier of Suffolk, and perhaps of England; this must be attributed to the skill of the monks of those times, who chose so beautiful a situation for the seat of their retirement; and who built here the greatest and in its time, the most flourishing monastery in all these parts of England, I mean the monastery of St Edmund the Martyr. It was, if we believe antiquity, a house of pleasure in more ancient times; or to speak more properly, a court of some of the Saxon or East-Angle kings; and as Mr Camden says, was even then called a royal village;[33] though it much better merits that name now; it being the town of all this part of England, in proportion to its bigness, most thronged with gentry, people of the best fashion, and the most polite conversation. This beauty and healthiness of its situation, was no doubt the occasion which drew the clergy to settle here, for they always chose the best places in the country to build in, either for richness of soil, or for health and pleasure in the situation of their religious houses.

For the like reason, I doubt not, they translated the bones of the martyred King St Edmund, to this place; for it is a vulgar error to say he was murthered here. His martyrdom, it is plain was at Hoxon or Henilsdon, near Harlston, on the Waveney, in the farthest northern verge of the county; but Segebert, King of the East Angles, had built a religious house in this pleasant rich part of the country; and as the monks began to taste the pleasure of the place, they procured the body of this saint to be removed hither, which soon increased the wealth and revenues of their house, by the zeal of that day, in going on pilgrimage to the shrine of the blessed St Edmund.

We read however, that after this, the Danes under King Sweno,[34] over-running this part of the country, destroyed this monastery and burnt it to the ground, with the church and town; but see the turn religion gives to things in the world. His son King Canutus, at first a pagan and a tyrant, and the most cruel ravager of all that crew, coming to turn Christian; and being touched in conscience for the soul of his father, in having robbed God and His holy martyr St Edmund, sacrilegiously destroying the church, and plundering the monastery; I say, touched with remorse, and, as the monks pretend terrified with a vision of St Edmund appearing to him, he rebuilt the house, the church, and the town also, and very much added to the wealth of the abbot and his fraternity, offering his crown at the feet of St Edmund, giving the house to the monks, town and all; so that they were absolute lords of the town, and governed it by their steward for many ages.

The abbey is demolished; its ruins are all that is to be seen of its glory. Out of the old building, two very beautiful churches are built, and serve the two parishes, into which the town is divided, and they stand both in one church-yard. Here it was, in the path-way between these two churches, that a tragical and almost unheard of act of barbarity [35] was committed, which made the place less pleasant for some time, than it used to be, when Arundel Coke, Esq; a barrister at law, of very ancient family, attempted, with the assistance of a barbarous assassin, to murther in cold blood, and in the arms of hospitality, Edward Crisp, Esq; his brother-in-law, leading him out from his own house, where he had invited him, his wife and children, to supper: I say, leading him out in the night, on pretence of going to see some friend that was known to them both; but in this church-yard, giving a signal to the assassin he had hired, he attacked him with a hedge bill, and cut him, as one might say, almost in pieces; and when they did not doubt of his being dead, they left him. His head and face was so mangled, that it may be said to be next to a miracle that he was not quite killed. Yet so Providence directed for the exemplary punishment of the assassins, that the gentleman recovered to detect them, who, (though he out-lived the assault) were both executed as they deserved, and Mr Crisp is yet alive. They were condemned on the statute for defacing and dismembering, called the Coventry Act. But this accident does not at all lessen the pleasure and agreeable delightful show of the town of Bury; it is crowded with nobility and gentry, and all sorts of the most agreeable company; and as the company invites, so there is the appearance of pleasure upon the very situation; and they that live at Bury, are supposed to live there for the sake of it.

The Duke of Grafton,[36] now Lord Lieutenant of Ireland, has also a stately house at Euston, near this town, which he enjoys in right of his mother, daughter to the Earl of Arlington, one of the chief ministers of state in the reign of King Charles II and who made the second letter in the word CABAL; a word formed by that famous satirist Andrew Marvell, to represent the five heads of the politics of that time.

I shall believe nothing so scandalous of the ladies of this

town and the county round it, as a late writer [37] insinuates. That the ladies round the country appear mighty gay and agreeable at the time of the fair in this town, I acknowledge; one hardly sees such a show in any part of the world; but to suggest they come hither as to a market, is so coarse a jest that the gentlemen that wait on them hither, (for they rarely come but in good company) ought to resent and correct him for it.

It is true, Bury-Fair, like Bartholomew-Fair, is a fair for diversion, more than for trade; and it may be a fair for toys and for trinkets, which the ladies may think fit to lay out some of their money in, as they see occasion. But to judge from thence, that the knights' daughters of Norfolk, Cambridge-shire, and Suffolk, come hither to be picked up, is a way of speaking I never before heard any author have the assurance to make use of in print. The assemblèe he justly commends for the bright appearance of the beauties; but with a sting in the tail of this compliment, where he says, they seldom end without some considerable match or intrigue; and yet he owns, that during the fair, these assemblèes are held every night. Now that these fine ladies go intriguing every night, and that too after the comedy is done, which is after the fair and raffling is over for the day; so that it must be very late. This is a terrible character for the ladies of Bury, and intimates in short, that most of them are whores, which is a horrid abuse upon the whole country.

Now, though I like not the assemblèes at all, and shall in another place give them something of their due; yet having the opportunity to see the fair at Bury, and to see that there were indeed abundance of the finest ladies, or as fine as any in Britain, yet I must own, the number of the ladies at the comedy, or at the assemblèe, is no way equal to the number that are seen in the town, much less are they equal to the whole body of the ladies in the three counties, and I must also add, that though it is far from true, that all that appear at the assemblèe, are there for matches or intrigues, yet I will venture to say, that they are not the worst of the ladies who stay away; neither are they the fewest in number, or the meanest in beauty, but just the contrary. And I do not at all doubt, but that the scandalous liberty some take at those assemblèes, will in time bring them out of credit with the virtuous part of the sex here, as it has done already in Kent and other places; and that those ladies who most value their reputation, will be seen less there than they have been; for though the institution of them has been innocent and virtuous, the ill use of them, and the scandalous behaviour of some people at them, will in time arm virtue against them, and they will be laid down as they have been set up, without much satisfaction. But the beauty of this town consists in the number of gentry who dwell in and near it, the polite conversation among them; the affluence and plenty they live in; the sweet air they breathe in, and the pleasant country they have to go abroad in.

This town is famous for two great events, one was that in the year 1447, in the 25th year of Henry the VIth, a Parliament was held here. The other was, that at the meeting of this Parliament, the great Humphry, Duke of Glocester,[38] regent of the kingdom, during the absence of King Henry the Vth, and the minority of Henry the VIth, and to his last hour, the safeguard of the whole nation, and darling of the people, was basely murthered here; by whose death, the gate was opened so that dreadful war between the Houses of Lancaster and York, which ended in the confusion of that very race, who are supposed to have contrived the murther.

From St Edmund's Bury I returned by Stow-Market and Needham, to Ipswich, that I might keep as near the coast as was proper to my designed circuit or journey; and from Ipswich, to visit the sea again, I went to Woodbridge, and from thence to Orford, on the sea-side. Woodbridge has nothing remarkable, but that it is a considerable market for butter and corn to be exported to London; for now begins that part which is ordinarily called High-Suffolk; which being a rich soil, is for a long tract of ground, wholly employed in dairies; and again famous for the best butter, and perhaps the worst cheese, in England. The butter is barrelled, or often pickled up in small casks, and sold, not in London only, but I have known a firkin of Suffolk butter sent to the West-Indies, and brought back to England again, and has been perfectly good and sweet, as at first. From hence turning down to the shore, we see Orford Ness, a noted point of land for the guide of the colliers and coasters, and a good shelter for them to ride under, when a strong north-east wind blows and makes a foul shore on the coast. Orford was once a good town, but is decayed, and as it stands on the land-side of the river, the sea daily throws up more land to it, and falls off itself from it, as if it was resolved to disown the place, and that it should be a sea port no longer. A little farther lies Albro', as thriving, though without a port, as the other is decaying, with a good river in the front of it.

From Albro' to Dunwich, there are no towns of note; even this town seems to be in danger of being swallowed up; for fame reports, that once they had fifty churches in the town; I saw but one left, and that not half full of people. This town is a testimony of the decay of public things, things of the most durable nature; and as the old poet expresses it,

> By numerous examples we may see,
> That towns and cities die, as well as we.

The ruins of Carthage, or the great city of Jerusalem, or of ancient Rome, are not at all wonderful to me; the ruins of Nineveh, which are so entirely sunk, as that 'tis doubtful where the city stood; the ruins of Babylon, or the great Persepolis, and many capital cities, which time and the change of monarchies have overthrown; these, I say, are not at all wonderful, because being the capitals of great and flourishing kingdoms, where those kingdoms were overthrown, the capital cities necessarily fell with them. But for a private town, a sea-port, and a town of commerce, to decay, as it were of itself (for we never read of Dunwich being plundered, or ruined, by any disaster, at least not of late years); this I must confess, seems owing to nothing but to the fate of things, by which we see that towns, kings, countries, families, and persons, have all their elevation, their medium, their declination, and even their destruction in the womb of time, and the course of nature. It is true, this town is manifestly decayed by the invasion of the waters, and as other towns seem sufferers by the sea, or the tide withdrawing from their ports, such as Orford just now named; Winchelsea in Kent, and the like: so this town is, as it were, eaten up by the sea, as above; and the still encroaching ocean seems to threaten it with a fatal immersion in a few years more.

Yet Dunwich, however ruined, retains some share of trade, as particularly for the shipping off butter, cheese, and corn, which is so great a business in this county, and it employs a great many people and ships also; and this port lies right against the particular part of the county for butter, as Framlingham, Halstead, &c. Also a very great quantity of corn is brought up hereabout for the London market; for I shall still touch that point, how all the counties in England contribute something towards the subsistence of the great city of London.

Hereabouts they begin to talk of herrings, and the fishery; and we find in the ancient records, that this town, which was then equal to a large city; paid, among other tribute to the Government, 50000 of herrings. Here also, and at Swole, or Southole, the next sea-port, they cure sprats in the same manner as they do herrings at Yarmouth; that is to say, speaking in their own language, they made red sprats; or to speak good English, they make sprats red. It is remarkable, that this town is now so much washed away by the sea, that what little trade they have, is carried on by Walderswick, a little town near Swole, the vessels coming in there, because the ruins of Dunwich make the shore there unsafe and uneasy to the boats; from whence the northern coasting seamen a rude verse of their own using, and I suppose of their own making; as follows,

Swoul and Dunwich, and Walderswick,
All go in at one lousie creek.

This lousy creek, in short, is a little river at Swoul, which our late famous atlas-maker calls a good harbour for ships, and rendezvous of the royal navy; but that by the bye; the author it seems knew no better.

From Dunwich, we came to Southwold, the town above-named; this is a small port-town upon the coast, at the mouth of a little river called the Blith. There is but one church in this town, but it is a very large one and well-built, as most of the churches in this county are, and of impenetrable flint; indeed there is no occasion for its being so large, for staying there one Sabbath-Day, I was surprised to see an extraordinary large church, capable of receiving five or six thousand people, and but twenty-seven in it besides the parson and the clerk; but at the same time the meeting-house of the dissenters was full to the very doors, having, as I guessed from 6 to 800 people in it.

This town is made famous for a very great engagement at sea, in the year 1672, between the English and Dutch fleets, in the bay opposite to the town; in which, not to be partial to ourselves, the English fleet was worsted; and the brave Montague [39] Earl of Sandwich, admiral under the Duke of York, lost his ship. The ship *Royal Prince*, carrying 100 guns, in which he was, and which was under him, was burnt, and several other ships lost, and about 600 seamen; part of those killed in the fight, were, as I was told, brought on shore here and buried in the church-yard of this town, as others also were at Ipswich.

At this town in particular, and so at all the towns on this coast, from Orford-Ness to Yarmouth, is the ordinary place where our summer friends the swallows, first land when they come to visit us; and here they may be said to embark for their return, when they go back into warmer climates; and, as I think the following remark, though of so trifling a circumstance, may be both instructing, as well as diverting, it may be very proper in this place. The case is this; I was some years before at this place, at the latter end of the year (viz.) about the beginning of October, and lodging in a house that looked into the church-yard, I observed in the evening an unusual multitude of birds sitting on the leads of the church; curiosity led me to go nearer to see what they were, and I found they were all swallows; that there was such an infinite number that they covered the whole roof of the church, and of several houses near, and perhaps might, of more houses which I did not see. This led me to enquire of a grave gentleman whom I saw near me, what the meaning was of such a prodigious multitude of swallows sitting there; O SIR, says he, turning towards the sea, you may see the reason, the wind is off sea. I did not seem fully informed by that expression; so he goes on: I perceive, sir, says he, you are a stranger to it; you must then understand first, that this is the season of the year when the swallows, their food here failing, begin to leave us, and return to the country, where-ever it be, from whence they came; and this being the nearest to the coast of Holland, they come here to embark; this he said smiling a little; and now, sir, says he, the weather being too calm, or the wind contrary, they are waiting for a gale, for they are all wind-bound. This was more evident to me, when in the morning I found the wind had come about to the north-west in the night, and there was not one swallow to be seen, of near a million, which I believe was there the night before.

How those creatures know that this part of the island of Great-Britain is the way to their home, or the way that they are to go; that this very point is the nearest cut over, or even that the nearest cut is best for them, that we must leave to the naturalists to determine, who insist upon it, that brutes cannot think. Certain it is, that the swallows neither come hither for warm weather, nor retire from cold, the thing is of quite another nature; they, like the shoals of fish in the sea, pursue their prey; they are a voracious creature, they feed flying; their food is found in the air, viz. the insects; of which in our summer evenings, in damp and moist places, the air is full; they come hither in the summer, because our air is fuller of fogs and damps than in other countries, and for that reason, feeds great quantities of insects; if the air be hot and dry, the gnats die of themselves, and even the swallows will be found famished for want, and fall down dead out of the air, their food being taken from them. In like manner, when cold weather comes in, the insects all die, and then of necessity, the swallows quit us, and follow their food where-ever they go; this they do in the manner I have mentioned above; for sometimes they are seen to go off in vast flights like a cloud. And sometimes again, when the wind grows fair, they go away a few and a few, as they come, not staying at all upon the coast.

I find very little remarkable on this side of Suffolk, but what is on the sea shore as above; the inland country is that which they properly call High-Suffolk, and is full of rich feeding-grounds and large farms, mostly employed in dairies for making the Suffolk butter and cheese, of which I have spoken already. Among these rich grounds stand some market-towns, though not of very considerable note; such as Framlingham, where was once a royal castle, to which Queen Mary [40] retired, when the Northumberland faction, in behalf of the Lady Jane, endeavoured to supplant her; and it was this part of Suffolk where the Gospellers,[41] as they were then called, preferred their loyalty to their religion, and complimented the popish line at expense of their share of the Reformation; but they paid dear for it, and their successors have learned better politics since.

In these parts are also several good market-towns, some in this county, and some in the other, as Becles, Bungay, Harlston, &c. And here in a bye-place, and out of common remark, lies the ancient town of Hoxon,[42] famous for being the place where St Edmund was martyred, for whom so many cells and shrines have been set up, and monasteries built; and in honour of whom, the famous monastery of St Edmund's Bury above-mentioned, was founded.

This part of England is also remarkable for being the first where the feeding and fattening of cattle, both sheep as well as black cattle with turnips, was first practised in England, which is made a very great part of the improvement of their lands to this day; and from whence the practice is spread over most of the east and south parts of England, to the great enriching of the farmers, and increase of fat cattle. And though some have objected against the goodness of the flesh thus fed with turnips, and have fancied it would taste of the root; yet upon experience 'tis found, that at market there is no difference nor can they that buy, single out one joint of mutton from another by the taste. So that the complaint which our nice palates at first made, begins to cease of itself; and a very great quantity of beef, and mutton also, is brought every year, and every week to London, from this side of England.

I can't omit, however little it may seem, that this county of Suffolk is particularly famous for furnishing the city of London and all the counties round, with turkeys; and that it is thought, there are more turkeys bred in this county, and the part of Norfolk that adjoins to it, than in all the rest of England, especially for sale. Nor will it be found so inconsiderable an article as some may imagine, if this be true which I received an account of from a person living on the place, (viz.) that they have counted 300 droves of turkeys (for they drive them all in droves on foot) pass in one season over Stratford-Bridge on the River Stour, on the road from Ipswich to London. These droves, as they say, generally contain from three hundred to a thousand each drove; so that one may suppose them to contain 500 one with another, which is 150000 in all; and yet this is one of the least passages, the numbers which travel by New Market-Heath, and the open country and the forest, and also by Sudbury and Clare, being many more.

For the further supplies of the markets of London with poultry, of which these countries particularly abound: they have within these few years found it practicable to make the geese travel on foot too, as well as the turkeys; and a prodigious number are brought up to London in droves from the farthest parts of Norfolk. They begin to drive them generally in August, by which time the harvest is almost over, and the geese may feed in the stubbles as they go. Thus they hold on to the end of October, when the roads begin to be too stiff and deep for their broad feet and short legs to march in. Besides these methods of driving these creatures on foot, they have of late also invented a new method of carriage, being carts formed on purpose, with four stories or stages, to put the creatures in one above another, by which invention one cart will carry a very great number and for the smoother going, they drive with two horses a-breast, like a coach, so quartering the road for the ease of the gentry that thus ride; changing horses they travel night and day; so that they bring the fowls 70, 80, or 100 miles in two days and one night. The horses in this new-fashioned voiture go two a-breast, as above, but no perch below as in a coach, but they are fastened together by a piece of wood lying cross-wise upon their necks, by which they are kept even and together, and the driver sits on the top of the cart, like as in the public carriages for the army, &c. In this manner they hurry away the creatures alive, and infinite numbers are thus carried to London every year.

In this part, which we call High-Suffolk, there are not so many families of gentry or nobility placed, as in the other side of the country. But 'tis observed that though their seats are not so frequent here, their estates are; and the pleasure of West Suffolk is much of it supported by the wealth of High-Suffolk; for the richness of the lands, and application of the people to all kinds of improvement, is scarce credible.

From High-Suffolk, I passed the Waveney into Norfolk, near Schole-Inn; in my passage I saw at Redgrave, (the seat of the family) a most exquisite monument of Sir John Holt,[43] Knight, late Lord Chief Justice of the King's-Bench, several years, and one of the most eminent lawyers of his time.

When we come into Norfolk, we see a face of diligence spread over the whole country; the vast manufactures carried on (in chief) by the Norwich weavers, employs all the country round in spinning yarn for them; besides many thousand packs of yarn which they receive from other countries, even from as far as Yorkshire, and Westmoreland, of which I shall speak in its place. This side of Norfolk is very populous, and thronged with great and spacious market-towns, more and larger than any other part of England so far from London, except Devonshire, and the West-riding of Yorkshire; for example, between the frontiers of Suffolk and the city of Norwich on this side, which is not above 22 miles in breadth, are the following market-towns, viz.

Thetford,	Hingham,	Harleston,
Dis,	West Deerham,	E. Deerham,
Harling,	Attleboro',	Watton,
Bucknam,	Windham,	Loddon, &c.

Most of these towns are very populous and large; but that which is most remarkable is, that the whole country round them is so interspersed with villages, and those villages so large, and so full of people, that they are equal to market-towns in other counties. An eminent weaver of Norwich, gave me a scheme of their trade on this occasion, by which, calculating from the number of looms at that time employed in the city of Norwich only, besides those employed in other towns in the same county, he made it appear very plain, that there were 120000 people employed in the woollen and silk manufactures of that city only, not that the people all lived in the city, though Norwich is a very large and populous city too: but I say, they were employed for spinning the yarn used for such goods as were all made in that city.

This shows the wonderful extent of the Norwich manufacture, or stuff-weaving trade, by which so many thousands of families are maintained. Their trade indeed felt a very sensible decay, and the cries of the poor began to be very loud, when the wearing of painted calicoes was grown to such an height in England, as was seen about two or three years ago. But an Act of Parliament[44] having been obtained, though not without great struggle, in the years 1720, and 1721, for prohibiting the use and wearing of calicoes, the stuff trade revived incredibly; and as I passed this part of the country in the year 1723, the manufacturers assured me, that there was not in all the eastern and middle part of Norfolk, any hand, unemployed, if they would work; and that the very children after four or five years of age, could every one earn their own bread.

This throng of villages continues through all the east part of the county, which is of the greatest extent, and where the manufacture is chiefly carried on. If any part of it be waste and thin of inhabitants, it is the west part, drawing a line from about Brand, or Brandon, south, to Walsingham, north. But put it all together, the county of Norfolk has the most people in the least tract of land of any county in England, except about London, and Exon, and the West-Riding of Yorkshire, as above. Add to this, that there is no single county in England, except as above, that can boast of three towns so populous, so rich, and so famous for trade and navigation, as in this county. By these three towns, I mean the city of Norwich, the towns of Yarmouth and Lynn; besides, that it has several other sea-ports of very good trade, as Wisbich, Wells, Burnham, Clye, &c.

Norwich is the capital of all the county and the centre of all the trade and manufactures which I have just mentioned; an ancient, large, rich, and populous city. If a stranger was only to ride through or view the city of Norwich for a day, he would have much more reason to think there was a town without inhabitants, than there is really to say so of Ipswich; but on the contrary, if he was to view the city, either on a Sabbath-day, or on any public occasion, he would wonder where all the people could dwell, the multitude is so great. But the case is this; the inhabitants being all busy at their manufactures, dwell in their garrets at their looms, and in their combing-shops, so they call them, twisting-mills, and other work-houses; almost all the works they are employed in, being done within doors. There are in this city thirty-two parishes besides the cathedral, and a great many meeting-houses of Dissenters of all denominations. The public edifices are chiefly the castle, ancient and decayed, and now for many years past made use of for a gaol. The Duke of Norfolk's house[45] was formerly kept well, and the gardens preserved for the pleasure and diversion of the citizens, but since feeling too sensibly the sinking circumstances of that once glorious family, who were the first peers and hereditary earl-marshals of England.

The walls of this city are reckoned three miles in circumference, taking in more ground than the city of London; but much of that ground lying open in pasture-fields and gardens; nor does it seem to be, like some ancient places, a decayed declining town, and that the walls mark out its ancient dimensions: but the walls seem to be placed, as if they expected that the city would in time increase sufficiently to fill them up with buildings. The cathedral of this city is a fine fabric, and the spire-steeple very high and beautiful. It is not ancient, the bishop's see having been first at Thetford; from whence it was not translated hither till the twelfth century; yet the church has so many antiquities in it, that our late great scholar and physician, Sir Tho. Brown,[46] thought it worth his while to write a whole book to collect the monuments and inscriptions in this church, to which I refer the reader.

Here is one thing indeed strange in itself, and more so, in that history seems to be quite ignorant of the occasion of it. The River Waveney is a considerable river, and of a deep and full channel, navigable for large barges as high as Beccles. It runs for a course of about fifty miles, between the two counties of Suffolk and Norfolk, as a boundary to both; and pushing on, though with a gentle stream, towards the sea, no one would doubt, but, that when they see the river growing broader and deeper and going directly towards the sea, even to the edge of the beach; that is to say, within a mile of the main ocean; no stranger, I say, but would expect to see its entrance into the sea at that place, and a noble harbour for ships at the mouth of it; when on a sudden, the land rising high by the sea-side, crosses the head of the river, like a dam, checks the whole course of it, and it returns, bending its course west, for two miles, or thereabouts; and then turning north, through another long course of meadows (joining to those just now mentioned) seeks out the River Yare, that it may join its water with her's, and find their way to the sea together.

Some of our historians tell a long fabulous story[47] of this river's being once open, and a famous harbour for ships belonging to the town of Leostof adjoining; but that the town of Yarmouth envying the prosperity of the said town of Leostof, made war upon them; and that after many bloody battles, as well by sea as by land, they came at last to a decisive action at sea with their respective fleets, and the victory fell to the Yarmouth men, the Leostof fleet being overthrown and utterly destroyed; and that upon this victory, the Yarmouth men either actually did stop up the mouth of the said river, or obliged the vanquished Leostof men to do it themselves, and bound them never to attempt to open it again. I believe my share of this story, and I recommend no more of it to the reader; adding, that I see no authority for the relation, neither do the relators agree either in the time of it, or in the particulars of the fact. So I satisfy myself with transcribing the matter of fact, and then leave it as I find it.

In this vast tract of meadows are fed a prodigious number of black cattle, which are said to be fed up for the fattest beef, though not the largest in England; and the quantity is so great, as that they not only supply the city of Norwich, the town of Yarmouth, and county adjacent, but send great quantities of them weekly in all the winter season, to London. And this in particular is worthy remark, that the gross of all the Scots cattle which come yearly into England, are brought hither, being brought to a small village lying north of the city of Norwich, called St Faiths, where the Norfolk graziers go and buy them. These Scots runts, so they call them, coming out of the cold and barren mountains of the Highlands in Scotland, feed so eagerly on the rich pasture in these marshes, that they thrive in an unusual manner, and grow monstrously fat; and the beef is so delicious for taste, that the inhabitants prefer 'em to the English cattle, which are much larger and fairer to look at, and they may very well do so.

Yarmouth is an ancient town, much older than Norwich; and at present, though not standing on so much ground, yet better built; much more complete; for number of inhabitants, not much inferior; and for wealth, trade, and advantage of its situation, infinitely superior to Norwich.

It is placed on a peninsula between the River Yare and the sea; the two last lying parallel to one another, and the town in the middle. The river lies on the west-side of the town, and being grown very large and deep, by a conflux of all the rivers on this side the county, forms the haven; and the town facing to the west also, and open to the river, makes the finest quay in England, if not in Europe, not inferior even to that of Marseilles itself.

The ships ride here so close, and as it were, keeping up one another, with their head-fasts on shore, that for half a mile together, they go across the stream with their bowsprits over the land, their bows, or heads, touching the very wharf; so that one may walk from ship to ship as on a floating bridge, all along by the shore-side. The quay reaching from the draw-bridge almost to the south-gate, is so spacious and wide, that in some places 'tis near one hundred yards from the houses to the wharf. In this pleasant and agreeable range of houses are some very magnificent buildings, and among the rest, some merchants' houses, which look like little palaces, rather than the dwelling-houses of private men.

The greatest defect of this beautiful town, seems to be, that though it is very rich and increasing in wealth and trade, and consequently in people, there is not room to enlarge the town by building; which would be certainly done much more than it is, but that the river on the land-side prescribes them, except at the north end without the gate; and even there the land is not very agreeable. But had they had a larger space within the gates, there would before now have been many spacious streets of noble fine buildings erected, as we see is done in some other thriving towns in England, as at Liverpool, Manchester, Bristol, Frome, &c.

The quay and the harbour of this town during the fishing-fair, as they call it, which is every Michaelmas, one sees the land covered with people, and the river with barks and boats, busy day and night, landing and carrying off the herrings, which they catch here in such prodigious quantities, that it is incredible. This fishing-fair begins on Michaelmas Day, and lasts all the month of October, by which time the herrings draw off to sea, shoot their spawn, and are no more fit for the merchants' business; at least not those that are taken thereabouts.

The quantity of herrings that are catched in this season are diversely accounted for; some have said, that the towns of Yarmouth and Leostof only, have taken forty thousand last in a season. I will not venture to confirm that report; but this I have heard the merchants themselves say, (viz.) that they have cured, that is to say, hanged and dried in the smoke 40,000 barrels of merchantable redherrings in one season, which is in itself (though far short of the other) yet a very considerable article; and it is to be added, that this is besides all the herrings consumed in the country towns of both those populous counties, for thirty miles from the sea, whither very great quantities are carried every tide during the whole season.

But this is only one branch of the great trade carried on in this town. Another part of this commerce, is in the exporting these herrings after they are cured; and for this their merchants have a great trade to Genoa, Leghorn, Naples, Messina, and Venice as also to Spain and Portugal also exporting with their herring very great quantities of worsted stuffs, and stuffs made of silk and worsted; camblets, &c. the manufactures of the neighbouring city of Norwich, and the places adjacent. Besides this, they carry on a very considerable trade with Holland, whose opposite neighbours they are; and a vast quantity of woollen manufactures they export to the Dutch every year. They have also a considerable trade to

Norway, and to the Baltic, from whence they bring back deals, and fir-timber, oaken plank, baulks, spar, oars, pitch, tar, hemp, flax, spruce canvas, and sail-cloth; with all manner of naval stores, which they generally have a consumption for in their own port, where they build a very great number of ships every year, besides re-fitting and repairing the old. Add to this the coal trade between Newcastle and the river of Thames, in which they are so improved of late years, that they have now a greater share of it than any other town in England.

For the carrying on all these trades, they must have a very great number of ships, either of their own, or employed by them; and it may in some measure be judged of by this, that in the year 1697, I had an account from the town register, that there was then 1123 sail of ships using the sea, and belonged to the town, besides such ships as the merchants of Yarmouth might be concerned in, and be part-owners of, belonging to any other ports. To all this I must add, without compliment to the town, or to the people, that the merchants, and even the generality of traders of Yarmouth, have a very good reputation in trade, as well abroad as at home, for men of fair and honourable dealing, punctual and just in their performing their engagements, and in discharging commissions; and their seamen, as well masters as mariners, are justly esteemed among the ablest and most expert navigators in England.

This town however populous and large, was ever contained in one parish, and had but one church; but within these two years they have built another very fine church, near the south-end of the town. This old church, is very large, and has a high spire, which is a useful sea-mark. Here is one of the finest market-places, and the best served with provisions, in England, London excepted, and the inhabitants are so multiplied in a few years, that they seem to want room in their town, rather than people to fill it, as I have observed above. The streets are all exactly straight from north to south, with lanes or alleys, which they call rows, crossing them in straight lines also from east to west; so that it is the most regular built town in England, and seems to have been built all at once. Or, that the dimensions of the houses, and extent of the streets, were laid out by consent.

They have particular privileges in this town, and a jurisdiction by which they can try, condemn, and execute in especial cases, without waiting for a warrant from above; and this they exerted once very smartly, in executing a captain of one of the king's ships of war in the reign of King Charles II, for a murther committed in the street.[48] It is also a very well governed town; and I have no where in England observed the Sabbath-Day so exactly kept, or the breach so continually punished as in this place, which I name to their honour. Among all these regularities, it is no wonder if we do not find abundance of revelling, or that there is little encouragement to assemblies, plays, and gaming-meetings at Yarmouth, as in some other places; and yet I do not see that the ladies here come behind any of the neighbouring counties, either in beauty, breeding, or behaviour; to which may be added too, not at all to their disadvantage, that they generally go beyond them in fortunes.

From Yarmouth I resolved to pursue my first design, (viz.) to view the sea-side on this coast, which is particularly famous for being one of the most dangerous and most fatal to the sailors in all England, I may say in all Britain; and the more so, because of the great number of ships which are continually going and coming this way, in their passage between London and all the northern coasts of Great-Britain. From Winterton Ness, which is the utmost northerly point of land in the county of Norfolk, and about four miles beyond Yarmouth, the shore falls off for near sixty miles to the west, as far as Lynn and Boston, till the shore of Lincolnshire tends north again for about sixty miles more, as far as the Humber, whence the coast of Yorkshire, or Holderness, which is the East Riding, shoots out again into the sea, to the Spurn, and to Flambro' Head, as far east almost as the shore of Norfolk had given back at Winterton, making a very deep gulf or bay, between those two points of Winterton and the Spurn Head; so that the ships going north, are obliged to stretch away to sea from Winterton Ness, and leaving the sight of land in that deep bay which I have mentioned, that reaches to Lynn, and the shore of Lincolnshire, they go, I say, N. or still N.N.W. to meet the shore of Holderness, which I said runs out into the sea again at the Spurn; this they leave also and the first land they make, or desire to make, is called as above, Flambro' Head; so that Winterton Ness and Flambro' Head, are the two extremes of this course, there is, as I said, the Spurn Head indeed between; but as it lies too far in towards the Humber, they keep out to the north to avoid coming near it.

In like manner the ships which come from the north, leave the shore at Flambro' Head, and stretch away S.S.E. for Yarmouth Roads; and the first land they make is Winterton Ness (as above). Now, the danger of the place is this: if the ships coming from the north are taken with a hard gale of wind from the S.E. or from any point between N.E. and S.E. so that they cannot, as the seamen call it, weather Winterton Ness, they are thereby kept in within that deep bay; and if the wind blows hard, are often in danger of running on shore upon the rocks about Cromer, on the north coast of Norfolk, or stranding upon the flat shore between Cromer and Wells. All the relief they have, is good ground tackle to ride it out, which is very hard to do there, the sea coming very high upon them, or if they cannot ride it out then, to run into the bottom of the great bay I mentioned, to Lynn or Boston, which is a very difficult and desperate push: so that sometimes in this distress whole fleets have been lost here all together.

The like is the danger to ships going northward, if after passing by Winterton they are taken short with a north-east wind, and cannot put back into the Roads, which very often happens, then they are driven upon the same coast, and embayed just at the latter. The dangers of this place being thus considered, 'tis no wonder, that upon the shore beyond

Yarmouth, there are no less than four light-houses kept flaming every night, besides the lights at Castor, north of the town, and at Goulston S, all which are to direct the sailors to keep a good offing, in case of bad weather, and to prevent their running into Cromer Bay, which the seamen call the Devil's Throat.

As I went by land from Yarmouth northward, along the shore towards Cromer aforesaid, and was not then fully master of the reason of these things, I was surprised to see, in all the way from Winterton, that the farmers, and country people had scarce a barn, or a shed, or a stable; nay, not the pales of their yards, and gardens, not a hogsty, not a necessary-house, but what was built of old planks, beams, wales and timbers, &c. the wrecks of ships, and ruins of mariners' and merchants' fortunes.

About the year 1692, (I think it was that year) there was a melancholy example of what I have said of this place; a fleet of 200 sail of light colliers (so they call the ships bound northward empty to fetch coals from Newcastle to London) went out of Yarmouth Roads with a fair wind, to pursue their voyage, and were taken short with a storm of wind at N.E., after they were past Winterton Ness, a few leagues; some of them, whose masters were a little more wary than the rest, or perhaps, who made a better judgement of things, or who were not so far out as the rest, tacked, and put back in time, and got safe into the roads; but the rest pushing on, in hopes to keep out to sea, and weather it, were by the violence of the storm driven back, when they were too far embayed to weather Winterton Ness, as above; and so were forced to run west, every one shifting for themselves, as well as they could. Some run away for Lyn Deeps but few of them, (the night being so dark) could find their way in there; some but very few rid it out, at a distance; the rest being above 140 sail were all driven on shore, and dashed to pieces, and very few of the people on board were saved. At the very same unhappy juncture, a fleet of loaden ships were coming from the north, and being just crossing the same bay, were forcibly driven into it, not able to weather the Ness, and so were involved in the same ruin as the light fleet was; also some coasting vessels loaden with corn from Lyn, and Wells, and bound for Holland, were with the same unhappy luck just come out, to begin their voyage, and some of them lay at anchor; these also met with the same misfortune, so that in the whole, above 200 sail of ships, and above a thousand people perished in the disaster of that one miserable night, very few escaping.

Cromer is a market town close to the shore of this dangerous coast, I know nothing it is famous for (besides it's being thus the terror of the sailors) except good lobsters, which are taken on that coast in great numbers, and carried to Norwich, and in such quantities sometimes too, as to be conveyed by sea to London.

Farther within the land, and between this place and Norwich, are several good market towns, and innumerable villages, all diligently applying to the woollen manufacture, and the country is exceeding fruitful and fertile, as well in corn as in pastures; particularly, (which was very pleasant to see) the pheasants were in such great plenty, as to be seen in the stubbles like cocks and hens; a testimony though (by the way) that the county had more tradesmen than gentlemen in it. Indeed this part is so entirely given up to industry, that what with the seafaring men on the one side, and the manufactures on the other, we saw no idle hands here, but every man busy on the main affair of life, that is to say, getting money.

From Cromer, we ride on the strand or open shore to Weyburn Hope, the shore so flat that in some places the tide ebbs out near two miles. From Weyburn west lies Clye, where there are large salt-works, and very good salt made, which is sold all over the county, and some times sent to Holland, and to the Baltick. From Clye, we go to Masham, and to Wells, all towns on the coast, in each whereof there is a very considerable trade carried on with Holland for corn, which that part of the county is very full of. I say nothing of the great trade driven here from Holland, back again to England, because I take it to be a trade carried on with much less honesty than advantage; especially while the clandestine trade, or the art of smuggling was so much in practice; what it is now, is not to my present purpose.

From hence we turn to the S.W. to Castle-Rising, an old decayed borough town with perhaps not ten families in it, which yet (to the scandal of our prescription right) sends two members to the British Parliament, being as many as the city of Norwich it self, or any town in the kingdom, London excepted can do.

On our left we see Walsingham, an ancient town, famous for the old ruins of a monastery of note there, and the shrine of our Lady, as noted as that of St Thomas-a-Becket at Canterbury, and for little else. Near this place are the seats of the two allied families of the Lord Viscount Townsend,[49] and Robert Walpole, Esq.; the latter at this time one of the Lords Commissioners of the Treasury, and minister of state, and the former one of the principal Secretaries of State to King GEORGE.

From hence we went to Lyn, another rich and populous thriving port-town. It stands on more ground than the town of Yarmouth, and has I think parishes, yet I cannot allow that it has more people than Yarmouth, if so many. It is a beautiful well built, and well situated town, at the mouth of the River Ouse, and has this particular attending it, which gives it a vast advantage in trade; namely, that there is the greatest extent of inland navigation here, of any port in England, London excepted. The reason whereof is this, that there are more navigable rivers empty themselves here into the sea, including the Washes which are branches of the same port, than at any one mouth of waters in England, except the Thames and the Humber. By these navigable rivers the merchants of Lynn supply about six counties wholly, and three counties in part, with their goods, especially wine and coals, which has given rise to this observation on the town of Lynn, that they bring in more coals, than any sea-port between London and Bristol.

Here are more gentry, and consequently is more gaiety in this town than in Yarmouth, or even in Norwich it self; the place abounding in very good company. The situation of this town renders it capable of being made very strong, and in the late wars it was so; a line of fortification being drawn round it at a distance from the walls; the ruins, or rather remains of which works appear very fair to this day; nor would it be a hard matter to restore the bastions, with the ravelins and counterscarp, upon any sudden emergency, to a good state of defence; and that in a little time, a sufficient number of workmen being employed, especially because they are able to fill all their ditches with water from the sea, in such a manner as that it cannot be drawn off.

They pass over here in boats into the fen-country, and over the famous washes into Lincolnshire, but the passage is very dangerous and uneasy, and where passengers often miscarry and are lost; but then it is usually on their venturing at improper times, and without the guides, which if they would be persuaded not to do, they would very rarely fail of going or coming safe.

From Lynn, I bent my course to Downham, where is an ugly wooden bridge over the Ouse; from whence we passed the fen country to Wisbech, but saw nothing that way to tempt our curiosity but deep roads, innumerable drains and dykes of water, all navigable, and a rich soil, the land bearing a vast quantity of good hemp; but a base unwholesome air. So we came back to Ely, whose cathedral, standing in a level flat country, is seen far and wide; and of which town, when the minster, so they call it, is described, every thing remarkable is said that there is room to say; and of the minster this is the most remarkable thing that I could hear, namely, that some of it is so ancient, totters so much with every gust of wind, looks so like a decay, and seems so near it, that when ever it does fall, all that 'tis likely will be thought strange in it, will be, that it did not fall a hundred years sooner.

From hence we came over the Ouse, and in a few miles to

Newmarket. In our way near Snaybell we saw a noble seat of the late Admiral Russel, now Earl of Orford,[50] a name made famous by the glorious victory obtained under his command over the French fleet, and the burning their ships at La Hogue; a victory equal in glory to, and infinitely more glorious to the English nation in particular, than that at Blenheim, and above all more to the particular advantage of the Confederacy, because it so broke the heart of the naval power of France, that they have not fully recovered it to this day.

Being come to Newmarket in the month of October, I had the opportunity to see the horse-races; and a great concourse of the nobility and gentry, as well from London as from all parts of England; but they were all so intent, so eager, so busy upon the sharping part of the sport, their wagers and bets, that to me they seemed just as so many horse-coursers in Smithfield, descending (the greatest of them) from their high dignity and quality, to picking one another's pockets, and biting one another as much as possible, and that with such eagerness, as that it might be said they acted without respect to faith, honour, or good manners.

There was Mr Frampton,[51] the oldest, and as some say, the cunningest jockey in England, one day he lost 1000 guineas, the next he won two thousand; and so alternately he made as light of throwing away five hundred or one thousand pounds at a time, as other men do of their pocket-money, and as perfectly calm, cheerful, and unconcerned, when he had lost one thousand pounds, as when he had won it. On the other side, there was Sir R—— Fagg,[52] of Sussex, of whom fame says he has the most in him and the least to show for it, relating to jockeyship, of any man there; yet he often carried the prize; his horses, they said, were all cheats, how honest soever their master was; for he scarce ever produced a horse but he looked like what he was not, and was what no body could expect him to be. If he was as light as the wind, and could fly like a meteor, he was sure to look as clumsy, and as dirty, and as much like a cart-horse as all the cunning of his master and the grooms could make him; and just in this manner he bit some of the greatest gamesters in the field.

Here I fancied myself in the Circus Maximus at Rome, seeing the ancient games, and the racings of the chariots and horsemen; and in this warmth of my imagination I pleased and diverted myself more and in a more noble manner, than I could possibly do in the crowds of gentlemen at the weighing and starting posts, and at their coming in; or at their meetings at the coffee-houses and gaming-tables after the races were over, where there was little or nothing to be seen, but what was the subject of just reproach to them, and reproof from every wise man that looked upon them. *N.B.* Pray take it with you as you go, you see no ladies at New-Market, except a few of their neighbouring gentlemen's families who come in their coaches on any particular day to see a race and so go home again directly.

From thence I went to Rushbrook, formerly the seat of the noble family of Jermyns, lately Lord Dover, and now of the house of Davers. Here Nature, for the time I was there, drooped, and veiled all the beauties of which she once boasted; the family being in tears, and the house shut up; Sir Robert Davers,[53] the head thereof, and knight of the shire for the county of Suffolk, and who had married the eldest daughter of the late Lord Dover, being just dead, and the corpse lying there in its funeral form of ceremony, not yet buried; yet all looked lovely in their sorrow, and a numerous issue promising and grown up, intimated that the family of Davers would still flourish, and that the beauties of Rushbrook, the mansion of the family, were not formed with so much art in vain, or to die with the present possessor.

After this we saw Brently, the seat of the Earl of Dysert,[54] with several others of exquisite situation, and adorned with the beauties both of art and nature; so that I think, any traveller from abroad, who would desire to see how the English gentry live, and what pleasures they enjoy, should come into Suffolk and Cambridgeshire, and take but a light circuit among the country seats of the gentlemen on this side only, and they would be soon convinced, that not France, no not Italy itself, can out-do them, in proportion to the climate they lived in.

We enter Cambridgeshire out of Suffolk with all the advantage in the world; the county beginning upon those pleasant and agreeable plains called New Market-Heath, where passing the Devil's Ditch, which has nothing worth notice but its name, and that but fabulous too, from the hills called Gogmagog, we see a rich and pleasant vale westward, covered with corn-fields, gentlemen's seats, villages, and at a distance, to crown all the rest, that ancient and truly famous town and university of Cambridge; capital of the county.

As my business is not to lay out the geographical situation of places, I say nothing of the buttings and boundings of this county. It lies on the edge of the great level, called by the people here the fen-country; and great part, if not all, the Isle of Ely, lies in this county and Norfolk. The rest of Cambridgeshire is almost wholly a corn country; and of that corn five parts in six of all they sow, is barley. As Essex, Suffolk, and Norfolk, are taken up in manufacturing, and famed for industry, this county has no manufacture at all; nor are the poor, except the husbandmen, famed for any thing so much as idleness and sloth, to their scandal be it spoken; what the reason of it is, I know not.

It is scarce possible to talk of anything in Cambridgeshire but Cambridge itself; whether it be that the county has so little worth speaking of in it, or that the town has so much, that I leave to others. I first had a view of Cambridge from Gogmagog Hills. As we descended westward, we saw the fen country on our right, almost all covered with water like a sea, the Michaelmas rains having been very great that year, they had sent down great floods of water from the upland countries, and those fens being, as may be very properly said, the sink of no less than thirteen counties; that is to say, that all the water, or most part of the water of thirteen counties, falls into them, they are often thus overflowed. The rivers which thus empty themselves into these fens, and which thus carry off the water, are the Cam or Grant, the Great Ouse, and Little Ouse, the Nene, the Welland, and the river which runs from Bury to Milden-Hall. In a word, all the water of the middle part of England which does not run into the Thames or the Trent, comes down into these fens.

In these fens are abundance of those admirable pieces of art called duckoys; that is to say, places so adapted for the harbour and shelter of wild-fowl, and then furnished with a breed of those they call decoy-ducks, who are taught to allure and entice their kind to the places they belong to, that it is incredible what quantities of wild-fowl of all sorts, duck, mallard, teal, widgeon, &c. they take in those duckoys every week, during the season. It may indeed be guessed at a little by this, that there is a duckoy not far from Ely, from which they assured me at St Ives, (a town on the Ouse, where the fowl they took was always brought to be sent to London;) that they generally sent up three thousand couple a week.

As these fens appear covered with water, so I observed too, that they generally at this latter part of the year appear also covered with fogs, so that when the Downs and higher grounds of the adjacent country were gilded by the beams of the sun, the Isle of Ely looked as if wrapped up in blankets, and nothing to be seen, but now and then, the lanthorn or cupola of Ely Minster.

One could hardly see this from the hills and not pity the many thousands of families that were bound to or confined in those fogs, and had no other breath to draw than what must be mixed with those vapours, and that steam which so universally overspread the country. But notwithstanding this, the people, especially those that are used to it, live unconcerned, and as healthy as other folks, except now and then an ague, which they make light of, and there are great numbers of very ancient people among them.

I now draw near to Cambridge, to which I fancy I look as if I was afraid to come, having made so many circumlocutions beforehand; but I must yet make another digression before I enter the town; I cannot omit, that I came necessarily through Sturbridge Fair, which was then in its height. If it is a diversion worthy a book to treat of trifles, such as the gaiety of Bury Fair, it cannot be very unpleasant, especially to the trading part of the world, to say something of this fair, which is not only the greatest in the whole nation, but in the world; nor, if I may believe those who have seen them all, is the fair at Leipsick in Saxony, the mart at Frankfort on the Main, or the fairs at Neuremberg, or Augsburg, any way to compare to this fair at Sturbridge. It is kept in a large corn-field, near Casterton, extending from the side of the River Cam, towards the road, for about half a mile square. If the husbandmen who rent the land, do not get their corn off before a certain day in August, the fair-keepers may trample it under foot and spoil it to build their booths, or tents; for all the fair is kept in tents, and booths. On the other hand, to balance that severity, if the fair-keepers have not done their business of the fair, and removed and cleared the field by another certain day in September, the ploughmen may come in again, with plough and cart, and overthrow all and trample it into the dirt; and as for the filth, dung, straw, &c. necessarily left by the fair-keepers, the quantity of which is very great, it is the farmers' fees, and makes them full amends for the trampling, riding, and carting upon, and hardening the ground.

It is impossible to describe all the parts and circumstances of this fair exactly; the shops are placed in rows like streets, whereof one is called Cheapside; and here, as in several other streets, are all sorts of trades, who sell by retail, and who come principally from London with their goods. Scarce any trades are omitted, goldsmiths, toyshops, braziers, turners, milliners, haberdashers, hatters, mercers, drapers, pewterers, china-warehouses, and in a word all trades that can be named in London; with coffee-houses, taverns, brandy-shops, and eating-houses, innumerable, and all in tents, and booths, as above.

This great street reaches from the road, which as I said goes from Cambridge to New-Market, turning short out of it to the right towards the river, and holds in a line near half a mile quite down to the river-side. In another street parallel with the road are like rows of booths, but larger, and more intermingled with wholesale dealers, and one side, passing out of this last street to the left hand, is a formal great square, formed by the largest booths, built in that form, and which they call the Duddery; whence the name is derived, and what its signification is, I could never yet learn, though I made all possible search into it. The area of this square is about 80 to a 100 yards, where the dealers have room before every booth to take down, and open their packs, and to bring in waggons to load and unload.

This place is separated, and peculiar to the wholesale dealers in the woollen manufacture. Here the booths, or tents, are of a vast extent, have different apartments, and the quantities of goods they bring are so great, that the insides of them look like another Blackwell-Hall, being as vast ware-houses piled up with goods to the top. In this Duddery, as I have been informed, there have been sold one hundred thousand pounds worth of woollen manufactures in less than a week's time, besides the prodigious trade carried on here, by wholesale-men, from London, and all parts of England, who transact their business wholly in their pocket-books, and meeting their chapmen from all parts, make up their accounts, receive money chiefly in bills, and take orders. These they say exceed by far the sales of goods actually brought to the fair, and delivered in kind; it being frequent for the London wholesale men to carry back orders from their dealers for ten thousand pounds worth of goods a man, and some much more.

Here are clothiers from Hallifax, Leeds, Wakefield and Huthersfield in Yorkshire, and from Rochdale, Bury, &c. in Lancashire, with vast quantities of Yorkshire cloths, kerseys, pennistons, cottons, &c. with all sorts of Manchester ware, fustians, and things made of cotton wool; of which the quantity is so great, that they told me there were near a thousand horse-packs of such goods from that side of the country, and these took up a side and half of the Duddery at least.

But all this is still outdone, at least in show, by two articles, which are the peculiars of this fair, and do not begin till the other part of the fair, that is to say for the woollen manufacture, begins to draw to a close. These are the WOOL, and the HOPS, as for the hops, there is scarce any price fixed for hops in England, till they know how they sell at Sturbridge Fair; the quantity that appears in the fair is indeed prodigious, and they, as it were, possess a large part of the field on which the fair is kept, to themselves.

Enquiring why this fair should be thus, of all other places in England, the centre of that trade; and so great a quantity of so bulky a commodity be carried thither so far: I was answered by one thoroughly acquainted with that matter thus: the hops, said he, for this part of England, grow principally in the two counties of Surrey and Kent, with an exception only to the town of Chelmsford in Essex, and there are very few planted any where else. There are indeed in the west of England some quantities growing; as at Wilton, near Salisbury; at Hereford and Broomsgrove, near Wales, and the like; but the quantity is inconsiderable, and the places remote, so that none of them come to London. As to the north of England they formerly used but few hops there, their drink being chiefly pale smooth ale, which required no hops, and consequently they planted no hops in all that part of England, north of Trent; nor did I ever see one acre of hop-ground planted beyond Trent, in my observations; but as for some years past, they not only brew great quantities of beer in the north; but also use hops in the brewing their ale much more than they did before; so they all come south of Trent to buy their hops; and here being vast quantities bought, 'tis great part of their back carriage into Yorkshire, and Northamptonshire, Derbyshire, Lancashire, and all those counties; nay, of late, since the Union, even to Scotland it self; for I must not omit here also to mention, that the river Grant, or Cam, which runs close by the N.W. side of the fair in its way from

Cambridge to Ely, is navigable, and that by this means, all heavy goods are brought even to the fair-field, by water carriage from London, and other parts; first to the port of Lynn, and then in barges up the Ouse, from the Ouse into the Cam, and so, as I say, to the very edge of the fair.

Now as there is still no planting of hops in the north, though a great consumption, and the consumption increasing daily, this, says my friend, is one reason why at Sturbridge Fair there is so great a demand for the hops: he added, that besides this, there were very few hops, if any worth naming, growing in all the counties even on this side Trent, which were above forty miles from London; those counties depending on Sturbridge Fair for their supply, so the counties of Suffolk, Norfolk, Cambridge, Huntingdon, Northampton, Lincoln, Leicester, Rutland, and even to Stafford, Warwick and Worcestershire, bought most if not all of their hops at Sturbridge Fair.

The next article brought hither, is wool, and this of several sorts, but principally fleece wool, out of Lincolnshire, where the longest staple is found; the sheep of those countries being of the largest breed. Here I saw what I have not observed in any other country of England, namely, a pocket of wool. This seems to be first called so in mockery, this pocket being so big, that it loads a whole waggon, and reaches beyond the most extreme parts of it, hanging over both before, and behind, and these ordinarily weigh a ton or 25 hundred weight of wool, all in one bag. The quantity of wool only, which has been sold at this place at one fair, has been said to amount to fifty or sixty thousand pounds in value, some say a great deal more.

I might go on here to speak of several other sorts of English manufactures, which are brought hither to be sold; as all sorts of wrought iron, and brass ware from Birmingham; edged tools, knives, &c. from Sheffield; glass ware, and stockings, from Nottingham, and Leicester; and an infinite throng of other things of smaller value, every morning.

To attend this fair, and the prodigious conflux of people, which come to it, there are sometimes no less than fifty hackney coaches, which come from London, and ply night and morning to carry the people to and from Cambridge; for there the gross of the people lodge. It is not to be wondered at, if the town of Cambridge cannot receive, or entertain the numbers of people that come to this fair; not Cambridge only, but all the towns round are full; nay, the very barns, and stables are turned into inns, and made as fit as they can to lodge the meaner sort of people. As for the people in the fair, they all universally eat, drink, and sleep in their booths, and tents; and the said booths are so intermingled with taverns, coffee-houses, drinking-houses, eating-houses, cooks-shops, &c. and all in tents too; that there's no want of any provisions of any kind, either dressed, or undressed. In a word, the fair is like a well fortified city, and there is the least disorder and confusion (I believe) that can be seen any where, with so great a concourse of people.

Towards the latter end of the fair, and when the great hurry of wholesale business begins to be over, the gentry come in, from all parts of the county round; and though they come for their diversion; yet 'tis not a little money they lay out; which generally falls to the share of the retailers, and some loose coins, they reserve for the puppet-shows, drolls, rope-dancers, and such like; of which there is no want, though not considerable like the rest. The last day of the fair is the horse-fair where the whole is closed with both horse and foot-races, to divert the meaner sort of people only, for nothing considerable is offered of that kind. Thus ends the whole fair and in less than a week more there is scarce any sign left that there has been such a thing there: except by the heaps of dung and straw; and other rubbish which is left behind, trod into the earth, and which is as good as a summer's fallow for dunging to the land; and as I have said above, pays the husbandmen well for the use of it.

I should have mentioned, that here is a court of justice always open, and held every day in a shed built on purpose in the fair; this is for keeping the peace, and deciding controversies in matters deriving from the business of the fair.

The magistrates of the town of Cambridge are judges in this court, as being in their jurisdiction, or they holding it by special privilege. Here they determine matters in a summary way, as is practised in those we call Pie-Powder Courts[55] in other places, or as a court of conscience; and they have a final authority without appeal.

I come now to the town, and university of Cambridge; I say the town and university, for though they are blended together in the situation, and the colleges, halls, and houses for literature are promiscuously scattered up and down among the other parts, and some even among the meanest of the other buildings; as Magdalen College over the bridge, is in particular; yet they are all incorporated together, by the name of the university, and are governed apart, and distinct from the town, which they are so intermixed with. The town is governed by a mayor, and aldermen. The university by a chancellor, and vice-chancellor, &c. Though their dwellings are mixed, and seem a little confused, their authority is not so; in some cases the vice-chancellor may concern himself in the town, as in searching houses for the scholars at improper hours, removing scandalous women, and the like. But as the colleges are many, and the gentlemen entertained in them are a very great number, the trade of the town very much depends upon them, and the tradesmen may just be said to get their bread by the colleges; and this is the surest hold the university may be said to have of the townsmen and by which they secure the dependence of the town upon them, and consequently their submission.

Thus I say, interest gives them authority; and there are abundance of reasons why the town should not disoblige the university, as there are some also on the other hand, why the university should not differ to any extremity with the town; nor, such is their prudence, do they let any disputes between them run up to any extremities, if they can avoid it. As for society; to any man who is a lover of learning, or of learned men, here is the most agreeable under heaven; nor is there any want of mirth and good company of other kinds. But 'tis to the honour of the university to say, that the governors so well understand their office, and the governed their duty, that here is very little encouragement given to those seminaries of crime the assemblies, which are so much boasted of in other places. Again, as dancing, gaming, intriguing, are the three principal articles which recommend those assemblies; and that generally the time for carrying on affairs of this kind, is the night, and sometimes all night; a time as unseasonable as scandalous; add to this, that the orders of the university admit no such excesses: I therefore say, as this is the case, 'tis to the honour of the whole body of the university, that no encouragement is given to them here.

The present vice-chancellor is Dr Snape,[56] formerly Master of Eaton School near Windsor; and famous for his dispute with and evident advantage over the late Bishop of Bangor, in the time of his government. The dispute between the university and the Master of Trinity College has been brought to a head, so as to employ the pens of the learned on both sides; but at last prosecuted in a judicial way, so as to deprive Dr Bently of all his dignities and offices in the university; but the Dr flying to the royal protection, the university is under a writ of mandamus, to shew cause why they do not restore the doctor again, to which it seems they demur, and that demur has not, that we hear, been argued, at least when these sheets were sent to the press; what will be the issue time must show.

From Cambridge the road lies north-west, on the edge of the fens, to Huntingdon, where it joins the Great North-Road; on this side, 'tis all an agreeable corn country, as above; adorned with several seats of gentlemen, but the chief is the noble house, seat, or mansion of Wimple, or Wimple-Hall, formerly built at a vast expense, by the late Earl of Radnor;[57] adorned with all the natural beauties of situation; and to which was added all the most exquisite contrivances which the best head could invent to make it artificially as well as naturally pleasant. However, the fate of the Radnor family so directing, it was bought with the whole estate about it, by the late Duke of Newcastle; in a partition of whose immense estate, it fell to the Right Honourable the Lord Harley, (son and heir apparent of the present Earl of Oxford and Mortimer) in right of the Lady Harriot Cavendish, only daughter of the said Duke of Newcastle, who is married to his lordship, and brought him this estate, and many other, sufficient to denominate her the richest heiress in Great-Britain.

From Cambridge, my design obliging me, and the direct road, in part concurring, I came back through the west part of the county of Essex, and at Saffron Walden I saw the ruins of the once largest and most magnificent pile in all this part of England, (viz.) Audley End; built by, and decaying with the noble Dukes and Earls of Suffolk.

As we came on this side we saw at a distance Braintree and Bocking, two towns, large, rich and populous, and made so originally by the bay trade, of which I have spoken at large at Colchester, and which flourishes still among them. The manor of Braintree I found descended by purchase, to the name of Olmeus,[58] the son of a London merchant of the same name; making good what I had observed before, of the great number of such who have purchased estates in this county. Near this town is Felsted, a small place, but noted for a free-school, of an ancient foundation; for many years under the mastership of the late reverend Mr Lydiat,[59] and brought by him to the meridian of its reputation; 'tis now supplied, and that very worthily, by the reverend Mr Hutchins. Near to this is the priory of Lees, a delicious seat of the late Dukes of Manchester, but sold by the present duke[60] to the Duchess Dowager of Bucks; his grace the Duke of Manchester removing to his yet finer seat of Kimbolton in Northamptonshire, the ancient mansion of the family.

From hence we crossed the country to the great forest, called Epping Forest, reaching almost to London. The country on that side of Essex is called the Roodings, I suppose because there are no less than ten towns almost together, called by the name of Roding, and is famous for good land, good malt, and dirty roads; the latter indeed in the winter are scarce passable for horse or man. In the midst of this we see Chipping Onger, Hatfield Broad-Oak, Epping, and many forest-towns, famed, as I have said, for husbandry and good malt; but of no other note. On the south-side of the county is Waltham-Abbey; the ruins of the abbey remain; and though antiquity is not my proper business, I could not but observe, that King Harold,[61] slain in the great battle in Sussex against William the Conqueror, lies buried here; his body being begged by his mother, the Conqueror allowed it to be carried hither; but no monument was, as I can find, built for him, only a flat grave-stone, on which was engraven, *Harold Infælix*.

From hence I came over the forest again, that is to say, over the lower or western part of it, where it is spangled with fine villages, and these villages filled with fine seats, most of them built by the citizens of London, as I observed before; but the lustre of them seems to be entirely swallowed up in the magnificent palace of the Lord Castlemain,[62] whose father, Sir Josiah Child, as it were, prepared it in his life for the design of his son, though altogether unforeseen by adding to the advantage of its situation innumerable rows of trees, planted in curious order for avenues and visto's, to the house, all leading up to the place where the old house stood, as to a centre.

In the place adjoining, his lordship, while he was yet Sir Richard Child only, and some years before he began the foundation of his new house, laid out the most delicious as well as most spacious pieces of ground for gardens that is to be seen in all this part of England. The green-house is an excellent building fit to entertain a prince; and these gardens have been so the just admiration of the world, that it has been the general diversion of the citizens to go out to see them, till the crowds grew too great, and his lordship was obliged to restrain his servants from showing them, except on one or two days in a week only. As the front of the house opens to a long row of trees, reaching to the great road at Leighton Stone; so the back-face, or front, if that be proper, respects the gardens, and with an easy descent lands you upon the terrace, from whence is a most beautiful prospect to the river, which is all formed into canals and openings, to answer the views from above, and beyond the river, the walks and wildernesses go on to such a distance, and in such a manner up the hill, as they before went down, that the sight is lost in the woods adjoining, and it looks all like one planted garden as far as the eye can see.

I shall cover as much as possible the melancholy part of a story, which touches too sensibly, many, if not most of the great and flourishing families in England. Pity and matter of grief is it to think that families, by estate, able to appear in such a glorious posture as this, should ever be vulnerable by so mean a disaster as that of stock-jobbing. But the general infatuation of the day is a plea for it; so that men are not now blamed on that account. South-Sea was a general possession; and if my Lord Castlemain was wounded by that arrow shot in the dark, 'twas a misfortune. But 'tis so much a happiness, that it was not a mortal wound, as it was to some men, who once seemed as much out of the reach of it; and that blow, be it what it will, is not remembered for joy of the escape; for we see this noble family, by prudence and management rise out of all that cloud, if it may be allowed such a name, and shining in the same full lustre as before.

This cannot be said of some other families in this county, whose fine parks and new-built palaces are fallen under forfeitures and alienations by the misfortunes of the times, and by the ruin of their masters' fortunes in that South-Sea deluge.

But I desire to throw a veil over these things, as they come in my way; 'tis enough that we write upon them as was written upon King Harold's tomb at Waltham-Abbey, INFÆLIX, and let all the rest sleep among things that are the fittest to be forgotten.

From my Lord Castlemain's house, I went south, towards

the great road over that part of the forest called the Flatts. By this turn I came necessarily on to Stratford, where I set out. And thus having finished my first circuit, I conclude my first letter;[63] and am,

SIR,

Your most humble,

And obedient servant.

Letter 2

Containing a description of the Sea-Coasts of Kent, Sussex, Hampshire, and of part of Surrey

SIR, – As in my first journey I went over the eastern counties of ENGLAND, and took my course on that side the River Thames, to view the sea-coasts, harbours, &c. so being now to traverse the southern counties, I begin with the other side of the Thames, and shall surround the sea-coast of KENT, as I did that of NORFOLK and SUFFOLK, and perhaps it is as fruitful of instructing and diverting observations as any of the other.

I took boat at Tower-Wharf, sending my horses round by land to meet me at Greenwich, that I might begin my journey at the beginning of the county, and here I had the advantage of making my first step into the county of Kent, at a place which is the most delightful spot of ground in Great-Britain; pleasant by situation, those pleasures increased by art, and all made completely agreeable by the accident of fine buildings, the continual passing of fleets of ships up and down the most beautiful river in Europe; the best air, best prospect, and the best conversation in England.

The Royal Hospital for Seamen, though not yet finished; the park, the Queen's House, the Observatory on the hill, commonly called Flamstead-House,[1] are all things so well known, they need no particular description. The ground, part of this hospital now stands upon, and is to stand upon, is the same on which formerly stood the royal palace of our kings. Here Henry VIII held his royal feasts with jousts and tournaments, and the ground which was called the Tilt-yard, is the spot on which the easternmost wing of the hospital is built; the park,[2] (for it was even then a park also) was enlarged, walled about, and planted with beautiful rows, or walks of trees by King Charles II soon after the Restoration; and the design or plan of a royal palace was then laid out, one wing of which was finished and covered in a most magnificent manner, and makes now the first wing of the hospital as you come to it from London. The building is regular, the lower part a strong Doric, the middle part a most beautiful Corinthian, with an Attic above all, to complete the height; the front to the water-side is extremely magnificent and graceful; embellished with rich carved work and fine devices, such as will hardly be outdone in this, or any age for beauty or art.

But the beauty of Greenwich is owing to the lustre of its inhabitants, where there is a kind of collection of gentlemen, rather than citizens, and of persons of quality and fashion, different from most, if not all, the villages in this part of England. Here several of the most active and useful gentlemen of the late armies, after having grown old in the service of their country, and covered with the honours of the field, are retired to enjoy the remainder of their time, and reflect with pleasure upon the dangers they have gone through, and the faithful services they have performed both abroad and at home.

Other gentlemen still in service, as in the navy ordnance, docks, yards, &c. as well while in business, as after laying down their employments, have here planted themselves, insomuch, that the town of Greenwich begins to out-swell its bounds, and extends itself not only on this side the park to the top of the heath, by the way called Crum-Hill, but now stretches out on the east-side, where Sir John Vanburg[3] has built a house castlewise, and where in a little time 'tis probable, several streets of like buildings will be erected, to the enlarging and beautifying the town, and increasing the inhabitants; who, as I have said, are already the chief beauty and ornament of the place.

The country behind Greenwich adds to the pleasure of the place: Black-Heath, both for beauty of situation, and an excellent air, is not out-done by any spot of ground so near the river and so near land in England. On the east-side stands an hospital [4] very particular for its foundation or design, though through the misfortunes of the times, the generous design of the founder has been much straitened, and in great part, defeated. It was built by Sir John Morden, a Turkey merchant of London; his first design, as I had it from his own mouth the year before he began to build, was to make apartments for forty decayed merchants, to whom he resolved to allow 40l. per annum, each; with coals, a gown, (and servants to look after their apartments) and many other conveniences so as to make their lives as comfortable as possible, and that, as they had lived like gentlemen, they might die so. Sir John Morden and his lady lie buried in a vault in the chancel of the chapel of this hospital. The chapel is a very neat building facing the entrance into the court; the lodgings for the merchants, are on either side two apartments in each stair case, with cellars for their conveniences, coals, beer, &c. and each apartment consists of a bed-chamber, and a study, or large closet, for their retreat, and to divert themselves in with books, &c. There is a velvet pall given, by her ladyship in particular, to be laid up in the chapel for the use of the gentlemen; as also a large quantity of communion-plate; and the chaplain is obliged to read prayers twice every day, viz. at eleven a clock, and at three at which all the pensioners are obliged to attend.

On the other side of the heath, north, is Charleton, a village famous, or rather infamous for the yearly collected rabble of mad-people, at Horn-Fair; the rudeness of which I cannot but think, is such as ought to be suppressed, and indeed in a civilized well governed nation, it may well be said to be unsufferable. The mob indeed at that time take all kinds of liberties, and the women are especially impudent for that day; as if it was a day that justified the giving themselves a loose to all manner of indecency and immodesty, without any reproach, or without suffering the censure which such behaviour would deserve at another time. The introduction of this rude assembly, or the occasion of it, I can meet with very little account of, in antiquity; and I rather recommend it to the public justice to be suppressed, as a nuisance and offence to all sober people, than to spend any time to inquire into its original. There are some very good houses lately built in this town, and abating the rabble and hurry of the 19th of October, as above, 'tis indeed a very pleasant village.

Through this town lies the road to Woolwich, a town on the bank of the same river, wholly taken up by, and in a manner raised from, the yards, and public works, erected there for the public service; here, when the business of the royal navy increased, and Queen Elizabeth built larger and greater ships of war than were usually employed before, new docks, and launches were erected, and places prepared for the building and repairing ships of the largest size; because, as here was a greater depth of water and a freer channel, than at Deptford, (where the chief yard in the river of Thames was before) so there was less hazard in the great ships going up and down.

At this dock the *Royal-Sovereign*[5] was built, once the largest ship in the whole royal navy, and in particular esteemed, for so large a ship, the best sailor in the world. Here also was rebuilt the *Royal Prince*, now called the *Queen*, a first rate, carrying a hundred guns, and several others. Close under the south-shore from the west-end of Woolwich, the Thames is very deep, and the men of war lie there moored, and as we call it, laid up; their topmasts, and all their small rigging taken down and laid in ware-houses; this reaches as high as the point over-against Bow-River and is called Bugby's-Hole.

Besides the building-yards, here is a large rope-walk where the biggest cables are made for the men of war; and on the east or lower part of the town is the gun-yard, or place set apart for the great guns belonging to the ships, commonly called the Park, or the Gun-Park; where is a prodigious quantity of all manner of ordnance-stores, such as are fit for sea-service, that is to say, cannon of all sorts for the ships of war, every ship's guns by themselves; heavy cannon for batteries, and mortars of all sorts and sizes. Here also is the house where the firemen and engineers prepare their fireworks, charge bombs, carcasses, and grenades for the public service, in time of war and here (if I remember right, it was in the time of a Dutch war) by mischance, the fire in the laboratory took hold of some combustibles, which spreading fired first a bomb or shell, and the bursting of that shell blew up all the works with such a terrible blast and noise, as shook and shattered the whole town of Woolwich almost in pieces, and terrified the people to the last degree, but killed no person as I heard of, except about eleven men who were in or near the fireworking house, where it first took hold.

In this park, close on the south bank of the river, a large battery of forty pieces of heavy cannon was raised, to have saluted the Dutch,[6] if they had thought fit to have ventured up the river in 1667, as was given out they would when they burnt our ships at Chatham; and large furnaces and forges were erected to have furnished the gunners with red hot bullets for that service; but the Dutch had no design that way and did their business with far less hazard, and as much to our disgrace in another place.

From this town there is little remarkable upon the river, till we come to Gravesend, the whole shore being low, and spread with marshes and unhealthy grounds, except with small intervals, where the land bends inward as at Erith, Greenwhich, North-Fleet, &c. in which places the chalk hills come close to the river, and from thence the city of London, the adjacent countries, and even Holland and Flanders, are supplied with lime, for their building, or chalk to make lime, and for other uses. Thus the barren soil of Kent, for such the chalky grounds are esteemed, make the Essex lands rich and fruitful, and the mixture of earth forms a composition, which out of two barren extremes, makes one prolific medium; the strong clay of Essex and Suffolk is made fruitful by the soft meliorating melting chalk of Kent, which fattens and enriches it.

On the back-side of these marshy grounds in Kent at a small distance, lies the road from London to Dover, and on that highway, or near it, several good towns; for example,

Eltham, formerly a royal palace when the Court was kept at Greenwich; and Queen Elizabeth, who was born at Greenwich,[7] was often carried, as they say, to Eltham by her nurses to suck in the wholesome air of that agreeable place; but at present there are few or no signs of the old palace to be seen.

It is now a pleasant town, very handsomely built, full of good houses, and many families of rich citizens inhabit here. So it is here, they bring a great deal of good company with them: also abundance of ladies of very good fortunes dwell here, and one sees at the church such an appearance of the sex, as is surprising. But 'tis complained of that the youths of these families where those beauties grow, are so generally or almost universally bred abroad, either in Turkey, Italy, or Spain, as merchants, or in the army or court as gentlemen; that for the ladies to live at Eltham, is, as it were, to live recluse and out of sight; since to be kept where the gentlemen do not come, is all one as to be kept where they cannot come. This they say threatens Eltham with a fatal turn, unless the scene alters in a few years, and they tell us, that all the ladies will abandon the place.

From this side of the country all pleasant and gay, we go over Shooter's Hill, where the face of the world seems quite altered; for here we have but a chalky soil, and indifferently fruitful, far from rich, much overgrown with wood, especially coppice-wood, which is cut for faggots and bavins, and sent up by water to London. Here they make those faggots which the wood-mongers call ostrey wood, and here in particular those small light bavins which are used in taverns in London to light their faggots, and are called in the taverns a brush, the woodmen call them pimps; 'tis incredible what vast quantities of these are laid up at Woolwich, Erith and Dartford; but since the taverns in London are come to make coal fires in their upper rooms, that cheat of a trade declines.

As I passed, I saw Gravesend from the hills, but having been often in the town, I know enough to be able to say, that there is nothing considerable in it; except first that it is the town where the great ferry (as they call it) is kept up between London and East-Kent, it is hardly credible what numbers of people pass here every tide, as well by night as by day, between this town and London. About 25 years ago one of these tilt-boats was cast away, occasioned by the desperate obstinacy and rudeness of the steersman or master, as they call him, who would tack again and stand over upon a wind, in the reach called Long-Reach, contrary to the advice and entreaties not of the passengers only but of his own rowers, who told him it blew a storm and she would founder; but he called them fools, bid the wind blow-devil, (a rude sailor's proverb) the more wind the better boat, till coming into the channel where the sea ran very high, he took in a wave, or a sea, as they call it, which run her down, and foundered her, as was foretold; and himself and three and fifty passengers were all drowned, only about five escaping by swimming.

The other thing for which this town is worth notice, is, that all the ships which go to sea from London, take, as we say, their departure from hence; for here all outward-bound ships must stop, come to an anchor, and suffer what they call a second clearing, (viz.) here a searcher of the customs comes on board, looks over all the coquets or entries of the cargo, and may, if he pleases, rummage the whole loading, to see if there are no more goods than are entered; which however they seldom do, though they forget not to take a compliment for their civility, and besides being well treated on board, have generally three or five guns fired in honour to them when they go off.

When a merchant-ship comes down from London ... as soon as they come among the ships that are riding in the road, the sentinel at the block-house, as they call it, on Gravesend side fires his musket, which is to tell the pilot he must bring too; if he comes on, as soon as the ship passes broad side with the block-house, the sentinel fires again, which is as much as to say, Why don't you bring too? if he drives a little farther, he fires a third time, and the language of that is, Bring to immediately, and let go your anchor, or we will make you. If the ship continues to drive down, and does not let go her anchor, the gunner of the fort is fetched, and he fires a piece of cannon though without ball; and that is still a threat, though with some patience, and is to say, Will you come to an anchor or won't you? If he still ventures to go on, by which he gives them to understand he intends to run for it; then the gunner fires again, and with a shot, and that shot is a signal to the fortress over the river, (viz.) Tilbury Fort, and they immediately let fly at the ship from the guns on the east bastion and after from all the guns they can bring to bear upon her; it is very seldom that a ship will venture their shot, because they can reach her all the way unto the Hope, and round the Hope-Point almost to Hole-Haven.

Yet I happened once to be upon the shore just by Tilbury-Fort, when a ship ventured to run off in spite of all those firings; and it being just at the first shoot of the ebb, and when a great fleet of light colliers and other ships were under sail too. By that time, the ship escaping came round the Hope-Point, she was so hid among the other ships, that the gunners on the bastion hardly knew who to shoot at; upon which they manned out several boats with soldiers, in hopes to overtake her or make signals to some men of war at the Nore, to man out their boats, and stop her, but she laughed at them all; for as it blew a fresh gale of wind at south-west, and a tide of ebb strong under her foot, she went three foot for their one, and by that time the boats got down to Hole Haven, the ship was beyond the Nore, and as it grew dark, they soon lost sight of her, nor could they ever hear to this day what ship it was, or on what account she ventured to run such a risk.

Another time I was with some merchants in a large yacht, bound to France; they had a great quantity of block-tin on board, and other goods, which had not been entered at the custom-house; and the master or captain told us, he did not doubt but he would pass by Gravesend without coming to an anchor. He lay, when this thought came into his head, at an anchor in Gray's Reach just above the Old Man's Head, which is a point or head of land on the Essex shore, which makes the upper end of Gravesend Reach. He observed that the mornings were likely to be exceeding foggy; particularly on the morning next after his resolution of trying there was so thick a fog, that it was scarce possible to see from the main-mast to the bow-sprit, even of a hoy; it being high water, he resolved to weigh and drive, as he called it, and so he did. When he came among the other ships and over against the town, his greatest danger was running foul of them, to prevent which he kept a man lying on his belly at the bow-sprit end, to look out, and so, though not without some danger too, he went clear. As for Gravesend or Tilbury-Fort, they could see no more of us than they could of London-Bridge; and we drove in this fog undiscerned by the forts of the custom-house men, as low as Hole-Haven, and went afterwards clear away to Caen in Normandy without being visited.

But such attempts as these, are what would very hardly be brought to pass again now, nor is the risk worth any body's running if the value be considerable that may be lost. As for ships coming in, they all go by here without any notice taken of them, unless it be to put waiters on board them, if they are not supplied before.

From Gravesend we see nothing remarkable on the road but GAD'S-HILL, a noted place for robbing of sea-men after they have received their pay at Chatham. Here it was that famous robbery was committed in the year 1676 or thereabouts; it was about four a clock in the morning when a gentleman was robbed by one Nicks on a bay mare, just on the declining part of the hill, on the west-side, for he swore to the spot and to the man. Mr Nicks [8] who robbed him, came away to Gravesend, immediately ferried over, and, as he said, was stopped by the difficulty of the boat, and of the passage, near an hour; which was a great discouragement to him, but was a kind of bait to his horse. From thence he rode cross the county of Essex, through Tilbury, Hornden, and Bilerecay to Chelmsford. Here he stopped about half an hour to refresh his horse, and gave him some balls; from thence to Braintre, Bocking, Wethersfield; then over the downs to Cambridge, and from thence keeping still the cross roads, he went by Fenny Stanton to Godmanchester, and Huntingdon, where he baited himself and his mare about an hour; and, as he said himself, slept about half an hour, then holding on the North Road, and keeping a full larger gallop most of the way, he came to York the same afternoon, put off his boots and riding clothes, and went dressed as if he had been an inhabitant of the place, not a traveller, to the bowling-green, where, among other gentlemen, was the Lord Mayor of the city; he singling out his lordship, studied to do something particular that the Mayor might remember him by, and accordingly lays some odd bets with him concerning the bowls then running, which should cause the Mayor to remember it the more particularly; and then takes occasion to ask his lordship what a clock it was; who, pulling out his watch, told him the hour, which was a quarter before, or a quarter after eight at night. Some other circumstances, it seems, he carefully brought into their discourse, which should make the Lord Mayor remember the day of the month exactly, as well as the hour of the day.

Upon a prosecution which happened afterwards for this robbery, the whole merit of the case turned upon this single point. The person robbed swore as above to the man, to the place, and to the time, in which the fact was committed: namely, that he was robbed on Gad's-Hill in Kent, on such a day, and at such a time of the day, and on such a part of the hill, and that the prisoner at the bar was the man that robbed him. Nicks, the prisoner, denied the fact, called several persons to his reputation, alleging that he was as far off as Yorkshire at that time, and that particularly the day whereon the prosecutor swore he was robbed, he was at bowls on the public green in the city of York; and to support this, he produced the Lord Mayor of York to testify that he was so, and that the mayor acted so and so with him there as above.

This was so positive, and so well attested, that the jury acquitted him on a bare supposition, that it was impossible the man could be at two places so remote on one and the same day. There are more particulars related of this story, such as I do not take upon me to affirm; namely, that King Charles II prevailed on him on assurance of pardon, and that he should not be brought into any further trouble about it, to confess the truth to him privately, and that he owned to his majesty that he committed the robbery, and how he rode the journey after it, and that upon this the king gave him the name or title of Swift Nicks, instead of Nicks; but these things, I say, I do not relate as certain: I return to the business in hand.

From Gad's-Hill we come to Rochester Bridge, the largest, highest, and the strongest built of all the bridges in England, except London-Bridge. Rochester, Stroud, and Chatham, are three distinct places, but contiguous, except the interval of the river between the two first, and a very small marsh or vacancy between Rochester and Chatham.

There's little remarkable in Rochester, except the ruins of a very old castle, and an ancient but not extraordinary cathedral; but the river, and its appendices are the most considerable of the kind in the world. This being the chief arsenal of the royal navy of Great-Britain. The buildings here are indeed like the ships themselves, surprisingly large, and in their several kinds beautiful. The ware-houses, or rather streets of ware-houses, and store-houses for laying up the naval treasure are the largest in dimension, and the most in number, that are any where to be seen in the world. The rope-walk for making cables, and the forges for anchors and other iron-work, bear a proportion to the rest as also the wet-dock for keeping masts, and yards of the greatest size, where they lie sunk in the water to preserve them, the boat-yard, the anchor yard; all like the whole, monstrously great and extensive, and are not easily described.

We come next to the stores themselves, for which all this provision is made; and first, to begin with the ships that are laid up there. The sails, the rigging, the ammunition, guns, great and small-shot, small-arms, swords, cutlasses, half pikes, with all the other furniture belonging to the ships that ride at their moorings in the river Medway. These take up one part of the place, where the furniture of every ship lies in particular ware-houses by themselves, and may be taken out on the most hasty occasion without confusion, fire excepted. N.B. The powder is generally carried away to particular magazines to avoid disaster. Besides these, there are store-houses for laying up the furniture and stores for ships; but which are not appropriated, or do not belong (as it is expressed by the officers) to any particular ship; but lie ready to be delivered out for the furnishing other ships to be built, or for repairing and supplying the ships already there, as occasion may require.

The particular government of these yards, as they are called is very remarkable, the commissioners, clerks, accomptants, &c. within doors, the store-keepers, yard-keepers, dock-keepers, watchmen, and all other officers without doors, with the subordination of all officers one to another respectively, as their degree and offices require, is admirable. In the river there is a guard-boat, which, as the main guard in a garrison, goes the grand-rounds at certain times, to see that every sentinel does his duty on board the ships; these go by every ship in the river, and see that the people on board are at their post. If the ship does not challenge, that is to say, if the man placed to look out does not call, Who comes there? the guard-boat boards them immediately, to examine who is deficient in their duty.

They told us an odd story of a guard-boat which having not been challenged by the person who ought to have been walking on the forecastle of the ship, boarded them on the bow, and as the boat's crew was entering the ship by the fore-chains they found a man fallen over board, but the lap of his coat catching in a block, was drawn so hard in by the running of the rope in the block, that it held the man fast; but he was fallen so low, that his head and arms hung in the water, and he was almost drowned. However it seems he was not quite dead; so that catching hold of him, and pulling him out of the water, they saved his life. But they added, as the main part of the story, that the man could never give any account of his disaster, or how he came to fall over-board, only said that it must be the Devil that threw him over-board, for nothing else could do it. How true this passage may be, I do not undertake to enter upon the debate of.

The expedition that has been sometimes used here in fitting out men of war, is very great, and as the workmen relate it, 'tis indeed incredible; particularly, they told us, that the *Royal Sovereign*,[9] a first rate of 106 guns, was riding at her moorings, entirely unrigged, and nothing but her three masts standing, as is usual when a ship is laid up, and that she was completely rigged, all her masts up, her yards put to, her sails bent, anchors and cables on board, and the ship sailed down to Black-Stakes in three days, Sir Cloudesly Shovell being then her captain. I do not vouch the thing, but when I consider, first, that every thing lay ready in her store-houses, and wanted nothing but to be fetched out and carried on board; a thousand or fifteen hundred men to be employed in it and more if they were wanted; and every man, knowing his business perfectly well, boats, carriages, pullies, tacklers, cranes, and hulk all ready, I do not know, but it might be done in one day if it was tried; certain it is, the dexterity of the English sailors in those things is not to be matched by the world.

The building-yards, docks, timber-yard, deal-yard, mast-yard, gun-yard, rope-walks and all the other yards and places, set apart for the works belonging to the navy, are like a well ordered city; and though you see the whole place as it were in the utmost hurry, yet you see no confusion, every man knows his own business; the master builders appoint the working, or converting, as they call it, of every piece of timber; and give to the other head workmen, or foremen their moulds for the squaring and cutting out of every piece, and placing it in its proper berth (so they call it) in the ship that is in building, and every hand is busy pursuing those directions, and so in all the other works.

It is about sixteen or eighteen miles from Rochester Bridge to Sheerness Fort by water on the River Medway, of this it is about fourteen miles to Black-Stakes, the channel is so deep all the way, the banks soft, and the reaches of the river so short, that in a word, 'tis the safest and best harbour in the world; and we saw two ships of eighty guns, each riding afloat at low water within musket-shot of Rochester Bridge. 'Tis as safe as in a wet-dock, nor did I ever hear of any accident that befell any of the king's ships here, I mean by storms and weather; except in that dreadful tempest [10] in 1703, when one ship, (viz) the *Royal Catherine* was driven on shore, and receiving some damage sunk, and the ship also being old, could not be weighed again; but this was such a storm as never was known before, and 'tis hoped the like may never be known again.

There are two castles on the shore of this river, the one at Upnore, which guards two reaches of the river, and is supposed to defend all the ships which ride above, between that and the bridge; also on the other shore is Gillingham Castle, formed for the same purpose, and well furnished with guns which command the river, besides which there is a fort or platform of guns at a place called the swamp and another at Cockham Wood. But all these are added, or at least additions made to them, since the time that the Dutch made that memorable attempt [11] upon the royal navy in this river (viz.) on the 22d of June, in the year 1667; for at that time all was left unguarded, and as it were, secure; there were but four guns that could be used at Upnore, and scarce so many at Gillingham, the carriages being rotten and broke; and in a word, every thing concurring to invite the enemy. There were about twelve guns at the Isle of Shepey, where since, Sheerness Fort is built; but the Dutch soon beat them from those guns, after which they went boldly up to Black-Stakes with their whole squadron; and after that seven of their biggest men of war went up as high as Upnore, where they did what mischief they could, and went away again, carrying off the *Royal Charles*, a first rate ship of 100 guns, and burning the *London*, and several others, besides the damaging most of the ships which were within their reach; and all things considered, it was a victory, that they went away without ruining all the rest of the navy that was in that river.

But as this is a dull story in it self, so it is none of my present business farther than to introduce what follows; namely, that this alarm gave England such a sense of the consequence of the river Medway, and of the docks and yards at Chatham, and of the danger the royal navy lay exposed to there, that all these doors which were open then, are locked up and sufficiently barred since that time; and 'tis not now in the power of any nation under heaven, no, though they should be masters at sea, unless they were masters at land too at the same time, to give us such another affront. For besides all the castles, lines of guns, and platforms on each side the river Medway, as we go up, as above there is now a royal fort built at the point of the Isle of Shepey, called Sheerness, which guards that entrance into the river. This is a regular, and so complete a fortification, and has such a line of heavy cannon commanding the mouth of the river, that no man of war, or fleet of men of war, would attempt to pass by as the Dutch did; or at least could not effect it without hazard of being torn to pieces by those batteries.

SHEERNESS is not only a fortress, but a kind of town, with several streets in it, and inhabitants of several sorts; but chiefly such whose business obliges them to reside here. The officers of the ordnance have here apartments, and an office, they being often obliged to be here many days together. This fort commands only the entrance into the Medway, or that branch of the Medway, properly, which they call West-Swayle. The East-Swayle, not navigable by ships of force, goes in by the town of Queenborough, passes east, makes the Isle of Shepey, parting it on the south side, and opens to the sea, near Feversham, and Swale-Cliff, and is therefore of small consequence.

At the south-west point of the Isle of Shepey, where the East-Swayle parts from the West, and passes on, as above, stands a town memorable for nothing, but that which is rather a dishonour to our country than otherwise: namely,

Queenborough,[12] a miserable, dirty, decayed, poor, pitiful, fishing town; yet vested with corporation privileges, has a mayor, aldermen, &c. and his worship the mayor has his mace carried before him to church, and attended in as much state and ceremony as the mayor of a town twenty times as good. I remember when I was there, Mr Mayor was a butcher, and brought us a shoulder of mutton to our inn himself in person, which we bespoke for our dinner, and afterwards he sat down and drank a bottle of wine with us. But that which is still worse, and which I meant in what I said before, is, that this town sends two burgesses to Parliament, as many as the borough of Southwark, or the city of Westminster: though it may be presumed all the inhabitants are not possessed of estates answerable to the rent of one good house in either of those places I last mentioned. The chief business of this town, as I could understand, consists in ale-houses, and oyster-catchers.

Here we took boat, and went up the East-Swayle to a town, which lies, as it were hid, in the country, and among the creeks; for 'tis out of the way, and almost out of sight, as well by water as by land, I mean Milton; it lies up so many creeks and windings of the water, that nobody sees it by water, but they who go on purpose out of the way to it; and yet it is a large town, has a considerable market, and especially for corn, and fruit and provisions, which they send to London by water.

From hence following the coast, and the great road together, for they are still within view of one another, we come to Feversham, a large populous, and as some say, a rich town: the principal business we found among them, was fishing for oysters, which the Dutch fetch hence in such extraordinary quantities, that when I was there, we found twelve large Dutch hoys and doggers lying there to load oyster; and some times, as they told us, there are many more.

It was at the mouth of this Swayle, namely, at Shell-Ness, so called from the abundance of oyster-shells always lying there, that the smack in which the late King James II was embarked for his escape into France,[13] ran on shore, and being boarded by the fishermen, the king was taken prisoner; and I must mention it to the reproach of the people of Feversham, let the conduct of that unfortunate prince be what it will, that the fishermen and rabble can never be excused, who treated the king, even after they were told who he was, with the utmost indecency, using his majesty; (for he was then their sovereign, even in the acknowledged sense of his enemies) I say, using him with such indignity in his person, such insolence in their behaviour, and giving him such opprobrious and abusive language, and searching him in the rudest and most indecent manner, and indeed rifling him; that the king himself said, he was never more apprehensive of his life than at that time. He was afterwards carried by them up to town, where he was not much better treated for some time, till some neighbouring gentlemen in the county came in, who understood their duty better, by whom he was at least preserved from farther violence, till coaches and a guard came from London, by the Prince of Orange's order, to bring him with safety and freedom to London; where he was at least for the present much better received.

While I was near this town some years ago, a most surprising accident happened, namely, the blowing up of a powder-mill, which stood upon the river, close to the town; the blast was not only frightful, but it shattered the whole town, broke the windows, blew down chimneys, and gable-ends not a few; also several people were killed at the powder-house it self, though not any, as I remember, in the town. I know nothing else this town is remarkable for, except the most notorious smuggling trade, carried on partly by the assistance of the Dutch, in their oyster-boats, and partly by other arts, in which they say, the people hereabouts are arrived to such a proficiency, that they are grown monstrous rich by that wicked trade; nay, even the owling trade (so they call the clandestine exporting of wool) has seemed to be transposed from Rumney Marsh to this coast. As to the landing goods here from Holland and France, such as wine and brandy from the latter, and pepper, tea, coffee, callicoes, tobacco, and such goods, (the duties of which being very high in England, had first been drawn back by debentures) that black trade has not only been carried on here, as I was informed, but on both sides the river, on the Essex as well as the Kentish shores.

From this East Swale, and particularly from these last three towns, Queenborough, Milton, and Feversham, the fish-market at Billingsgate is supplied with several sorts of fish; but particularly with the best and largest oysters, such as they call stewing oysters: which are generally called also Milton Oysters; some of which are exceeding large.

This leads me to cross the hills from Milton to Maidstone, about ten miles distant. This is a considerable town, very populous, and the inhabitants generally wealthy; 'tis the county town, and the river Medway is navigable to it by large hoys, of fifty to sixty tons burthen, the tide flowing quite up to the town. Round this town are the largest cherry orchards, and the most of them that are in any part of England; and the gross of the quantity of cherries, and the best of them which supply the whole city of London come from hence, and are therefore called Kentish cherries.

Here likewise, and in the country adjacent, are great quantities of hops planted, and this is called the Mother of Hop Grounds in England; being the first place in England where hops were planted in any quantity, and long before any were planted at Canterbury, though that be now supposed to be the chief place in England. These were the hops, I suppose, which were planted at the beginning of the Reformation, and which gave occasion to that old distich:

Hops, Reformation, bays, and beer,
Came into England all in a year.

From this town, and the neighbouring parts, London is supplied with more particulars than from any single market town in England.

1. From the wild of Kent, which begins but about six miles off, and particularly from that part which lies this way; they

bring the large Kentish bullocks, famed for being generally all red, and with their horns crooked inward, the two points standing one directly against the other, they are counted the largest breed in England.

2. From the same country are brought great quantities of the largest timber for supply of the king's yards at Chatham, and often to London; most of which comes by land carriage to Maidstone.

3. From the country adjoining to Maidstone also, is a very great quantity of corn brought up to London, besides hops and cherries, as above.

4. Also a kind of paving stone, about eight to ten inches square, so durable that it scarce ever wears out; 'tis used to pave court-yards, and passages to gentlemen's houses, being the same the Royal Exchange at London is paved with, which has never yet wanted the least repair.

5. Also fine white sand for the glass-houses, esteemed the best in England for melting into flint-glass, and looking glass-plates; and for the stationer's use also, vulgarly called writing-sand.

6. Also very great quantities of fruit, such as Kentish pippins, runnets, &c. which come up as the cherries do, whole hoy-loads at a time to the wharf, called the Three Cranes,[14] in London; which is the greatest pippin market perhaps in the world.

At Maidstone you begin to converse with gentlemen, and persons of rank of both sexes, and some of quality. All that side of the county which I have mentioned already, as it is marshy, and unhealthy, by its situation among the waters; so it is embarrassed with business, and inhabited chiefly by men of business, such as ship-builders, fisher-men, seafaring-men, and husband-men, or such as depend upon them, and very few families of note are found among them. But as soon as we descend from the poor chalky downs, and deep foggy marshes, to the wholesome rich soil, the well wooded, and well watered plain on the banks of the

Medway, we find the country every where spangled with populous villages, and delicious seats of the nobility and gentry; and especially on the north-side of the river, beginning at Aylesford, on the Medway, and looking east towards the sea.

This neighbourhood of persons of figure and quality, makes Maidstone a very agreeable place to live in, and where a man of letters, and of manners, will always find suitable society, both to divert and improve himself; so that here is, what is not often found, namely, a town of very great business and trade, and yet full of gentry, of mirth, and of good company. It is to be recorded here for the honour of the gentry in this part of England; that though they are as sociable and entertaining as any people are, or can be desired to be, and as much famed for good manners, and good humour; yet the new mode of forming assemblies so much, and so fatally now in vogue, in other parts of England, could never prevail here; and that though there was an attempt made by some loose persons, and the gentlemen, and ladies, did for a little while appear there; yet they generally disliked the practice, soon declined to give their company, as to a thing scandalous, and so it dropped of course.

There is not much manufacturing in this county; what is left, is chiefly at Canterbury, and in this town of Maidstone, and the neighbourhood. At Cranbrook, Tenterden, Goudhurst, and other villages thereabout, on the other side the Medway, there was once a very considerable clothing trade carried on, and the yeomen of Kent, of which so much has been famed, were generally the inhabitants on that side, and who were much enriched by that clothing trade; but that trade is now quite decayed, and scarce ten clothiers left in all the county. These clothiers and farmers, and the remains of them, upon the general elections of members of parliament for the county, show themselves still there, being ordinarily 14 or 1500 freeholders brought from this side of the county; and who for the plainness of their appearance, are called the gray coats of Kent; but are so considerable, that who ever they vote for is always sure to carry it, and therefore the gentlemen are very careful to preserve their interest among them.

In prosecution of my journey east, I went from hence to Canterbury; of which town and its antiquities so much has been said, and so accurately, that I need do no more than mention it by recapitulation. However I observe here.

1. That the first Christian bishop, if not the first Christian preacher, that ever came to England, (for I know not what to say to the story of Joseph of Arimathea, and his holy thorn at Glassenbury) landed in this country, and settled in this place; I mean St Augustin,[15] sent over by Gregory, Bishop of Rome. This Gregory it seems was a true primitive Christian Bishop of Rome; not such as since are called so; long before they assumed the title of popes, or that usurped honour of Universal Bishop.

2. That, seven Bishops of Canterbury, from St Augustine, inclusive of himself, lie buried here in one vault.

3. That Thomas Becket, or Thomas a Becket, as some call him, archbishop of this see, and several archbishops before him, plagued, insulted, and tyrannized over the Kings of England, their sovereigns, in an unsufferable manner.

4. That the first of these, having made himself intolerable to King Henry II, by his obstinacy, pride and rebellion, was here murthered by the connivance, and as some say, by the express order of the king, and that they show his blood upon the pavement to this day.

5. That he was afterwards canonized, and his shrine made the greatest idol of the world; and they show the stone-steps ascending to his shrine, worn away to a slope, by the knees of the pilgrims, and ignorant people who came thither to pray to him, and to desire him to pray for them.

6. That the bodies of King Henry IV and of Edward the Black Prince are buried here, and the magnificent effigies of the latter very curiously carved and engraved, lies on his tomb, or monument; also that King Stephen [16] should have lain here, but on some scruple of the monks, the corpse was

stopped short on the road, and was afterwards buried at Feversham, about seven miles off. What the monks objected, or whether they had no money offered them, is not recorded with the rest of the story.

7. That the immense wealth offered by votaries, and pilgrims, for several ages to the altar, or shrine of this mock saint, Thomas Becket, was such, that Erasmus Roterdamus,[17] who was in the repository and saw it, relates of it, that the whole place glittered and shone with gold and diamonds.

8. That all this immense treasure, with the lands and revenues of the whole monastery were seized upon, and taken away by King Henry VIII, at the general suppression of religious houses, except such as are annexed to the Dean and Chapter, and to the revenue of the arch-bishopric, which are not large.

Under the church is a large Protestant French church, given first by Queen Elizabeth to the Walloons,[18] who fled hither from the persecution of the Duke D'Alva, and the King of France; and whose number has been since very much increased by the particular cruelty of Louis XIV.

As for the town, its antiquity seems to be its greatest beauty. The houses are truly ancient, and the many ruins of churches, chapels, oratories, and smaller cells of religious people, makes the place look like a general ruin a little recovered. The city will scarce bear being called populous, were it not for two or three thousand French Protestants, which, including men, women and children, they say there are in it, and yet they tell me the number of these decreases daily. The employment of those refugees was chiefly broad silk weaving; but that trade was so decayed before the first Act [19] for Prohibiting the Wearing of East India Silks passed, that there were not twenty broad looms left in the city, of near three hundred, that had formerly been there; upon the passing that Act, the trade revived again and the number of master workmen increased, and the masters increased; and the masters which were there before, increasing their works also, the town filled again, and a great many looms were employed; but after this by the encroaching of the printed callicoes, chintz, &c. and the prevailing of the smuggling trade as above, the silk trade decayed a second time. But now the use and wear of printed callicoes and chintz, being by Act of Parliament severely prohibited, 'tis expected the silk trade at Canterbury will revive a third time, and the inhabitants promise themselves much from it.

But the great wealth and increase of the city of Canterbury, is from the surprising increase of the hop-grounds all round the place. It is within the memory of many of the inhabitants now living, and that none of the oldest neither, that there was not an acre of ground planted with hops in the whole neighbourhood, or so few as not to be worth naming; whereas I was assured that there are at this time near six thousand acres of ground so planted, within a very few miles of the city; I do not vouch the number, and I confess it seems incredible, but I deliver it as I received it. The river Stour was made navigable to this city, by virtue of an Act of Parliament in the reign of King Henry VIII,[20] but the person who undertook it, not meeting with encouragement, and failing in the carrying it on, the locks and sluices are all run to decay.

In the neighbourhood of this city are some ancient families, as Sir Tho. Hales,[21] the Lord Strangford, Sir Henry Oxenden, and several others, the two former Roman; also Sir George Rook, famous for his services at sea against the French; the last of which was in the Streights, where the French fleet was commanded by the Count de Tourville, Admiral of France; where both sides fought with such equal gallantry, and resolution, and the strength of the fleets were so equal, though the French the most in number of the two, that neither seemed to seek a second engagement; and of which the following lines were made by some of the merry wits of that time.

The great Tourville Sir George did beat,
The great Sir George beat him;
But if they chance again to meet,
George will his jacket trim:

They both did fight, they both did beat,
They both did run away;
They both did strive again to meet,
The clean contrary way.

On the north-east point of this land, is the promontory, or head-land, called the North Foreland; which, by a line drawn due north to the Nase in Essex, about six miles short of Harwich, makes the mouth of the river of Thames, and the Port of London. As soon as any vessels pass this Foreland from London, they are properly said to be in the open sea.

From this point westward, the first town of note is Ramsgate, a small port, the inhabitants are mighty fond of having us call it Roman's-Gate; pretending that the Romans under Julius Caesar made their first attempt to land here, when he was driven back by a storm; but soon returned, and coming on shore, with a good body of troops beat back the Britains, and fortified his camp, just at the entrance of the creek, where the town now stands. All which may be true for ought any one knows, but is not to be proved, either by them or any one else; and is of so little concern to us, that it matters nothing whether here or at Deal, where others pretend it was.

It was from this town of Ramsgate, that a fellow of gigantic strength, though not of extraordinary stature, came abroad in the world, and was called the English Sampson, and who suffered men to fasten the strongest horse they could find to a rope, and the rope round his loins, sitting on the ground, with his feet straight out against a post, and no horse could stir him; several other proofs of an incredible strength he gave before the king, and abundance of the nobility at Kensington, which no other man could equal; but his history was very short, for in about a year he disappeared, and we heard no more of him since.

Sandwich is the next town, lying in the bottom of a bay, at the mouth of the river Stour, an old, decayed, poor, miserable town, of which when I have said that it is an ancient town, one of the Cinque Ports, and sends two members to

Parliament; I have said all that I think can be worth anybody's reading of the town of Sandwich.

From hence to Deal is about —— miles.[22] This place is famous for the road for shipping, so well known all over the trading world, by the name of the Downs, and where almost all ships which arrive from foreign parts for London, or go from London to foreign parts, and who pass the Channel, generally stop; the homeward-bound to dispatch letters, send their merchants and owners the good news of their arrival, and set their passengers on shore, and the like; and the outward-bound to receive their last orders, letters, and farewells from owners, and friends, take in fresh provisions, &c.

This place would be a very wild and dangerous road for ships, were it not for the South Foreland, a head of land, forming the east point of the Kentish shore; and is called, the South, as its situation respects the North Foreland; and which breaks the sea off, which would otherwise come rolling up from the west. And yet on some particular winds, and especially, if they over-blow, the Downs proves a very wild road; ships are driven from their anchors, and often run on shore, or are forced on the said sands, or into Sandwich-Bay, or Ramsgate-Peer, as above, in great distress; this is particularly when the wind blows hard at S.E. or at E. by N. or E.N.E. and some other points; and terrible havoc has been made in the Downs at such times.

But the most unhappy account that can be given of any disaster in the Downs, is in the time of that terrible tempest, which we call by way of distinction, the Great Storm,[23] being on 27th of November 1703, unhappy in particular; for that there chanced just at that time to be a great part of the royal navy under Sir Cloudesly Shovel, just come into the Downs, in their way to Chatham, to be laid up. There remained in the Downs about twelve sail when this terrible blast began, at which time England may be said to have received the greatest loss that ever happened to the royal navy at one time; either by weather, by enemies, or by any accident whatsoever;

the short account of it, as they showed it me in the town, I mean of what happened in the Downs, is as follows.

The *Northumberland*, a third rate, carrying 70 guns, and 353 men; the *Restoration*, a second rate, carrying 76 guns, and 386 men; the *Sterling-Castle*, a second rate, carrying 80 guns, and 400 men, but had but 349 men on board; and the *Mary*, a third rate, of 64 guns, having 273 men on board; these were all lost, with all their men, high and low; except only one man out of the *Mary*, and 70 men out of the *Sterling-Castle*, who were taken up by boats from Deal. All this was besides the loss of merchants' ships, which was exceeding great, not here only, but in almost all the ports in the south, and west of England; and also in Ireland, which I shall have occasion to mention again in another place.

From hence we pass over a pleasant champaign country, with the sea, and the coast of France, clear in your view; and by the very gates of the ancient castle (to the town) of Dover. As we go, we pass by Deal Castle, and Sandown Castle, two small works, of no strength by land, and not of much use by sea; but however maintained by the government for the ordinary services of salutes, and protecting small vessels, which can lie safe under their cannon from picaroons, privateers, &c. in time of war.

Neither Dover nor its castle has any thing of note to be said of them, but what is in common with their neighbours; the castle is old, useless, decayed, and serves for little; but to give the title and honour of government to men of quality, with a salary, and sometimes to those that want one. The town is one of the Cinque Ports, sends members to Parliament, who are called barons, and has it self an ill repaired, dangerous, and good for little harbour and pier, very chargeable and little worth. The packets for France go off from here, as also those for Nieuport, with the mails for Flanders, and all those ships which carry freights from New-York to Holland, and from Virginia to Holland, come generally hither, and unlade their goods, enter them with, and show them to the custom-house officers, pay the duties, and then enter them again by certificate, reload them, and draw back the duty by debenture, and so they go away for Holland.

From this place the coast affords nothing of note; but some other small Cinque-Ports, such as Hith and Rumney, and Rye; and as we pass to them Folkstone, eminent chiefly for a multitude of fishing-boats belonging to it, which are one part of the year employed in catching mackerel for the city of London. The Folkstone men catch them, and the London and Barking mackerel-smacks, of which I have spoken at large in Essex, come down and buy them, and fly up to market with them, with such a cloud of canvas, and up so high that one would wonder their small boats could bear it and should not overset.

As I rode along this coast, I perceived several dragoons riding, officers, and others armed and on horseback, riding always about as if they were huntsmen beating up their game; upon inquiry I found their diligence was employed in quest of the owlers, as they call them, and sometimes they catch some of them; but when I came to enquire farther, I found too, that often times these are attacked in the night, with such numbers, that they dare not resist, or if they do, they are wounded and beaten, and sometimes killed; and at other times are obliged, as it were, to stand still, and see the wool carried off before their faces, not daring to meddle. But I find so many of these desperate fellows are of late taken up, by the courage and vigilance of the soldiers, that the knots are very much broken, and the owling-trade much abated, at least on that side the French also finding means to be supplied from Ireland with much less hazard, and at very little more expense.

From Rumney-Marsh the shore extends it self a great way into the sea, and makes that point of land, called Dengey-Ness. Between this point of land and Beachy,[24] it was that the French in the height of their naval glory took the English and Dutch fleets at some disadvantage, offering them battle, when the French were so superior in number, that it was not consistent with human prudence to venture an engagement, the French being ninety-two ships of the line of battle, and the English and Dutch, put together, not sixty sail; the French ships also generally bigger: yet such was the eagerness of both the English and Dutch seamen, and commanders, that it was not without infinite murmurings, that Admiral Herbert stood away, and called off the Dutch, who had the van, from engaging; the English it seems believed themselves so superior to the French when they came to lie broad-side and broad-side, yard-arm and yard-arm, as the seamen call it in an engagement, that they would admit of no excuse for not fighting; though according to all the rules of war, no admiral could justify hazarding the royal navy on such terms; and especially the circumstances of the time then considered, for the king was in Ireland, and King James ready in France, if the English and Dutch fleets had received a blow, to have embarked with an army for England, which perhaps would have hazarded the whole Revolution; so that wise men afterwards, and as I have been told the king himself upon a full hearing justified the conduct of Admiral Herbert, and afterwards created him Earl of Torrington.

The towns of Rye, Winchelsea, and Hastings, have little in them to deserve more than a bare mention; Rye would flourish again, if her harbour, which was once able to receive the royal navy, could be restored; but as it is, the bar is so loaded with sand cast up by the sea, that ships of 200 ton choose to ride it out under Dengey or Beachy, though with the greatest danger, rather than to run the hazard of going into Rye for shelter.

From a little beyond Hastings to Bourn, we ride upon the sands in a straight line for eighteen miles, all upon the coast of Sussex, passing by Pemsey, or Pevensey Haven. This is that famous strand where William the Norman landed with his whole army; and near to which, namely, at the town of Battle, which is about nine miles off, he fought that memorable fight with Harold, then King of England; in which the fate of this nation was determined, and where victory gave the crown to the Conqueror and his race, of the particulars of all which, our histories are full; this town of Battle is remarkable for little now, but for making the finest gun-powder, and the best perhaps in Europe.

From hence it was that, turning north, and traversing the deep, dirty, but rich part of these two counties, I had the curiosity to see the great foundries, or iron-works, which are in this county, and where they are carried on at such a prodigious expense of wood, that even in a country almost all over-run with timber, they begin to complain of the consuming it for those furnaces, and leaving the next age to want timber for building their navies. I must own however, that I found that complaint perfectly groundless, the three counties of Kent, Sussex, and Hampshire, (all which lie contiguous to one another) being one inexhaustible store-house of timber [25] never to be destroyed, but by a general conflagration, and able at this time to supply timber to rebuild all the royal navies in Europe, if they were all to be destroyed, and set about the building them together.

After I had fatigued my self in passing this deep and heavy part of the country, I thought it would not be foreign to my design, if I refreshed my self with a view of Tunbridge-Wells, which were not then above twelve miles out of my way. When I came to the wells, I found a great deal of good company there, and that which was more particular, was, that it happened to be at the time when his Royal Highness the Prince of Wales [26] was there with abundance of the nobility, and gentry of the country, who to honour the prince's coming, or satisfy their own curiosity, thronged to that place; so that at first I found it very difficult to get a lodging. The prince appeared upon the walks, went into the raffling shops, and to every public place, saw every thing, and let every body see him, and went away, with the Duke of Dorset, and other of his attendance for Portsmouth; so in two or three days, things returned all to their ancient channel, and Tunbridge was just what it used to be.

The ladies that appear here, are indeed the glory of the place; the coming to the Wells to drink the water is a mere matter of custom; some drink, more do not, and few drink physically. But company and diversion is in short the main business of the place; and those people who have nothing to do any where else, seem to be the only people who have any thing to do at Tunbridge. After the appearance is over at the Wells, (where the ladies are all undressed) and at the chapel, the company go home; and as if it was another species of people, or a collection from another place, you are surprised to see the walks covered with ladies completely dressed and gay to profusion; where rich clothes, jewels, and beauty not to be set out by (but infinitely above) ornament, dazzles the eyes from one end of the range to the other.

Here you have all the liberty of conversation in the world, and any thing that looks like a gentleman, has an address agreeable, and behaves with decency and good manners, may single out whom he pleases, that does not appear engaged, and may talk, rally, be merry, and say any decent thing to them; but all this makes no acquaintance, nor is it taken so, or understood to mean so; if a gentleman desires to be more intimate, and enter into any acquaintance particular, he must do it by proper application, not by ordinary meeting on the walks, for the ladies will ask no gentlemen there, to go off the walk, or invite any one to their lodgings, except it be a sort of ladies of whom I am not now speaking.

As for gaming, sharping, intriguing; as also fops, fools, beaux, and the like, Tunbridge is as full of these, as can be desired, and it takes off much of the diversion of those persons of honour and virtue, who go there to be innocently recreated. However a man of character, and good behaviour cannot be there any time, but he may single out such company as may be suitable to him, and with whom he may be as merry as heart can wish. In a word, Tunbridge wants nothing that can add to the felicities of life, or that can make a man or woman completely happy, always provided they have money; for without money a man is no-body at Tunbridge, any more than at any other place; and when any man finds his pockets low, he has nothing left to think of, but to be gone, for he will have no diversion in staying there any longer.

And yet Tunbridge also is a place in which a lady however virtuous, yet for want of good conduct may as soon shipwreck her character as in any part of England; and where, when she has once injured her reputation, 'tis as hard to restore it; nay, some say no lady ever recovered her character at Tunbridge, if she first wounded it there. But this is to be added too, that a lady very seldom suffers that way at Tunbridge, without some apparent folly of her own; for that they do not seem so apt to make havoc of one another's reputation here, by tattle and slander, as I think they do in some other places in the world; particularly at Epsome, Hampstead, and such like places; which I take to be, because the company who frequent Tunbridge, seem to be a degree or two above the society of those other places, and therefore are not so very apt, either to meddle with other people's affairs, or to censure if they do; both which are the properties of that more gossiping part of the world.

In this I shall be much misunderstood, if it is thought I mean the ladies only, for I must own I look just the other way; and if I may be allowed to use my own sex so coarsely, it is really among them that the ladies' characters first, and oftenest receive unjust wounds; and I must confess the malice, the reflections, the busy meddling, the censuring, the tattling from place to place, and the making havoc of the characters of innocent women, is found among the men gossips more than among their own sex, and at the coffee-houses more than at the teatable; then among the women themselves, what is to be found of it there, is more among the chambermaids, than among their mistresses; slander is a meanness below persons of honour and quality, and to do injustice to the ladies, especially, is a degree below those who have any share of breeding and sense. On this account you may observe, 'tis more practised among the citizens than among the gentry, and in country towns and villages, more than in the city, and so on, till you come to the mere *canail*, the common mob of the street, and there, no reputation, no character can shine without having dirt thrown upon it every day: but this is a digression.

I left Tunbridge, for the same reason that I give, why others should leave it, when they are in my condition; namely, that I found my money almost gone; and though I had bills of credit to supply my self in the course of my intended journey; yet I had none there; so I came away, or as they call it there, I retired; and came to Lewes, through the deepest, dirtiest, but many ways the richest, and most profitable country in all that part of England. The timber I saw here was prodigious, as well in quantity as in bigness, and sometimes I have seen one tree on a carriage, which they call there a tug drawn by two and twenty oxen, and even then, 'tis carried so little a way, and then thrown down, and left for other tugs to take up and carry on, that sometimes 'tis two or three year before it gets to Chatham; for if once the rains come in, it stirs no more that year, and sometimes a whole summer is not dry enough to make the roads passable. Here I had a sight, which indeed I never saw in any other part of England: namely, that going to church at a country village, not far from Lewis, I saw an ancient lady, and a lady of very good quality, I assure you, drawn to church in her coach with six oxen; nor was it done in frolic or humour, but mere necessity, the way being so stiff and deep, that no horses could go in it.

Lewis is a fine pleasant town, well built, agreeably situated in the middle of an open champaign country, and on the edge of the South Downs, the pleasantest, and most delightful of their kind in the nation; it lies on the bank of a little wholesome fresh river, within twelve miles of the sea; but that which adds to the character of this town, is, that both the town and the country adjacent, is full of gentlemen of good families and fortunes, of which the Pelhams may be named with the first. Here are also the ancient families of Gage, Shely, &c. formerly Roman, but now Protestant, with many others.

From this town, following still the range of the South Downs, west; we ride in view of the sea, and on a fine carpet ground for about twelve miles to Bright Helmston,[27] commonly called Bredhemston, a poor fishing town, old built, and on the very edge of the sea. The sea is very unkind to this town, and has by its continual encroachments, so gained upon them, that in a little time more they might reasonably expect it would eat up the whole town, above 100 houses having been devoured by the water in a few years past; they are now obliged to get a brief granted them, to beg money all over England, to raise banks against the water; the expense of which, the brief expressly says, will be eight thousand pounds which if one were to look on the town, would seem to be more than all the houses in it are worth.

From hence, still keeping the coast close on the left, we come to Shoreham, a sea-faring town, and chiefly inhabited by ship-carpenters, ship-chandlers, and all the several trades depending upon the building and fitting up of ships, which is their chief business; and they are famed for neat building, and for building good sea-boats. Here in the compass of about six miles are three borough [28] towns, sending members to Parliament, (viz) Shoreham, Bramber, and Stenning: and Shoreham, Stenning are tolerable little market-towns; but Bramber (a little ruin of an old castle excepted) hardly deserves the name of a town, having not above fifteen or sixteen families in it, and of them not many above asking you an alms as you ride by; the chiefest house in the town is a tavern, and here, as I have been told, the vintner, or alehouse-keeper rather, for he hardly deserved the name of a vintner, boasted, that upon an election, just then over, he had made 300*l.* of one pipe of canary.

This is the second town in this country, where the elections have been so scandalously mercenary; and of whom it is said, there was in one king's reign more money spent at elections, than all the lands in the parishes were worthy, at twenty years purchase. The other town I mean is Winchelsea, a town, if it deserves the name of a town, which is rather the skeleton of an ancient city than a real town, where the ancient gates stand near three miles from one another over the fields, and where the ruins are so buried, that they have made good corn fields of the streets, and the plough goes over the foundations, nay over the first floors of the houses, and where nothing of a town[29] but the destruction of it seems to remain; yet at one election for this town the strife was such between Sir John Banks, father-in-law to the Earl of Aylesford, and Colonel Draper, a neighbouring gentleman, that I was told in the country the latter spent 1100l. at the election, and yet lost it too; what the other spent who opposed him, may be guessed at, seeing he that spent most was always sure to carry it in those days.

Near Steyning, the famous Sir John Fagg[30] had a noble ancient seat, now possessed with a vast estate by his grandson, Sir Robert Fagg; but I mention the ancient gentleman on this occasion, that being entertained at his house, in the year 1697, he showed me in his park four bullocks of his own breeding, and of his own feeding, of so prodigious a size, and so excessively overgrown by fat, that I never saw any thing like them. While I continued at Sir John's some London butchers came down to see them, and in my hearing offered Sir John six and twenty pound a head for them, but he refused it; and when I moved him afterward to take the money, he said No, he was resolved to have them to Smithfield himself, that he might say he had the four biggest bullocks in England at market.

He continued positive, and did go up to Smithfield-Market with them; but whether it was that they sunk a little in the driving, or that the butchers played a little upon him, I cannot tell; but he was obliged to sell them for twenty five pound a head when he came there. I knew of one of the butchers that bought them, and on a particular occasion enquired of him what they weighed when killed, and he assured me that they weighed eighty stone a quarter, when killed and cut-out; which is so incredible, that if I had not been well assured of the truth of it, I should not have ventured thus to have recorded it. But by this may be judged something of the largeness of the cattle in the Wild of Kent and Sussex.

From hence we come to Arundel, a decayed town also; but standing near the mouth of the good river, called Arun, which signifies, says Mr Cambden, the swift, though the river it self is not such a rapid current as merits that name; at least it did not seem to be so to me. This river, and the old decayed, once famous castle at Arundel, which are still belonging to the family of Howards, Earls of Arundel, a branch of the Norfolk family, is all that is remarkable here; except it be that in this river are catched the best mullets, and the largest in England, a fish very good in it self, and much valued by the gentry round, and often sent up to London.

From hence to the city of Chichester are twelve miles, and the most pleasant beautiful country in England, whether we go by the hill, that is the Downs, or by the plain, (viz.) the enclosed country. To the north of Arundel, and at the bottom of the hills, and consequently in the Wild, is the town of Petworth, a large handsome country market-town, and very populous, and as it stands upon an ascent, and is dry and healthy, it is full of gentlemen's families, and good well built houses both in the town and neighbourhood. But the beauty of Petworth, is the ancient seat of the old family of Peircy, Earls of Northumberland, now extinct; whose daughter, the sole heiress of all his vast estates, married the present Duke of Somerset:[31] of the noble and ancient family of Seymour, and among other noble seats brought his grace this of Petworth.

The Duke pulled down the ancient house, and on the same spot has built from the ground, one of the finest piles of building, and the best modelled houses then in Britain. It has had the misfortune to be once almost demolished by fire, but the damage is fully repaired; but another disaster to the family can never be repaired, which has happened to it, even while these sheets were writing; namely, the death of the

Duchess, who died in November 1722, and lies buried in the burying place of the family of Seymor, Dukes of Somerset, in the cathedral church of Salisbury.

The Duke's house at Petworth, is certainly a complete building in it self, and the apartments are very noble, well contrived, and richly furnished; but it cannot be said, that the situation of the house is equally designed, or with equal judgement as the rest; the avenues to the front want space, the house stands as it were with its elbows to the town, its front has no visto answerable, and the west front looked not to the parks or fine gardens, but to the old stables. To rectify this, when it was too late to order it any other way, the duke was obliged to pull down those noble buildings; I mean the mews, or stables, the finest of their kind in all the south of England, and equal to some noblemen's whole houses, and yet even the demolishing the pile has done no more than opened a prospect over the country.

From Petworth west, the country is a little less woody than the Wild, and there begin to show their heads above the trees, a great many fine seats of the nobility and gentlemen of the country, as the Duke of Richmond's seat at Goodwood, near Chichester. (This family also in tears, at the writing these sheets, for the death of her grace the duchess,[32] who died the beginning of the month of December, and is buried in Westminster Abbey; and since the above was written, and sent to the press, the Duke of Richmond himself is also dead.) These and a great many more lying so near together, make the country hereabout much more sociable and pleasant than the rest of the woody country, called the Wild, and yet I cannot say much for the city of Chichester, in which, if six or seven good families were removed, there would not be much conversation, except what is to be found among the canons, and dignitaries of the cathedral.

The cathedral here is not the finest in England, but is far from being the most ordinary. The spire is a piece of excellent workmanship, but it received such a shock about —— years ago, that it was next to miraculous, that the whole steeple did not fall down; which in short, if it had, would almost have demolished the whole church.

It was a fire-ball, if we take it from the inhabitants, or, to speak in the language of nature, the lightning broke upon the steeple, and such was the irresistible force of it, that it drove several great stones out of the steeple, and carried them clear off, not from the roof of the church only, but of the adjacent houses also, and they were found at a prodigious distance from the steeple, so that they must have been shot out of the places where they stood in the steeple, as if they had been shot out of a cannon, or blown out of a mine. One of these stones of at least a ton weight, by estimation, was blown over the south side, or row of houses in the West-Street, and fell on the ground in the street at a gentleman's door, on the other side of the way; and another of them almost as big was blown over both sides of the said West-Street, into the same gentleman's garden, at whose door the other stone lay, and no hurt was done by either of them whereas if either of those stones had fallen upon the strongest built house in the street, it would have dashed it all to pieces, even to the foundation. This account of the two stones, I relate from a person of undoubted credit, who was an eye-witness, and saw them, but had not the curiosity to measure them, which he was very sorry for. The breach it made in the spire, though within about forty five foot of the top, was so large, that as the workmen said to me, a coach and six horses might have driven through it, and yet the steeple stood fast, and is now very substantially repaired; withal, showing that it was before, an admirable sound and well finished piece of workmanship.

They have a story in this city, that when ever a bishop of that diocese is to die, a heron comes and sits upon the pinnacle of the spire of the cathedral. This accordingly happened, about —— when Dr —— Williams was bishop.[33] A butcher standing at his shop-door, in the South-Street, saw it, and ran in for his gun, and being a good marks-man shot the heron, and killed it at which his mother was very angry with him, and said he had killed the bishop, and the next day news came to the town that Dr Williams, the last bishop was dead; this is affirmed by many people inhabitants of the place.

This city is not a place of much trade, nor is it very populous; but they are lately fallen into a very particular way of managing the corn trade here, which it is said turns very well to account; the farmers generally speaking, carried all their wheat to Farnham, to market, which is very near forty miles by land-carriage, and from some parts of the country more than forty miles. But some monied men of Chichester, Emsworth, and other places adjacent, have joined their stocks together, built large granaries near the Crook, where the vessels come up, and here they buy and lay up all the corn which the country on that side can spare; and having good mills in the neighbourhood, they grind and dress the corn, and send it to London in the meal about by Long Sea, as they call it; nor now the war is over do they make the voyage so tedious as to do the meal any hurt, as at first in the time of war was sometimes the case for want of convoys.

From hence we descend gradually to Portsmouth, the largest fortification, beyond comparison, that we have in England. The situation of this place is such, that it is chosen, as may well be said, for the best security to the navy above all the places in Britain; the entrance into the harbour is safe, but very narrow, guarded on both sides by terrible platforms of cannon, particularly on the Point; which is a suburb of Portsmouth properly so called, where there is a brick platform built with two tier of guns, one over another, and which can fire so in cover, that the gunners cannot be beaten from their guns, or their guns easily dismounted; the other is from the point of land on the side of Gosport, which they call Gilkicker, where also they have two batteries.

Before any ships attempt to enter this port by sea, they must also pass the cannon of the main platform of the garrison, and also another at South-Sea-Castle; so that it is next to impossible that any ships could match the force of all those cannon, and be able to force their way into the harbour; in which I speak the judgment of men well acquainted with such matters, as well as my own opinion, and of men whose opinion leads them to think the best of the force of naval batteries too; and who have talked of making no difficulty to force their way through the Thames, in the teeth of the line of guns at Tilbury; I say, they have talked of it, but it was but talk, as any one of judgment would imagine, that knew the works at Tilbury, of which I have spoken in its place. The reasons, however, which they give for the difference, have some force in them, as they relate to Portsmouth, though not as they relate to Tilbury. But to avoid comparing of strengths, or saying what may be done in one place, and not done in another; 'tis evident, in the opinion of all that I have met with, that the greatest fleet of ships that ever were in the hands of one nation at a time, would not pretend, if they had not an army also on shore, to attack the whole work, to force their entrance into the harbour at Portsmouth.

As to the strength of the town by land, the works are very large and numerous, and besides the battery at the Point aforesaid, there is a large hornwork on the south-side, running out towards South-Sea Castle; there is also a good counterscarp, and double moat, with ravelins in the ditch, and double pallisadoes, and advanced works to cover the place from any approach, when it may be practicable. The strength of the town is also considerably augmented on the land-side, by the fortifications raised in King William's time about the docks and yards, which are now perfected, and those parts made a particular strength by themselves. These docks and yards are now like a town by themselves, and are a kind of marine corporation, or a government of their own kind within themselves; there being particular large rows of dwellings, built at the public charge, within the new works, for all the principal officers of the place. The tradesmen likewise have houses here, and many of the labourers are allowed to live in the bounds as they can get lodging.

The town of Portsmouth, besides its being a fortification,

is a well inhabited, thriving, prosperous corporation; and hath been greatly enriched of late by the fleet's having so often and so long lain there, as well as large fleets of merchantmen, as the whole navy during the late war; besides the constant fitting out of men here, and the often paying them at Portsmouth, has made a great confluence of people thither on their private business, with other things, which the attendance of those fleets hath required. These things have not only been a great advantage to the town, but has really made the whole place rich, and the inhabitants of Portsmouth are quite another sort of people than they were a few years before the Revolution; it may be said, there is as much to do at Portsmouth now in time of peace, as there was then in time of war, and more too.

There is also this note to be put upon the two great arsenals of England, Portsmouth, and Chatham; namely, that they thrive by a war, as the war respects their situation (viz.) that when a war with France happens, or with Spain, then Portsmouth grows rich, and when a war with Holland, or any of the powers of the north, then Chatham, and Woolwich, and Deptford are in request.

The government of the place is by a mayor and aldermen, &c. as in other corporations, and the civil government is no more interrupted by the military, than if there was no garrison there, such is the good conduct of the governors, and such it has always been, since our sovereigns have ceased to encourage the soldiery to insult the civil magistrates. And we have very seldom had any complaint on either side, either of want of discipline among the soldiers, or want of prudence in the magistrates. The inhabitants indeed necessarily submit to such things as are the consequence of a garrison town, such as being examined at the gates, such as being obliged to keep garrison hours, and not be let out, or let in after nine o'clock at night, and the like; but these are things no people will count a burthen, where they get their bread by the very situation of the place, as is the case here.

From Portsmouth west, the country lies low and flat, and

is full of creeks and inlets of the sea and rivers, all the way to Southampton, so that we ferry over three times in about eighteen miles; besides going over on bridge, namely, at Tichfield. From hence when we come opposite to Southampton, we pass another creek, being the mouth of the river Itchen which comes down from Winchester, and is both very broad and deep, and the ferry men having a very sorry boat, we found it dangerous enough passing it. On the other bank stands the ancient town of Southampton, and on the other side of Southampton comes down another large river, entering Southampton Water by Red-Bridge; so that the town of Southampton stands upon a point running out into the sea, between two very fine rivers, both navigable, up some length into the country, and particularly useful for the bringing down timber out of one of the best wooded counties in Britain; for the river on the west side of the town in particular comes by the edge of the great forest, called New-Forest.

In riding over the south part of Hampshire, I made this observation about that growth of timber, which I mention in supplement to what I said before concerning our timber being wasted and decayed in England (viz.) that notwithstanding the very great consumption of timber in King William's reign, by building or rebuilding almost the whole navy; and notwithstanding so many of the king's ships were built hereabouts, besides abundance of large merchant ships, which were about that time built yet I saw the gentlemen's estates, within six, eight, or ten miles of Southampton, so over-grown with wood, and their woods so full of large full grown timber, that it seemed as if they wanted sale for it, and that it was of little worth to them. In one estate at Hursely in particular near Winchester, the estate since bought by Mr Cardonell,[34] late manager for the Duke of Marlborough, and formerly belonging to Mr Cromwell, grandson to Oliver Cromwell, the whole estate not above 800l. per ann. in rent, they might have cut twenty thousand pounds worth of timber down, and yet have left the woods in a thriving condition. Farther west it is the like, and as I rode through New-Forest, I could see the ancient oaks of many hundred years standing, perishing with their withered tops advanced up in the air, and grown white with age, and that could never yet get the favour to be cut down, and made serviceable to their country. These in my opinion are no signs of the decay of our woods, or of the danger of our wanting timber in England; on the contrary, I take leave to mention it again, that if we were employed in England, by the rest of the world, to build a thousand sail of three deck ships, from 80 to 100 guns, it might be done to our infinite advantage, and without putting us in any danger of exhausting the nation of timber.

Southampton is a truly ancient town, for 'tis in a manner dying with age; the decay of the trade is the real decay of the town; and all the business of moment that is transacted there, is the trade between us and the islands of Jersey and Guernsey, with a little of the wine trade, and much smuggling. The building of ships also is much stopped of late; however, the town is large, has many people in it, a noble fair High-Street, a spacious quay; and if its trade should revive, is able to entertain great numbers of people. There is a French church, and no inconsiderable congregation, which was a help to the town, and there are still some merchants who trade to Newfoundland, and to the Streights with fish; but for all other trade, it may be said of Southampton as of other towns, London has eaten it up.

Whatever the fable of Bevis of Southampton,[35] and the giants in the woods thereabouts may be derived from, I found the people mighty willing to have those things pass for true; and at the north gate of the town, the only entrance from the land side, they have the figures of two eminent champions, who might pass for giants if they were alive now, but they can tell us very little of their history, but what is all fabulous like the rest, so I say no more of them.

I was now at the extent of my intended journey west, and thought of looking no farther this way for the present, so I came away north east, leaving Winchester a little on the left, and came into the Portsmouth road at Petersfield, a town eminent for little, but its being full of good inns, and standing in the middle of a country, still over-grown with a prodigious quantity of oak-timber. From hence we came to Alton, and in the road thither, began a little to taste the pleasure of the Western Downs, which reach from Winchester almost to Alton.

Alton is a small market-town, of no note, neither is there any considerable manufacture in all this part of England; except a little drugget and shalloon making, which begins hereabout, otherwise the whole counties of Kent, Sussex, Surrey, and Hampshire, are not employed in any considerable woollen manufacture.

From Alton we came to Farnham, of which I can only say, that it is a large populous market-town, the farthest that way in the county of Surrey, and without exception the greatest corn-market in England, London excepted; that is to say, particularly for wheat, of which so vast a quantity is brought every market-day to this market, that a gentleman told me, he once counted on a market-day eleven hundred teams of horse, all drawing waggons, or carts, loaden with wheat at this market; every team of which is supposed to bring what they call a load, that is to say, forty bushel of wheat to market; which is in the whole, four and forty thousand bushel; but I do not take upon me to affirm this relation, or to say whether it be a probable opinion or not.

At this town is a castle [36] eminent for this, that it was built by a Bishop of Winchester. Here the said Bishops of Winchester usually keep their ordinary residence, and though the county of Surrey, be generally speaking within the diocese, they may be truly said to reside in the middle of their ecclesiastical dominion. The Farnham people it seems, or some of the country folks, notwithstanding the liberality and bounty of the several bishops, who, if some people may be believed, have very good benefactors to the town; I say, notwithstanding all this, have of late been very unkind to the bishop, in pulling down the pale of his park, and plundering it of the deer, killing, wounding, and disabling, even those they could not carry away.

From Farnham, that I might take in the whole county of Surrey, I took the coach-road, over Bagshot-Heath, and that great forest, as 'tis called, of Windsor. Those that despise Scotland, and the north part of England, for being full of waste and barren land, may take a view of this part of Surrey, and look upon it as a foil to the beauty of the rest of England; or a mark of the just resentment showed by Heaven upon the Englishmen's pride; I mean the pride they show in boasting of their country, its fruitfulness, pleasantness, richness, the fertility of the soil, &c. whereas here is a vast tract of land, some of it within seventeen or eighteen miles of the capital city; which is not only poor, but even quite sterile, given up to barrenness, horrid and frightful to look on, not only good for little, but good for nothing. Much of it is a sandy desert, and one may frequently be put in mind here of Arabia Deserta, where the winds raise the sands, so as to overwhelm whole caravans of travellers, cattle and people together; for in passing this heath, in a windy day, I was so far in danger of smothering with the clouds of sand, which were raised by the storm, that I could neither keep it out of my mouth, nose or eyes; and when the wind was over, the sand appeared spread over the adjacent fields of the forest some miles distant, so as that it ruins the very soil. This sand indeed is checked by the heath, or heather, which grows in it, and which is the common product of barren land, even in the very Highlands of Scotland; but the ground is otherwise so poor and barren, that the product of it feeds no creatures, but some very small sheep, who feed chiefly on the said heather, and but very few of these, nor are there any villages worth remembering, and but few houses, or people for many miles far and wide; this desert lies extended so much, that some say, there is not less than a hundred thousand acres of this barren land that lies all together, reaching out every way in the three counties of Surrey, Hampshire and Berkshire.

Through this desert, for I can call it no less, we come into the great western road, leading from London to Salisbury, Exeter, &c. and pass the Thames at Stanes; and here upon viewing the beautiful prospect of the river, and of the meadows, on the banks of the river, on the left hand of the road, I could not but call to mind those two excellent lines of Sir John Denham,[37] in his poem, called *Cooper's Hill*, viz.

> Tho' deep, yet clear, tho' gentle, yet not dull,
> Strong without rage, without o'erflowing full.

Here I remembered that I had yet left the inland towns of the two counties of Kent and Sussex, and almost all the county of Surrey out of my account; and that having as it were taken a circuit round the coast only, I had a great many places worth viewing to give an account of; I therefore left Windsor, which was within my view, on one side of the river, and Hampton Court on the other, as being the subject of another letter; and resolved to finish my present view, in the order I had begun it; that is to say, to give an account of the whole country as I come on; that I may make no incongruous transitions from one remote part of England to another, at least as few as may be.

From Stanes therefore I turned S. and S.E. to Chertsey, another market-town, and where there is a bridge over the Thames. This town was made famous, by being the burial place of Henry VI till his bones were after removed to Windsor by Henry VII, also by being the retreat of the incomparable Cowley,[38] where he lived withdrawn from the hurries of the Court and town, and where he died so much a recluse. From this town wholly employed, either in malting, or in barges to carry it down the river to London; I went away south to Woking, a private country market-town, so out of all road, or thorough-fare, as we call it, that 'tis very little heard of in England; it claims however some honour, from its being once the residence of a royal branch of the family of Plantagenet, the old Countess of Richmond,[39] mother to King Henry VII, who made her last retreat here.

From hence we came to Guilford, a well known and considerable market-town. It has the name of being the county town, though it cannot properly be called so; neither the county gaol being here, or the assizes, any more than in common with other towns. But the election indeed for Parliament men for the county is always held here. The river which according to Mr Camden is called the Wey, and which falls into the Thames at Oatlands, is made navigable to this town, which adds greatly to its trade. This navigation is also a mighty support to the great cornmarket at Farnham, which I have mentioned so often.

Here is a small remainder of an old manufacture, that is to say, of the clothing trade, and it extends it self to Godalming, Haselmeer, and the vale country, on the side of the Holmwood. This clothing trade, however small, is very assistant to the poor of this part of the country, where the lands, as I have noted, are but indifferent.

From this town of Guilford, the road to Farnham is very remarkable, for it runs along west from Guilford, upon the ridge of a high chalky hill, so narrow that the breadth of the road takes up the breadth of the hill, and the declivity begins on either hand, at the very hedge that bounds the highway, and is very steep, as well as very high. From this hill is a prospect either way, so far that 'tis surprising; and one sees to the north, or N.W. over the great black desert, called Bagshot-Heath, mentioned above, one way, and the other way south east into Sussex, almost to the South Downs, and west to an unbounded length, the horizon only restraining the eyes. This hill being all chalk, a traveller feels the effect of it in a hot summer's day, being scorched by the reflection of the sun from the chalk, so as to make the heat almost insupportable; and this I speak by my own experience. This hill reaches from Guilford town's end to within a mile and half of Farnham. The hill, or the going up to it from Guilford rather, is called St Katharine's-Hill, and at the top of the ascent from the town stands the gallows, which is so placed, respecting the town, that the towns people from the High-

Street may sit at their shop doors, and see the criminals executed.

The ten miles from Guilford to Leatherhead make one continued line of gentlemen's houses, lying all, or most of them, on the west side of the road, and their parks, or gardens almost touching one another. Here are pleasantly seated several very considerable persons, as the posterity of Sir Tho. Bludworth,[40] once Lord Mayor of London, a person famous for the implacable passion he put the people of London in, by one rash expression at the time of the Great Fire: (viz.) 'That is nothing, and they might piss it out'; which was only spoken at the beginning of the fire, when neither Sir Thomas or the citizens themselves could foresee the length it would go; and without any design to lessen their endeavours to quench it. But this they never forgot, or forgave to him, or his family after him; but fixed the expression on him, as a mark of indelible reproach, even to this day.

At the north east end of this range of fine seats, is Letherhead, a little thorough-fare town, with a stone-bridge over the river Mole; this river is called the Mole, from its remarkable sinking into the earth, at the foot of Box-Hill, near a village called Mickleham, and working its way under ground like a mole, rising again at or near this town of Leatherhead, where its wandering streams are united again, and form a pretty large river, as they were before, running together under Leatherhead Bridge, and from thence to Cobham, and so it pursues its course to the Thames, which it joins at Molesy, which takes its name to be sure from the name of the river Mole.

And here I cannot but take notice of an unaccountable error, which all the writers I have met with fall unwarily into, on account of this little river hiding itself in the earth, and finding its way under ground, from the foot of Beechworth, more properly Betsworth-Castle, near Box-Hill, and then rising again at Letherhead, as above; as if the water had at once engulfed itself in a chasm of the earth, or sunk in a whirlpit, as is said of the Caspian-Sea, which they say rises again in the Persian Gulph with the same violence that it engulfs it self. 'Tis strange this error should prevail in this manner, and with men of learning too, and in a case so easily discovered and so near. But thus it is, nor is it at all remote from the true design of this work, to undeceive the world in the false or mistaken accounts, which other men have given of these things, especially when those mistakes are so demonstrably gross; and when the subject is significant too, as in this part now in hand.

The accounts are so positive, that many curious people have rid thither to see this place, called Swallow, and to see this Beechworth Castle, at the foot of which the river is swallowed up, not doubting but they should see some wonderful gulf, in which a whole river should be at once as it were buried alive; for Mr Camden says, 'Swallow is the place'. The bishop [41] says, 'near Beechworth-Castle the river is swallowed up'; nay, and to make the wonder appear more conformable to the relation, the map of the county of Surrey, placed in Mr Camden, makes a large blank between the river as swallowed up, a little off at Darking, and is rising again as at Leatherhead, breaking the river off abruptly, as if pouring its waters all at once into a great gulf, like one of the common-shores of the streets of London, and bringing it out again at once, just as the water of the brook running into Fleet-Ditch, comes out from under Holbourn-Bridge.

Now after all these plausible stories, the matter of fact is this, and no more; and even of this, the thing is wonderful enough too. But I say, it is thus, and no more, (viz.)

The River Mole passes by Beechworth Castle in a full stream; and for near a mile further on the west of the castle, it takes into its stream Darking-Brook, as they call it, and has upon it a large cornmill, called Darking-Mill; below this it runs close at the foot of Box-Hill, near that part of the hill, which is called the Stomacher; then, as if obstructed by the hill, it turns a little south, and runs cross the road which leads from Darking to Leatherhead, where it is apparently rapid and strong; and then fetches a circuit round a park, within sight of Leatherhead, and so keeps a continued channel to the very town of Leatherhead; so that there is no such thing as a natural bridge, or a river lost, no, not at all; and in the winter, in time of floods the stream will be very large, and rapid all the way above ground, which I affirm of my own knowledge, having seen it so, on many occasions.

But the true state of the case is this, the current of the river being much obstructed by the interposition of those hills, called Box-Hill, which though descending in a kind of vale, as if parted to admit the river to pass, and making that descent so low as to have the appearance of a level, near a village called Mickleham; I say, these hills yet interrupting the free course of the river, it forces the waters as it were to find their way through as well as they can; and in order to this, beginning, I say, where the river comes close to the foot of the precipice of Box-Hill, called the Stomacher, the waters sink insensibly away, and in some places are to be seen (and I have seen them) little channels which go out on the sides of the river, where the water in a stream not so big as would fill a pipe of a quarter of an inch diameter, trills away out of the river, and sinks insensibly into the ground.

In this manner it goes away, lessening the stream for above a mile, near two, and these they call the Swallows; and the whole ground on the bank of the river, where it is flat and low, is full of these subterraneous passages; so that if on any sudden rain the river swells over the banks, it is observed not to go back into the channel again when the flood abates, but to sink away into the earth in the meadows, where it spreads.

But now take this with you as you go, that these Swallows, though they diminish the stream much, do not so drink it up as to make it disappear. But that, where it crosses the road near Mickleham, it runs, as I have said, very sharp and broad, nor did I ever know it dry in the driest summer in that place, though I lived in the neighbourhood several years. On the contrary I have known it so deep, that waggons and carriages have not dared to go through, but never knew it, I say, dry in the greatest time of drought.

Below this place the hills rise again on the other side very high, and particularly on the ridge, which the country people call the Ashcom-Hills, and they seem to force the river again west; so it surrounds most of the park I mentioned above, and has several bridges upon it, and by this time indeed, so much of it is sunk away, that in a very dry summer the channel, though full of water in pits and holes cannot be perceived to run; but this must be, I say, in a very dry season, and still there is the channel visible where it runs at other times fiercely enough.

This part which I say has the least water, continuing about half a mile, we then perceive the channel insensibly to have more water than before. That is to say, that as it sunk in gradually and insensibly, so it takes vent again in the like manner in thousands of little springs, and unseen places, very few in any quantity, till in another half mile, it is a full river again, and passes in full streams under Leatherhead-Bridge, as above, and for the truth of this, I appeal to the knowledge of the inhabitants of Darking, Mickleham, Leatherhead, and all the country round.[42]

The town of Darking is eminent for several little things worth observation; as first, for the great Roman highway, called Stonny-street, which Mr Cambden says, passes through the very church-yard of this town. Secondly, for a little common or heath, called the Cottman Dean, or the dean or heath of poor cottagers, for so the word signifies, belonging to the town; and where their alms-house stands; which some learned physicians have singled out for the best air in England. Thirdly, for Mr Howard's house and garden, called Deaden, the garden is so naturally mounded with hills, that it makes a complete amphitheatre, being an oblong square, the area about eighty yards by forty, and at the south end, the ancient possessor, Mr Howard,[43] by what we call perforation, caused a vault or cave to be made quite through the hill, which came out again into a fine vineyard, which he planted the same year, on the south side, or slope of the hill, and which they say has produced since most excellent good wines, and a very great quantity of them.

At this town lived another ancient gentleman and his son, of a very good family; (viz.) Augustin Bellson, Esq: the father was measured seven foot and half an inch high, allowing all that he might have sunk, for his age, being seventy one years old; and the son measured two inches taller than his father.

The market of Darking . . . is of all the markets in England famous for poultry; and particularly for the fattest geese, and the largest capons, the name of a Darking Capon being well known among the poulterers in Leaden-Hall Market. In a word, they are brought to this market from as far as Horsham in Sussex; and 'tis the business of all the country, on that side for many miles, to breed and fatten them up, insomuch, that 'tis like a manufacture to the country people; and some of these capons are so large, as that they are little inferior to turkeys; and I have seen them sold for 4*s*. to 4*s*. 6*d*. each, and weighing from 4*l*. to 5 or 6*l*. a piece.

On the top of Box-Hill, and in view of this town, grows a very great beech-tree, which by way of distinction is called the Great Beech, and a very great tree it is; but I mention it on the following account, under the shade of this tree, was a little vault or cave, and here every Sunday, during the summer season, there used to be a rendezvous of coaches and horsemen, with abundance of gentlemen and ladies from Epsome to take the air, and walk in the box-woods; and in a word, divert, or debauch, or perhaps both, as they thought fit, and the game increased so much, that it began almost on a sudden, to make a great noise in the country.

A vintner who kept the King's-Arms-Inn, at Darking, taking notice of the constant and unusual flux of company thither, took the hint from the prospect of his advantage, which offered, and obtaining leave of Sir Adam Brown[44] whose manor and land it was, furnished this little cellar or vault with tables, chairs, &c. and with wine and eatables to entertain the ladies and gentlemen on Sunday nights, as above; and this was so agreeable to them as that it increased the company exceedingly. In a word, by these means, the concourse of gentry, and in consequence of the country people, became so great, that the place was like a little fair; so that at length the country began to take notice of it, and it was very offensive, especially to the best governed people; this lasted some years, I think two or three, and though complaint was made of it to Sir Adam Brown, and the neighbouring justices; alleging the revelling, and the indecent mirth that was among them, and on the Sabbath Day too, yet it did not obtain a suitable redress. Whereupon a certain set of young men, of the town of Darking, and perhaps prompted by some others, resenting the thing also, made an unwelcome visit to the place once on a Saturday night, just before the usual time of their wicked mirth, and behold when the coaches and ladies, &c. from Epsome appeared the next afternoon, they found the cellar and vault, and all that was in it, blown up with gun-powder; and so secret was it kept, that upon the utmost enquiry it could never be heard, or found out who were the persons that did it. That action put an end to their revels for a great while; nor was the place ever repaired that I heard of, at least it was not put to the same wicked use that it was employed in before.

The vale beneath this hill is for many miles east and west, called the Holmward, by some the Holm-Wood, others Holmsdale but more vulgarly the Homeward: in the woody part of which are often found outlying red deer, and in the days of King James II or while he was Duke of York, they have hunted the largest stags here that have been seen in England; the Duke took great care to have them preserved for his own sport, and they were so preserved for many years; but have since that been most of them destroyed.

It is suggested that this place was in ancient times so unpassable a wild, or overgrown waste, the woods so thick, and the extent so large, reaching far into Sussex, that it was the retreat for many ages of the native Britons, who the Romans could never drive out; and after that it was the like to the Saxons, when the Danes harrassed the nation with their troops, and ravaged the country wherever they came. But this is a piece of history, which I leave as I find it; the country though wild still, and perhaps having the same countenance now in many places, as it had above a thousand years ago; yet in other places is cultivated, and has roads passable enough in the summer quite through it, on every side, and the woods are cleared off in a great measure as above.

Here travelling east at the foot of the hills, we came to Rygate, a large market-town with a castle, and a mansion-house, inhabited for some years by Sir John Parsons,[45] once Lord Mayor of London, and whose son is in a fair way to be so also; being one of the aldermen and sheriffs of the said city at the writing these sheets. Here are two miserable borough towns too, which nevertheless send each of them two members to Parliament, to wit, Gatton under the side of the hill, almost at Rygate; and Bleechingly, more eastward on the same cross-road, which we were upon before. The last was for many years, the estate of Sir Robert Clayton,[46] a known citizen, and benefactor to the city of London, whose posterity still enjoy it; and at either town the purchasers seem to buy the election with the property.

From hence, crossing still the roads leading from London into Sussex, keeping on (east) we come to Westerham, the first market town in Kent on that side. This is a neat handsome well built market-town, and is full of gentry, and consequently of good company. All this part of the country is very agreeably pleasant, wholesome and fruitful, I mean quite from Guilford to this place; and is accordingly overspread with good towns, gentlemen's houses, populous villages, abundance of fruit, with hop-grounds and cherry orchards, and the lands well cultivated; but all on the right-hand, that is to say, south, is exceedingly grown with timber, has abundance of waste and wild grounds, and forests, and woods, with many large iron-works, at which they cast great quantities of iron cauldrons, chimney-backs, furnaces, retorts, boiling pots, and all such necessary things of iron; besides iron cannon, bomb-shells, stink-pots, hand-grenadoes, and cannon ball, &c. in an infinite quantity, and which turn to very great account; though at the same time the works are prodigiously expensive, and the quantity of wood they consume is exceeding great, which keeps up that complaint I mentioned before; that timber would grow scarce, and consequently dear, from the great quantity consumed in the iron-works in Sussex.

From hence going forward east, we come to Riverhead, a town on the road from London to Tunbridge; and then having little to speak of in Kent, except some petty market-towns, such as Wrotham, commonly called Rootham, Town-Malling, Cranbrook, and the like; I turned north, and came to Bromley, a market-town, made famous by an hospital, lately built there by Dr Warner,[47] Lord Bishop of Rochester, for the relief of the widows of clergy-men, which was not only well endowed at first, but has had many gifts and charities bestowed on it since, and is a very noble foundation for the best of charities in the world; besides it has been an example, and an encouragement to the like in other places, and has already been imitated, by the Bishops of Winchester and Salisbury in their dioceses.

Near this town we turned away by Beckenham, and through Norwood to Croydon; in the way we saw Dullige or Sydenham Wells, where great crowds of people throng every summer from London to drink the waters, as at Epsome and Tunbridge, they go more for the diversion of the season, for the mirth and the company; for gaming, or intriguing, and the like, here they go for mere physic, and this causes another difference; namely, that as the nobility and gentry go to Tunbridge, the merchants and rich citizens to Epsome; so the common people go chiefly to Dullwich and Stretham; and the rather also, because it lies so near London, that they can walk to it in the morning, and return at night; which abundance do; that is to say, especially of a Sunday, or on holidays, which makes the better sort also decline the place; the crowd on those days being both unruly and unmannerly.

Croydon is a great corn-market, but chiefly for oats and oatmeal, all for London still; the town is large and full of citizens from London, which makes it so populous. It is the ancient palace of the Archbishops of Canterbury, and several of them lie buried here; particularly that great man, Archbishop Whitgift, who not only repaired the palace, but built the famous hospital and school, which remains there to this day, to the singular honour of the giver. In the gardens of this episcopal palace, the Lady Dowager Onslow,[48] mother of the present lord of that name, was very unhappily drowned about two year since, in one of the fish-ponds, whether she did it herself, or whether by accident, or how, 'tis not the business of such a work as this to enquire.

I am sorry to record it to the reproach of any person in their grave, that the ancestor of this family, though otherwise a very honest gentleman, if fame lies not, was so addicted to gaming, and so unfortunately over-matched in his play, that he lost this noble seat and parks, and all the fine addenda which were then about it, at one night's play, some say, at one cast of dice, to Mr Harvey of Comb, near Kingston. What misery had befallen the family, if the right of the winner had been prosecuted with rigour, as by what I have heard it would have been, is hard to write. But God had better things in store for the gentleman's posterity than he took thought for himself; and the estate being entailed upon the heir, the loser died before it came into possession of the winner, and so it has been preserved, and the present gentleman has not only recovered the disaster, but as above, has exceedingly improved it all.

From hence it is but a little mile to Cashalton, a country village situate among innumerable springs of water, which all together, form a river in the very street of the town, and joining the other springs which come from Croydon and Bedington, make one stream, which are called the river Wandell. This village seated among such delightful springs, is yet all standing upon firm chalk; and having the Downs close adjoining, makes the most agreeable spot on all this side of London, as is abundantly testified by its being, as it were, crowded with fine houses of the citizens of London; some of which are built with such a profusion of expense, that they look rather like seats of the nobility, than the country houses of citizens and merchants; particularly those of Sir William Scawen, lately deceased; who besides an immense estate in money has left, as I was told, one article of nine thousand pounds a year to his heir; and was himself since the Fire of London, only Mr Scawen,[49] a Hamborough merchant, dealing by commission, and not in any view of such an increase of wealth, or any thing like it.

The other house is that of Sir John Fellows, late sub-governor of the South-Sea Company, who having the misfortune to fall in the general calamity of the late directors, lost all his unhappy wealth, which he had gained in the company, and a good and honestly gotten estate of his own into the bargain: I cannot dwell on the description of all the fine houses in this and the neighbouring villages; but I must take a trip here cross the downs of Epsome.

Banstead Downs need no description other than this, that their being so near London, and surrounded as they are with pleasant villages, and being in themselves perfectly agreeable, the ground smooth, soft, level and dry; (even in but a few hours after rain) they conspire to make the most delightful spot of ground, of that kind in all this part of Britain.

When on the public race days they are covered with coaches and ladies, and an innumerable company of horsemen, as well gentlemen as citizens, attending the sport; and then adding to the beauty of the sight, the racers flying over the course, as if they either touched not, or felt not the ground they run upon; I think no sight, except that of a victorious army, under the command of a Protestant King of Great Britain could exceed it.

About four miles, over those delicious downs, brings us to Epsome, and if you will suppose me to come there in the month of July, or thereabouts, you may think me to come in the middle of the season, when the town is full of company, and all disposed to mirth and pleasantry; for abating one unhappy stock jobbing year,[50] when England took leave to act the frantic, for a little while; and when every body's heads were turned with projects and stocks, I say, except this year, we see nothing of business in the whole conversation of Epsome. Even the men of business, who are really so when in London; whether it be at the Exchange, the Alley, or the Treasury-Offices, and the Court; yet here they look as if they had left all their London thoughts behind them, and had separated themselves to mirth and good company; as if they came hither to unbend the bow of the mind, and to give themselves a loose to their innocent pleasures; I say, innocent, for such they may enjoy here, and such any man may make his being here, if he pleases.

As, I say, this place seems adapted wholly to pleasure, so the town is suited to it; 'tis all rural, the houses are built at large, not many together, with gardens and ground about them; that the people who come out of their confined dwellings in London, may have air and liberty, suited to the design of country lodgings. You have no sooner taken lodgings, and entered the apartments, but if you are any thing known, you walk out, to see who and who's together; for 'tis the general language of the place, Come let's go see the town, folks don't come to Epsome to stay within doors. The next morning you are welcomed with the music under your chamber window; but for a shilling or two you get rid of them, and prepare for going to the Wells.

Here you have the compliment of the place, are entered into the list of the pleasant company, so you become a citizen of Epsome for that summer; and this costs you another shilling, or if you please, half a crown. Then you drink the waters, or walk about as if you did; dance with the ladies, though it be in your gown and slippers; have music and company of what kind you like, for every man may sort himself as he pleases; the grave with the grave, and the gay with the gay, the bright, and the wicked; all may be matched if they seek for it, and perhaps some of the last may be over-matched, if they are not upon their guard.

After the morning diversions are over, and every one are walked home to their lodgings, the town is perfectly quiet again; nothing is to be seen, the Green, the Great Room, the raffling-shops all are (as if it was a trading town on a holiday) shut up; there's little stirring, except footmen, and maid servants, going to and fro of errands, and higglers and butchers, carrying provisions to people's lodgings.

This takes up the town till dinner is over, and the company have reposed for two or three hours in the heat of the day; then the first thing you observe is, that the ladies come to the shady seats, at their doors, and to the benches in the groves, and covered walks; (of which, every house that can have them, is generally supplied with several). Here they refresh with cooling liquors, agreeable conversation, and innocent mirth.

Those that have coaches, or horses (as soon as the sun declines) take the air on the downs, and those that have not, content themselves with staying a little later, and when the air grows cool, and the sun low, they walk out under the shade of the hedges and trees, as they find it for their diversion. In the mean time, towards evening the bowling-green begins to fill, the music strikes up in the Great Room, and company draws together a-pace. And here they never fail of abundance of mirth, every night being a kind of ball; the gentlemen bowl, the ladies dance, others raffle, and some rattle; conversation is the general pleasure of the place, till it grows late, and then the company draws off; and, generally speaking, they are pretty well as to keeping good hours; so that by eleven a clock the dancing generally ends, and the day closes with good wishes, and appointments to meet the next morning at the Wells, or somewhere else.

The retired part of the world, of which also there are very many here, have the waters brought home to their apartments in the morning, where they drink and walk about a little, for assisting the physical operation, till near noon, then dress, dinner, and repose for the heat as others do; after which they visit, drink tea, walk abroad, come to their lodgings to supper, then walk again till it grows dark, and then to bed. The greatest part of the men, I mean of this grave sort, may be supposed to be men of business, who are at London upon business all the day, and thronging to their lodgings at night, make the families, generally speaking, rather provide suppers than dinners; for 'tis very frequent for the trading part of the company to place their families here, and take their horses every morning to London, to the Exchange, to the Alley, or to the warehouse, and be at Epsome again at night; and I know one citizen that practised it for several years together, and scarce ever lay a night in London during the whole season. Nor are these which I call the more retired part of the company, the least part of those that fill up the town of Epsome, nor is their way of living so retired, but that there is a great deal of society, mirth, and good manners, and good company among these too.

The pleasures of nature are so many round the town, the shady trees so every where planted, and now generally well grown, that it makes Epsome like a great park filled with little groves, lodges and retreats for coolness of air, and shade from the sun; and I believe, I may say, it is not to be matched in the world, on that account; at least, not in so little a space of ground.

In the winter this is no place for pleasure indeed; as it is full of mirth and gaiety in the summer, so the prospect in the winter presents you with little, but good houses shut up, and windows fastened; the furniture taken down, the families removed, the walks out of repair, the leaves off of the trees, and the people out of the town; and which is still worse, the ordinary roads both to it, and near it, except only on the side of the downs, are deep, stiff, full of sloughs, and, in a word, unpassable; so that there's no riding in the winter without the utmost fatigue, and some hazard, and this is the reason that Epsome is not (like Hampstead or Richmond) full of company in winter as well as summer.

From Epsome that I might thoroughly visit the county of Surrey, I rode over those clays, and through very bad roads to Kingstone, and from thence to Oatland, that I might see the famous place where Julius Caesar passed the river Thames in the sight of the British army, and notwithstanding they had stuck the river full of sharp stakes for three miles together.

The people said several of those stakes were still to be seen in the bottom of the river, having stood there for now above 1760 years; but they could show me none of them, though they call the place Coway Stakes to this day; I could make little judgment of the thing, only from this, that it really seems probable, that this was the first place where Caesar at that time could find the river fordable, or any way passable to him, who had no boats, no pontoons, and no way to make bridges over, in the teeth of so powerful, and so furious an enemy; but the Roman valour and discipline surmounted all difficulties, and he passed the army, routing the Britons; whose king and general, Cassibellanus,[51] never offered a pitched battle to the Romans afterward.

Satisfied with what little I could see here, which indeed was nothing at all, but the mere place, said to be so; and which it behoved me to believe, only because it was not unlikely to be true; I say, satisfied with this, I came back directly to Kingstone, a good market-town, but remarkable for little, only that they say, the ancient British and Saxon kings were usually crowned here in former times, which I will neither assert or deny.

But keeping the river now on my left, drawing near to London, we came to Hame and Peterson, little villages; the first, famous for a most pleasant palace of the late Duke of Lauderdale,[52] close by the river; a house King Charles II used to be frequently at, and be exceedingly pleased with; the avenues of this fine house to the land side, come up to the end of the village of Peterson, where the wall of New Park comes also close to the town, on the other side; in an angle of which stood a most delicious house, built by the late Earl of Rochester, Lord High Treasurer in King James II's reign, as also in part of Queen Ann's reign, which place he discharged so well, that we never heard of any misapplications, so much as suggested, much less inquired after.

I am obliged to say only, that this house *stood* here; for

even while this is writing the place seems to be but smoking with the ruins of a most unhappy disaster,[53] the whole house being a few months ago burnt down to the ground with a fire, so sudden, and so furious, that the family who were all at home, had scarce time to save their lives.

Nor was the house, though so exquisitely finished, so beautiful within and without, the greatest loss sustained; the rich furniture, the curious collection of paintings; and above all, the most curious collection of books, being the library of the first Earl of Clarendon, Lord Chancellor of England, and author of that most excellent History of the Rebellion, of which the world knows so much; I say, this library, as I am assured, was here wholly consumed; a loss irreparable, and not to be sufficiently regretted by all lovers of learning, having among other valuable things, several manuscripts relating to those times, which both for their rarity, antiquity, and authority, were of an inestimable value.

From hence we come to Richmond, the delightful retreat of their royal highnesses, the Prince and Princess of Wales, and where they have spent the fine season every summer for some years. The prince's court being so near must needs have filled Richmond, which was before a most agreeable retreat for the first and second rate gentry, with a great deal of the best company in England. This town and the country adjacent, increase daily in buildings, many noble houses for the accommodation of such, being lately raised and more in prospect: but 'tis feared should the prince come, for any cause that may happen to quit that side of the country, those numerous buildings must abate in the value which is now set upon them.

Here are wells likewise, and a mineral-water, which though not so much as that at Epsome and Tunbridge, are yet sufficient to keep up the forms of the place, and bring the company together in the morning, as the music does in the evening; and as there is more of quality in and about the place than is ordinarily to be seen at Epsome, the company is more shining, and sometimes even illustriously bright. Mr

Temple[54] created Baron Temple, of the kingdom of Ireland, even since this circuit was performed; and who is the son and successor to the honour, estate, and great part of the character of the great Sir William Temple, has a fine seat and gardens (hard by) at Shene. The gardens are indeed exquisitely fine, being finished, and even contrived by the great genius of Sir William, his father; and as they were his last delight in life, so they were every way suited to be so, to a man of his sense and capacity, who knew what kind of life was best fitted to make a man's last days happy.

It is not easy to describe the beauty with which the banks of the Thames shine on either side of the river, from hence to London, much more than our ancestors, even of but one age ago, knew any thing of. If for pleasant villages, great houses, palaces, gardens, &c. it was true in Queen Elizabeth's time, according to the poet, that

> The Thames with royal Tyber may compare.

I say, if this were true at that time, what may be said of it now? when for one fine house that was to be seen then, there are a hundred; nay, for ought I know, five hundred to be seen now, even as you sit still in a boat, and pass up and down the river.

First beginning from Ham-House, as above, the prince's palace salutes the eye, being formerly no more than a lodge in the park. I have seen many of the seats of the nobility in France, and some larger, but none finer than this, except such as had been laid out at the royal expense.

From Richmond to London, the river sides are full of villages, and those villages so full of beautiful buildings, charming gardens, and rich habitations of gentlemen of quality, that nothing in the world can imitate it; no, not the country for twenty miles round Paris, though that indeed is a kind of prodigy. To enumerate the gentlemen's houses in their view, would be too long for this work to describe them, would fill a large folio; it shall suffice to observe something, concerning the original of the strange passion, for fine gardens, which has so commendably possessed the English gentlemen of late years, for 'tis evident it is but of late years.

It is since the Revolution that our English gentlemen, began so universally, to adorn their gardens with those plants, we call ever greens, which leads me to a particular observation that may not be improper in this place; King William and Queen Mary introduced each of them two customs, which by the people's imitating them became the two idols of the town, and indeed of the whole kingdom; the queen brought in (1.) the love of fine East-India callicoes, such as were then called Masslapatan chintz, atlasses, and fine painted callicoes, which afterward descended into the humours of the common people so much, as to make them grievous to our trade, and ruining to our manufacturers and the poor; so that the Parliament were obliged at last to prohibit the use of them: (2.) The queen brought in the custom or humour, as I may call it, of furnishing houses with china-ware, which increased to a strange degree afterwards, piling their china upon the tops of cabinets, scrutores, and every chimney-piece, to the tops of the ceilings, and even setting up shelves for their china-ware, where they wanted such places, till it became a grievance in the expense of it, and even injurious to their families and estates.

The good queen far from designing any injury to the country where she was so entirely beloved, little thought she was in either of these laying a foundation for such fatal excesses, and would no doubt have been the first to have reformed them had she lived to see it.

The king on his part introduced (1.) the love of gardening; and (2.) of painting. In the first his majesty was particularly delighted with the decoration of ever greens, as the greatest addition to the beauty of a garden, preserving the figure in the place even in the roughest part of an inclement and tempestuous winter.

With the particular judgment of the king, all the gentlemen in England began to fall in; and in a few years fine gardens, and fine houses began to grow up in every corner;

the king began with the gardens at Hampton-Court and Kensington, and the gentlemen followed every where, with such a gust that the alteration is indeed wonderful throughout the whole kingdom.

But I find none has spoken of what I call the distant glory of all these buildings. There is a beauty of these things at a distance, taking them *en passant*, and in perspective, which few people value, and fewer understand; and yet here they are more truly great, than in all their private beauties whatsoever. Here they reflect beauty, and magnificence upon the whole country, and give a kind of a character to the island of Great Britain in general. The banks of the Sein are not thus adorned from Paris to Roan, or from Paris to the Loign above the city: the Danube can show nothing like it above and below Vienna, or the Po above and below Turin; the whole country here shines with a lustre not to be described. Take them in a remote view, the fine seats among the trees as jewels shine in a rich coronet; in a near sight they are mere pictures and paintings; at a distance they are all nature, near hand all art; but both in the extremest beauty. In a word, nothing can be more beautiful; here is a plain and pleasant country, a rich fertile soil, cultivated and enclosed to the utmost perfection of husbandry, then bespangled with villages; those villages filled with these houses, and the houses surrounded with gardens, walks, vistas, avenues, representing all the beauties of building, and all the pleasures of planting. It is impossible to view these countries from any rising ground and not be ravished with the delightful prospect. For example, suppose you take your view from the little rising hills about Clapham, there you see the pleasant villages of Peckham and Camberwell, with some of the finest dwellings about London; with all the villages mentioned above, and the country adjoining filled with the palaces of the British nobility and gentry already spoken of; looking north, behold, to crown all, a fair prospect of the whole city of London it self; the most glorious sight without exception, that the whole world at present can show, or perhaps ever could show since the sacking of Rome in the European, and the burning the Temple of Jerusalem in the Asian part of the world.

Add to all this, that these fine houses and innumerable more, which cannot be spoken of here, are not, at least very few of them, the mansion houses of families, the ancient residences of ancestors, the capital messuages of the estates; nor have the rich possessors any lands to a considerable value about them; but these are all houses of retreat, like the Bastides of Marseilles, gentlemen's mere summer-houses, or citizen's country-houses; whither they retire from the hurries of business, and from getting money, to draw their breath in a clear air, and to divert themselves and families in the hot weather; and they that are shut up, and as it were stripped of their inhabitants in the winter, who return to smoke and dirt, sin and seacoal, (as it was coarsely expressed) in the busy city; so that in short all this variety, this beauty, this glorious show of wealth and plenty, is really a view of the luxuriant age which we live in, and of the over-flowing riches of the citizens, who in their abundance make these gay excursions, and live thus deliciously all the summer, retiring within themselves in the winter, the better to lay up for the next summer's expense.

If this then is produced from the gay part of the town only, what must be the immense wealth of the city it self, where such a produce is brought forth? where such prodigious estates are raised in one man's age; instances of which we have seen in those of Sir Josiah Child,[55] Sir John Lethulier, Sir James Bateman, Sir Robert Clayton, Sir William Scawen, and hundreds more; whose beginnings were small, or but small compared, and who have exceeded even the greatest part of the nobility of England in wealth, at their death, and all of their own getting.

It would also take up a large chapter in this book, to but mention the overthrow, and catastrophe of innumerable wealthy city families, who after they have thought their houses established, and have built their magnificent country seats, as well as others, have sunk under the misfortunes of business, and the disasters of trade, after the world has thought them passed all possibility of danger; such as Sir Joseph Hodges,[56] Sir Justus Beck, the widow Cock at Camberwell, and many others; besides all the late South-Sea directors, all which I choose to have forgotten, as no doubt they desire to be, in recording the wealth and opulence of this part of England, which I doubt not to convince you infinitely outdoes the whole world.

I am come now to Southwark, a suburb to, rather than a part of London; but of which this may be said with justice.

A royal city were not London by.

To give you a brief description of Southwark, it might be called a long street, of about nine miles in length, as it is now built on eastward; reaching from Vaux-Hall to London-Bridge, and from the bridge to Deptford, all up to Deptford-Bridge, which parts it from Greenwich, all the way winding and turning as the river winds and turns; except only in that part, which reaches from Cuckold's-Point to Deptford, which indeed winds more than the river does. In the centre, which is opposite to the bridge, it is thickened with buildings, and may be reckoned near a mile broad; (viz.) from the bridge to the end of Kent-street and Blackman-street, and about the Mint;[57] but else the whole building is but narrow, nor indeed can it be otherwise; considering the length of it.

The principal beauty of the borough of Southwark, consists in the prodigious number of its inhabitants. Take it as it was anciently bounded, it contained nine parishes; but as it is now extended, and, as I say, joins with Deptford, it contains eleven large parishes. According to the weekly bills, for the year 1722, the nine parishes only buried 4166, which is about one sixth part of the whole body, called London; the bill of mortality for that year, amounting in all to 25750.

The first thing we meet with considerable, is at the Spring-Garden, just at the corner, where the road turns away to go from Vaux-Hall Turnpike, towards Newington, there are the remains of the old lines cast up in the times of the Rebellion, to fortify this side of the town; and at that corner was a very large bastion, or rather a fort, and such indeed they call it; which commanded all the pass on that side, and farther on, where the openings near St George's-Fields are, which they now call the Ducking-Pond, there was another. From hence they turned south east, and went to the windmill, at the end of Blackman-street, where they crossed the road, and going to the end of Kent-street, we see another great bastion; and then turning S.E. till they come to the end of Barnaby-street, or rather beyond, among the tanners, and there you see another fort, so plain, and so undemolished, the grass growing now over the works, that it is as plain as it was, even when it was thrown down. Here is also another remain of antiquity, the vestiges of which are easy to be traced; (viz.) the place where by strength of men's hands, they turned the channel of this great river of Thames, and made a new course for the waters, while the great bridge, which is now standing, was built: here it is evident they turned the waters out. A farther description of Southwark, I refer till I come to speak of London, as one general appellation for the two cities of London and Westminster; and all the borough of Southwark, and all the buildings and villages included within the bills of mortality, make but one London, in the general appellation, of which in its order. I am, &c.

Letter 3

Containing a description of the South Coasts of Hampshire, Wilts, Dorsetshire, Somersetshire, Devonshire, and Cornwall

SIR, – I find so many things to say in every part of England, that my journey cannot be barren of intelligence, which way soever I turn; no, though I were to oblige myself to say nothing of any thing that had been spoken of before.

I intended once to have gone due west this journey; but then I should have been obliged to crowd my observations so close, (to bring Hampton-Court, Windsor, Blenheim, Oxford, the Bath and Bristol, all into one letter; all those remarkable places lying in a line, as it were, in one point of the compass) as to have made my letter too long, or my observations too light and superficial, as others have done before me.

This letter will divide the weighty task, and consequently make it fit lighter on the memory, be pleasanter to the reader, and make my progress the more regular: I shall therefore take in Hampton-Court and Windsor in this journey; the first at my setting out, and the last at my return, and the rest as their situation demands.

As I came down from Kingston, in my last circuit, by the south bank of the Thames, so I go up to Hampton-Court, now, on the north bank, which I mention, because as the sides of the country bordering on the river, lie parallel, so the beauty of the country, the pleasant situations, the glory of innumerable fine buildings, noblemen's and gentlemen's houses, and citizen's retreats, are so equal a match to what I had described on the other side, that one knows not which to give the preference to.

Hampton-Court lies on the north bank of the river Thames, about two small miles from Kingston, and on the road from Stanes to Kingston Bridge; so that the road straightening the parks a little, they were obliged to part the parks, and leave the Paddock, and the Great Park, part on the other side the road, a testimony of that just regard that the kings of England always had, and still have, to the common good, and to the service of the country, that they would not interrupt the course of the road, or cause the poor people to go out of the way of their business, to or from the markets and fairs, for any pleasure of their own whatsoever.

The palace of Hampton-Court[1] was first founded, and built from the ground, by that great statesman, and favourite of King Henry VIII, Cardinal Wolsey. If there be a situation on the whole river between Stanes-Bridge and Windsor-Bridge, pleasanter than another, it is this of Hampton; close to the river, yet not offended by the rising of its waters in floods, or storms, near to the reflux of the tides, but not quite so near as to be affected with any foulness of the water, which the flowing of the tides generally is the occasion of. The gardens extend almost to the bank of the river, yet are never overflowed; nor are there any marshes on either side the river to make the waters stagnate, or the air unwholesome on that account. The river is high enough to be navigable, and low enough to be a little pleasantly rapid; so that the stream looks always cheerful, not slow and sleeping, like a pond. This keeps the waters always clear and clean, the bottom in view, the fish playing, and in sight; and, in a word, it has every thing that can make an inland; or, as I may call it, a country river pleasant and agreeable.

I shall sing you no songs here of the river in the first person of a water nymph, a goddess, (and I know not what) according to the humour of the ancient poets. I shall talk nothing of the marriage of old Isis, the male river, with the beautiful Thame, the female river, a whimsy as simple as the subject was empty, but I shall speak of the river as occasion presents, as it really is made glorious by the splendour of its shores, gilded with noble palaces, strong fortifications, large hospitals, and public buildings; with the greatest bridge, and the greatest city in the world, made famous by the opulence of its merchants, the increase and extensiveness of its commerce; by its invincible navies, and by the innumerable fleets of ships sailing upon it, to and from all parts of the world.

As I meet with the river upwards in my travels through the inland country, I shall speak of it, as it is the channel for conveying an infinite quantity of provisions from remote counties to London, and enriching all the counties again that lie near it, by the return of wealth and trade from the city; and in describing these things I expect both to inform and divert my readers, and speak, in a more masculine manner, more to the dignity of the subject, and also more to their satisfaction, than I could do any other way.

The Prince and Princess,[2] I remember came once down by water, upon the occasion of Her Royal Highness's being great with child, and near her time; so near, that she was delivered within two or three days after. But this passage being in the royal barges, with strength of oars, and the day exceeding fine, the passage, I say, was made very pleasant, and still the more so for being short. Again this passage is all the way with the stream, whereas, in the common passage, upwards, great part of the way is against the stream, which is slow and heavy.

The situation of Hampton-Court being thus mentioned, and its founder, 'tis to be mentioned next, that it fell to the Crown in the forfeiture of his eminence the cardinal, when the king seized his effects and estate, by which this and Whitehall, another house of his own building also, came to King Henry VIII. Two palaces fit for the Kings of England, erected by one cardinal, are standing monuments of the excessive pride, as well as the immense wealth of that prelate, who knew no bounds of his insolence and ambition, till he was overthrown at once by the displeasure of his master.

Whoever knew Hampton-Court before it was begun to be rebuilt, or altered, by the late King William, must acknowledge it was a very complete palace before, and fit for a king; and though it might not, according to the modern method of building, or of gardening, pass for a thing exquisitely fine;

yet it had this remaining to itself, and perhaps peculiar; namely, that it showed a situation exceedingly capable of improvement, and of being made one of the most delightful palaces in Europe.

This Her Majesty Queen Mary was so sensible of, that while the king had ordered the pulling down the old apartments, and building it up in that most beautiful form, which we see them now appear in, her majesty, impatient of enjoying so agreeable a retreat, fixed upon a building formerly made use of chiefly for landing from the river, and therefore called the Water Gallery. The Queen had here her gallery of beauties, being the pictures, at full length, of the principal ladies attending upon her majesty, or who were frequently in her retinue; and this was the more beautiful sight, because the originals were all in being, and often to be compared with their pictures. Her majesty had here a fine apartment, with a set of lodgings, for her private retreat only, but most exquisitely furnished; particularly a fine chintz bed, then a great curiosity; another of her own work, while in Holland, very magnificent, and several others; and here was also her majesty's fine collection of Delft ware, which indeed was very large and fine; and here was also a vast stock of fine china ware, the like whereof was not then to be seen in England; the long gallery, as above, was filled with this china, and every other place, where it could be placed, with advantage.

All these things were finished with expedition, that here their majesties might repose while they saw the main building go forward. While this was doing, the gardens were laid out, the plan of them devised by the King himself; and especially the amendments and alterations were made by the King, or the Queen's particular special command, or by both; for their majesties agreed so well in their fancy, and had both so good judgment in the just proportions of things, which are the principal beauties of a garden, that it may be said they both ordered every thing that was done.

The ground on the side of the other front, has received

some alterations since the taking down the water gallery; but not that part immediately next the lodgings. The orange trees, and fine Dutch bays, are placed within the arches of the building under the first floor: so that the lower part of the house was all one as a green house for some time. Here stands advanced, on two pedestals of stone, two marble vases, or flower pots, of most exquisite workmanship; the one done by an Englishman, and the other by a German. 'Tis hard to say which is the best performance, though the doing of it was a kind of trial of skill between them; but it gives us room, without partiality, to say they were both masters of their art.

The fine scrolls and bordure of these gardens were at first edged with box; but on the Queen's disliking the smell, those edgings were taken up, but have since been planted again, at least in many places, nothing making so fair and regular an edging as a box, or is so soon brought to its perfection.

On the north side of the house, where the gardens seemed to want screening from the weather, or the view of the chapel, and some part of the old building required to be covered from the eye; the vacant ground, which was large, is very happily cast into a wilderness, with a labyrinth, and espaliers so high, that they effectually take off all that part of the old building, which would have been offensive to the sight.

I hinted in my last that King William brought into England the love of fine paintings, as well as that of fine gardens; and you have an example of it in the cartoons, as they are called, being five pieces of such paintings, as, if you will believe men of nice judgment and great travelling, are not to be matched in Europe. The stories are known, but especially two of them,[3] (viz.) that of St Paul preaching on Mars-Hill to the self-wise Athenians, and that of St Peter passing sentence of death on Ananias; I say, these two strike the mind with the utmost surprise; the passions are so drawn to the life, astonishment, terror and death in the face of Ananias; zeal and a sacred fire in the eyes of the blessed apostle; fright and surprise upon the countenances of the beholders in the piece of Ananias; all these describe themselves so naturally, that you cannot but seem to discover something of the like passions, even in seeing them.

'Tis reported, but with what truth I know not, that the late French king offered an hundred thousand louis d'ors for these pictures; but this, I say, is but a report. The King brought a great many other fine pieces to England, and with them the love of fine paintings so universally spread itself among the nobility and persons of figure all over the kingdom, that it is incredible what collections have been made by English gentlemen since that time; and how all Europe has been rummaged, as we say, for pictures to bring over hither, where, for twenty years, they yielded the purchasers, such as collected them for sale, immense profit. But the rates are abated since that, and we begin to be glutted with the copies and frauds of the Dutch and Flemish painters, who have imposed grossly upon us. But to return to the palace of Hampton-Court: Queen Mary lived not to see it completely finished; and her death, with the other difficulties of that reign, put a stop to the works for some time, till the King reviving his good liking of the place, set them to work again, and it was finished, as we see it. But I have been assured, that had the peace continued, and the King lived to enjoy the continuance of it, his majesty had resolved to have pulled down all the remains of the old building; and to have built up the whole palace after the manner of those two fronts already done. In these would have been an entire set of rooms of state for the receiving, and, if need had been, lodging, and entertaining any foreign prince, with his retinue; also offices for all the Secretaries of State, Lords of the Treasury, and of trade; as also apartments for all the great officers of the household. But the King's death put an end to all these things.

Since the death of King William, Hampton-Court seemed abandoned of its patron. They have gotten a kind of proverbial saying relating to Hampton-Court, (viz.) that it has been generally chosen by every other prince, since it became a house of note. King Charles I was not only a prince that delighted in country retirements, but knew how to make choice of them by the beauty of their situation, the goodness of the air, &c. He took great delight here, and, had he lived to enjoy it in peace, had purposed to make it another thing than it was. But we all know what took him off from that felicity. and all others; and this house was at last made one of his prisons by his rebellious subjects.

His son, King Charles II may well be said to have an aversion to the place, for the reason just mentioned, namely, the treatment his royal father met with there; and particularly that the rebel and murtherer of his father, Cromwell, afterwards possessed this palace, and revelled here in the blood of the royal party, as he had done in that of his sovereign; King Charles II therefore chose Windsor, and bestowed a vast sum in beautifying the castle there, and which brought it to the perfection we see it in at this day.

King William, for King James is not to be named as to his choice of retired palaces, his delight running quite another way; I say, King William fixed upon Hampton-Court; and it was in his reign that Hampton-Court put on new clothes, and being dressed gay and glorious, made the figure we now see it in.

The late Queen, taken up for part of her reign in her kind regards to the Prince her spouse,[4] was obliged to reside where her care of his health confined her, and in this case kept for the most part at Kensington, where he died; but her majesty always discovered her delight to be at Windsor, where she chose the little house, as 'twas called, opposite to the castle, and took the air in her chaise in the parks and forest, as she saw occasion.

Now Hampton-Court, by the like alternative, is come into request again; and we find his present majesty, who is a good judge too of the pleasantness and situation of a place of that kind, has taken Hampton-Court into his favour, and has made it much his choice for the summer's retreat of the

Court, and where they may best enjoy the diversions of the season.

From Hampton-Court I directed my course for a journey into the south west part of England; and I crossed to Chertsey on the Thames, a town I mentioned before; from whence crossing the Black Desert, as I called it, of Bagshot-Heath, I directed my course for Hampshire, or Hantshire.

Before we reach Basingstoke, we get rid of that unpleasant country, which I so often call a desert, and enter into a pleasant fertile country, enclosed and cultivated like the rest of England; and passing a village or two, we enter Basingstoke, in the midst of woods and pastures, rich and fertile, and the country accordingly spread with the houses of the nobility and gentry, as in other places. Basingstoke has a good market for corn, and lately, within a very few years, is fallen into a manufacture, (viz.) of making druggets and shalloons, and such slight goods, which, however, employs a good number of the poor people, and enables them to get their bread, which knew not how to get it before.

From hence the great western road goes to Whitchurch and Andover, two market towns, and sending members to Parliament; at the last of which, the Downs, or open country, begins, which we in general, though falsely, call Salisbury-Plain. But I was obliged to go off to the left hand, to Alresford and Winchester. Alresford was a flourishing market town, and remarkable for this: that though it had no great trade, and particularly very little, if any manufactures, yet there was no collection in the town for the poor, nor any poor low enough to take alms of the parish, which is what I do not think can be said of any town in England besides.

But this happy circumstance, which so distinguished Alresford from all her neighbours, was brought to an end in the year ——, when, by a sudden and surprising fire,[5] the whole town, with both the church and the market-house, was reduced to a heap of rubbish; and, except a few poor huts at the remotest ends of the town, not a house left standing. The town is since that very handsomely rebuilt, and the neighbouring gentlemen contributed largely to the relief of the people, especially, by sending in timber towards their building; also their market-house is handsomely built; but the church not yet, though we hear there is a fund raising likewise for that.

Here is a very large pond, or lake of water, kept up to a head, by a strong *batterd'eau*, or dam, which the people tell us was made by the Romans; and that it is to this day part of the great Roman highway, which leads from Winchester to Alton, and, as 'tis supposed, went on to London.

From hence, at the end of seven miles over the downs, we come to the very ancient city of Winchester; not only the great church, which is so famous all over Europe, and has been so much talked of, but even the whole city has, at a distance, the face of venerable, and looks ancient afar off; and yet here are many modern buildings too, and some very handsome; as the college schools; with the bishop's palace,[6] built by Bishop Morley, since the late wars; the old palace of the bishop having been ruined by that known church incendiary, Sir William Waller, and his crew of plunderers; who, if my information is not wrong, as I believe it is not, destroyed more monuments of the dead, and defaced more churches, than all the Round-heads in England beside.

The outside of the church is as plain and coarse, as if the founders had abhorred ornaments, or that William of Wickham had been a Quaker, or at least a Quietist. There is neither statue, or a niche for a statue, to be seen on all the outside; no carved work, no spires, towers, pinnacles, balustrades or any thing; but mere walls, buttresses, windows, and coins, necessary to the support and order of the building. It has no steeple, but a short tower covered flat, as if the top of it had fallen down, and it had been covered in haste to keep the rain out, till they had time to build it up again.

But the inside of the church has many very good things in it, and worth observation; it was for some ages the burying place of the English Saxon kings; whose relics, at the repair of the church, were collected by Bishop Fox,[7] and, being put together into large wooden chests, lined with lead, were again interred at the foot of the great wall in the choir, three on one side, and three on the other; with an account whose bones are in each chest, whether the division of the relics might be depended upon, has been doubted, but is not thought material, so that we do but believe they are all there.

The choir of the church appears very magnificent; the roof is very high, and the Gothic work in the arched part is very fine, though very old; the painting in the windows is admirably good, and easy to be distinguished by those that understand those things.

The choir is said to be the longest in England; and as the number of prebendaries, canons, &c. are many, it required such a length. The ornaments of the choir are the effects of the bounty of several bishops; the fine altar (the noblest in England by much) was done by Bishop Morley; the roof, and the coat of arms of the Saxon and Norman kings, were done by Bishop Fox; and the fine throne, for the bishop in the choir, was given by Bishop Mew,[8] in his life-time; and it was well it was; for if he had ordered it by will, there is reason to believe it had never been done. That reverend prelate, notwithstanding he enjoyed so rich a bishopric, scarce leaving money enough behind him, to pay for his coffin.

There are a great many persons of rank buried in this church, besides the Saxon kings, mentioned above; and besides several of the most eminent bishops of the see. Just under the altar lies a son of William the Conqueror, without any monument. The monument of Sir John Cloberry is extraordinary, but more, because it puts strangers upon enquiring into his story, than for any thing wonderful in the figure, it being cut in a modern dress; the habit gentlemen wore in those times, which, being now so much out of fashion, appears mean enough.

The body of the church was built by the famous William of Wickham;[9] whose monument, intimating his fame, lies in the middle of that part, which was built at his expense. He was a courtier before a bishop; his natural genius was much beyond his acquired parts, and his skill in politics beyond his ecclesiastic knowledge. He is said to have put his master, King Edward III, to whom he was Secretary of State, upon the two great projects which made his reign so glorious, viz. first, upon setting up his claim to the crown of France, and pushing that claim by force of arms, which brought on the war with France, in which that prince was three times victorious in battle. (2) Upon setting up, or instituting the Order of the Garter; in which he (being before that made Bishop of Winchester) obtained the honour for the Bishops of Winchester, of being always prelates of the Order, as an appendix to the bishopric; and he himself was the first prelate of the Order, and the ensigns of that honour are joined with his episcopal ornaments, in the robing of his effigy on the monument above.

To the honour of this bishop, there are other foundations of his, but particularly the college in this city, which is a noble foundation indeed. The building consists of two large courts, in which are the lodgings for the masters and scholars, and in the centre a very noble chapel; beyond that, in the second court, are the schools, with a large cloister beyond them, and some enclosures laid open for the diversion of the scholars. There also is a great hall, where the scholars dine. The funds for the support of this college are very considerable; the masters live in a very good figure, and their maintenance is sufficient to support it: they have all separate dwellings in the house, and all possible conveniences appointed them. The scholars have exhibitions at a certain time of continuance here, if they please to study, in the New College at Oxford, built by the same noble benefactor.

This school has fully answered the end of the founder, who, though he was no great scholar, resolved to erect a house for the making the ages to come more learned than those that went before; and it had, I say, fully answered the end, for many learned and great men have been raised here, some of whom we shall have occasion to mention as we go on.

Among the many private inscriptions in this church, we

found one made by an eminent physician in this city, on a mother and child, who, being his patients, died together, and were buried in the same grave, and which intimate, that one died of a fever, and the other of a dropsy.

At the west gate of this city was anciently a castle, known to be so by the ruins, more than by any extraordinary notice taken of it in history. What they say of it, that the Saxon kings kept their Court here, is doubtful, and must be meant of the West Saxons only; and as to the tale of King Arthur's round table, which, they pretend, was kept here for him, and his two dozen of knights; which table hangs up still, as a piece of antiquity, to the tune of 1200 years, and has, as they pretend, the names of the said knights in Saxon characters, and yet such as no man can read. All this story I see so little ground to give the least credit to, that I look upon it, and 't shall please you, to be no better than a FIB.

Where this castle stood, or whatever else it was, for some say there was no castle there, the late King Charles II marked out, a very noble design;[10] which had he lived, would certainly have made that part of the country, the New-Market of the ages to come.

The building is begun, and the front next the city carried up to the roof, and covered; but the remainder is not begun. There was a street of houses designed from the gate of the palace down to the town, but it was never begun to be built; all hope of seeing this design perfected, or the house finished, is now vanished.

I cannot omit that there are several public edifices in the neighbourhood; towards the north, a piece of an old monastery undemolished, and which is still preserved to the religion, being the residence of some private Roman Catholic gentlemen, where they have an oratory, and, as they say, live still according to the rules of St Benedict. This building is called Hide-House; and, as they live very usefully and, to the highest degree, obliging among their neighbours they meet with no obstruction or disturbance from any body.

Winchester is a place of no trade, other than is naturally

occasioned by the inhabitants of the city and neighbouring villages, one with another. Here is no manufacture, no navigation; here is a great deal of good company; and abundance of gentry being in the neighbourhood, it adds to the sociableness of the place. The clergy also here are, generally speaking, very rich, and very numerous.

As there is such good company, so they are gotten into that new-fashioned way of conversing by assemblies: they are pleasant and agreeable to the young people, and some times fatal to them, of which, in its place. Winchester has its share of the mirth: may it escape the ill consequences.

The hospital [11] on the south of this city, at a mile's distance on the road to Southampton, is worth notice. 'Tis said to be founded by King William Rufus, but was not endowed or appointed till later times by Cardinal Beaufort. Every traveller that knocks at the door of this house, in his way, and asks for it, claims the relief of a piece of white bread and a cup of beer; and this donation is still continued; a quantity of good beer is set apart every day to be given away; and what is left, is distributed to other poor, but none of it kept to the next day.

How the revenues of this hospital, which should maintain the master and thirty private gentlemen, who they call fellows, but ought to call brothers, is now reduced to maintain only fourteen, while the master lives in a figure equal to the best gentleman in the country, would be well worth the enquiry of a proper visitor, if such can be named. 'Tis a thing worthy of complaint, when public charities, designed for the relief of the poor, are embezzled and deprecated by the rich, and turned to the support of luxury and pride.

From Winchester, is about 25 miles, and over the most charming plains that can any where be seen, (far in my opinion) excelling the plains of Mecca, we come to Salisbury; the vast flocks of sheep, which one every where sees upon these downs, and the great number of those flocks, is a sight truly worth observation.

But 'tis more remarkable still; how a great part of these downs comes by a new method of husbandry, to be not only made arable, which they never were in former days, but to bear excellent wheat, and great crops too, though otherwise poor barren land, and never known to our ancestors to be capable of any such thing; nay, they would perhaps have laughed at any one that would have gone about to plough up the wild downs and hills, where the sheep were wont to go. But experience has made the present age wiser, and more skilful in husbandry; for by only folding the sheep upon the ploughed lands, those lands, which otherwise are barren, and where the plough goes within three or four inches of the solid rock of chalk, are made fruitful, and bear very good wheat, as well as rye and barley.

This plain country continues in length from Winchester to Salisbury 25 miles, from thence to Dorchester 22 miles, thence to Weymouth 6 miles, so that they lie near 50 miles in length, and breadth; they reach also in some places 35 to 40 miles. They who would make any practicable guess at the number of sheep usually fed on these downs, may take it from a calculation made, as I was told, at Dorchester, that there were 600000 sheep fed within 6 miles of that town, measuring every way round, and the town in the centre.

As we passed this plain country, we saw a great many old camps, as well Roman as British, and several remains of the ancient inhabitants of this kingdom, and of their wars, battles, entrenchments, encampments, buildings, and other fortifications, which are indeed very agreeable to a traveller, that has read any thing of the history of the country. Old Sarum is as remarkable as any of these, where there is a double entrenchment, with a deep graffe, or ditch, to either of them; the area about 100 yards in diameter, taking in the whole crown of the hill, and thereby rendering the ascent very difficult. Near this, there is one farm house, which is all the remains I could see of any town in or near the place, for the encampment has no resemblance of a town; and yet this is called the borough of Old Sarum, and sends two members to Parliament, who, those members can justly say, they represent, would be hard for them to answer.

Salisbury itself is indeed a large and pleasant city; though I do not think it at all the pleasanter for that which they boast so much of; namely, the water running through the middle of every street, or that it adds any thing to the beauty of the place, but just the contrary; it keeps the streets always dirty, full of wet and filth, and weeds, even in the middle of summer.

As the city of Winchester is a city without trade, that is to say, without any particular manufactures; so this city of Salisbury, and all the county of Wilts, of which it is the capital, are full of a great variety of manufactures; and those some of the most considerable in England; namely, the clothing trade, and the trade of flannels, druggets, and several other sorts of manufactures.

The city of Salisbury has two remarkable manufactures carried on in it, and which employ the poor of great part of the country round; namely, fine flannels, and long cloths for the Turkey trade, called Salisbury Whites. The people of Salisbury are gay and rich, and have a flourishing trade; and there is a great deal of good manners and good company among them; I mean, among the citizens, besides what is found among the gentlemen.

The cathedral is famous for the height of its spire, which is without exception the highest, and the handsomest in England, being from the ground 410 foot,[12] and yet the walls so exceeding thin, that at the upper part of the spire upon a view made by the late Sir Christopher Wren, the wall was found to be less than five inches thick; upon which a consultation was had, whether the spire, or at least the upper part of it should be taken down, it being supposed to have received some damage by the great storm in the year 1703; but it was resolved in the negative, and Sir Christopher ordered it to be strengthened with bands of iron plates, as has effectually secured it; and I have heard some of the best architects say, it is stronger now than when it was first built.

They tell us, this church was 40 years a building, and cost an immense sum of money, but it must be acknowledged that the inside of the work is not answerable in the decoration of things, to the workmanship without; the painting in the choir [13] is mean, and more like the ordinary method of common drawing room, or tavern painting, than that of a church; the carving is good, but very little of it, and it is rather a fine church than finely set off. The ordinary boast of this building, that there were as many gates as months, as many windows as days, as many marble pillars as hours in the year, is now no recommendation at all. However the mention of it must be preserved.

> As many days as in one year there be,
> So many windows in one church we see;
> As many marble pillars there appear,
> As there are hours throughout the fleeting year;
> As many gates as moons one year do view:
> Strange tale to tell, yet not more strange than true.

Among other monuments of noble men in this cathedral they show you one that is very extraordinary, and to which there hangs a tale: there was in the reign of Philip and Mary a very unhappy murther committed by the then Lord Sturton,[14] or Stourton, a family since extinct, but well known till within a few years in that country. This Lord Stourton being guilty of the said murther, which also was aggravated with very bad circumstances, could not obtain the usual grace of the Crown, (viz.) to be beheaded, but Queen Mary positively ordered that like a common malefactor he should die at the gallows. After he was hanged, his friends desiring to have him buried at Salisbury, the bishop would not consent that he should be buried in the cathedral, unless as a farther mark of infamy, his friends would submit to this condition (viz.) that the silken halter in which he was hanged should be hanged up over his grave in the church, as a monument of his crime; which was accordingly done, and there it is to be seen to this day. The putting this halter up here, was not so wonderful to me as it was, that the posterity of that lord, who remained in good rank sometime after, should never prevail to have that mark of infamy taken off from the memory of their ancestor.

From hence directing my course to the sea-side, I left the great road, and went down the east side of the river towards New-Forest, and Lymington; and here I saw the ancient house and seat of Clarendon, the mansion of the ancient family of Hide, ancestors of the great Earl of Clarendon.

Being happily fixed by the favour of a particular friend at so beautiful a spot of ground as this of Clarendon Park, I made several little excursions from hence to view the northern parts of this county; a county so fruitful of wonders, that though I do not make antiquity my chief search, yet I must not pass it over entirely, where so much of it, and so well worth observation is to be found, which would look as if I either understood not the value of the study, or expected my readers should be satisfield with a total omission of it.

I have mentioned that this county is generally a vast continued body of high chalky hills, whose tops spread themselves into fruitful and pleasant downs and plains, upon which great flocks of sheep are fed, &c. But the reader is desired to observe these hills and plains are most beautifully intersected, and cut through by the course of divers pleasant and profitable rivers; in the course, and near the banks, of which there always is a chain of fruitful meadows, and rich pastures, and those interspersed with innumerable pleasant towns, villages, and houses, and among them many of considerable magnitude; so that while you view the downs, and think the country wild and uninhabited; yet when you come to descend into these vales you are surprised with the most pleasant and fertile country in England.

There are no less than four of these rivers which meet all together, at, or near the city of Salisbury, especially the waters of three of them run through the streets of the city; and the course of these three lead us through the whole mountainous part of the country, the two first join their waters at Wilton the shire-town, though a place of no great notice now; and these are the waters which run through the canal, and the gardens of Wilton House, the seat of that ornament of nobility and learning, the Earl of Pembroke.[15]

One cannot be said to have seen any thing that a man of curiosity would think worth seeing in this county, and not have been at Wilton House; but not the beautiful building, not the ancient trophy of a great family, not the noble situation, not all the pleasures of the gardens, parks, fountains, hare-warren, or of whatever is rare either in art or nature are equal to, that yet more glorious sight, of a noble princely palace, constantly filled with its noble and proper inhabitants; viz. the lord and proprietor, who is indeed a true patriarchal monarch, reigns here with an authority agreeable to all his subjects (family); and his reign is made agreeable, by his first practising the most exquisite government of himself, and then guiding all under him by the rules of honour and virtue; being also himself perfectly master of all the needful arts of family government.

Here an exalted genius is the instructor, a glorious example the guide, and a gentle well directed hand the governor and law-giver to the whole; and the family like a well governed city appears happy, flourishing and regular, groaning under no grievance, pleased with what they enjoy, and enjoying every thing which they ought to be pleased with. Nor is the blessing of this noble resident extended to the family only, but even to all the country round, who in their degree feel the effects of the general beneficence; and where the neighbourhood, however poor, receive all the good they can expect, and are sure to have no injury, or oppression.

As the present Earl of Pembroke, the lord of this fine palace, is a nobleman of great personal merit, many other ways; so he is a man of learning, and reading, beyond most men of his lordship's high rank in this nation, if not in the world; and as his reading has made him a master of antiquity, and judge of such pieces of antiquity,[16] as he has had opportunity to meet with in his own travels, and otherwise in the world; so it has given him a love of the study, and made him a collector of valuable things, as well in painting as in sculpture, and other excellencies of art, as also of nature; in so much that Wilton-House is now a mere museum, a chamber of rarities, and we meet with several things there, which are to be found no where else in the world.

As his lordship is a great collector of fine paintings; so I know no nobleman's house in England, so prepared, as if built on purpose to receive them; the largest, and the finest pieces that can be imagined extant in the world, might have found a place here capable to receive them. I say, they might have found, as if they could not now, which is in part true; for at present the whole house is so completely filled, that I see no room for any new piece to crowd in, without displacing some other fine piece that hung there before; as for the value of the piece, that might so offer to succeed the displaced, that the great judge of the whole collection, the earl himself, must determine, and as his judgement is perfectly good, the best picture would be sure to possess the place. The piece of our Saviour washing His disciples' feet, which they show you in one of the first rooms you go into, must be spoken of by every body that has any knowledge of painting, and is an admirable piece indeed.

When you are entered the apartments, such variety seizes you every way, that you scarce know to which hand to turn your self. First, on one side you see several rooms filled with paintings, as before, all so curious, and the variety such, that 'tis with reluctance, that you can turn from them; while looking another way, you are called off by a vast collection of busto's, and pieces of the greatest antiquity of the kind, both Greek, and Romans; among these, there is one of the Roman emperor, Marcus Aurelius in *basso relievo*. I never saw any thing like what appears here, except in the chamber of rarities at Munick in Bavaria.

Passing these, you come into several large rooms, as if contrived for the reception of the beautiful guests that take them up; one of these is near 70 foot long and the ceiling 26 foot high, with another adjoining of the same height, and breadth, but not so long. Those together might be called the Great

Gallery of Wilton, and might vie for paintings with the gallery of Luxemburg in the Fauxbourg of Paris.

These two rooms are filled with the family pieces of the house of Herbert, most of them by Lilly, or Vandyke, and one in particularly, out does all that ever I met with, either at home, or abroad, 'tis done, as was the mode of painting at that time, after the manner of a family piece of King Charles I with his queen, and children, which before the burning of White-Hall, I remember to hang at the east end of the Long Gallery in the palace.

It would be endless to describe the whole set of the family pictures, which take up this room, unless we would enter into the roof-tree of the family, and set down a genealogical line of the whole house.

After we have seen this fine range of beauties, for such indeed they are; far from being at an end of your surprise, you have three or four rooms still upon the same floor, filled with wonders, as before. Nothing can be finer than the pictures themselves, nothing more surprising than the number of them; at length you descend the back-stairs, which are in themselves large, though not like the other. However, not a hand's breadth is left to crowd a picture in of the smallest size, and even the upper rooms, which might be called garrets, are not naked, but have some very good pieces in them.

From this pleasant and agreeable day's work, I returned to Clarendon, and the next day took another short tour to the hills, to see that celebrated piece of antiquity, the wonderful Stone-Henge, and upon the side of the river Avon, near the town of Amesbury. 'Tis needless, that I should enter here into any part of the dispute about which our learned antiquaries have so puzzled themselves, that several books, and one of them, in folio, has been published about it; some alleging it to be a heathen, or pagan temple, and altar, or place of sacrifice, as Mr Jones;[17] others, a monument, or trophy of victory; others a monument for the dead, as Mr Aubury, and the like. Again, some will have it be British, some Danish, some Saxon, some Roman, and some before them all, Phenician.

I shall suppose it, as the majority of all writers do, to be a monument for the dead, and the rather, because men's bones have been frequently dug up in the ground near them. The common opinion that no man could ever count them, that a baker carried a basket of bread, and laid a loaf upon every stone, and yet could never make out the same number twice: this, I take, as a mere country fiction, and a ridiculous one too; the reason why they cannot easily be told, is, that many of them lie half, or part buried in the ground, and a piece here, and a piece there, only appearing above the grass, it cannot be known easily, which belong to one stone, and which to another, or which are separate stones, and which are joined under ground to one another; otherwise, as to those which appear, they are easy to be told, and I have seen them told four times after one another, beginning every time at a different place, and every time they amounted to 72 in all.

The form of this monument is not only described but delineated in most authors, and indeed 'tis hard to know the first, but by the last; the figure was at first circular, and there were at least four rows or circles, within one another; the main stones were placed upright, and they were joined on the top by cross stones, laid from one to another, and fastened with vast mortices and tenants. Length of time has so decayed them, that not only most of the cross stones which lay on the top are fallen down, but many of the upright also, notwithstanding the weight of them is so prodigious great. How they came thither, or from whence, no stones of that kind being now to be found in any part of England near it, is still the mystery, for they are of such immense bulk that no engines, or carriages which we have in use in this age could stir them.

These stones at Stonehenge, as Mr Cambden describes them, were very large, the upright stones 24 foot high, 7 foot broad, 16 foot round; and weight 12 ton each; and the cross stones on the top, which he calls coronets, were 6 or 7 ton, but this does not seem equal, for if the cross stones weighed six, or seven ton, the others, as they appear now, were at least 5 or 6 times as big, and must weigh in proportion. And therefore, I must think their judgement much nearer the case who judge the upright stones at 16 ton, or thereabouts, supposing them to stand a great way into the earth, as 'tis not doubted but they do; and the coronets, or cross stones, at about two ton, which is very large too, and as much as their bulk can be thought to allow. Upon the whole, we must take them as our ancestors have done; namely, for an erection, or building so ancient, that no history has handed down to us the original, as we find it then uncertain, we must leave it so. 'Tis indeed a reverend piece of antiquity, and 'tis a great loss that the true history of it is not known.

The downs and plains in this part of England being so open, and the surface so little subject to alteration, there are more remains of antiquity to be seen upon them, than in other places; for example, I think they tell us there are three and fifty ancient encampments, or fortifications to be seen in this one county, some whereof are exceeding plain to be seen, some of one form, some of another; some of one nation, some of another, British, Danish, Saxon, Roman.

Also the barrows, as we all agree to call them, are very many in number in this county, and very obvious, having suffered very little decay. These are large hillocks of earth cast up, as the ancients agree, by the soldiers over the bodies of their dead comrades slain in battle; several hundreds of these are to be seen, especially in the north part of this county, about Marlbro' and the downs, from thence to St Ann's-Hill, and even every way, the downs are full of them.

I am now to pursue my first design, and shall take the west part of Wiltshire in my return, where are several things very well worth our stay. From hence in my way to the sea-side I came to New-Forest of which I have said something already.

This waste and wild part of the country was, as some record, laid open, and waste for a forest, and for game, by that violent tyrant William the Conqueror, and for which purpose he unpeopled the country, pulled down the houses, and which was worse, the churches of several parishes or towns, and of abundance of villages, turning the poor people out of their habitations, and possessions, and laying all open for his deer. The same histories likewise record that two of his own blood and posterity, and particularly his immediate successor William Rufus lost their lives in this forest: one (viz.) the said William Rufus being shot with an arrow directed at a deer, which the king, and his company were hunting, and the arrow glancing on a tree, changed his course and struck the king full on the breast, and killed him. This they relate as a just judgment of God on the cruel devastation made here by the Conqueror. Be it so or not, as heaven pleases; but that the king was so killed, is certain, and they show the tree, on which the arrow glanced, to this day.

I cannot omit to mention here a proposal [18] made a few years ago to the late Lord Treasurer, Godolphin, for re-peopling this forest, which for some reasons I can be more particular in, than any man now left alive, because I had the honour to draw up the scheme, and argue it before that noble lord, and some others who were principally concerned at that time in bringing over, or rather providing for when they were come over, the poor inhabitants of the Palatinate; a thing in it self commendable, but as it was managed, made scandalous to England, and miserable to those poor people.

Some persons being ordered by that noble lord, above mentioned, to consider of measures, how the said poor people should be provided for, and whether they could be provided for, or no, without injury to the public. The answer was grounded upon this maxim, that the number of inhabitants is the wealth and strength of a kingdom, provided those inhabitants were such, as by honest industry applied themselves to live by their labour, to whatsoever trades, or employments they were brought up. In the next place it was enquired, what employments those poor people were brought up to? It was answered. there were husbandmen, and artificers of all sorts, upon which the proposal was as follows.

New Forest in Hampshire was singled out to be the place.

Here it was proposed to draw a great square-line, containing four thousand acres of land, marking out two large highways, or roads through the centre, crossing both ways, so that there should be a thousand acres in each division, exclusive of the land contained in the said cross roads.

Then it was proposed to single out twenty men, and their families, who should be recommended as honest industrious men, expert in, or at least capable of being instructed in husbandry, curing and cultivating of land, breeding and feeding cattle, and the like. To each of these should be parcelled out in equal distributions, two hundred acres of this land, so

The form of the several farms would be laid out thus.

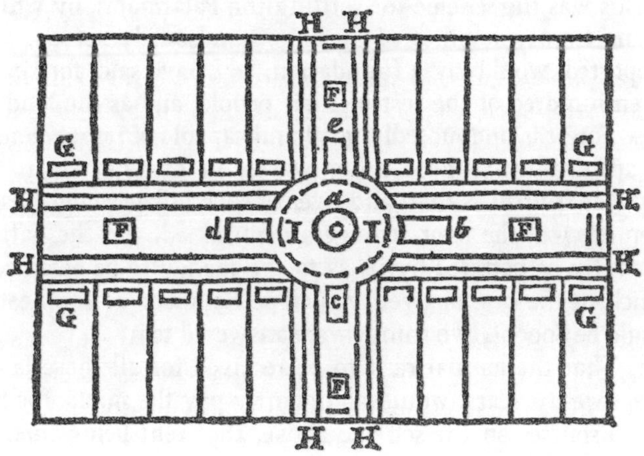

a the church, *b* the shambles, *c* the market house, *d* a town hall, *e* a conduit with stocks, &c. F the conduits, or wells, G houses, H the lands enclosed behind, *I* streets of houses for tradesmen.

that the whole four thousand acres should be fully distributed to the said twenty families, for which they should have no rent to pay, and be liable to no taxes, but such as provided for their own sick or poor, repairing their own roads, and the like; this exemption from rent and taxes, to continue for twenty years, and then to pay each 50*l.* a year to the queen: that is to say, to the crown.

To each of these families, who I would now call farmers, it was proposed to advance 200*l.* in ready money, as a stock to set them to work, to furnish them with cattle, horses, cows, hogs, &c. and to hire and pay labourers, to enclose, clear, and cure the land; which it would be supposed the first year would not be so much to their advantage as afterwards; allowing them timber out of the forest to build themselves houses, and barns, sheds, and offices, as they should have occasion; also for carts, waggons, ploughs, harrows and the like necessary things, care to be taken that the men and their families went to work forthwith according to the design.[19]

This was the scheme for settling the Palatinates, by which means twenty families of farmers, handsomely set up, and supported, would lay a foundation, as I have said, for six or seven hundred of the rest of their people; and as the land in New Forest is undoubtedly good and capable of improvement by such cultivation, so other wastes in England are to be found as fruitful as that; and twenty such villages might have been erected, the poor strangers maintained, and the nation evidently be bettered by it; as to the money to be advanced, which in the case of twenty such settlements, at 400*l.* each, would be 80000*l.* two things were answered to it.

1. That the annual rent to be received for all those lands after twenty years, would abundantly pay the public for the first disburses on the scheme above, that rent being then to amount to 40000*l.* per ann.

2. More money than would have done this, was expended or rather thrown away upon them here, to keep them in suspense, and afterwards starve them; sending them a begging all over the nation, and shipping them off to perish in other

countries. Where the mistake lay, is none of my business to enquire.

I reserved this account for this place, because I passed in this journey over the very spot where the design was laid out; namely, near Lindhurst, in the road from Rumsey to Limington, whither I now directed my course.

Limington is a little but populous sea port, standing opposite to the Isle of Wight, in the narrow part of the strait, which ships some times pass through in fair weather, called the Needles; and right against an ancient town of that island called Yarmouth, and which, in distinction from the great town of Yarmouth in Norfolk, is called South Yarmouth. Limington sends two members to Parliament and this and her salt trade is all I can say to her; for though she is very well situated, as to the convenience of shipping, I do not find they have any foreign commerce, except it be what we call smuggling, and roguing; which, I may say, is the reigning commerce of all this part of the English coast, from the mouth of the Thames to the Land's End of Cornwall.

From hence there are but few towns on the sea coast west, nor are there any harbours, or sea ports of any note, except Pool. As for Christ Church, though it stands at the mouth of the Avon, which, as I have said, comes down from Salisbury, and receives also the Stour and Piddle, two Dorsetshire rivers, which bring with them all the waters of the north part of Dorsetshire; yet it is a very inconsiderable poor place, scarce worth seeing, and less worth mentioning in this account; only, that it sends two members to Parliament, which many poor towns in this part of England do, as well as that.

From hence I stept up into the country north-west, to see the ancient town of Wimburn, or Wimburnminster. There I found nothing remarkable; but the church, which is indeed a very great one, ancient, and yet very well built, with a very firm strong square tower, considerably high; but was, without doubt, much finer, when on the top of it, stood a most exquisite spire, finer and taller, if fame lies not, than that at Salisbury and, by its situation, in a plainer, flatter country, visible, no question, much farther. But this most beautiful ornament was blown down by a sudden tempest of wind as they tell us in the year 1622.

The church remains a venerable piece of antiquity, and has in it the remains of a place, once, much more in request than it is now; for here are the monuments of several noble families; and in particular of one king, viz. King Ethelred,[20] who was slain in battle by the Danes. He was a prince famed for piety and religion, and, according to the zeal of these times, was esteemed as a martyr; because venturing his life against the Danes, who were heathens, he died fighting for his religion and his country. The inscription upon his grave is preserved, and has been carefully repaired, so as to be easily read, and is as follows:

> In hoc loco quiescit Corpus S. Etheldredi, Regis West Saxonum, Martyris, qui Anno Dom. DCCCLXXII. xxiii. Aprilis per Manus Danorum Paganorum Occubuit.

In English thus:

> Here rests the body of Holy Etheldred, King of the West Saxons, and martyr, who fell by the hands of the pagan Danes, in the year of our Lord 872, the 23d of April.

South of this town, over a sandy wild and barren country, we came to Pool, a considerable sea-port, and indeed the most considerable in all this part of England; for here I found some ships, some merchants, and some trade; especially, here were a good number of ships fitted out every year to the Newfoundland fishing, in which the Pool men were said to have been particularly successful for many years past.

The town sits in the bottom of a great bay, or inlet of the sea, which entering at one narrow mouth opens to a very great breadth within the entrance, and comes up to the very shore of this town. This place is famous for the best, and biggest oysters in all this part of England, which the people of Pool pretend to be famous for pickling, and they are barrelled up here, and sent not only to London, but to the West Indies, and to Spain, and Italy, and other parts. 'Tis observed more pearl are found in the Pool oysters, and larger than in any other oysters about England.

Wareham is a neat town, and full of people, having a share of trade with Pool it self, it shows the ruins of a large town, and 'tis apparent has had eight churches, of which they have three remaining. South of Wareham, and between the bay I have mentioned and the sea, lies a large tract of land, which being surrounded by the sea, except on one side is called an island, though it is really what should be called a peninsula. This tract of land is better inhabited than the sea coast of this west end of Dorsetshire generally is, and the manufacture of stockings is carried on there also; it is called the Isle of Purbeck, and has in the middle of it a large market-town, called Corf, and from the famous castle there, the whole town is now called Corf-Castle, it is a corporation, sending members to Parliaments.

This part of the country is eminent for vast quarries of stone, which is cut out flat, and used in London in great quantities for paving court-yards, alleys, avenues to houses, kitchens, foot-ways on the sides of the high-streets, and the like; and is very profitable to the place, as also in the number of shipping employed in bringing it to London. There are also several rocks of very good marble, only that the veins in the stone are not black and white, as the Italian, but grey, red, and other colours.

From hence to Weymouth, we rode in view of the sea; the country is open, and in some respects pleasant, but not like the northern parts of the county, which are all fine carpet ground, soft as velvet. I cannot omit here a small adventure, which was very surprising to me on this journey; passing this plain country, we came to an open piece of ground where a neighbouring gentleman had at a great expense laid out a proper piece of land for a Decoy, or Duck-coy, as some call it; the works were but newly done, the planting young, the ponds very large, and well made; but the proper places for shelter of the fowl not covered, the trees not being grown, and men were still at work improving, and enlarging, and planting on the adjoining heath, or common. Near the decoy keeper's house, were some places where young decoy-ducks were hatched, or otherwise kept to fit them for their work; to preserve them from vermin, polecats, kites, and such like, they had set traps, as is usual in such cases, and a gibbet by it, where abundance of such creatures as were taken were hanged up for show.

While the decoy man was busy showing the new-works, he was alarmed with a great cry about this house for Help, Help, and away he run, like the wind, guessing, as we supposed that something was catched in the trap. It was a good big boy about 13 or 14 year old, that cried out, for coming to the place, he found a great fowl catched by the leg in the trap, which yet was so strong, and so outrageous, that the boy going too near him, he flew at him, and frighted him, bit him, and beat him with his wings, for he was too strong for the boy. As the master ran from the decoy, so another man-servant ran from the house, and finding a strange creature fast in the trap, not knowing what it was, laid at him with a great stick; the creature fought him a good while, but at length he struck him an unlucky blow, which quieted him; after this we all came up to see what was the matter, and found a monstrous eagle caught by the leg in the trap, and killed by the fellow's cudgel, as above.

When the master came to know what it was, and that his man had killed it, he was ready to kill the fellow for his pains, for it was a noble creature indeed, and would have been worth a great deal to the man to have it shown about the country, or to have sold to any gentleman curious in such things; but the eagle was dead, and there we left it. 'Tis probable this eagle had flown over the sea from France, either there, or at the Isle of Weight, where the Channel is not so wide; for we do not find that any eagles are known to breed in those parts of Britain.

From hence we turned up to Dorchester, the county town, though not the largest town in the county; Dorchester[21] is indeed a pleasant agreeable town to live in, and where I thought the people seemed less divided into factions and parties, than in other places; for though here are divisions and the people are not all of one mind, either as to religion, or politics, yet they did not seem to separate with so much animosity as in other places. Here I saw the Church of England clergymen, and the Dissenting minister, or preacher drinking tea together, and conversing with civility and good neighbourhood, like catholic Christians, and men of a catholic, and extensive charity. The town is populous, though not large, the streets broad, but the buildings old, and low; however, there is good company and a good deal of it; and a man that coveted a retreat in this world might as agreeably spend his time, and as well in Dorchester, as in any town I know in England.

The downs round this town are exceeding pleasant, and come up on every side, even to the very street's end; and here it was that they told me, that there were 600 thousand sheep fed on the downs, within six miles of the town. This I say, I was told, I do not affirm it to be true; but when I viewed the country round, I confess I could not but incline to believe it.

The grass, or herbage of these downs is full of the sweetest, and the most aromatic plants, such as nourish the sheep to a strange degree, and the sheep's dung again nourishes that herbage to a strange degree; so that the valleys are rendered extremely fruitful, by the washing of the water in hasty showers from off these hills. An eminent instance of this is seen at Amesbury in Wiltshire, the next county to this, for it is the same thing in proportion over this whole county: I was told that at this town there was a meadow on the bank of the river Avon, which runs thence to Salisbury, which was let for 12*l.* a year per acre for the grass only. This I enquired particularly after, at the place, and was assured by the inhabitants as one man, that the fact was true, and was showed the meadows; the grass which grew on them was such as grew to the length of ten or twelve foot, rising up to a good height, and then taking root again, and was of so rich a nature as to answer very well such an extravagant rent. The reason they gave for this was the extraordinary richness of the soil, made so, as above, by the falling, or washing of the rains from the hills adjacent.

From Dorchester it is six miles to the sea side south, and the ocean in view almost all the way. The first town you come to is Weymouth, or Weymouth and Melcomb, two towns lying at the mouth of a little rivulet, which they call the Wey, but scarce claims the name of a river; however, the entrance makes a very good, though small harbour, and they are joined by a wooden bridge; so that nothing but the harbour parts them; yet they are separate corporations, and choose each of them two Members of Parliament, just as London and Southwark.

Weymouth is a sweet, clean, agreeable town, considering its low situation, and close to the sea; 'tis well built, and has a great many good substantial merchants in it; who drive a considerable trade, and have a good number of ships belonging to the town. They carry on now, in time of peace, a trade with France; but besides this, they trade also to Portugal, Spain, Newfoundland, and Virginia.

While I was here once, there came a merchant ship into that road, called Portland Road, under a very hard storm of wind; she was homeward bound from Oporto for London, laden with wines, and as she came in, she made signals of distress to the town, firing guns for help, and the like, as is usual in such cases.

The venturous Weymouth-men went off, even before it was light, with two boats to see who she was, and what condition she was in, and found she was come to an anchor, and had struck her top-masts; but that she had been in bad weather, had lost an anchor and cable before, and had but one cable to trust to, which did hold her, but was weak; and as the storm continued to blow, they expected every hour to go on shore, and split to pieces.

Upon this, the Weymouth boats came back with such diligence, that, in less than three hours, they were on board them again with an anchor and cable, which they immediately bent in its place, and let go to assist the other, and thereby secured the ship. 'Tis true, that they took a good price of the master for the help they gave him; for they made him draw a bill on his owners at London for 12*l*. for the use of the anchor, cable, and boat, besides some gratuities to the men. But they saved the ship and cargo by it, and in three or four days the weather was calm, and he proceeded on his voyage, returning the anchor and cable again; so that, upon the whole, it was not so extravagant as at first I thought it to be.

The Isle of Portland lies right against this port of Weymouth. Hence it is, that our best and whitest free stone comes, with which the cathedral of St Paul's, the Monument, and all the public edifices in the city of London, are chiefly built; and 'tis wonderful, and well worth the observation of a traveller to see the quarries in the rocks, from whence they are cut out, what stones, and of what prodigious a size are cut out there.

The sea off of this island, and especially to the west of it, is counted the most dangerous part of the British Channel. Due south, there is almost a continued disturbance in the waters, by reason of what they call two tides meeting, which I take to be no more than the sets of the currents from the French coast, and from the English shore meeting. This they call Portland Race; and several ships, not aware of these currents, have been embayed to the west of Portland, and been driven on shore on the beach, (of which I shall speak presently) and there lost.

To prevent this danger, and guide the mariner in these distresses, they have, within these few months, set up two light-houses [22] on the two points of that island; and they had not been many months set up, with the directions given to the public for their bearings, but we found three outward-bound East-India ships which were in distress in the night, in a hard extreme gale of wind, were so directed by those lights, that they avoided going on shore by it, which, if the lights had not been there, would inevitably happened to their destruction.

This island, though seemingly miserable, and thinly inhabited, yet the inhabitants being almost all stone-cutters, we found there was no very poor people among them; and when they collected money for the rebuilding St Paul's, they got more in this island than in the great town of Dorchester, as we were told.

From hence we went on to Bridport, a pretty large corporation town on the sea shore, though without a harbour. Here we saw boats all the way on the shore fishing for mackerel, which they take in the easiest manner imaginable. As soon as the boats had brought their fish on shore, we observed a guard, or watch, placed on the shore in several places, who we found had their eye not on the fishermen, but on the country people, who came down to the shore to buy their fish; and very sharp we found they were; and some that came with small carts were obliged to go back empty, without any fish. When we came to enquire into the particulars of this, we found, that these were officers placed on the shore by the justices and magistrates of the towns about, who were ordered to prevent the country farmers buying the mackerel to dung their land with them, which was thought to be dangerous, as to infection. In short, such was the plenty of fish that year, that mackerel, the finest and largest I ever saw, were sold at the sea side a hundred for a penny.

From Bridport, a town in which we see nothing remarkable, we came to Lime, the town particularly made famous by the landing of the Duke of Monmouth,[23] and his unfortunate troop, in the time of King James II, of which I need say nothing, the history of it being so recent in the memory of so many living. This is a town of good figure, and has in it several eminent merchants, who carry on a considerable trade to France, Spain, Newfoundland, and the Streights; and though they have neither creek or bay, road, or river, they have a good harbour; but 'tis such a one as is not in all Britain besides, if there is such a one in any part of the world.

It is a massy pile of building, consisting of high and thick walls of stone. The walls are raised in the main sea, at a good distance from the shore; it consists of one main and solid wall of stone, large enough for carts and carriages to pass on the top, and to admit houses and ware houses to be built on it; so that it is broad as a street; opposite to this, but farther into the sea, is another wall of the same workmanship, which crosses the end of the first wall, and comes about with a tail, parallel to the first wall. Between the point of the first or main wall, is the entrance into the port, and the second, or opposite wall, breaking the violence of the sea from the entrance, the ships go into the basin, as into a pier, or harbour, and ride there as secure as in a mill pond, or as in a wet dock.

This work is called the COBB. The custom-house officers have a lodge and warehouse upon it, and there were several ships of very good force, and rich in value, in the basin of it when I was there. It might be strengthened with a fort, and the walls themselves are firm enough to carry what guns they please to plant upon it; but they did not seem to think it needful; and as the shore is convenient for batteries, they have some guns planted in proper places, both for the defence of the COBB, and the town also.

It was in sight of these hills that Queen Elizabeth's fleet, under the command of the Lord Howard of Effingham,[24] then admiral, began first to engage in a close, and resolved fight with the invincible Spanish Armada, in 1588. Maintaining the fight, the Spaniards making eastward, till they came the length of Portland Race, where they gave it over; the Spaniards having received considerable damage.

While we stayed here some time viewing this town and coast, we had opportunity to observe the pleasant way of conversation, as it is managed among the gentlemen of this county, and their families, which are without reflection some of the most polite and well bred people in the isle of Britain. As their hospitality is very great, and their bounty to the poor remarkable, so their generous friendly way of living with, visiting, and associating one with another is as hard to be described, as it is really to be admired; they seem to have a mutual confidence in, and friendship with one another, as if they were all relations. Nor did I observe the sharping tricking temper, which is too much crept in among the gaming and horse-racing gentry in some parts of England, to be so much known among them, any otherwise than to be abhorred; and yet they sometimes play too, and make matches, and horse-races, as they see occasion.

The ladies here do not want the help of assemblies to assist in match-making; or half-pay officers to run away with their daughters, which the meetings, called assemblies in some other parts of England, are recommended for. Here's no Bury Fair, where the women are scandalously said to carry themselves to market, and where every night they meet at the play, or at the assembly for intrigue, and yet I observed that the women do not seem to stick on hands so much in this country, as in those countries, where those assemblies are so lately set up; the reason of which I cannot help saying, if my opinion may bear any weight, is, that the Dorsetshire ladies are equal in beauty, and may be superior in reputation. And yet the Dorsetshire ladies, I assure you, are not nuns, they do not go veiled about streets, or hide themselves when visited; but a general freedom of conversation, agreeable, mannerly, kind, and good runs through the whole body of the gentry of both sexes, mixed with the best of behaviour, and yet governed by prudence and modesty; such as I no where see better in all my observation, through the whole isle of Britain. In this little interval also I visited some of the biggest towns in the north-west part of this county, as Blandford, a handsome well built town, but chiefly famous for making the finest bonelace in England.

From thence I went west to Stourbridge, vulgarly called Strabridge; the town, and the country round is employed in the manufacture of stockings, and which was once famous for making the finest, best, and highest prized knit stockings in England; but that trade now is much decayed by the increase of the knitting-stocking engine, or frame, which has destroyed the hand knitting-trade for fine stockings through the whole kingdom.

From hence I came to Shireburn, a large and populous town, with one collegiate, or conventual church, and may properly claim to have more inhabitants in it than any town in Dorsetshire, though it is neither the county town, or does it send members to Parliament; the church is still a reverend pile, and shows the face of great antiquity.

Shaftesbury is also on the edge of this county, adjoining to Wiltshire and Dorsetshire, being 14 miles from Salisbury, over that fine down or carpet ground, which they call particularly, or properly Salisbury Plain. It has neither house or town in view all the way, but there is a certain never failing assistance upon all these downs for telling a stranger his way, and that is the number of shepherds keeping their vast flocks of sheep, which are every where in the way, and who, with a very little pains, a traveller may always speak with. Nothing can be like it, the Arcadians' plains of which we read so much pastoral trumpery in the poets, could be nothing to them.

This Shaftesbury is now a sorry town, upon the top of a high hill, and which closes the plain, or downs, and whence nature presents you a new scene or prospect, (viz.) of Somerset and Wiltshire, where 'tis all enclosed, and grown with woods, forests, and planted hedge-rows. The country rich, fertile and populous of inhabitants, and those inhabitants fully employed in the richest and most valuable manufacture in the world, (viz.) the English clothing, as well, the medley, or mixed clothing, as whites.

In my return to my western progress, I passed some little part of Somersetshire, as through Evil, or Yeovil, upon the river Ivil, in going to which we go down a long steep hill, which they call Babylon-Hill; but from what original I could find none of the country people to inform me. It cannot pass my observation here, that when we are come this length from London, the dialect of the English tongue, or the country way of expressing themselves is not easily understood, it is so strangely altered; it is true, that it is so in many parts of England besides, but in none so gross a degree as in this part. This way of boorish country speech, as in Ireland, it is called the brogue upon the tongue; so here 'tis called *jouring* and 'tis certain, that though the tongue be all mere natural English, yet those that are but a little acquainted with them, cannot understand one half of what they say. It is not possible to explain this fully by writing, because the difference is not so much in the orthography of words, as in the tone, and diction; their abridging the speech, *cham* for *I am, chil* for *I will, don,* for *put on,* and *doff,* for *put off,* and the like. And I cannot omit a short story here on this subject; coming to a relation's house, who was a school-master at Martock in Somersetshire, I went into his school to beg the boys a play day, as is usual in such cases, I should have said to beg the master a play day, but that by the way; coming into the school, I observed one of the lowest scholars was reading his lesson to the usher, which lesson it seems was a chapter in the Bible, so I sat down by the master, till the boy had read out his chapter. I observed the boy read a little oddly in the tone of the country, which made me the more attentive, because on enquiry, I found that the words were the same, and the orthography the same as in all our Bibles. I observed also the boy read it out with his eyes still on the book, and his head like a mere boy, moving from side to side, as the lines reached cross the columns of the book; his lesson was in the Cant. [Song of Solomon] 5. 3. of which the words are these,

'I have washed my coat, how shall I put it on, I have washed my feet, how shall I defile them?'

The boy read thus, with his eyes, as I say, full on the text.

'Chava doffed my cooat, how shall I don't, chav a washed my veet, how shall I moil'em?'

How the dexterous dunce could form his mouth to express so readily the words, (which stood right printed in the book) in his country jargon, I could not but admire.

I could give many more accounts of the different dialects of the people of this country, in some of which they are really not to be understood, but the particulars have little or no diversion in them, they carry it such a length, that we see their jouring speech upon their monuments, and grave-stones; as for example, even in some of the church-yards of the city of Bristol, I saw this excellent poetry after some other lines—

And when that thou doest hear of thick,
Think of the glass that runneth quick.

But I proceed into Devonshire, from Evil we came to Crookorn, thence to Chard, and from thence into the same road I was in before at Honiton. This is a large and beautiful market-town, very populous, and well built, and is so very remarkably paved with small pebbles, that on either sides the way a little channel is left shouldered up on the sides of it; so that it holds a small stream of fine clear running water with a little square dipping place left at every door, so that every family in the town has a clear clean running river, (as it may be called) just at their own door.

Here we see the first of the great serge manufacture of Devonshire, a trade too great to be described in miniature, as it must be, if I undertake it here; and which takes up this whole county, which is the largest and most populous in England, Yorkshire excepted, (which ought to be esteemed three counties, and is indeed divided as such into the East, West and North Riding;) but Devonshire one entire county, is so full of great towns, and those towns so full of people, and those people so universally employed in trade, and manufactures, that not only it cannot be equalled in England, but perhaps not in Europe.

In my travel through Dorsetshire, I ought to have observed that the biggest towns in that county sent no members to Parliament, and that the smallest did; that is to say, that Sherborn, Blandford, Winbornminster, Sturminster, and several other towns choose no members, whereas Weymouth,

Melcom, and Bridport, were all burgess towns; but now we come to Devonshire, we find almost all the great towns, and some smaller choosing members also. It is true, there are some large populous towns that do not choose, but then there are so many that do, that the county seems to have no injustice, for they send up six and twenty members.

I cannot but recommend it to any gentlemen that travel this road, that if they please to observe the prospect for half a mile, till their coming down the hill, and to the entrance into Honiton, the view of the country is the most beautiful landskip in the world, a mere picture; and I do not remember the like in any one place in England; 'tis observable that the market of this town was kept originally on the Sunday, till it was changed by the direction of King John.

From Honiton the country is exceeding pleasant still, and on the road they have a beautiful prospect almost all the way to Exeter, which is twelve miles; on the left hand of this road lies also the town of St Mary Oterey, commonly called St Mary Autree. They tell us the name is derived from the river Ottery, and that, from the multitude of otters found always in that river, which however to me seems fabulous; nor does there appear to be any such great number of otters in that water, or in the county about, more than is usual in other counties, or in other parts of the county about them; they tell us they send 20000 hogsheads of cider hence every year to London, and which is still worse, that it is most of it bought there by the merchants to mix with their wines, which if true, is not much to the reputations of the London vintners; but that by the by.

From hence we came to Exeter, a city famous for two things, which we seldom find unite in the same town, (viz.) that 'tis full of gentry, and good company, and yet full of trade and manufactures also; the serge market held here every week is very well worth a stranger's seeing, and next to the Brigg-Market at Leeds in Yorkshire, is the greatest in England. The people assured me that at this market is generally sold from 60 to 70 to 80, and sometimes a hundred thousand pounds value in serges in a week. I think 'tis kept on Mondays.

This city drives a very great correspondence with Holland, as also directly to Portugal, Spain and Italy; shipping off vast quantities of the woollen-manufactures, especially, to Holland, the Dutch giving very large commissions here for the buying of serges, perpetuan's, and such goods; which are made not only in and about Exeter, but especially at Tiverton, Cullumbton, Bampton, and all the north east part of the county, which part of the county is, as it may be said, fully employed, the people made rich, and the poor that are properly so called, well subsisted, and employed by it.

Excester is a large rich, beautiful, populous, and was once a very strong city; but as to the last, as the castle, the walls, and all the old works are demolished so were they standing, the way of managing sieges, and attacks of towns is such now, and so altered from what it was in those days, that Excester in the utmost strength it could ever boast, would not now hold out five days open trenches; nay, would hardly put an army to the trouble of opening trenches against it at all. This city was famous in the late civil unnatural war, for its loyalty to the king, and for being a sanctuary to the queen.

The cathedral church of this city is an ancient beauty, or as it may be said, it is beautiful for its antiquity. But it has been so fully, and often described that it would look like a mere copying from others to mention it. This county, and this part of it in particular, has been famous for the birth of several eminent men, as well for learning, as for arts, and for war, as particularly: (1.) Sir William Petre,[25] who was Secretary of State, and Privy Counsellor to King Henry VIII, Edward VI, Queen Mary, and Queen Elizabeth, and seven times sent ambassador into foreign countries.

2. Sir Thomas Bodley, famous, and of grateful memory to all learned men, and lovers of letters, for his collecting, and establishing, the best library in Britain; which is now at Oxford, and is called after his name the Bodleian Library to this day.

3. Also Sir Francis Drake, born at Plymouth.

4. Sir Walter Raleigh, of both those I need say nothing. Fame publishes their merit upon every mention of their names.

5. That great patron of learning – Hooker, author of the *Ecclesiastical Polity*, and of several other valuable pieces.

[6.] Peter Blundel, a clothier, who built the free-school at Tiverton, and endowed it very handsomely, of which in its place.

[7.] Sir John Glanvill, a noted lawyer, and one of the judges of the Common Pleas.

[8.] Sergeant Glanvill his son, as great a lawyer as his father. These were born at Tavistock.

[9.] Sir Peter King, the present Lord Chief Justice of the Common Pleas, and many others.

I must now lean to the south, that is to say, to the south coast, for in going on indeed, we go south west.

About 22 miles from Excester we go to Totness, on the river Dart. This is a very good town; of some trade, but has more gentlemen in it than tradesmen of note; they have a very fine stone-bridge here over the river, which being within seven or eight miles of the sea, is very large, and the tide flows 10 or 12 foot at the bridge. Here was had the diversion of seeing them catch fish, with the assistance of a dog. The case is this, on the south side of the river, and on a slip, or narrow cut or channel made on purpose for a mill, there stands a corn-mill; the mill tail, or floor for the water below the wheels is wharfed up on either side with stone, above high-water mark, and for above 20 or 30 foot in length below it, on that part of the river towards the sea; at the end of this wharfing is a grating of wood, the cross-bars of which stand bearing inward, sharp at the end, and pointing inward towards one another, as the wires of a mouse-trap.

When the tide flows up, the fish can with ease go in between the points of these cross-bars, but the mill being shut down they can go no farther upwards; and when the water ebbs again, they are left behind, not being able to pass the points of the grating, as above, outwards; which like a mouse-trap keeps them in, so that they are left at the bottom with about a foot, or a foot and half water. We were carried hither at low water, where was saw about 50 or 60 small salmon, about 17 to 20 inches long, which the country people call salmon peal, and to catch these, the person who went with us, who was our landlord at a great inn next the bridge, put in a net on a hoop at the end of a pole, the pole going cross the hoop, which we call in this country a shove net: the net being fixed at one end of the place they put in a dog, who was taught his trade before hand, at the other end of the place, and he drives all the fish into the net, so that only holding the net still in its place, the man took up two or three and thirty salmon peal at the first time.

From hence we went still south about seven miles, (all in view of this river) to Dartmouth, a town of note, seated at the mouth of the river Dart, and where it enters into the sea at a very narrow, but safe entrance. The opening into Dartmouth Harbour is not broad, but the channel deep enough for the biggest ship in the royal navy; the sides of the entrance are high mounded with rocks; without which just at the first narrowing of the passage, stands a good strong fort without a platform of guns, which commands the port.

The narrow entrance is not much above half a mile, when it opens and makes a basin, or harbour able to receive 500 sail of ships of any size, and where they may ride with the greatest safety, even as in a mill-pond, or wet-dock. I had the curiosity here with the assistance of a merchant of the town to go out to the mouth of the haven in a boat to see the entrance, and castle, or fort that commands it; and coming back with the tide of flood, I observed some small fish to skip, and play upon the surface of the water, upon which I asked my friend what fish they were; immediately one of the rowers or seamen starts up in the boat, and throwing his arms abroad, as if he had been bewitched, cried out as loud as he could bawl, 'a school, a school.' The word was taken to the shore as hastily as it would have been on land if he had cried fire; and by that time we reached the quays, the town was all in a kind of an uproar.

The matter was, that a great shoal, or as they call it a *school* of pilchards came swimming with the tide of flood directly, out of the sea into the harbour. My friend whose boat we were in, told me this was a surprise which he would have been very glad of, if he could have had a day's or two's warning, for he might have taken 200 ton of them, and the like was the case of other merchants in town; for in short, no body was ready for them, except a small fishing boat, or two; one of which went out into the middle of the harbour, and at two or three hauls, took about forty thousand of them. We sent our servant to the quay to buy some, who for a half-penny, brought us seventeen, and if he would have taken them, might have had as many more for the same money; with these we went to dinner; the cook at the inn broiled them for us, which is their way of dressing them, with pepper and salt, which cost us about a farthing; so that two of us, and servant dined, and at a tavern too, for three farthings, dressing and all, and this is the reason for telling the tale. What drink, wine, or beer we had, I do not remember, but whatever it was, that we paid for by it self; but for our food we really dined for *three farthings*, and very well too.

In observing the coming in of those pilchards, as above, we found that out at sea, in the offing, beyond the mouth of the harbour there was a whole army of porpoises, which as they told us pursued the pilchards, and 'tis probable drove them into the harbour, as above.

Round the west side of this basin, or harbour in a kind of a semicircle, lies the town of Dartmouth, a very large and populous town, though but meanly built, and standing on the side of a steep hill; yet the quay is large, and the street before it spacious. Here are some very flourishing merchants, who trade very prosperously, and to the most considerable trading ports of Spain, Portugal, Italy, and the plantations; but especially, they are great traders to Newfoundland, and from thence to Spain, and Italy with fish.

A little to the southward of this town, and to the east of the port, is Torbay, of which I know nothing proper to my observation, more than that it is a very good road for ships. I suppose I need not mention, that they had from the hilly part of this town, and especially from the hills opposite to it, the noble prospect, and at that time particularly delightful, of the Prince of Orange's fleet, when he came to that coast, and as they entered into Torbay, to land; the prince and his army being in a fleet of about 600 sail of transport ships, besides 50 sail of men of war of the line, all which with a fair wind, and fine weather came to an anchor there at once.

From hence we went to Plympton, a poor and thinly inhabited town, though blessed with the privilege of sending members to the Parliament; of which I have little more to say, but that from thence the road lies to Plymouth, distance about six miles.

Plymouth is indeed a town of consideration, and of great importance to the public. The situation of it between two very large inlets of the sea, and in the bottom of a large bay, which is very remarkable for the advantage of navigation. The Sound, or bay is compassed on every side with hills, and the shore generally steep and rocky, though the anchorage is good, and it is pretty safe riding. In the entrance to this bay, lies a large and most dangerous rock, which at high-water is covered, but at low-tide lies bare, where many a good ship has been lost, even in the view of safety, and many a ship's crew drowned in the night, before help could be had for them.

Upon this rock, which was called the Eddystone, from its situation, the famous Mr Winstanley[26] undertook to build a light-house for the direction of sailors, and with great art, and expedition finished it; which work considering its height, the magnitude of its building, and the little hold there was, by which it was possible to fasten it to the rock, stood to admiration, and bore out many a bitter storm.

Mr Winstanley often visited, and frequently strengthened the building, by new works, and was so confident of its firmness, and stability, that he usually said, he only desired to be in it when a storm should happen for many people had told him, it would certainly fall, if it came to blow a little harder than ordinary.

But he happened at last to be in it once too often; namely, when that dreadful tempest blew, Nov. the 27, 1703. This tempest began on the Wednesday before, and blew with such violence, and shook the light-house so much, that as they told me there, Mr Winstanley would fain have been on shore, and made signals for help, but no boats durst go off to him; and to finish the tragedy, on the Friday, Nov. 26, when the tempest was so redoubled, that it became a terror to the whole nation; the first sight there seaward, that the people of Plymouth, were presented with in the morning after the storm, was the bare Eddystone, the light-house being gone; in which Mr Winstanley, and all that were with him perished, and were never seen, or heard of since. But that which was a worse loss still, was, that a few days after a merchant's ship called the *Winchelsea* homeward bound from Virginia, not knowing the Eddystone light-house was down; for want of the light that should have been seen run foul of the rock it self, and was lost with all her lading, and most of her men, but there is now another light-house built on the same rock.

One thing, which I was a witness to, on a former journey to this place, I cannot omit. It was the next year after that great storm, and but a little sooner in the year, being in August, I was at Plymouth, and walking on the Hoo, which is a plain on the edge of the sea, looking to the road, I observed the evening so serene, so calm, so bright, and the sea so smooth, that a finer sight, I think, I never saw; there was very little wind, but what was, seemed to be westerly; and, about an hour after, it blew a little breeze at south west, with which wind there came into the Sound, that night, and the next morning, a fleet of fourteen sail of ships, from Barbados; richly loaden, for London. Having been long at sea, most of the captains and passengers came on shore to refresh themselves, as is usual, after such tedious voyages, and the ships rode all in the Sound on that side next to Catwater: as is customary, upon safe arriving to their native country, there was a general joy and rejoicing, both on board and on shore.

The next day the wind began to freshen, especially in the afternoon, and the sea to be disturbed, and very hard it blew at night, but all was well for that time; but the night after it blew a dreadful storm, not much inferior, for the time it lasted, to the storm mentioned above, which blew down the light-house on the Eddy Stone; about midnight the noise was very dreadful, what with the roaring of the sea, and of the wind, intermixed with the firing of guns for help from the ships, the cries of the seamen and people on shore, and, which was worse, the cries of those, which were driven on shore by the tempest, and dashed in pieces. In a word, all the fleet, except three, or thereabouts, were dashed against the rocks, and sunk in the sea, most of the men being drowned. Those three, who were saved, received so much damage, that their lading was almost all spoiled. One ship in the dark of the night, the men not knowing where they were, run into Catwater, and run on shore there, by which she was however saved from shipwreck, and the lives of her crew were saved also.

This was a melancholy morning indeed; nothing was to be seen but wrecks of the ships, and a foaming furious sea, in that very place where they rode all in joy and triumph, but the evening before. The captains, passengers and officers who were, as I have said, gone on shore, between the joy of saving their lives, and the affliction of having lost their ships, their cargoes, and their friends, were objects indeed worth our compassion and observation; and there was a great variety of the passions to be observed in them: now lamenting their losses, then giving thanks for their deliverance, many of the passengers had lost their all, and were, as they expressed themselves, utterly undone; then again in tears for such as were drowned; the various cases were indeed very affecting, and, in many things, very instructing.

On the shore, over-against this island, is the citadel of Plymouth, a small, but regular fortification, inaccessible by sea, but not exceeding strong by land, except that they say the works are of a stone, hard as marble, and would not soon yield to the batteries of an enemy. But that is a language our modern engineers now laugh at. The town stands above this, upon the same rock, and lies sloping on the side of it, towards the east; the inlet of the sea, which is called Catwater, and which is a harbour, capable of receiving any number of ships, and of any size, washing the eastern shore of the town.

The other inlet of the sea, as I term it, is on the other side of the town, and is called Ham-Oze, being the mouth of the river Tamar, a considerable river, which parts the two counties of Devon and Cornwall. Here the war with France making it necessary that the ships of war should have a retreat nearer hand than at Portsmouth, the late King William ordered a wet dock, with yards, dry docks, launches, and conveniences of all kinds for building, and repairing of ships to be built; and with these followed necessarily the building of store-houses and ware-houses, for the rigging, sails, naval and military stores, &c. of such ships as may be appointed to be laid up there, as now several are, with very handsome houses for the commissioners, clerks, and officers of all kinds usual in the king's yard, to dwell in. It is in short, now become as complete an arsenal, or yard, for building and fitting men of war as any of the government are masters of, and perhaps much more convenient than some of them, though not so large. The building of these things, with the addition of rope walks, and mast-yards, &c. as it brought abundance of trades-people, and workmen to the place, so they began by little and little to build houses on the lands adjacent, till at length there appeared a very handsome street, spacious and large, and as well inhabited, and so many houses are since added, that it is become a considerable town,[27] and must of consequence in time draw abundance of people from Plymouth it self.

However, the town of Plymouth is, and will always be a

very considerable town, while the excellent harbour makes it such a general port for the receiving all the fleets of merchants' ships from the southward, as from Spain, Italy, the West-Indies, &c. who generally make it the first port to put in for refreshment, or safety, from either weather or enemies.

The town is populous and wealthy, having, as above, several considerable merchants, and abundance of wealthy shop-keepers, whose trade depends upon supplying the sea-faring people, that upon so many occasions put into that port. As for gentlemen, I mean those that are such by family, and birth, and way of living, it cannot be expected to find many such in a town, merely depending on trade, shipping and sea-faring business, yet I found here some men of value, persons of liberal education, general knowledge, and excellent behaviour, whose society obliges me to say, that a gentleman might find very agreeable company in Plymouth.

From Plymouth we pass the Tamar, over a ferry to Saltash, a little poor shattered town, the first we sat foot on in the county of Cornwall. The Tamar here is very wide, and the ferry boats bad, so that I thought my self well escaped, when I got safe on shore in Cornwall.

Saltash seems to be the ruins of a larger place, and we saw many houses as it were falling down, and I doubt not but the mice and rats have abandoned many more, as they say they will, when they are likely to fall; yet this town is governed by a mayor and alderman, has many privileges, sends members to Parliament, takes toll of all vessels that pass the river, and have the sole oyster fishing in the whole river, which is considerable. Mr Carew,[28] tells us a strange story of a dog in this town, of whom it was observed, that if they gave him any large bone, or piece of meat, he immediately went out of doors with it, and after having disappeared for some time, would return again, upon which after some time they watched him, when to their great surprise they found that the poor charitable creature carried what he so got to an old decrepit mastiff, which lay in a nest that he had made among the brakes a little way out of the town, and was blind; so that he could not help himself, and there this creature fed him. He adds, also, that on Sundays, or holidays, when he found they made good cheer in the house, where he lived, he would go out, and bring this old blind dog to the door, and feed him there till he had enough, and then go with him back to his habitation in the country again, and see him safe in. If this story is true, it is very remarkable indeed, and I thought it worth telling, because the author was a person, who they say might be credited.

They talk of some merchants beginning to trade here, and they have some ships that use the Newfoundland fishery; but I could not hear of any thing considerable they do in it.

From Saltash I went to Liskard, about 7 miles. This is a considerable town, well built, has people of fashion in it, and a very great market; it also sends two members to Parliament, and is one of the five towns, called Stannary Towns, that is to say, where the blocks of TIN are brought to the coinage, of which by it self. This coinage of tin is an article very much to the advantage of the towns where it is settled, though the money paid goes another way.[29] This town of Liskard was once eminent, had a good castle, and a large house, where the ancient Dukes of Cornwall kept their court in those days.

The only public edifices they have now to show, are the guild, or town-hall, a very good free-school, well provided; a very fine conduit in the market-place; an ancient large church, and which is something rare, for the county of Cornwall, a large new built meeting-house for the Dissenters, which I name, because they assured me there was but three more, and those very inconsiderable in all the county of Cornwall; whereas in Devonshire, which is the next county, there are reckoned about seventy, some of which are exceeding large and fine.

This town is also remarkable for a very great trade in all manufactures of leather, and some spinning of late years is set up here, encouraged by the woollen manufacturers of Devonshire.

Between these two towns of Saltash and Liskard, is St

Germans, now a village, decayed, and without any market, but the largest parish in the whole county; in the bounds of which is contained, as they report, 17 villages, and the town of Saltash among them, for Saltash has no parish church it seems of it self but as a chapel of ease to St Germans.

On the hills north of Liskard, and in the way between Liskard and Lanceston, there are many tin mines, and as they told us some of the richest veins of that metal are found there, that are in the whole country; the metal when cast at the blowing houses into blocks, being as above, carried to Liskard to be coined.

On this south side we come to Foy, or Fowey, an ancient town, and formerly very large; nay, not large only, but powerful and potent for the Foyens, as they were then called, were able to fit out large fleets not only for merchant's ships, but even of men of war; and with these not only fought with, but several times vanquished, and routed the squadron of the Cinque Port men, who in those days were thought very powerful.

Edward IV favoured them much, and because the French threatened them, to come up their river with a powerful navy to burn their town, he caused two forts to be built at the public charge, for security of the town and river, which forts at least some show of them remain there still, but the same King Edward was some time after so disgusted at the townsmen for officiously falling upon the French after a truce was made, and proclaimed, that he effectually disarmed them, took away their whole fleet, ships, tackle apparel and furniture; and since that time we do not read of any of their naval exploits, nor that they ever recovered, or attempted to recover their strength at sea. However, Foy, at this time, is a very fair town, it lies extended on the east side of the river for above a mile, the buildings fair; and there are a great many flourishing merchants in it, who have a great share in the fishing trade, especially for pilchards.

The river Fowey, which is very broad and deep here, was formerly navigable by ships of good burthen as high as Lestwithiel an ancient, and once flourishing, but now a decayed town, and as to trade and navigation quite destitute, which is occasioned by the river being filled up with sands, which some say, the tides drive up in stormy weather from the sea. This town of Lestwithiel, retains however several advantages, which support its figure, as first, that it is one of the Coinage Towns, as I call them, or Stannary Towns, as others call them. (2.) The common gaol for whole Stannary is here, as are also the county courts for the whole county of Cornwall. There is a mock cavalcade[30] which is very remarkable.

Behind Foye, and nearer to the coast at the mouth of a small river, which some call Lowe, though without any authority, there stand two towns opposite to one another, bearing the name of the river Loe, that is to say, distinguished by the addition of East Loe, and West Loe. These are both good trading towns, and especially fishing towns and which is very particular, are like Weymouth and Melcomb, in Dorsetshire, separated only by the creek, or river; and yet each of them send members to Parliaments. These towns are joined together by a very beautiful and stately stone bridge having fifteen arches. Were they put together, they would make a very handsome seaport town. They have a great fishing trade here, as well for supply of the country, as for merchandise, and the towns are not despisable; but as to sending four members to the British Parliament, which is as many as the city of London chooses, that I confess seems a little scandalous, but to who, is none of my business to enquire.

The sea making several deep bays here, they who travel by land are obliged to go higher into the country to pass above the water, especially at Trewardreth Bay. The next inlet of the sea, is the famous firth, or inlet, called Falmouth Haven. It is certainly next to Milford Haven in South Wales, the fairest and best road for shipping that is in the whole of Britain, when there be considered the depth of water for above twenty miles within land; the safety of riding, sheltered from all kind of winds or storms, the good anchorage, and the many creeks, all navigable, where ships may run in and be safe, so that the like is no where to be found.

St Mawes and Pendennis are two fortifications placed at the points, or entrance of this haven, opposite to one another, though not with a communication, or view; they are very strong; the first principally by sea, having a good platform of guns, pointing thwart the channel, and planted on a level with the water; but Pendennis Castle is strong by land as well as by water, is regularly fortified, has good out works, and generally a strong garrison. St Mawes, otherwise called St Mary's has a town annexed to the castle, and is a borough, sending members to the Parliament.

The town of Falmouth is by much the richest, and best trading town in this county, though not so ancient as its neighbour town of Truro; and indeed, is in some things obliged to acknowledge the seigniorty; namely, that in the corporation of Truro, the person who they choose to be their mayor of Truro, is also mayor of Falmouth of course. But let these advantages be what they will, the town of Falmouth has gotten the trade, at least the best part of it from the other, which is chiefly owing to the situation, for that Falmouth lying upon the sea, but within the entrance, ships of the greatest burthen come up to the very quays, and the whole royal navy might ride safely in the road, whereas the town of Truro lying far within, and at the mouth of two fresh rivers, is not navigable for vessels of above 150 tons, or thereabouts.

But let this be as it will, the trade is now in a manner wholly gone to Falmouth, the trade at Truro, being now chiefly if not only for shipping off of block TIN and copper ore, the latter being lately found in large quantities in some of the mountains between Truro, and St Michaels, and which is much improved since the several mills are erected at Bristol, and other parts, for the manufactures of battery ware or, as 'tis called, brass, which is made out of English copper, most of it dug in these parts; the ore it self also being found very rich and good.

Falmouth is well built, has abundance of shipping belonging to it, is full of rich merchants, and has a flourishing and increasing trade. I say increasing, because by the late setting up the English packets between this port and Lisbon, there is a new commerce [31] between Portugal and this town, carried on to a very great value.

It is true, part of this trade was founded in a clandestine commerce, carried on by the said packets at Lisbon, where being king's ships, and claiming the privilege of not being searched, or visited by the custom-house officers, they found means to carry off great quantities of British manufactures, which they sold on board to the Portuguese merchants, and they conveyed them on shore, as 'tis supposed without paying custom. But the government there, getting intelligence of it, and complaint being made in England also, where it was found to be very prejudicial to the fair merchant, that trade has been effectually stopped, but the Falmouth merchants having by this means gotten a taste of the Portuguese trade, have maintained it ever since in ships of their own. This is a specimen of the Portugal trade, and how considerable it is in it self, as well as how advantageous to England, but as that is not to the present case, I proceed.

Truro is however a very considerable town too; it stands up the water north and by east from Falmouth in the utmost extended branch of the haven, in the middle, between the conflux of two rivers, which though not of any long course, have a very good appearance for a port, and make a large wharf between them in the front of the town; and the water here makes a good port for small ships, though it be at the influx, but not for ships of burthen. This is the particular town where the Lord Warden of the Stannaries always holds his famous Parliament of Miners, and for stamping of TIN. There are at least three churches in it, but no Dissenter's meeting house, that I could hear of.

Tregony, is upon the same water north east from Falmouth, distance about sixteen miles from it, but is a town of very little trade but what is carried on under the merchants of Falmouth, or Truro; the chief thing that is to be said of this town, is, that it sends members to Parliament.

Penryn, is up the same branch of the haven, as Falmouth, but stands four miles higher towards the west, yet ships come to it of as great a size, as can come to Truro it self; it is a very pleasant agreeable town, and for that reason has many merchants in it, who would perhaps otherwise live at Falmouth. The chief commerce of these towns, as to their sea affairs, is the pilchards, and Newfoundland fishing, which is very profitable to them all. It had formerly a conventional church, with a chantry, and a religious house, a cell to Kirton, but they are all demolished, and scarce the ruins of them distinguishable enough to know one part from another.

Quitting Falmouth Haven from Penryn west, we came to Helsten, about 7 miles, and stands upon the little river Cober, which however admits the sea so into its bosom as to make a tolerable good harbour for ships a little below the town. It is the fifth town, allowed for the coining TIN, and several of the ships called 'tin' ships are loaden here.

At Helford is a small, but good harbour between Falmouth and this port, where many times the TIN ships go in to load for London; also here are a good number of fishing vessels for the pilchard trade, and abundance of skilful fishermen.

Pensance is the farthest town of any note west, being 254 miles from London, and within about ten miles of the promontory, called the Lands End. The town of Pensance is a place of good business, well built and populous, has a good trade, and a great many ships belonging to it, notwithstanding it is so remote. Here are also a great many good families of gentlemen, though in this utmost angle of the nation; and, which is yet more strange, the veins of lead, tin, and copper ore, are said to be seen, even to the utmost extent of land at low water mark, and in the very sea; so rich, so valuable a treasure is contained in these parts of Great Britain, though they are supposed to be so poor, because so very remote from London, which is the centre of our wealth.

Between this town and St Burien stands a circle of great

stones, not unlike those at Stonehenge in Wiltshire, with one bigger than the rest in the middle; they stand about 12 foot asunder, but have no inscription, neither does tradition offer to leave any part of their history upon record; as whether it was a trophy, or a monument of burial, or an altar for worship, or what else; so that all that can be learned of them, is, that here they are.

Near Pensance, but open to the sea, is that gulf they call Mounts Bay, named so from a high hill standing in the water, which they call St Michael's Mount; the seamen call it only, the Cornish Mount. It has been fortified, though the situation of it makes it so difficult of access, that like the Bass in Scotland, there needs no fortification; like the Bass too, it was once made a prison for prisoners of State, but now it is wholly neglected.

I am now at my journey's end. I must now return *sur mes pas*, as the French call it; though not literally so, for I shall not come back the same way I went; but I shall come back by the north coast, and my observations in my return will furnish very well materials for a fourth letter.

I am, &c.

Appendix to Letter 3

I HAVE ended this account at the utmost extent of the island of Great Britain west, without visiting those excrescences of the island, as I think I may call them, (viz.) the rocks of Scilly, of which, what is most famous, is their infamy, or reproach; namely, how many good ships are, almost *continually* dashed in pieces there, and how many brave lives lost, in spite of the mariners' best skills, or the light-houses, and other sea-marks best notice.

These islands lie so in the middle between the two vast openings of the north and south narrow seas, or as the sailors call them, the Bristol Channel, and The Channel, (so called by way of eminence) that it cannot, or perhaps never will be avoided, but that several ships in the dark of the night, and in stress of weather may by being out in their reckonings, or other unavoidable accidents mistake, and if they do, they are sure, as the sailors call it, to run bump a shore upon Scilly, where they find no quarter among the breakers, but are beat to pieces, without any possibility of escape.

One can hardly mention the Bishop and his Clerks, as they are called, or the rocks of Scilly, without letting fall a tear to the memory of Sir Cloudesly Shovel,[1] and all the gallant spirits that were with him at one blow, and without a moment's warning dashed into a state of immortality; the admiral with three men of war, and all their men (running upon these rocks, right afore the wind, and in a dark night) being lost there, and not a man saved.

They tell us of eleven sail of merchant ships homeward-bound, and richly laden from the southward, who had the like fate, in the same place, a great many years ago; and that some of them coming from Spain, and having a great quantity of bullion, or pieces of eight on board, the money frequently drives on shore still, and that in good quantities, especially after stormy weather.

Nor is it seldom that the voracious country people scuffle and fight about the right to what they find, and that in a desperate manner, so that this part of Cornwall may truly be said to be inhabited by a fierce and ravenous people; for they are so greedy, and eager for the prey, that they are charged with strange, bloody, and cruel dealings, even sometimes with one another; but especially with poor distressed seamen when they come on shore by force of a tempest, and seek help for their lives, and where they find the rocks themselves not more merciless than the people who range about them for their prey.

Upon a former accidental journey into this part of the country, during the war with France,[2] it was with a mixture of pleasure and horror that we saw from the hills at the Lizard, which is the southernmost point of this land, an obstinate fight between three French-men of war, and two English, with a privateer, and three merchant-ships in their company. The English had the misfortune, not only to be fewer ships of war in number, but of less force; so that while the two biggest French ships engaged the English, the third in the mean time took the two merchant-ships, and went off with them; as to the picaroon, or privateer, she was able to do little in the matter, not daring to come so near the men of war, as to take a broadside, which her thin sides would not have been able to bear, but would have sent her to the bottom at once; so that the English men of war had no assistance from her, nor could she prevent the taking the two merchant-ships; yet we observed that the English captains managed their fight so well, and their seamen behaved so briskly, that in about three hours both the Frenchmen stood off, and being sufficiently banged, let us see that they had no more stomach to fight; after which the English, having damage enough too no doubt, stood away to the eastward, as we supposed, to refit.

Nor is the Lizard Point less useful (though not so far west) than the other, which is more properly called the Land's End; but if we may credit our mariners, it is more frequently, first discovered from the sea. So that the Lizard is the general guide, and of more use in these cases than the other point, and is therefore the land which the ships choose to make first, for then also they are sure that they are past Scilly, and all the dangers of that part of the island.

Nature has fortified this part of the island of Britain in a strange manner, and so as is worth a traveller's observation, as if she knew the force and violence of the mighty ocean, which beats upon it, and which indeed, if the land was not made firm in proportion, could not withstand, but would have been washed away long ago.

First, there are the islands of Scilly, and the rocks about them, these are placed like outworks to resist the first assaults of this enemy, and so break the force of it; as the piles, or starlings (as they are called) are placed before the solid stone-work of London-Bridge, to fence off the force, either of the water, or ice, or any thing else that might be dangerous to the work.

Then there are a vast number of sunk rocks, (so the seamen call them,) besides such as are visible, and above water; which gradually lessen the quantity of water, that would otherwise lie with an infinite weight and force upon the land; 'tis observed, that these rocks lie under water for a great way off into the sea on every side the said two horns of land; so breaking the force of the water, and as above lessening the weight of it.

But besides this, the whole terra firma, or body of the land, which makes this part of the isle of Britain, seems to be one solid rock, as if it was formed by Nature to resist the otherwise irresistible power of the ocean; and indeed if one was to observe with what fury the sea comes on sometimes against the shore here, especially at the Lizard Point, where there are but few, if any outworks, (as I call them) to resist it. How high the waves come rolling forward, storming on the neck of one another; particularly when the wind blows off sea, one would wonder, that even the strongest rocks themselves should be able to resist, and repel them.

And yet, as if all this was not enough, Nature has provided another strong fence, and that is, that these vast rocks are, as it were, cemented together by the solid and weighty ore of TIN and copper, especially the last, which is plentifully found upon the very outmost edge of the land, and with which the stones may be said to be soldered together, lest the force of the sea should separate and disjoint them, and so break in upon these fortifications of the island, to destroy its chief security.

Upon this remote part of the island we saw great numbers of that famous kind of crows, which is known by the name of the Cornish cough, or chough, so the country people call them. They are the same kind, which are found in Switzerland among the Alps, and which Pliny pretended, were peculiar to those mountains, and calls the Pyrrhocorax; the body is black, the legs, feet, and bill of a deep yellow, almost to a red. It is counted little better than a kite, for it is of ravenous quality, and is very mischievous; it will steal and carry away any thing it finds about the house, that is not too heavy, though not fit for its food; as knives, forks, spoons and linen cloths, or whatever it can fly away with, sometimes they say it has stolen bits of firebrands, or lighted candles, and lodged them in the stacks of corn, and the thatch of barns and houses, and set them on fire; but this I only had by oral tradition.

I might take up many sheets in describing the valuable curiosities of this little Cherosonese,[3] or neck land, called the Land's End. But I am too near the end of this letter. If I have opportunity, I shall take notice of some part of what I omit here, in my return by the northern shore of the county.

PREFACE TO THE SECOND VOLUME

THE reception which the first part of this work has met with has not been so mean as to discourage the performance of the second volume, nor to slacken the diligence in our endeavours to perform it well. It is not an easy thing to travel over a whole kingdom, and in so critical a manner too, as will enable the traveller to give an account of things fit for the use of those that shall come after him.

To describe a country by other men's accounts of it, would soon expose the writer to a discovery of the fraud; and to describe it by survey, requires a preparation too great for any thing but a public purse, and persons appointed by authority. But to describe a country by way of journey, in a private capacity, as has been the case here, though it requires a particular application, to what may be learned from due enquiry and from conversation, yet it admits not the observer to dwell upon every nicety, to measure the distances, and determine exactly the site, the dimensions, or the extent of places, or read the histories of them. But it is giving an account by way of essay, or, as the moderns call it, by memoirs of the present state of things, in a familiar manner.

This we have performed in the best manner we could, and have taken care to have it come fully up to our proposals. We are not to boast of the performance, but are content to have it compared with any that have gone before it; if it may be done with impartiality and a fair design of determining according to truth. Our manner is plain, and suited to the nature of familiar letters; our relations have no blusters, no rhodomontadoes of our own abilities; but we keep close to the first design of giving, as near as possible, such an account of things, as may entertain the reader, and give him a view of our country, such as may tempt him to travel over it himself, in which case it will be not a little assisting to him, or qualify him to discourse of it, as one that had a tolerable knowledge of it, though he stayed at home.

As we observed in the first volume, there will always be something new, for those that come after; and if an account of Great Britain was to be written every year, there would be something found out, which was overlooked before, or something to describe, which had its birth since the former accounts. New foundations are always laying, new buildings always raising, highways repairing, churches and public buildings erecting, fires and other calamities happening, fortunes of families taking different turns, new trades are every day erected, new projects enterprised, new designs laid; so that as long as England is a trading, improving nation, no perfect description either of the place, the people, or the conditions and state of things can be given.

We have now finished the whole south of Trent, which being the most populous part of the country, and infinitely fuller of great towns, of people, and of trade, has also the greatest variety of incidents in its passing over. But the northern part being also to include Scotland, and being the greatest in extent, will have its beauties, we can assure you; and though the country may in some respects, be called barren, the history of it will not be so.

The great and once wasted countries of Northumberland, Cumberland, and Durham, shall be truly and not slightly described, with their real improvements, without loading our work with fragments of antiquity, and dressing up the wilds of the borders as a paradise, which are indeed but a wilderness.

In the mean time we recommend our performance to the candour of the reader, and whatever may be objected, we doubt not to have obtained the just reputation of having written with impartiality and with truth.

Letter 4

Containing a description of the North Shore of the counties of Cornwall, and Devon, and some parts of Somersetshire, Wiltshire, Dorsetshire, Gloucestershire, Buckinghamshire and Berkshire

SIR, – My last letter ended the account of my travels, where Nature ended her account, when she meted out the island, and where she fixed the utmost western bounds of Britain; and, being resolved to see the very extremity of it, I set my foot into the sea, as it were, beyond the farthest inch of dry land west, as I had done before near the town of Dover, at the foot of the rocks of the South-Foreland in Kent, which, I think, is the farthest point east in a line; and as I had done, also, at Leostoff in Suffolk, which is another promontory on the eastern coast, and is reckoned the farthest eastward of the island in general: likewise, I had used the same ceremony at Selsy near Chichester, which I take to be the farthest land south, except at Portland only, which, as it is not really an island, may be called, the farthest land south; so, in its place, I shall give you an account of the same curiosity at John a Grot's House in Caithness, the farthest piece of ground in Great Britain, north.

I had once, indeed, resolved to have coasted the whole circuit of Britain by sea, as 'tis said, Agricola [1] the Roman general, did; and in this voyage I would have gone about every promontory, and into the bottom of every bay, and had provided myself a good yacht, and an able commander for that purpose; but I found it would be too hazardous an undertaking for any man to justify himself in the doing it upon the mere foundation of curiosity, and having no other business at all; so I gave it over.

I now turned about to the east. The first place, of any note, we came to, is St Ives, a pretty good town, and grown rich by the fishing-trade; it is situated on the west side of a deep bay, called St Ives Bay, trom the name of the town. It is a very pleasant view we have at Madern Hills, and the plain by them, in the way from the Land's-End to St Ives, where, at one sight, there is a prospect of the ocean at the Land's-End west; of the British Channel at Mount's Bay south; and the Bristol Channel, or Severn Sea, north. At St Ives, neither of the two seas are above three miles off, and very plain to be seen; and also, in a clear day, the islands of Scilly, though above thirty miles off.

From this town and port of St Ives, we have no town of any note on the coast; no, not a market town, except Redruth, which is of no consideration, 'till we come to Padstow-Haven, which is near thirty miles. The country is, indeed, both fruitful and pleasant, and several houses of gentlemen are seen as we pass; the sands, also, are very pleasant to the eye, and to travel upon; also a good house belonging to the ancient family of Trefusis.

In viewing these things, we observed the hills fruitful of tin, copper, and lead, all the way on our right hand, the product of which, is carried all to the other shore; so that we shall have little to say of it here. The chief business on this shore, is in the herring fishing; the herrings, about October, come driving up the Severn Sea, and from the coast of Ireland, in prodigious shoals, and beat all upon this coast as high as Biddeford, and Barnstable, in Devonshire, and are caught in great quantities by the fishermen.

Padstow is a large town, and stands on a very good harbour for such shipping as use that coast, that is to say, for the Irish trade. The harbour is the mouth of the river Camel, or Camal, which rising at Camelford, runs down by Bodmyn to Wodbridge, or Wardbridge, a large stone bridge of eight arches, or thereabouts, built by the general good will of the country gentlemen; the passage over the river there, before, being very dangerous, and having been the loss of some lives, as well as goods. The passage from this town of Padstow to Ireland, is called, by writers, to be no more than twenty-four hours, but not justly. It is true, that Padstow being the first, and best, if not the only haven on this shore, the trade from Ireland settled here of course, and a great many ships in this harbour, are employed in the commerce; but to say, they make the voyage in four-and-twenty hours, is to say, it has been so, or, on extraordinary gales of fair wind, it may be done; but not one in twenty-four ships makes its voyage in twenty-four hours; and, I believe, it may be said, they are oftener five or six days in the passage.

Higher within the land, lies the town of Bodmyn, once one of the coining towns for tin, but lost it to Lestwithyel: however, this town enjoys several privileges, some of which are also tokens of its antiquity.

The coinage towns were, in Queen Elizabeth's time, four; namely, Leskeard, Lestwithyel, Truro, Helston.

Since that, in King James's time, was added, Pensance.

Tintagel Castle lies upon this coast a little farther, a mark of great antiquity, and every writer has mentioned it; but as antiquity is not my work, I leave the ruins of Tintagel to those that search into antiquity; little or nothing, that I could hear, is to be seen at it; and as for the story of King Arthur [2] being both born and killed there, 'tis a piece of tradition, only on oral history, and not any authority to be produced for it.

The game called the Hurlers, is a thing the Cornish men value themselves much upon; I confess, I see nothing in it, but that it is a rude violent play among the boors, or country people; brutish and furious, and a sort of an evidence, that they were, once, a kind of barbarians. It seems, to me, something to resemble the old way of play, as it was then called, with whirle-bats,[3] with which Hercules slew the giant, when he undertook to clean the Augean stable. The wrestling in Cornwall, is, indeed, a much more manly and generous exercise, and that closure, which they call the Cornish Hug, has made them eminent in the wrestling rings all over England, as the Norfolk and Suffolk men, are for their dexterity at the hand and foot, and throwing up the heels of their adversary, without taking hold of him.

I came out of Cornwall by passing the river Tamar at Launceston, the last, or rather, the first, town in the county, the town shewing little else, but marks of its antiquity; for great part of it is so old, as it may, in a manner, pass for an old, ragged, decayed place, in general. In the time when Richard, Earl of Cornwall,[4] had the absolute government of this county, and was, we might say, king of the country, it was a frontier town, walled about, and well fortified, and had, also a strong castle to defend it; but these are seen, now, only in their old clothes, and lie all in ruins and heaps of rubbish.

It is a principal gain to the people of this town, that they let lodgings to the gentlemen, who attend here in the time of the assizes, and other public meetings; as particularly, that of electing knights of the shire, and at the county sessions, which are held here; for which purposes, the town's people have their rooms better furnished than in other places of this country, though their houses are but low; or do they fail to make a good price to their lodgers, for the conveniences they afford them.

There is a fine image, or figure of Mary Magdalen, upon the tower of the church, which the Catholics fail not to pay their reverences to, as they pass by. There is no tin, or copper, or lead, found hereabouts, as I could find, nor any manufacture in the place; there are a pretty many attorneys here, who manage business for the rest of their fraternity at the assizes. As to trade, it has not much to boast of, and yet there are people enough in it to excuse those who call it a populous place. Passing the river Tamar, about two miles from Launceston, we enter the great county of Devon, and as we enter Devonshire, in the most wild and barren part of the county, and where, formerly, tin mines were found, though now they are either quite exhausted, or not to be found without more charge than the purchase, if found, would be worth; so we must expect it a little to resemble its neighbour country for a while.

The river Tamar, here, is so full of fresh salmon, and those so exceeding fat, and good, that they are esteemed, in both counties, above the fish, of the same kind, found in other places; and the quantity is so great, as supplies the country in abundance, which is occasioned by the mouth of the river being so very large, and the water so deep for two leagues before it opens into Plymouth Sound, so that the fish have a secure retreat in the salt water for their harbour and shelter, and from thence they shoot up into the fresh water, in such vast numbers to cast their spawn, that the country people cannot take too many.

As we are just entered Devonshire, as I said above, it seems, at first sight, a wild, barren, poor country; but we ride but a few miles, 'till we find an alteration in several things: 1. More people; 2. Larger towns; 3. The people all busy, and in full employ upon their manufactures.

At the uppermost, and extreme part of the county, N.W. there runs a huge promontory, a mountain like proboscis, into the sea, beyond all the land on either side, whether of Devonshire, or of Cornwall. This they would fain have called Hercules's Promontory, and Mr Cambden calls it Herculis Promontorium; but the honest sailors, and after them, the plain country people, call it, in down-right modern English, Hartland Point, or, Hearty Point, from the town of Hartland, which stands just within the shore, and is on the very utmost edge of the county of Devon. It is a market town, though so remote, and of good resort too, the people coming to it out of Cornwall, as well as out of Devonshire; and particularly the fisher-boats of Barnstaple, Bidiford, and other towns on the coast, lying often under the lee, as they call it, of these rocks, for shelter from the S.W. or S.E. winds.

From this point or promontory, the land, falling away for some miles, makes a gulf or bay, which, reaching to the head land, or point of Barnstable River or Haven, is called from thence, Barnstable Bay. Into this bay, or at the W. end of this bay, the rivers Taw and Tower empty themselves at one mouth, that is to say, in one channel; and it is very particular, that as two rivers join in one channel, so here are two great trading towns in one port, a thing which as it is not usual, so

I cannot say 'tis any advantage to either of them; for it naturally follows, that they rival one another, and lessen both; whereas, had they been joined together in one town, or were it possible to join them, they would make the most considerable town, or city rather, in all this part of England.

These are the towns of Barnstable and Biddiford, or, as some write it, Bediford; the first of these is the most ancient, the last the most flourishing; the harbour or river is in its entrance the same to both, and when they part, the Tower turning to the right, or south west, and the Taw to the S.E. yet they seem to be both so safe, so easy in the channel, so equally good with respect to shipping, so equi-distant from the sea, and so equally advantageous, that neither town complains of the bounty of the sea to them, or their situation by land; and yet, of late years, the town of Biddiford has flourished, and the town of Barnstable rather declined.

Biddiford is a pleasant, clean, well-built town; the more ancient street which lies next the river, is very pleasant, where is the bridge, a very noble quay, and the custom-house. But besides this, there is a new spacious street, broad as the High Street of Excester, well-built, and, which is more than all, well inhabited, with considerable and wealthy merchants, who trade to most parts of the trading world.

Here, as is to be seen in almost all the market towns of Devonshire, is a very large, well-built, and well-finished meeting-house, and, by the multitude of people which I saw come out of it, and the appearance of them, I thought all the town had gone thither, and began to enquire for the church. But when I came to the church, I found that also, large, spacious, and well filled too, and that with people of the best fashion. The person who officiates at the meeting-house in this town, I happened to have some conversation with, and found him to be not only a learned man, and master of good reading; but a most acceptable gentlemanly person, and one, who, contrary to our received opinion of those people, had not only good learning, and good sense, but abundance of good manners, and good humour; nothing sour, cynical, or morose in him, and, in a word, a very valuable man. And as such a character always recommends a man to men of sense and good breeding, so I found this gentleman was very well received in the place, even by those who he differed from in matters of religion, and those differences did not, as is usual, make any breach in their conversing with him. His name, as I remember, was Bartlet.[5] But this is a digression: I wish I could say the like of all the rest of his brethren.

There is indeed, a very fine stone bridge over the river here; the arches are beautiful and stately; but as for saying one of them is so big, that a ship of 60 tons may sail under it, &c. as a late author asserts, I leave that where I find it, for the people of Bidiford to laugh at. If it had been said the hull of such a ship might pass under the bridge, it might have been let go. But, as he says, It may SAIL under it, which must suppose some or one of its masts standing too; this puts it past all possibility of belief, at least to those who judge of such things by rules of mechanism, or by what is to be seen in other parts of the world, no such thing being practicable either at London Bridge, Rochester Bridge, or even at York, where the largest arch in England is supposed to be.

As Biddiford has a fine bridge over the Tower or Towridge, so Barnstable has a very noble bridge over the Taw, and though not longer, is counted larger and stronger than the other. These two rival towns are really very considerable; both of them have a large share in the trade to Ireland, and in the herring fishery, and in a trade to the British colonies in America; if Biddiford cures more fish, Barnstable imports more wine, and other merchandises; they are both established ports for landing wool from Ireland; of which by itself.

If Biddiford has a greater number of merchants, Barnstable has a greater commerce within land, by its great market for Irish wool and yarn, &c. with the serge-makers of Tiverton and Excester, who come up hither to buy. So that, in a word, Barnstable, though it has lost ground to Biddiford, yet, take it in all its trade completely, is full as considerable as Biddiford; only, that perhaps, it was formerly far superior to it, and the other has risen up to be a match to it. Barnstable is a large, spacious, well built town, more populous than Biddiford, but not better built, and stands lower; insomuch, that at high water in spring tides, it is, as it were, surrounded with water.

Behind Biddiford, that is as we come from Launceston, are several good towns, though I observed that the country was wild and barren; as Tavistock, belonging to the house of Bedford; the town of Torrington, on the same river Towridge that Biddiford stands on. The title of Earl of Torrington, was first given to the late General Monk,[6] Duke of Albemarle, for a reward of his loyalty, in restoring King Charles II, and the line being extinct in his son, it was given by King William III to Admiral Herbert, who came over with him, and was immediately made admiral of the British fleet, to defend the possession of the crown in the person of that prince; and since that to Sir George Bing, one of our present admirals, and one who asserted the authority and power of the British navy against the Spaniards, at the late sea fight near Cape Passaro in Sicily: so that the town of Torrington, seems to be appropriated to the honour of the defenders of the British sovereignty at sea.

Another town in this part of the country is Okehampton, vulgarly Okington, a good market town, and sends two members to the Parliament; it is a manufacturing town, as all the towns this way now are, and pretty rich; and having said this, I have said all, unless it be, that in the records of antiquity, it appears to have been much more considerable than it is now, having 92 knights fees belonging to it.

A little above Barnstable, N.E. upon the coast, stands a good market and port town, called Ilfar-Comb, a town of good trade, populous and rich, all which is owing to its having a very good harbour and road for ships, and where ships from Ireland often put in, when, in bad weather, they cannot, without the extremest hazard, run into the mouth of the Taw, which they call Barnstable Water.

Antiquity tells us long stories, of the Danes landing on this coast. All this may be true, for ought we know, but I could neither find or hear of any thing of the ruins or remains of them in the country; so I shall trouble you no farther about them.

Leaving the coast, we came, in our going southward, to the great river Ex, or Isca, which rises in the hills on this north side of the county; the country it rises in, is called Exmore, Cambden calls it a filthy, barren, ground, and, indeed, so it is; but as soon as the Ex comes off from the moors and hilly country, and descends into the lower grounds, we found the alteration; for then we saw Devonshire in its other countenance, viz. cultivated, populous, and fruitful; and continuing so 'till we came to Tiverton.

Next to Excester, this is the greatest manufacturing town in the county, and, of all the inland towns, is next to it in wealth, and in numbers of people; it stands on the river Ex, and has over it, a very fine bridge, with another over the little river Loman. Antiquity says, before those bridges were built, there were two fords here, one through each river, and that the town was from thence called Twyford-ton, that is, the town upon the two fords, and so by abbreviating the sounds Twy-for-ton, then Tiverton; but that I leave to the learned searchers into ancient things.

But the beauty of Tiverton is the Free-School, a noble building, but a much nobler foundation; it was erected by one Peter Blundel,[7] a clothier, and a lover of learning, who used the saying of William of Wickham to the king when he founded the royal school at Winchester, viz. that if he was not himself a scholar, he would be the occasion of making more scholars, than any scholar in England; to which end he founded this school. He has endowed it with so liberal a maintenance, that, as I was informed, the school-master has, at least, sixty pounds per annum, besides a very good house to live in, and the advantage of scholars not on the foundation, and the usher in proportion.

As this is a manufacturing country, as above, we found the people, here, all fully employed, and very few, if any, out of work, except such as need not be unemployed, but were so from mere sloth and idleness, of which, some will be found every where.

From this town, there is little belonging to Devonshire, but what has been spoken of, except what lies in the road to Taunton, which we took next. Entering Wellington, the first town we came at in Somersetshire, though partly employed in manufacturing too, we were immediately surrounded with beggars, to such a degree, that we had some difficulty to keep them from under our horse heels.

It was our misfortune at first, that we threw some farthings, and halfpence, such as we had, among them; for thinking by this to be rid of them, on the contrary, it brought out such a crowd of them, as if the whole town was come out into the street, and they ran in this manner after us through the whole street, and a great way after we were quite out of the town; so that we were glad to ride as fast as we could through the town to get clear of them; I was, indeed, astonished at such a sight, in a country where the people were so generally full of work, as they were here; for in Cornwall, where there are hardly any manufactures, and where there are, indeed, abundance of poor, yet we never found any thing like this.

Before I quite leave Devonshire, I must mention one thing, which I observed at my first setting out; namely, that I would take notice how every county in England furnished something of its produce towards the supply of the city of London : now I must allow, that Cornwall is, in some respects, an exception to this rule, because, though it is fruitful enough for the supply of its own inhabitants, yet, in the first place, the waste grounds are so many, the inhabitants so numerous, and the county so narrow, that, except the herrings, a few of which may be brought to London for sale, they have not much overplus to furnish other parts with; but then they make amends by sending up an immense wealth in their tin, lead, and copper, from the bowels of their barren mountains, and the export of the pilchards, and herrings, from both their shores to

Spain and Italy, from whence much of the returns are again brought to London for their vent and consumption.

In like manner, the county of Devon has been rich in mines of tin and lead, though they seem at present, wrought out; and they had their stannery towns and coinage, as well as in Cornwall; nay, so numerous were the miners or tinners, as they are called in this county, that they were, on occasion of a national muster, or defence, regimented by themselves, armed, and officered by themselves, and were, in short, a separate militia from the trained bands, or militia of the county; but now we see the tin works in Devonshire is quite laid aside, not one tin mine being at work in the whole county.

But there is one article in the produce of Devonshire, which makes good what I have written before, that every county contributes something towards the supply of London; and this is, the cider which takes up the south part of the county, between Topsham and Axminster, where they have so vast a quantity of fruit, and so much cider made, that sometimes they have sent ten, or twenty thousand hogsheads of it in a year to London, and at a very reasonable rate too.

The county of Somerset joins to the N.E. part of Devonshire. I entered the county, as I observed above, by Wellington, where we had the entertainment of the beggars; from whence we came to Taunton, vulgarly called Taunton Dean upon the River Ton; this is a large, wealthy, and exceedingly populous town. One of the chief manufacturers of the town told us, that there was at that time so good a trade in the town, that they had then eleven hundred looms going for the weaving of sagathies, du roys, and such kind of stuffs, which are made there; and that which added to the thing very much, was, that not one of those looms wanted work. He farther added, that there was not a child in the town, or in the villages round it; of above five years old, but, if it was not neglected by its parents, and untaught, could earn its own bread.

This town chooses two Members of Parliament, and their

way of choosing is, by those who they call 'pot-walloners,' that is to say, every inhabitant, whether house-keeper or lodger, that dresses their own victuals; to make out which, several inmates, or lodgers, will, sometime before the election, bring out their pots, and make fires in the street, and boil their victuals in the sight of their neighbours, that their votes may not be called in question.

There are two large parish churches in this town, and two or three meeting-houses, whereof one, is said to be the largest in the county. The inhabitants have been noted for the number of Dissenters; for among them it was always counted a seminary of such. They suffered deeply in the Duke of Monmouth's rebellion, but paid King James home for the cruelty exercised by Jeffries among them; for when the Prince of Orange arrived, the whole town ran in to him, with so universal a joy, that, 'twas thought, if he had wanted it, he might have raised a little army there, and in the adjacent part of the country. There was, and, I suppose, is still, a private college, or academy, for the Dissenters in this town; the tutor, who then managed it, was named Warren,[8] who told me, that there were threescore and twelve ministers then preaching, whereof six had conformed to the Church, the rest were among the Dissenters, who had been his scholars.

From this town of Taunton, which is by far the greatest in all this part of the country, we went north to take a view of the coast. Exmore lies in the way, part of it in this country, and extending to the sea side. It gives, indeed, but a melancholy view, being a vast tract of barren, and desolate lands; yet on the coast, there are some very good sea-ports. As, 1. Porlock, on the very utmost extent of the country; it has a small harbour, but of no importance, nor has it any thing of trade, so I need but name it. 2. Minhead, the best port, and safest harbour, in all these counties, at least, on this side: and they told me, that in the great storm anno 1703, when in all the harbours and rivers in the county, the ships were blown on shore, wrecked, and lost, they suffered little or no damage in this harbour.

The trade of this town lies chiefly with Ireland, and this was, for many years, the chief port in this part of England, where wool from Ireland was allowed to be imported; but that liberty is since enlarged to several other ports by Act of Parliament. This corporation sends two members to the Parliament, which are chosen also, as at Taunton, by the pot-walloners; the town is well built, is full of rich merchants, and has some trade also to Virginia, and the West Indies.

There are some very good families, and of very ancient standing, in this part of the county. The Mohuns in particular were anciently lords of Dunstar Castle, at a small distance from the sea, and very strong. Here formerly was the ancient mansion, or inheritance, of the Lords Mohun. Who it will now descend to, that ancient family being extinct in the person of the late unhappy Lord Mohun,[9] who was killed in a duel with Duke Hamilton, I could not learn.

From hence the coast bears back west to Watchet, a small port also, but, 'tis of no importance now; for if we may calculate things present, by things past, the town of Minhead is risen out of the decay of the towns of Porlock and Watchet, which were once important places; and the reason is clear, since the increase of shipping and trade, bigger ships being brought into use, than were formerly built; and the harbour at Minhead being fairer, and much deeper, than those at Watchet and Porlock, and therefore able to secure those greater ships, which the others were not, the merchants removed to it.

From hence the winding shore brings us to Bridgewater. This is an ancient and very considerable town and port, it stands at the mouth of the river Parrat, or Perot, which comes from the south, after having received the river Tone from the west, which is made navigable up to Taunton, by a very fine new channel, cut at the expense of the people of Taunton, and which, by the navigation of it, is infinitely advantageous to that town, and well worth all their expense.

This town of Bridgewater, is a populous, trading town, is well built, and as well inhabited, and has many families of good fashion dwelling in it, besides merchants. The famous Admiral Blake,[10] was a native of this town. Here it was, that the Duke of Monmouth,[11] finding himself defeated in his expectation of the city of Bristol, and repulsed at the city of Bath, made his retreat; where, finding the King's troops followed him, and seemed resolved to attack him, he went up to the top of the steeple, with some officers, and viewing the situation of the King's army, by the help of perspectives, resolved to make an attempt upon them the same night, by way of prevention, and accordingly marched out of the town in the dead of the night to attack them, and had he not, either by the treachery, or mistake of his guides, been brought to an unpassable ditch, where he could not get over, in the interval of which, the King's troops took the alarm, by the firing a pistol among the Duke's men, whether, also, by accident, or treachery, was not known; I say, had not those accidents, and his own fate, conspired to his defeat, he had certainly cut the Lord Feversham's [12] army all to pieces; but by these circumstances, he was brought to a battle on unequal terms, and defeated. The rest I need not mention.

This town was regularly fortified in the late civil wars, and sustained two sieges, if not more; the situation of it renders it easy to be fortified, the river and haven taking one chief part of the circumference. Over the river, they have a very good bridge of stone, and the tide rises here, at high water, near six fathoms, whereof, sometimes it comes in with such furious haste, as to come two fathoms deep at a time, and when it does so, by surprise, it often does great damage to ships, driving them foul of one another, and oftentimes oversetting them. This sudden rage of the tide, is called, the 'bore,' and is frequent in all the rivers of this channel, especially in the Severn itself.

In this town of Bridgewater, besides a very large church, there is a fine new-built meeting-house, in which 'tis remarkable, that they have an advanced seat for the mayor and aldermen, when any of the magistrates should be of their communion, as sometimes has happened. Here, also, is a college, or private academy, for the Dissenters to breed up their preaching youth; the tutor was one Mr Moor,[13] a man who, it is owned, was a master of good literature; what talent he had at erudition, I can give no account of, for it is not every master of learning, that makes a good instructor of others.

From Bridgewater, there is a road to Bristol, which they call the Lower Way; the Upper Way, and which is the more frequented road, being over Mendip Hills. This Lower Way also is not always passable, being subject to floods, and dangerous inundations, I mean, dangerous to travel through, especially for strangers. This low part of the country, between Bridgewater and Bristol, suffered exceedingly in that terrible inundation of the sea, which was occasioned by the violence of the wind in the great storm, anno 1703, and the country people have set up marks upon their houses and trees, with this note upon them, 'Thus high the waters came in the great storm'; 'Thus far the great tide flowed up in the last violent tempest'; and the like. And in one place they showed us, where a ship was, by the force of the water, and the rage of the tempest, driven up upon the shore, several hundred yards from the ordinary high water mark, and was left in that surprising condition upon dry land.

As this country is all a grazing, rich, feeding soil, so a great number of large oxen are fed here, which are sent up to London; no county in England furnishes more effectual provisions, nor, in proportion, a greater value than this. These supplies are in three articles.

1. Fat oxen (as above) as large, and good, as any in England.

2. Large Cheddar cheese, the greatest, and best of the kind in England.

3. Colts bred in great numbers in the moors, and sold into the northern counties, where the horse copers, as they are called, in Staffordshire, and Leicestershire, buy them again, and sell them to London for cart horses, and coach horses, the breed being very large.

As the low part of this county is thus employed in grazing

and feeding cattle, so all the rest of this large extended country is employed in the woollen manufactures, and in the best, and most profitable part of it, viz.

In Taunton - -	The serges, druggets, &c. and several other kinds of stuffs.
In Wells, Shepton, Glastenbury, &c.	Knitting of stockings, principally for the Spanish trade.
In Bristol, and many towns on the Somersetshire side - - - -	Druggets, cantaloons, and other stuffs.
In Froom, Philips-Norton, and all the country bordering upon Wiltshire - - -	Fine Spanish medley cloths, especially on that part of the county from Wincanton, and Meer, to Warminster, Bruton, Castlecary, Temple Comb, down to Gillingham, and Shaftsbury, in Dorsetshire.

As I made a little trip from Bridgewater north, into the body of the county, I must take notice of what I observed in that part of it. The first place I came to was Glastenbury, where indeed, the venerable marks of antiquity, however I have declined the observation of them, struck me with some unusual awe, and I resolved to hear all that could be told me upon that subject; and first they told me (for there are two pieces of antiquity, which were to be inquired of in this place) that King Arthur was buried here, and that his coffin had been found here.

Secondly, that Joseph of Arimathea [14] was here, and that when he fixed his staff in the ground, which was on Christmas Day, it immediately took root, budded, put forth whitethorn leaves, and the next day, was in full blossom, white as a sheet, and that the plant is preserved, and blows every Christmas Day, as at first, to this very day.

I took all this *ad referendum*, but took guides afterwards, to see what demonstrations there could be given of all these things; they went over the ruins of the place with me, telling me, which part every particular piece of building had been; and as for the white-thorn, they carried me to a gentleman's garden in the town, where it was preserved, and I brought a piece of it away in my hat, but took it upon their honour, that it really does blow in such manner, as above, on Christmas Day. However, it must be confessed, that it is universally attested.[15]

As to the burial of King Arthur, Mr Cambden[16] makes no doubt of it, and gives us from Giraldus Cambrensis, an account how King Henry II caused search to be made for his tomb, and before they had dug seven foot, they came to a great stone, having a cross of lead on the inside of it, and the subsequent letters, or inscription upon it, and in the following rude character; which the said Giraldus Cambrensis, Mr Cambden says, was an eye-witness of, as well as of a coffin of hollowed oak, which they found by digging nine foot deeper than the inscription, wherein were deposited the bones of that great prince. On the top of a high hill, near a mile from the town, stands an old tower, which the people vulgarly call the TOR; what it was, we are not certain. I must confess, that I cannot so much blame the Catholics in those early days, for reverencing this place as they did, or, at least, 'till they came to found idolatry upon their respect, if they really believed all these things; but my business is to relate, rather than make remarks.

The inscription on King Arthur's coffin, is as follows:

Four miles from Glastonbury, lies the little city of Wells, where is one of the neatest, and, in some respects, the most beautiful, cathedrals in England, particularly the west front of it, is one complete draught of imagery, very fine, and yet very ancient. This is a neat, clean city, and the clergy, in particular, live very handsomely. Here are no less than seven-and-twenty prebends, and nineteen canons, belonging to this church, besides a dean, a chancellor, a precentor, and three arch deacons; a number which very few cathedrals in England have, besides this. The city lies just at the foot of the mountains called Mendip Hills, and is itself built on a stony foundation. Its manufacture is chiefly of stockings, as is mentioned already; 'tis well built, and populous, and has several good families in it; so that there is no want of good company there.

Near this city, and just under the hills, is the famous, and so much talked of Wokey Hole, which, to me, that had been in Pool's Hole, in the Peak of Derby, has nothing of wonder or curiosity in it. The chief thing I observed in this, is, what is generally dropping from the roof of the vault, petrifies, and hangs in long pieces like icicles, as if it would, in time, run into a column to support the arch. As to the stories of a witch dwelling here, as of a giant dwelling in the other (I mean in Pool's Hole) I take them to be equally fabulous, and worth no notice.

In the low country, on the other side Mendip Hills, lies Chedder, a village pleasantly situated under the very ridge of the mountains; before the village is a large green, or common, a piece of ground, in which the whole herd of the cows, belonging to the town, do feed; the ground is exceeding rich, and as the whole village are cowkeepers, they take care to keep up the goodness of the soil, by agreeing to lay on large quantities of dung for manuring, and enriching the land.

The milk of all the town cows, is brought together every day in a common room, where the persons appointed, or trusted for the management, measure every man's quantity, and set it down in a book; when the quantities are adjusted, the milk is all put together, and every meal's milk makes one cheese, and no more; so that the cheese is bigger, or less, as the cows yield more, or less, milk. By this method, the goodness of the cheese is preserved and, without all dispute, it is the best cheese that England affords, if not, that the whole world affords.

Here is a deep, frightful chasm in the mountain, in the hollow of which, the road goes, by which they travel towards Bristol; and out of the same hollow, springs a little river, which flows with such a full stream, that, it is said, it drives twelve mills within a quarter of a mile of the spring; but this is not to be understood, without supposing it to fetch some winding reaches in the way; there would not, otherwise, be room for twelve mills to stand, and have any head of water above the mill, within so small a space of ground.

I come now to that part of the country, which joins itself to Wiltshire, which I reserved, in particular, to this place, in order to give some account of the broad-cloth manufacture. As the east, and south parts of Wiltshire are, as I have already observed, all hilly, spreading themselves far and wide, in plains, and grassy downs, for breeding, and feeding, vast flocks of sheep, and a prodigious number of them. And as the west and north parts of Somersetshire are, on the contrary, low, and marshy, or moorish, for feeding, and breeding, of black cattle, and horses or for lead-mines, &c. so all the south west part of Wiltshire, and the east part of Somersetshire, are low and flat, being a rich, enclosed country, full of rivers and towns, and infinitely populous, insomuch, that some of the market towns are equal to cities in bigness and superior to them in number of people.

In this extent of country, we have the following market towns, which are principally employed in the clothing trade, that is to say, in that part of it, which I am now speaking of; namely, fine medley, or mixed cloths, such as are usually worn in England by the better sort of people; and also, exported in great quantities to Holland, Hamburgh, Sweden, Denmark, Spain, Italy, &c. The principal clothing towns in this part of the country are these,

Somersetshire	Frome, Pensford, Philip's Norton, Bruton, Shepton Mallet, Castle Carey, and Wincanton.
Wiltshire	Malmsbury, Castlecomb, Chippenham, Caln, Devizes, Bradford, Trubridge, Westbury, Warminster, Meer.
Dorsetshire	Gillingham, Shaftesbury, Bemister, and Bere, Sturminster, Shireborn.
Gloucester	Cirencester, Tetbury, Marshfield, Minchinghampton, and Fairford.

These towns, as they stand thin, and at considerable distance from one another; for, except the two towns of Bradford and Trubridge, the other stand at an unusual distance; I say these towns are interspersed with a very great number of villages, I had almost said, innumerable villages, hamlets, and scattered houses, in which, generally speaking, the spinning work of all this manufacture is performed by the poor people; the master clothiers who generally live in the greater towns, sending out the wool weekly to their houses, by their servants and horses, and, at the same time, bringing back the yarn that they have spun and finished, which then is fitted for the loom.

The increasing and flourishing circumstances of this trade, are happily visible by the great concourse of people to, and increase of buildings and inhabitants in these principal clothing towns where this trade is carried on, and wealth of the clothiers. The town of Froom, or, as it is written in our maps, Frome Sellwood, is a specimen of this, which is so prodigiously increased within these last twenty or thirty years, that they have built a new church, and so many new streets of houses, and those houses are so full of inhabitants, that Frome is now reckoned to have more people in it, than the city of Bath, and some say, than even Salisbury itself, and it is very likely to be one of the greatest and wealthiest inland towns in England.

I call it an inland town, because it is particularly distinguished as such, being, not only no sea-port, but not near any sea-port, having no manner of communication by water, no navigable river at it, or near it. Its trade is wholly clothing, and the cloths they make, are, generally speaking, all conveyed to London; and, if we may believe common fame, there are above ten thousand people in Frome now, more than lived in it twenty years ago, and yet it was a considerable town then too. Here are, also, several large meeting-houses, as well as churches, as there are, generally, in all the manufacturing, trading towns in England, especially in the western counties.

The Devizes is, next to this, a large and important town, and full of wealthy clothiers; but this town has, lately, run pretty much into the drugget-making trade; a business, which has made some invasion upon the broad-cloth trade, and great quantities of druggets are worn in England, as also, exported beyond the seas, even in the place of our broad-cloths, and where they usually were worn and exported; but this is much the same as to the trade still; for as it is a woollen maufacture, and that the druggets may properly be called cloth, though narrow, and of a different make, so the makers are all called clothiers.

From these towns south, to Westbury, and to Warminster, the same trade continues, and the finest medley Spanish cloths, not in England only, but in the whole world, are made in this part. They told me at Bradford, that it was no extraordinary thing to have clothiers in that country worth, from ten thousand, to forty thousand pounds a man, and many of the great families, who now pass for gentry in those counties, have been originally raised from, and built up by this truly noble manufacture.

It may be worth enquiry, by the curious, how the manufacturers, in so vast a consumption of the wool, as such a trade must take up, can be supplied with wool for their trade; and, indeed, it would be something strange, if the answer were not at hand.

1. We may reasonably conclude, that this manufacture was at first seated in this county, or, as we may say, planted itself here at first, because of the infinite numbers of sheep, which were fed at that time upon the downs and plains of Dorset, Wilts, and Hampshire, all adjoining. The first planters of the clothing manufacture, doubtless, chose this delightful vale for its seat, because of the neighbourhood of those plains, which might be supposed to be a fund of wool for the carrying it on. Thus the manufacture of white cloth was planted in Stroud Water in Gloucestershire, for the sake of the excellent water there for the dying scarlets, and all

colours that are dyed in grain, which are better dyed there, than in any other place of England, some towns near London excepted. Hence, therefore, we first observe, they are supplied yearly with the fleeces of two or three millions of sheep.

2. But as the number of sheep fed on these downs is lessened, rather than increased, because of the many thousand acres of the carpet ground being, of late years turned into arable land, and sowed with wheat...

I say, the number of sheep, and consequently the quantity of wool, decreasing, and at the same time the manufacture, as has been said, prodigiously increasing, the manufacturers applied themselves to other parts for a supply, and hence began the influx of north-country wool to come in from the counties of Northampton, Leicester, and Lincoln, the centre of which trade, is about Tetbury and Cirencester, where are the markets for the north-country wool and where, as they say, several hundred packs of wool are sold every week, for the supply of this prodigious consumption.

3. From London, they have great quantities of wool, which is generally called Kentish wool, in the fleece, which is brought up from thence by the farmers, since the late severe Acts[17] against their selling it within a certain number of miles of the sea, also fell-wool for the combers, bought of the woolstaplers in Barnabystreet, and sent back by the carriers, which bring up the cloths to market.

4. They have also, sometimes, large quantities of Irish wool, by the way of Bristol, or of Mynhead, in Somersetshire; but this is uncertain, and only on extraordinary occasions. I omit the Spanish wool, as being an article by itself.

And yet, notwithstanding the whole country is thus employed in the broad-cloth manufacture, as above, I must not omit to mention, that here is a very great application to another trade or two. As the spinning is generally the work of the women and children, and that the land is here exceeding rich and fertile, so it cannot be supposed, but that here are farmers in great numbers, whose business is to cultivate the land, and supply the rest of the inhabitants with provisions; and this they do so well, that notwithstanding the county is so exceeding populous.

All the lower part of this county, and also of Gloucestershire, adjoining, is full of large feeding farms, which we call dairies, and the cheese they make, as it is excellent good of its kind, so being a different kind from the Cheshire, being soft and thin, is eaten newer than that from Cheshire. Of this, a vast quantity is every week . . . carried to the river of Thames, by land carriage, and so by barges to London.

Again, in the spring of the year, they make a vast quantity of that we call green cheese, which is a thin, and very soft cheese, resembling cream cheeses, only thicker, and very rich. These are brought to market new, and eaten so; but then this holds only for the two first summer months of the year, May and June, or little more.

Besides this, the farmers in Wiltshire, and the part of Gloucestershire adjoining, send a very great quantity of bacon up to London, which is esteemed as the best bacon in England, Hampshire only excepted. This bacon is raised in such quantities here, by reason of the great dairies, as above, the hogs being fed with the vast quantity of whey, and skimmed milk, which so many farmers have to spare, and which must, otherwise, be thrown away. But this is not all, for as the north part of Wiltshire, as well the downs, as the vales, border upon the river Thames, and, in some places, comes up even to the banks of it; so most of that part of the county being arable land they sow a very great quantity of barley, which is carried to the markets of Abingdon, at Farrington, and such places, where it is made into malt, and carried to London.

Thus Wiltshire itself helps to supply London with cheese, bacon, and malt, three very considerable articles, besides that vast manufacture of fine Spanish cloths, and I may, without being partial, say, that it is thereby rendered one of the most important counties in England, that is to say, important to the public wealth of the kingdom. The bare product is in itself prodigious great; the downs are an inexhausted store-house of wool, and of corn, and the valley, or low part of it, is the like for cheese and bacon.

One thing here is worth while to mention, for the observation of those counties in England, where they are not yet arrived to that perfection of husbandry, as in this county, and I have purposely reserved it to this place. The case is this, the downs or plains, which are generally called Salisbury Plain, were formerly all left open to be fed by the large flocks of sheep so often mentioned; but now, so much of these downs are ploughed up, as has increased the quantity of corn produced in this county, in a prodigious manner, and lessened their quantity of wool, as above; all of which has been done by folding their sheep upon the ploughed lands, removing the fold every night to a fresh place, 'till the whole piece of ground has been folded on; this, and this alone, has made these lands, which in themselves are poor, and where, in some places, the earth is not above six inches above the solid chalk rock, able to bear as good wheat, as any of the richer lands in the vales, though not quite so much.

If this way of folding sheep upon the fallows, and ploughed lands, were practised, in some parts of England, and especially in Scotland, they would find it turn to such account, and so effectually improve the waste lands, which now are useless and uncultivated, that the sheep would be more valuable, and lands turn to a better account than was ever yet known among them.

I am come now to Marlborough. On the downs, about two or three miles from the town, are abundance of loose stones, lying scattered about the plain; some whereof are very large, and appear to be of the same kind with those at Stonehenge, and some larger. They are called by the country people, not for want of ignorance, the Gray Weathers. I do not find any account given of them in history, or by the greatest of our antiquaries, so I must leave them as I find them.

At Marlborough, and in several villages near, as well as on the downs, there are several of those round rising mounts, which the country people call barrows, and which all our writers agree, were monuments of the dead, and particularly of soldiers slain in fight. This is an ancient town, and, at present, has a pretty good shop-keeping trade, but not much of the manufacturing part. The river Kennet, lately made navigable by Act of Parliament,[18] rises just by this town, and running from hence to Hungerford, and Newbery, becomes a large stream, and passing by Reading, runs into the Thames near the town. This river is famous for craw-fish, which they help travellers to at Newbery; but they seldom want for price.

Between this town of Marlborough, and Abingdon, westward, is the Vale of White Horse. The inhabitants tell a great many fabulous stories of the original of its being so called; but there is nothing of foundation in them all, that I could see; the whole of the story is this looking south from the vale, we see a trench cut on the side of a high green hill, this trench is cut in the shape of a horse, and not ill-shaped I assure you. The trench is about two yards wide on the top, about a yard deep, and filled almost up with chalk, so that at a distance, for it is seen many miles off, you see the exact shape of a White Horse; but so large, as to take up near an acre of ground, some say, almost two acres. From this figure the hill is called, in our maps, White Horse Hill, and the low, or flat country under it, the Vale of White Horse.

I must here take the liberty to look round upon some passages in later times, which have made this part of the country more famous than before. 1. On the hills on this side the Devizes, is Roundway Down,[19] where the Lord Wilmot, and the king's forces, beat, and entirely routed, the famous Sir William Waller, in the late Rebellion, or Civil War; from whence the place is called, by some, Runaway Down to this day. A little nearer towards Marlborough, is St Ann's Hill, where, notwithstanding several high hills between, and the distance of twenty-two miles, or more, is a fair view of Salisbury-steeple, or spire, which is, without all dispute, the highest in England.

At Newbery there was another, or rather a double scene of blood;[20] for here were two obstinate, and hard fought, battles, at two several times, between the king's army, and the Parliament's, the king being present at them both, and both fought almost upon the same spot of ground. In these two battles, said an old experienced soldier, that served in the king's army, there was more generalship shown on both sides, than in any other battle through the whole course of the war. His meaning was, that the generals, on both sides, showed the most exquisite skill in the managing, posting, bringing up, and drawing off their troops; and as the men fought with great bravery on both sides, so the generals, and officers, showed both their bravery, and their judgment. In the first of these battles, the success was doubtful, and both sides pretended to the advantage. In the last, the king's army had apparently the worst of it, and yet the king, in a very few days, with a great body of horse, fetched off his cannon, which he had, in the close of the battle, thrust into Dunnington Castle, and carried them away to Oxford, the head quarter of his army, or his place of arms, as it would be called now; and this he did in the sight of the victorious army, facing them at the same time with a body of six thousand horse, and they, on the other hand, did not think fit to draw out to attack him. That retreat, in point of honour, was equal to a victory, and gave new courage, as well as reputation, to the king's troops.

But this is not my business. This town of Newbery is an ancient clothing town, though, now, little of that part remains to it; but it retains still a manufacturing genius, and the people are generally employed in making shalloons, a kind of stuff, which, though it be used only for the lining and insides of men's clothes, for women use but little of it, nor the men for any thing but as above, yet it becomes so generally worn, both at home and abroad, that it is increased to a manufacture by itself, and is more considerable, than any single manufacture of stuffs in the nation.

Though out of the road that I was in, I must digress to tell you, that the town of Andover lies on the very edge of the downs which I have so often mentioned, and is in the road from Newbery to Salisbury, as it is from London to Taunton, and all the manufacturing part of Somersetshire; 'tis a handsome town, well built, populous, and much enriched by the manufacture, and may be called a thriving town. It sends two members to Parliament, and is an ancient corporation.

But the chief reason of my making this digression, is to mention, that within a mile, or thereabouts, of this town, at the place where the open down country begins, is Wey-Hill, where the greatest fair for sheep is kept, that this nation can show. I confess, though I once saw the fair, yet I could make no estimate of the number brought thither for sale; but asking the opinion of a grazier, who had used to buy sheep there, he boldly answered, he believed there were five hundred thousand sheep sold there in one fair. Now, though this might, I believe, be too many, yet 'tis sufficient to note, that there are a prodigious quantity of sheep sold here; nor can it be otherwise, if it be considered, that the sheep sold here, are not for immediate killing, but are generally ewes for store sheep for the farmers. The custom of these farmers, is, to send one farmer in behalf of (perhaps) twenty, and so the sheep come up together, and they part them when they come home. These ewes have also this property, that they generally bring two lambs at a time.

But to go back to Newbery: not to insist upon the famous Jack of Newbery,[21] who was so great a clothier, that when King James met his waggons loaden with cloths going to London, and inquiring whose they were, was answered by them all, they were Jack of Newbery's, the king returned, if the story be true, that this Jack of Newbery was richer than he. But not to insist upon this man's story, which is almost grown fabulous, yet another story is fact, and to be proved, viz. that this is one of the two legatee towns (as they were called) in the will of the late famous Mr Kenrick,[22] who being the son of a clothier of Newbery, and afterwards a merchant in London, left four thousand pounds to Newbery, and seven thousand five hundred pounds to Reading, to encourage the clothing trade, and set the poor at work, besides other gifts of extraordinary value to the poor, as such.

This extraordinary will is to be seen at large in Stow's *Survey of London*, to which I refer. It seems he died a bachelor, or, at least, without children, and his legacies, all in ready money, cannot amount to less than forty thousand to fifty thousand pounds, besides what might be included in the general clause of leaving all the rest of his estate to him who he made his universal heir; which estate, as I have heard, amounted to a very great value. That forty or fifty thousand pounds also, being considered at the time it was left, might well be rated at four times the value, as the rate of things goes now, it being in the year 1624.

Here it was that the vanguard, or first line of the Prince of Orange's army, was posted, when the Irish dragoons, who were posted in Reading, finding they should be attacked in a few days, had put the town's people into such a fright, by threatening to burn and plunder the town, and cut all the people's throats, that they sent express messengers to the Dutch general officer Grave Van Nassau for help; who sent them a detachment of but two hundred and eighty dragoons, though the troops in the town were near seven hundred men. What success they met with, I shall mention presently.

The next town of note, I say, is Reading, a very large and wealthy town, handsomely built, the inhabitants rich, and driving a very great trade. The town lies on the River Kennet, but so near the Thames, that the largest barges which they use, may come up to the town bridge, and there they have wharfs to load, and unload them. Their chief trade is by this water-navigation to and from London.

They send from hence to London by these barges, very great quantities of malt, and meal, and these are the two principal articles of their loadings, of which, so large are those barges, that some of them, as I was told, bring a thousand, or twelve hundred quarters of malt at a time, which, according to the ordinary computation of tonnage in the freight of other vessels, is from a hundred, to an hundred and twenty ton, dead weight.

Here was a large manufacture of sail-cloth set up in this

town, by the late Sir Owen Buckingham,[23] Lord Mayor of London, and many of the poor people were, profitably (to them) employed in it; but Sir Owen himself dying, and his son being unhappily killed in a duel, a little while after, that manufacture died also. There is, however, still a remnant of the woollen manufacture here; I say a remnant, because this was once a very considerable clothing town, much greater than it is now.

It was here that the Dutch with two hundred and eighty horse and dragoons, attacked the forces of the late King James, in aid of the distressed town's-men, who they threatened to murther and plunder that very day. It was on a Sunday morning, that the Irish dragoons had resolved on the designed mischief, if they really intended it. In order to it, they posted a guard at the principal church in the piazza there, and might, indeed, easily have locked all the people in, and have cut their throats; also they placed a company of foot in the church-yard of another church, over-against the Bear Inn; so that if they really did not intend to massacre the people, as their officers said they did not, yet that way of posting their men, joined to the loud oaths and protestations, that they would do it, made it look as like such a design, as any thing unexecuted, or unattempted, could do.

In this posture things stood when the Dutch entered the town. The Irish had placed a sentinel on the top of the steeple of the great church, with orders, if he saw any troops advance, to fire his piece, and ring the bell; the fellow, being surprised with the sight, for he discovered the Dutch but a little before they reached the town, fired his musket, but forgot to ring the bell, and came down. However, his firing gave the alarm sufficiently, and the troops in the town, who were all under arms before, whether for the designed execution, or not, I will not determine; but, I say, being under arms before, they had little more to do, but to post their troops, which they did with skill enough, and had the men done their duty, they might easily have repulsed the few troops that attacked them; but the Dutch entering the town in two places, forced both the posts, and entered the market place, where the main body of the Irish troops were drawn up.

The first party of the Dutch found a company of foot drawn up in the church-yard over-against the Bear Inn, and a troop of dragoons in the Bear Inn yard; the dragoons hearing the Dutch were at hand, their officer bravely drew them out of the inn yard, and faced the Dutch in the open road, the church-yard wall being lined with musketeers to flank the street; the Dutch, who came on full gallop, fell in upon the dragoons, sword in hand, and with such irresistible fury, that the Irish were immediately put into confusion, and after three or four minutes bearing the charge, they were driven clear out of the street. At the very same instant, another party of the Dutch dragoons, dismounting, entered the church-yard, and the whole body posted there, fled also, with little or no resistance, not sufficient, indeed, to be called resistance. After this, the dragoons, mounting again, forced their squadrons, and entered the market place.

Here the troops being numerous, made two or three regular discharges; but finding themselves charged in the rear by the other Dutchmen, who had by this time entered Broad Street, they not knowing the strength, or weakness of their enemy, presently broke, and fled by all the ways possible.

The Dutch having cleared the town, pursued some of them as far as Twyford, and such was the terror that they were in, that a person, from whom I had this part of the relation, told me, he saw one Dutch trooper chase twelve of the Irish dragoons to the river near Twyford, and ride into the water a good way after them; nor durst Sir John Lanier's [24] regiment of horse, and Sir John Fenwick's, advance to relieve their friends, though they, having had the alarm, stood drawn up on the hill on Twyford side of the river, where they might see by what a contemptible number their numerous party was pursued; for there were not above five and forty, or fifty at most, of the Dutch, that pursued about three hundred of the Irish dragoons to Twyford. Thus the town of Reading was delivered from the danger they were threatened with, and which they as really expected as they expected the sun would rise.

I cannot omit to observe one thing here, to which I was an eye-witness, and which will resolve a difficulty that to this day has puzzled the understandings of a great many people, if not the whole nation; namely, that here began the universal alarm that spread over the whole kingdom (almost at the same time) of the Irish being coming to cut every bodies' throats. The brief account of which, because it has something curious in it, I believe will be agreeable to you.

As the terror which the threatenings of these Irishmen had brought upon the whole town of Reading, obliged the magistrates, and chief of the inhabitants, to apply to the Prince of Orange's army for immediate help, so you cannot doubt, but that many of the inhabitants fled for their lives by all the ways that they could; and this was chiefly in the night; for in the day, the soldiers, who had their eyes every where, stopped them, and would not permit them to stir, which still increased their terror.

Those that got away, you may be sure, were in the utmost fright and amazement, and they had nothing less in their mouths, but that the Irish would (and by that time had) burnt the town, and cut the throats of all the people, men, women, and children. I was then at Windsor, and in the very interval of all this fright, King James being gone, and the army retreated from Salisbury, the Lord Feversham calls the troops together, and causing them to lay down their arms, disbands them, and gives them leave, every man, to go whither they would.

The Irish dragoons, which had fled from Reading, rallied at Twyford, and having not lost many of their number (for there were not above twelve men killed) they marched on for Maidenhead, swearing, and cursing, after most soldierly a manner, that they would burn all the towns where-ever they came, and cut the throats of all the people. However, they did not offer to take quarters at Maidenhead, the town also being full of King James's troops, so they marched on for

Colebrook, blustering in the same manner, of what they would do when they came there. The town of Colebrook had notice of their coming, and how they had publicly threatened to burn the town, and murther all the people; but, happily for them, they had quartered there a regiment of Scots foot, of those regiments which King James had caused to march from Scotland to his aid on this occasion; and they had with them, as was the usage of all the foot in those times, two pieces of cannon, that is to say, field-pieces, and they stood just in the market-place, pointing westward to the street where these gentlemen were to come.

The people of Colebrook applied immediately to the Scots colonel, whose name I am very sorry I cannot remember, because it is to his honour that I should mention it, and begged his protection. The colonel calling together a council of his officers, immediately resolved, they would make good their quarters, unless they received orders from their superior officers to quit them, and that they would defend the town from plunder; and upon this, immediately the drums beat to arms, and the regiment came together in a few moments. It was in the depth of winter, and, by consequence, was night, and being a wet day, the evening was exceeding dark, when some advanced sentinels gave notice, that they heard the drums beat the dragoons march, at some distance upon the road.

Upon this the colonel ordered a lieutenant, with thirty musketeers, to make an advanced guard at the extreme part of the town, and he was supported by another party of forty men, most pikes, at a small distance, who were to advance upon a signal; and if these last should engage, the drums of the whole regiment were to beat a march, and half the battalion, to advance with the two pieces of cannon.

It was near ten a clock at night before the dragoons reached the town, when the two advanced dragoons were challenged by the sentinels placed by the lieutenant, and they told the officer what regiment they belonged to, and that they had orders to stop any troops from entering the town, 'till their colonel should be acquainted with it, and give farther orders.

The dragoons, as the ground would admit, drew up in front, and their officers began to huff and threaten, that they were the king's troops. [They] insulted and menaced the major and that at such rate, that he gave orders immediately to acquaint the colonel of it, who instantly advanced, in full march, with the whole regiment, having about one hundred links lighted to let them see the way, the night being exceeding dark. When the dragoons saw this, and having no stomach to engage, they desisted; but raged and stormed at such a rate, as I cannot express, and taking the road to Stanes, swore, they would go thither, and burn the town, and kill man, woman and child.

Those blusters were so loud, and the fellows, by nation, such as from whom it might be expected, as put the people of Colebrook into concern for their neighbours at Stanes, and some of them showed the concern to be so real, that they sent express upon express to Stanes, to acquaint the people there of their danger, knowing there was, at that time, only two companies of foot, of Colonel ——'s regiment, in the town. When these messengers came here, they found the people already alarmed by others, who had come from the same town of Colebrook, in the first fright, with the news, that the Irish were coming to burn the said town of Colebrook, and that, by that time, they did not question but they had done it, and they were surprised to hear now, that it was not done; but upon the arriving of these messengers, bringing word, that they had burnt Colebrook, but for the assistance of the Scots regiment; and that they were coming to Stanes, and swore, they would kill man, woman and child; it is impossible to express the consternation of the people. Away they run out of the town, dark, and rainy, and midnight as it was, some to Kingston, some over the heath to Hounslow, and Brentford, some to Egham, and some to Windsor, with the dreadful news; and by that time they reached those places, their fears had turned their story from saying, they would burn and kill, to they had burned and killed, and were coming after you to do the like.

The same alarm was carried by others from Colebrook to Uxbridge; for thither the dragoons were for marching at first; and thus, some one way, and some another, it spread like the undulations of the water in a pond, when a flat stone is cast upon the surface. From Brentford and Kingston, and from Uxbridge, it came severally, and by different roads, to London, and so, as I may say, all over England; nor is it wonderful, that it seemed to be all over the nation in one day, which was the next after this beginning. Fear gave wings to the news, no post could carry it as it flew from town to town, and still every messenger had two articles with him. 1. Not that such and such towns were to be burnt and plundered by them; but that they were already burnt; and 2. That the Irish were at their heels to do the like.

This, I think, is a clear account of this alarm, and what can be more natural? I rode the next morning to Maidenhead. At Slough they told me, Maidenhead was burnt, and Uxbridge, and Reading, and I know not how many more, were destroyed; and when I came to Reading, they told me, Maidenhead and Okingham were burnt, and the like. From thence I went to Henley, where the Prince of Orange, with the second line of his army, entered that very afternoon, and there they had had the same account, with the news of King James's flight;[25] and thus is spread every way insensibly. The manner is too recent in memory, to need my giving any description of it.

My next stage from Reading, was to Great Marlow in Buckinghamshire, which ... is a town of very great embarkation on the Thames, not so much for goods wrought here, (for the trade of the town is chiefly in bone-lace) but for goods from the neighbouring towns, and particularly, a very great quantity of malt, and meal, is brought hither from High-Wickham.

Between High Wickham and Marlow, is a little river called

the Loddon, on which are a great many mills, and particularly corn mills, and paper mills; the first of these, grind and dress the wheat, and then the meal is sent to Marlow, and loaded on board the barges for London. And the second makes great quantities of printing paper, and that, very good of its kind, and cheap, such as generally is made use of in printing our news papers, journals, &c. and smaller pamphlets; but not much fine, or large, for bound books, or writing.

On the river of Thames, just by the side of this town, though on the other bank, are three very remarkable mills, which are called the Temple-Mills, and are called also, the Brass-Mills, and are for making Bisham Abbey battery work, as they call it, viz. brass kettles, and pans, &c. of all sorts. They have first a foundry, where, by the help of *lapis caliminaris*, they convert copper into brass, and then, having cast the brass in large broad plates, they beat them out by force of great hammers, wrought by the water mills, into what shape they think fit for sale. Those mills went on by the strength of a good stock of money in a company or partnership, and with very good success, 'till at last, they turned it into what they call a bubble, brought it to Exchange-Alley, set it a stock-jobbing in the days of our South Sea madness, and brought it up to be sold at one hundred pounds per share, whose intrinsic worth was perhaps ten pounds, 'till, with the fall of all those things together, it fell to nothing again. Their treasurer, a tradesman in London, failed, having misapplied about thirty thousand pounds of their money, and then, as it is usual where want of success goes before, quarrelling among themselves followed after, and so the whole affair sunk into a piece of mere confusion and loss, which otherwise was certainly a very beneficial undertaking.

Next to these are two mills, one for making of thimbles, a work excellently well finished, and which performs to admiration, and another for pressing of oil from rape-seed, and flax-seed, both which, as I was told, turn to very good account to the proprietors. Here is also brought down a vast quantity of beech wood, which grows in the woods of Buckinghamshire. This is the most useful wood, for some uses, that grows, and without which, the city of London would be put to more difficulty, than for any thing of its kind in the nation.

1. For fellies for the great cars, as they are called, which ply in London streets for carrying of merchandises, and for coal-carts, dust-carts, and such like sorts of voiture, which are not, by the city laws, allowed to draw with shod wheels, or wheels tyred with iron.

2. For billet wood for the king's palaces, and for the plate and flint glass houses, and other such nice purposes.

3. Beech quarters for divers uses, particularly chairmakers, and turnery wares.

At Bisham, over against this town, was formerly an abbey, and the remains of it are still to be seen there. The estate belongs to the ancient family of the name of Hobby. Some of the heads of this family, were very eminent in former days. A little higher, on the same side of the river, is Hurley, an ancient seat of the Lord Lovelace,[26] and that family being extinct, it came, by the daughter and heiress, to Sir Henry Johnson of Blackwall, near Ratcliff, who originally was only a shipwright, or master-builder, at the great yard and dock there. There are two other towns on the Thames, viz. Henly and Maidenhead, which have little or nothing remarkable in them; but that they have great business also, by the trade for malt and meal and timber for London, which they ship, or load, on their great barges for London, as the other towns do.

And now I am, by just degree, come to Windsor, where I must leave talking of trade, river, navigation, meal, and malt, and describe the most beautiful, and most pleasantly situated castle and royal palace, in the whole isle of Britain.

Windsor Castle, founded, as some say, by William the Conqueror, if there was any thing in that part, was at least rebuilt, by Edward III. But the truth of the story is this, William the Conqueror did pitch upon it as a pleasant situation, in a delightful sporting country, and agreeable to him, who delighted much in hunting. He also had several little lodges, or hunting houses, in the forest adjoining, and frequently lodged, for the conveniency of his game, in a house which the monks before enjoyed, near, or in the town of Windsor, for the town is much more ancient than the castle. But to pass over the antiquity or history of the town, this is certain, that King Edward III took an extreme liking to the place, because of its beautiful situation, and pleasing prospect, which, indeed, is not to be out-done in any part of the kingdom. Here, at length, the king resolved to fix his summer residence, and himself laid out the plan of a most magnificent palace, the same, as to the outward form and building, as we now see it; for whatever has been done for beautifying, altering, or amending the inside and apartments, there has nothing been added to the building itself, except that noble terrace, which runs under the north front, and leads to the green on the park, at the east side, or end of it, along which east end, the fine lodgings, and royal apartments, were at first built, all the north part being then taken up in rooms of state, and halls for public balls, &c. The house itself was, indeed, a palace, and without any appearance of a fortification; but when the building was brought on to the slope of the hill on the town side, the king added ditches, ramparts, the round tower, and several addenda of strength; and so it was immediately called a castle.

But to pass over this fiction, this is certain, King Edward was the founder of the whole work, and the plan of it was much of his own contrivance; but he committed the overseeing, and direction of the works, to William of Wickham, or, if you please, William of Wickham was the Sir Christopher Wren of that Court; for William was then a layman, not having had a liberal education, but had a good genius, a mighty lover of building, and had applied his head much that way; nor, indeed, does the building itself fail to do the head, or master-builder, a great deal of honour.

The only addition in the inside, is a fine equestrian statue of King Charles II which stands over the great well, sunk, as may be supposed, in the first building, for the supply of the castle with water, and in which was an engine for raising the water, notwithstanding the great depth, by very little labour. On the outside was added, the terrace walk, built by Queen Elizabeth, and where she usually walked for an hour every day before her dinner, if not hindered by windy weather, which she had a peculiar aversion to; for as to rainy weather, it would not always hinder her; but she rather loved to walk in a mild, calm rain, with an umbrella over her head.

This noble walk is covered with fine gravel, and has cavities, with drains, to carry off all the water; so that let it rain as it will, not a drop of it is seen to rest on the walk, but it is dry, hard, and fit to walk on immediately. The breadth of this walk is very spacious on the north side, on the east side it is narrower; but neither at Versailles, or at any of the royal palaces in France, or at Rome, or Naples, have I ever seen any thing like it. The grand seignior's terrace in the outer court of the Seraglio, next the sea, is the nearest to it, that I have read of, and yet not equal to it, if I may believe the account of those who have seen it; for that, I acknowledge, I have not seen. At the north-east corner of this terrace, where it turns south, to run on by the east side of the castle, there are steps, by which you go off upon the plain of the park, which is kept smooth as a carpet, and on the edge of which, the prospect of the terrace is doubled by a vista, south over the park, and quite up to the great park, and towards the forest.

On that side of the building which looks out upon the terrace, are all the royal apartments, King Edward III's were on the east side. The east side is now allotted to great officers of state, who are obliged to attend whenever the Court removes to Windsor, such as the Lord Treasurers, Secretaries of State, Lord High Chancellor, Lord Archbishop of Canterbury, and the like; and below they have proper offices for business, if they please to order any to be done there.

You mount into the royal apartments, by several back stairs; but the public way is up a small ascent to a flat, or half pace (for I love to make my account speak English) where there are two entries of state, by two large stair-cases, one on the left hand to the royal apartments, and the other, on the right, to St George's-Hall, and the royal chapel. Before the entrance to these, on either side, you pass through the guard chambers, where you see the walls furnished with arms, and the king's beef-eaters, as they call the yeomen of the guard, keep their station.

In the chimney-piece of one of these apartments, is a piece of needle-work exquisitely fine, performed, as they say, by the Queen of Scots, during the time of her confinement in Fotheringay Castle. There are several family pieces in the chimney-pieces, and other parts of those lodgings, that are valuable, because of the persons they represent. But the finery of painting is to come.

These rooms look all out north towards the terrace, and over part of the finest, and richest, vale in the world; for the same vale attending the course of the River Thames, with very little interruption, reaches to, and includes the city of London east, and the city of Oxford west. The river, with a winding, and beautiful stream, gliding gently through the middle of it, and enriching by its navigation, both the land and the people on every side.

It may be proper here to say something to the beauties and ornaments of St George's Hall, though nothing can be said equal to what the eye would be witness to; 'tis surprising, at the first entrance, to see at the upper end, the picture of King William on horseback, under him, an ascent with marble steps, a balustrade, and a half pace, which, formerly was actually there with room for a throne, or chair of state, for the sovereign to sit on, when on public days he thought fit to appear in ceremony.

No man that had seen the former steps or ascent, and had gone up to the balustrade and throne, as I had done, could avoid supposing, they were there still; and as on a casual view, having been absent some years out of the nation, I was going forward towards the end of the hall, intending to go up the steps, as I had done formerly, I was confounded, when

I came nearer, to see that the ascent was taken down, the marble steps gone, the chair of state, or throne, quite away, and that all I saw, was only painted upon the wall below the king and his horse. Indeed it was so lively, so bright, so exquisitely performed, that I was perfectly deceived, though I had some pretension to judgment in pictures too; nor was my eye alone deceived, others were under the same deception, who were then with me.

When I came to the farther end, and looked from the throne, as I called it, down the hall, I was again surprised, though most agreeably, I confess, viz. the painting on the side of the hall, which was the representation of Prince Edward's triumph, in imitation of Caesar's glorious entry into Rome, and which was drawn marching from the lower end of the room, to the upper, that is to say, from the door, which is in the corner on the north side of the hall, was now wholly inverted, and the same triumph was performed again; but the march turned just the other way.

That this could be done no other way, but by wiping the whole work out, and painting it all over again,[27] was easy to conclude, seeing it was not done upon cloth, but upon the mere plaster of the wall, as appeared by the salts of the lime in the wall, having worked out, and spoiled a great piece of the paint; besides, the nature of the thing forbids; for if it had been a canvas, turning it would have been impracticable, for then all the imagery would have stood heels up, unless it had been carried on to the directly opposite part of the hall, and that could not be, because there were the windows, looking all into the inner court of the castle.

At the west end of the hall, is the Chapel Royal, the neatest and finest of the kind in England; the carved work is beyond any that can be seen in England, the altar-piece is that of the institution, or, as we may call it, our Lord's first supper. I remember, that going with some friends to show them this magnificent palace, it chanced to be at the time when the Dissenters were a little uneasy at being obliged to kneel at the Sacrament; one of my friends, who, as I said, I carried to see Windsor Castle, was a Dissenter, and when he came into the chapel, he fixed his eyes upon the altar-piece with such a fixed, steady posture, and held it so long, that I could not but take notice of it, and asked him, Whether it was not a fine piece? Yes, says he, it is; but, whispering to me, he added, How can your people prosecute us for refusing to kneel at the Sacrament? Don't you see there, that though our Saviour himself officiates, they are all sitting about the table? I confess it surprised me, and, at first, I knew not what answer to make to him; but I told him, That was not a place for him and I to dispute it, we would talk of it afterwards, and so we did, but brought it to no conclusion, so 'tis needless to mention it any more here.

I might go back here to the history of the Order of the Garter, the institution of which by King Edward III not only had its original here, but seems to be seated here, as a native of the place; and that this is the place where the ceremonies of it, the instalments, feasts, &c. are always to be performed. But this is done so fully in other authors, and by so many, that it would be falling into that error, which I condemn in others, and making my accounts be, what I resolved, from the beginning, they should not be; namely, a copy of other men's performances.[28]

The lower court, as I mentioned, of the castle, though not so beautiful, for the stately lodgings, rooms of state, &c. is particularly glorious for this fine chapel of the Order, a most beautiful and magnificent work, and which shows the greatness, not only of the court in those days, but the spirit and genius of the magnanimous founder. The chapel is not only fine within, but the workmanship without is extraordinary; nothing so ancient is to be seen so very beautiful. The chapel of St Stephen's in Westminster-Abby, called Henry VIIth's Chapel, and King's College Chapel at Cambridge, built by Henry VI are fine buildings; but they are modern, compared to this, which was begun, as by the inscribed dates upon the works appears, in the year 1337. The coats of arms, and the various imagery &c. even inside and outside, not only of the king, but of several of the first Knights Companions, are most admirably finished, and the work has stood out the injury of time to admiration; the beauty of the building remains without any addition, and, indeed, requiring none.

In the choir are the stalls for the knights of the Order, with a throne for the sovereign; also stalls in the middle of it for the poor knights pensioners, who live in their house or hospital on the south side of the square or court which the church stands in.

Here are to be seen, the banners of the knights who now enjoy the honour of the Garter. When they die, those banners are taken down, and the coat of arms of the deceased knight set up in the place allotted for those arms over the same stall, so that those coats of arms are a living history, or rather a record of all the knights that ever have been since the first institution of the Order, and how they succeeded one another; by which it appears, that kings, emperors and sovereign princes, have not thought it below them to accept of the honour of being Knights Companions of this Order; while, at the same time, it must be noted to the honour of the English Crown, that our kings have never thought fit to accept of any of their Orders abroad, of what kind soever, whether Popish or Protestant; that of the Cordon Blue, or the Cordon Blanc, the Cordon Noir, or the Cordon Rouge, the Golden Fleece of Spain, the Holy Ghost of France, or the Black Eagle of Prussia, or any other.

As the upper court and building are fronted with the fine terrace as above, so the lower court, where this fine chapel stands, is walled round with a very high wall, so that no buildings, if there was room for any, could overlook it.

The parks about Windsor are very agreeable, and suitable to the rest; the little park, which is so, only compared to the great park, is above three miles round, the great one fourteen, and the forest above thirty. This park is particular to the court, the other[s] are open for riding, hunting, and taking the air for any gentlemen that please.

The lodges in those parks, are no more lodges, though they

retain the name, but palaces, and might pass for such in other countries; but as they are all eclipsed by the palace itself, so it need only be added, that those lodges are principally beautified by the grandeur of the persons to whom the post of rangers has been assigned, who, having been enriched by other advancements, honours and profitable employments, thought nothing too much to lay out to beautify their apartments, in a place, which it was so much to their honour, as well as conveniency, to reside; such is the lodge, which belongs to Admiral Churchill,[29] the Duchess of Marlborough and others.

I cannot leave Windsor, without taking notice, that we crossed the Thames upon a wooden bridge, for all the bridges on the river, between London and Oxford, are of timber, for the conveniency of the barges. Here we saw Eaton College, the finest school for what we call grammar learning, for it extends only to the humanity class, that is in Britain, or, perhaps, in Europe.

The building, except the great school room, is ancient, the chapel truly Gothic; but all has been repaired, at a very great expense, out of the college stock, within these few years. This college was founded by King Henry VI, a prince munificent in his gifts, for the encouragement of learning, to profusion. This college has a settled revenue of about five thousand pounds per annum, and maintains as follows.

A provost.
A vice provost, who is also a fellow.
Seven fellows, inclusive of the vice provost.
Seventy scholars on the foundation, besides a full choir for the chapel, with officers, and servants usual.

The school is divided into the upper and lower, and each into three classes. Each school has one master, and each master four assistants, or ushers. None are received into the upper school, 'till they can make Latin verse, and have a tolerable knowledge of the Greek. In the lower school, the children are received very young, and are initiated into all school-learning. Besides the seventy scholars upon the foundation, there are always abundance of children, generally speaking, of the best families, and of persons of distinction, who are boarded in the houses of the masters, and within the college. The number of scholars instructed here, is from 400 to 550; but has not been under 400 for many years past. The elections of scholars for the university out of this school, is worth taking notice of: it being a time of jubilee to the school.

The election is once every year, and is made on the first Tuesday in August. In order to the election, there are deputed from King's College in Cambridge, three persons, viz. the provost of King's College for the time being, with one senior, and one junior poser, fellows of the same college. To these are joined, on the part of Eaton College, the provost, the vice provost, and the head master.

When a scholar from Eaton, comes to King's College, he is received upon the foundation, and pursues his studies there for three years, after which, he claims a fellowship, unless forfeited in the terms of the statutes; that is to say, by marriage, accepting of ecclesiastic preferments, &c.

N.B. The Provost has a noble house and garden, besides the use of the college gardens, at his pleasure.

And now being come to the edge of Middlesex, which is a county too full of cities, towns, and palaces, to be brought in at the close of a letter, and with which I purpose to begin my next travels; I conclude this letter, and am,

SIR,

Your most humble servant.

Letter 5

Containing a description of the City of London, as taking in the City of Westminster, Borough of Southwark, and the buildings circumjacent

SIR, – As I am now near the centre of this work, so I am to describe the great centre of England, the city of London, and parts adjacent. This great work is infinitely difficult in its particulars, though not in itself; not that the city is so difficult to be described, but to do it in the narrow compass of a letter, which we see so fully takes up two large volumes in folio,[1] and which, yet, if I may venture to give an opinion of it, is done but by halves neither.

London, as a city only, and as its walls and liberties line it out, might, indeed, be viewed in a small compass; but when I speak of London, now in the modern acceptation, you expect I shall take in all that vast mass of buildings, reaching from Black-Wall in the east, to Tot-Hill Fields[2] in the west; and extended in an unequal breadth, from the bridge, or river, in the south, to Islington north; and from Peterburgh House on the bank side in Westminster, to Cavendish Square, and all the new buildings by, and beyond, Hannover Square, by which the city of London, for so it is still to be called, is extended to Hide Park Corner in the Brentford Road, and almost to Maribone in the Acton Road, and how much farther it may spread, who knows? New squares, and new streets rising up every day to such a prodigy of buildings, that nothing in the world does, or ever did, equal it, except old Rome in Trajan's time, when the walls were fifty miles in compass, and the number of inhabitants six million eight hundred thousand souls.

It is the disaster of London, as to the beauty of its figure, that it is thus stretched out in buildings, just at the pleasure of every builder, or undertaker of buildings, and as the convenience of the people directs, whether for trade, or otherwise; and this has spread the face of it in a most straggling, confused manner, out of all shape, uncompact, and unequal; neither long or broad, round or square; whereas the city of Rome, though a monster for its greatness, yet was, in a manner, round, with very few irregularities in its shape.

At London, including the buildings on both sides the water, one sees it, in some places, three miles broad, as from St George's in Southwark, to Shoreditch in Middlesex; or two miles, as from Peterburgh House to Montague House; and in some places, not half a mile, as in Wapping; and much less, as in Redriff.

We see several villages, formerly standing, as it were, in the country, and at a great distance, now joined to the streets by continued buildings, and more making haste to meet in the like manner; for example, Deptford, this town was formerly reckoned, at least two miles off from Redriff, and that over the marshes too, a place unlikely ever to be inhabited; and yet now, by the increase of buildings in that town itself, and the many streets erected at Redriff, and by the docks and building-yards on the riverside, which stand between both, the town of Deptford, and the streets of Redriff, or Rotherhith (as they write it) are effectually joined, and the buildings daily increasing; and were the town of Deptford now separated, and rated by itself, I believe it contains more people, and stands upon more ground, than the city of Wells.

The town of Islington, on the north side of the city, is in like manner joined to the streets of London, excepting one small field, and which is in itself so small, that there is no doubt, but in a very few years, they will be entirely joined, and the same may be said of Mile-End, on the east end of the town.

Newington, called Newington-Butts, in Surrey, reaches out her hand north, and is so near joining to Southwark, that it cannot now be properly called a town by itself, but a suburb to the Burrough, and if, as they now tell us is undertaken, St George's Fields should be built into squares and streets, a very little time will show us Newington, Lambeth, and the Burrough all making but one Southwark. That Westminster is in a fair way to shake hands with Chelsea, as St Gyles's [3] is with Marybone; and Great Russel Street by Montague House,[4] with Tottenham-Court: all this is very evident, and yet all these put together, are still to be called London. Whither will this monstrous city then extend? and where must a circumvallation or communication line of it be placed?

I have, as near as I could, caused a measure to be taken of this mighty, I cannot say uniform, body; and for the satisfaction of the curious, I have here given as accurate a description of it, as I can do in so narrow a compass, as this of a letter, or as I could do without drawing a plan, or map of the places.

A Line of Measurement, drawn about all the Continued Buildings of the City of London, and Parts adjacent, including Westminster and Southwark, etc.

The line begins, for the Middlesex side of the buildings,

	Miles	Fur.	Rods
1. At Peterborough House, the farthest house west upon the River Thames, and runs N.W. by W. by the marshes to Tutthill Fields, and passing by the Neat Houses, and Arnold's Brewhouse, ends at Chelsea Road, measured - - -	1	6	16
2. Then, allowing an interval from Buckingham House cross the park, about one furlong and half to the corner of my Lord Godolphin's [5] garden wall, the line goes north behind the stable-yard buildings, and behind Park-Place, and on the park wall behind the buildings; on the west side of St James's Street, to the corner in Soho, or Pickadilly, then crossing the road, and goes along the north side of the road west to Hide Park Gate	1	2	11

	Miles	Fur.	Rods
3. Then the line turns N.E. by E. and taking in the buildings and streets, called May-Fair, and holds on east till the new streets formed out of Hide House Garden, cause it to turn away north, a point west reaching to Tyburn-Road, a little to the east of the great mother conduit; then it goes north, and crossing the road, takes in the west side of Cavendish Square, and the streets adjoining, and leaving Marybone, goes away east, 'till it reaches to Hampstead-Road, near a little village called Tottenham Court - - - -	2	5	20
4. From Tottenham Court, the line comes in a little south, to meet the Bloomsbury buildings, then turning east, runs behind Montague and Southampton Houses, to the N.E. corner of Southampton House, then crossing the path, meets the buildings called Queen's Square, then turning north, 'till it comes to the N.W. corner of the square, thence it goes away east behind the buildings on the north side of Ormond Street, 'till it comes to Lamb's Conduit - - -	1	1	13
5. Here the line turns south, and indents to the corner of Bedford Row, and leaving some few houses, with the cock-pit, and bowling green, goes on the back of Gray's Inn Wall, to Gray's Inn Lane, then turns on the outside of the buildings, which are on the west side of Gray's Inn Lane, going north to the stones end, when turning east, it passes to the new river bridge without Liquor-pond Street, so taking in the Cold Bath and the Bear Garden; but leaving out Sir John Old-Castle's and the Spaw, goes on east by the Ducking-Pond to the end of New Bridewell, and crossing the Fairfield, comes into the Islington Road by the Distiller's House, formerly Justice Fuller's - - - - - - - -	1	2	6

	Miles	Fur.	Rods
6. Here to take in all the buildings which join Islington to the streets, the line goes north on the east side of the road to the Turk's Head ale-house; then turning north west, passes to the New River House, but leaving it to the west, passes by Sadler's Well, from thence to Bussby's House, and keeping on the west side of Islington, 'till it comes opposite to Cambray House-Lane, turns into the road, and passes south almost to the lane which turns east down to the lower street, but then turns east without the houses, and goes to the Cow-keeper's in the low street crossing the road, and through the Cow-keeper's Yard into Frog-lane, then running west on the south side of the town, just without the buildings, joins again to the buildings on the west side of Wood's-close, passing behind the Sheep-market wall - -	2	4	39
7. From Wood's-Close, the line goes due east to Mount Hill, where, leaving several buildings to the north, it passses on, crossing all the roads to Brick-lane, to the north side of the great new square in Old-street, and taking in the Pest-house wall, turns south at the north-east corner of the said wall, to Old-street Road; then going away east till it meets the buildings near Hoxton Square, it turns north to the north west corner of the wall of Ask's Hospital, then sloping north east, it passes by Pimlico, the Cyder House, and the two walls to the north end of Hoxton, when it turns east, and enclosing the garden walls, comes into the Ware road, just at the King's Head in the new buildings by the Land of Promise - -	2	0	16
8. From the King's Head, the line turns south, running to the stones end in Shoreditch, then turning east, it takes in a burying ground and some buildings in the Hackney road, when slop-			

	Miles	Fur.	Rods
ing south east by south, it goes away by the Virginia House to a great brewhouse, and then still more east to the back of Wheeler-street, and then east by south, to Brick-lane, crossing which, it goes away east towards Bethnal Green; but then turning short south, it goes towards White Chapel Mount, but being intercepted by new streets, it goes quite up to the south end of the Dog-Row at Mile End - - - -	1	6	10
9. From the Dog-Row, the line crosses the road, and takes in a little hamlet of houses, called Stepney, though not properly so, and coming back west to the streets end at White Chapel Mill, goes away south by the Hog-houses into Church Lane, and to Rag Fair, when turning again east, it continues in a straight line on the north side of Ratcliff High-way, 'till it comes almost to the farther glass-houses, then turning north, it surrounds all Stepney and Stepney causeway to Mile End Road, then turning east again, and afterwards south, comes back to the new streets on the north side of Lime-house, and joining the marsh, comes down to the water side at the lower shipwright dock in Lime-house Hole - - -	3	7	01
	18	4	21

N.B. This line leaves out all the north side of Mile End town, from the end of the Dog-Row, to the Jews Burying Ground, which is all built; also all the north part of the Dog-Row, and all Bethnal Green: also all Poplar and Black-Wall, which are, indeed, contiguous.

For the Southwark side of the buildings, the line is as follows;

I allow an interval of two miles, from Poplar, cross the Isle of Dogs, and over the Thames, to the lower water-gate at Deptford, and though in measuring the circumference of all cities, the river, where any such runs through any part of the buildings, is always measured, yet; that I may not be said to stretch the extent of the buildings which I include in this account, I omit the river from Limehouse to Deptford.

	Miles	Fur.	Rods
1. From the said upper water-gate at Deptford, the line goes east to the corner next the Thames, where the shipwright's yard now is, and where I find a continued range of buildings begins by the side of a little creek or river, which runs into the Thames there, and reaches quite up the said river, to the bridge in the great Kentish road, and over the street there, taking in the south side of the street, to the west corner of the buildings in that street, and then measuring down on the west side of the long street, which runs to the Thames side, 'till you come to the new street which passes from Deptford to Rederiff, then turning to the left, passing on the back side of the king's yard to Mr Evelin's house, including the new church of Deptford, and all the new streets or buildings made on the fields side, which are very many, this amounts in the whole, to - - - - - -	3	1	16
2. From Mr Evelin's garden gate, the line goes north west, taking in all the new docks and yards, the Red-house, and several large streets of houses, which have been lately built, and by which the said town of Deptford is effectually joined to the buildings, reaching from Cuckold's Point, eastward, and which are carried out, as if Rederiff stretched forth its arm to embrace Deptford; then for some length, the said street of Rederiff con-			

Miles Fur. Rods

tinues narrow 'till you come to Church-street, where several streets are also lately built south, and others parallel with the street, till gradually, the buildings thicken, and extend farther and farther to the south and south by east, 'till they cross over the east end of Horslydown to Bermondsey Church, and thence east to the sign of the World's End, over against the great fort, being the remains of the fortifications drawn round these parts of Southwark in the late civil wars. This extent is, by computation, four miles; but being measured, as the streets indented, the circuit proved - - - - - - - 5 6 12

3. From this fort, to the corner of Long Lane, and through Long Lane to the Lock, at the end of Kent-street, is - - - - - - 1 7 02

4. From the corner of Kent-street to the town of Newington Butts, drawing the line behind all the buildings as they stand, and round the said village of Newington, to the Haberdashers Alms Houses, and thence by the road to the windmill, at the corner of Blackman-street, is - - - - 3 2 16

5. From the windmill crossing St George's Fields, on the back of the Mint, to the Fighting Cocks, thence to the Restoration Gardens, and thence on the outside of all the buildings to Lambeth-Wells, and on to Faux-Hall Bridge, over against the other fort of the old fortifications, being just the same length that those old fortifications extended, though infinitely fuller of buildings; this last circuit measures - - 3 5 12

17 6 18

Thus the extent or circumference of the continued buildings of the cities of London and Westminster and borough of Southwark, all which, in the common acceptation, is called London, amounts to thirty-six miles, two furlongs, thirty nine rods.

N.B. The town of Greenwich, which may, indeed, be said to be contiguous to Deptford, might be also called a part of this measurement; but I omit it, as I have the towns of Chelsea and Knights Bridge on the other side, though both may be said to join the town, and in a very few years will certainly do so.

The guesses that are made at the number of inhabitants, have been variously formed; Sir William Petty,[6] famous for his political arithmetic, supposed the city, at his last calculation, to contain a million of people, and this he judges from the number of births and burials; and by this rule, as well by what is well known of the increase of the said births and burials, as of the prodigious increase of buildings, it may be very reasonable to conclude, the present number of inhabitants within the circumference I have mentioned, to amount to, at least, fifteen hundred thousand,[7] with this addition, that it is still prodigiously increasing.

The government of this great mass of building, and of such a vast collected body of people, though it consists of various parts, is, perhaps, the most regular and well-ordered government that any city, of above half its magnitude, can boast of. The government of the city of London in particular, and abstractedly considered, is, by the Lord Mayor, twenty-four aldermen, two sheriffs, the recorder and common council; but the jurisdiction of these is confined to that part only, which they call the city and its liberties, which are marked out, except the Borough, by the walls and the bars, as they are called. The government of the out parts, is by justices of the peace, and by the sheriffs of London, who are, likewise, sheriffs of Middlesex; and the government of Westminster is, by a high bailiff, constituted by the Dean and Chapter, to whom the civil administrations is so far committed. The remaining part of Southwark side, when the city jurisdiction is considered, is governed, also by a bench of justices, and their proper substituted peace officers; excepting out of this the privileges of the Marshalseas, or of the Marshal's Court, the privilege of the Marshal of the King's Bench, the Mint, and the like.

To enter here, into a particular description of the city of London, its antiquities, monuments, &c. would be only to make an abridgment of Stow and his continuators,[8] and would make a volume by itself; but I write in manner of a letter and in the person of an itinerant, and give a cursory view of its present state, and to the reader, who is supposed to be upon the spot, or near it, and who has the benefit of all the writers, who have already entered upon the description.

By London, as I shall discourse of it, I mean, all the buildings, places, hamlets, and villages contained in the line of circumvallation, if it be proper to call it so, by which I have computed the length of its circumference as above.

We ought, with respect to this great mass of buildings, to observe, in every proper place, what it is now, and what it was within the circumference of a few years past.

It is, in the first place, to be observed, as a particular and remarkable crisis, singular to those who write in this age, and very much to our advantage in writing, that the great and more eminent increase of buildings, in, and about the city of London, and the vast extent of ground taken in, and now become streets and noble squares of houses, by which the mass, or body of the whole, is become so infinitely great, has been generally made in our time, not only within our memory, but even within a few years, and the description of these additions, cannot be improper to a description of the whole, as follows.

A Brief Description of the New Buildings erected in and about the Cities of London and Westminster and Borough of Southwark, since the Year 1666

This account of new buildings is to be understood,

1. Of houses re-built after the great fires in London and Southwark, &c.

2. New foundations, on ground where never any buildings were erected before.

It is true, that before the Fire of London, the streets were narrow, and public edifices, as well as private, were more crowded, and built closer to one another; for soon after the Fire, the king, by his proclamation, forbid all persons whatsoever, to go about to re-build for a certain time, viz. till the Parliament (which was soon to sit) might regulate and direct the manner of building, and establish rules for the adjusting every man's property, and yet might take order for a due enlarging of the streets, and appointing the manner of building, as well for the beauty as the conveniency of the city, and for safety, in case of any future accident; for though I shall not inquire, whether the city was burnt by accident, or by treachery, yet nothing was more certain, than that as the city stood before, it was strangely exposed to the disaster which happened, and the buildings looked as if they had been formed to make one general bonfire, whenever any wicked party of incendiaries should think fit.

The streets were not only narrow, and the houses all built of timber, lath and plaster, or, as they were very properly called paper work. But the manner of the building in those days, one story projecting out beyond another, was such, that in some narrow streets, the houses almost touched one another at the top, and it has been known, that men, in case of fire, have escaped on the tops of the houses, by leaping from one side of a street to another; this made it often, and almost always happen, that if a house was on fire, the opposite house was in more danger to be fired by it, according as the wind stood, than the houses next adjoining on either side.

How this has been regulated, how it was before, and how much better it now is, I leave to be judged, by comparing the old unburnt part of the city with the new.

But though by the new buildings after the fire, much ground was given up, and left unbuilt, to enlarge the streets, yet 'tis to be observed, that the old houses stood severally upon more ground, were much larger upon the flat, and in many places, gardens and large yards about them, all which, in the new buildings, are, at least, contracted, and the ground generally built up into other houses, so that notwithstanding all the ground given up for beautifying the streets, yet there are many more houses built than stood before upon the same ground; so that taking the whole city together, there are more inhabitants in the same compass, than there was before. So many great houses were converted into streets and courts, alleys and buildings, that there are, by estimation, almost 4000 houses now standing on the ground which the Fire left desolate, more than stood on the same ground before.

Another increase of buildings in the city, is to be taken from the inhabitants in the unburnt parts following the same example of pulling down great old buildings, which took up large tracks of ground in some of the well inhabited places, and buildings on the same ground, not only several houses, but even whole streets of houses, which are since fully inhabited.

All those palaces of the nobility, formerly making a most beautiful range of buildings fronting the Strand, with their gardens reaching to the Thames, where they had their particular water-gates and stairs, one of which remains still, viz. Somerset House, have had the same fate, such as Essex, Norfolk, Salisbury, Worcester, Exceter, Hungerford, and York Houses; in the place of which, are now so many noble streets and beautiful houses, erected, as are, in themselves, equal to a large city, and extend from the Temple to Northumberland-House; Somerset House and the Savoy, only intervening and the latter of these may be said to be, not a house, but a little town, being parted into innumerable tenements and apartments. These are prodigious enlargements to the city, even upon that which I call inhabited ground, and where infinite numbers of people now live, more than lived upon the same spot of ground before.

But all this is a small matter, compared to the new foundations raised within that time, in those which we justly call the out parts; and not to enter on a particular description of the buildings, I shall only take notice of the places where such enlargements are made; as, first, within the memory of the writer hereof, all those numberless ranges of building, called Spittle Fields, reaching from Spittle-yard, at Northern Fall-gate, and from Artillery Lane in Bishopsgate-street, with all the new streets, beginning at Hoxton, and the back of Shore-ditch Church, north, and reaching to Brick-Lane, and to the end of Hare-street, on the way to Bethnal Green, east; then sloping away quite to White Chapel Road, south east, containing, as some people say, who pretend to know, by good observation, above three hundred and twenty acres of ground, which are all now close built, and well inhabited with an infinite number of people, I say, all these have been built new from the ground, since the year 1666.

The lanes were deep, dirty, and unfrequented, that part now called Spittlefields-Market, was a field of grass with cows feeding on it, since the year 1670. Brick-Lane, which is now a long well-paved street, was a deep dirty road, frequented by carts fetching bricks that way into White-Chapel from Brick-Kilns in those fields, and had its name on that account; in a word, it is computed, that about two hundred thousand inhabitants dwell now in that part of London, where, about fifty years past, there was not a house standing.

On the more eastern part, the same increase goes on in proportion, namely, all Goodman's Fields, the name gives evidence for it, and the many streets between White-Chapel and Rosemary Lane, all built since the year 1678. Well Close, now called Marine Square, was so remote from houses, that it used to be a very dangerous place to go over after it was dark, and many people have been robbed and abused in passing it; a well standing in the middle, just where the Danish church is now built, there the mischief was generally done; beyond this, all the hither or west end of Ratcliff-high-way, from the corner of Gravel-Lane, to the east end of East Smithfield, was a road over the fields.

To come to the north side of the town, and beginning at Shoreditch, west, and Hoxton-Square, and Charles's-Square adjoining, and the streets intended for a market-place, those were all open fields, from Anniseed-clear to Hoxton Town, till the year 1689, or thereabouts. Farther west, the like addition of buildings begins at the foot way, by the Pest-house, and includes the French hospital, Old street two squares, and several streets, extending from Brick-Lane to Mount-Mill, and the road to Islington, and from the road, still west, to Wood's Close, and to St John's, and Clerkenwell, all which streets and squares are built since the year 1688 and 1689, and were before that, and some for a long time after, open fields or gardens, and never built on till after that time.

From hence we go on still west, and beginning at Gray's-Inn, and going on to those formerly called Red Lyon Fields, and Lamb's Conduit Fields, we see there a prodigious pile of buildings; it begins at Gray's-Inn Wall towards Red-Lyon Street, from whence, in a straight line, 'tis built quite to Lamb's Conduit Fields, north, including a great range of buildings yet unfinished, reaching to Bedford Row and the Cockpit, east; this pile of buildings is very great, the houses so magnificent and large, that abundance of persons of quality, and some of the nobility are found among them, particularly in Ormond Street, is the D—— of Powis's[9] house, built at the expense of France, on account of the former house being burnt, while the Duke D'Aumont, the French Ambassador Extraordinary lived in it; it is now a very noble structure, and is said to be, next the Banqueting House, the most regular building in this part of England. Here is also a very convenient church, built by the contribution of the gentry inhabitants of these buildings, though not yet made parochial, being called St George's Chapel.

Farther west, in the same line, is Southampton great Square, called Bloomsbury, with King-street on the east side of it, and all the numberless streets west of the square, to the market place, and through Great-Russel-street by Montague House, quite into the Hampstead road, all which buildings, except the old building of Southampton House and some of the square, has been formed from the open fields, since the time above-mentioned, and must contain several thousands of houses.

From hence, let us view the two great parishes of St Giles's and St Martin's in the Fields, the last so increased, as to be above thirty years ago, formed into three parishes, and the other about now to be divided also. The increase of the buildings here, is really a kind of prodigy; all the buildings north of Long Acre, up to the Seven Dials, all the streets, from Leicester-Fields and St Martin's-Lane, both north and west, to the Hay-Market and Soho, and from the Hay-Market to St James's-street inclusive, and to the park wall; then all the buildings on the north side of the street, called Picadilly, and the road to Knight's-Bridge, and between that and the south side of Tyburn Road, including Soho-Square, Golden-Square, and now Hanover-Square, and that new city on the north side of Tyburn Road, called Cavendish-Square, and all the streets about it. This last addition, is, by calculation, more in bulk than the cities of Bristol, Exeter and York, if they were all put together; all which places were, within the time mentioned, mere fields of grass, and employed only to feed cattle as other fields are.

This is enough to give a view of the difference between the present and the past greatness of this mighty city, called London.

N.B. Three projects have been thought of, for the better regulating the form of this mighty building, which though not yet brought to perfection, may, perhaps, in time, be brought forwards, and if it should, would greatly add to the beauty.

1. Making another bridge over the Thames.

2. Making an Act of Parliament, abrogating the names as well as the jurisdictions of all the petty privileged places, and joining or uniting the whole body, Southwark and all, into one city, and calling it by one name, London.

3. Forbidding the extent of the buildings in some particular places, where they too much run it out of shape, and letting the more indented parts swell out on the north and south side a little, to balance the length, and bring the form of the whole more near to that of a circle, as particularly stopping the running out of the buildings at the east and west ends, as at Ratcliff and Deptford, east, and at Tyburn and Kensington roads, west, and encouraging the building out at Moor-fields, Bunhil-fields, the west side of Shoreditch, and such places, and the north part of Gray's-Inn, and other adjacent parts, where the buildings are not equally filled out, as in other places, and the like in St George's Fields and behind Redriff on the other side of the water.

But these are speculations only, and must be left to the wisdom of future ages. Hitherto I have been upon the figure and extent of the city and its out-parts; I come now to speak of the inside, the buildings, the inhabitants, the commerce, and the manner of its government, &c.

It should be observed, that the city being now re-built, has occasioned the building of some public edifices, even in the place which was inhabited, which yet were not before, and the re-building others in a new and more magnificent manner than ever was done before.

1. That beautiful column, called the Monument, erected at the charge of the city, to perpetuate the fatal burning of the whole, cannot be mentioned but with some due respect to the building itself, as well as to the city; it is two hundred and two feet high, and in its kind, out does all the obelisks and pillars of the ancients, at least that I have seen, the top is fashioned like an urn.

2. The canal or river, called Fleet-ditch,[10] was a work of great magnificence and expense; but not answering the de-

sign, and being now very much neglected, and out of repair, is not much spoken of, yet it has three fine bridges over it, and a fourth, not so fine, yet useful as the rest, and the tide flowing up to the last; the canal is very useful for bringing of coals and timber, and other heavy goods but the wharfs in many places are decayed and fallen in, which make it all look ruinous.

The Royal Exchange,[11] the greatest and finest of the kind in the world, is the next public work of the citizens, the beauty of which answers for itself, and needs no description here; 'tis observable, that though this Exchange cost the citizens an immense sum of money re-building, some authors say, eighty thousand pounds, being finished and embellished in so exquisite a manner, yet it was so appropriated to the grand affair of business, that the rent or income of it for many years, fully answered the interest of the money laid out in building it. Whether it does so still or not, I will not say, but those shops, of which there were eight double rows above, and the shops and offices round it below, with the vaults under the whole, did at first, yield a very great sum.

Among other public edifices, that of the hospital of Bethlehem, or Bedlam, should not be forgot, which is at the very time of writing this, appointed to be enlarged with two new wings, and will then be the most magnificent thing of its kind in the world.

The churches in London are rather convenient than fine, not adorned with pomp and pageantry as in Popish countries; but, like the true Protestant plainness, they have made very little of ornament either within them or without, nor, excepting a few, are they famous for handsome steeples, a great many of them are very mean, and some that seem adorned, are rather deformed than beautified by the heads that contrived, or by the hands that built them.

Some, however, hold up their hands with grandeur and magnificence, and are really ornaments to the whole, I mean by these, such as Bow, St Brides, the new church in the Strand [St Mary's], Rood-Lane Church, or St Margaret Pattons, St

Antholins, St Clement Danes, and some others, and some of the fifty churches,[12] now adding to the bounty and charity of the government, are like to be very well adorned. Three or four Gothic towers have been rebuilt at the proper expenses of the fund appointed, and are not the worst in all the city, namely St Michael at Cornhill, St Dunstan in the East, St Christophers, St Mary Aldermary, and at St Sepulchre's.

But the beauty of all the churches in the city, and of all the Protestant churches in the world, is the cathedral of St Paul's; a building exceeding beautiful and magnificent; though some authors are pleased to expose their ignorance, by pretending to find fault with it. 'Tis easy to find fault with the works even of God Himself, when we view them in the gross, without regard to the particular beauties of every part separately considered, and without searching into the reason and nature of the particulars; but when these are maturely inquired into, viewed with a just reverence, and considered with judgment, then we fly out in due admirations of the wisdom of the Author from the excellency of His works.

The vast extent of the dome, that mighty arch, on which so great a weight is supported (meaning the upper towers or lanthorn of stone work seventy feet high) may well account for the strength of the pillars and butments below; yet those common observers of the superficial parts of the building, complain, that the columns are too gross, that the work looks heavy, and the lower figures near the eye are too large, as if the Doric and the Attic were not each of them as beautiful in their place as the Corinthian.

The wise architect, like a complete master of his business, had the satisfaction, in his lifetime, of hearing those ignorant reprovers of his work confuted, by the approbation of the best masters in Europe; and the church of St Peter's in Rome, which is owned to be the most finished piece in the world, only exceeds St Paul's in the magnificence of its inside work; the paintings, the altars, the oratories, and the variety of its imagery; things, which, in a Protestant church, however ornamental, are not allowed of.

If all the square columns, the great pilasters, and the flat panel work, as well within as without, which they now allege are too heavy and look too gross, were filled with pictures, adorned with carved work and gilding, and crowded with adorable images of the saints and angels, the kneeling crowd would not complain of the grossness of the work; but 'tis the Protestant plainness, that divesting those columns, &c. of their ornaments, makes the work, which in itself is not so large and gross as that of St Peter's, be called gross and heavy; whereas neither by the rules of order, or by the necessity of the building, to be proportioned and sufficient to the height and weight of the work, could they have been less, or any otherwise than they are.

When all these things are considered complexly, no man that has the least judgment in building, that knows any thing of the rules of proportion, and will judge impartially, can find any fault in this church; on the contrary, those excellent lines of Mr Dryden,[13] which were too meanly applied in allegory to the praise of a paltry play, may be, with much more honour to the author, and justice to this work, applied here to St Paul's Church.

Strong Dorick pillars form the base,
Corinthian fills the upper space;
So all below is strength, and all above is grace.

Sir Christopher [Wren]'s design was, indeed, very unhappily baulked in several things at the beginning, as well in the situation as in the conclusion of this work, which, because very few may have heard of, I shall mention in public, from the mouth of its author.

1. In the situation: he would have had the situation of the church removed a little to the north. By this situation, the east end of the church, which is very beautiful, would have looked directly down the main street of the city, Cheapside; and for the west end, Ludgate having been removed a little north, the main street called Ludgate-street and Ludgate-Hill, would only have sloped a little W.S.W. as they do now irregularly two ways, one within, and the other without the gate,

and all the street beyond Fleet-Bridge would have received no alteration at all.

By this situation, the common thorough-fare of the city would have been removed at a little farther distance from the work, and we should not then have been obliged to walk just under the very wall as we do now, which makes the work appear quite out of all perspective, and is the chief reason of the objections I speak of; whereas, had it been viewed at a little distance, the building would have been seen infinitely to more advantage.

But the circumstance of things hindered this noble design, and the city being almost rebuilt before he obtained an order and provision for laying the foundation; he was prescribed to the narrow spot where we see it now stands, in which the building, however magnificent in itself, stands with infinite disadvantage as to the prospect of it; the inconvenience of which was so apparent when the church was finished, that leave was at length, though not without difficulty, obtained, to pull down one whole row of houses on the north side of the body of the church, to make way for the baluster that surrounds the cemetery or church-yard, and, indeed, to admit the light into the church, as well as to preserve it from the danger of fire.

Another baulk which Sir Christopher met with, was in the conclusion of the work, namely, the covering of the dome, which Sir Christopher would have had been of copper double gilded with gold; but he was over-ruled by party, and the city thereby, deprived of the most glorous sight that the world ever saw, since the temple of Solomon.

Yet with all these disadvantages, the church is a most regular building, beautiful, magnificent, and beyond all the modern works of its kind in Europe, St Peter's at Rome, as above, only excepted.

It is true, St Peter's, besides its beauty in ornament and imagery, is beyond St Paul's in its dimensions, is every way larger; but it is the only church in the world that is so; and it was a merry hyperbole of Sir Christopher Wren's, who, when some gentlemen in discourse compared the two churches, and in compliment to him, pretended to prefer St Paul's, and when they came to speak of the dimensions, suggested, that St Paul's was the biggest: I tell you, says Sir Christopher, you might set it in St Peter's, and look for it a good while, before you could find it.

Having thus spoken of the city and adjacent buildings of London, and of the particulars which I find chiefly omitted by other writers, I have not room here to enter into all the articles needful to a full description. However, I shall touch a little at the things most deserving a stranger's observation.

Supposing now, the whole body of this vast building to be considered as one city, London, and not concerning myself or the reader with the distinction of its several jurisdictions; we shall then observe it only as divided into three, viz. the city, the Court, and the out-parts.

The city is the centre of its commerce and wealth. The Court of its gallantry and splendour. The out-parts of its numbers and mechanics; and in all these, no city in the world can equal it. Between the Court and city, there is a constant communication of business to that degree, that nothing in the world can come up to it. As the city is the centre of business, there is the Custom-house, an article, which, as it brings in an immense revenue to the public, so it cannot be removed from its place, all the vast import and export of goods being, of necessity, made there.

Here, also, is the Excise Office, the Navy Office, the Bank, and almost all the offices where those vast funds are fixed, in which so great a part of the nation are concerned, and on the security of which so many millions are advanced.

Here are the South Sea Company, the East India Company, the Bank, the African Company, &c. whose stocks support that prodigious paper commerce, called stock jobbing; a trade, which once bewitched the nation to its ruin, and which, though reduced very much, and recovered from that terrible infatuation which once overspread the whole body of the people, yet is still a negotiation, which is so vast in its extent, that almost all the men of substance in England are more or less concerned in it, and the property of which is so very often alienated, that even the tax upon the transfers of stock, though but five shillings for each transfer, brings many thousand pounds a year to the government; and some have said, that there is not less than a hundred millions of stock transferred forward or backward from one hand to another every year, and this is one thing which makes such a constant daily intercourse between the Court part of the town, and the city; and this is given as one of the principal causes of the prodigious conflux of the nobility and gentry from all parts of England to London, more than ever was known in former years, viz. that many thousands of families are so deeply concerned in those stocks, and find it so absolutely necessary to be at hand to take advantage of buying and selling, as the sudden rise or fall of the price directs, and the loss they often sustain by their ignorance of things when absent, and the knavery of brokers and others, whom, in their absence, they are bound to trust, that they find themselves obliged to come up and live constantly here, or at least, most part of the year.

But let the citizens and inhabitants of London know, and it may be worth the reflection of some of the landlords, and builders especially, that if peace continues, and the public affairs continue in honest and upright management, there is a time coming, at least the nation hopes for it, when the public debts being reduced and paid off, the funds or taxes on which they are established, may cease, and so fifty or sixty millions of the stocks, which are now the solid bottom of the South-Sea Company, East-India Company, Bank, &c. will cease, and be no more; by which the reason of this conflux of people being removed, they will of course, and by the nature of the thing, return again to their country seats, to avoid the expensive living at London, as they did come up hither to share the extravagant gain of their former business here.

What will be the condition of this overgrown city in such a case, I must leave to time; but . . . in time, 'tis to be hoped, all our taxes may cease, and the ordinary revenue may, as it always used to do, again supply the ordinary expense of the government.

Then, I say, will be a time to expect the vast concourse of people to London, will separate again and disperse as naturally, as they have now crowded hither. What will be the fate then of all the fine buildings in the out parts, in such a case, let any one judge.

There has formerly been a great emulation between the Court end of the town, and the city; and it was once seriously proposed in a certain reign, how the Court should humble the city; nor was it so impracticable a thing at that time, had the wicked scheme been carried on. Indeed, it was carried farther than consisted with the prudence of a good government, or of a wise people; for the Court envied the city's greatness, and the citizens were ever jealous of the Court's designs. The most fatal steps the Court took to humble the city, were, 1. The shutting up the Exchequer,[14] and, 2. The bringing a *quo warranto* against their charter; but these things can but be touched at here; the city has outlived it all, and both the attempts turned to the discredit of the Court party, who pushed them on. But the city, I say, has gained the ascendant, and is now made so necessary to the Court (as before it was thought rather a grievance) that now we see the Court itself the daily instrument to encourage and increase the opulence of the city, and the city again, by its real grandeur, made not a glory only, but an assistance and support to the Court, on the greatest and most sudden emergencies. Nor can a breach be now made on any terms, but the city will have the advantage; for while the stocks, and Bank, and trading companies remain in the city, the centre of the money, as well as of the credit and trade of the kingdom, will be there.

The Council, the Parliament, and the Courts of Justice, are all kept at the same part of the town; but as all suits among the citizens are, by virtue of their privileges, to be tried within the liberty of the city, so the term is obliged to be (as it were) adjourned from Westminster-Hall to Guild-Hall, to try causes there, also criminal cases are in like manner tried monthly at the Old Baily, where a special commission is granted for that purpose to the judges but the Lord Mayor always presides, and has the chair.

The equality, however, being thus preserved, and a perfect good understanding between the Court and city having so long flourished, this union contributes greatly to the flourishing circumstances of both, and the public credit is greatly raised by it; for it was never known, that the city, on any occasion, was so assistant to the government, as it has been since this general good agreement. No sum is so great, but the Bank has been able to raise. Here the Exchequer bills are at all times circulated, money advanced upon the funds as soon as laid, and that at moderate interest, not encroaching on the government, or extorting large interest to eat up the nation, and disappoint the sovereign, and defeat his best designs, as in King William's time was too much the practice.

By this great article of public credit, all the king's business is done with cheerfulness, provisions are now bought to victual the fleets without difficulty, and at reasonable rates. The several yards where the ships are built and fitted out, are currently paid: the magazines of military and naval stores kept full: in a word, by this very article of public credit, of which the Parliament is the foundation (and the city, are the architectures or builders) all those great things are now done with ease, which, in the former reigns, went on heavily, and were brought about with the utmost difficulty.

But, to return to the city; besides the companies and public offices, which are kept in the city, there are several particular offices and places, as,

Here are several great offices for several societies of insurers; for here almost all hazards may be insured; the four principal are called, 1. Royal Exchange Ensurance: 2. The London Ensurers: 3. The Hand in Hand Fire Office: 4. The Sun Fire Office. In the two first of those, all hazard by sea are insured, that is to say, of ships or goods, not lives; as also houses and goods are insured from fire. In the last, only houses and goods. In all which offices, the *premio* is so small, and the recovery, in case of loss, so easy and certain, where no fraud is suspected, that nothing can be shown like it in the whole world; especially that of insuring houses from fire, which has now attained such an universal approbation, that I am told, there are above seventy thousand houses thus insured in London, and the parts adjacent.

The East-India House is in Leadenhall-Street, an old, but spacious building; very convenient, though not beautiful, and I am told, it is under consultation to have it taken down, and rebuilt with additional buildings for warehouses and cellars for their goods, which at present are much wanted.

The Bank[15] is kept in Grocer's Hall, a very convenient place, and, considering its situation, so near the Exchange, a very spacious, commodious place.

Here business is dispatched with such exactness, and such expedition and so much of it too, that it is really prodigious; no confusion, nobody is either denied or delayed payment, the merchants who keep their cash there, are sure to have their bills always paid, and even advances made on easy terms, if they have occasion. No accounts in the world are more exactly kept, no place in the world has so much business done, with so much ease.

In the next street (the Old Jury) is the Excise Office. In this one office is managed an immense weight of business, and they have in pay, as I am told, near four thousand officers. The whole kingdom is divided by them into proper districts, and to every district, a collector, a supervisor, and a certain number of gaugers, called, by the vulgar title excise men.

Nothing can be more regular, than the methods of this office, by which an account of the whole excise is transmitted from the remotest parts of the kingdom, once every six weeks, which is called a sitting, and the money received, or prosecutions commenced for it, in the next sitting.

Under the management of this office, are now brought, not only the excise upon beer, ale, and other liquors, as formerly, but also the duties on malt and candles, hops, soap, and leather, all which are managed in several and distinct classes, and the accounts kept in distinct books; but, in many places, are collected by the same officers, which makes the charge of the collection much easier to the government. Nor is the like duty collected in any part of the world, with so little charge, or so few officers.

The South-Sea House is situate in a large spot of ground, between Broad-Street and Threadneedle-Street, two large houses having been taken in, to form the whole office; but, as they were, notwithstanding, straitened for room, so they have now resolved to erect a new and complete building for the whole business, which is to be exceeding fine and large, and to this end, the company has purchased several adjacent buildings, so that the ground is enlarged towards Threadneedle-Street.

As the company are enlarging their trade to America, and have also engaged in a new trade, namely, that of the Greenland whale fishing, they are like to have an occasion to enlarge their offices. This building, they assure us, will cost the company from ten to twenty thousand pounds, that is to say, a very great sum.

The Post Office, a branch of the revenue formerly not much valued, but now, by the additional penny upon the letters, and by the visible increase of business in the nation, is grown very considerable. This office maintains now, packet boats to Spain and Portugal, which never was done before: so the merchants' letters for Cadiz or Lisbonne, which were before two and twenty days in going over France and Spain to Lisbonne, oftentimes arrive there now, in nine or ten days from Falmouth. They have also a packet from England to the West-Indies; but I am not of opinion, that they will keep it up for much time longer, if it be not already let fall.

The penny post, a modern contrivance of a private person, one Mr William Dockraw,[16] is now made a branch of the general revenue by the Post Office; and though, for a time, it was subject to miscarriages and mistakes, yet now it is come also into so exquisite a management, that nothing can be more exact, and 'tis with the utmost safety and dispatch, that letters are delivered at the remotest corners of the town, almost as soon as they could be sent by a messenger, and that from four, five, six, to eight times a day, according as the distance of the place makes it practicable; and you may send a letter from Ratcliff or Limehouse in the East, to the farthest part of Westminster for a penny, and that several times in the same day. Nor are you tied up to a single piece of paper, as in the General Post-Office, but any packet under a pound weight, goes at the same price. We see nothing of this at Paris, at Amsterdam, at Hamburgh, or any other city, that ever I have seen, or heard of.

The Custom House I have just mentioned before, but must take up a few lines to mention it again. The stateliness of the building, showed the greatness of the business that is transacted there: the Long Room is like an Exchange every morning, and the crowd of people who appear there, and the business they do, is not to be explained by words, nothing of that kind in Europe is like it. Yet it has been found, that the business of export and import in this port of London, is so prodigiously increased, and the several new offices, which they are bound to erect for the managing the additional parts of the customs, are such, that the old building, though very spacious, is too little, and as the late Fire burnt or demolished some part of the west end of the Custom House, they have had the opportunity in rebuilding,[17] to enlarge it very much, buying in the ground of some of the demolished houses, to add to the Custom House, which will be now a most glorious building.

The quays, or wharfs, next the river, fronting not the Custom House only, but the whole space from the Tower stairs, or dock, to the bridge, ought to be taken notice of as a public building; nor are they less an ornament to the city, as they are a testimony of the vast trade carried on in it, than the Royal Exchange itself. The revenue, or income, brought in by these wharfs, inclusive of the warehouses belonging to them, and the lighters they employ, is said to amount to a prodigious sum; and, as I am told, seldom so little as forty thousand pounds per annum: and abundance of porters, watchmen, wharfingers, and other officers, are maintained here by the business of the wharfs; in which, one thing is very remarkable, that here are porters, and poor working men, who, though themselves not worth, perhaps, twenty pounds in the world, are trusted with great quantities of valuable goods, sometimes to the value of several thousand pounds, and yet 'tis very rarely to be heard, that any loss or embezzlement is made.

From these public places, I come next to the markets, which, in such a mass of building, and such a collection of people, and where such business is done, must be great, and very many. To take a view of them in particular;

First, Smithfield Market for living cattle, which is, without question, the greatest in the world no description can be given of it, no calculation of the numbers of creatures sold there, can be made. This market is every Monday and Friday. There is also a great market, or rather fair for horses, in Smithfield every Friday in the afternoon, where very great numbers of horses, and those of the highest price, are to be sold weekly.

The flesh markets are as follow: Leaden-Hall, Honey-Lane, Newgate, Clare, Shadwell, Southwark, Westminster, Spittle Fields, Hoxton (forsaken) Brook, Bloomsbury Newport, St James's, Hungerford.

Fish markets	Billingsgate, Fishstreet Hill, and Old Fish-street.
Herb markets	Covent Garden, and Stocks Market.
N.B. Cherry market and apple market - - -	At the Three Cranes
Corn markets	Bear Key, and Queen Hith.
Meal markets	Queen Hith, Hungerford, Ditch-Side, and Whitecross-Street.
Hay markets	Whitechapel, Smithfield, Southwark, the Hay-Market-Street, Westminster, and Bloomsbury.

Leather market	Leaden Hall.
Hides and skins	Leaden Hall, and Wood's Close.
Coal markets	Billingsgate, Room Land.
Bay market	Leaden Hall.
Broad cloth market - - -	Blackwell Hall.

N.B. The last three are, without doubt, the greatest in the world of those kinds.

Bubble market	Exchange Alley.

Of the fourteen flesh markets, or markets for provisions, seven of them are of ancient standing, time out of mind. But the other seven are erected since the enlargement of buildings mentioned above. The old ones are, Leaden-Hall, Honey-Lane, Newgate Market, Southwark, Clare, St James's, and Westminster; and these are so considerable, such numbers of buyers, and such an infinite quantity of provisions of all sorts, flesh, fish, and fowl, that, especially the first, no city in the world can equal them. 'Tis of the first of these markets, that a certain Spanish ambassador said, there was as much meat sold in it in one month, as would suffice all Spain for a year.

This great market, called, Leaden-Hall, though standing in the middle of the city, contains three large squares, every square having several outlets into divers streets, and all into one another. Every Wednesday is kept a market for raw hides, tanned leather, and shoemakers' tools; and in the warehouses, up stairs on the east and south sides of the square, is the great market for Colechester bays.

All the other markets follow the same method in proportion to the room they have for it; and there is an herb market in every one but the chief markets in the whole city for herbs and garden-stuff, are the Stocks and Covent Garden.

There are but two corn markets in the whole city and out parts; but they are monsters for magnitude, and not to be matched in the world. These are Bear Key, and Queen Hith. To the first comes all the vast quantity of corn that is brought into the city by sea, and here corn may be said, not to be sold by cart loads, or horse loads, but by ship loads, and, except the corn chambers and magazines in Holland, when the fleets come in from Dantzick and England, the whole world cannot equal the quantity bought and sold here.

The other, which I call a corn market too, is at Queen Hith; but this market is chiefly, if not wholly, for malt; as to the whole corn, as the quantity of malt brought to this market is prodigious great, so I must observe too, that this place is the receiver of all the malt, the barley of which, takes up the ground of so many hundred thousand acres of land in the counties of Surrey, Bucks, Berks, Oxford, Southampton, and Wilts, and is called west country malt.

The vessels which bring this malt and meal to Queen Hith, are worth the observation of any stranger that understands such things. They are remarkable for the length of the vessel, and the burthen they carry, and yet the little water they draw; in a word, some of those barges carry over a thousand quarter of malt at a time, and yet do not draw two foot of water. Some of these large barges come as far as from Abbington, which is above one hundred and fifty miles from London, if we measure by the river.

The next market, which is more than ordinary remarkable, is the coal market at Billingsgate. This is kept every morning on the broad place just at the head of Billingsgate Dock, and the place is called Room Land from what old forgotten original it has that name, history is silent. I need not, except for the sake of strangers, take notice, that the city of London, and parts adjacent, as also all the south of England, is supplied with coals, called therefore sea-coal, from Newcastle upon Tyne, and from the coast of Durham, and Northumberland. This trade is so considerable, that it is esteemed the great nursery of our best seamen. The quantity of coals, which it is supposed are, *communibus annis*, burnt and consumed in and about this city, is supposed to be about five hundred thousand chalder, every chalder containing thirty-six bushels, and generally weighing about thirty hundred weight.

All these coals are bought and sold on this little spot of

Room Land, and, though sometimes, especially in case of a war, or of contrary winds, a fleet of five hundred to seven hundred sail of ships, comes up the river at a time, yet they never want a market. The brokers, or buyers of these coals, are called crimps, for what reason, or original, is likewise a mystery peculiar to this trade; for these people are noted for giving such dark names to the several parts of their trade; so the vessels they load their ships with at New Castle, are called keels, and the ships that bring them, are called cats, and hags, or hag boats, and fly boats, and the like.

It must be observed, that as the city of London occasions the consumption of so great a quantity of corn and coals, so the measurement of them is under the inspection of the Lord Mayor and court of aldermen, and for the direction of which, there are allowed a certain number of corn meters, and coal meters, whose places are for life, and bring them in a very considerable income. These places are in the gift of the Lord Mayor for the time being, and are generally sold for three or four thousand pounds a piece, when they fall. They have abundance of poor men employed under them, who are called, also, meters, and are, or ought to be, freemen of the city.

There is one great work yet behind, which, however, seems necessary to a full description of the city of London, and that is the shipping and the Pool; but in what manner can any writer go about it, to bring it into any reasonable compass? The thing is a kind of infinite, and the parts to be separated from one another in such a description, are so many, that it is hard to know where to begin.

The whole river, in a word, from London-Bridge to Black Wall, is one great arsenal, nothing in the world can be like it. The great building-yards at Schedam near Amsterdam, are said to out-do them in the number of ships which are built there, and they tell us, that there are more ships generally seen at Amsterdam, than in the Thames. As to the building part, I will not say, but that there may be more vessels built at Schedam, and the parts adjacent, than in the River Thames; but then it must be said;

1. That the English build for themselves only, the Dutch for all the world.

2. That almost all the ships the Dutch have, are built there, whereas, not one fifth part of our shipping is built in the Thames; but abundance of ships are built at all the sea-ports in England, such as at New-Castle, Sunderland, Stockton, Whitby, Hull, Gainsborough, Grimsby, Lynn, Yarmouth, Alborough, Walderswick, Ipswich and Harwich, upon the east coast; and at Shoram, Arundel, Brighthelmston, Portsmouth, Southampton, Pool, Weymouth, Dartmouth, Plymouth, besides other places, on the south coast.

3. That we see more vessels in less room at Amsterdam; but the setting aside their hoys, bilanders and schoots, which are in great numbers always there, being vessels particular to their inland and coasting navigation; you do not see more ships, nor near so many ships of force, at Amsterdam as at London.

4. That you see more ships there in less room, but, perhaps, not so many ships in the whole.

That part of the river of Thames which is properly the harbour, and where the ships usually deliver or unload their cargoes, is called the Pool, and begins at the turning of the river out of Lime-house Reach, and extends to the Custom-house-Keys. In this compass I have had the curiosity to count the ships as well as I could, *en passant*, and have found above two thousand sail of all sorts, not reckoning barges, lighters or pleasure-boats, and yachts; but vessels that really go to sea.

In the river, as I have observed, there are from Battle-Bridge on the Southwark side, and the Hermitage-Bridge on the city-side, reckoning to Black-Wall, inclusive,

Three wet docks for laying up	merchant ships.
Twenty-two dry docks for repairing	
Thirty-three yards for building	

To enter into any description of the great magazines of all manner of naval stores, for the furnishing those builders, would be endless, and I shall not attempt it; 'tis sufficient to add, that England, as I have said elsewhere, is an inexhaustible store-house of timber, and all the oak timber, and generally the plank also, used in the building these ships, is found in England only, nay, and which is more, it is not fetched from the remoter parts of England, but these southern counties near us are the places where 'tis generally found. But I must land, lest this part of the account seems to smell of the tar, and I should tire the gentlemen with leading them out of their knowledge.

No where in the world is so good care taken to quench fires as in London; I will not say the like care is taken to prevent them for I must say, that I think the servants, nay, the masters too in London, are the most careless people in the world about fire, and this, no doubt, is the reason why there are frequently more fires in London and in the out-parts, than there are in all the cities of Europe put them together; nor are they the more careful, as I can learn, either from observation or report, I say, they are not made more cautious, by the innumerable fires which continually happen among them.

And this leads me back to what I just now said, that no city in the world is so well furnished for the extinguishing fires when they happen.

1. By the great convenience of water which being every where laid in the streets in large timber pipes, as well from the Thames as the New-River, those pipes are furnished with a fire plug, which the parish officers have the key of, and when opened, let out not a pipe, but a river of water into the streets, so that making but a dam in the kennel, the whole street is immediately under water to supply the engines.

2. By the great number of admirable engines, of which, almost, every parish has one, and some halls also, and some private citizens have them of their own, so that no sooner does a fire break out, but the house is surrounded with engines, and a flood of water poured upon it, 'till the fire is, as it were, not extinguished only, but drowned.

3. The several insurance offices, of which I have spoken above, have each of them a certain set of men, who they keep

in constant pay, and who they furnish with tools proper for the work, and to whom they give jack-caps of leather, able to keep them from hurt, if brick or timber, or any thing not of too great a bulk, should fall upon them; these men make it their business to be ready at call, all hours, and night or day, to assist in case of fire; and it must be acknowledged, they are very dextrous, bold, diligent, and successful. These they call fire-men, but with an odd kind of contradiction in the title, for they are really most of them water-men.

However, the New-River,[18] which is brought by an aqueduct or artificial stream from Ware, continues to supply the greater part of the city with water, only with this addition by the way, that they have been obliged to dig a new head or basin at Islington on a higher ground than that which the natural stream of the river supplies, and this higher basin they fill from the lower, by a great engine worked formerly with six sails, now by many horses constantly working; so from that new elevation of the water, they supply the higher part of the town with the same advantage, and more ease than the Thames engines do it.

There was a very likely proposal set on foot by some gentlemen, whose genius seemed equal to the work, for drawing another river, rather larger than that now running, and bringing it to a head on some rising grounds beyond Mary le Bonne. This water was proposed to be brought from the little Coln or Cole near St Albans, and the river, called Two Waters, near Rickmansworth, and as I have seen the course of the water, and the several supplies it was to have, and how the water-level was drawn for containing the current, I must acknowledge it was a very practical undertaking, and merited encouragement; but it was opposed in Parliament, and dropped for the present.

However, though this be laid aside, yet it cannot be denied, that the city of London is the best supplied with water of any great city in the world, and upon as easy terms to its inhabitants.

There were formerly several beautiful conduits of running-water in London, which water was very sweet and good, and was brought at an infinite expense, from several distant springs, in large leaden pipes to those conduits, and this was so lately, that several of those conduits were re-built since the Fire, as one on Snow-Hill and one at Stocks-Market, which serves as a pedestal for the great equestrian statue of King Charles II, erected there at the charge of Sir Robert Viner,[19] then Lord Mayor, and who was then an eminent banker in Lombard-street; but his loyalty could not preserve him from being ruined by the common calamity, when the king shut up the Exchequer.

The gates of the city are seven, besides posterns, and the posterns that remain are four, besides others that are demolished. The gates are all remaining, two of them which were demolished at the fire, being beautifully re-built. These are Ludgate and Newgate; the first a prison for debt for freemen of the city only, the other a prison for criminals, both for London and Middlesex, and for debtors also for Middlesex, being the county gaol.

Moregate is also re-built, and is a very beautiful gateway, the arch being near twenty foot high, which was done to give room for the city Trained Bands to go through to the Artillery Ground, where they muster, and that they might march with their pikes advanced, for then they had pikemen in every regiment, as well in the army as in the militia, which since that, is quite left off; this makes the gate look a little out of shape, the occasion of it not being known. Cripplegate and Bishopsgate are very old, and make but a mean figure; Aldersgate is about one hundred and twenty years old, and yet being beautified, as I have said, on the occasion of King James's entry, looks very handsome.

Aldgate was very ancient and decayed, so that *as old as Aldgate*, was a city proverb for many years; but this gate was re-built also, upon the triumphant entry of K. James I and looks still very well.

Temple-Bar is the only gate which is erected at the extent of the city liberties, and this was occasioned by some needful ceremonies at the proclaiming any King or Queen of England, at which time the gates are shut; the Herald at Arms knocks hard at the door, the sheriffs of the city call back, asking who is there? Then the herald answers, 'I come to proclaim,' &c. at which the sheriffs open, and bid them welcome, and so they go on to the Exchange, where they make the last proclamation. This gate is adorned with the figures of kings below, and traitors above, the heads of several criminals executed for treason being set up there; the statues below are of Queen Elizabeth and King James I, King Charles I and II.

There are in London, notwithstanding we are a nation of liberty, more public and private prisons, and houses of confinement, than any city in Europe, perhaps as many as in all the capital cities of Europe put together; for example:

PUBLIC GAOLS[20]

The Tower.
Newgate.
Ludgate.
King's Bench.
The Fleet.
Bridewell.
Marshalseas.
The Gatehouse.
Two Counters in the city.
One Counter in the Burrough.
St Martin's le Grand.
The Clink, formerly the prison to the Stews.
Whitechapel.
Finsbury.
The Dutchy.
St Katherines.
Bale-Dock.
Little-Ease.
New-Prison.
New-Bridewell.
Tottil-Fields Bridewell.
Five night prisons, called round-houses, &c.

TOLERATED PRISONS

Bethlem or Bedlam.
One hundred and nineteen Spunging Houses.
Fifteen Private Mad-Houses.
The King's Messengers-Houses.
The Sergeant at Arms's Officers Houses.
The Black Rod Officers-Houses.
Cum aliis.
Three Pest-houses.
The Admiralty Officers-Houses.
Tip-staffs Houses.
Chancery Officers Houses.

N.B. All these private houses of confinement, are pretended

to be little purgatories, between prison and liberty, places of advantage for the keeping prisoners at their own request, till they can get friends to deliver them, and so avoid going into public prisons; though in some of them, the extortion is such, and the accommodation so bad, that men choose to be carried away directly.

This has often been complained of, and hopes had of redress; but the rudeness and avarice of the officers prevails, and the oppression is sometimes very great; but that by the way.

To sum up my description of London, take the following heads; there are in this great mass of buildings thus called London,

Two cathedrals.
Four choirs for music-worship.
One hundred and thirty-five parish churches.
Nine new churches unfinished, being part of fifty appointed to be built.
Sixty-nine chapels where the Church of England service is performed.
Two churches at Deptford, taken into the limits now described.
Twenty-eight foreign churches.
Besides Dissenters meetings of all persuasions;
Popish chapels; and
One Jews' synagogue.
There are also, thirteen hospitals, besides lesser charities, called Alms-houses, of which they reckon above a hundred, many of which have chapels for divine service.
Three colleges.
Twenty-seven public prisons.
Eight public schools, called Free Schools.
Eighty-three Charity Schools.
Fourteen markets for flesh.
Two for live cattle, besides two herb-markets.
Twenty-three other markets, as described.
Fifteen Inns of Court.
Four fairs.
Twenty-seven squares, besides those within any single building, as the Temple, Somerset House, &c.
Five public bridges.
One town-house, or Guild-Hall.
One Royal Exchange.
Two other Exchanges only for shops.
One custom-house.
Three Artillery Grounds.
Four pest-houses.
Two bishop's palaces;
and
Three royal palaces.

Having dwelt thus long in the city, I mean properly called so, I must be the shorter in my account of other things.

The Court end of the town, now so prodigiously increased, would take up a volume by itself. The king's palace, though the receptacle of all the pomp and glory of Great Britain, is really mean, in comparison of the rich furniture within, I mean the living furniture, the glorious Court of the King of Great Britain: the splendour of the nobility, the wealth and greatness of the attendants, the economy of the house, and the real grandeur of the whole royal family, out-does all the Courts of Europe, even that of France itself, as it is now managed since the death of Lewis the Great. But the palace of St James's is, I say, too mean, and only seems to be honoured with the Court, while a more magnificent fabric may be erected, where the King of England usually resided, I mean at White-Hall.

The ruins of that old palace, seem to predict, that the time will come, when that Phœnix shall revive, and when a building shall be erected there, suiting the majesty and magnificence of the British princes, and the riches of the British nation. Many projects have been set on foot for the rebuilding the ancient palace [21] of White-hall; but most of them have related rather to a fund for raising the money, than a model for the building.

But I return to the description of things which really exist, and are not imaginary: as the Court is now stated, all the offices and places for business are scattered about.

The Parliament meets, as they ever did, while the Court was at Westminster, in the king's old palace, and there are the courts of justice also, and the officers of the Exchequer, nor can it be said, however convenient the place is made for them; but that it has a little an air of venerable, though ruined antiquity. What is the Court of Requests, the Court of Wards, and the Painted Chamber, though lately repaired, but the corpse of the old English grandeur laid in state?

The whole, it is true, was anciently the king's palace or royal house, and it takes up full as much ground as the new palace would do, except only the gardens and parks, the space before it, which is still called Palace-yard, is much greater than that which would be at the north gate of the palace of White-hall, as proposed.

But, alas! as I say, though they seem now even in their ruins, great; yet compared to the beauty and elegancy of modern living, and of royal buildings in this age, what are they! The royal apartments, the prince's lodgings, the great officers' apartments, what are they now, but little offices for clerks, rooms for coffee-houses, auctions of pictures, pamphlet and toy-shops?

Even St Stephen's Chapel, formerly the royal chapel of the palace, but till lately beautified for the convenience of the House of Commons, was a very indifferent place, old and decayed. The House of Lords is a venerable old place, indeed; but how mean, how incoherent, and how straitened are the several avenues to it, and rooms about it? the matted gallery, the lobby, the back ways the king goes to it, how short are they all of the dignity of the place, and the glory of a King of Great Britain, with the Lords and Commons, that so often meet there?

Some attempts were made lately, to have restored the decrepit circumstances of this part of the building, and orders were given to Mr Benson,[22] then surveyor of the king's buildings, to do his part towards it; but it was directed so ill, or understood so little, that some thought he was more likely to throw the old fabric down, than to set it to rights, for which ignorance and vanity, 'tis said, some have not fared as they deserved.

It is true, the sitting of the Parliament is by the order of the Houses themselves, accommodated as well as the place will admit; but how much more beautiful it would be in such a building, as is above contrived, I leave to the contriver to describe and to other people to judge.

Come we next to Westminster-Hall; 'tis true, it is a very noble Gothic building, ancient, vastly large, and the finest roof of its kind in England, being one hundred feet wide; but what a wretched figure does it make without doors; the front, a vast pinnacle or pediment, after the most ancient and almost forgotten part of the Gothic way of working; the building itself, resembles nothing so much as a great barn of three hundred feet long, and really looks like a barn at a distance.

Nay, if we view the whole building from without doors, 'tis like a great pile of something, but a stranger would be much at a loss to know what; and whether it was a house, or a church, or, indeed, a heap of churches being huddled all together, with differing and distant roofs, some higher, some lower, some standing east and west, some north and south, and some one way, and some another.

The Abbey, or Collegiate Church of Westminster, stands next to this; a venerable old pile of building, it is indeed, but so old and weak, that had it not been taken in hand some years ago, and great cost bestowed in upholding and repairing it, we might, by this time, have called it a heap, not a pile, and not a church, but the ruins of a church. But it begins to stand upon new legs now, and as they continue to work upon the repairs of it, the face of the whole building will, in a short while, be entirely new.

This is the repository of the British kings and nobility, and very fine monuments are here seen over the graves of our ancient monarchs; the particulars are too long to enter into here, and are so many times described by several authors, that it would be a vain repetition to enter upon it here; besides, we have by no means any room for it. The monarchs of Great Britain are always crowned here, even King James II submitted to it, and to have it performed by a Protestant bishop. It is observable, that our kings and queens make always two solemn visits to this church, and very rarely, if ever, come here any more, viz. to be crowned and to be buried.

It is become such a piece of honour to be buried in Westminster-Abbey, that the body of the church begins to be crowded with the bodies of citizens, poets, seamen, and parsons, nay, even with very mean persons, if they have but any way made themselves known in the world; so that in time, the royal ashes will be thus mingled with common dust, that it will leave no room either for king or common people, or at least not for their monuments, some of which also are rather pompously foolish, than solid and to the purpose.

Near to this church is the Royal Free-School, the best of its kind in England, not out-done either by Winchester or Eaton, for a number of eminent scholars.

'Tis remarkable, that the whole city, called properly, Westminster, and standing on the S. side of the park, is but one parish, and is the only city of one parish in England. There is now another great church erected, or rather erecting, by the commissioners for building fifty new churches; but they have been strangely mistaken in the situation, which is a fenny marshy ground, and it is not found so able to support the weight as, perhaps, they were told it would; I say no more. The building was very curious, especially the roof; but the towers are not so beautiful as it is thought was intended, the foundation not being to be trusted.

The Cottonian Library [23] is kept here in an ancient building, near Westminster-Hall gate; we were told it would be removed to the royal library, and then, that it would be removed to a house to be built on purpose; but we see neither yet in hand. This is one of the most valuable collections in Britain, and, the Bodleian Library excepted, is, perhaps, the best. It has in it some books and manuscripts invaluable for their antiquity; but I have not room so much as to enter upon giving an account of the particulars.

This part of Westminster has but one street, which gives it a communication with London, and this is called King-street, a long, dark, dirty and very inconvenient passage; but there seems to be no remedy for it, for most passengers get out of it through the Privy Garden, and some by private passages into the park, as at Locket's, at the Cock-Pit, and the new gate from Queen's-Square; but these are all upon sufferance.

Having mentioned White-Hall already, I have nothing more to say of it, but that it was, and is not, but may revive.

There is, doubtless, a noble situation, fit to contain a royal palace, equal to Versailles but I have given you my thoughts on that subject at large.

Nor can I dwell here upon a description of His Majesty's Court, or an account of the politics managed there; it does not relate to this work; let it suffice to say, His Majesty resides, especially all the winter, at St James's; but the business of the government, is chiefly carried on at the Cock-pit. This is a royal building, was once part of White-hall, first the Duke of Monmouth lived in it, then Prince George of Denmark and his princess, afterwards Queen Ann, and since the fire at White-Hall, the Treasury, the Secretary's office, the Council Chamber, the Board of Trade, and the Lord Chamberlain, hold all their particular offices here and here there is also, a by-way out of Duke-street into the park.

From thence we come to the Horse Guards, a building commodious enough, built on purpose, as a barrack for a large detachment of the Horse-Guards, who keep their post here, while attending on duty; over it are offices for payment of the troops, and a large court of judicature, for holding councils of war, for trial of deserters and others, according to the articles of war.

In the same range of buildings, stood the Admiralty Office, built by the late King William; but though in itself a spacious building, is found so much too narrow now the business is so much increased, and as there is a sufficient piece of spare ground behind it, to enlarge the building, we find a new and spacious office is now building in the same place, which shall be sufficient to all the uses required. This office is, perhaps, of the most importance of any of the public parts of the administration, the royal navy being the sinews of our strength, and the whole direction of it being in the hands of the commissioners for executing this office.

From this part of the town, we come into the public streets, where nothing is more remarkable than the hurries of the people; Charing-Cross is a mixture of Court and city; Man's Coffee-house is the Exchange Alley of this part of the town, and 'tis perpetually thronged with men of business, as the others are with men of play and pleasure.

From hence advancing a little, we see the great equestrian statue of King Charles the First in brass, a costly, but a curious piece; however, it serves sufficiently, to let us know who it is, and why erected there. The circumstances are two, he faces the place where his enemies triumphed over him, and triumphs, that is, tramples in the place where his murtherers were hanged.

On the right side of the street, coming from White-Hall, is Northumberland-House, so called, because belonging to the Northumberland family for some ages but descending to the Duke of Somerset in right of marriage, from the late Duchess, heiress of the house of Piercy.

'Tis an ancient, but a very good house, the only misfortune of its situation is, its standing too near the street; the back part of the house is more modern and beautiful than the front, and when you enter the first gate, you come into a noble square fronting the fine lodgings. 'Tis a large and very well designed building, and fit to receive a retinue of one hundred in family; nor does the Duke's family come so far short of the number, as not very handsomely to fill the house.

Advancing thence to the Hay-Market, we see, first, the great new theatre,[24] a very magnificent building, and perfectly accommodated for the end of which it was built, though the entertainment there of late, has been chiefly operas and balls. These meetings are called BALLS, the word *masquerade* not being so well relished by the English, who, though at first fond of the novelty, began to be sick of the thing on many accounts. However, as I cannot in justice say any thing to recommend them, I choose to say no more; but go on.

From hence westward and northward, lie those vastly extended buildings, which add so exceedingly to the magnitude of the whole body, and of which I have already said so much. It would be a task too great for this work, to enter into a description of all the fine houses, or rather palaces of the nobility in these parts.

The hospitals in and about the city of London, deserve a little further observation, especially those more remarkable for their magnitude, as,

I. Bethlem[25] or Bedlam: this and Bridewell, indeed, go together, for though they are two several houses, yet they are incorporated together, and have the same governors; also the president, treasurer, clerk, physician and apothecary are the same; but the stewards and the revenue are different, and so are the benefactions; but to both very great.

The orders for the government of the hospital of Bethlem are exceedingly good, and a remarkable instance of the good disposition of the gentlemen concerned in it, especially these that follow;

1. That no person, except the proper officers who tend them, be allowed to see the lunatics of a Sunday.

2. That no person be allowed to give the lunatics strong drink, wine, tobacco or spirits, or to sell any such thing in the hospital.

3. That no servant of the house shall take any money given to any of the lunatics to their own use; but that it shall be carefully kept for them till they are recovered, or laid out for them in such things as the committee approves.

4. That no officer or servant shall beat or abuse, or offer any force to any lunatic; but on absolute necessity. The rest of the orders are for the good government of the house.

This hospital was formerly in the street now called Old Bedlam, and was very ancient and ruinous. The new building was erected at the charge of the city in 1676, and is the most beautiful structure for such a use that is in the world, and was finished from its foundation in fifteen months; it was said to be taken ill at the Court of France, that it was built after the fashion of one of the King of France's palaces. The number of people who are generally under cure in this hospital, is from 130 to 150 at a time. There are great additions now making to this hospital, particularly for the relief and subsistence of incurables, of which no full account can be given, because they are not yet finished.

II. The hospital of Bridewell, as it is an hospital, so it is also a house of correction. The house was formerly the king's city palace; but granted to the city to be in the nature of what is now called a work-house, and has been so employed, ever since the year 1555. As idle persons, vagrants, &c. are committed to this house for correction, so there are every year, several poor lads brought up to handicraft trades, as apprentices, and of these the care is in the governors, who maintain them out of the standing revenues of the house.

There are two other Bridewells, properly so called, that is to say, houses of correction; one at Clarkenwell, called New Prison, being the particular Bridewell for the county of Middlesex, and another in Tuttle-fields, for the city of Westminster.

The other city hospitals, are the Blue-coat Hospital for poor freemen's orphan children, and the two hospitals for sick and maimed people, as St Bartholomew's and St Thomas's. These three are so well known by all people that have seen the city of London, and so universally mentioned by all who have written of it, that little can be needful to add; however I shall say something as an abridgment.

III. Christ's Hospital was originally constituted by King Edward VI who has the honour of being the founder of it, as also of Bridewell; but the original design was, and is owing to the Lord Mayor and aldermen of London, and the Christian endeavours of that glorious martyr, Dr Ridley [26] then Bishop of London. The design is for entertaining, educating, nourishing and bringing up the poor children of the citizens, such as, their parents being dead, or fathers, at least, have no way to be supported, but are reduced to poverty.

Of these, the hospital is now so far increased in substance, by the benefactions of worthy gentlemen contributors, they now maintain near a thousand, who have food, clothing and instruction, useful and sufficient learning, and exceeding good discipline; and at the proper times they are put out to trades, suitable to their several genius's and capacities, and near five thousand pounds a year are expended on this charity.

IV. St Bartholomew's Hospital adjoins to Christ Church. The first founder is esteemed to be King Henry VIII whose statue in stone and very well done, is, for that very reason, lately erected in the new front, over the entrance to the Cloyster in West-Smithfield.

From this small beginning, this hospital rose to the greatness we now see it arrived at, of which take the following account for one year, viz. 1718;

Cured and discharged, of sick, maimed and wounded, from all parts	3088
Buried at the expense of the house	198
Remaining under cure	513

V. St Thomas's Hospital in Southwark, has a different foundation, but to the same purpose; it is under the same government, viz. the Lord Mayor, aldermen and commanalty of the city of London, and had a revenue of about 2000*l.* per annum, about 100 years ago.

This hospital has received greater benefactions than St Bartholomew's; but then 'tis also said to have suffered greater losses, especially by several great fires in Southwark and elsewhere, as by the necessity of expensive buildings, which, notwithstanding the charitable gifts of divers great benefactors, has cost the hospital great sums. The state of this hospital is so advanced at this time, that in the same year as above, viz. 1718, the state of the house was as follows;

Cured and discharged of sick, wounded and maimed, from all parts	3608
Buried at the expense of the house	216
Remaining under cure	566

Adjoining to this of St Thomas's, is lately laid a noble foundation of a new hospital, by the charitable gift and single endowment of one person, and, perhaps, the greatest of its kind, that ever was founded in this nation by one person, whether private or public, not excepting the kings themselves.

This will, I suppose, be called Guy's Hospital, being to be built and endowed at the sole charge of one Mr Thomas Guy,[27] formerly a bookseller in Lombard Street, who lived to see the said hospital not only designed, the ground purchased and cleared, but the building begun, and a considerable progress made in it, and died while these sheets were in the press.

It was generally understood to have been intended for a ward, or an addition to the old hospital of St Thomas's, for the reception of such as were accounted incurable. But when Mr Guy died, his will being made public, it appeared, that it was really a separate, independent and distinct hospital, under distinct governors, and for a separate purpose, to wit, for receiving such poor persons as have been dismissed from other hospitals as incurable.

What the revenue, when settled, will be; what the building will amount to when finished; what the purchase of the land, and what the expense of finishing and furnishing it, cannot be estimated, 'till it be further looked into but we are told without doors, that besides all the expense of purchase, building, furnishing and finishing as above there will be left more than two hundred thousand pounds for endowing the hospital with a settled revenue, for maintaining the said poor, and yet the charitable founder was so immensely rich, that besides leaving four hundred pounds a year to the Blue-coat Hospital of London, and besides building an hospital for fourteen poor people at Tamworth in Staffordshire, where he was chosen representative; and besides several considerable charities which he had given in his life-time; he also gave away, in legacies, to his relations and others, above a hundred thousand pound more, so that he cannot, as has been said by some, be said to give a great charity to the poor, and forget his own family.

How Mr Guy amassed all this wealth, having been himself in no public employment or office of trust, or profit, and only carrying on the trade of a bookseller, till within a few years of his death, that is not the business of this book; 'tis enough to say, he was a thriving, frugal man, who God was pleased exceedingly to bless, in whatever he set his hand to, knowing to what good purposes he laid up his gains. He was never married, and lived to be above eighty years old; so that the natural improvements of this money, by common interest, after it was first grown to a considerable bulk, greatly increased the sum.

Next to these hospitals, whose foundations are so great and magnificent, is the work-house, or city work-house, properly so called, which being a late foundation, and founded upon mere charity, without any settled endowment, is the more remarkable, for here are a very great number of poor children taken in, and supported and maintained, fed, clothed, taught, and put out to trades, and that at an exceeding expense, and all this without one penny revenue.

It is established, or rather the establishment of it, is supported by an old Act of Parliament, 13. 14. Car. II empowering the citizens to raise contributions for the charge of employing the poor, and suppressing vagrants and beggars, and it is now, by the voluntary assistance and bounty of benefactors, become so considerable, that in the year 1715 they gave the following state of the house, viz.

Vagabonds, beggars, &c. taken into the house, including fifty-five which remained at the end of the preceding year	418
Discharged, including such as were put out to trades	356
Remaining in the house	62
Not one buried that whole year.	

There are three considerable charities given by private persons in the city of Westminster, viz.

1. The Gray-coat Hospital, founded by a generous subscription or contribution. It maintains 70 boys and 40 girls, clothed, fed, and taught, and in some measure provided for, by being put out to trades.

2. The Green-coat Hospital, in the same Fields, founded by King Charles I for poor fatherless children of St Margaret's

parish; and next to this hospital is the house of correction, or the Westminster Bridewell.

3. The Emanuel Hospital, founded by the Lady Ann Dacres,[28] for ten poor men, and ten poor women, in the forty-third year of Queen Elizabeth.

There has been, also, a very noble hospital erected by contribution of the French refugees, for the maintenance of their poor. It stands near the Pest-house, in the foot-way to Islington in the parish of Cripplegate.

The hospital called the Charter House, or Sutton's Hospital, is not by this supposed to be forgot, or the honour of it lessened. On the other hand, it must be recorded for ever, to be the greatest and noblest gift that ever was given for charity, by any one man, public or private, in this nation, since history gives us any account of things. The revenue of Mr Sutton's hospital being, besides the purchase of the place, and the building of the house, and other expenses, little less than 6000*l.* per annum revenue.

These are the principal hospitals, but it will not be useless observation, nor altogether improper to take notice of it here, that this age has produced some of the most eminent acts of public charity; and of the greatest value, I mean from private persons, that can be found in any age within the reach of our English history, excepting only that of Sutton's Hospital.

These, added to the innumerable number of alms-houses which are to be seen in almost every part of the city, make it certain, that there is no city in the world can show the like number of charities from private hands, there being, as I am told, not less than twenty thousand people maintained of charity, besides the charities of schooling for children, and besides the collections yearly at the annual feasts of several kinds, where money is given for putting out children apprentices, &c. so that the Papists have no reason to boast, that there were greater benefactions and acts of charity to the poor given in their times, than in our Protestant times; and this is indeed, one of the principal reasons for my making mention of it in this place.

I come now to an account of new edifices and public buildings erected or erecting in and about London, since the writing the foregoing account; and with this I conclude.

1. The fine new church of St Martin's in the Fields,[29] with a very fine steeple, which they tell us is 215 feet high, all wholly built by the contribution of that great parish, and finished with the utmost expedition.

2. The new Admiralty Office near White-hall, being on the same ground where the old office stood but much larger, being both longer in front and deeper backward, not yet finished.

3. Mr Guy's new hospital for incurables, mentioned above, situated on ground purchased for that purpose, adjoining to St Thomas's Hospital in Southwark, being a most magnificent building not yet quite finished.

4. Two large wings to the hospital of Bedlam, appointed also for incurables; this also not yet finished.

5. A large new meeting-house in Spittle-fields, for the sect of Dissenters, called Baptists, or Antepædo Baptists.

6. The South-Sea House in Threadneedle-street, the old house being entirely pulled down, and several other houses adjoining being purchased, the whole building will be new from the foundation; this not finished.

7. Several very fine new churches,[30] being part of the fifty churches appointed by Act of Paliament, viz. one in Spittle-fields, one in Radcliff-High-way, one in Old-street, one at Lime-house, with a very beautiful tower, and one in Bloomsbury, and five more not finished.

8. The parish church of St Botolph without Bishopsgate, pulled down and re-building, by the contribution of the inhabitants, not as one of the fifty churches.

9. The Custom-house, which since the late fire in Thames-street, is ordered to be enlarged; but is not yet finished.

All these buildings are yet in building, and will all, in their several places, be very great ornaments to the city.

10. A new street or range of houses taken out of the south side of the Artillery Ground near Morefields, also an enlarge-

ment to the new burying ground as it was formerly called, on the north side of the same ground.

11. The iron balustrade, or others call it, balcony, on the lanthorn upon the cupola of St Paul's, gilded.

12. A new bear-garden, called Figg's Theatre,[31] being a stage for the gladiators or prize-fighters, and is built on the Tyburn Road.

N.B. The gentlemen of the science, taking offence at its being called Tyburn Road, though it really is so, will have it called the Oxford Road; this public edifice is fully finished, and in use.

I conclude this account of London, with mentioning something of the Account of Mortality, that is to say, the births and burials, and I shall only take notice, that whereas, the general number of the burials in the year 1666, and farther back, were from 17000 to 19000 in a year, the last yearly bill for the year 1723, amounted as follows,

Christenings 19203. Burials 29197.

Here is to be observed, that the number of burials exceeding so much the number of births, is, because as it is not the number born, but the number christened that are set down, which is taken from the parish register; so all the children of Dissenters of every sort, Protestant, Popish and Jewish are omitted, also all the children of foreigners, French, Dutch, &c. which are baptized in their own churches, and all the children of those who are so poor, that they cannot get them registered: so that if a due estimate be made, the births may be very well supposed to exceed the burials one year with another by many thousands.

It is not that I have no more to say of London, that I break off here; but that I have no room to say it, and though some things may be taken notice of by others, which I have passed over; yet I have also taken notice of so many things which others have omitted, that I claim the balance in my favour.

I am, SIR,

Yours, &c.

Letter 6

Containing a description of part of the counties of Middlesex, Hertford, Bucks, Oxford, Wilts, Somerset, Gloucester, Warwick, Worcester, Hereford, Monmouth, and the several counties of South and North-Wales

I HAVE spent so much time, and taken up so much room in my description of London, and the adjacent parts, that I must be the more cautious, at least, as to needless excursions in the country near it. The villages round London partake of the influence of London, so much, that it is observed as London is increased, so they are all increased also, and from the same causes.

Hackney and Bromley are the first villages which begin the county of Middlesex, east; for Bow as reckoned to Stepney, is a part of the great mass. This town of Hackney is of a great extent, containing no less than 12 hamlets or separate villages.

All these, are within a few years so increased in buildings, and so fully inhabited, that there is no comparison to be made between their present and past state. Every separate hamlet is increased, and some of them more than treble as big as formerly; indeed as this whole town is included in the bills of mortality,[1] though no where joining to London, it is in some respects to be called a part of it.

This town is so remarkable for the retreat of wealthy citizens, that there is at this time near a hundred coaches kept in it; though I will not join with a certain satirical author,[2] who said of Hackney, that there were more coaches than Christians in it.

Newington, Tottenham, Edmonton, and Enfield stand all in a line N. from the city; the increase of buildings is so great in them all, that they seem to a traveller to be one continued street; especially Tottenham and Edmunton, and in them all, the new buildings so far exceed the old, especially in the value of them, and figure of the inhabitants, that the fashion of the towns are quite altered.

There is not any thing more fine in their degree, than most of the buildings this way; only with this observation, that they are generally belonging to the middle sort of mankind, grown wealthy by trade, and who still taste of London; some of them live both in the city, and in the country at the same time: yet many of these are immensely rich.

High-gate and Hamstead are next on the north-side. At the first is a very beautiful house built by the late Sir William Ashurst,[3] on the very summit of the hill, and with a view from the very lowest windows over the whole vale, to the city: and that so eminently, that they see the very ships passing up and down the river for 12 or 15 miles below London. The Jews have particularly fixed upon this town for their country retreats, and some of them are very wealthy; they live there in good figure, and have several trades particularly depending upon them, and especially, butchers of their own to supply them with provisions killed their own way; also, I am told, they have a private synagogue here.

In the chase, at Enfield[4] is a fine lodge formerly possessed by the Earl of Denbigh: now we are told that General Pepper is fixed ranger of the chase, and resides there. This chase was once a very beautiful place, and when King James I resided at Theobalds, which he loved for the pleasure of his hunting; it was then very full of deer, and all sorts of game; but it has suffered several depredations since that, and particularly in the late Protector's usurpation, when it was utterly stripped, both of game, and timber, and let out in farms to tenants, for the use of the public. After the Restoration, it was reassumed, and laid open again. Woods and groves were every where planted, and the whole chase stored with deer. But the young timber which indeed began to thrive, was so continually plundered, and the deer-stealers have so harassed the deer, and both perhaps by those who should have preserved it, as well as by others, that the place was almost ruined for a forest, and little but hares and bushwood was to be found in it. But now we hear, that by the vigilance of General Pepper, the chase is much recovered, and likely to be a place fit for the diversion of a prince, as it has been before.

The Mineral Waters, or Barnet Wells, are on the declivity of a hill; they were formerly in great request, being very much approved by physicians; but of late, they began to decline, and are now almost forgotten : other waters at Islington, and at Hampstead having grown popular in their stead.

Hampstead indeed is risen from a little country village, to a city, not upon the credit only of the waters, though 'tis apparent, its growing greatness began there; but company increasing gradually, and the people liking both the place and the diversions together; it grew suddenly populous, and the concourse of people was incredible. This consequently raised the rate of lodgings, and that increased buildings, till the town grew up from a little village, to a magnitude equal to some cities; nor could the uneven surface, inconvenient for building, uncompact, and unpleasant, check the humour of the town, for even on the very steep of the hill, where there's no walking twenty yards together, without tugging up a hill, or straddling down a hill, yet 'tis all one, the buildings increased to that degree, that the town almost spreads the whole side of the hill.

On the top of the hill indeed, there is a very pleasant plain, called the Heath, which on the very summit, is a plain of about a mile every way and in good weather 'tis pleasant airing upon it, and some of the streets are extended so far, as that they begin to build, even on the highest part of the hill. But it must be confessed, 'tis so near heaven, that I dare not say it can be a proper situation, for any but a race of mountaineers, whose lungs have been used to a rarified air, nearer the second region, than any ground for 30 miles round it.

Here is a most beautiful prospect indeed, for we see here Hanslop Steeple one way, which is within eight miles of Northampton, N.W. to Landown-Hill in Essex another way, east, at least 66 miles from one another; the prospect to London, and beyond it to Bansted Downs, south; Shooters-Hill, S.E. Red-Hill, S.W. and Windsor-Castle, W. is also uninterrupted. Indeed due north, we see no farther than to Barnet, which is not above six miles; but the rest is sufficient.

At the foot of this hill is an old seat of the Earls of Chesterfields, called Bellsize; which for many years had been neglected, and as it were forgotten. But being taken lately by a certain projector to get a penny, and who knew by what handle to take the gay part of the world, he has made it a true house of pleasure.[5] This brought a wonderful concourse of people to the place, for they were so effectually gratified in all sorts of diversion, that the wicked part at length broke in, till it alarmed the magistrates, and I am told it has been now in a manner suppressed by the hand of justice. Here was a great room fitted up with abundance of dexterity for their balls. One saw pictures and furniture there beyond what was to have been expected in a mere public house; and 'tis hardly credible how it drew company to it. But it could not be, no British government could be supposed to bear long with the liberties taken on such public occasions. So as I have said, they are reduced, at least restrained from liberties which they could not preserve by their prudence.

Yet Hampstead is not much the less frequented for this. But as there is (especially at the Wells) a conflux of all sorts of company, even Hampstead itself has suffered in its good name; and you see sometimes more gallantry than modesty: so that the ladies who value their reputation, have of late more avoided the wells and walks at Hampstead, than they had formerly done.

I could not be at Hampstead, and not make an excursion to Edgworth, a little market town. From Hide-Park Corner, just where Tyburn stands, the road makes one straight line without any turning, even to the very town of St Albans. In this road lies the town of Edgworth, some will have it that it was built by King Edgar the Saxon monarch, and called by his name, and so will have the town called Edgar, and that it was built as a garrison on the said Watling-street, to preserve the high-way from thieves: but all this I take to be fabulous, and without authority.

Near this town, and which is the reason for naming it, the present Duke of Chandos [6] has built a most magnificent palace or mansion house, I might say, the most magnificent in England. This palace is so beautiful in its situation, so lofty, so majestic the appearance of it, that a pen can but ill describe it, the pencil not much better; 'tis only fit to be talked of upon the very spot, when the building is under view, to be considered in all its parts.

The fronts are all of freestone, the columns and pilasters are lofty and beautiful, the windows very high, with all possible ornaments. In a word, the whole structure is built with such a profusion of expense, and all finished with such a brightness of fancy, goodness of judgment; that I can assure you, we see many palaces of sovereign princes abroad, which do not equal it, which yet pass for very fine too either within or without. No ornament is wanting to make it the finest house in England. The plastering and gilding is done by the famous Pargotti an Italian, said to be the finest artist in those particular works now in England. The great salon or hall is painted by Paolucci,[7] for the Duke spared no cost to have every thing as rich as possible. The pillars supporting the building are all of marble: the great staircase is the finest by far of any in England; and the steps are all of marble, every step being of one whole piece, about 22 foot in length.

Nor is the splendour which the present Duke lives in at this place, at all beneath what such a building calls for, and yet, so far is the Duke from having exhausted himself by this prodigy of building; that we see him since that laying out a scheme, and storing up materials for building another house for his city convenience, on the north side of the new square, called Oxford or Cavendish Square,[8] near Maribone; and if that is discontinued it seems to be so, only because the Duke found an opportunity to purchase another much more to his advantage; namely, the Duke of Ormond's house in St James's Square.

It is in vain to attempt to describe the beauties of this building at Cannons; the whole is a beauty, and as the firmament is a glorious mantle filled with, or as it were made up of a concurrence of lesser glories the stars; so every part of this building adds to the beauty of the whole. The avenue is spacious and majestic, and as it gives you the view of two fronts, joined as it were in one, the distance not admitting you to see the angle, which is in the centre; so you are agreeably drawn in, to think the front of the house almost twice as large as it really is. And yet when you come nearer you are again surprised, by seeing the winding passage opening as it were a new front to the eye, of near 120 feet wide, which you had not seen before, so that you are lost a while in looking near hand for what you so evidently saw a great way off.

The great palaces in Italy, are either the work of sovereign princes, or have been ages in their building; one family laying the design, and ten succeeding ages and families being taken up, in carrying on the building. But Cannons had not been three years in the Duke's possession, before we saw this prodigy rise out of the ground, as if he had been resolved to merit that motto which the French king assumed, He saw, and it was made.

The inside of this house is as glorious, as the outside is fine; the lodgings are indeed most exquisitely finished, and if I may call it so, royally furnished; the chapel is a singularity, not only in its building, and the beauty of its workmanship, but in this also, that the Duke maintains there a full choir, and has the worship performed there with the best music, after the manner of the Chapel Royal, which is not done in any other noble man's chapel in Britain; no not the Prince of Wales's, though heir apparent to the crown.

Nor is the chapel only furnished with such excellent music, but the Duke has a set of them to entertain him every day at dinner.

In his gardens and out-houses the Duke keeps a constant night-guard, who take care of the whole place, duly walk the rounds, and constantly give the hour to the family at set appointed places and times; so that the house has some waking eyes about it, to keep out thieves and spoilers night and day. In a word, no nobleman in England, and very few in Europe, lives in greater splendour, or maintains a grandeur and magnificence, equal to the Duke of Chandos. Here are continually maintained, and that in the dearest part of England, as to house expenses, not less than one hundred and twenty in family, and yet a face of plenty appears in every part of it; nothing needful is with-held, nothing pleasant is restrained; every servant in the house is made easy, and his life comfortable; and they have the felicity that it is their lord's desire and delight that it should be so.

Two mile from hence, we enter a spacious heath or common called Bushy-Heath, where, again, we have a very agreeable prospect.

I cannot but remember, with some satisfaction, that having two foreign gentlemen in my company, in our passing over this heath, I say I could not but then observe, and now remember it with satisfaction, how they were surprised at the beauty of this prospect, and how they looked at one another, and then again turning their eyes every way in a kind of wonder, one of them said to the other, that England was not like other countries, but it was all a planted garden.

They had there on the right hand, the town of St Albans in their view; and all the spaces between, and further beyond it, looked indeed like a garden. The enclosed corn-fields made one grand parterre, the thick planted hedge rows, like a wilderness or labyrinth, divided in espaliers; the villages interspersed, looked like so many several noble seats of gentlemen at a distance. In a word, it was all nature, and yet looked all like art; on the left hand we see the west-end of London, Westminster-Abbey, and the Parliament-House, but the body of the city was cut off by the hill, at which Hampstead intercepted the sight on that side. More to the south we had Hampton Court, and S.W. Windsor, and between both, all those most beautiful parts of Middlesex and Surrey, on the bank of the Thames.

At the farther end of this heath, is the town of Bushy, and at the end of the town, the Earl of Essex[9] has a very good old seat, situate in a pleasant park, at Cashiobery; a little farther, is the town of Hemstead, noted for an extraordinary corn-market, and at Ashridge, near Hemstead, is an ancient mansion house of the Duke of Bridge-water.

St Albans is the capital town, though not the county town of Hertfordshire, it has a great corn market, and is famous for its ancient church, built on the ruins, or part of the ruins of the most famous abbey of Verulam; the greatness of which, is to be judged by the old walls, which one sees for a mile before we come to town.

In this church as some workmen were digging for the repairs of the church, they found some steps which led to a door in a very thick stone wall, which being opened, there was discovered an arched stone vault, and in the middle of it a large coffin near 7 foot long, which being opened, there was in it the corpse of a man, the flesh not consumed, but discoloured; by the arms and other paintings on the wall, it appeared that this must be the body of Humphry Duke of Gloucester, commonly called the good Duke of Gloucester, one of the sons of Henry IV and brother to King Henry V, and by the most indisputable authority, must have lain buried there 277 years.

But I must travel no farther this way, till I have taken a journey west from London, and seen what the country affords that way; the next towns adjacent to London, are, Kensington, Chelsea, Hammersmith, Fulham, Twickenham, &c. all of them near, or adjoining to the river of Thames, and which, by the beauty of their buildings, make good the north shore of the river, answerable, to what I have already described.

Kensington cannot be named without mentioning the king's palace[10] there; a building which may now be called entirely new, though it was originally an old house of the Earl of Nottingham's of whom the late King William bought it, and then enlarged it as we see; some of the old building still remaining in the centre of the house.

The house itself fronts to the garden three ways, the gardens being now made exceeding fine, and enlarged to such a degree, as to reach quite from the great road to Kensington town, to the Acton road north, more than a mile. The first laying out of these gardens was the design of the late Queen Mary, who finding the air agreed with, and was necessary to the health of the king, resolved to make it agreeable to her self too, and gave the first orders for enlarging the gardens: the author of this account, having had the honour to attend her majesty, when she first viewed the ground, and directed the doing it, speaks this with the more satisfaction.

But this house has lost much of its pleasantness on one account, namely, that all the princes that ever might be said to single it out for their delight, had the fate to die in it; namely, King William, Prince George of Denmark,[11] and lastly, Queen Anne her self; since which it has not been so much in request, King George having generally kept his summer, when in England, at Hampton Court.

This south wing was burnt down by accident, the king and queen being both there, the queen was a little surprised at first, apprehending some treason, but King William a stranger to fears smiled at the suggestion, cheered her majesty up, and being soon dressed, they both walked out into the garden, and stood there some hours till they perceived the fire by the help that came in, and by the diligence of the foot guards, was gotten under foot.

It is no wonder if the Court being so much at Kensington, that town has increased in buildings, so I do not place that to the same account as of the rest. On the south side of the street over against the palace, is a fair new large street, and a little way down a noble square full of very good houses, but since the Court has so much declined the palace, the buildings have not much increased.

South of this town stands Chelsea, a town of palaces, and which by its new extended buildings seems to promise itself to be made one time or other a part of London, I mean London in its new extended capacity, which if it should once happen, what a monster must London be, extending (to take it in a line) from the farther end of Chelsea, west, to Deptford-Bridge east, which I venture to say, is at least eleven miles.

Here is the noblest building, and the best foundation of its kind in the world, viz. for the entertainment of maimed and old soldiers. If we must except the hospital called Des Invalids at Paris, it must be only that the number is greater there, but I pretend to say that the economy of the invalids there, is not to compare with this at Chelsea; and as for the provisions, the lodging and attendance given, Chelsea infinitely exceeds that at Paris. Here the poor men are lodged, well clothed, well furnished, and well fed, and I dare say there are thousands of poor families in England who are said to live well too, and do not feed as the soldiers there are fed; and as for France, I may add, they know nothing there what it is to live so. The like may be said of the invalid sea men at the hospital of Greenwich.

Near this hospital or college, is a little palace, I had almost called it a paradise, of the late Earl of Ranelagh.[12] It is true that his lordship was envied for the work, but had it been only for the beauties of the building, and such things as these, I should have been hardly able to censure it, the temptation would have been so much. In a word, the situation, the house, the gardens, the pictures, the prospect, and the lady, all is such a charm; who could refrain from coveting his neighbour's . . . &c.

Let it suffice to tell you that there's an incredible number of fine houses built in all these towns within these few years, and that England never had such a glorious show to make in the world before. In a word, being curious in this part of my enquiry, I find two thousand houses which in other places would pass for palaces, and most, if not all the possessors whereof, keep coaches in the little towns or villages of the county of Middlesex, west of London only; and not reckoning any of the towns within three miles of London. Among all these three thousand houses I reckon none but such, as are built since the year 1666, and most of them since the Revolution.

Among these, that is to say, among the first two thousand new foundations, there are very many houses belonging to the nobility, and to persons of quality, (some of whom) have been in the ministry; which excel all the rest; such as Secretary Johnson's,[13] and others. This last is a seat so exquisitely finished, that his majesty was pleased to dine there, to view the delightful place, and honour it with his presence, that very day, that I was writing this account of it. The king was pleased to dine in the green house, or rather in a pleasant room which Mr Johnson built, joining to the green house; from whence is a prospect every way into the most delicious gardens. Here is a complete vineyard, and Mr Johnson who is a master of gardening, perhaps the greatest master now in England, has given a testimony that England notwithstanding the changeable air and uncertain climate, will produce most excellent wines, if due care be taken in the gardening or cultivating, as also in the curing and managing part; and without due care in these, not France it self will do it.

In the village of Hammersmith, which was formerly a long scattering place, full of gardeners' grounds, with here and there an old house of some bulk: I say, in this village we see now not only a wood of great houses and palaces, but a noble square built as it were in the middle of several handsome streets, as if the village seemed inclined to grow up into a city. Here we are told they design to obtain the grant of a market, though it be so near to London, and some talk also of building a fine stone bridge over the Thames; but these things are yet but in embryo, though it is not unlikely but they may be both accomplished in time, and also Hammersmith and Chiswick joining thus, would in time be a city indeed.

I have now ranged the best part of Middlesex, a county made rich, pleasant, and populous by the neighbourhood of London. The borders of the county indeed have three market towns; which I shall but just mention, Stanes, Colebrook, and Uxbridge. This last, a pleasant large market town, famous in particular, for having abundance of noble seats of gentlemen and persons of quality in the neighbourhood. This town is also famous in story, for being the town where an attempt was in vain made in the late war, to settle the peace of these nations, by a treaty. Some say both sides were sincerely inclined to peace; some say neither side; all I can say of it is, in the words of blessed St Paul,[14] Sathan hindered.

On the right hand as we ride from London to Uxbridge, or to Colebrook, we see Harrow, a little town on a very high hill, and is therefore called Harrow on the Hill. The church of this town standing upon the summit of the hill, and having a very handsome and high spire, they tell us, King Charles, ridiculing the warm disputes among some critical scripturalists of those times, concerning the visible church of Christ upon earth; used to say of it, that if there was e'er a visible church upon earth, he believed this was one.

From hence, we proceeded on the road towards Oxford; but first turned to the right to visit Aylesbury. This is the principal market town in the county of Bucks; though Buckingham a much inferior place, is called the county town. Here also is held the election for Members of Parliament, or knights of the shire for the county, and county gaol, and the assizes. It is a large town, has a very noble market for corn, and is famous for a large tract of the richest land in England, extended for many miles round. It was my hap formerly, to be at Aylesbury, when there was a mighty confluence of noblemen and gentlemen, at a famous horse race at Quainton-Meadow, not far off, where was then the late Duke of Monmouth,[15] and a great many persons of the first rank, and a prodigious concourse of people.

Were there not in every part of England at this time so many fine palaces, and so many curious gardens, that it would but be a repetition of the same thing to describe them; I should enter upon that task with great cheerfulness here, as at Clifden, the Earl of Orkney's [16] fine seat near Windsor, and at several other places, but I proceed. We went on from Aylesbury to Thame or Tame, a large market town on the

River Thames. This brings me to mention the Vale of Aylesbury; which is eminent for the richest land, and perhaps the richest graziers in England. But it is more particularly famous for the head of the River Thame or Thames, which rises in this vale near a market town called Tring, and waters the whole vale either by itself or the several streams which run into it, and when it comes to the town of Tame, is a good large river.

At Tring abovenamed is a most delicious house, built *à la moderne*, as the French call it, by the late Mr Guy,[17] who was for many years Secretary of the Treasury, and continued it till near his death; when he was succeeded by the late Mr Lowndes. There was an eminent contest here between Mr Guy, and the poor of the parish, about his enclosing part of the common to make him a park; Mr Guy presuming upon his power, set up his pales, and took in a large parcel of open land, called Wiggington-Common; the cottagers and farmers opposed it, by their complaints a great while; but finding he went on with his work, and resolved to do it, they rose upon him, pulled down his banks, and forced up his pales, and carried away the wood, or set it on a heap and burnt it; and this they did several times, till he was obliged to desist. After some time he began again, offering to treat with the people, and to give them any equivalent for it. But that not being satisfactory, they mobbed him again. How they accommodated it at last, I know not: I mention this as an instance of the popular claim in England; which we call right of commonage, which the poor take to be as much their property, as a rich man's land is his own.

From Thame, a great corn market, the Thame joins the other branch called also the Thames, at a little town called Dorchester. I observe that most of our historians reject the notion that Mr Cambden makes so many flourishes about, of the marriage of Thame and Isis; that this little river was called the Thame, and the other, the Isis; and that being joined, they obtained the united name of Thamisis: I may say they reject it, and so do I.

From hence I came to Oxford, a name known throughout the learned world; a city famous in our English history for several things, besides its being an university.

1. So eminent for the goodness of its air, and healthy situation; that our Courts have no less than three times, if my information is right, retired hither, when London has been visited with the pestilence; and here they have been always safe.

2. It has also several times been the retreat of our princes, when the rest of the kingdom has been embroiled in war and rebellion; and here they have found both safety and support; at least, as long as the loyal inhabitants were able to protect them.

3. It was famous for the noble defence of religion, which our first reformers and martyrs made here, in their learned and bold disputations against the Papists, in behalf of the Protestant religion; and their triumphant closing the debates, by laying down their lives for the truths which they asserted.

4. It was likewise famous for resisting the attacks of arbitrary power, in the affair of Magdalen College,[18] in King James's time; and the Fellows laying down their fortunes, though not their lives, in defence of liberty and property.

This, to use a scripture elegance, is that city of Oxford; the greatest (if not the most ancient) university in this island of Great-Britain; and perhaps the most flourishing at this time, in men of polite learning, and in the most accomplished masters in all sciences, and in all the parts of acquired knowledge in the world.

I know there is a long contest, and yet undetermined between the two English universities, about the antiquity of their foundation; and as they have not decided it themselves, who am I? and what is this work? that I should pretend to enter upon that important question, in so small a tract?

It is out of question, that in the largeness of the place, the beauty of situation, the number of inhabitants, and of scholars, Oxford has the advantage. But fame tells us, that as great and applauded men, as much recommended, and as much recommending themselves to the world, and as many of them have been produced from Cambridge, as from Oxford.

Oxford has several things as a university, which Cambridge has not; and Cambridge ought not to be so meanly thought of, but that it has several things in it, which cannot be found in Oxford. For example, the theatre, the museum, or chamber of rarities, the Bodleian Library, the number of colleges, and the magnificence of their buildings are on the side of Oxford, yet King's College Chapel, and College, is in favour of Cambridge; for as it is now edifying, it is likely to be the most admired in a few years of all the colleges of the world.

I have said something of Cambridge; I'll be as brief about Oxford as I can. It is a noble flourishing city, so possessed of all that can contribute to make the residence of the scholars easy and comfortable, that no spot of ground in England goes beyond it. The situation is in a delightful plain, on the bank of a fine navigable river, in a plentiful country, and at an easy distance from the capital city, the port of the country.

To enter into the detail or description of all the colleges, halls, &c. would be to write a history of Oxford, which in so little a compass as this work can afford, must be so imperfect, so superficial, and so far from giving a stranger a true idea of the place; that it seems ridiculous, even to think it can be to anyone's satisfaction.

As therefore I did in the speaking of Cambridge, I shall now give a summary of what a traveller may be supposed to observe in Oxford, *en passant*, and leave the curious inquirer to examine the histories of the place. There are in Oxford 17 colleges, and seven halls, some of these colleges as particularly, Christ Church, Magdalen, New College, Corpus Christi, Trinity and St John's will be found to be equal, if not superior to some universities abroad; whether we consider the number of the scholars, the greatness of their revenues, or the magnificence of their buildings.

Besides the colleges, some of which are extremely fine and magnificent; there are some public buildings which make a most glorious appearance. The first and greatest of all is the theatre, a building not to be equalled by any thing of its kind in the world; no, not in Italy itself. Not that the building of the theatre here is as large as Vespasian's or that of Trajan at Rome; neither would any thing of that kind be an ornament at this time, because not at all suited to the occasion, the uses of them being quite different.

We see by the remains that those amphitheatres, as they were for the exercise of their public shows, and to entertain a vast concourse of people, to see the fighting of the gladiators, the throwing criminals to the wild beasts, and the like, were rather great magnificent bear-gardens, than theatres, for the actors of such representations, as entertained the polite part of the world; consequently, those were vast piles of building proper for the uses for which they were built.

The theatre at Oxford prepared for the public exercises of the schools, and for the operations of the learned part of the English world only, is in its grandeur and magnificence, infinitely superior to any thing in the world of its kind; it is a finished piece, as to its building, the front is exquisitely fine, the columns and pilasters regular, and very beautiful; 'tis all built of freestone. The model was approved by the best masters of architecture at that time, in the presence of K. Charles II, who was himself a very curious observer, and a good judge; Sir Christopher Wren was the director of the work, as he was the person that drew the model: Archbishop Sheldon,[19] they tell us, paid for it, and gave it to the university. There is a world of decoration in the front of it, and more beautiful additions, by way of ornament, besides the ancient inscription, than is to be seen any where in Europe; at least, where I have been.

The Bodleian Library is an ornament in it self worthy of Oxford, where its station is fixed, and where it had its birth. The old library, the first public one in Oxford, was afterward joined to another, and both enlarged by the bounty of Humphry Duke of Gloucester, founder of the divinity schools: these libraries being lost, and the books embezzled by the many changes and hurries of the suppressions in the reign of Henry VIII the commissioners appointed by King Edward VI to visit the universities, and establish the Reformation; found very few valuable books or manuscripts left in them.

In this state of things, one Sir Thomas Bodley,[20] a wealthy and learned knight, zealous for the encouragement both of learning and religion, resolved to apply, both his time, and estate, to the erecting and furnishing a new library for the public use of the university.

In this good and charitable undertaking, he went on so successfully, for so many years, and with such a profusion of expense, and obtained such assistances from all the encouragers of learning in his time, that having collected books and manuscripts from all parts of the learned world; he got leave of the university, (and well they might grant it) to place them in the old library room, built as is said, by the good Duke Humphry.

To this great work, great additions have been since made in books, as well as contributions in money, and more are adding every day; and thus the work was brought to a head, the 8th of Nov. 1602, and has continued increasing by the benefactions of great and learned men to this day. To remove the books once more and place them in beauty and splendour suitable to so glorious a collection, the late Dr Radcliff [21] has left a legacy of 40000*l*. say some, others say not quite so much, to the building a new repository or library for the use of the university. This work is not yet built, but I am told 'tis likely to be such a building as will be greater ornament to the place than any yet standing in it.

Other curious things in Oxford are, the museum, the chamber of rarities, the collection of coins, medals, pictures and ancient inscriptions, the physic-garden, &c.

It is no part of my work to enter into the dispute between the two universities about the antiquity of their foundation. But this I shall observe for the use of those who insist that it was the piety of the Popish times to which we owe the first institution of the university it self, the foundation and endowment of the particular colleges, and the encouragement arising to learning from thence, all which I readily grant; but would have them remember too, that though those foundations stood as they tell us eight hundred years, and that the Reformation as they say, is not yet of 200 years standing, yet learning has more increased and the universities flourished more; more great scholars been produced, greater libraries been raised, and more fine buildings been erected in these 200 years than in the 800 years of Popery; and I might add, as many great benefactions have been given, notwithstanding this very momentous difference; that the Protestant's gifts are merely acts of charity to the world, and acts of bounty, in reverence to learning and learned men, without the grand excitement of the health of their souls, and of the souls of their fathers, to be prayed out of purgatory and get a ready admission into heaven, and the like.

Oxford, had for many ages the neighbourhood of the Court, while their kings kept up the royal palace at Woodstock; which though perhaps it was much discontinued, for the fate of the fair Rosamond,[22] mistress to Henry Fitz Empress, or Henry II, of which history tells us something, and fable much more; yet we after find that several of the kings of England made the house and park at Woodstock, which was always famed for its pleasant situation, the place of their summer retreat for many years.

It is still a most charming situation, and 'tis still disputable after all that has been laid out, whether the country round gives more lustre to the building, or the building to the country. It has now changed masters, 'tis no more a royal house or palace for the king; but a mark of royal bounty to a great, and at that time powerful subject, the late Duke of Marlborough.[23]

The magnificence of the building does not here as at Canons, at Chatsworth, and at other palaces of the nobility, express the genius and the opulence of the possessor, but it represents the bounty, the gratitude, or what else posterity pleases to call it, of the English nation, to the man whom they delighted to honour. Posterity when they view in this house the trophies of the Duke of Marlborough's fame, and the glories of his great achievements will not celebrate his name only; but will look on Blenheim House, as a monument of the generous temper of the English nation; who in so glorious a manner rewarded the services of those who acted for them as he did. Nor can any nation in Europe show the like munificence to any general, no nor the greatest in the world.

Again, it is to be considered, that not this house only, built at the nation's expense, was thus given; but lands and pensions to the value of above one hundred thousand pounds sterl. and honours the greatest England can bestow. These are all honours indeed to the Duke, but infinitely more to the honour of the nation.

The magnificent work then is a national building, and must for ever be called so. Nothing else can justify the vast design, a bridge or *ryalto* rather, of one arch costing 20000l. and this, like the bridge at the Escurial in Spain, without a river. Gardens of near 100 acres of ground. Offices fit for 300 in family. Out-houses fit for the lodgings of a regiment of guards, rather than of livery servants. Also the extent of the fabric, the avenues, the salons, galleries, and royal apartments; nothing below royalty and a prince, can support an equipage suitable to the living in such a house. And one may without a spirit of prophecy, say, it seems to intimate, that some time or other Blenheim may and will return to be as the old Woodstock once was, the palace of a king.

I shall enter no farther into the description, because 'tis yet a house unfurnished, and it can only be properly said what it is to be, not what it is: but as the Duke is dead, the Duchess old, and the heir abroad, when and how it shall be all performed, requires more of the gift of prophecy than I am master of.

From Woodstock I could not refrain taking a turn a little northward as high as Banbury to the banks of the Charwell, to see the famous spot of ground where a vigorous rencounter happened between the Royalists in the grand Rebellion, and the Parliament's forces, under Sir William Waller; I mean at Croprady Bridge,[24] near Banbury. It was a vigorous action, and in which the king's forces may be said fairly to outgeneral their enemies, which really was not always their fate. I had the plan of that action before me, which I have had some years, and found out every step of the ground as it was disputed on both sides by inches, where the horse engaged and where the foot, where Waller lost his cannon, and where he retired; and it was evident to me the best thing Waller could do, (though superior in number) was to retreat as he did, having lost half his army.

From thence, being within eight miles of Edge-Hill,[25] where the first battle in that war happened, I had the like pleasure of viewing the ground about Keinton, where that bloody battle was fought; it was evident, and one could hardly think of it without regret, the king with his army had an infinite advantage by being posted on the top of the hill, that he knew that the Parliament's army were under express orders to fight, and must attack him lest his majesty who had got two days' march of them, should advance to London, where they were out of their wits for fear of him.

The king I say knowing this, 'tis plain he had no business but to have entrenched, to fight upon the eminence where he was posted, or have detached 15000 men for London, while he had fortified himself with a strong body upon the hill. But on the contrary, his majesty scorning to be pursued by his subjects, his army excellently appointed, and full of courage, not only halted, but descended from his advantages and offered them battle in the plain field, which they accepted.

Here I cannot but remark that this action is perhaps the only example in the world, of a battle so furious, so obstinate, managed with such skill, every regiment behaving well, and doing their duty to the utmost, often rallying when disordered, and indeed fighting with the courage and order of veterans; and yet not one regiment of troops that had ever seen the face of an enemy, or so much as been in arms before. It's true, the king had rather the better of the day; and yet the rebel army though their left wing of horse was entirely defeated, behaved so well, that at best it might be called a drawn battle; and the loss on both sides was so equal, that it was hard to know who lost most men.

But to leave the war, 'tis the place only I am taking notice of. From hence I turned south, for I was here on the edge both of Warwickshire, and Gloucestershire. But I turned south, and coming down by and upon the west side of Oxfordshire, to Chipping-Norton, we were showed Roll-Richt-Stones, a second Stone-Henge; being a ring of great stones standing upright, some of them from 5 to 7 foot high. I leave the debate about the reason and antiquity of this ancient work to the dispute of the learned, who yet cannot agree about them any more than about Stone-Henge in Wiltshire.

We were very merry at passing through a village called Bloxham, on the occasion of a meeting of servants for hire, which the people there call a Mop; 'tis generally in other places vulgarly called a Statute, because founded upon a statute law [26] in Q. Elizabeth's time for regulating of servants. This I christened by the name of a Jade-Fair, at which some of the poor girls began to be angry, but we appeased them with better words. I have observed at some of these fairs, that the poor servants distinguish themselves by holding something in their hands, to intimate what labour they are particularly qualified to undertake; as the carters a whip, the labourers a shovel, the wood man a bill, the manufacturers a wool comb, and the like. But since the ways and manners of servants are advanced as we now find them to be, those Jade Fairs are not so much frequented as formerly.

Here we saw also the famous parish of Brightwell, of which it was observed, that there had not been an alehouse nor a dissenter from the church, nor any quarrel among the inhabitants that rise so high as to a suit of law within the memory of man. But they could not say it was so still, especially as to the alehouse part; though very much is still preserved, as to the unity and good neighbourhood of the parishioners, and their conformity to the church.

Hence we came to the famous Cotswold-Downs, so eminent for the best of sheep, and finest wool in England: it was of the breed of these sheep. And fame tells us that some were sent by King Richard I into Spain, and that from thence the breed of their sheep was raised, which now produce so fine a wool, that we are obliged to fetch it from thence, for the making our finest broad cloths; and which we buy at so great a price.

Upon these downs we had a clear view of the famous old Roman high-way, called the Fosse, which evidently crosses all the middle part of England, and is to be seen and known (though in no place plainer than here,) quite from the Bath to Warwick, and thence to Leicester, to Newark, to Lincoln, and on to Barton, upon the bank of Humber.

Here it is still the common road, and we followed it over the downs to Cirencester. We observed also how several cross roads as ancient as it self, and perhaps more ancient, joined it, or branched out of it; some of which the people have by ancient usage though corruptly called also Fosses, making the word Fosse as it were a common name for all roads. For example, the Ackemanstreet which is an ancient Saxon road leading from Buckinghamshire through Oxfordshire to the Fosse, and so to the Bath; this joins the Fosse between Burford and Cirencester. It is worth observing how this is said to be called Ackeman's Street; namely, by the Saxon way of joining their monosyllables into significant words, as thus, *ackman* or *achman*, a man of aching limbs, in English a *cripple* travelling to the Bath for cure. So Achmanstreet was the road or street for diseased people going to the Bath; and the city of Bath was on the same account called Achmanchester, or the city of diseased people; or, *Urbs Ægrotorum hominum*. Thus much for antiquity.

In passing this way we very remarkably crossed four rivers within the length of about 10 miles, and enquiring their names, the country people called them every one the Thames, which moved me a little to enquire the reason, which is no more than this; namely, that these rivers, which are, the Lech, the Coln, the Churn, and the Isis; all rising in the Cotswold Hills and joining together and making a full stream at Lechlade near this place, they become one river there, and are all called Thames, or vulgarly Temms; also beginning there to be navigable, you see very large barges at the key, taking in goods for London, which makes the town of Lechlade a very populous large place.

On the Churne one of those rivers stands Cirencester, or Ciciter for brevity, a very good town, populous and rich, full of clothiers, and driving a great trade in wool; which as likewise at Tetbury, is brought from the midland counties of Leicester, Northampton, and Lincoln, where the largest sheep in England are found, and where are few manufactures; it is sold here in quantities, so great, that it almost exceeds belief.

As we go on upon the Fosse, we see in the vale on the left hand, the ancient town of Malmsbury, famous for a monastery, and a great church, built out of the ruins of it. We next arrived at Marshfield, a Wiltshire clothing town, very flourishing and in the evening keeping still the Fosse-Way, we arrived at Bath.

My description of this city would be very short, and indeed it would have been a very small city, (if at all a city) were it not for the hot baths here, which give both name and fame to the place.

The antiquity of this place, and of the baths here, is doubtless very great, though I cannot come in to the inscription under the figure, said to be of a British king, placed in that called the King's Bath, which says that this King Bladud [27] found out the use of these baths, 300 years before our Saviour's time. I say, I cannot come into this, because even the discovery is ascribed to the magic of the day, not their judgment in the physical virtue of minerals, and mineral-waters.

There remains little to add, but what relates to the modern customs, the gallantry and diversions of that place, in which

I shall be very short. It has been observed before, that in former times this was a resort hither for cripples; and we see the crutches hang up at the several baths, as the thank-offerings of those who have come hither lame, and gone away cured. But now we may say it is the resort of the sound, rather than the sick; the bathing is made more a sport and diversion, than a physical prescription for health; and the town is taken up in raffling, gaming, visiting, and in a word, all sorts of gallantry and levity.

The whole time indeed is a round of the utmost diversion. In the morning you (supposing you to be a young lady) are fetched in a close chair, dressed in your bathing clothes, that is, stripped to the smock, to the Cross-Bath. There the music plays you into the bath, and the women that tend you, present you with a little floating wooden dish, like a basin; in which the lady puts a handkerchief, and a nosegay, of late the snuff-box is added, and some patches; though the bath occasioning a little perspiration, the patches do not stick so kindly as they should.

Here the ladies and the gentlemen pretend to keep some distance, and each to their proper side, but frequently mingle here too, as in the King and Queens Bath, though not so often; and the place being but narrow, they converse freely, and talk, rally, make vows, and sometimes love; and having thus amused themselves an hour, or two, they call their chairs and return to their lodgings.

The rest of the diversion here, is the walks in the great church, and at the raffling shops, which are kept (like the cloister at Bartholomew Fair,) in the churchyard, and ground adjoining. In the afternoon there is generally a play, though the decorations are mean, and the performances accordingly; but it answers, for the company here (not the actors) make the play, to say no more. In the evening there is a ball, and dancing at least twice a week, which is commonly in the great town hall, over the market-house; where there never fails in the season to be a great deal of very good company.

There is one thing very observable here, which though it

brings abundance of company to the Bath, more than ever used to be there before; yet it seems to have quite inverted the use and virtue of the waters, (viz.) that whereas for seventeen hundred or two thousand years, if you believe King Bladud, the medicinal virtue of these waters had been useful to the diseased people by bathing in them, now they are found to be useful also, taken into the body; and there are many more come to drink the waters, than to bathe in them; nor are the cures they perform this way, less valuable than the outward application; especially in colics, ill digestion, and scorbutic distempers.

This discovery they say, is not yet above fifty years old, and is said to be owing to the famous Dr Radcliff, but I think it must be older, for I have my self drank the waters of the Bath above fifty years ago. But be it so, 'tis certain, 'tis a modern discovery, compared to the former use of these waters.

On the N.W. of this city up a very steep hill, is the King's Down, where sometimes persons of quality who have coaches go up for the air. But very few people care to have coaches here, it being a place where they have but little room to keep them, and less to make use of them. And the hill up to the Downs is so steep, that the late Queen Anne was extremely frighted in going up, her coachman stopping to give the horses breath, and the coach wanting a dragstaff, run back in spite of all the coachman's skill; the horses not being brought to strain the harness again, or pull together for a good while, and the coach putting the guards behind it into the utmost confusion, till some of the servants setting their heads and shoulders to the wheels, stopped them by plain force.

Following the course of the river Avon, which runs through Bath, we come in ten miles to the city of Bristol, the greatest, the richest, and the best port of trade in Great Britain, London only excepted. The merchants of this city not only have the greatest trade, but they trade with a more entire independency upon London, than any other town in Britain. And 'tis evident in this particular, (viz.) that whatsoever exportations they make to any part of the world, they are able to bring the full returns back to their own port, and can dispose of it there. This is not the case in any other port in England. But they are often obliged to ship part of the effects in the ports abroad, on the ships bound to London; or to consign their own ships to London, in order both to get freight, as also to dispose of their own cargoes.

But the Bristol merchants as they have a very great trade abroad, so they have always buyers at home, for their returns, and that such buyers that no cargo is too big for them. To this purpose, the shopkeepers in Bristol who in general are all wholesale men, have so great an inland trade among all the western counties, that they maintain carriers just as the London tradesmen do, to all the principal countries and towns from Southampton in the south, even to the banks of the Trent north; and though they have no navigable river that way, yet they drive a very great trade through all those counties.

The greatest inconveniences of Bristol, are, its situation, and the tenacious folly of its inhabitants; who by the general infatuation, the pretence of freedoms and privileges, that corporation-tyranny, which prevents the flourishing and increase of many a good town in England, continue obstinately to forbid any, who are not subjects of their city sovereignty, (that is to say, freemen,) to trade within the chain of their own liberties; were it not for this, the city of Bristol, would before now, have swelled and increased in buildings and inhabitants, perhaps to double the magnitude it was formerly of.

This is evident by this one particular. There is one remarkable part of the city where the liberties extend not at all, or but very little without the city gate. Here and no where else, they have an accession of new inhabitants; and abundance of new houses, nay, some streets are built, and the like 'tis probable would have been at all the rest of the gates, if liberty had been given. As for the city itself, there is hardly room to set another house in it, 'tis so close built, except in the great square, the ground about which is a little too subject to the hazard of inundations: so that people do not so freely enlarge that way.

The Tolsey[28] of this city, (so they call their Exchange where their merchants meet,) has been a place too of great business, yet so straitened, so crowded, and so many ways inconvenient, that the merchants have been obliged to do less business there, than indeed the nature of their great trade requires. They have therefore long solicited, a sufficient authority of Parliament, empowering them to build a Royal Exchange; but there is not much progress yet made in this work, though if finished, it would add much to the beauty of the city of Bristol.

There are in Bristol 21 parish churches, many meeting-houses, especially Quakers, one (very mean) cathedral, the reason of which, may be, that it is but a very modern bishopric. It is supposed they have an hundred thousand inhabitants in the city, and within three miles of its circumference; and they say above three thousand sail of ships belong to that port, but of the last I am not certain.

'Tis very remarkable, that this city is so plentifully supplied with coals though they are all brought by land carriage, that yet they are generally bought by the inhabitants, laid down at their doors, after the rate of from seven to nine shillings per chaldron.

The situation of the city is low, but on the side of a rising hill. The ground plat of it is said very much to resemble that of old Rome, being circular, with something greater diameter one way than another, but not enough to make it oval: and the river cutting off one small part, as it were, a sixth, or less from the rest. They draw all their heavy goods here on sleds, or sledges without wheels, which kills a multitude of horses; and the pavement is worn so smooth by them, that in wet-weather the streets are very slippery, and in frosty-weather 'tis dangerous walking.

From this city I resolved to coast the marshes or border of Wales, especially South-Wales, by tracing the rivers Wye, and Lug, into Monmouth and Herefordshire. But I changed this resolution on the following occasion; namely, the badness and danger of the ferries over the Severn, besides, having formerly traversed these counties, I can without a re-visit, speak to every thing that is considerable in them, and shall do it in a letter by itself. But in the mean time, I resolved to follow the course of the famous River Severn, by which I should necessarily see the richest, most fertile, and most agreeable part of England; the bank of the Thames only excepted.

From Bristol West, you enter the county of Gloucester, and keeping the Avon in view, you see King Road, where the ships generally take their departure. There is also a little farther, an ugly, dangerous, and very inconvenient ferry over the Severn, to the mouth of Wye; namely, at Aust; the badness of the weather, and the sorry boats, at which, deterred us from crossing there.

As we turn north towards Gloucester, we lose the sight of the Avon, and in about two miles exchange it for an open view of the Severn Sea, which you see on the west side, and which is as broad as the ocean there; except, that looking N.W. you see plainly the coast of South Wales; and particularly a little nearer hand, the shore of Monmouthshire. Then as you go on, the shores begin to draw towards one another, and the coasts to lie parallel; so that the Severn appears to be a plain river, or an *æstuarium*, somewhat like the Humber, or as the Thames is at the Nore, being 4 to 5 and 6 miles over; and to give it no more than its just due, a most raging, turbulent, furious place. This is occasioned by those violent tides called the Bore, which flow here sometimes six or seven foot at once, rolling forward like a mighty wave: so that the stern of a vessel shall on a sudden be lifted up six or seven foot upon the water, when the head of it is fast a ground.

After coasting the shore about 4 miles farther, the road being by the low salt marshes, kept at a distance from the river: we came to the ferry called Aust Ferry, from a little dirty village called Aust; near which you come to take boat.

When we came to Aust, the hither side of the passage, the

sea was so broad, the fame of the Bore of the tide so formidable, the wind also made the water so rough, and which was worse, the boats to carry over both man and horse appeared (as I have said above) so very mean, that in short none of us cared to venture: so we came back, and resolved to keep on the road to Gloucester. By the way we visited some friends at a market-town, a little out of the road, called Chipping-Sodbury, a place of note for nothing that I saw, but the greatest cheese market in all that part of England; or, perhaps, any other, except Atherstone, in Warwickshire.

Hence we kept on north, passing by Dursley to Berkley-Castle; the ancient seat of the Earls of Berkley, a noble though ancient building, and a very fine park about it. I say nothing of the dark story of King Edward II of England;[29] who, all our learned writers agree, was murthered in this castle: as Richard II was in that of Pontefract, in Yorkshire; I say I take no more notice of it here, for history is not my present business. 'Tis true, they show the apartments where they say that king was kept prisoner: but they do not admit that he was killed there. The place is rather ancient, than pleasant or healthful, lying low, and near the water; but 'tis honoured by its present owner, known to the world for his many services to his country.

From hence to Gloucester, we see nothing considerable, but a most fertile, rich country, and a fine river, but narrower as you go northward, 'till a little before we come to Gloucester it ceases to be navigable by ships of burthen, but continues to be so, by large barges, above an hundred miles farther; not reckoning the turnings and windings of the river. Besides that, it receives several large and navigable rivers into it.

Gloucester is an ancient middling city, tolerably built, but not fine; was fortified and stood out obstinately against its lord King Charles the 1st, who besieged it to his great loss in the late Rebellion, for which it had all its walls and works demolished; for it was then very strong. Here is a large stone bridge over the Severn, the first next the sea; and this, and the cathedral is all I see worth recording of this place.

The cathedral is an old venerable pile, with very little ornament within or without, yet 'tis well built; and though plain, it makes together, especially the tower, a very handsome appearance. The inhabitants boast much of its antiquity, and tell us, that a bishop and preachers were placed here, in the very infancy of the Christian religion; namely, in the year 189. But this I take *ad referendum*. The cathedral they tell us has been three times burnt to the ground.

The whispering place in this cathedral, has for many years passed for a kind of wonder; but since, experience has taught us the easily comprehended reason of the thing: and since there is now the like in the church of St Paul, the wonder is much abated. However, the verses written over this whispering place, intimate, that it has really passed for something miraculous; and as the application rather shows religion, than philosophy in the author, the reader may not like them the worse.

> Doubt not, that God who sits on high,
> Thy secret prayers can hear;
> When a dead wall thus cunningly,
> Conveys soft whispers to thine ear.

From Gloucester we kept the east shore of the Severn, and in twelve miles came to Tewksbury, a large and very populous town situate upon the River Avon, this is called the Warwickshire Avon, to distinguish it from the Avon at Bristol and others, for there are several rivers in England of this name; and some tell us that *avona* was an old word in the British tongue signifying a river. This town is famous for a great manufacture of stockings, as are also, the towns of Pershore and Evesham, or Esham; on the same river.

The great old church at Tewksbury may indeed be called the largest private parish church in England; I mean, that is not a collegiate or cathedral church. This town is famous for the great, and as may be said, the last battle,[30] fought between the two houses of Lancaster and York, in which Edward IV was conqueror; and in, or rather after which, Prince Edward the only surviving son of the House of Lancaster, was killed by the cruel hands of Richard the king's brother; the same afterwards Richard III or Crookback Richard. In this place begins that fruitful and plentiful country which was called the Vale of Esham, which runs all along the banks of the Avon, to Stratford upon Avon, and in the south part of Warwickshire; and so far, (viz. to Stratford,) the River Avon is navigable.

At this last town, going into the parish church, we saw the monument of old Shakespear, the famous poet, and whose dramatic performances so justly maintain his character among the British poets; and perhaps will do so to the end of time. The busto of his head is in the wall on the north side of the church, and a flat grave-stone covers the body, in the aisle just under him. On which grave-stone these lines are written.

> Good friend, for Jesus's sake, forbear
> To move the dust that resteth here.
> Blest be the man that spares these stones,
> And curst be he, that moves my bones.

The navigation of this River Avon is an exceeding advantage to all this part of the country, and also to the commerce of the city of Bristol. For by this river they drive a very great trade for sugar, oil, wine, tobacco, iron, lead, and in a word, all heavy goods which are carried by water almost as far as Warwick; and in return the corn and especially the cheese, is brought back from Gloucestershire and Warwickshire, to Bristol.

Gloucestershire must not be passed over, without some account of a most pleasant and fruitful vale which crosses part of the country, from east to west on that side of the Cotswold, and which is called Stroud-Water; famous not for the finest cloths only, but for dying those cloths of the finest scarlets, and other grain colours that are any where in England; perhaps in any part of the world. The clothiers lie all along the banks of this river for near 20 miles, and in the town of

Stroud, which lies in the middle of it, as also at Paynswick, which is a market-town at a small distance north.

From Tewkesbury we went north 12 miles, to Worcester, all the way still on the bank of the Severn; and here we had the pleasing sight of the hedge-rows, being filled with apple trees and pear trees, and the fruit so common, that any passenger as they travel the road may gather and eat what they please; and here, as well as in Gloucestershire, you meet with cider in the public-houses sold as beer and ale is in other parts of England, and as cheap.

Worcester is a large, populous, old, though not a very well built city; I say not well built because the town is close and old, the houses standing too thick. The north part of the town is more extended and also better built. There is a good old stone bridge over the Severn, which stands exceeding high from the surface of the water. But as the stream of the Severn is contracted here by the buildings on either side, there is evident occasion sometimes for the height of the bridge, the waters rising to an incredible height in the winter-time.

It narrowly escaped burning, but did not escape plundering at the time when the Scots army commanded by King Ch. II in person, was attacked here by Cromwel's forces;[31] 'twas said some of the Royalist's officers themselves, proposed setting the city on fire, when they saw it was impossible to avoid a defeat, that they might the better make a retreat; which they proposed to do over the Severn, and so to march into Wales: but that the king, a prince from his youth, of a generous and merciful disposition would by no means consent to it.

I went to see the town-house, which afforded nothing worth taking notice of, unless it be how much it wants to be mended with a new one; which the city, they say, is not so much inclined, as they are able and rich to perform.

The cathedral of this city is an ancient, and indeed, a decayed building; the body of the church is very mean in its aspect, nor did I see the least ornament about it, I mean in the outside. The tower is low, without any spire, only four very small pinnacles on the corners; and yet the tower has some little beauty in it more than the church itself, too; and the upper part has some images in it, but decayed by time.

The inside of the church has several very ancient monuments in it, particularly some royal ones; as that of King John, who lies interred between two sainted bishops, namely, St Oswald, and St Woolstan.[32] Whether he ordered his interment in that manner, believing that they should help him *up* at the last call, and be serviceable to him for his salvation I know not; it is true they say so, but I can hardly think the king himself so ignorant, whatever the people might be in those days of superstition; nor will I say but that it may be probable, they may all three go together at last (as it is) and yet, without being assistant to, or acquainted with one another at all.

Here is also a monument for that famous Countess of Salisbury, who dancing before, or with K. Edward III in his great hall at Windsor, dropped her garter, which the king taking up, honoured it so much as to make it the denominating ensign of his new order of knighthood,[33] which is grown so famous, and is called the *most Noble* Order of the Garter. What honour, or that any honour redounds to that most noble order, from its being so derived from the garter of a - - - for 'tis generally agreed, she was the king's mistress, I will not enquire.

There are several other ancient monuments in this church, too many to be set down here. They reckon up 99 bishops of this diocese, beginning at the year 980, out of which catalogue they tell us have been furnished to the world, 1 Pope, 4 Saints, 7 High-Chancellors of England, 11 Arch-Bishops, 2 Lord Treasurers of England, 1 Chancellor to the Queen, 1 Lord President of Wales, and 1 Vice President.

This city is very full of people, and the people generally esteemed very rich, being full of business, occasioned chiefly by the clothing trade, of which the city and the country round carries on a great share, as well for the Turkey trade as for the home trade.

The salt springs in this county which were formerly

esteemed as next to miraculous, have since the discovery of the mines of rock salt in Lancashire, Cheshire, &c. lost all of wonder that belonged to them, and much of the use also; the salt made there being found to be much less valuable than what is now made of the other. So I need say little to them.

Near this city are the famous Maulvern Hills, or Mauvern Hills, and they say they are seen from the top of Salisbury steeple, which is above 50 miles. There was a famous monastery at the foot of these hills, on the S.W. side, and the ruins are seen to this day; the old legend of wonders performed by the witches of Mauvern, I suppose they mean the religieuse of both kinds, are too merry, as well as too ancient for this work.

They talk much of mines of gold and silver, which are certainly to be found here, if they were but looked for, and that Mauvern would outdo Potosi [34] for wealth; but 'tis probable if there is such wealth, it lies too deep for this idle generation to find out, and perhaps to search for.

There are three or four especial manufactures carried on in this country, which are peculiar to it self, or at least to this county with the two next adjoining; namely, Chester, and Warwick.

1. Monmouth cups sold chiefly to the Dutch seamen, and made only at Beawdly.

2. Fine stone pots for the glass-makers melting their metal, of which they make their fine flint glass, glass plates, &c. not to be found any where but at Stourbridge in this county, the same clay makes crucibles and other melting pots.

3. The Birmingham iron works: the north indeed claims a share or part of this trade, but it is only a part.

4. Kidderminster stuffs called lindsey woolseys, they are very rarely made any where else.

At Stourbridge also they have a very great manufacture for glass of all sorts.

From Worcester I took a tour into Wales, which though, it was not at the same time with the rest of my journey; my account I hope will be as effectual.

A little below Worcester the Severn receives a river of a long course and deep channel, called the Teme, and going from Worcester we passed this river at a village called Broadways; from whence keeping a little to the north, we come to Ludlow-Castle, on the bank of the same river. On another journey I came from Stourbridge, thence to Kidderminster, and passing the Severn at Bewdley we came to Ludlow, on the side of Shropshire.

The castle of Ludlow shows in its decay, what it was in its flourishing estate. It is the palace of the Princes of Wales, that is, to speak more properly, it is annexed to the principality of Wales; which is the appanage of the heir apparent, and this is his palace in right of his being made Prince of Wales.

The situation of this castle is most beautiful indeed; there is a most spacious plain or lawn in its front, which formerly continued near two miles; but much of it is now enclosed. The country round it is exceeding pleasant, fertile, populous, and the soil rich; nothing can be added by nature to make it a place fit for a royal palace. It only wants the residence of its princes, but that is not now to be expected.

The castle itself is in the very perfection of decay, all the fine courts, the royal apartments, halls, and rooms of state, lie open, abandoned and some of them falling down; for since the Courts of the President and Marches are taken away, here is nothing to do that requires the attendance of any public people; so that time, the great devourer of the works of men, begins to eat into the very stone walls, and to spread the face of royal ruins upon the whole fabric.

The town of Ludlow is a tolerable place, but it decays to be sure with the rest. King Henry VIII established the Court of the President here, and the Council of the Marches and all causes of *nisi prius*, or of civil right were tried here, before the Lord President and Council; but this Court was entirely taken away by Act of Parliament in our days,[35] and this, as above, tends to the sensible decay of the town as well as of the castle.

From Ludlow we took our course due south to Lemster, or Leominster, a large and good trading town on the River Lug. This river is lately made navigable by Act of Parliament, to the very great profit of the trading part of this country, who have now a very great trade for their corn, wool, and other products of this place, into the river Wye, and from the Wye, into the Severn, and so to Bristol.

Leominster has nothing very remarkable in it, but that it is a well built, well inhabited town. The church which is very large, has been in a manner rebuilt, and is now, especially in the inside, a very beautiful church. This town, besides the fine wool, is noted for the best wheat, and consequently the finest bread; whence Lemster bread, and Weobly ale, is become a proverbial saying.

The country on our right as we came from Ludlow is very fruitful and pleasant, and is called the Hundred of Wigmore, from which the late Earl of Oxford [36] at his creation, took the title of Baron of Wigmore. And here we saw two ancient castles, (viz.) Brampton-Brian, and Wigmore-Castle, both belonging to the Earl's father, Sir Edward Harley; Brampton is a stately pile, but not kept in full repair, the fate of that ancient family not permitting the rebuilding it as we were told was intended.

We were now on the borders of Wales, properly so called; for from the windows of Brampton-Castle, you have a fair prospect into the county of Radnor, which is, as it were, under its walls; nay, even this whole county of Hereford, was, if we may believe antiquity, a part of Wales, and was so esteemed for many ages. The people of this county too, boast that they were a part of the ancient Silures, who for so many ages withstood the Roman arms, and who could never be entirely conquered. But that's an affair quite beyond my enquiry. I observed they are a diligent and laborious people, chiefly addicted to husbandry, and they boast, perhaps, not without reason, that they have the finest wool, and the best hops, and the richest cider in all Britain.

Indeed the wool about Leominster, and in the Hundred of

Wigmore observed above, and the Golden Vale as 'tis called, for its richness on the banks of the river Dove, (all in this county) is the finest without exception, of any in England, the South Down wool not excepted. As for hops, they plant abundance indeed all over this county, and they are very good. And as for cider, here it was, that several times for 20 miles together, we could get no beer or ale in their public houses, only cider; and that so very good, so fine, and so cheap, that we never found fault with the exchange; great quantities of this cider are sent to London, even by land carriage, though so very remote, which is an evidence for the goodness of it, beyond contradiction.

One would hardly expect so pleasant, and fruitful a country as this, so near the barren mountains of Wales; but 'tis certain, that not any of our southern counties, the neighbourhood of London excepted, comes up to the fertility of this county.

From Lemster it is ten miles to Hereford, the chief city, not of this county only, but of all the counties west of Severn. 'Tis a large and a populous city, and in the time of the late Rebellion, was very strong, and being well fortified, and as well defended, supported a tedious and very severe siege; for besides the Parliament's forces, who could never reduce it, the Scots army was called to the work, who lay before it, 'till they laid above 4000 of their bones there, and at last, it was rather taken by the fate of the war, than by the attacks of the besiegers.

Coming to Hereford, we could not but enquire into the truth of the story; of the removing the two great stones near Sutton, which the people confirmed to us. The story is thus, between Sutton and Hereford, is a common meadow called the Wergins, where were placed two large stones for a watermark; one erected upright, and the other laid a-thwart. In the late Civil Wars, about the Year 1652, they were removed to about twelve score paces distance, and no body knew how; which gave occasion to a common opinion, that they were carried thither by the Devil. When they were set in their places again, one of them required nine yoke of oxen to draw it.

It is truly an old, mean built, and very dirty city, lying low, and on the bank of Wye, which sometimes incommodes them very much, by the violent freshes that come down from the mountains of Wales; for all the rivers of this county, except the Driffin-Doe, come out of Wales.

The chief thing remarkable next to the cathedral, is the college, which still retains its foundation laws, and where the residentiaries are still obliged to celibacy, but otherwise, live a very happy, easy, and plentiful life; being furnished upon the foot of the foundation, besides their ecclesiastical stipends.

The great church is a magnificent building, however ancient, the spire is not high, but handsome, and there is a fine tower at the west end, over the great door or entrance. The choir is very fine, though plain, and there is a very good organ. The revenues of this bishopric are very considerable, but lie under some abatement at present, on account of necessary repairs.

From Hereford keeping the bank of Wye as near as we could, we came to Ross, a good old town, famous for good cider, a great manufacture of iron ware, and a good trade on the River Wye, and nothing else as I remember, except it was a monstrous fat woman, who they would have had me gone to see. But I had enough of the relation, and so I suppose will the reader, for they told me she was more than three yards about her waist; that when she sat down, she was obliged to have a small stool placed before her, to rest her belly on, and the like.

From hence we came at about 8 miles more into Monmouthshire, and to the town of Monmouth. It is an old town situate at the conflux of the Wye and of Munnow, whence the town has its name; it stands in the angle where the rivers join, and has a bridge over each river, and a third over the River Trothy, which comes in just below the other.

This town shows by its reverend face, that it is a place of

great antiquity, and by the remains of walls, lines, curtains, and bastions, that it has been very strong, and by its situation that it may be made so again. This place is made famous, by being the native place of one of our most ancient historians Jeoffry of Monmouth.[37] At present 'tis rather a decayed than a flourishing town, yet, it drives a considerable trade with the city of Bristol, by the navigation of the Wye.

Near Monmouth the Duke of Beaufort has a fine old seat, called Troy; but since the family has had a much finer place at Badminton, near the Bath; this though a most charming situation seems to be much neglected.

Lower down upon the Wye stands Chepstow, the sea port for all the towns seated on the Wye and Lug, and where their commerce seems to centre. Here is a noble bridge over the Wye: to this town ships of good burthen may come up, and the tide runs here with the same impetuous current as at Bristol; the flood rising from six fathom, to six and a half at Chepstow Bridge. This is a place of very good trade, as is also Newport, a town of the like import upon the River Uske, a great river, though not so big as Wye, which runs through the centre of the county, and falls also into the Severn Sea.

This county furnishes great quantities of corn for exportation, and the Bristol merchants frequently load ships here, to go to Portugal, and other foreign countries with wheat; considering the mountainous part of the west of this county, 'tis much they should have such good corn, and so much of it to spare; but the eastern side of the county, and the neighbourhood of Herefordshire, supplies them.

I am now at the utmost extent of England west, and here I must mount the Alps, traverse the mountains of Wales, (and indeed, they are well compared to the Alps in the inmost provinces;) but with this exception, that in abundance of places you have the most pleasant and beautiful valleys imaginable, and some of them, of very great extent, far exceeding the valleys so famed among the mountains of Savoy, and Piedmont.

The two first counties which border west upon Monmouthshire, are Brecknock, and Glamorgan, and as they are very mountainous, so that part of Monmouthshire which joins them, begins the rising of the hills. Kyrton-Beacon, Tumberlow, Blorench, Penvail, and Skirridan, are some of the names of these horrid mountains, and are all in this shire; and I could not but fancy my self in view of Mount Brennus, Little Barnard, and Great Barnard, among the Alps.

We now entered South Wales. We began with Brecknock, being willing to see the highest of the mountains, which are said to be hereabouts; and indeed, except I had still an idea of the height of the Alps, and of those mighty mountains of America, the Andes, which we see very often in the South-Seas, 20 leagues from the shore: I say except that I had still an idea of those countries on my mind, I should have been surprised at the sight of these hills; nay, (as it was) the Andes and the Alps, though immensely high, yet they stand together, and they are as mountains, piled upon mountains, and hills upon hills; whereas sometimes we see these mountains rising up at once, from the lowest valleys, to the highest summits which makes the height look horrid and frightful, even worse than those mountains abroad; which though much higher, rise as it were, one behind another: so that the ascent seems gradual, and consequently less surprising.

Brecknockshire is a mere inland county, as Radnor is; the English jestingly (and I think not very improperly) call it Breakneckshire. 'Tis mountainous to an extremity, except on the side of Radnor, where it is something more low and level. It is well watered by the Wye, and the Uske, two rivers mentioned before; upon the latter stands the town of Brecknock, the capital of the county. The most to be said of this town, is what indeed I have said of many places in Wales, (viz.) that it is very ancient, and indeed to mention it here for all the rest, there are more tokens of antiquity to be seen every where in Wales, than in any particular part of England, except the counties of Cumberland, and Northumberland. Here we saw Brecknock-Mere, a large or long lake of water, two or three miles over. They take abundance of good fish in this lake, so that as is said of the river Thysse in Hungary; they say this lake is two thirds water, and one third fish. The country people affirm, there stood a city once here, but, that by the judgment of Heaven, for the sin of its inhabitants, it sunk into the earth, and the water rose up in the place of it.

It was among the mountains of this county that the famous Glendower[38] sheltered himself, and taking arms on the deposing Richard II proclaimed himself Prince of Wales; and they show us several little refuges of his in the mountains, whither he retreated, and from whence, again, he made such bold excursions into England.

Though this county be so mountainous, provisions are exceeding plentiful, and also very good all over the county; nor are these mountains useless, even to the city of London, as I have noted of other counties; for from hence they send yearly, great herds of black cattle to England, and which are known to fill our fairs and markets, even that of Smithfield it self.

The yellow mountains of Radnorshire are the same, and their product of cattle is the same; nor did I meet with any thing new, and worth noticing, except monuments of antiquity, which are not the subject of my enquiry. The stories of Vortigern, and Roger of Mortimer,[39] are in every old woman's mouth here. There is a kind of desert too, on that side, which is scarce habitable or passable, so we made it our north boundary for this part of our journey, and turned away to Glamorganshire.

Entering this shire, from Radnor and Brecknock, we were saluted with Monuchdenny-Hill on our left, and the Black-Mountain on the right, and all a ridge of horrid rocks and precipices between, over which, if we had not had trusty guides, we should never have found our way; and indeed, we began to repent our curiosity, as not having met with any thing worth the trouble; and a country looking so full of horror, that we thought to have given over the enterprise, and have left Wales out of our circuit. But after a day and a night conversing thus with rocks and mountains, our guide brought us down into a most agreeable vale, opening to the south, and a pleasant river running through it, called the Taaffe; and following the course of this river, we came in the evening to the ancient city of Landaff, and Caerdiff, standing almost together.

Landaff is the seat of the episcopal see, and a city; but Cardiff which is lower on the river, is the port and town of trade; and has a very good harbour opening into the Severn Sea, about 4 miles below the town. The cathedral is a neat building, but very ancient; they boast that this church was a house of religious worship many years before any church was founded in England, and that the Christian religion flourished here in its primitive purity, from the year 186, till the Pelagian heresy overspread this country; which being afterwards rooted out by the care of the orthodox bishop, they placed St Dobricius [40] as the first bishop in this town of Landaff, then called Launton.

The south part of this country is a pleasant and agreeable place, and is very populous; 'tis also a very good, fertile, and rich soil, and the low grounds are so well covered with grass, and stocked with cattle, that they supply the city of Bristol with butter in very great quantities salted and barrelled up, just as Suffolk does the city of London.

The chief sea port is Swanzey, a very considerable town for trade, and has a very good harbour. Here is also a very great trade for coals, and culm, which they export to all the ports of Sommerset, Devon, and Cornwal, and also to Ireland itself; so that one sometimes sees a hundred sail of ships at a time loading coals here; which greatly enriches the country, and particularly this town of Swanzey, which is really a very thriving place; it stands on the River Tawye, or Taw. 'Tis very remarkable, that most of the rivers in this county chime upon the letters T, and Y, as Taaf, Tawy, Tuy, Towy, Tyevy. Neath is another port, where the coal trade is also considerable, though it stands farther within the land.

Having thus touched at what is most curious on this coast, we passed through the land of Gowre, and going still west, we came to Caermarthen, or Kaer-Vyrdhin, as the Welsh call it, the capital of the county of Kaermardhinshire.

This is an ancient but not a decayed town, pleasantly situated on the River Towy, or Tovy, which is navigable up to the town, for vessels of a moderate burthen. The town indeed is well built, and populous, and the country round it, is the most fruitful, of any part of all Wales, considering that it continues to be so for a great way; namely, through all the middle of the county, and a great way into the next; nor is this county so mountainous and wild, as the rest of this part of Wales: but it abounds in corn, and in fine flourishing meadows, as good as most are in Britain, and in which are fed, a very great number of good cattle.

The chancery, and exchequer of the principality, was usually kept at this town, till the jurisdiction of the Court and Marches of Wales was taken away. This town was also famous for the birth of the old British prophet Merlin, of whom so many things are fabled, that indeed nothing of its kind ever prevailed so far, in the delusion of mankind, and who flourished in the year 480. And here also the old Britains often kept their parliament or assemblies of their wise men, and made their laws. The town was fortified in former times, but the walls are scarcely to be seen now, only the ruins of them.

We found the people of this county more civilised and more courteous, than in the more mountainous parts, where the disposition of the inhabitants seems to be rough, like the country. But here as they seem to converse with the rest of the world, by their commerce, so they are more conversible than their neighbours.

The next county west, is Pembrokeshire, which is the most extreme part of Wales on this side, in a rich, fertile, and plentiful country, lying on the sea coast, where it has the benefit of Milford Haven, one of the greatest and best inlets of water in Britain. Mr Cambden says it contains 16 creeks, 5 great bays, and 13 good roads for shipping, all distinguished as such by their names; and some say, a thousand sail of ships may ride in it, and not the topmast of one be seen from another; but this last, I think, merits confirmation.

Before we quitted the coast, we saw Tenbigh, the most agreeable town on all the sea coast of South Wales, except Pembroke, being a very good road for shipping, and well frequented. Here is a great fishery for herring in its season, a great colliery, or rather export of coals, and they also drive a very considerable trade to Ireland.

From hence, we crossed over the isthmus to Pembroke, which stands on the E. shore of the great haven of Milford. This is the largest and richest, and at this time, the most flourishing town of all S. Wales. Here are a great many English merchants, and some of them men of good business; and they told us, there were near 200 sail of ships belonged to the town, small and great; in a word, all this part of Wales is a rich and flourishing country, but especially this part is so very pleasant, and fertile, and is so well cultivated, that 'tis called by distinction, Little England, beyond Wales.

This is the place also made particularly famous for the landing of King Henry VII, then Duke of Richmond.[41] From hence, being resolved to see the utmost extent of the country west, we ferried over the haven and went to Haverford, or by some called Haverford-West. Haverford is a better town than we expected to find, in this remote angle of Britain; 'tis strong, well built, clean, and populous.

From hence to St Davids, the country begins to look like Wales again, dry, barren, and mountainous; St Davids is not a bishop's see only, but was formerly an arch-bishop's, which they tell us, was by the Pope transferred to Dole in Britany, where it still remains.

The venerable aspect of this cathedral church, shows that it has been a beautiful building, but that it is much decayed. The west end or body of the church is tolerably well; the choir is kept neat, and in tolerable repair, the S. aisle without the choir, and the Virgin Mary's chapel, which makes the E. end of the church, are in a manner demolished, and the roofs of both fallen in.

There are a great many eminent persons buried here, besides such, whose monuments are defaced by time. There is St Davids monument, to whom the church is dedicated, the monument of the Earl of Richmond, as also of the famous Owen Tudor.

This St David[42] they tell us was uncle to King Arthur, that he lived to 146 years of age, that he was bishop of this church 65 years, being born in the year 496, and died ann. 642; that he built 12 monasteries, and did abundance of miracles.

Here the weather being very clear, we had a full view of Ireland, though at a very great distance. The land here is called St Davids Head, and from hence, there has some time ago, gone a passage boat constantly between England and Ireland, but that voiture is at present discontinued.

From hence we turned N. keeping the sea in our W. prospect, and a rugged mountainous country on the E. where the hills even darkened the air with their height; as we went on, we past by Newport, on the River Nevern, a town having a good harbour, and consequently a good trade with Ireland.

Here we left Pembrokeshire, and after about 22 miles, came to the town of Cardigan, an old and well inhabited town, on the River Tivy. 'Tis a very noble river indeed, and famous for its plenty of the best and largest salmon in Britain. The country people told us, that they had beavers here, which bred in the lakes among the mountains, and came down the stream of Tivy to feed; that they destroyed the young fry of salmon, and therefore the country people destroyed them; but they could shew us none of them, or any of their skins, neither could the countrymen describe them, or tell us that they had ever seen them; so that we concluded they only meant the otter, till I found after our return, that Mr Cambden mentions also, that there were beavers seen here formerly.

The town is not large, has been well fortified, but that part is now wholly neglected. It has a good trade with Ireland, and is enriched very much, as is all this part of the country, by the famous lead mines, formerly discovered by Sir Carbery

Price,[43] which are the greatest, and perhaps the richest in England; and particularly as they require so little labour and charge to come at the ore, which in many places lies within a fathom or two of the surface, and in some, even bare to the very top.

Going N. from the Tyvy about 25 miles, we came to Abrystwyth, that is to say, the town at the mouth of the River Ystwyth. This town is enriched by the coals and lead which is found in its neighbourhood, and is a populous, but a very dirty, black, smoky place, and we fancied the people looked as if they lived continually in the coal or lead mines. However, they are rich, and the place is very populous.

The whole county of Cardigan is so full of cattle, that 'tis said to be the nursery, or breeding-place for the whole kingdom of England, S. by Trent; but this is not a proof of its fertility, for though the feeding of cattle indeed requires a rich soil, the breeding them does not, the mountains and moors being as proper for that purpose as richer land.

Now we entered N. Wales, only I should add, that as we passed, we had a sight of the famous Plymlymon-Hill, out of the east side of which, rises the Severn, and the Wye; and out of the west side of it, rises the Rydall and the Ystwyth. This mountain is exceeding high, and though it is hard to say which is the highest hill in Wales, yet I think this bids fair for it; nor is the county for 20 miles round it, any thing but a continued ridge of mountains: so that for almost a whole week's travel, we seemed to be conversing with the upper regions; for we were often above the clouds, I'm sure, a very great way, and the names of some of these hills seemed as barbarous to us, who spoke no Welch, as the hills themselves.

In passing Montgomery-shire, we were so tired with rocks and mountains, that we wished heartily we had kept close to the sea shore, but it not much mended the matter if we had, as I understood afterwards. The River Severn is the only beauty of this country, which rising I say, out of the Plymlymon Mountain, receives instantly so many other rivers into its bosom, that it becomes navigable before it gets out of the county; namely, at Welch Pool, on the edge of Shropshire. This is a good fashionable place, and has many English dwelling in it, and some very good families; but we saw nothing farther worth remarking.

The vales and meadows upon the bank of the Severn, are the best of this county, I had almost said, the only good part of it; some are of opinion, that, the very water of the Severn, like that of Nile, impregnates the valleys, and when it overflows, leaves a virtue behind it, particularly to itself; and this they say is confirmed, because all the country is so fruitful, wherever this river does overflow, and its waters reach. The town, or rather as the natives call it, the city of Montgomery, lies not far from this river, on the outer edge of the country next to Herefordshire. This was, it seems, a great frontier town in the wars between the English and the Welch, and was beautified and fortified by King Henry III; the town is now much decayed.

This county is noted for an excellent breed of Welch horses, which, though not very large, are exceeding valuable, and much esteemed all over England; all the North and West part of the county is mountainous and stony. We saw a great many old monuments in this country, and Roman camps wherever we came, and especially if we met any person curious in such things, we found they had many Roman coins; but this was none of my enquiry, as I have said already.

Merionithshire, or Merionydshire, lies west from Montgomeryshire; it lies on the Irish Sea, or rather the ocean; for St George's Chanel does not begin till further north, and it is extended on the coast, for near 35 miles in length, all still mountainous and craggy. The principal river is the Tovy, which rises among the unpassable mountains, which range along the centre of this part of Wales, and which we call unpassable, for that even the people themselves called them so; we looked at them indeed with astonishment, for their rugged tops, and the immense height of them. Some particular hills have particular names, but otherwise we called them all the Black Mountains, and they well deserved the name; some think 'tis from the unpassable mountains of this county, that we have an old saying, that the devil lives in the middle of Wales, though I know there is another meaning given to it.

There is but few large towns in all this part, nor is it very populous; indeed much of it is scarce habitable, but 'tis said, there are more sheep in it, than in all the rest of Wales. On the sea shore however, we see Harleigh-Castle, which is still a garrison, and kept for the guard of the coast, but 'tis of no great strength, but by its situation.

Here among innumerable summits, and rising peaks of nameless hills, we saw the famous Kader-Idricks, which some are of opinion, is the highest mountain in Britain, another called Rarauvaur, another called Mowylwynda, and still every hill we saw, we thought was higher than all that ever we saw before.

We enquired here after that strange phenomenon which was not only seen, but fatally experienced by the country round this place, namely, of a livid fire, coming off from the sea; and setting on fire, houses, barns, stacks of hay and corn, and poisoning the herbage in the fields; of which there is a full account given in the Philosophical Transactions.[44]

But to return to the face of things, as they appeared to us, the mountainous country spoken of runs away N. through this county and almost the next, I mean Caernarvonshire, where Snowden Hill is a monstrous height, and according to its name, had snow on the top in the beginning of June; and perhaps had so till the next June, that is to say, all the year. These unpassable heights were doubtless the refuges of the Britains, when they made continual war with the Saxons and Romans, and retreated on occasion of their being over powered, into these parts where, in short, no enemy could pursue them.

That side of the country of Carnarvon, which borders on the sea, is not so mountainous, and is both more fertile and more populous. The principal town in this part, is Carnarvon, a good town, with a castle built by Edward I to curb and reduce the wild people of the mountains, and secure the passage into Anglesea. As this city was built by Edward I so he kept his Court often here, and honoured it with his presence very much; and here his eldest son and successor, though unhappy, (Ed. II) was born, who was therefore called Edward of Caernarvon.[45] This Edward was the first Prince of Wales; that is to say, the first of the Kings of England's sons, who was vested with the title of Prince of Wales. It is a small, but strong town, clean and well built, and considering the place, the people are very courteous and obliging to strangers. It is seated on the firth or inlet called Menai, parting the isle of Anglesea, or Mona, from the main land; and here is a ferry over to the island called Abermenai Ferry: and from thence a direct road to Holly Head, where we went for no purpose, but to have another view of Ireland, though we were disappointed, the weather being bad and stormy.

Whoever travels critically over these mountains, I mean of S. Wales, and Merionithshire, will think Stone-henge in Wiltshire, and Roll-Rich Stones in Oxfordshire no more a wonder, seeing there are so many such, and such like, in these provinces; that they are not thought strange of at all, nor is it doubted, but they were generally monuments of the dead, as also are the single stones of immense bulk any other, of which we saw so many, that we gave over remarking them; some we saw from 7, 8, to 10, and one 16 foot high, being a whole stone, but so great, that the most of the wonder is, where they were found and how dragged to the place; since, besides the steep ascents to some of the hills on which they stand, it would be impossible to move some of them, now, with 50 yoke of oxen. And yet a great many of these stones are found confusedly lying one upon another on the utmost summit or top of the Glyder, or other hills, in Merionith and Carnarvonshire; to which it is next to impossible, that all the power of art, and strength of man and beast could carry them, and the people make no difficulty of saying the devil set them up there.

One of these monumental stones is to be seen a little way from Harleigh-Castle. It is a large stone lying flat, supported by three other stones at 3 of the 4 angles, though the stone is rather oval than square, it is almost 11 foot long, the breadth unequal, but in some places it's from 7 to 8 foot broad, and it may be supposed has been both longer and broader; 'tis in some places above 2 foot thick, but in others 'tis worn almost to an edge by time. The three stones that support it, are about 20 inches square, 'tis supposed there has been four, two of which that support the thickest end, are near 8 foot high, the other not above 3 foot, being supposed to be settled in the ground, so that the stone lies sloping, like the roof of a barn. There are also two circles of stones in that island, such as Stone-henge, but the stones much larger.

These mountains are indeed so like the Alps, that except the language of the people, one could hardly avoid thinking he is passing from Grenoble to Susa, or rather passing the country of the Grisons. The lakes also, which are so numerous here, make the similitude the greater, nor are the fables which the country people tell of these lakes, much unlike the stories which we meet with among the Switzers, of the famous lakes in their country.

There is nothing of note to be seen in the Isle of Anglesea but the town, and the castle of Beaumaris, which was also built by King Edward I and called Beau-Marsh, or the Fine Plain; for here the country is very level and plain, and the land is fruitful and pleasant. As we went to Holly Head, by the S. part of the island from Newborough, and came back through the middle to Beaumaris, we saw the whole extent of it, and indeed, it is a much pleasanter country, than any part of N. Wales, that we had yet seen; and particularly is very fruitful for corn and cattle.

Here we crossed the Fretum, or strait of Meneu again ... to Bangor, a town noted for its antiquity, its being a bishop's see, and an old, mean looking, and almost despicable cathedral church.

This church claims to be one of the most ancient in Britain, the people say, 'tis the most ancient; that St Daniel (to whom this church was dedicated) was first bishop here, in the year

512. They allow that the pagans, perhaps of Anglesea, ruined the church, and possessed the bishopric after it was first built, for above 100 years; nor is there any account of it from the year 512, to 1009. After this, the bishopric was ruined again by dilapidation, by one of its own bishops, whose name was Bulkeley,[46] who, not only sold the revenues, but even the very bells, for which sacrilege he was struck blind; but this last is tradition only.

It is certainly at present a poor bishopric, and has but a poor cathedral; yet the bishops are generally allowed to hold some other good benefice *in commendam*, and the preferment seems to be a grateful introduction to the clergy, as the bishops are generally translated from hence, to a more profitable bishopric.

From Bangor we went north, (keeping the sea on our left hand) to Conway. This is the poorest but pleasantest town in all this county for the bigness of it; it is seated on the bank of a fine river, which is not only pleasant and beautiful, but is a noble harbour for ships, had they any occasion for them there; the stream is deep and safe, and the river broad, as the Thames at Deptford. It only wants a trade suitable to so good a port, for it infinitely out does Chester or Leverpool itself.

In this passage, we went over the famous precipice called Penmen-muir, which indeed fame has made abundance more frightful, than it really is; for though the rock is indeed very high, and if any one should fall from it, it would dash them in pieces, yet, on the other hand, there is no danger of their falling; and besides, there is now a wall built all the way, on the edge of the precipice, to secure them.

We have but little remarkable in the road from Conway to Hollywell, but crags and rocks all along the N. shore of Denbeigh, till we come to Denbeigh town. This is the county town, and is a large populous place, which carries something in its countenance of its neighbourhood to England, but that which was most surprising, after such a tiresome and fatiguing journey, over the unhospitable mountains of Merioneth, and Carnarvonshire, was, that descending now from the hills, we came into a most pleasant, fruitful, populous, and delicious vale, full of villages and towns, the fields shining with corn, just ready for the reapers, the meadows green and flowery, and a fine river, with a mild and gentle stream running through it: nor is it a small or casual intermission, but we had a prospect of the country open before us, for above 20 miles in length, and from 5 to 7 miles in breadth, all smiling with the same kind of complexion; which made us think our selves in England again, all on a sudden.

In this pleasant vale, turning N. from Denbeigh, and following the stream of the river, we came to S. Asaph, a small city, with a cathedral, being a bishopric of tolerable good value, though the church is old. It is but a poor town, and ill built, though the country is so pleasant and rich round it. There are some old monuments in this church, but none of any note, nor could we read the Welch inscriptions.

From hence we come to Holly-well. The stories of this Well of S. Winifrid are, that the pious virgin, being ravished and murthered, this healing water sprung out of her body when buried; but this smells too much of the legend, to take up any of my time; the Romanists indeed believe it, as 'tis evident, from their thronging hither to receive the healing sanative virtue of the water, which they do not hope for as it is a medicinal water, but as it is a miraculous water, and heals them by virtue of the intercession and influence of this famous virgin, St Winifrid; of which I believe as much as comes to my share.

There is a little town near the well, which may, indeed, be said to have risen from the confluence of the people hither, for almost all the houses are either public houses, or let into lodgings; and the priests that attend here, and are very numerous, appear in disguise. Sometimes they are physicians, sometimes surgeons, sometimes gentlemen, and sometimes patients, or any thing as occasion presents. No body takes notice of them, as to their profession, though they know them well enough, no not the Roman Catholics themselves; but in private, they have their proper oratories in certain places, whither the votaries resort; and good manners has prevailed so far, that however the Protestants know who and who's together; no body takes notice of it, or enquires where one another goes, or has been gone.

From hence we passed by Flint-Castle, and then in a few hours we crossed the River Dee, and arrived at the city of West Chester, from whence, I shall give a farther account of my journey in my next.

I am,
SIR,
Yours, &c.

Letter 7

Containing a description of part of Cheshire, Shropshire, Wales, Staffordshire, Warwickshire, Northamptonshire, Leicestershire, Lincolnshire, Rutlandshire, and Bedfordshire

SIR, – My last from West Chester, gave you a full account of my progress through Wales, and my coming to Chester, at the end of that really fatiguing journey: I must confess, I that have seen the Alps, on so many occasions, have gone under so many of the most frightful passes in the country of the Grisons, and in the mountains of Tirol, never believed there was any thing in this island of Britain that came near, much less that exceeded those hills, in the terror of their aspect, or in the difficulty of access to them. But certainly, if they are out done any where in the world, it is here: even Hannibal himself would have found it impossible to have marched his army over Snowden, or over the rocks of Merioneth and Montgomery shires; no, not with all the help that fire and vinegar could have yielded, to make way for him.

The only support we had in this heavy journey, was, (1.) that we generally found their provisions very good and cheap, and very good accommodations in the inns. And (2.) that the Welsh gentlemen are very civil, hospitable, and kind; the people very obliging and conversible, and especially to strangers; but when we let them know, we travelled merely in curiosity to view the country, and be able to speak well of them to strangers, their civility was heightened to such a degree, that nothing could be more friendly, willing to tell us every thing that belonged to their country, and to show us every thing that we desired to see.

They value themselves much upon their antiquity. The ancient race of their houses, and families, and the like; and above all, upon their ancient heroes: their King Caractacus,[1] Owen ap Tudor, Prince Lewellin, and the like noblemen and princes of British extraction; and as they believe their country to be the pleasantest and most agreeable in the world, so you cannot oblige them more, than to make them think you believe so too.

I continued at Chester for some time, except that I made two or three excursions into the neighbouring country, and particularly into that part of Shropshire, which I had not viewed as I went; as also into the north, and north west part of Cheshire.

The first trip I made, was into the Cestria Chersonesus,[2] as I think we may properly call it, (viz.) a piece of the country, which runs out a great way into the Irish Sea, and is bounded by the two great firths, or arms of the sea, the one called the mouth of the Dee, and the other of two rivers, the Mersey, and the Wever; this isthmus or neck of land, is about 16 miles long, and about 6 or 7 miles over, and has not one market town in it, though 'tis exceeding rich and fertile; the last occasioned possibly by the neighbourhood of two such great towns, or cities rather: I mean Chester and Leverpool.

We crossed over that fruitful level I mentioned before, and coming to the other water, we ferried over to Leverpool.[3] This town is now become so great, so populous, and so rich, that it may be called the Bristol of this part of England. It had formerly but one church, but upon the increase of inhabitants, and of new buildings in so extraordinary a manner, they have built another very fine church in the north part of the town; and they talk of erecting two more.

This part of the town may indeed be called New Leverpool, for that, they have built more than another Leverpool that way, in new streets, and fine large houses for their merchants. Besides this, they have made a great wet dock,[4] for laying up their ships, and which they greatly wanted; for though the Mersey is a noble harbour, and is able to ride a thousand sail of ships at once, yet those ships that are to be laid up, or lie by the walls all the winter, or longer, as sometimes may be the case; must ride there, as in an open road, or (as the seamen call it,) be haled a shore; neither of which would be practicable in a town of so much trade. And in the time of the late great storm, they suffered very much on that account. This is the only work of its kind in England, except what is in the river Thames, I mean for the merchants; nor is it many years since there was not one wet dock in England for private use, except Sir Henry Johnson's at Black Wall.

This is still an increasing flourishing town, and if they go on in trade, as they have done for some time, 'tis probable it will in a little time be as big as the city of Dublin. The houses here are exceedingly well built, the streets straight, clean, and spacious, and they are now well supplied with water. The merchants here have a very pretty Exchange, standing upon 12 free-stone columns, but it begins to be so much too little, that 'tis thought they must remove or enlarge it. 'Tis already the next town to Bristol, and in a little time may probably exceed it, both in commerce, and in numbers of people.

We went no farther this way at that time, but came back to Chester, by the same ferry as we went over.

As I am now at Chester, 'tis proper to say something of it, being a city well worth describing: Chester has four things very remarkable in it. 1. Its walls, which are very firm, beautiful, and in good repair. 2. The castle, which is also kept up, and has a garrison always in it. 3. The cathedral. 4. The River Dee, and 5. the bridge over it.

It is a very ancient city, and to this day, the buildings are very old; nor do the Rows as they call them, add any thing, in my opinion, to the beauty of the city; but just the contrary, they serve to make the city look both old and ugly. These Rows are certain long galleries, up one pair of stairs, which run along the side of the streets, before all the houses, though joined to them, and as is pretended, they are to keep the people dry in walking along. This they do indeed effectually, but then they take away all the view of the houses from the street, nor can a stranger, that was to ride through Chester, see any shops in the city; besides, they make the shops themselves dark, and the way in them is dark, dirty, and uneven.

The best ornament of the city, is, that the streets are very broad and fair, and run through the whole city in straight lines, crossing in the middle of the city, as at Chichester. The walls as I have said, are in very good repair, and it is a very pleasant walk round the city, upon the walls, and within the battlements, from whence you may see the country round; and particularly on the side of the Roodee,[5] which is a fine large low green, on the bank of the Dee. In the winter this green is often under water by the inundations of the river, and a little before I came there, they had such a terrible land flood, which flowed 8 foot higher than usual so that it not only overflowed the said green, called the Roodee, but destroyed a fine new wharf and landing-place for goods, a little below the town, bore down all the warehouses, and other buildings, which the merchants had erected for securing their goods, and carried all away goods and buildings together, to the irreparable loss of the persons concerned.

The castle of Chester is a good firm building, and strong, though not fortified, with many out works. There is always a good garrison kept, and here the prisoners taken at Preston,[6] in the late time of Rebellion, were kept a great while, till compassion to their misery, moved the clemency of the conqueror to deliver them.

The great church here is a very magnificent building, but 'tis built of a red, sandy, ill looking stone, which takes much from the beauty of it, and which yielding to the weather, seems to crumble, and suffer by time, which much defaces the building. It was formerly a part of the diocese of Litchfield, and was not made a bishop's see till the year 1541; when King Henry VIII divided it from Litchfield; nor has there even been above 19 bishops of this see from its foundation. The short account of it is thus. Hugh Lupus [7] gave the old monastery dedicated to St Werburge, to a society of monks, after which, they say, King Edgar who conquered all this part of Britain, and was rowed up the Dee, in his royal barge, by four kings, founded the great church; and Hugh Lupus the great, Earl of Chester, finished and endowed it.

Here is a noble stone bridge over the Dee, very high and

strong built, and 'tis needful it should be so, indeed; for the Dee is a most furious stream at some seasons, and brings a vast weight of water with it from the mountains of Wales. Here it was that the first army of King William,[8] designed for the war in Ireland, encamped, for a considerable time before they embarked, ann. 1689.

There are 11 parishes in this city, and very good churches to them, and it is the largest city in all this side of England that is so remote from London. When I was formerly at this city, about the year 1690, they had no water to supply their ordinary occasions, but what was carried from the River Dee upon horses, in great leather vessels, like a pair of bakers' paniers; just the very same for shape and use, as they have to this day in the streets of Constantinople, and at Belgrade, in Hungary; to carry water about the streets to sell, for the people to drink. But at my coming there this time, I found a very good water-house in the river, and the city plentifully supplied by pipes, just as London is from the Thames; though some parts of Chester stands very high from the river.

Though this is not an ancient bishopric, 'tis an ancient city, and was certainly a frontier of the Roman Empire this way; and its being so afterwards to the English Empire also, has doubtless been the reason of its being so well kept, and the castle continued in repair, when most of the other castles on the frontiers were slighted and demolished.

This county, however remote from London, is one of those which contributes most to its support, as well as to several other parts of England, and that is by its excellent cheese, which they make here in such quantities, and so exceeding good, that as I am told from very good authority, the city of London only take off 14000 ton every year; besides 8000 ton which they say goes every year down the Rivers Severn and Trent, the former to Bristol, and the latter to York including all the towns on both these large rivers. And besides the quantity shipped both here, and at Leverpool, to go to Ireland, and Scotland. Indeed, the whole county is employed in it, and part of its neighbourhood too; for though 'tis called by the name of Cheshire cheese, yet great quantities of it are made in Shropshire, Staffordshire and Lancashire, that is to say, in such parts of them as border upon Cheshire.

The soil is extraordinary good, and the grass they say, has a peculiar richness in it, which disposes the creatures to give a great quantity of milk, and that very sweet and good; and this cheese manufacture, for such it is, increases every day, and greatly enriches all the county; raises the value of the lands, and encourages the farmers to the keeping vast stocks of cows; the very number of the cattle improving and enriching the land.

I now resolved to direct my course east, and making the Wever and the Trent, my northern boundary in this circuit; I came forward to view the midland counties of England. I had taken a little trip into the N.E. parts of Cheshire before, seen a fine old seat of the Lord Delamere's,[9] and which is beyond it all, the fine forest, which bears the name of that noble family; intending to see the salt pits at Northwich, which are odd indeed, but not so very strange as we were made to believe. So we came away not extremely gratified in our curiosity.

From Northwich we turned S. and following the stream of the river by Middle Wich, we crossed the great London road at Nantwich, or as some write it Namptwych; these are the three salt making towns of this county; there is a fourth which is called Droitwych, in Worcestershire; the nature of the thing is this, they boil the brine into fine salt, which is much prized for the beauty of its colour, and fineness of the grain, but the salt is not so strong, as what we now make from the rock salt, and therefore loses of its value.

Hence we turned a little W. to Whitchurch, in Shropshire. But before I leave Cheshire, I must note two things of it. (1.) That there is no part of England, where there are such a great number of families of gentry, and of such ancient and noble extraction. (2) That it is a County Palatine, and has been for so many ages, that its government is distinct from any other and very particular; it is administered by a chamberlain, a judge special, two barons of the exchequer, three sergeants at law, a sheriff, and attorney, and escheator, and all proper and useful subordinate officers; and the jurisdiction of all these offices are kept up, and preserved very strictly, only we are to note, that the judge special as he is called, tries only civil causes, not criminal, which are left to the ordinary judges of England, who go the circuits here, as in other places.

Whitchurch is a pleasant and populous town, and has a very good church, in which is the famous monument of the great Talbot,[10] first Earl of Shrewsbury, who, perhaps, and not unworthily, was called in his time, the English ACHILLES.

But the most to be said of this town now, is, that they have a good market, and a great many gentry near it, whereof some are Roman Catholics. They tell us that this town when King Charles I removed his standard from Nottingham to Shrewsbury,[11] raised a whole regiment for the king. Nor has this town lost its old loyal principle, to this time; though now it may run a little another way.

From hence we went towards Wales again, and crossed the Dee, at Bangor Bridge; I could not satisfy myself to omit seeing this famous town, which was once so remarkable, but was surprised when I came there, to see there was a stone-bridge over the Dee, and indeed, a very fine one. But as for the town or monastery, scarce any of the ruins were to be seen, and as all the people spoke Welch, we could find no body that could give us any intelligence. So effectually had time in so few years, razed the very foundations of the place. I will not say, as some do, that this is miraculous, and that it is the particular judgment of God upon the place, for being the birth-place of that arch heretic Pelagius,[12] who from hence also began to broach his heretical opinions, which afterwards so terribly overspread the Church: I say I will not insist upon this. That Pelagius was a monk of Bungor, or Banchor, is not doubted; but for the rest I leave it where I find it.

The place is now (I say) a poor contemptible village. From thence we visited Wrexham, having heard much of a fine church there, but we were greatly disappointed. There is indeed a very large tower steeple, if a tower may be called a steeple, and 'tis finely adorned with imagery; but far from fine: the work is mean, the statues seem all mean and in dejected postures, without any fancy or spirit in the workmanship, and as the stone is of a reddish crumbling kind like the cathedral at Chester, Time has made it look gross and rough. There are a great many ancient monuments in this church, and in the church-yard also; but none of note, and almost all the inscriptions are in Welch.

This town is large, well built and populous, and besides the church there are two large meeting-houses, in one of which we were told they preach in Welch one part of the day, and in English the other. Here is a great market for Welch flannel which the factors buy up of the poor Welch people, who manufacture it; and thence it is sent to London; and it is a very considerable manufacture indeed through all this part of the country, by which the poor are very profitably employed.

From hence we turned south, and passing by Wem, the title given by King James II to the late Lord Chancellor Jefferies,[13] we saw the house where his father, then but a private gentleman lived, and in but middling circumstances. Thence we came to Ellsmere, famous for a great lake or mere, which the people pretend has in some places no bottom. This place is remarkable for good fish. From hence we came the same night to Shrewsbury. This is indeed a beautiful, large, pleasant, populous, and rich town; full of gentry and yet full of trade too; for here too, is a great manufacture, as well of flannel, as also of white broad-cloth, which enriches all the country round it. The Severn surrounds this town, just as the Thames does the Isle of Dogs; so that it makes the form of an horse-shoe, over which there are two fine stone bridges, upon one of which is built a very noble gate, and over the arch of the gate the statue of the great Lewellin, the idol of the Welch, and their last Prince of Wales.

This is really a town of mirth and gallantry, something

like Bury in Suffolk, or Durham in the north, but much bigger than either of them, or indeed than both together. They speak all English in the town, but on a market-day you would think you were in Wales.

Here is the greatest market, the greatest plenty of good provisions, and the cheapest that is to be met with in all the western part of England; the Severn supplies them here with excellent salmon, but 'tis also brought in great plenty from the River Dee, which is not far off, and which abounds with a very good kind, and is generally larger than that in the Severn.

Near this place was fought the bloody battle [14] between Henry Hotspur and Henry IV King of England, in which the former was killed, and all his army overthrown, and the place is called Battlefield to this day. This town will for ever be famous for the reception it gave to King Charles the I who, after setting up his standard at Nottingham,[15] and finding no encouragement there, removed to Shrewsbury, being invited by the gentry of the town and country round, where he was received with such a general affection, and hearty zeal by all the people, that his majesty recovered the discouragement of his first step at Nottingham, and raised and completed a strong army in less time than could be imagined; insomuch that to the surprise of the Parliament, and indeed of all the world, he was in the field before them, and advanced upon them so fast, that he met them two-thirds onward of his way to London, and gave them battle at Edge-hill near Banbury.

But the fate of the war turning afterward against the king, the weight of it fell heavy upon this town also, and almost ruined them. But they are now fully recovered, and it is at this time one of the most flourishing towns in England. The walls and gates are yet standing, but useless, and the old castle is gone to ruin, as is the case of almost all the old castles in England.

It should not be forgotten here, that notwithstanding the healthiness of the place, one blot lies upon the town of

Shrewsbury, and which, though nothing can be charged on the inhabitants, yet it seems they are the most obliged when 'tis least spoken of; namely that here broke out first that unaccountable plague, called the sweating sickness;[16] which at first baffled all the sons of art, and spread itself through the whole kingdom of England: this happened in the year 1551. It afterwards spread itself into Germany, and several countries abroad.

Here is an ancient free-school,[17] the most considerable in this part of England; built and endowed by Queen Elizabeth, with a very sufficient maintenance for a chief or head-master, and three under-masters or ushers. The buildings are very spacious, and particularly the library is a fine building, and has a great many books in it; but I saw nothing curious or rare among them, and no manuscripts.

Here I was showed a very visible and remarkable appearance of the great ancient road or way called Watling-Street, which comes from London to this town, and goes on from hence to the utmost coast of Wales; where it crossed the Severn, there are remains of a stone bridge to be seen in the bottom of the river, when the water is low. On this road we set out now for Litchfield in our way towards London; and I would gladly have kept to this old road, if it had been possible, because I knew several remarkable places stood directly upon it. But we were obliged to make many excursions, and sometimes quit the street for a great way together. And first we left it to go away south to the edge of Stafford-shire, to see the old house called White Ladies, and the royal oak, the famous retreat of King Charles II [18] after the Battle of Worcester. The tree is surrounded with a palisadoe, to preserve it from the fate which threatened it from curiosity; for almost every body that came to see it for several years, carried away a piece of it, so that the tree was literally in danger not to die of age, but to be pulled limb from limb; but the veneration of that kind is much abated, and as the palisadoes are more decayed than the tree, the latter seems likely to stand safe without them.

Entering Stafford-shire we quitted the said Street-way, a little to the left, to see Stafford the county town, and the most considerable except Litchfield in the county. In the way we were surprised in a most agreeable manner, passing through a small but ancient town called Penkrige, vulgarly Pankrage, where happened to be a fair. We expected nothing extraordinary; but was I say surprised to see the prodigious number of horses brought hither, and those not ordinary and common draught-horses, and such kinds as we generally see at county-fairs remote from London. But here were really incredible numbers of the finest and most beautiful horses that can any where be seen; being brought hither from Yorkshire, the bishopric of Durham, and all the horse-breeding countries. We were told that there were not less than an hundred jockeys and horse-copers, as they call them there, from London, to buy horses for sale. Also an incredible number of gentlemen attended with their grooms to buy gallopers, or race-horses, for their Newmarket sport.

We stayed 3 days here to satisfy our curiosity, and indeed the sight was very agreeable, to see what vast stables of horses there were, which never were brought out or shown in the fair. How dextrous the northern grooms and breeders are in their looking after them, and ordering them. Those fellows take such indefatigable pains with them, that they bring them out like pictures of horses, not a hair amiss in them; they lie constantly in the stables with them, and feed them by weight and measure; keep them so clean, and so fine, I mean in their bodies, as well as their outsides, that, in short, nothing can be more nice. Here were several horses sold for 150 guineas a horse; but then they were such as were famous for the breed, and known by their race, almost as well as the Arabians know the genealogy of their horses.

From hence we came in two hours easy riding to Stafford, on the River Sow; 'tis an old and indeed ancient town, and gives name to the county; but we thought to have found something more worth going so much out of the way in it.

The town is however neat and well built, and is lately much increased; nay, as some say, grown rich by the clothing trade, which they have fallen into but within the reach of the present age and which has not enriched this town only, but Tamworth also, and all the country round.

The people of this county have been particularly famous, and more than any other county in England, for good footmanship, and there have been, and still are among them, some of the fleetest runners in England; which I do not grant to be occasioned by any particular temperature of the air or soil, so much as to the hardy breed of the inhabitants, especially in the moorlands or northern part of the county, and to their exercising themselves to it from their child-hood; for running foot-races seems to be the general sport or diversion of the country.

From hence to Litchfield, a city, and the principal, next to Chester, of all the N.W. part of England; neither indeed is there any other, but this and Coventry, in the whole road from London to Carlisle on the edge of Scotland.

Litchfield is a fine, neat, well-built, and indifferent large city; there is a little lake or lough of water in the middle of it, out of which runs a small stream of water, which soon becomes a little rivulet, and save that it has but 4 or 5 miles to the Trent, would soon become a river. This lake parts Litchfield, as it were, into two cities, one is called the town, and the other the close; in the first is the market-place, a fine school, and a very handsome hospital well-endowed. This part is much the largest and most populous: but the other is the fairest, has the best buildings in it, and, among the rest, the cathedral-church, one of the finest and most beautiful in England, especially for the outside, the form and figure of the building, the carved worked, imagery, and the three beauitful spires; the like of which are not to be seen in one church, no not in Europe.

There are two fine causeways which join the city and the close, with sluices to let the water pass, but those were cut through in the time of the late intestine wars in England; and the close, which is walled about, and was then fortified for the king, was very strong, and stood out several vigorous attacks against Cromwell's men, and was not at last taken without great loss of blood on both sides, being gallantly defended to the last drop, and taken by storm.

There are in the close, besides the houses of the clergy residentiaries, a great many very well-built houses, and well inhabited too; which makes Litchfield a place of good conversation and good company, above all the towns in this county or the next.

They told us there a long story of St Chad,[19] formerly bishop of this church, and how he lived in a little hovel or cell in the church-yard, instead of a bishop's palace. But the bishops, since that time, have, I suppose, thought better of it, and make shift with a very fine palace in the close and the residentiaries live in proportion to it.

The church I say is indeed a most beautiful building; the west prospect of it is charming, the two spires on the corner towers being in themselves perfect beauties of architecture, in the old Gothic way of building, but made still more shining and glorious by a third spire, which rising from the main tower in the body of the church, surmounts the other two, and shews itself exactly between them.

It is not easy to describe the beauty of the west end; you enter by three large doors in the porch or portico, which is as broad as the whole front; the spaces between the doors are filled with carved work and imagery, no place being void, where (by the rules of architecture) any ornament could be placed. The great window over the middle door is very large, and the pediment over it finely adorned, a large cross finishing the top of it; on either corner of the west front are two very fine towers, not unlike the two towers on the west end of St Peter's Church at Westminster, only infinitely finer. Even with the battlement of the porch, and adjoining to the towers, are large pinnacles at the outer angles, and on the top of the towers are to each tower eight more, very beautiful and fine; between these pinnacles, on the top of each tower, rises a spire equal in height, in thickness, and in workmanship, but so beautiful no pen can describe them.

The imagery and carved work on the front as above, has suffered much in the late unhappy times; and they told us the cross over the west window was frequently shot at by the rude soldiers; but that they could not shoot it down, which however they do not say was miraculous.

From Litchfield we came to Tamworth, a fine pleasant trading town, eminent for good ale and good company, of the middling sort; from whence we came into the great road again at Coleshill in Warwickshire. This is a small but very handsome market-town; it chiefly, if not wholly belongs to the Lord Digby,[20] who is lord of the manor, if not real owner of almost all the houses in the town, and as that noble person is at present a little on the wrong side as to the government, not having taken the oaths to King George, so the whole town are so eminently that way too, that they told me there was but one family of Whigs, as they called them, in the whole town, and they hoped to drive them out of the place too very quickly.

The late incumbent[21] of this parish quitted his living, which is very considerable, because he would not take the oaths, and his successor was the famous — who, when I was there, was newly proscribed by proclamation, and the reward of 1000l. ordered to whoever should apprehend him; so their instructors being such, 'tis no wonder the people have followed their leader.

From Coles-hill we came to Coventry, the sister city to Litchfield, and joined in the title of the see. It was a very unhappy time when I first came[22] to this city; for their heats and animosities for election of members to serve in Parliament, were carried to such a height, that all manner of method being laid aside, the inhabitants (in short) enraged at one another, met, and fought a pitched battle in the middle of the street, where they did not take up the breadth of the street, as two rabbles of people would generally do; in which case no more could engage, but so many as the breadth of the street would admit in the front; but, on the contrary, the two parties meeting in the street, one party kept to one side of the way, and one side to the other, the kennel in the middle only parting them, and so marching as if they intended to pass by one another, 'till the front of one party was come opposite to the rear of the other, and then suddenly facing to one another, and making a long front, where their flanks were before, upon a shout given, as the signal on both sides, they fell on with such fury with clubs and staves, that in an instant the kennel was covered with them, not with slain, but with such as were knocked down on both sides, and, in a word, they fought with such obstinacy that 'tis scarce credible. Nor were these the scum and rabble of the town but in short the burgesses and chief inhabitants, nay even magistrates, aldermen, and the like. Nor was this one skirmish a decision of the quarrel, but it held for several weeks, and they had many such fights; nor is the matter much better among them to this day, only that the occasion does not happen so often.

Coventry is a large and populous city, and drives a very great trade; the manufacture of tammies is their chief employ, and next to that weaving of ribbons of the meanest kind, chiefly black. The buildings are very old, and in some places much decayed; the city may be taken for the very picture of the city of London, on the south side of Cheapside before the Great Fire; the timber-built houses, projecting forwards and towards one another, till in the narrow streets they were ready to touch one another at the top.

The tale of the Lady Godiva, who rode naked through the High Street of the city to purchase her beloved city of Coventry exemption from taxes, is held for so certain a truth, that they will not have it questioned upon any account whatever; and the picture of the poor fellow that peeped out of the window to see her, is still kept up, looking out of a garret in the High Street of the city. But Mr Cambden says positively no body looked at her at all.

Here is no cathedral, as some have falsely said, neither is the great church, so called, either collegiate or conventual. In

King Henry 8th's time, the priory being dissolved, the church which they would have called a cathedral, was reduced to a private parish-church, and continues so to this day.

From Coventry we could by no means pass the town of Warwick, the distance too being but about six miles, and a very pleasant way on the banks of the River Avon. 'Tis famous for being the residence of the great Guy Earl of Warwick,[23] known now only by fame, which also has said so much more than the truth of him, that even what was true is become a kind of romance, and the real history of his actions is quite lost to the world.

As to the town of Warwick, it is really a fine town, pleasantly situated on the bank of the Avon, over which there is a large and stately bridge, the Avon being now grown a pretty large river, Warwick was ever esteemed a handsome, well-built town, and there were several good houses in it, but the face of it is now quite altered; for having been almost wholly reduced to a heap of rubbish, by a terrible fire [24] about two and twenty years ago, it is now rebuilt in so noble and so beautiful a manner, that few towns in England make so fine an appearance. The new church also is a fine building, but all the old monuments, which were very many, are entirely defaced, and lost by the fire.

The castle is a fine building, beautiful both by situation and its decoration; it stands on a solid rock of free-stone, from whose bowels it may be said to be built, as likewise is the whole town; the terrace of the castle, like that of Windsor, overlooks a beautiful country, and sees the Avon running at the foot of the precipice, at above 50 foot perpendicular height: the building is old, but several times repaired and beautified by its several owners, and 'tis now a very agreeable place both within and without. One finds no irregularity in the whole place, notwithstanding its ancient plan, as it was a castle not a palace, and built for strength rather than pleasure.

Being at Warwick, I took a short circuit through the S.E. part of the county, resolving after viewing a little the places of note, that lay something out of my intended route, to come back to the same place. Three miles from Warwick we passed over the Foss Way, which goes on to Leicester; then we came by Southam to Daventry, a considerable market town, but which subsists chiefly by the great concourse of travellers on the old Watling-street way, which lies near it; and the road being turned by modern usage, lies now through the town itself, then runs on to Dunsmore Heath.

It is a most pleasant curiosity to observe the course of these old famous highways the Icknild Way, the Watling-street, and the Foss, in which one sees so lively a representation of the ancient British, Roman and Saxon governments, that one cannot help realizing those times to the imagination; and though I avoid meddling with antiquity as much as possible in this work, yet in this case a circuit or tour through England would be very imperfect, if I should take no notice of these ways, seeing in tracing them we necessarily come to the principal towns, either that are or have been in every county.

From Daventry we crossed the country to Northampton, the handsomest and best built town in all this part of England; but here, as at Warwick, the beauty of it is owing to its own disasters, for it was so effectually and suddenly burnt down,[25] that very few houses were left standing, and this, though the fire began in the day-time; 'tis now finely rebuilt with brick and stone, and the streets made spacious and wide.

The great new church, the town-hall, the gaol, and all their public buildings, are the finest in any country town in England, being all new built. But he took very little notice of Northampton,[26] or rather had never seen it, who told us of a cathedral, a chapter-house and a cloister. The great inn at the George, the corner of the High Street, looks more like a palace than an inn, and the cost above 2000*l.* building; and so generous was the owner, that, as we were told, when he had built it, he gave it to the poor of the town. This is counted the centre of all the horse-markets and horse-fairs in England, there being here no less than four fairs in a year. Here they buy horses of all sorts, as well for the saddle as for the coach and cart, but chiefly for the two latter.

Near this town is the ancient royal house of Holmby, which was formerly in great esteem, and by its situation is capable of being made a royal palace indeed. But the melancholy reflection of the imprisonment of King Charles the First [27] in this house, and his being violently taken hence again by the mutinous rebels, has cast a kind of odium upon the place, so that it has been, as it were, forsaken and uninhabited.

The Earl of Sunderland's [28] house at Althorp, on the other hand, has within these few years changed its face to the other extreme, and had the late Earl lived to make some new apartments, which, as we were told, were designed as two large wings to the buildings, it would have been one of the most magnificent palaces in Europe. The gardens are exquisitely fine, and add, if it be possible, to the natural beauty of the situation.

From hence we went north to Harborough, and in the way, in the midst of the deep dismal roads, the dirtiest and worst in all that part of the country, we saw Boughton, the noble seat of the Duke of Mountague,[29] a house built at the cost and by the fancy of the late Duke, very much after the model of the Palace of Versailles.

From hence we went on to Harborough intending to go forward to Leicester; but curiosity turned us west a little to see an old town called Lutterworth, famous for being the birth-place of honest John Wickliff,[30] the first preacher of the Reformation in England, whose disciples were afterwards called Lollards; when we came there we saw nothing worth notice, nor did the people, as I could find, so much as know in general, that this great man was born amongst them.

Being thus got a little out of our way, we went on with it, and turning into the great Watling-street way, at High Cross, where the Foss crosses it, and which I suppose occasioned the name, we kept on the street way to Non-Eaton, a manufacturing town on the River Anker, and then to Atherstone, a town famous for a great cheese fair on the 8th of September.

From Atherston we turned N. to see Bosworth-Field,[31]

famous for the great battle which put an end to the usurpation of Richard III and to the long and bloody contention between the red rose and the white, or the two royal houses of York and Lancaster, which, as fame tells us, had cost the lives of eleven princes, three and twenty earls and dukes, three thousand noblemen knights, and gentlemen, and two hundred thousand of the common people. They showed us the spot of ground where the battle was fought, and at the town they showed us several pieces of swords, heads of lances, barbs of arrows, pieces of pole-axes, and such like instruments of death, which they said were found by the country people in the several grounds near the place of battle, as they had occasion to dig, or trench, or plough up the ground.

Having satisfied° our curiosity in these points, we turned east towards Leicester. Leicester is an ancient large and populous town, containing about five parishes, 'tis the capital of the county of Leicester, and stands on the River Soar, which rises not far from that High Cross I mentioned before. They have considerable manufacture carried on here, and in several of the market towns round for weaving of stockings by frames; and one would scarce think it possible so small an article of trade could employ such multitudes of people as it does; for the whole county seems to be employed in it.

Warwickshire and Northamptonshire are not so full of antiquities, large towns, and gentlemen's seats, but this county of Leicester is as empty. The whole county seems to be taken up in country business, such as the manufacture above, but particularly in breeding and feeding cattle; the largest sheep and horses in England are found here, and hence it comes to pass too, that they are in consequence a vast magazine of wool for the rest of the nation; even most of the gentlemen are graziers, and in some places the graziers are so rich, that they grow gentlemen: 'tis not an uncommon thing for graziers here to rent farms from 500*l.* to two thousand pounds a year rent.

The sheep bred in this county and Lincolnshire, which joins to it, are, without comparison, the largest, and bear not only the greatest weight of flesh on their bones but also the greatest fleeces of wool on their backs of any sheep of England: nor is the fineness of the wool abated for the quantity; but as 'tis the longest staple, (so the clothiers call it) so 'tis the finest wool in the whole island, some few places excepted, where the quantity is small and insignificant, compared to this part of the country. These are the funds of sheep which furnish the city of London with their large mutton in so incredible a quantity.

The horses produced here, or rather fed here, are the largest in England, being generally the great black coach horses and dray horses, of which so great a number are continually brought up to London, that one would think so little a spot as this of Leicestershire could not be able to supply them.

Leicester was formerly a very strong and well fortified town, being situated to great advantage for strength, the river compassing it half about, so it was again fortified in the late unhappy wars, and being garrisoned by the Parliament forces, was assaulted by the Royalists,[32] and being obstinately defended, was taken sword in hand, with a great slaughter, and not without the loss also of several of the inhabitants, who too rashly concerned themselves in opposing the conquerors. They preserve here a most remarkable piece of antiquity, being a piece of mosaic work at the bottom of a cellar; 'tis the story of Actæon, and his being killed by his own hounds, wrought as a pavement in a most exquisite manner; the stones are small, and of only two colours, white and brown, or chestnut, and very small.

The Foss Way leads us from hence through the eastern and north east part of the county, and particularly through the vale of Belvoir, to Newark in Nottinghamshire. In all this long tract we pass a rich and fertile country, fruitful fields, and the noble River Trent, for twenty miles together, often in our view; the towns of Mount Sorrel, Loughborough, Melton Mowbray, and Waltham in the Would, that is to say, on the Downs; all these are market towns, but of no great note.

At Newark one can hardly see without regret the ruins of

that famous castle, which maintained itself through the whole Civil War in England, and keeping a strong garrison there for the king to the last, cut off the greatest pass into the north that is in the whole kingdom; nor was it ever taken, 'till the king, pressed by the calamity of his affairs, put himself into the hands of the Scots army, which lay before it, and then commanded the governor to deliver it up,[33] after which it was demolished, that the great road might lie open and free; and it remains in rubbish to this day. Newark is a very handsome well-built town, the market place a noble square, and the church is large and spacious, with a curious spire, which, were not Grantham so near, might pass for the finest and highest in all this part of England: the Trent divides itself here, and makes an island, and the bridges lead just to the foot of the castle wall; so that while this place was in the hands of any party, there was no travelling but by their leave.

From Newark, still keeping the Foss Way, which lies as strait as a line can mark it out, we went on to Lincoln, having a view of the great church called the minster all the way before us, the River Trent on the left, and the downs called Lincoln Heath on the right. Lincoln is an ancient, ragged, decayed, and still decaying city; it is so full of the ruins of monasteries and religious houses, that, in short, the very barns, stables, out-houses and as they showed me some of the very hog-sties were built church-fashion; that is to say, with stone walls and arched windows and doors. There are here 13 churches, but the meanest to look on that are any where to be seen; the cathedral indeed and the ruins of the old castle are very venerable pieces of antiquity.

The situation of the city is very particular; one part is on the flat and in a bottom, so that the Wittham, a little river that runs through the town, flows sometimes into the street, the other part lies upon the top of a high hill, where the cathedral stands, and the very steepest part of the ascent of the hill is the best part of the city for trade and business. Nothing is more troublesome than the communication of the upper and lower town, the street is so steep and so straight, the coaches and horses are obliged to fetch a compass another way, as well on one hand as on the other.

The River Wittham, which as I said runs through the city, is arched over, so that you see nothing of it as you go through the main street; but it makes a large lake on the west side, and has a canal, by which it has a communication with the Trent, by which means the navigation of the Trent is made useful for trade to the city; this canal is called the Foss-dike.

There are some very good buildings, and a great deal of very good company, in the upper city, and several families of gentlemen have houses there, besides those of the prebendaries and other clergy belonging to the cathedral.

This cathedral is in itself a very noble structure, and is counted very fine, though I thought it not equal to some that I have already described. Its situation is infinitely more to advantage, than any cathedral in England, for it is seen far and wide; it stands upon an exceeding high hill, and is seen into five or six counties.

The building in general is very noble, and the church itself is very large; it has a double cross, one in the nave or centre on which the great tower stands, and one at the east end of the choir, under which are several ancient monuments; the length of the church is near 500 foot, the breadth 126; so that it is much larger than that at Litchfield; but the spires on the towers at the angles of the west end are mean, small, and low, and not to be named with those at Litchfield. The tower also is very plain, and has only four very ill-proportioned spires, or rather pinnacles, at the four corners small and very mean.

The church, as it is the seat of the bishopric, is not ancient, but the city is ancient, and the ruins of it tell us as much; it was certainly a flourishing city in the time of the Romans, and continued so after the fall of their empire.

The city was a large and flourishing place at the time of the Norman Conquest, though neither the castle or the great church were then built; there were then three and fifty parish churches in it, of which I think only thirteen remain; and by the Domesday Book they tell us it must be one of the greatest cities in England, whence perhaps that old English proverbial line:

Lincoln was, London is, and York shall be.[34]

It is certain William the Conqueror built the castle, and, as 'tis said, to curb the potent citizens; and the ruins show that it was a most magnificent work, well fortified, and capable of receiving a numerous garrison.

The bishopric of Lincoln at that time contained all that now is contained in the dioceses of Ely, Peterborough, and Oxford, besides what is now the diocese of Lincoln. This see, though of no longer date than since the conquest, has produced to the Church and State

Three Saints,
One Cardinal, (namely Wolsey)
Six Lord Chancellors,
One Lord Treasurer,
One Lord Privy Seal,
Four Chancellors of Oxford,
Two ditto, of Cambridge.

But all this relates to times past, and is an excursion, which I shall atone for by making no more. Such is the present state of Lincoln, that it is an old dying, decayed, dirty city; and except that part, which, as above, lies between the castle and the church on the top of the hill, it is scarce tolerable to call it a city.

Yet it stands in a most rich, pleasant, and agreeable country; for on the north, and again on the south east, the noble plain, called Lincoln Heath extends itself, like the plains about Salisbury, for above fifty miles; namely, from Sleeford and Ancaster south to the bank of the Humber north, though not with a breadth equal to the vast stretched out length; for the plain is hardly any where above three or four miles broad.

As the middle of the country is all hilly, and the west side low, so the east side is the richest, most fruitful, and best cultivated of any county in England, so far from London; one part is all fen or marsh grounds, and extends itself south to the Isle of Ely, and here it is that so vast a quantity of sheep are fed, as makes this county and that of Leicester an inexhaustible fountain of wool for all the manufacturing counties in England.

There are abundance of very good towns too in this part, especially on the sea coast, as Grimsby, in the utmost point of the county north east, facing the Humber and the ocean, and almost opposite to Hull. A little farther within Humber is Barton, a town noted for nothing that I know of, but an ill-favoured dangerous passage, or ferry, over the Humber to Hull; where in an open boat, in which we had about fifteen horses, and ten or twelve cows, mingled with about seventeen or eighteen passengers, called Christians; we were about four hours tossed about on the Humber, before we could get into the harbour at Hull; whether I was sea-sick or not, is not worth notice, but that we were all sick of the passage, any one may suppose, and particularly I was so uneasy at it, that I chose to go round by York, rather than return to Barton, at least for that time.

Grimsby is a good town, but I think 'tis but an indifferent road for shipping; and in the great storm, (ann. 1703) it was proved to be so, for almost all the ships that lay in Grimsby road were driven from their anchors, and many of them lost.

Here within land we see Brigg, Castor, Louth, Horncastle, Bolingbroke, Spilsby, Wainfleet, and Boston. As these are all, except the last, inland towns they afford little remarkable, only to intimate that all this country is employed in husbandry, in breeding and feeding innumerable droves and flocks of black cattle and sheep. Indeed I should not have said black cattle. I should have called them red cattle; for it was remarkable, that almost all their cows for 50 miles together are red, or pied red and white, and consequently all the cattle raised there, are the same.

The Fen Country begins about Wainfleet, which is within twenty miles of Grimsby, and extends itself to the Isle of Ely south, and to the grounds opposite to Lynn Regis in Norfolk east. This part is indeed very properly called Holland, for 'tis a flat, level, and often drowned country, like Holland itself; here the very ditches are navigable, and the people pass from town to town in boats, as in Holland. Here we had the uncouth music of the bittern, a bird formerly counted ominous and presaging, and who, as fame tells us, (but as I believe no body knows) thrusts its bill into a reed, and then gives the dull, heavy groan or sound, like a sigh, which it does so loud, that with a deep bass like the sound of a gun at a great distance, 'tis heard two or three miles, (say the people) but perhaps not quite so far.

Here we first saw Boston, a handsome well-built sea port town, at the mouth of the River Wittham. The tower of this church is, without question, the largest and highest in England; and, as it stands in a country, which (they say) has no bottom, nothing is more strange, than that they should find a foundation for so noble and lofty a structure; it had no ornament, spire, or pinnacle on the top, but it is so very high, that few spires in England, can match it, and it is not only beautiful by land but is very useful at sea to guide pilots into that port, and even into the mouth of the River Ouse; for in clear weather 'tis seen quite out at sea to the entrance of those channels, which they call Lynn Deeps, and Boston Deeps, which are as difficult places as most upon the whole eastern shore of Britain.

The town of Boston is a large, populous, and well-built town, full of good merchants, and has a good share of foreign trade, as well as Lynn. Here is held one of those annual fairs, which preserve the ancient title of a mart, whereof I remember only four in England of any considerable note, viz. Lynn, Gainsborough, Beverly, and Boston.

The country round this place is all fen and marsh grounds, the land very rich, and which feeds prodigious numbers of large sheep, and also oxen of the largest size, the overplus and best of which goes all to London market; and from this part, as also from the downs or heath above-mentioned, comes the greatest part of the wool, known, as a distinction for its credit, because of its fineness, by the name of Lincolnshire wool; which is sent in great quantities into Norfolk and Suffolk, for the manufacturers of those counties, and indeed to several other of the most trading counties in England.

From Boston we came on through the fen country to Spalding, which is another sea port in the level, but standing far within the land on the River Welland. Here was nothing very remarkable to be seen as to antiquity, but the ruins of an old famous monastery. There is a bridge over the Welland, and vesels of about fifty or sixty ton may come up to the town and that is sufficient for the trade of Spalding, which is chiefly in corn and coal.

We must not pass by Crowland, another place of great religious antiquity, here being once a famous monastery, the remains of which are still to be seen. The monks of Crowland were eminent in history, and a great many stories are told of the devils of Crowland also, and what conversation they had with the monks, which tales are more out of date now, than they were formerly; for they tell us, that in ancient times those things were as certainly believed for truths, as if they had been done before their faces.

There is one thing here that is curious indeed, and very remarkable, and which is not to be seen in any other place in Britain, if it be in Europe; namely, a triangular bridge. The case is this; the River Welland and another river, or rather branch from the River Nyne, join together just at Crowland, and the bridge being fixed at the very point where they join, stands upon a centre in the middle of the united waters, and then parting into two bridges, lands you one to the right upon Thorney, and one to the left upon Holland; and yet they tell us there is a whirlpool, or bottomless pit, in the middle too; but that part I see no reason to give credit to.

The town of Spalding is not large, but pretty well built and well inhabited; but for the healthiness or pleasantness of it, I have no more to say than this, that I was very glad when I got out of it, and out of the rest of the fen country; for 'tis a horrid air for a stranger to breathe in.

The history of the draining those fens, by a set of gentlemen called the Adventurers,[35] the several laws for securing and preserving the banks, and dividing the lands; how they were by the extraordinary conflux of waters from all the inland counties of England frequently overflowed, and sometimes lay under water most part of the year; how all the water in this part of England, which does not run into the Thames, the Trent, or the Severn, falls together into these low grounds, and empty themselves into the sea by those drains as though a sink; and how by the skill of these Adventurers, and, at a prodigious expense, they have cut new channels, and even whole rivers, with particular drains from one river to another, to carry off the great flux of waters, when floods or freshes come down either on one side or on the other; and how notwithstanding all that hands could do, or art contrive, yet sometimes the waters do still prevail, the banks break, and whole levels are overflowed together; all this though it would be very useful and agreeable to have it fully and geographically described, yet it would take up so much room, and be so tedious here, where you are expecting a summary description of things, rather than the history and reasons of them that I cannot think of entering any farther into it.

Here are also an infinite number of wild fowl, such as duck and mallard, teal and widgeon, brand geese, wild geese, &c. and for the taking of the four first kinds, here are a great number of decoys or duckoys, call them which you please, from all which the vast number of fowls they take are sent up to London; the quantity indeed is incredible, and the accounts which the country people give of the numbers they sometimes take, are such, that one scarce dares to report it from them. But this I can say, of my certain knowledge, that some of these decoys are of so great an extent, and take such great quantities of fowl, that they are let for great sums of money by the year, viz. from 100l. to 3, 4, and 500l. a year rent.[36]

There are many particulars in the managing and draining these levels, throwing off the water by mills and engines, and cultivating the grounds in an unusual manner, which would be very useful to be described.

1. That here are some wonderful engines for throwing up water, and such as are not to be seen any where else, whereof one in particular threw up, (as they assured us) twelve hundred ton of water in half an hour, and goes by wind-sails, 12 wings or sails to a mill. This I saw the model of, but I must own I did not see it perform.

2. Here are the greatest improvements by planting of hemp, that, I think, is to be seen in England; particularly on the Norfolk and Cambridge side of the Fens, as about Wisbech, Well, and several other places where we saw many hundred acres of ground bearing great crops of hemp.

3. Here is a particular trade carried on with London, which is no where else practised in the whole kingdom, that I have met with, or heard of, (viz.) for carrying fish alive by land-carriage; this they do by carrying great butts filled with water in waggons, as the carriers draw other goods. The butts have a little square flap, instead of a bung, about ten, twelve, or fourteen inches square which, being opened gives air to the fish and every night, when they come to the inn, they draw off the water, and let more fresh and sweet water run into them again. In these carriages they chiefly carry especially tench and pike, of which here are some of the largest in England.

From the Fens, longing to be delivered from fogs and stagnate air, and the water of the colour of brewed ale, like the rivers of the Peak, we first set foot on dry land, as I called it, at Peterborough. This is a little city, and indeed 'tis the least in England; for Bath, or Wells, or Ely, or Carlisle, which are all called cities are yet much bigger; yet Peterborough is no contemptible place neither; there are some good houses in it, and the streets are fair and well-built; but the glory of Peterborough is the cathedral, which is truly fine and beautiful.

In this church was buried the body of the unhappy Mary Queen of Scots, mother to King James the First, who was beheaded not far off[37] in Fotheringay Castle in the same county; but her body was afterwards removed by King James the First, her son, into Westminster Abbey, where a monument is erected for her, in King Henry VIIth's chapel; though some do not stick to tell us, that though the monument was erected, the body was never removed. Here also lies interred another unhappy queen, namely, the Lady Katherine of Spain,[38] the divorced wife of King Henry VIII and mother to Queen Mary: who reigned immediately after King Edward VI. Her monument is not very magnificent, but 'tis far from mean.

'Tis remarkable, that as this church, when a monastery, was famous for its great revenues, so now, as reduced, 'tis one of the poorest bishoprics in England, if not the meanest.

Coming to this little city landed us in Northamptonshire; but as great part of Lincolnshire, which is a vastly extended large county, remained yet unseen, we were obliged to turn north from Peterborough, and take a view of the fens again, though we kept them at some distance too. Here we passed the Welland at Market Deeping, an old, ill-built and dirty town; then we went through Bourn to Folkingham.

From hence we crossed part of the great heath mentioned before, and came into the high road again at Ankaster, a small but ancient Roman village, and full of remnants of antiquity. This place and Panton, a village near it, would afford great subject of discourse, if antiquity was my present province, for here are found abundance of Roman coins, urns, and other remains of antiquity, as also in several parts here about; and at this town of Ankaster there was a station or colony settled of Romans, which afterwards swelled up into a city, but is now sunk again out of knowledge.

From hence we came to Grantham, famous for a very fine church and spire steeple, so finely built, and so very high, that I do not know many higher and finer built in Britain. The vulgar opinion, that this steeple stands leaning, is certainly a vulgar error. I had no instrument indeed to judge it by, but, according to the strictest observation, I could not perceive it, or anything like it, and am much of opinion with that excellent poet:[39]

'Tis height makes Grantham steeple stand awry.

This is a neat, pleasant, well-built and populous town, has a good market, and the inhabitants are said to have a very good trade, and are generally rich. There is also a very good free-school here. This town lying on the great northern road is famous, as well as Stamford, for abundance of very good inns, some of them fit to entertain persons of the greatest quality and their retinues, and it is a great advantage to the place.

From a hill, about a mile beyond this town north west, being on the great York road, we had a prospect again into the Vale of Bever, or Belvoir, also here we had a distant view of Bever, or Bellevoir Castle, which 'tis supposed took its name from the situation, from whence there is so fine a prospect, or Bellevoir over the country; so that you see from the hill into six counties, namely, into Lincoln, Nottingham, Darby, Leicester, Rutland, and Northampton shires. The castle or palace (for such it now is) of Bevoir, is now the seat of the noble family of Mannors, Dukes of Rutland, who have also a very noble estate, equal to the demesnes of some sovereign princes, and extending itself into Nottingham and Darbyshire far and wide, and in which estate they have an immense subterranean treasure, never to be exhausted; I mean the lead mines and coal-pits, of which I shall say more in its place.

Turning southward from hence we entered Rutlandshire, remarkable for being the least county in England, having but two market towns in it, viz. Okeham and Uppingham, but famous for abundance of fine seats of the gentlemen, and some of the first rank, as particularly the Earls of Gainsborough and Nottingham;[40] the latter has at a very great expense, and some years labour, rebuilt the ancient seat of Burleigh on the Hill, near Okeham, and on the edge of the vale of Cathross. This house would indeed require a volume of itself, to describe the pleasant situation, and magnificent structure, the fine gardens, the perfectly well-finished apartments, the curious paintings, and well-stored library: all these merit a particular view, and consequently an exact description; but it is not the work of a few pages, and it would be to lessen the fame of this palace, to say any thing by way of abstract, where every part calls for a full account: at present, all I can say of it is, there may be some extraordinary palaces in England, but I do not know a house in Britain, which excels all the rest in so many particulars, or that goes so near to excelling them all in every thing.

From hence we came to Stamford; the town is placed in a kind of an angle of the county of Lincoln, just upon the edge of three counties, viz. Lincoln, Northampton, and Rutland: this town boasts greatly too of its antiquity, and indeed it has evident marks of its having been a very great place in former days. History tells us it was burnt by the Danes above 1500 years ago, being then a flourishing city. Tradition tells us, it was once a university, and that the schools were first erected by Bladud King of the Britains; the same whose figure stands up at the King's Bath in the city of Bath, and who lived 300 years before our Saviour's time. But the famous camps and military ways, which still appear at and near this town, are a more visible testimony of its having been a very ancient town, and that it was considerable in the Romans' time.

It is at this time a very fair, well-built, considerable and wealthy town, consisting of six parishes, including that of St Martin in Stamford-Baron; that is to say, in that part of the town which stands over the river. The government of this town is not, it seems, as most towns of such note are, by a mayor and aldermen, but by an alderman, who is chief magistrate, and twelve comburgesses, and twenty-four capital burgesses, which, abating their worships' titles, is, to me, much the same thing as a mayor, aldermen, and common council. They boast in this town of very great privileges, especially to their alderman, who is their chief magistrate, and his comburgesses; such as being freed from the sheriff's jurisdiction, and from being impanneled on juries out of the town; to have the return of all writs, to be freed from all lords lieutenants, and from their musters, and for having the militia of the town commanded by their own officers.

There are two constant weekly markets here, viz. on Mondays and Fridays, but the last is the chief market. They have also three fairs, viz. St Simon and Jude, St James's, and Green-goose Fair, and a great Midlent mart; but the latter is not now so considerable, as it is reported to have formerly been.

But the beauty of Stamford is the neighbourhood of the noble palace of the Earl of Excester, called Burleigh House, built by the famous Sir William Cecil,[41] Lord Burleigh, and Lord High Treasurer to Queen Elizabeth. This house, built all of free-stone, looks more like a town than a house, at which avenue soever you come to it; the towers and the pinnacles so high, and placed at such a distance from one another, look like so many distant parish-churches in a great town, and a large spire covered with lead, over the great clock in the centre, looks like the cathedral, or chief church of the town.

The house stands on an eminence, which rises from the north entrance of the park, coming from Stamford. As you mount the hill, you come to a fine esplanade, before the great gate or first entrance of the house, where there is a small but very handsome semi-circle, taken in with an iron balustrade, and from this, rising a few steps, you enter a most noble hall, but made infinitely more noble by the invaluable paintings, with which it is so filled, that there is not room to place any thing between them.

The late Earl of Excester,[42] father of his present lordship, had a great genius for painting and architecture, and a superior judgment in both, as every part of this noble structure will testify; for he changed the whole face of the building; he pulled down great part of the front next the garden, and turned the old Gothic windows into those spacious sashes which are now seen there; and though the founder or first builder, who had an exquisite fancy also, (as the manner of buildings then was) had so well ordered the situation and avenues of the whole fabric, that nothing was wanting of that kind, and had also contrived the house itself in a most magnificent manner; the rooms spacious, well directed, the ceilings lofty, and the decorations just, yet the late Earl found room for alterations, infinitely to the advantage of the whole; as particularly, a noble stair case, a whole set of fine apartments, with rooms of state, fitting for the entertainment of a prince, especially those on the garden side; though at present a little out of repair again.

As this admirable genius, the late Earl, loved paintings, so he had infinite advantage in procuring them; for he not only travelled three times into Italy, and stayed every time a considerable while at Florence, but he was so entertained at the Court of Tuscany, and had, by his most princely deportment and excellent accomplishments, so far obtained upon the great duke, that he might be said indeed to love him, and his highness showed the Earl many ways that esteem; and more particularly, in assisting him to purchase many excellent pieces at reasonable prices; and not only so, but his highness presented him with several pieces of great value.

Besides the pictures, which, as above, were brought from abroad, the house itself, at least the new apartments may be said to be one entire picture. The stair-case, the ceilings of all the fine lodgings, the chapel, the hall, the late Earl's closet, are all finely painted by VARRIO,[43] of whose work I need say no more than this, that the Earl kept him twelve years in his family, wholly employed in painting those ceilings and stair-cases, &c. and allowed him a coach and horses, and equipage, a table, and servants and a very considerable pension.

N.B. The character this gentleman left behind him at this town, is, that he deserved it all for his paintings; but for nothing else; his scandalous life, and his unpaid debts, it seems, causing him to be but very meanly spoken of in the town of Stamford.

By the park wall, adjoining to Burleigh House, passed an old Roman highway, beginning at Castor, a little village near Peterborough; but which was anciently a Roman station, or colony, called Durobrevum; this way is still to be seen, and is now called the 40 Foot Way, passing from Gluniworth Ferry (and Peterborough) to Stamford. This was, as the antiquaries are of opinion, the great road into the north, which is since turned from Stilton in Huntingdonshire to Wandsworth or Wandsford, where there is a very good bridge over the River Nyne; which coming down from Northampton, as I have observed already, passes thence by Peterborough, and so into the Fen country. But if I may straggle a little into antiquity, (which I have studiously avoided) I am of opinion, neither this or Wandsford was the ancient northern road in use by the Romans; for 'tis evident, that the great Roman causeway is still seen on the left hand of that road, and passing the Nyne at a place called Water Neuton, went directly to Stamford, and passed the Welland, just above that town, not in the place where the bridge stands now: and this Roman way is still to be seen, both on the south and the north side of the Welland, stretching itself on to Brig Casterton, a little town about three miles beyond Stamford; which was, as all writers agree, another Roman station; whence it went on to Panton, another very considerable colony, and so to Newark, where it crossed the Foss. This Forty Foot Way then must be a cross road from Castor, and by that from the Fen Country, so leading into the great highway at Stamford.

Lord Fitzwilliams lately built a very fine stone bridge over the Nyne. I was very much applauding this generous action of my lord's, knowing the inconvenience of the passage there before, especially if the waters of the Nyne were but a little swelled, and I thought it a piece of public charity; but my applause was much abated, when coming to pass the bridge (being in a coach) we could not be allowed to go over it, without paying 2*s.* 6*d.* of which I shall only say this, that I think 'tis the only half crown toll that is in Britain.

On the other side of the river is a fine new-built house, all of free stone, possessed by Sir Francis St John,[44] Bart. which affords a very beautiful prospect to travellers, as they pass from the hill beyond Stilton to Wansford Bridge. This Wansford has obtained an idle addition to its name, from a story so firmly believed by the country people, that they will hardly allow any room for contradiction; namely, that a great flood coming hastily down the River Nyne, in hay-making-time, a country fellow, having taken up his lodging on a cock of hay in the meadow, was driven down the stream in the night, while he was fast asleep; and the hay swimming, and the fellow sleeping, they drove together towards Wisbech in the Fens, whence he was fairly going on to the sea; when being wakened, he was seen and taken up by some fishermen, almost in the open sea; and being asked, who he was? he told them his name; and where he lived? he answered, at Wansford in England. From this story the town is called Wansford in England and we see at the great inn, by the south end of the bridge, the sign of a man floating on a cock of hay, and over him written, Wansford in England.

Coming south from hence we passed Stilton, a town famous for cheese, which is called our English Parmesan, and is brought to table with the mites, or maggots round it, so thick, that they bring a spoon with them for you to eat the mites with, as you do the cheese.

Hence we came through Sautrey Lane, a deep descent between two hills, in which is Stangate Hole, famous for being the most noted robbing-place in all this part of the country. Hence we passed to Huntingdon, the county town, otherwise not considerable; it is full of very good inns, is a strong pass upon the Ouse, and in the late times of rebellion it was esteemed so by both parties. Here are the most beautiful meadows on the banks of the River Ouse, that I think are to be seen in any part of England; and to see them in the summer season, covered with such innumerable stocks of cattle and sheep, is one of the most agreeable sights of its kind in the world. This town has nothing remarkable in it; 'tis a long continued street, pretty well built, has three parish churches, and a pretty good market-place; but the bridge, or bridges rather, and causeway over the Ouse is a very great ornament to the place.

Hence we went a little north to see Oundle, being told that the famous drum was to be heard just at that time in the well; but when we came there, they showed us indeed the well and the town, but as for the drum, they could only tell us they heard of it, and that it did drum; but we could meet with no person of sufficient credit, that would say seriously they had heard it: so we came away dissatisfied.

From Oundle we crossed the county of Northampton into Bedfordshire, and particularly to the town of Bedford, the chief town of the county; for this county has no city in it, though even this town is larger and more populous, than several cities in England, having five parish-churches, and a great many, and those wealthy and thriving inhabitants. This is one of the seven counties, which they say lie together, and have not one city among them; namely, Huntington, Bedford, Bucks, Berks, Hertford, Essex, and Suffolk.

But here I must do a piece of justice to the usage of England in denominating of cities, namely, that it is not here as in France, and Flanders, and Holland, where almost all their towns of note are called cities and where the gentry chiefly live in those cities, and the clergy also. But as we have no authority, but ancient usage and custom, for the distinguishing places by the names of towns and cities, so since that ancient usage or authority had the titles of places, 'tis observable some places, formerly of note, are considerably decayed, and scarce preserve the face of their ancient greatness; as Lincoln, Old Sarum, Carlisle, Verulam, and others; and several towns which in those times scarce deserved the name of cities are now, by the increase of commerce and numbers of inhabitants, become greater, more populous and wealthy, than others, which are called cities.

Nor is this all but several towns, which Mr Cambden tells us, were called cities in his time, are now sunk from the dignity, and are only called towns, and yet still retain a greatness, wealth, and populousness superior to many cities, such as Colchester, Ipswich, Shrewsbury, Cambridge, Stamford, Leicester, and others which are without all comparison greater now than Wells, Peterborough, Ely, or Carlisle, and yet have lost the title of cities, which the other retain.

Thus we have at this time the towns of Froom, Taunton, Tiverton, Plymouth, Portsmouth, and others in the west, and towns of Liverpool, Manchester, Leeds, Sheffield, Birmingham, Hull, and several others in the north, that are much larger, richer, and more populous than Rochester, Peterborough, Carlisle, Bath, and even than York itself, and yet these retain but the name of towns, nay even of villages, in some of which the chiefest magistrate is but a constable, as in Manchester, for example.

Another thing is scarce to be equalled in the whole isle of Britain; namely, that though the Ouse, by a long and winding course, cuts through the county, and by its long reachings, so as to make above seventy miles between Oulney and St Neots, though not above twenty by land, yet in all that course it receives but one river into it, namely the little River Ivel.

Bedford, as I have said, is a large, populous, and thriving town, and a pleasant well-built place; it has five parish churches, a very fine stone bridge over the Ouse, and the High Street, (especially) is a very handsome fair street, and very well-built; and though the town is not upon any of the great roads in England, yet it is full of very good inns, and many of them; and in particular we found very good entertainment here.

Here is the best market for all sorts of provisions, that is to be seen at any country town in all these parts of England; and this occasions, that though it is so far from London, yet the higglers or carriers buy great quantities of provisions here for London markets; also here is a very good trade down the river to Lynn.

Here is also a great corn market, and great quantities of corn are bought here, and carried down by barges and other boats to Lynn, where it is again shipped, and carried by sea to Holland. The soil hereabouts is exceeding rich and fertile, and particularly produces great quantities of the best wheat in England. There are but ten market towns in the whole county, and yet 'tis not a small county neither. The towns are,

Bedford,	Ampthill,	Potton,
Biggleswood,	Shefford,	Tuddington,
Leighton,	Luton,	Wooburn.
Dunstable,		

The last of these was almost demolished by a terrible fire,[45] which happened here just before my writing this account; but as this town has the good luck to belong to a noble family, particularly eminent for being good landlords; that is to say, bountiful and munificent to their poor tenants, I mean the ducal house of Bedford; there is no doubt but that the trustees, though his grace the present Duke[46] is in his minority, will preserve that good character to the family, and re-edify the town, which is almost all their own.

The Duke's house, called Wooburn Abbey, is just by the town, a good old house, but very ancient, spacious and convenient rather than fine but exceedingly pleasant by its situation; and for the great quantity of beech woods which surround the parks and cover the hills, and also for great woods of oak too, as rich and valuable, as they are great and magnificent.

Ampthill is graced like Wooburn; for though in itself, like the other, it is not a considerable town, and has no particular manufacture to enrich it, yet by the neighbourhood of that great and noble family of Bruce Earls of Ailesbury, the very town is made both rich and honourable. From hence, through the whole south part of this county, as far as the border of Buckinghamshire and Hertfordshire, the people are taken up with the manufacture of bone-lace, in which they are wonderfully increased and improved within these few years past. Also the manufactures of straw-work, especially straw hats, spreads itself from Hertfordshire into this county, and is wonderfully increased within a few years past. Having thus viewed this county in all its most considerable towns, we came from Dunstable to St Albans, and so into London, all which has been spoken of before; I therefore break off this circuit here, and subscribe,

SIR,
Your most obedient servant.

Appendix to the Second Volume[1]

In travelling this latter part of this second tour, it has not been taken notice of, though it very well deserves mention; that the soil of all the midland part of England, even from sea to sea, is of a deep stiff clay, or marly kind, and it carries a breadth of near 50 miles at least, in some places much more; nor is it possible to go from London to any part of Britain, north, without crossing this clayey dirty part. For example:

1. Suppose we take the great northern post road from London to York, and so into Scotland; you have tolerable good ways and hard ground, 'till you reach Royston about 32, and to Kneesworth, a mile farther. But from thence you enter upon the clays, which beginning at the famous Arrington-Lanes, and going on to Caxton, Huntington, Stilton, Stamford, Grantham, Newark, Tuxford (called for its deepness Tuxford in the Clays) holds on 'till we come almost to Bautree, which is the first town in Yorkshire, and there the country is hard and sound, being part of Sherwood Forest.

2. Suppose you take the other northern road, namely, by St Albans, Dunstable, Hockley, Newport Pagnel, Northampton, Leicester and Nottingham or Darby. On this road after you are passed Dunstable, which, as in the other way, is about 30 miles, you enter the deep clays, which are so surprisingly soft that it is perfectly frightful to travellers, and it has been the wonder of foreigners, how, considering the great numbers of carriages which are continually passing with heavy loads, those ways have been made practicable; indeed the great number of horses every year killed by the excess of labour in those heavy ways, has been such a charge to the country, that new building of causeways, as the Romans did of old, seems to me to be a much easier expense. From Hockley to Northampton, thence to Harborough, and Leicester, and thence to the very bank of Trent these terrible clays con-

tinue; at Nottingham you are passed them, and the forest of Sherwood yields a hard and pleasant road for 30 miles together.

3. Take the same road as it leads to Coventry, and from thence to West Chester, the deep clays reach through all the towns of Brickhill, Fenny and Stony Stratford, Towcester, Daventry, Hill Morton, or Dunchurch, Coventry, Coleshill, and even to Birmingham for very nearly 80 miles.

4. If we take the road to Worcester it is the same through the vale of Aylesbury to Buckingham, and westward to Banbury, Keynton, and the vale of Evesham, where the clays reach, with some intermissions, even to the bank of Severn, as they do more northernly quite to West Chester.

The reason of my taking notice of this badness of the roads, through all the midland counties, is this; that as these are counties which drive a very great trade with the city of London, and with one another, perhaps the greatest of any counties in England; and that, by consequence, the carriage is exceeding great, and also that all the land carriage of the northern counties necessarily goes through these counties, so the roads had been ploughed so deep, and materials have been in some places so difficult to be had for repair of the roads, that all the surveyors rates have been able to do nothing; nay, the very whole country has not been able to repair them; that is to say, it was a burthen too great for the poor farmers; for in England it is the tenant, not the landlord, that pays the surveyors of the highways.

This necessarily brought the country to bring these things before the Parliament; and the consequence has been, that turnpikes or toll-bars [2] have been set up on the several great roads of England, beginning at London, and proceeding through almost all those dirty deep roads, in the midland counties especially; at which turn-pikes all carriages, droves of cattle, and travellers on horseback, are obliged to pay an easy toll; that is to say, a horse a penny, a coach three pence, a cart four pence, at some six pence to eight pence, a waggon six pence. in some a shilling, and the like; cattle pay by the score, or by the head, in some places more, in some less; but in no place is it thought a burthen that ever I met with, the benefit of a good road abundantly making amends for that little charge the travellers are put to at the turn-pikes.

Several of these turn-pikes and tolls had been set up of late years, and great progress had been made in mending the most difficult ways, and that with such success as well deserves a place in this account. And this is one reason for taking notice of it in this manner; for as the memory of the Romans, which is so justly famous, is preserved in nothing more visible to common observation, than in the remains of those noble causeways and highways, which they made through all parts of the kingdom, and which were found so needful, even then, when there was not the five hundredth part of the commerce and carriage that is now. How much more valuable must these new works be, though nothing to compare with those of the Romans, for the firmness and duration of their work?

The causeways and roads, or streetways of the Romans, were perfect solid buildings, the foundations were laid so deep, and the materials so good, however far they were obliged to fetch them, that if they had been vaulted and arched, they could not have been more solid: I have seen the bottom of them dug up in several places, where I have observed flint-stones, chalk-stones, hard gravel, solid hard clay, and several other sorts of earth, laid in layers, like the veins of ore in a mine; a laying of clay of a solid binding quality, then flint-stones, then chalk, then upon the chalk rough ballast or gravel, 'till the whole work has been raised six or eight foot from the bottom; then it has been covered with a crown or rising ridge in the middle, gently sloping to the sides, that the rain might run off every way, and not soak into the work. This I have seen as fair and firm, after having stood, as we may conclude, at least 12 or 1600 years, as if it had been made but the year before.

And that I may not be charged with going beyond the most exact truth, I refer the curious to make their observations upon that causeway, called the Fosse, which is now remaining, and to be seen between Cirencester and Marshfield in Wiltshire, on the road to the Bath, or between the same Cirencester and Birdlip Hill in Gloucestershire, on the road to Gloucester; but more particularly, between Castleford Bridge, near Pontefract in Yorkshire, upon the River Aire, and the town of Aberford, in the road to Tadcaster and York.

In several parts of this causeway, the country being hard, and the way good on either side, travellers have not made much use of the causeway, it being very high, and perhaps exposing them too much to the wind and weather, but have rather chosen to go on either side, so that the causeway in some places, lies as flat and smooth on the top, as if it had never been made use of at all; and perhaps it has not, there being not so much as the mark of a wheel upon it, or of a horse foot for a good way together, for which I refer to the curious traveller that goes that way.

It is true the Romans being lords of the world, had the command of the people, their persons and their work, their cattle, and their carriages; even their armies were employed in these noble undertakings; and if the materials they wanted, were to fetch 20, nay 30 to 40 miles off, if they wanted them, they would have them, and the works were great and magnificent like themselves: witness the numberless encampments, lines, castles and fortifications, which we see the remains of to this day.

But now the case is altered, labour is dear, wages high, no man works for bread and water now; our labourers do not work in the road, and drink in the brook; so that as rich as we are, it would exhaust the whole nation to build the edifices, the causeways, the aqueducts, lines, castles, fortifications, and other public works, which the Romans built with very little expense.

But to return to this new method of repairing the highways at the expense of the turn-pikes; that is to say, by the product of funds raised at those turn-pikes; I shall give some examples here of those which have been brought to perfection already, and of others which are now carrying on.

First, that great county of Essex, of which our first tour gives an ample account. The great road from London, through this whole county towards Ipswich and Harwich, is the most worn with waggons, carts, and carriages; and with infinite droves of black cattle, hogs, and sheep, of any road (that leads through no larger an extent of country) in England. The length of it from Stratford-bridge by Bow, to Streetford-bridge over the Stour, on the side of Suffolk, is 50 miles, and to Harwich above 65 miles.

These roads were formerly deep, in time of floods dangerous, and at other times, in winter, scarce passable; they are now so firm, so safe, so easy to travellers, and carriages as well as cattle, that no road in England can yet be said to equal them; this was first done by the help of a turnpike, set up by Act of Parliament,[3] about the year 1697, at a village near Ingerstone. Since that, another turnpike, set up at the corner of the Dog Row, near Mile-end; with an additional one at Rumford, which is called a branch, and paying at one, passes the person through both. This I say, being set up since the other, completes the whole, and we are told, that as the first expires in a year or two, this last will be sufficient for the whole, which will be a great ease to the country. The first toll near Ingerstone, being the highest rated public toll in England for they take 8*d*. for every cart, 6*d*. for every coach, and 12*d*. for every waggon; and in proportion for droves of cattle. For single horsemen indeed, it is the same as others pay, viz. 1*d*. per horse, and we are told, while this is doing, that the gentlemen of the county, design to petition the Parliament, to have the commissioners of the last Act, whose turnpike, as above, is at Mile-end and Rumford, empowered to place other turnpikes, on the other most considerable roads, and so to undertake, and repair all the roads in the whole county, I mean all the considerable roads.

But to come back to the counties which I am now speaking of, some very good attempts have been made of this kind on the northern roads, through those deep ways I mentioned, in the high post road; for example. That an Act of Parliament was obtained about 30 years since, for repairing the road between Ware and Royston, and a turnpike was erected for it at Wade's-mill, a village so called, about a mile and a half beyond Ware. This proved so effectual, that the road there, which was before scarce passable, is now built up in a high, firm causeway; the most like those mentioned above, of the Romans, of any of these new undertakings. And, though this road is continually worked upon, by the vast number of carriages, bringing malt and barley to Ware, for whose sake indeed, it was obtained; yet, with small repairs it is maintained, and the toll is reduced from a penny, to a half-penny, for the ease of the country, and so in proportion.

Beyond this, two grants have been obtained; one for repair of those wretched places, called Arrington Lanes, and all the road beyond Royston, to Caxton and Huntington; and another, for repairing the road from Stukely to Stilton, including the place called Stangate-Hole, and so on, towards Wansford and Santry Lane and Peterborough; by which these roads, which were before intolerable, are now much mended, but I cannot say, they are yet come up to the perfection of that road from London to Colchester.

One great difficulty indeed here, is, that the country is so universally made up of a deep, stiff clay; that 'tis hard to find any materials to repair the ways with, that may be depended upon. In some places they have a red sandy kind of a slate or stone, which they lay with timber and green faggots, and puts them to a very great expense; but this stone does not bind like chalk and gravel, or endure like flint and pebbles, but wears into clay from whence it proceeds; and this is the reason why they cannot expect those roads can reach up, however chargeable the repairs are to the goodness of the roads in Essex.

We see also a turnpike set up at a village very justly called Foul Mire near Cambridge, for the repair of the particular roads to the university, but those works are not yet brought to any pefection.

There is another road, which is a branch of the northern

road, and is properly called the coach road, and which comes into the other near Stangate Hole; and this indeed is a most frightful way, if we take it from Hatfield, or rather the park corners of Hatfield House, and from thence to Stevenage, to Baldock, to Biggleswade, and Bugden. Here is that famous lane called Baldock Lane, famous for being so unpassable, that the coaches and travellers were obliged to break out of the way even by force, which the people of the country not able to prevent, at length placed gates, and laid their lands open, setting men at the gates to take voluntary toll, which travellers always chose to pay, rather than plunge into sloughs and holes, which no horse could wade through. This terrible road is now under cure by the same methods, and probably may in time be brought to be firm and solid, the chalk and stones being not so far to fetch here, as in some of those other places I have just now mentioned.

But the repair of the roads in this county, namely Bedfordshire, is not so easy a work, as in some other parts of England. The drifts of cattle, which come this way out of Lincolnshire and the fens of the Isle of Ely, of which I have spoken already, are so great, and so constantly coming up to London markets, that it is much more difficult to make the ways good, where they are continually treading by the feet of the large heavy bullocks, of which the numbers that come this way are scarce to be reckoned up, and which make deep impressions, where the ground is not very firm, and often work through in the winter what the commissioners have mended in the summer.

But leaving these undertakings to speak for themselves when finished; for they can neither be justly praised or censured before; it ought to be observed, that there is another road branching out from this deep way at Stevenage, and goes thence to Hitchin, to Shefford, and Bedford. Hitchin is a large market town, and particularly eminent for its being a great corn market for wheat and malt, but especially the first, which is brought here for London market. The road to Hitchin, and thence to Bedford, though not a great thorough-fare for travellers, yet is a very useful highway for the multitude of carriages, which bring wheat from Bedford to that market, and from the country round it, even as far as Northamptonshire, and the edge of Leicestershire; and many times the country people are not able to bring their corn for the mere badness of the ways.

This road, I hear, will be likewise repaired, by virtue of a turn-pike to be placed near Hitchin on this side, and at the two bridges over the Ouse, namely Barford Bridge and Bedford Bridge, on the other side; as also at Temsford, where they drive through the river without the help of a bridge.

But to leave what may be, I return to what is. The next turnpikes are on the great north west road, or, as I have distinguished it already, the Watling-street Way; which, to describe it once for all, begins at Islington near London, and leads to Shrewsbury, West Chester, and Hollyhead in Wales; with other branches breaking out from it to the north, leading to Nottingham, Darby, Burton on the Trent, and Warrington, and from them all, farther north, into the north west parts of Great Britain.

Upon this great road there are wonderful improvements made and making, which no traveller can miss the observation of, especially if he knew the condition these ways were formerly in; nor can my account of these counties be perfect, without taking notice of it; for certainly no public edifice, almshouse, hospital, or nobleman's palace, can be of equal value to the country with this, no nor more an honour and ornament to it.

The first attempt upon this road was at Brickhill in Buckinghamshire, and the turn-pike was set up on the hill, near the town called Little Brickhill, by virtue of which, they repaired the road from thence to Stony Stratford, for about ten miles, and with very good success; for that road was broad, and capable of giving room for such a work; and though materials were hard to come at, and far to fetch, yet we soon found a large firm causeway, or highway, and of a full breadth, reaching from Fenny Stratford to Stony Stratford, which is six miles, and where the way was exceeding bad before.

This encouraged the country to set about the work in good earnest; and we now see the most dismal piece of ground for travelling, that ever was in England, handsomely repaired namely, from the top of the chalky hill beyond Dunstable down into Hockley Lane,[4] and through Hockley, justly called Hockley in the Hole, to Newport Pagnall, being a bye branch of the great road, and leading to Northampton, and was called the coach road; but such a road for coaches, as worse was hardly ever seen.

The next (to come southward) was the road from St Albans to South Mims, a village beyond Barnet. Soon after this road parts from the great coach road to the north beginning at Hatfield. This road is so well mended, the work so well done, and the materials so good, so plentifully furnished, and so faithfully applied, that, in short, if possible, it out-does the Essex road mentioned before; for here the bottom is not only repaired, but the narrow places are widened, hills levelled, bottoms raised, and the ascents and descents made easy, to the inexpressible ease and advantage of travellers, and especially of the carriers, who draw heavy goods and hard loads, who find the benefit in the health and strength of their cattle.

From hence, to come still more towards London, another undertaking reaches from the foot of Barnet Hill, called formerly the Blockhouse, to Whetstone, and so over the great heath, called Finchley Common, to Highgate Hill, and up the hill to the gatehouse at Highgate, where they had their turnpike; as also at the Blockhouse; and this work is also admirably well performed, and through a piece of ground, which was very full of sloughs and deep places before.

But from Highgate to London still required help; the road branched into two, at the top of Highgate Hill, or just at the gatehouse there; one came to London by Islington, and there branched again into two, one coming by the north end of Islington, and another on the back of the town, and entering the town at the south west end near the Angel Inn, there dividing again, one branch entered London at Goswell-street and Aldersgate street; and this was the principal road for waggons and pack-horses: the other going directly to St John-street and into Smithfield; and this way was the chief road for Cattle to Smithfield Market. The other road parting off at Highgate, came down the hill and thence passing through Kentish Town, entered London by two ways: one by Grays Inn Lane, and the other by Clerkenwell.

All these roads were to the last extremity run to ruin, and grew worse and worse so evidently, that it was next to impossible, the country should be able to repair them: upon which an Act of Parliament was obtained for a turnpike, which is now erected at Islington aforesaid, as also all the other branches by the Kentish Town way, and others; so that by this new toll, all these roads are now likely to be made good, which were before almost a scandal to the city of London.

Another turnpike, and which was erected before this, was on the great north road, beginning at Shoreditch, and extending to Enfield Street, in the way to Ware; though this road is exceedingly thronged, and raises great sums, yet I cannot say, that the road itself seems to be so evidently improved, and so effectually repaired, as the others last mentioned, notwithstanding no materials are wanting; even on the very verge of the road itself, whether it be, that the number of carriages, which come this way, and which are indeed greater than in any other road about London, is the occasion, or whether the persons concerned do not so faithfully, or so skilfully perform, I will not undertake to determine.

After so many encouraging examples on this great Watling-street road, as I have mentioned above, they have now begun the like on the same way farther down, and particularly from Stony Stratford to Daventry and Dunchurch, and so on to Coventry and Coles-hill; all those parts of it are at this time repairing, and they promise themselves that in a few years those roads will be completely sound and firm, as Watling-street was in its most ancient and flourishing state.

I come next to mention other works of the same kind in remoter places, also more westerly, but within the compass of this midland circuit; as particularly the road from Birdlip Hill to Gloucester, formerly a terrible place for poor carriers and travellers out of Wales, &c. but now repaired very well. Likewise the road from Sandy Lane Hill in Wiltshire to the Bath, which began to be repaired by the direction of Her late Majesty Queen Anne.

By the same happy example, turnpikes are erected at the west end of the town, for repairing that horrid road, formerly also a part of the Watling-street Way, from St Giles Church to Paddington, and thence to Edgworth, obtained first by the interest and motion of his grace the Duke of Chandos.

On the other side of the river is another turnpike erected, or rather two turnpikes, one at the north end of the town of Newington, called Newington Buts, which has two or three collateral branches, viz. one at Vaux-Hall, at the bridge near the Spring Garden corner, and another at Croydon, besides smaller toll-bars on the bye-lanes. This undertaking has been very well prosecuted, and the great Sussex road, which was formerly unsufferably bad, is now become admirably good; and this is done at so great an expense, that they told me at Strettham, that one mile between the two next bridges south of that town, cost a thousand pounds repairing, including one of the bridges, and yet it must be acknowledged, that the materials are very near hand, and very good all the way to Croydon.

The other turnpike on that side is placed near New Cross on the road into Kent, a little before the road to Lusum parts from the road to Deptford Bridge; so that all the road to Lee and Eltham, the road to Bromley and Tunbridge, as well as the great road to Rochester and Canterbury, are taken in there; and this undertaking, they tell us, is likewise very well performed.

So that upon the whole, this custom prevailing, 'tis more than probable, that our posterity may see the roads all over England restored in their time to such a perfection, that travelling and carriage of goods will be much more easy both to man and horse, than ever it was since the Romans lost this island.

Nor will the charge be burthensome to any body; as for trade, it will be encouraged by it every way; for carriage of all kind of heavy goods will be much easier, the waggoners will either perform in less time, or draw heavier loads, or the same load with fewer horses; the pack-horses will carry heavier burthens, or travel farther in a day, and so perform their journey in less time; all which will tend to lessen the rate of carriage, and so bring goods cheaper to market.

The fat cattle will drive lighter, and come to market with less toil, and consequently both go farther in one day, and not waste their flesh, and heat and spoil themselves, in wallowing through the mud and sloughs, as is now the case.

The sheep will be able to travel in the winter, and the city not be obliged to give great prizes to the butchers for mutton, because it cannot be brought up out of Leicestershire and Lincolnshire, the sheep not being able to travel: the graziers and breeders will not be obliged to sell their stocks of wethers cheap in October to the farmers within 20 miles of London, because after that they cannot bring them up.

Another benefit of these new measures for repairing the roads by turnpikes, is the opening of drains and water-courses, and building bridges, especially over the smaller waters, which are oftentimes the most dangerous to travellers on hasty rains, and always most injurious to the roads, by lying in holes and puddles, to the great spoiling the bottom, and making constant sloughs, sometimes able to bury both man and horse.

This improving of the roads is an infinite improvement to the towns near London, in the convenience of coming to them, which makes the citizens flock out in greater numbers than ever to take lodgings and country-houses, which many, whose business called them often to London, could not do, because of the labour of riding forward and backward, when the roads were but a little dirty, and this is seen in the difference in the rents of houses in those villages upon such repaired roads, from the rents of the like dwellings and lodgings in other towns of equal distance, where they want those helps, and particularly the increase of the number of buildings in those towns, as above.

There are indeed some very deep roads in many places of England, and that south by Trent too, where no such provision is yet made for repair of the roads, as particularly in and through the vale of Aylesbury, and to Buckingham, and beyond it into Oxfordshire; also beyond Northampton to Harborough and Leicester; also in Lincolnshire, beyond what we named to be from Huntington to Stilton, the road from Stamford to Grantham, Newark, and Tuxford, in the clays, all which remain very deep, and in some seasons dangerous.

Likewise the roads in Sussex, and that in particular which was formerly a Roman work, called Stony-street or Stone-street: going from Leatherhead to Darking, and through Darking church-yard, then cross a terrible deep country, called the Homeward, and so to Petworth and Arundel. But we see nothing of it now; and the country indeed remains in the utmost distress for want of good roads. So also all over the Wild of Kent and Sussex it is the same, where the corn is cheap at the barn, because it cannot be carried out; and dear at the market, because it cannot be brought in.

The benefit of these turnpikes appears now to be so great, and the people in all places begin to be so sensible of it, that it is incredible what effect it has already had upon trade in the countries where it is more completely finished; even the carriage of goods is abated in some places, 6*d*. per hundred weight, in some places 12*d*. per hundred, which is abundantly more advantage to commerce, than the charge paid amounts to, and yet at the same time the expense is paid by the carriers too, who make the abatement; so that the benefit in abating the rate of carriage is wholly and simply the tradesmen's, not the carrier's.

Yet the advantage is evident to the carriers also another way; for, as was observed before, they can bring more weight with the same number of horses, nor are their horses so hard worked and fatigued with their labour as they were before; in which one particular 'tis acknowledged by the carriers, they perform their work with more ease, and the masters are at less expense.

The advantage to all other kinds of travelling I omit here; such as the safety and ease to gentlemen travelling up to London on all occasions, whether to the term, or to Parliament, to Court, or on any other necessary occasion, which is not a small part of the benefit of these new methods. Also the riding post, as well for the ordinary carrying of the mails, or for the gentlemen riding post, when their occasions require speed; I say, the riding post is made extremely easy, safe, and pleasant, by the alteration of the roads.

I mention so often the safety of travelling on this occasion, because, as I observed before, the commissioners for these repairs of the highways have ordered, and do daily order, abundance of bridges to be repaired and enlarged, and new ones built, where they find occasion, which not only serve to carry the water off, where it otherwise often spreads, and lies as it were, dammed up upon the road, and spoils the way; but where it rises sometimes by sudden rains to a dangerous height; for it is to be observed, that there is more hazard, and more lives lost, in passing, or attempting to pass little brooks and streams, which are swelled by sudden showers of rain, and where passengers expect no stoppage, than in passing great rivers, where the danger is known, and therefore more carefully avoided.

In many of these places the commissioners have built large and substantial bridges for the benefit of travelling, as is said already, and in other places have built sluices to stop, and opened channels to carry off the water, where they used to swell into the highway. We have two of these sluices near London, in the road through Tottenham High-Cross and Edmonton, by which the waters in those places, which have sometimes been dangerous, are now carried off, and the road cleared; and as for bridges I have been told, that the several commissioners, in the respective districts where they are concerned, have already built about three hundred new ones, where there were none before, or where the former were small and insufficient to carry the traveller safe over the waters; many of these are within a few miles of London.

And for farther confirmation of what I have advanced above, namely, that we may expect, according to this good beginning, that the roads in most parts of England will in a few years be fully repaired, and restored to the same good condition, (or perhaps a better, than) they were in during the Roman government, we may take notice, that there are no less than twelve bills, or petitions for bills, depending before the Parliament, at this time sitting, for the repair of the roads, in several remote parts of England, or for the lengthening the time allowed in former Acts, some of which give us hopes, that the grants, when obtained, will be very well managed, and the country people greatly encouraged by them in their commerce; for there is no doubt to be made, but that the inland trade of England has been greatly obstructed by the exceeding badnesss of the roads.

This is evidenced to a demonstration in the counties of Essex and Suffolk, from whence they already bring their fat cattle, and particularly their mutton in droves, from sixty, seventy, or eighty miles, without fatiguing, harassing, or sinking the flesh of the creatures, even in the depth of winter.

I might give examples of other branches of inland commerce, which would be quite altered for the better, by this restoring the goodness of the roads, and particularly that of carrying cheese, a species of provision so considerable, that nothing, except that of live cattle, can exceed it.

I could enlarge here upon the convenience that would follow such a restoring the ways, for the carrying of fish from the sea coasts to the inner parts of the kingdom, where, by reason of the badness of the ways, they cannot now carry them sweet. This would greatly increase the consumption of fish in its season, which now for that very reason, is but small, and would employ an innumerable number of horses and men, as well as increase the shipping by that consumption.

These, and many others, are the advantages of our inland commerce, which we may have room to hope for upon the general repair of the roads, and which I shall have great occasion to speak of again in my northern circuit, which is yet to come.

INTRODUCTION TO THE THIRD VOLUME[1]

SIR, – I have now finished my account of the several circuits which I took the last year, completing the southern parts of the isle of Britain; my last brought me to the banks of the River Trent, and from thence back to London, where I first set out.

I have yet the largest, though not the most populous, part of Britain to give you an account of; nor is it less capable of satisfying the most curious traveller. Though, as in some places things may stand more remote from one another, and there may, perhaps, be more waste ground to go over; yet 'tis certain a traveller spends no waste hours, if his genius will be satisfied with just observations. The wildest part of the country is full of variety, the most mountainous places have their rarities to oblige the curious, and give constant employ to the enquiries of a diligent observer, making the passing over them more pleasant than the traveller could expect, or than the reader perhaps at first sight will think possible.

The people in these northern climes will increase the variety; their customs and genius differing so much from others, will add to our entertainment; the one part of them being, till now, a distinct nation, the inhabitants thereof will necessarily come in as a part of what we are to describe. Scotland is neither so considerable, that we should compliment her at the expense of England; or so inconsiderable, that we should think it below us to do her justice; I shall take the middle of both extremes.

I shall be tempted very often to make excursions here on account of the history and antiquities of persons and places both private and public. For the northern parts of Britain, especially of England, as they were long the seat of war between the several nations; such as the Britains, Scots, Picts, Romans, Saxons, and Danes, so there are innumerable remains of antiquity left behind them, and those more visible in those parts, and less defaced by time, and other accidents than in any other part of the island.

The north part of Great Britain, I mean Scotland, is a country which will afford a great variety to the observation, and to the pen of an itinerate; a kingdom so famous in the world for great and gallant men, as well states-men as soldiers, but especially the last, can never leave us barren of subject, or empty of somewhat to say of her.

The Union [2] has seemed to secure her peace, and to increase her commerce. But I cannot say she has raised her figure in the world at all since that time, I mean as a body. She was before considered as a nation, now she appears no more but as a province, or at best a dominion; she has not lost her name as a place; but as a state, she may be said to have lost it, and that she is now no more than a part of Great Britain in common with other parts of it, of which England it self is also no more. I might enlarge here upon the honour it is to Scotland to be a part of the British Empire, and to be incorporated with so powerful a people under the crown of so great a monarch; their being united in name as one, Britain, and their enjoying all the privileges of, and in common with, a nation who have the greatest privileges, and enjoy the most liberty of any people in the world. But I should be told, and perhaps justly too, that this was talking like an Englishman, rather than like a Briton; that I was gone from my declared impartiality, and that the Scots would perhaps talk a different style when I came among them. Nor is it my business to enquire which nation have the better end of the staff in the late coalition, or how the articles on which it is established, are performed on one side or other.

My business is rather to give a true and impartial description of the place; a view of the country, its present state as to fertility, commerce, manufacture, and product; with the manners and usages of the people, as I have done in England; and to this I shall confine my self as strictly as the nature of a journey through the country requires.

I shall, in doing this, come indeed of course to make frequent mention of the various turns and revolutions which have happened in those northern parts; for Scotland has changed its masters, and its forms of government, as often as other nations; and, in doing this, it will necessarily occur to speak of the Union, which is the last, and like to be the last revolution of affairs in Scotland for, we hope, many ages. But I shall enter no farther into this, than is concerned in the difference between the face of things there now, and what was there before the said Union, and which the Union has been the occasion or cause of; as particularly the division and government of the countries, and towns, and people in particular places; the communication of privileges, influence of government, and enlarging of the liberty of trade.

This will also bring on the needful account of alterations and improvements, in those counties, which, by reason of the long and cruel wars between the two nations in former reigns, lay waste and unimproved, thinly inhabited, and the people not only poor because of the continual incursions of the troops on either side; but barbarous and ravenous themselves, as being inured to rapine, and living upon the spoil of one another for several ages; all which is now at an end, and those counties called the marches or borders, are now as well peopled and cultivated as other counties, or in a fair way to be so.

This alteration affords abundance of useful observations, and 'tis hoped they shall be fruitfully improved in this work; and as it is a subject which none have yet meddled with, so we believe it will not be the less acceptable for its novelty, if tolerably well handled, as we hope it shall be.

Letter 8

SIR, – As I am to begin this circuit from the River Trent, and to confine my observations to that part of Britain which the Scots and Northumberlanders, and others on that side, call North by Trent, it seems necessary (at least it cannot be improper) to give some description of the river it self, and especially the course which it runs.

The River Trent is rated by ancient writers as the third river in England, the two greater being the Thames and the Severn. It is also one of the six principal rivers which running across the island from the west to the east, all begin with the letter *T*; namely, the Thames, Trent, Tees, Tine, Tweed, and Tay. The Trent is not the largest river of the six; yet it may be said to run the longest course of any of them, and rises nearer to the west verge of the island than any of the other; also it is the largest, and of the longest course of any river in England, which does not empty its waters immediately into the sea; for the Trent runs into the Humber, and so its waters lose their name before they reach to the ocean.

It rises in the hills or highlands of Staffordshire, called the Moorlands, receiving, from the edge of Cheshire, and towards Lancashire, a great many (some say thirty, and that thence it had its name) little rivulets into it, very near its head, all which may claim a share in being the originals of the Trent; thus it soon becomes one large river, and comes down from the hills with a violent current into the flat country; where, being increased by several other little rivers, it carries a deeper channel, and a stiller current; and having given its name to Trentham, a small market town in the same county, it goes on to Stone, a considerable town on the great road to West-Chester.

One branch of the Trent rises within a quarter of a mile of the Dane, (viz.) from a moor adjoining to, or part of a little ridge of hills called Molecop Hill, near Congleton, and is within twenty-two miles of the Irish Sea, or that arm or inlet of the sea which the Mersee makes from Frodsham to Liverpool and Hyle-lake; and as the Dane runs into the Weaver, and both into that arm of the sea, and the Trent into the Humber, which opens into the great German Ocean, those rivers may be said to cut the island across in the middle.

It is true, the northern part is much larger than the southern, now Scotland is united; otherwise the country south by Trent, including Wales, is by far the largest. But it must be allowed still, that the country south by Trent is the richest by far, and most populous; occasioned chiefly by the city of London, and the commerce of the Thames; as for the cities of Bristol, Exceter, and Norwich, which are large and very populous, and in some things drive a prodigious trade, as well in merchandise as manufacture, we shall find them matched, if not out-done, by the growing towns of Liverpool, Hull, Leeds, Newcastle, and Manchester, and the cities of Edinburgh and Glasgow, as shall be shown in its place.

The Trent runs a course of near two hundred miles, through the four counties of Stafford, Derby, Nottingham, and Lincoln; it . . . is navigable [1] by ships of good burthen as high as Gainsbrough, which is near 40 miles from the Humber by the river. The barges without the help of locks or stops go as high as Nottingham, and farther by the help of art, to Burton upon Trent in Staffordshire. The stream is full, the channel deep and safe, and the tide flows up a great way between Gainsborough and Newark. This, and the navigation lately,[2] reaching up to Burton and up the Derwent to Derby, is a great support to, and increase of the trade of those counties which border upon it; especially for the cheese trade from Cheshire and Warwickshire, which have otherwise no navigation but about from West Chester to London; whereas by this river it is brought by water to Hull, and from thence to all the south and north coasts on the east side of Britain. 'Tis calculated that there is about four thousand ton of Cheshire cheese only, brought down the Trent every year from those parts of England to Gainsborough and Hull; and especially in time of the late war, when the seas on the other side of England were too dangerous to bring it by long-sea.

The counties north by Trent are few; but most of them large; I mean on the side of England, (viz.) York, which I shall call three counties, as it is divided into three Ridings, and are large counties too; and Lancashire, which is very large, Derbyshire and Nottinghamshire, which are the most southerly, are but small; I shall begin there, and take them together.

As I am travelling now cross the island, and begin at the mouth of Trent, the first town of note that I meet with is Nottingham, the capital of that shire, and is the most considerable in all that part of England. The county is small, but, like the Peak, 'tis full of wonders; and indeed there are abundance of remarkables in it. (1.) 'Tis remarkable for the soil, which on the south part is the richest and most fruitful; and on the north part the most wild and waste, and next to barren of any part of England within many miles of it. (2.) For the fine seats of noblemen and gentlemen, not a few; such as the Dukes of Shrewsbury, Kingston, Rutland, Newcastle, and several others.

Nottingham is one of the most pleasant and beautiful towns in England. The situation makes it so, though the additions to it were not to be named. It is seated on the side of a hill overlooking a fine range of meadows about a mile broad, a little rivulet running on the north side of the meadows, almost close to the town; and the noble River Trent parallel with both on the further or south side of the meadows. Over the Trent there is a stately stone-bridge of nineteen arches, and the river being there joined into one united stream, is very large and deep.

The town of Nottingham is situated upon the steep ascent of a sandy rock; which is consequently remarkable, for that it is so soft that they easily work into it for making vaults and cellars, and yet so firm as to support the roofs of those cellars two or three under one another; the stairs into which, are all cut out of the solid, though crumbling rock; and we must not fail to have it be remembered that the bountiful inhabitants generally keep these cellars well stocked with excellent ALE; nor are they uncommunicative in bestowing it among their friends, as some in our company experienced to a degree not fit to be made matter of history.

They tell us there, speaking of the antiquity of Nottingham, that the hill where it was built, was called the Dolorous Hill, or the Golgotha of ancient time; because of a great slaughter of the Britains there by King Humber,[3] a northern monarch; the same who, being afterwards drowned in the passage of the sea between Hull and Barton, gave name to that arm of the sea which is now called the Humber, and which receives the Trent, and almost all the great rivers of Yorkshire into it.

Besides the situation of Nottingham towards the river; it is most pleasantly seated to the land side; that is to say, to the side of the forest on the north of the town. And here they have (1.) a most pleasant plain to accommodate the gentlemen who assemble once a year (at least) for the manly noble diversion of racings, and chiefly horse-races; 'tis a most glorious show they have here when the running season begins; for here is such an assembly of gentlemen of quality, that not Bansted Down, or New Market Heath, produces better company, better horses, or shows the horse and master's skill better.

At the west end of the town there is a very steep hill, and the south side of it a cliff, which descends in a precipice towards the river; on this hill stood an old castle, but when, we know not; so that if we may plead its antiquity, 'tis only because we have no account of its beginning; the oldest thing that we read of it is, that there was a tower here[4] which the Danes obstinately defended against King Alfred, and his brother Æthelred.

This castle, or some other building in the room of it, remained till the time of the late wars; 'tis evident it was standing in the reign of Queen Elizabeth. It was so strong, it seems, that it had not been subject to the ordinary fate of other fortified places; namely, to be often taken and retaken; for it was never stormed, that is to say, never taken sword in hand; once it was indeed taken by surprise in the Barons' Wars by Robert Earl Ferrers,[5] who also plundered the town, (city 'twas then called.)

The stories that people tell us here, of one of the Davids, King of Scotland, kept prisoner in it, I believe little of, any more than I do that of Roger Mortimore[6] Earl of March, and his being hid in a vault under ground in this castle, whence being discovered, he was taken, brought to justice, and hanged for treason; yet the place where they say he was taken, is showed still to strangers, and is called Mortimer's Hole, to this day.

Whoever built this great castle (for the dispute lies only between William the Conqueror and William de Peverell, his bastard son [7]), we know not; but we know who pulled it down; namely, the government, upon the Restoration, because it had been forfeited, and held out against the Royalists. After the Restoration Cavendish, late Marquis of Newcastle,[8] entirely bought it of King Charles II or of the Duke of Buckingham, to whom he would have sold it; and, having bought it, went to work immediately with it, in order to pull it quite down; for it lay, as it were, waste to him, and useless. In the year 1674 he cleared the old foundations, a small part excepted, and founded the noble structure which we see now standing; and which, through several successions, has revolved to the present branch of the house of Pelham, now Duke of Newcastle; who has beautified if not enlarged the building, and has laid out a plan of the finest gardens that are to be seen in all that part of England; but they are not yet finished.

The beauties of Nottingham, next to its situation, are the castle, the market-place, and the gardens of Count Tallard;[9] who, in his confinement here as prisoner of war taken by the Duke of Marlborough at the great Battle of Blenheim, amused himself with making a small, but beautiful parterre, after the French fashion. But it does not gain by English keeping.

There was once a handsome town-house[10] here for the sessions or assizes, and other public business; but it was very old, and was either so weak, or so ill looked after, that, being overcrowded upon occasion of the assizes last year, it cracked, and frighted the people, and that not without cause. As it happened, no body was hurt, nor did the building fall directly down. But it must be said, (I think) that Providence had more care of the judges, and their needful attendants, than the townsmen had, whose business it was to have been well assured of the place, before they suffered a throng of people to come into it; and therefore we cannot deny, but it was a seasonable justice in the court to amerce or fine the town, as they did as well for the omission, as for the repair of the place. We are told now that they are collecting money, not for the repair of the old house, but for erecting a new one, which will add to the beauty of the town.

The Trent is navigable here for vessels or barges of great burthen, by which all their heavy and bulky goods are brought from the Humber, and even from Hull; such as iron, block-tin, salt, hops, grocery, dyers' wares, wine, oil, tar, hemp, flax, &c. and the same vessels carry down lead, coal, wood, corn; as also cheese in great quantities, from Warwickshire and Staffordshire.

Nottingham, notwithstanding the navigation of the Trent, is not esteemed a town of very great trade, other than is usual to inland towns; the chief manufacture carried on here is frame-work knitting for stockings, the same as at Leicester, and some glass, and earthen ware-houses; the latter much increased since the increase of tea-drinking;[11] for the making fine stone-mugs, tea-pots, cups, &c. The glass-houses, I think, are of late rather decayed.

As they brew a very good liquor here, so they make the best malt, and the most of it of any town in this part of England, which they drive a great trade for, sending it by land-carriage to Derby through all the Peak as far as Manchester, and to other towns in Lancashire, Cheshire, and even into Yorkshire itself; to which end all the lower lands of this county, and especially on the banks of Trent, yield prodigious crops of barley.

The forest of Sherwood is an addition to Nottingham for the pleasure of hunting, and there are also some fine parks and noble houses in it, as Welbeck, the late Duke of Newcastle's, and Thoresby, the present noble seat of the Pierrepont's, Dukes of Kingston, which lies at the farthest edge of the forest. But this forest does not add to the fruitfulness of the county, for 'tis now, as it were, given up to waste; even the woods which formerly made it so famous for thieves, are wasted; and if there was such a man as Robin Hood, a famous out-law and deer-stealer, that so many years harboured here, he would hardly find shelter for one week, if he was now to have been there. Nor is there any store of deer, compared to the quantity which in former times they tell us there usually was.

Having thus passed the Rubicon (Trent) and set my face northward, I scarce knew which way to set forward, in a country too so full of wonders, and on so great a journey, and yet to leave nothing behind me to call on as I came back, at least not to lead me out of my way in my return. But then considering that I call this work, a Tour, and the parts of it, Letters; I think that though I shall go a great length forward, and shall endeavour to take things with me as I go; yet I may take a review of some parts as I came back, and so may be allowed to pick up any fragments I may have left behind in my going out.

I resolved indeed first for the Peak, which lay on my left-hand north east; but, as I say, to leave as little behind me as possible, I was obliged to make a little excursion into the forest, where, in my way, I had the diversion of seeing the annual meeting of the gentry at the horse-races near Nottingham. I could give a long and agreeable account of the sport it self, how it brought into my thoughts the Olympic Games among the Greeks; and the Circus Maximus at Rome; where the racers made a great noise, and the victors made great boasts and triumphs: but where they chiefly drove in chariots, not much unlike our chaises, and where nothing of the speed, or of skill in horsemanship could be shown, as is in our races.

It is true, in those races the young Roman and Grecian gentlemen rode, or rather drove themselves; whereas in our races the horses, not the riders, make the show; and they are generally ridden by grooms and boys, chiefly for lightness; sometimes indeed the gentlemen ride themselves, as I have often seen the Duke of Monmouth, natural son to King Charles II ride his own horses at a match, and win it too, though he was a large man, and must weigh heavy.

But the illustrious company at the Nottingham races was, in my opinion, the glory of the day; for there we saw, besides eleven or twelve noblemen, an infinite throng of gentlemen from all the countries round, nay, even out of Scotland it self; the appearance, in my opinion, greater, as it was really more numerous, than ever I saw at Newmarket, except when the king have been there in ceremony. Nor is the appearance of the ladies to be omitted, as fine and without comparison more bright and gay, though they might a little fall short in number of the many thousands of nobility and gentry of the other sex; in short, the train of coaches filled with the beauties of the north was not to be described; except we were to speak of the garden of the Tulleries at Paris, or the Prado at Mexico, where they tell us there are 4000 coaches with six horses each, every evening taking the air.

From hence I was called aside to take a view of the most famous piece of church history in this part of the whole island, I mean the collegiate church of Southwell. Paulinus, Archbishop of York, was (so ancient record supplies the tale) the founder of this church, having preached to the people of the country round, and baptized them in the River Trent; the ancient words imports Christianized them, by dipping them in the River Trent. Whether our Antipedo-Baptists will take any advantage of the word, I know not but I cannot see any doubt but that anciently baptism was performed in the water; whether it was performed there by immersion, putting the person into the water, or pouring the water upon him, we know not; neither do I see any extraordinary, much less any essential difference in it, be it one way or the other; but that is not my business, especially not here. The reason of naming it, is to give you the pious occasion which made the good bishop[12] build this church, namely, that having converted a whole province, or part of one at least, he was desirous they should not want a place of worship to serve God in.

Hence crossing the forest I came to Mansfield, a market town, but without any remarkables. In my way I visited the noble seat of the Duke of Kingston[13] at Thoresby, of the Duke of Newcastle at Welbeck, and the Marquis of Hallifax at Rufford, of Rugeford Abbey, all very noble seats, though ancient, and that at Welbeck especially, beautified with large additions, fine apartments, and good gardens; but particularly the park, well stocked with large timber, and the finest kind, as well as the largest quantity of deer that are any where to be seen; for the late Duke's delight being chiefly on horseback and in the chase, it is not to be wondered if he rather made his parks fine than his gardens, and his stables than his mansion-house; yet the house is noble, large, and magnificent.

From hence leaving Nottinghamshire, the west part abounding with lead and coal, I crossed over that fury of a river called the Derwent, and came to Derby, the capital of the county. This is a fine, beautiful, and pleasant town; it has more families of gentlemen in it than is usual in towns so remote, and therefore here is a great deal of good and some gay company. Perhaps the rather, because the Peak being so near, and taking up the larger part of the county, and being so inhospitable, so rugged and so wild a place, the gentry choose to reside at Derby, rather than upon their estates, as they do in other places.

It must be allowed, that the twelve miles between Nottingham and this town, keeping the mid-way between the Trent on the left, and the mountains on the right, are as agreeable with respect to the situation, the soil, and the well planting of the country, as any spot of ground, at least that I have seen of that length, in England.

The town of Derby is situated on the west bank of the Derwent, over which it has a very fine bridge, well built, but ancient, and a chapel upon the bridge, now converted into a dwelling-house. Here is a curiosity in trade worth observing, as being the only one of its kind in England, namely, a throwing or throwster's mill, which performs by a wheel turned by the water; and though it cannot perform the doubling part of a throwster's work, which can only be done by a handwheel, yet it turns the other work, and performs the labour of many hands. Whether it answers the expense or not, that is not my business.

This work was erected by one Soracule,[14] a man expert in making mill-work, especially for raising water to supply towns for family use. But he made a very odd experiment at this place; for going to show some gentlemen the curiosity, as he called it, of his mill, and crossing the planks which lay just above the mill-wheel; regarding, it seems, what he was to show his friends more than the place where he was, and too eager in describing things, keeping his eye rather upon what he pointed at with his fingers than what he stepped upon with his feet, he stepped awry and slipped into the river. He was so very close to the sluice which let the water out upon the wheel, and which was then pulled up, that though help was just at hand, there was no taking hold of him, till by the force of the water he was carried through, and pushed just under the large wheel, which was then going round at a great rate. The body being thus forced in between two of the plashers of the wheel, stopped the motion for a little while, till the water pushing hard to force its way, the plasher beyond him gave way and broke; upon which the wheel went again, and, like Jonah's whale, spewed him out, not upon dry land, but into that part they call the apron, and so to the mill-tail, where he was taken up, and received no hurt at all.

Derby, as I have said, is a town of gentry, rather than trade; yet it is populous, well built, has five parishes, a large marketplace, a fine town-house, and very handsome streets. In the church of Allhallows, or, as the Spaniards call it, *De Todos los Santos*, All Saints, is the Pantheon, or burial-place of the noble, now ducal family of Cavendish, now Devonshire, which was first erected by the Countess of Shrewsbury.[15] By an inscription upon this church, it was erected, or at least the steeple, at the charge of the maids and bachelors of the town; on which account, whenever a maid, native of the town, was married, the bells were rung by bachelors. How long the custom lasted, we do not read; but I do not find that it is continued, at least not strictly.

It is observable, that as the Trent makes the frontier or bounds of the county of Derby south, so the Dove and the Erwash make the bounds east and west, and the Derwent runs through the centre; all of them beginning and ending their course in the same county; for they rise in the Peak, and end in the Trent.

I that had read Cotton's *Wonders of the Peak*,[16] in which I always wondered more at the poetry than at the Peak; and in which there was much good humour, though but little good verse, could not satisfy my self to be in Derbyshire, and not see the River Dove, which that gentleman has spent so much doggerel upon, and celebrated to such a degree for trout and grayling. So from Derby we went to Dove-Bridge, or, as the country people call it, Dowbridge, where we had the pleasure to see the river drowning the low-grounds by a sudden shower, and hastening to the Trent with a most outrageous stream, in which there being no great diversion, and travelling being not very safe in a rainy season on that side.

Hence we kept the Derwent on our right-hand, but kept our distance, the waters being out; for the Derwent is a frightful creature when the hills load her current with water; I say, we kept our distance, and contented our selves with hearing the roaring of its waters, till we came to Quarn or Quarden, a little ragged, but noted village, where there is a famous chalybeate spring, to which abundance of people go in the season to drink the water, as also a cold bath. We found the wells, as custom bids us call them, pretty full of company, the waters good, and very physical, but wretched lodging and entertainment; so I resolved to stay till I came to the south, and make shift with Tunbridge or Epsom.

From Quarden we advanced due north, and, mounting the hills gradually for four or five miles, we soon had a most frightful view indeed among the black mountains of the Peak; however, as they were yet at a distance, and a good town lay on our left called Wirksworth, we turned thither for refreshment. Here indeed we found a specimen of what I had heard before, (viz.) that however rugged the hills were, the vales were every where fruitful, well inhabited, the markets well supplied, and the provisions extraordinary good; not forgetting the ale, which every where exceeded, if possible, what was passed, as if the farther north the better the liquor, and that the nearer we approached to Yorkshire, as the place for the best, so the ale advanced the nearer to its perfection.

Wirksworth is a large well-frequented market town, and market towns being very thin placed in this part of the county, they have the better trade, the people generally coming twelve or fifteen miles to a market, and sometimes much more; though there is no very great trade to this town but what relates to the lead works, and to the subterranean wretches, who they call Peakrills, who work in the mines, and who live all round this town every way.

The inhabitants are a rude boorish kind of people, but they are a bold, daring, and even desperate kind of fellows in their search into the bowels of the earth; for no people in the world out-do them; and therefore they are often entertained by our engineers in the wars to carry on the sap, and other such works, at the sieges of strong fortified places.

This town of Wirksworth is a kind of a market for lead; the like not known any where else that I know of, except it be at the custom-house quays in London. The Barmoot Court, kept here to judge controversies among the miners, that is to say, to adjust subterranean quarrels and disputes, is very remarkable. Here they summon a master and twenty-four jurors, and they have power to set out the bounds of the works under ground, when any man has found a vein of ore in another man's ground, except orchards and gardens; they may appoint the proprietor cartways and passage for timber, &c. This court also prescribes rules to the mines, and limits their proceedings in the works under ground; also they are judges of all their little quarrels and disputes in the mines, as well as out, and, in a word, keep the peace among them; which, by the way, may be called the greatest of all the wonders of the Peak, for they are of a strange, turbulent, quarrelsome temper, and very hard to be reconciled to one another in their subterraneous affairs.

And now I am come to this wonderful place, the Peak, where you will expect I should do as some others have, (I think, foolishly) done before me, viz. tell you strange long stories of wonders as (I must say) they are most weakly called.

Now to have so great a man as Mr Hobbes,[17] and after him Mr Cotton, celebrate the trifles here, the first in a fine Latin poem, the last in English verse, as if they were the most exalted wonders of the world: I cannot but, after wondering at their making wonders of them, desire you, my friend, to travel with me through this howling wilderness in your imagination, and you shall soon find all that is wonderful about it.

Near Wirksworth, and upon the very edge of Derwent, is, as above, a village called Matlock, where there are several warm springs, lately one of these being secured by a stone wall on every side, by which the water is brought to rise to a due height, is made into a very convenient bath; with a house built over it, and room within the building to walk round the water or bath, and so by steps to go down gradually into it.

This bath would be much more frequented than it is, if two things did not hinder; namely, a base, stony, mountainous road to it, and no good accommodation when you are there. They are intending, as they tell us, to build a good house to entertain persons of quality, or such who would spend their money at it; but it was not so far concluded or directed when I was there, as to be any where begun. The bath is milk, or rather blood warm, very pleasant to go into, and very sanative, especially for rheumatic pains, bruises, &c.

Over against this warm bath, and on the other, or east side of the Derwent, stands a high rock, which rises from the very bottom of the river (for the water washes the foot of it, and is there in dry weather very shallow); I say, it rises perpendicular as a wall, the precipice bare and smooth like one plain stone, to such a prodigious height, it is really surprising yet what the people believed of it surmounted all my faith too, though I looked upon it very curiously, for they told me it was above four hundred foot high, which is as high as two of our Monuments, one set upon another; that which adds most to my wonder in it is, that as the stone stands, it is smooth from the very bottom of the Derwent to the uppermost point, and nothing can be seen to grow upon it. The prodigious height of this tor, (for it is called Matlock Tor) was to me more a wonder than any of the rest in the Peak, and, I think, it should be named among them, but it is not. So it must not be called one of the wonders.

A little on the other side of Wirksworth, begins a long plain called Brassington Moor, which reaches full twelve miles in length. The Peak people, who are mighty fond of having strangers showed every thing they can, and of calling everything a wonder, told us here of another high mountain, where a giant was buried, and which they called the Giant's Tomb.

This tempted our curiosity, and we presently rode up to the mountain in order to leave our horses, dragoon-like, with a servant, and to clamber up to the top of it, to see this Giant's Tomb. Here we missed the imaginary wonder, and found a real one; the story of which I cannot but record, to show the discontented part of the rich world how to value their own happiness, by looking below them, and seeing how others live, who yet are capable of being easy and content, which content goes a great way towards being happy, if it does not come quite up to happiness. The story is this:

As we came near the hill, which seemed to be round, and a precipice almost on every side, we perceived a little parcel of ground hedged in, as if it were a garden, it was about twenty or thirty yards long, but not so much broad, parallel with the hill, and close to it; we saw no house, but, by a dog running out and barking, we perceived some people were thereabout; and presently after we saw two little children, and then a third run out to see what was the matter. When we came close up we saw a small opening, not a door, but a natural opening into the rock, and the noise we had made brought a woman out with a child in her arms, and another at her foot. N.B. The biggest of these five was a girl, about eight or ten years old.

We asked the woman some questions about the tomb of the giant upon the rock or mountain. She told us, there was a broad flat stone of a great size lay there, which, she said, the people called a gravestone; and, if it was, it might well be called a giant's, for she thought no ordinary man was ever so tall, and she described it to us as well as she could, by which it must be at least sixteen or seventeen foot long; but she could not give any farther account of it, neither did she seem to lay any stress upon the tale of a giant being buried there, but said, if her husband had been at home he might have shown it to us. I snatched at the word, at home! says I, good wife, why, where do you live. Here, sir, says she, and points to the hole in the rock. Here! says I; and do all these children live here too? Yes, sir, says she, they were all born here. Pray how long have you dwelt here then? said I. My husband was born here, said she, and his father before him. Will you give me leave, says one of our company, as curious as I was, to come in and see your house, dame? If you please, sir, says she, but 'tis not a place fit for such as you are to come into, calling him, your worship, forsooth; but that by the by. I mention it, to show that the good woman did not want manners, though she lived in a den like a wild body.

However, we alighted and went in. There was a large hollow cave, which the poor people by two curtains hanged cross, had parted into three rooms. On one side was the chimney, and the man, or perhaps his father, being miners, had found means to work a shaft or funnel through the rock to carry the smoke out at the top, where the giant's tombstone was. The habitation was poor, 'tis true, but things within did not look so like misery as I expected. Every thing was clean and neat, though mean and ordinary. There were shelves with earthen ware, and some pewter and brass. There was, which I observed in particular, a whole flitch or side of bacon hanging up in the chimney, and by it a good piece of another. There was a sow and pigs running about at the door, and a little lean cow feeding upon a green place just before the door, and the little enclosed piece of ground I mentioned, was growing with good barley; it being then near harvest.

To find out whence this appearance of substance came, I asked the poor woman, what trade her husband was? She said, he worked in the lead mines. I asked her, how much he could earn a day there? she said, if he had good luck he could earn about five pence a day, but that he worked by the dish (which was a term of art I did not understand, but supposed, as I afterwards understood it was, by the great, in proportion to the ore, which they measure in a wooden bowl, which they call a dish). Then I asked, what she did, she said, when she was able to work she washed the ore. But, looking down on her children, and shaking her head, she intimated, that they found her so much business she could do but little, which I easily granted must be true. But what can you get at washing the ore, said I, when you can work? She said, if she worked hard she could gain three-pence a day. So that, in short, here was but eight-pence a day when they both worked hard, and that not always, and perhaps not often, and all this to maintain a man, his wife, and five small children, and yet they seemed to live very pleasantly, the children looked plump and fat, ruddy and wholesome; and the woman was tall, well shaped, clean, and (for the place) a very well looking, comely woman; nor was there any thing looked like the dirt and nastiness of the miserable cottages of the poor; though many of them spend more money in strong drink than this poor woman had to maintain five children with.

This moving sight so affected us all, that, upon a short conference at the door, we made up a little lump of money, and I had the honour to be almoner for the company; and though the sum was not great, being at most something within a crown, as I told it into the poor woman's hand, I could perceive such a surprise in her face, that, had she not given vent to her joy by a sudden flux of tears, I found she would have fainted away. She was some time before she could do any thing but cry; but after that was abated, she expressed her self very handsomely (for a poor body) and told me, she had not seen so much money together of her own for many months.

We asked her, if she had a good husband; she smiled, and said, Yes, thanked God for it, and that she was very happy in that, for he worked very hard, and they wanted for nothing that he could do for them; and two or three times made mention of how contented they were. In a word, it was a lecture to us all, and that such, I assure you, as made the whole company very grave all the rest of the day. And if it has no effect of that kind upon the reader, the defect must be in my telling the story in a less moving manner than the poor woman told it her self.

From hence inquiring no farther after the giant, or his tomb, we went, by the direction of the poor woman, to a valley on the side of a rising hill, where there were several grooves, so they call the mouth of the shaft or pit by which they go down into a lead mine; and as we were standing still to look at one of them, admiring how small they were, and scarce believing a poor man that showed it us, when he told us, that they went down those narrow pits or holes to so great a depth in the earth; I say, while we were wondering, and scarce believing the fact, we were agreeably surprised with seeing a hand, and then an arm, and quickly after a head, thrust up out of the very groove we were looking at. It was the most surprising as not we only, but not the man that we were talking to, knew any thing of it, or expected it.

Immediately we rode closer up to the place, where we see the poor wretch working and heaving himself up gradually, as we thought, with difficulty; but when he showed us that it was by setting his feet upon pieces of wood fixed cross the angles of the groove like a ladder, we found that the difficulty was not much; and if the groove had been larger they could not either go up or down so easily, or with so much safety, for that now their elbows resting on those pieces as well as their feet, they went up and down with great ease and safety.

Those who would have a more perfect idea of those grooves, need do no more than go to the church of St Paul's, and desire to see the square wells which they have there to go down from the top of the church into the very vaults under it, to place the leaden pipes which carry the rain water from the flat of the roof to the common-shore, which wells are square, and have small iron bars placed cross the angles for the workmen to set their feet on, to go up and down to repair the pipes; the manner of the steps are thus described:

When this subterranean creature was come quite out, with all his furniture about him, we had as much variety to take us up as before, and our curiosity received full satisfaction without venturing down.

First, the man was a most uncouth spectacle; he was clothed all in leather, had a cap of the same without brims, some tools in a little basket which he drew up with him, not one of the names of which we could understand but by the help of an interpreter. Nor indeed could we understand any of the man's discourse so as to make out a whole sentence; and yet the man was pretty free of his tongue too.

For his person, he was lean as a skeleton, pale as a dead corpse, his hair and beard a deep black, his flesh lank, and, as we thought, something of the colour of the lead itself, and being very tall and very lean he looked, or we that saw him ascend *ab inferis*, fancied he looked like an inhabitant of the dark regions below, and who was just ascended into the world of light.

Besides his basket of tools, he brought up with him about three quarters of a hundred weight of ore, which we wondered at, for the man had no small load to bring, considering the manner of his coming up; and this indeed made him come heaving and struggling up, as I said at first, as if he had great difficulty to get out; whereas it was indeed the weight that he brought with him.

If any reader thinks this, and the past relation of the woman and the cave, too low and trifling for this work, they must be told, that I think quite otherwise; and especially considering what a noise is made of wonders in this country, which, I must needs say, have nothing in them curious, but much talked of, more trifling a great deal.

We asked him, how deep the mine lay which he came out of. He answered us in terms we did not understand; but our interpreter, as above, told us, it signified that he was at work 60 fathoms deep, but that there were five men of his party, who were, two of them, eleven fathoms, and the other three, fifteen fathoms deeper. He seemed to regret that he was not at work with those three; for that they had a deeper vein of ore than that which he worked in, and had a way out at the side of the hill, where they passed without coming up so high as he was obliged to do.

If we blessed ourselves before, when we saw how the poor woman and her five children lived in the hole or cave in the mountain, with the giant's grave over their heads; we had much more room to reflect how much we had to acknowledge to our Maker, that we were not appointed to get our bread thus, one hundred and fifty yards under ground, or in a hole as deep in the earth as the cross upon St Paul's cupola is high out of it. Nor was it possible to see these miserable people without such reflections, unless you will suppose a man as stupid and senseless as the horse he rides on. But to leave moralizing to the reader, I proceed.

We then looked on the ore, and got the poor man's leave to bring every one a small piece of it away with us, for which we gave him two small pieces of better metal, called shillings, which made his heart glad and, as we understood by our interpreter, was more than he could gain at sixty fathoms under ground in three days; and we found soon after the money was so much, that it made him move off immediately towards the alehouse, to melt some of it into good Pale Derby; but, to his farther good luck, we were gotten to the same alehouse before him; where, when we saw him come, we gave him some liquor too, and made him keep his money, and promise us to carry it home to his family, which they told us lived hard by.

From hence entering upon Brassington Moor, we had eight mile smooth green riding to Buxton bath, which they call one of the wonders of the Peak; but is so far from being a wonder, that to us, who had been at Bath in Somersetshire, and at Aix la Chapelle in Germany, it was nothing at all; nor is it any thing but what is frequent in such mountainous countries as this is, in many parts of the world.

But though I shall not treat this warm spring as a wonder, for such it is not; I must nevertheless give it the praise due to the medicinal virtue of its waters; for it is not to be denied, but that wonderful cures have been wrought by them, especially in rheumatic, scorbutic and scrofulous distempers, aches of the joints, nervous pains, and also in scurvy and leprous maladies.

The waters are temperately hot, or rather warm, and operate rather as a cold bath, without that violent attack which the cold bath makes upon all nature at once; you feel a little chillness when you first dip or plunge into the water, but it is gone in a moment; and you find a kind of an equality in the warmth of your blood and that of the water, and that so very pleasant, that far from the fainting and weakening violence of the hot baths; on the contrary, here you are never tired, and can hardly be persuaded to come out of the bath when you are in.

The Duke of Devonshire[18] is lord of the village, and consequently of the bath itself; and his grace has built a large handsome house at the bath, where there is convenient lodging, and very good provisions, and an ordinary well served for one shilling per head; but it is but one. And though some other houses in the town take in lodgers upon occasion, yet the conveniences are not the same; so that there is not accommodation for a confluence of people, as at the bath-house it self. If it were otherwise, and that the nobility and gentry were suitably entertained, I doubt not but Buxton would be frequented, and with more effect as to health, as well as much more satisfaction to the company; where there is an open and healthy country, a great variety of view to satisfy the curious, and fine down or moor for the ladies to take a ring upon in their coaches, all much more convenient than in a close city as the Bath is, which, more like a prison than a place of diversion, scarce gives the company room to converse out of the smell of their own excrements, and where the very city it self may be said to stink like a general common-shore.

South west from hence, about a quarter of a mile, or not so much, on the side, or rather at the foot of a very high ridge of mountains, is a great cave or hole in the earth, called Poole's Hole, another of the wonderless wonders of the Peak. The wit that has been spent upon this vault or cave in the earth, had been well enough to raise the expectation of strangers, and bring fools a great way to creep into it but is ill bestowed upon all those that come to the place with a just curiosity, founded upon ancient report; when these go in to see it, they generally go away, acknowledging that they have seen nothing suitable to their great expectation, or to the fame of the place.

It is a great cave, or natural vault, ancient doubtless as the mountain itself, and occasioned by the fortuitous position of the rocks at the creation of all things, or perhaps at the great absorption or influx of the surface into the abyss at the great rupture of the earth's crust or shell, according to Mr Burnet's theory;[19] and to me it seems a confirmation of that hypothesis of the breaking in of the surface. But that by the way.

The utmost you meet with after this, is the extraordinary height of the arch or roof; which, however, is far from what a late flaming author has magnified it to, (viz.) a quarter of a mile perpendicular. That it is very high, is enough to say for it is so far from a quarter of a mile, that there seems nothing admirable in it.

Dr Leigh[20] spends some time in admiring the spangled roof. Cotton and Hobbes are most ridiculously and outrageously witty upon it. Dr Leigh calls it fret work, organ, and choir work. The whole of the matter is this, that the rock being every where moist and dropping, the drops are some fallen, those you see below; some falling, those you have glancing by you *en passant*; and others pendant in the roof. Now as you have guides before you and behind you, carrying every one a candle, the light of the candles reflected by the globular drops of water, dazzle upon your eyes from every corner; like as the drops of dew in a sunny-bright morning reflect the rising light to the eye, and are as ten thousand rainbows in miniature; whereas were any part of the roof or arch of this vault to be seen by a clear light, there would be no more beauty on it than on the back of a chimney; for, in short, the stone is coarse, slimy, with the constant wet, dirty and dull; and were the little drops of water gone, or the candles gone, there would be none of these fine sights to be seen for wonders, or for the learned authors above to show themselves foolish about.

Let any person therefore, who goes into Poole's Hole for the future, and has a mind to try the experiment, take a long pole in his hand, with a cloth tied to the end of it, and mark any place of the shining spangled roof which his pole will reach to; and then, wiping the drops of water away, he shall see he will at once extinguish all those glories; then let him sit still and wait a little, till, by the nature of the thing, the drops swell out again, and he shall find the stars and spangles rise again by degrees, here one, and there one, till they shine with the same fraud, a mere *deceptio visus*, as they did before. As for the Queen of Scots pillar, as 'tis called, because her late unfortunate majesty, Mary, Queen of Scots, was pleased to have it be called so, it is a piece of stone like a kind of spar, which is found about the lead; and 'tis not improbable in a country where there is so much of the ore, it may be of the same kind, and, standing upright, obtained the name of a pillar of which almost every body that comes there, carries away a piece, in veneration of the memory of the unhappy princess that gave it her name. Nor is there any thing strange or unusual in the stone, much less in the figure of it, which is otherwise very mean, and in that country very common.

As to the several stones called Mr Cotton's, Haycock's, Poole's Chair, Flitches of Bacon, and the like, they are nothing but ordinary stones; and the shapes very little resemble the things they are said to represent; but the fruitful imagination of the country carls, who fancy to call them so, will have them to look like them; a stranger sees very little even of the similitude, any more than when people fancy they see faces and heads, castles and cities, armies, horses and men, in the clouds, in the fire, and the like. So that, in short, there is nothing in Poole's Hole to make a wonder of, any more than as other things in nature, which are rare to be seen, however easily accounted for, may be called wonderful.

Having thus accounted for two of the seven things, called wonders in this country, I come to two more of them, as wonderless, and empty of every thing that may be called rare or strange, as the others; and indeed much more so.

The first of these is Mam Tor, or, as the word in the mountain jargon signifies, the Mother Rock, upon a suggestion that the soft crumbling earth, which falls from the summit of the one, breeds or begets several young mountains below. The sum of the whole wonder is this, that there is a very high hill, nay, I will add (that I may make the most of the story, and that it may appear as much like a wonder as I can) an exceeding high hill. But this in a country which is all over hills, cannot be much of a wonder, because also there are several higher hills in the Peak than that, only not just there.

The south side of this hill is a precipice, and very steep from the top to the bottom; and as the substance of this hill is not a solid stone, or rocky, as is the case of all the hills thereabouts, but a crumbling loose earth mingled with small stones, it is continually falling down in small quantities, as the force of hasty showers, or solid heavy rains, loosens and washes it off, or as frosts and thaws operate upon it in common with other parts of the earth; now as the great hill, which is thick, as well as high, parts with this loose stuff, without being sensibly diminished, yet the bottom which it falls into, is more easily perceived to swell with the quantity that falls down; the space where it is received being small, comparatively to the height and thickness of the mountain Here the pretended wonder is formed, namely, that the little heap below, should grow up into a hill, and yet the great hill not be the less for all that is fallen down; which is not true in fact, any more than, as a great black cloud pouring down rain as it passes over our heads, appears still as great and as black as before, though it continues pouring down rain over all the country. But nothing is more certain than this, that the more water comes down from it, the less remains in it; and so it certainly is of Mam Tor, in spite of all the poetry of Mr Cotton or Mr Hobbes, and in spite of all the women's tales in the Peak.

This hill lies on the north side of the road from Buxton to Castleton, where we come to the so famed wonder called, saving our good manners, *The Devil's A——e in the Peak.*[21] Now notwithstanding the grossness of the name given it, and that there is nothing of similitude or coherence either in form and figure, or any other thing between the thing signified and the thing signifying; yet we must search narrowly for any thing in it to make a wonder, or even any thing so strange, or odd, or vulgar, as the name would seem to import.

The short of this story is; that on the steep side of a mountain there is a large opening very high, broad at bottom, and narrow, but rounding, on the top, almost the form of the old Gothic gates or arches, which come up, not to a half circle or half oval at the top, but to a point; though this being all wild and irregular, cannot be said to be an arch, but a mere chasm, entering horizontally the opening being upwards of thirty foot perpendicular, and twice as much broad at the bottom at least.

As you go on, the roof descends gradually, and is so far from admitting houses to stand in it, that you have not leave to stand upright your self, till stooping for a little way, and passing over another rill of water, you find more room over your head. But going a little farther you come to a third water, which crosses your way; and the rock stopping, as it were, down almost to the surface of the water, forbids any farther enquiry into what is beyond.

This is the whole wonder, unless it may be called so, that our ancestors should give it so homely a surname; and give us no reason for it, but what we must guess at from the uncouth entrance of the place, which being no guide in the case, leave us to reflect a little upon their modesty of expression; but it seems they talked broader in those days than we do now.

To conclude: if there were no such vaults and arches any where but in the Peak, or indeed if they were not frequent in such mountainous countries, as well here, as in other nations, we might call this a wonder. But as we know they are to be found in many places in England, and that we read of them in the description of other countries, and even in the Scripture, we cannot think there is any room to call it a wonder. We read of the cave of Adullam,[22] and of the cave of Mackpelah, in the Scripture, able to receive David, and his whole troop of four hundred men. We read of the persecuted worthies in the 12th of the Hebrews, who wandered about in dens and caves of the earth. We read of a cave in the Apenine Mountains near to Florence, which was able to receive an army; there are also many such caves, as I have observed above, in the Alpes, and the hills of Dauphine and Savoy, and in other parts of the world, too many to run over; and some of them, such as this is not worthy to be named among them.

The next wonder, which makes up number five, is called Tideswell, or a spring of water which ebbs and flows, as they will have it, as the sea does. A poor thing indeed to make a wonder of; and therefore most of the writers pass it over with little notice only that they are at a loss to make up the number seven without it.

This well or spring is called Weeden Well; the basin or receiver for the water is about three foot square every way; the water seems to have some other receiver within the rock, which, when it fills by the force of the original stream, which is small, the air being contracted or pent in, forces the water out with a bubbling noise, and so fills the receiver without; but when the force is spent within, then it stops till the place is filled again and, in the mean time, the water without runs off or ebbs, till the quantity within swells again, and then the same causes produce the same effects, as will always be while the world endures. So that all this wonder is owing only to the situation of the place, which is a mere accident in nature; and if any person were to dig into the place, and give vent to the air, which fills the contracted space within, they would soon see Tideswell turned into an ordinary running stream, and a very little one too.

So much for fictitious wonders. The two real wonders which remain, are first, Elden Hole, and secondly, the Duke of Devonshire's fine house at Chatsworth; one a wonder of nature, the other of art. I begin with the last.

Chatsworth is indeed a most glorious and magnificent house, and, as it has had two or three founders, may well be said to be completely designed and finished. It was begun on a much narrower plan that it now takes up, by Sir William

Cavendish,[23] of Cavendish in Suffolk, who married the Countess Dowager of Shrewsbury, and with her came into a noble and plentiful fortune in this country. Sir William died, having done little more than build one end of the fabric, and laid out the plan, as I have said, or ichnography of the whole. But the lady, who, it seems, was the mover of the first design, finished the whole in the magnificent manner which it appeared in, when it was first christened a *wonder*, and ranked among the *marvelleux* of the Peak.

It is indeed a palace for a prince, a most magnificent building, and, in spite of all the difficulties or disadvantages of situation, is a perfect beauty nay, the very obstructions and, as I called them, disadvantages of its situation, serve to set off its beauty, and are, by the most exquisite decoration of the place, made to add to the lustre of the whole. But it would take up a volume by itself to describe it.

The front to the garden is the most regular piece of architect I have seen in all the north part of England; the pilaster seventy two foot high to the foot of the baluster on the top; the frieze under the cornish is spacious, and has the motto of the family upon it. The sashes of the second story we were told are seventeen foot high, the plates polished looking-glass, and the woodwork double gilded; which, I think, is no where else to be seen in England. Under this front lie the gardens exquisitely fine, and, to make a clear vista or prospect beyond into the flat country, towards Hardwick, another seat of the same owner, the Duke, to whom what others thought impossible, was not only made practicable, but easy, removed, and perfectly carried away a great mountain that stood in the way, and which interrupted the prospect.

This was so entirely gone, that, having taken a strict view of the gardens at my first being there, and retaining an idea of them in my mind, I was perfectly confounded at coming there a second time, and not knowing what had been done; for I had lost the hill, and found a new country in view, which Chatsworth it self had never seen before. The house indeed had received additions, as it did every year, and perhaps would to this day, had the Duke lived, who had a genius for such things beyond the reach of the most perfect masters, and was not only capable to design, but to finish. The gardens, the water-works, the cascades, the statues, vasa, and painting, though they are but very imperfectly described by any of the writers who have yet named them, and more imperfectly by one author, who has so lately pretended to view them; yet I dare not venture to mention them here, least, for want of time, and having so long a journey to go, I should, like those who have gone before me, do it imperfectly, or leave no room to do justice to other persons and places, which I am still to mention. I shall therefore, as I said above, only touch at what others have omitted.

First, 'tis to be observed that on the east side rises a very high mountain, on the top of which they dig mill-stones, and it begins so close to, and so overlooks the house, being prodigiously high that, should they roll down a pair of those stones coupled with a wooden axis, as is the way of drawing them, they would infallibly give a shock to the building; yet this mountain is so planted, and so covered with a wood of beautiful trees, that you see no hill, only a rising wood, as if the trees grew so much higher than one another, and was only a wall of trees, whose tops join into one another so close, as nothing is seen through them.

Upon the top of that mountain begins a vast extended moor or waste, which, for fifteen or sixteen miles together due north, presents you with neither hedge, house or tree, but a waste and howling wilderness, over which when strangers travel, they are obliged to take guides, or it would be next to impossible not to lose their way.

Nothing can be more surprising of its kind, than for a stranger coming from the north, suppose from Sheffield in Yorkshire, for that is the first town of note, and wandering or labouring to pass this difficult desert country, and seeing no end of it, and almost discouraged and beaten out with the fatigue of it, (just such was our case) on a sudden the guide brings him to this precipice, where he looks down from a frightful height, and a comfortless, barren, and, as he thought, endless moor, into the most delightful valley, with the most pleasant garden, and most beautiful palace in the world. If contraries illustrate, and the place can admit of any illustration, it must needs add to the splendour of the situation, and to the beauty of the building, and I must say (with which I will close my short observation) if there is any wonder in Chatsworth, it is, that any man who had a genius suitable to so magnificent a design, who could lay out the plan for such a house, and had a fund to support the charge, would build it in such a place where the mountains insult the clouds, intercept the sun, and would threaten, were earthquakes frequent here, to bury the very towns, much more the house, in their ruins.

On the top of that mountain, that is to say, on the plain which extends from it, is a large pond or basin for water, spreading, as I was told, near thirty acres of ground, which, from all the ascents round it, receives, as into a cistern, all the water that falls, and from which again by pipes, the cascades, waterworks, ponds, and canals in the gardens, are plentifully supplied.

But I must dwell no longer here, however pleasant and agreeable the place. The remaining article, and which, I grant, we may justly call a WONDER, is Elden Hole. The description of it, in brief, is thus: in the middle of a plain open field, gently descending to the south, there is a frightful chasm, or opening in the earth, or rather in the rock, for the country seems thereabouts to be all but one great rock; this opening goes directly down perpendicular into the earth, and perhaps to the centre; it may be about twenty foot over one way, and fifty or sixty the other; it has no bottom, that is to say, none that can yet be heard of. Mr Cotton says, he let down eight hundred fathoms of line into it, and that the plummet drew still; so that, in a word, he sounded about a mile perpendicular.[24]

This I allow to be a wonder, and what the like of is not to be found in the world, that I have heard of, or believe. And would former writers have been contented with one wonder instead of seven, it would have done more honour to the Peak, and even to the whole nation, than the adding five imaginary miracles to it that had nothing in them, and which really depreciated the whole.

What Nature meant in leaving this window open into the infernal world, if the place lies that way, we cannot tell. But it must be said, there is something of horror upon the very imagination, when one does but look into it.

Having then viewed those things with an impartial mind, give me leave to reduce the wonders of the Peak to a less number, and of a quite different kind.

1. Elden Hole I acknowledge to be a wonderful place, as I have said above; but to me the greatest surprise is, that, after such a real wonder, any of the trifles added to it could bear the name of wonders.

2. Of Buxton; the wonder to me is, that in a nation so full of chronical diseases as we are, such as our scorbutics, rheumatics, cholics, and nephritics, there should be such a fountain of medicine sent from heaven, and no more notice taken of it, or care to make it useful.

3. That in a nation so curious, so inquiring, and so critical as this, any thing so unsatisfying, so foolish and so weak, should pass for wonders as those of Mam Tor, Tideswell, Poole's Hole, &c.

4. As to Chatsworth, the wonder, as I said before, seems to me; not that so noble and magnificent a palace should be built, but that it should be built in such a situation, and in such a country so out of the way, so concealed from the world, that whoever sees it must take a journey on purpose.

The Peak concludes the northern part of Derbyshire; nor are there any towns on that side worth noting. So we left the peak, and went to Chesterfield, a handsome market town at the northernmost border of the county, north east from Chatsworth.

There is indeed an extended angle of this county, which runs a great way north west by Chappel in the Frith, and which they call High Peak. This, perhaps, is the most desolate, wild, and abandoned country in all England. The mountains of the Peak, of which I have been speaking, seem to be but the beginning of wonders to this part of the country, and but the beginning of mountains, or, if you will, as the lower rounds of a ladder. The tops of these hills seem to be as much above the clouds, as the clouds are above the ordinary range of hills.

Nor is this all; but the countenance of these mountains is such, that we know no bounds set to them, but they run on in a continued ridge or ledge of mountains from one to another, till they are lost in the southern parts of Scotland, and even through that to the Highlands; so that they may be said to divide Britain, as the Appenine Mountains divide Italy. Thus these hills joining to Blackstone Edge divide Yorkshire from Lancashire, and going on north divides the Bishopric of Durham from Westmoreland, and so on. It is from this ridge of mountains that all the rivers in the north of England take their rise, I may say ALL, for it is so to a very trifle, not a considerable river north of this county, nay, and in this county too, but begin here; those on the east side run into the German Ocean, those on the west side into the Irish. I shall begin the observation here; the Dove and the Derwent rise both at this south end of them, and come away south to the Trent; but all the rivers afterwards run, as above, east or west; and first the Mersee rises on the west side, and the Don on the east, the first runs to Warrington, and into the sea at Liverpoole; the other to Doncaster, and into the sea at Humber. But to return to my progress.

Chesterfield is a handsome populous town, well-built and well inhabited, notwithstanding it stands in the farthest part of this rocky country. Here is, however, nothing remarkable in this town but a free school, and a very good market, well stored with provisions; for here is little or no manufacture.

From hence we entered the great country of York, uncertain still which way to begin to take a full view of it, for as 'tis a country of a very great extent, my business is not the situation or a mere geographical description of it; I have nothing to do with the longitude of places, the antiquities of towns, corporation, buildings, charters, &c., but to give you a view of the whole in its present state, as also of the commerce, curiosities and customs, according to my title.

The county is divided into three ridings; as I entered it from the south, it follows, I went in, by what they call the West Riding, which, as it is by much the largest, so it is the wealthiest and the most populous, has the greatest towns in it, and the greatest number of them; the greatest manufactures, and consequently the greatest share of wealth, as it has also of people.

Two eminent towns, though only mere market towns, and one of them no corporation, open the door into the West Riding of Yorkshire; these are Sheffield and Doncaster. It is true, there is a little market town, at the very first entrance into the county before we come to Doncaster, called Bautry, a town blessed with two great conveniences which assists to its support, and making it a very well frequented place.

1. That it stands upon the great post highway, or road from London to Scotland; and this makes it be full of very good inns and houses of entertainment.

2. That the little but pleasant River Idle runs through, or rather just by, the side of it, which, contrary to the import of its name, is a full and quick, though not rapid and unsafe stream, with a deep channel, which carries hoys, lighters, barges, or flat-bottomed vessels, out of its channel into the Trent, and from thence, in fair weather, quite to Hull.

By this navigation, this town of Bautry becomes the centre of all the exportation of this part of the country, especially for heavy goods, which they bring down hither from all the adjacent countries, such as lead, from the lead mines and smelting-houses in Derbyshire, wrought iron and edge-tools, of all sorts, from the forges at Sheffield, and from the country called Hallamshire, being adjacent to the towns of Sheffield and Rotherham, where an innumerable number of people are employed.

From hence to Doncaster is a pleasant road, and good ground, and never wants any repair, which is very hard to be said in any part of this lower side of the country. Doncaster is a noble, large, spacious town, exceeding populous, and a great manufacturing town, principally for knitting; also as it stands upon the great northern post-road, it is very full of great inns; and here we found our landlord at the post-house was mayor of the town as well as post-master, that he kept a pack of hounds, was company for the best gentlemen in the town or in the neighbourhood, and lived as great as any gentleman ordinarily did. Here we saw the first remains or ruins of the great Roman highway, which, though we could not perceive it before, was eminent and remarkable here, just at the entrance into the town; and soon after appeared again in many places.

This town, Mr Cambden says, was burnt entirely to the ground, anno 759, and is hardly recovered yet; but I must say, it is so well recovered, that I see no ruins appear, and indeed, being almost a thousand years ago, I know not how there should; and besides, the town seems as if it wanted another conflagration, for it looks old again, and many of the houses ready to fall.

Strange! that of two several authors [25] writing a description of Yorkshire but very lately, and pretending to speak positively of the places, which they ought not to have done, if they had not been there, both of them should so strangely mistake, as one to say of Doncaster, that there was a large church with a high spire steeple; and the other to say of the cathedral at York, that from the spire of the cathedral at York, you have an unbounded prospect. Whereas neither has the tower of York, or the tower at Doncaster, any spire, unless they will pretend any of the small pinnacles at the four corners of the two towers at the west end of the church at York, are to be called THE SPIRE of THE cathedral; so fit are such men to write descriptions of a country.

Leaving Doncaster, we turned out of the road a little way to the left, where we had a fair view of that ancient whittle making, cutlering town, called Sheffield; the antiquity, not of the town only, but of the trade also, is established by those famous lines of Geoffry Chaucer [26] on the Miller of Trumpington, which, however they vary from the print in Chaucer, as now extant, I give you as I find it:

> At Trumpington, not far from Cambridge,
> There dwelt a miller upon a bridge;
> With a rizzl'd beard, and a hooked nose,
> And a Sheffield whittl in his hose.

This town of Sheffield is very populous and large, the streets narrow, and the houses dark and black, occasioned by the continued smoke of the forges, which are always at work. Here they make all sorts of cutlery-ware, but especially that of edged-tools, knives, razors, axes, &c. and nails; and here the only mill of the sort, which was in use in England for some time was set up, (viz.) for turning their grindstones, though now 'tis grown more common.

Here is a very spacious church, with a very handsome and high spire; and the town is said to have at least as many, if not more people in it than the city of York. Whether they have been exactly numbered one against the other, I cannot tell. The manufacture of hard ware, which has been so ancient in this town, is not only continued, but much increased; insomuch that they told us there, the hands employed in it were a prodigious many more than ever dwelt, as well in the town, as in the bounds of that they call Hallamshire; and they talked of 30000 men employed in the whole; but I leave it upon the credit of report.

Here is a fine engine or mill also for raising water to supply the town, which was done by Mr Serocoal,[27] the same who fell into the river at the throwing-mill at Derby, as is said in its place. Here is also a very large and strong bridge over the Don, as there is another at Rotherham, a market town six miles lower. Here is also a very fine hospital, with the addition of a good revenue.

But the remains of the Roman fortification or encampment

between Sheffield and Rotherham, is there still, and very plain to be seen, and, I suppose, may remain so to the end of time.

Here is also the famous bank or trench which some call Devil's Bank, others Danes Bank; but 'tis frequent with us to give the honour of such great trenches, which they think was never worth the while for men to dig, to the devil, as if he had more leisure, or that it was less trouble to him than to a whole army of men.

Rotherham was the next town of any bulk in which, however, I saw nothing of note, except a fine stone bridge over the Don, which is here increased by the River Rother, from whence the town, I suppose, took its name, as the famous Bishop Rotherham [28] did his from the town: I will not say he was a foundling child in the streets, and so was surnamed from the place, as is often suggested in such cases, though if he was so, it did not diminish his character, which was that of a great and good man. He was Archbishop of York, and was a great benefactor to this town, having founded a college here; but it seems it has been a long while ago.

Thence over vast moors, I had almost said waste moors, we entered the most populous part of this county, I mean of the West Riding, only passing a town called Black Barnsley, eminent still for the working in iron and steel; and indeed the very town looks as black and smoky as if they were all smiths that lived in it; though it is not, I suppose, called Black Barnsley on that account, but for the black hue or colour of the moors, which, being covered with heath, (or heather, as 'tis called in that country) look all black, like Bagshot Heath, near Windsor; after, I say, we had passed these moors, we came to a most rich, pleasant and populous country, and the first town of note we came to in it was Wakefield, a large, handsome, rich clothing town, full of people, and full of trade.

The Calder passes through this town under a stately stone bridge of twelve arches, upon which is a famous building, by some called a chapel, by others a castle; the former is the most likely. It was built by Edward IV in memory of the fatal Battle of Wakefield, wherein his father, Richard, Duke of York, was killed by the Lancastrian army, under the command of Margaret, queen to Henry VI anno 1460. It was indeed a fatal battle; but as that is not any part of this work, I leave it to the historians to give a fuller account of it. The chapel on the bridge at Wakefield, the other monument of this battle, is now made use of for civil affairs; for we do not now pray for the souls of those slain in battle, and so the intent of that building ceases.

Wakefield is a clean, large, well-built town, very populous and very rich; here is a very large church, and well filled it is, for here are very few Dissenters; the steeple is a very fine spire, and by far the highest in all this part of the country, except that at Sheffield. They tell us, there are here more people also than in the city of York, and yet it is no corporation town; and the highest magistrate, as I understand, was a constable.

Here also is a market every Friday for woollen cloths, after the manner of that at Leeds, though not so great; yet as all the clothing trade is increasing in this country, so this market too flourishes with the rest; not but that sometimes, as foreign markets receive interruption either by wars, by a glut of the goods, or by any other incident, there are interruptions of the manufacture too, which, when it happen, the clothiers are sure to complain of loss of trade; but when the demand comes again they are not equally forward with their acknowledgments; and this, I observed, was the case every where else, as well as here.

The River Calder, of which I shall give an account by and by, having traced it from its beginning, receiving a mighty confluence of rivers into it, is now, as I have said, become a large river, and the first town it comes near of note is Huthersfield, another large clothing place; it passes also by Eland, where there is a very fine stone bridge. Huthersfield is one of the five towns which carry on that vast clothing trade by which the wealth and opulence of this part of the country has been raised to what it now is, and there those woollen manufactures are made in such prodigious quantities, which are known by the name of Yorkshire kerseys. Whether the scandal upon this country be just or not, (viz.) shrinking cloth and sharping k[nave]s, that I will not take upon me to determine; at this town there is a market for kerseys every Tuesday.

As the Calder rises in Blackstone Edge, so the Aire, another of the Yorkshire rivers, rises, though in the same ridge of hills, yet more particularly at the foot of the mountain Pennigent, on the edge of Lancashire, of which 'tis said proverbially:

> Pendle-Hill and Pennigent,
> Are the highest hills between Scotland and Trent.[29]

As the Calder runs by Hallifax, Huthersfield, and through Wakefield; so the Aire runs by Skippon, Bradforth and through Leeds, and then both join at Castleford Bridge, near Pontefract, so in an united stream forming that useful navigation from this trading part of Yorkshire to Hull; to the infinite advantage of the whole country, and which, as I took a singular satisfaction in visiting and enquiring into, so I believe you will be no less delighted in reading the account of it, which will be many ways both useful and very instructive.

It is not easy to take a view of this populous and wealthy part, called the West Riding, at one, no, nor at two journeys, unless you should dwell upon it, and go cross the country backward and forward, on purpose to see this or that considerable place. This is perhaps the reason why, as I hinted above, the other writers of journeys and travels this way might not see how to go about it. But, as I was resolved to have a perfect knowledge of the most remarkable things, and especially of the manufactures of England, which I take to be as well worth a traveller's notice, as the most curious thing he can meet with, and which is so prodigious great in this quarter, I made no less than three journeys into, and through, this part of the country.

If, by all these circuits, and traversing the country so many ways, which I name for the reasons above, I am not furnished to give a particular account of the most remarkable things, I must have spent my time very ill, and ought not to let you know how often I went through it.

In my second journey, I came from Lancashire, where you are to note, that all this part of the country is so considerable for its trade, that the Post-Master General had thought fit to establish a cross-post [30] through all the western part of England into it, to maintain the correspondence of merchants and men of business, of which all this side of the island is so full; this is a confirmation of what I have so often repeated, and may still repeat many times on farther occasion, of the greatness of the trade carried on in this part of the island. This cross-post begins at Plymouth, in the south west part of England, and, leaving the great western post road of Excester behind, comes away north to Taunton, Bridgwater and Bristol; from thence goes on through all the great cities and towns up the Severn; such as Gloucester, Worcester, Bridgnorth, and Shrewsbury, thence by West-Chester to Liverpool and Warrington, from whence it turns away east, and passes to Manchester, Bury, Rochdale, Hallifax, Leeds, and York, and ends at Hull.

By this means the merchants at Hull have immediate advice of their ships which go out of the channel, and come in; by their letters from Plymouth, as readily as the merchants at London, and without the double charge of postage. The shopkeepers and manufacturers can correspond with their dealers at Manchester, Liverpool and Bristol, nay, even with Ireland directly; without the tedious interruption of sending their letters about by London, or employing people at London to forward their packets.

I followed this post-road, from Liverpool to Bury and Rochdale, both manufacturing towns in Lancashire, and the last very considerable, for a sort of coarse goods, called half-thicks and kerseys, and the market for them is very great, though otherwise the town is situated so remote, so out of the way, and so at the very foot of the mountains, that we may suppose it would be but little frequented.

Here, for our great encouragement, though we were but at the middle of August, and in some places the harvest was hardly got in, we saw the mountains covered with snow, and felt the cold very acute and piercing; but even here we found, as in all those northern counties is the case, the people had an extraordinary way of mixing the warm and the cold very happily together; for the store of good ale which flows plentifully in the most mountainous part of this country, seems abundantly to make up for all the inclemencies of the season, or difficulties of travelling, adding also the plenty of coals for firing, which all those hills are full of.

We mounted the hills, fortified with the same precaution, early in the morning, and though the snow which had fallen in the night lay a little upon the ground, yet we thought it was not much; and the morning being calm and clear, we had no apprehension of an uneasy passage, neither did the people at Rochdale, who kindly directed us the way, and even offered to guide us over the first mountains, apprehend any difficulty for us; so we complimented our selves out of their assistance, which we afterwards very much wanted.

It was, as I say, calm and clear, and the sun shone when we came out of the town of Rochdale; but when we began to mount the hills, which we did within a mile, or little more of the town, we found the wind began to rise, and the higher we went the more wind; by which I soon perceived that it had blown before, and perhaps all night upon the hills, though it was calm below; as we ascended higher it began to snow again, that is to say, we ascended into that part where it was snowing, and had, no doubt, been snowing all night, as we could easily see by the thickness of the snow.

It is not easy to express the consternation we were in when we came up near the top of the mountain; the wind blew exceeding hard, and blew the snow directly in our faces, and that so thick, that it was impossible to keep our eyes open to see our way. The ground also was so covered with snow, that we could see no track, or when we were in the way, or when out; except when we were showed it by a frightful precipice on one hand, and uneven ground on the other; even our horses discovered their uneasiness at it; and a poor spaniel dog that was my fellow traveller, and usually diverted us with giving us a mark for our gun, turned tail to it and cried.

In the middle of this difficulty, and as we began to call to one another to turn back again, not knowing what dangers might still be before us, came a surprising clap of thunder, the first that ever I heard in a storm of snow, or, I believe, ever shall; nor did we perceive any lightning to precede the thunder, as must naturally be the case; but we supposed the thick falling of the snow might prevent our sight.

I must confess I was very much surprised at this blow; and one of our company would not be persuaded that it was thunder, but that it was some blast of a coal-pit, things which do sometimes happen in the country, where there are many coal mines. But we were all against him in that, and were fully satisfied that it was thunder, and, as we fancied, at last we were confirmed in it, by hearing more of it at a distance from us.

Upon this we made a full stop, and coming altogether, for we were then three in company, with two servants, we began to talk seriously of going back again to Rochdale; but just then one of our men called out to us, and said, he was upon the top of the hill, and could see over into Yorkshire, and that there was a plain way down on the other side.

We rode all up to him, and found it as the fellow had said, all but that of a plain way; there was indeed the mark or face of a road on the side of the hill, a little turning to the left north; but it was so narrow, and so deep a hollow place on the right, whence the water descending from the hills made a channel at the bottom, and looked as the beginning of a river, that the depth of the precipice, and the narrowness of way, looked horrible to us; after going a little way in it, the way being blinded too by the snow, the hollow on the right appeared deeper and deeper, so we resolved to alight and lead our horses, which we did for about a mile, though the violence of the wind and snow continuing, it was both very troublesome and dangerous.

At length, to our great joy, we found too the wind abated, as well as the snow, that is to say, the hills being so high behind us, they kept back the wind, as is the case under a high wall, though you are on the windward side of it, yet the wind having no passage through, is not felt, as it would be on the top where the space is open for it to pass.

All this way the hollow on our right continued very deep, and just on the other side of it a parallel hill continued going on east, as that did which we rode on the side of; the main hill which we came down from, which is properly called Blackstone Edge, or, by the country people, the Edge, without any surname or addition, ran along due north, crossing and shutting up those hollow gulls and valleys between, which were certainly originally formed by the rain and snow water running into them, and forcing its way down, washing the earth gradually along with it, till, by length of time, it wore down the surface to such a depth.

We continued descending still, and as the weather was quieter, so the way seemed to mend and be broader, and, to our great satisfaction, inclining more to the hill on the left; the precipice and hollow part where the water run, as I have said, went a little off from us, and by and by, to our no small comfort, we saw an enclosed piece of ground, that is enclosed with a stone wall, and soon after a house, where we asked our way, and found we were right.

Soon after this we came to the bottom, by another very steep descent, where we were obliged to alight again, and lead our horses. At the bottom, we found the hollow part, which I have so often mentioned as a precipice, was come to a level with us, that is to say, we were come down to a level with it, and it turning to the left toward us, we found a brook of water running from it, which crossed our way to the north, you shall hear of it again presently; when we crossed this brook, which, by reason of the snow on the hills which melted, was risen about knee deep, and run like a sluice for strength, we found a few poor houses, but saw no people, no not one; till we called at a door, to get directions of our way, and then we found, that though there was no body to be seen without doors, they were very full of people within, and so we found it on several occasions afterward, of which we shall speak again.

We thought now we were come into a Christian country again, and that our difficulties were over; but we soon found our selves mistaken in the matter; for we had not gone fifty yards beyond the brook and houses adjacent, but we found the way began to ascend again, and soon after to go up very steep, till in about half a mile we found we had another mountain to ascend, in our apprehension as bad as the first, and before we came to the top of it, we found it began to snow too, as it had done before.

But, to cut short the tedious day's work, the case was this; the hill was very high, and, in our opinion, not inferior to the Edge which we came just down from; but the sun being higher, and the wind not blowing so hard, what snow fell upon the hill melted as it fell, and so we saw our way plainer, and mastered the hill, though with some labour, yet not any terror or apprehensions of losing our way, falling down precipices, and the like.

But our case was still this; that as soon as we were at the top of every hill, we had it to come down again on the other side; and as soon as we were down we had another to mount, and that immediately; for I do not remember that there was one bottom that had any considerable breadth of plain ground in it, but always a brook in the valley running from those gulls and deep between the hills, with this remark, that they always crossed our way in the bottoms from the right-hand to the left, the reason of which you shall see presently.

From Blackstone Edge to Hallifax is eight miles, and all the way, except from Sorby to Hallifax, is thus up hill and down; so that, I suppose, we mounted to the clouds and descended to the water level about eight times, in that little part of the journey.

But now I must observe to you, that after having passed the second hill, and come down into the valley again, and so still the nearer we came to Hallifax, we found the houses thicker, and the villages greater in every bottom; and not only so, but the sides of the hills, which were very steep every way, were spread with houses, and that very thick; for the land being divided into small enclosures, that is to say, from two acres to six or seven acres each, seldom more; every three or four pieces of land had a house belonging to it.

Then it was I began to perceive the reason and nature of the thing, and found that this division of the land into small pieces, and scattering of the dwellings, was occasioned by, and done for the convenience of the business which the people were generally employed in, and that, as I said before, though we saw no people stirring without doors, yet they were all full within; for, in short, this whole country, however mountainous, and that no sooner we were down one hill but we mounted another, is yet infinitely full of people; these people all full of business; not a beggar, not an idle person to be seen, except here and there an alms-house, where people ancient, decrepit, and past labour, might perhaps be found; for it is observable, that the people here, however laborious, generally live to a great age, a certain testimony to the goodness and wholesomeness of the country, which is, without doubt, as healthy as any part of England; nor is the health of the people lessened, but helped and established by their being constantly employed, and, as we call it, their working hard; so that they find a double advantage by their being always in business.

This business is the clothing trade, for the convenience of which the houses are thus scattered and spread upon the sides of the hills, as above, even from the bottom to the top; the reason is this; such has been the bounty of nature to this otherwise frightful country, that two things essential to the business, as well as to the ease of the people are found here, and that in a situation which I never saw the like of in any part of England; and, I believe, the like is not to be seen so contrived in any part of the world; I mean coals and running water upon the tops of the highest hills. This seems to have been directed by the wise hand of Providence for the very purpose which is now served by it, namely, the manufactures, which otherwise could not be carried on; neither indeed could one fifth part of the inhabitants be supported without them, for the land could not maintain them. After we had mounted the third hill, we found the country, in short, one continued village, though mountainous every way, as before; hardly a house standing out of a speaking distance from another, and (which soon told us their business) the day clearing up, and the sun shining, we could see that almost at every house there was a tenter, and almost on every tenter a piece of cloth, or kersey, or shalloon, for they are the three articles of that country's labour; from which the sun glancing, and, as I may say, shining (the white reflecting its rays) to us, I thought it was the most agreeable sight that I ever saw, for the hills, as I say, rising and falling so thick, and the valleys opening sometimes one way, sometimes another, so that sometimes we could see two or three miles this way, sometimes as far another; sometimes like the streets near St Giles's,[31] called the Seven Dials; we could see through the glades almost every way round us, yet look which way we would, high to the tops, and low to the bottoms, it was all the same; innumerable houses and tenters, and a white piece upon every tenter.

But to return to the reason of dispersing the houses, as above; I found, as our road passed among them, for indeed no road could do otherwise, wherever we passed any house we found a little rill or gutter of running water, if the house was above the road, it came from it, and crossed the way to run to another; if the house was below us, it crossed us from some other distant house above it, and at every considerable house was a manufactory or work-house, and as they could not do their business without water, the little streams were so parted and guided by gutters or pipes, and by turning and dividing the streams, that none of those houses were without a river, if I may call it so, running into and through their work-houses.

Then, as every clothier must keep a horse, perhaps two, to fetch and carry for the use of his manufacture, (viz.) to fetch home his wool and his provisions from the market, to carry his yarn to the spinners, his manufacture to the fulling mill, and, when finished, to the market to be sold, and the like; so every manufacturer generally keeps a cow or two, or more, for his family, and this employs the two, or three, or four pieces of enclosed land about his house, for they scarce sow corn enough for their cocks and hens; and this feeding their grounds still adds by the dung of the cattle, to enrich the soil.

Having thus fire and water at every dwelling, there is no need to enquire why they dwell thus dispersed upon the highest hills, the convenience of the manufactures requiring it. Among the manufacturers' houses are likewise scattered an infinite number of cottages or small dwellings, in which dwell the workmen which are employed, the women and children of whom, are always busy carding, spinning, &c. so that no hands being unemployed, all can gain their bread, even from the youngest to the ancient; hardly any thing above four years old, but its hands are sufficient to it self.

This is the reason also why we saw so few people without doors; but if we knocked at the door of any of the master manufacturers, we presently saw a house full of lusty fellows, some at the dye-fat, some dressing the cloths, some in the loom, some one thing, some another, all hard at work, and full employed upon the manufacture, and all seeming to have sufficient business.

Having thus described the country, and the employment of the people, I am to tell you, that this part of it which I mentioned, is all belonging to and in the parish of Hallifax, and that brings me on towards the town.

I must only say a word or two of the River Calder, to complete the description of the country I thus passed through. I hinted to you, that all the rills or brooks of water which we crossed, one at least in every bottom, went away to the left or north side of us as we went forward east. I am to add, that following those little brooks with our eye, we could observe, that at some distance to the left there appeared a larger valley than the rest, into which not only all the brooks which we passed emptied themselves, but abundance more from the like hollow deep bottoms, among the hills on the north side of it, which emptied this way south, as those on our side run that way north, so that it was natural to conclude, that in this larger valley the waters of all those brooks joining, there must be some pretty large stream which received them all, and ran forward east, parallel to the way we were in.

After some time we found that great opening seemed to bend southward towards us, and that probably it would cross our road, or our road would rather cross the valley; and so it was natural to expect we should pass that larger water, either by a bridge or a ford; but we were soon convinced it was not the latter; for the snow, as is said, having poured down a quantity of water, we soon found at the next opening, that there was a considerable river in the larger valley, which, having received all those little brooks, was risen to a little flood; and at the next village we passed it over a stately stone bridge of several great arches. This village is called Sorby or Sowreby; and this was the main River Calder, which I mentioned at Wakefield, where it begins to be navigable, and which, without any spring or fountain, to be called the head or source of it, is formed on the declivity of these mountains, merely by the continued fall of rains and snows, which the said mountains intercepting the clouds, are seldom free from.

Having passed the Calder at Sorby Bridge, I now began to approach the town of Hallifax; in the description of which, and its dependencies, all my account of the commerce will come in, for take Hallifax, with all its dependencies, it is not to be equalled in England. First, the parish or vicarage, for it is but a vicarage; is, if not the largest, certainly the most populous in England; in short, it is a monster, I mean, for a country parish, and a parish so far out of the way of foreign trade, courts, or sea ports.

The extent of the parish, they tell us, is almost circular, and is about twelve miles in diameter. There are in it twelve or thirteen chapels of ease, besides about sixteen meeting-houses, which they call also chapels, and are so, having bells to call the people, and burying grounds to most of them, or else they bury within them. I think they told me, the Quakers' meetings, of which there are several too, are not reckoned into the number. In a word, it is some years ago that a reverend clergyman of the town of Hallifax, told me, they reckoned that they had a hundred thousand communicants in the parish, besides children.

History tells us also, that in Queen Elizabeth's time . . . no less than twelve thousand young men went out armed from this one parish, and, at her majesty's call, joined her troops to fight the Popish army, then in rebellion under the Earl of Westmorland.

If they were so populous at that time, how much must they be increased since? and especially since the late Revolution, the trade having been prodigiously encouraged and increased by the great demand of their kerseys for clothing the armies abroad, insomuch that it is the opinion of some that know the town, and its bounds very well, that the number of people in the vicarage of Hallifax, is increased one fourth, at least, within the last forty years, that is to say, since the late Revolution.[32] Nor is it improbable at all, for besides the number of houses which are increased, they have entered upon a new manufacture which was never made in those parts before, at least, not in any quantities, I mean, the manufactures of shalloons, of which they now make, if fame does not belie them, a hundred thousand pieces a year in this parish only, and yet do not make much fewer kerseys than they did before.

But it is evident that the trade must be exceeding great, in that it employs such a very great number of people, and that in this one town only; for, this is not what I may call the eldest son of the clothing trade in this county; the town of Leeds challenges a pre-eminence, and I believe, merits the dignity it claims, besides the towns of Huthersfield, Bradforth, Wakefield, and others.

But I must not leave Hallifax yet, as the vicarage is thus far extended, and the extent of it so peopled, what must the market be, and where must this vast number of people be supplied? For, as to corn, I have observed already, they sow little and hardly enough to feed their poultry, if they were to be corn fed; and as to beef and mutton, they feed little or none; and as they are surrounded with large, populous, manufacturing towns on every side, all of them employed as these are, in the clothing trade, they must then necessarily have their provisions from other parts of the country.

This then is a subsistence to the other part of the country, and so it is for us, the West Riding is thus taken up, and the lands occupied by the manufacture; the consequence is plain, their corn comes up in great quantities out of Lincoln, Nottingham, and the East Riding, their black cattle and horses from the North Riding, their sheep and mutton from the adjacent counties every way, their butter from the East and North Riding, their cheese out of Cheshire and Warwickshire, more black cattle also from Lancashire. And here the breeders and feeders, the farmers and county people find money owing in plenty from the manufacturers and commerce.

Upon this foot, 'tis ordinary for a clothier that has a large family, to come to Hallifax on a market-day, and buy two or three large bullocks from eight to ten pounds a piece. These he carries home and kills for his store. And this is the reason that the markets at all those times of the year are thronged with black cattle, as Smithfield is on a Friday; whereas all the rest of the year there is little extraordinary sold there.

Thus this one trading, manufacturing part of the country supports all the countries round it, and the numbers of people settle here as bees about a hive. As for the town of Hallifax it self, there is nothing extraordinary except on a market-day, and then indeed it is a prodigious thing.

But I must not quit Hallifax, till I give you some account of the famous course of justice anciently executed here, to prevent the stealing of cloth. The case was thus: the erecting the woollen manufacture here was about the year 1480, when King Henry VII by giving encouragement to foreigners to settle in England, and to set up woollen manufactures, caused an Act to pass prohibiting the exportation of wool into foreign parts, unwrought, and to encourage foreign manufacturers to come and settle here, of whom several coming over settled the manufactures of cloths in several parts of the kingdom, as they found the people tractable, and as the country best suited them; as the bays at Colchester, the says at Sudbury, the broad-cloth in Wilts, and other counties; so the trade of kerseys and narrow cloth fixed at this place, and other adjacent towns.

When this trade began to settle, nothing was more frequent than for young workmen to leave their cloths out all night upon the tenters, and the idle fellows would come in upon them, and tearing them off without notice, steal the cloth. Now as it was absolutely necessary to preserve the trade in its infancy, this severe law was made, giving the power of life and death so far into the hands of the magistrates of Hallifax, as to see the law executed upon them. As this law was particularly pointed against the stealing of cloth, and no other crime, so no others were capable of being punished by it, and the conditions of the law intimate as much; for the power was not given to the magistrates to give sentence, unless in one of these three plain cases:

1. Hand napping, that is, to be taken in the very fact, or, as the Scots call it in the case of murther, red hand.

2. Back bearing, that is, when the cloth was found on the person carrying it off.

3. Tongue confessing, that part needs no farther explanation.

This being the case, if the criminal was taken, he was

brought before the magistrates of the town, who at that time were only a bailie and the eoaldermen, how many we do not read, and these were to judge, and sentence, and execute the offender, or clear him, within so many days. The country people were, it seems, so terrified at the severity of this proceeding, that hence came that proverbial saying, which was used all over Yorkshire, (viz)

From Hell, Hull, and Hallifax,
Good Lord, deliver us.

How Hull came to be included in this petition, I do not find; for they had no such law there, as I read of.

The manner of execution was very remarkable; the engine indeed is carried away, but the scaffold on which it stood is there to this time, and may continue many ages; being not a frame of wood, but a square building of stone, with stone steps to go up, and the engine it self was made in the following manner.

They tell us of a custom which prevailed here, in the case of a criminal being to be executed, (viz.) that if after his head was laid down, and the signal given to pull out the pin, he could be so nimble as to snatch out his head between the pulling out the pin and the falling down of the axe and could get up upon his feet, jump off the scaffold, run down a hill that lies just before it, and get through the river before the executioner could overtake him, and seize upon him, he was to escape; and though the executioner did take him on the other side the river, he was not to bring him back, at least he was not to be executed.

But as they showed me the form of the scaffold, and the weight of the axe, it was, in my opinion, next to impossible, any man should be so quick-eyed as to see the pulling out the pin, and so quick with his head, as to snatch it out; yet they tell a story of one fellow that did it, and was so bold after he had jumped off the scaffold, and was running down the hill, with the executioner at his heels, to turn about and call to the people to give him his hat. But this story is said to be too long ago to have any vouchers, though the people indeed all receive it for truth.

The force of this engine is so strong, the head of the axe being loaded with a weight of lead to make it fall heavy, and the execution is so sure, that it takes away all possibility of its failing to cut off the head; and to this purpose, the Hallifax people tell you another story of a country woman, who was riding by upon her doffers or hampers to Hallifax Market, for the execution was always on a market day (the third after the fact) and passing just as the axe was let fall upon the neck of the criminal, it chopped it through with such force, that the head jumped off into one of her hampers, and that the woman not perceiving it, she carried it away to the market.

All the use I shall make of this unlikely story, is this, that it seems executions were so frequent, that it was not thought a sight worth the peoples running out to see; that the woman should ride along so close to the scaffold, and that she should go on, and not so much as stop to see the axe fall, or take any notice of it. But those difficulties seem to be much better solved, by saying, that 'tis reasonable to think the whole tale is a little Yorkshire, which, I suppose, you will understand well enough. This engine was removed, as we are told, in the year 1620, during the reign of King James the First, and the usage and custom of prosecution abolished, and criminals or felons left to the ordinary course of justice, as it is still; and yet they do not find the stealing cloth from the tenters is so frequent now as it was in those times.

From Hallifax it is twelve miles to Leeds north east, and about as many to Wakefield; due east, or a little southerly, between Hallifax and Leeds, is a little town called Burstall. Here the kersey and shalloon trade being, as it were, confined to Hallifax, and the towns already named, of Huthersfield and Bradforth, they begin to make broad cloth.

This town is famed for dying, and they make a sort of cloths here in imitation of the Gloucester white cloths, bought for the Dutch and the Turkey trades; and though their cloths here may not be as fine, they told us their colours are as good. But that is not my business to dispute, the west country clothiers deny it; and so I leave it as I find it.

From hence to Leeds, and every way to the right hand and the left, the country appears busy, diligent, and even in a hurry of work, they are not scattered and dispersed as in the vicarage of Hallifax, where the houses stand one by one; but in villages, those villages large, full of houses, and those houses thronged with people, for the whole country is infinitely populous.

A noble scene of industry and application is spread before you here, and which, joined to the market at Leeds, where it chiefly centres, is well worth the curiosity of a stranger to go on purpose to see; and many travellers and gentlemen have come over from Hamburgh, nay, even from Leipsick in Saxony, on purpose to see it.

And this brought me from the villages where this manufacture is wrought, to the market where it is sold, which is at Leeds.

Leeds is a large, wealthy and populous town, it stands on the north bank of the River Aire, or rather on both sides the river, for there is a large suburb or part of the town on the south side of the river, and the whole is joined by a stately and prodigiously strong stone bridge, so large, and so wide, that formerly the cloth market [33] was kept in neither part of the town, but on the very bridge it self; and therefore the refreshment given the clothiers by the inn-keepers, of which I shall speak presently is called the brigg-shot to this day.

The increase of the manufacturers and of the trade, soon made the market too great to be confined to the brigg or bridge, and it is now kept in the High-street, beginning from the bridge, and running up north almost to the market-house, where the ordinary market for provisions begins, which also is the greatest of its kind in all the north of England, except Hallifax. The street is a large, broad, fair, and well-built street, beginning, as I have said, at the bridge, and ascending gently to the north.

Early in the morning, there are trestles placed in two rows in the street, sometimes two rows on a side, but always one row at least; then there are boards laid cross those trestles, so that the boards lie like long counters on either side, from one end of the street to the other. The clothiers come early in the morning with their cloth; and as few clothiers bring more than one piece, the market being so frequent, they go into the inns and public-houses with it, and there set it down.

At seven a clock in the morning, the clothiers being supposed to be all come by that time, even in the winter, the market bell rings; it would surprise a stranger to see in how few minutes, without hurry or noise, and not the least disorder, the whole market is filled; all the boards upon the trestles are covered with cloth, close to one another as the pieces can lie long ways by one another, and behind every piece of cloth, the clothier standing to sell it.

This indeed is not so difficult, when we consider that the whole quantity is brought into the market as soon as one piece, because as the clothiers stand ready in the inns and shops just behind, and that there is a clothier to every piece, they have no more to do, but, like a regiment drawn up in line, every one takes up his piece, and has about five steps to march to lay it upon the first row of boards, and perhaps ten to the second row; so that upon the market bell ringing, in half a quarter of an hour the whole market is filled, the rows of boards covered, and the clothiers stand ready.

As soon as the bell has done ringing, the merchants and factors, and buyers of all sorts, come down, and coming along the spaces between the rows of boards, they walk up the rows, and down as their occasions direct. Some of them have their foreign letters of orders, with patterns sealed on them, in rows, in their hands; and with those they match colours, holding them to the cloths as they think they agree to; when they see any cloths to their colours, or that suit their occasions, they reach over to the clothier and whisper, and in the fewest words imaginable the price is stated; one asks, the other bids; and 'tis agree, or not agree, in a moment.

The merchants and buyers generally walk down and up twice on each side of the rows, and in little more than an hour all the business is done; in less than half an hour you will perceive the cloths begin to move off, the clothier taking it up upon his shoulder to carry it to the merchant's house; and by half an hour after eight a clock the market bell rings again; immediately the buyers disappear, the cloth is all sold, or if here and there a piece happens not to be bought, 'tis carried back into the inn, and, in a quarter of an hour, there is not a piece of cloth to be seen in the market. Thus, you see, ten or twenty thousand pounds value in cloth, and sometimes much more, bought and sold in little more than an hour, and the laws of the market the most strictly observed as ever I saw done in any market in England.

By nine a clock the boards are taken down, the trestles are removed, and the street cleared, so that you see no market or goods any more than if there had been nothing to do; and this is done twice a week. By this quick return the clothiers are constantly supplied with money, their workmen are duly paid, and a prodigious sum circulates through the county every week.

If you should ask upon all this, where all these goods, as well here as at Wakefield, and at Hallifax, are vented and disposed of? It would require a long treatise of commerce to enter into that part. But that I may not bring you into the labyrinth, and not show you the way out, I shall, in three short heads, describe the consumption, for there are three channels by which it goes:

1. For the home consumption; their goods being, as I may say, every where made use of, for the clothing the ordinary people, who cannot go to the price of the fine medley cloths made, as I formerly gave you an account, in the western counties of England. There are for this purpose a set of travelling merchants in Leeds, who go all over England with droves of pack horses, and to all the fairs and market towns over the whole island, I think I may say none excepted. Here they supply not the common people by retail, which would de-

nominate them pedlars indeed, but they supply the shops by wholesale or whole pieces; and not only so, but give large credit too, so that they are really travelling merchants, and as such they sell a very great quantity of goods.

2. Another sort of buyers are those who buy to send to London; either by commissions from London, or they give commissions to factors and warehouse-keepers in London to sell for them; and these drive also a very great trade. These factors and warehouse-keepers not only supply all the shop-keepers and wholesale men in London, but sell also very great quantities to the merchants, as well for exportation to the English colonies in America, which take off great quantities of those coarse goods, especially New England, New York, Virginia, &c. as also to the Russia merchants, who send an exceeding quantity to Petersburgh, Riga, Dantzic, Narva, and to Sweden and Pomerania.

3. The third sort of buyers, and who are not less considerable than the other, are truly merchants, that is to say, such as receive commissions from abroad to buy cloth for the merchants chiefly in Hamburgh, and in Holland, and from several other parts; and these are not only many in number, but some of them are very considerable in their dealings, and correspond as far as Nuremberg, Frankfort, Leipsick, and even to Vienna and Ausburgh, in the farthest provinces of Germany.

On account of this trade it was, that some years ago an Act of Parliament [34] was obtained for making the Rivers Aire and Calder navigable; by which a communication by water was opened from Leeds and Wakefield to Hull, and by which means all the woollen manufactures which those merchants now export by commission, as above, is carried by water to Hull, and there shipped for Holland, Bremen, Hamburgh, and the Baltic. And thus you have a brief account, by what methods this vast manufacture is carried off, and which way they find a vent for it.

There is another trade in this part of the country, which is now become very considerable since the opening the navigation of these rivers, and that is, that from hence they carry coals down from Wakefield (especially) and also from Leeds, at both which they have a very great quantity, and such, as they told me, could never be exhausted. These they carry quite down into the Humber, and then up the Ouse to York, and up the Trent, and other rivers, where there are abundance of large towns, who they supply with coals; with this advantage too, that whereas the Newcastle coals pay four shillings per chaldron duty to the public; these being only called river borne coal, are exempted, and pay nothing; though, strictly speaking, they are carried on the sea too, for the Humber is properly the sea. But they have been hitherto exempted from the tax, and so they carry on the trade to their very great profit and advantage.

The town of Leeds is very large, and, as above, there are abundance of wealthy merchants in it. Here are two churches, and two large meeting-houses of Dissenters, and six or seven chapels of ease, besides Dissenters' chapels, in the adjacent, depending villages; so that Leeds may not be much inferior to Hallifax in numbers of people. It is really a surprising thing to see what numbers of people are thronged together in all the villages about these towns, and how busy they all are, being fully employed in this great manufacture.

Before I go forward from hence, I should tell you, that I took a little trip to see the ancient town of Pontefract, with that dismal place called the Castle, a place that was really dismal on many accounts, having been a scene of blood in many several ages; for here Henry, the great Earl of Lancaster,[35] who was at the same time lord of the castle, and whose ancestors had beautified and enlarged it exceedingly, and fortified it too, was beheaded, in King Edward the IId's time, with three or four more of the English barons. Here Richard IId, being deposed and imprisoned, was barbarously murthered, and, if history lies not, in a cruel manner; and here Anthony, Earl Rivers, and Sir Richard Gray, the first uncle, and the last brother-in-law to King Edward the Fifth, were beheaded by that tyrant Richard III.

The town is large and well built, but much smaller than it has been; the castle lies in its ruins, though not demolished; within a mile of it is Ferry Bridge, where there is a great stone bridge over the Aire and Calder (then united) and a large stone causeway, above a mile in length, to a town called Brotherton, where Queen Margaret,[36] wife of King Edward the First, was delivered of a son, being surprised as she was abroad taking the air, some histories say, a hunting; but, I must confess, it seems not very probable, that queens big with child, and within a few hours of their time, should ride a hunting. Be that as it will, here her majesty was catched (as the women call it) and forced to take up, and brought forth a son, who afterwards was a famous man, and was made Earl of Norfolk, and Earl Marshal of England; which office is hereditary to the title of Norfolk to this day. A little on the south side of this village the road parts, and one way goes on to the right towards Tadcaster, and so to York, of which in its order; the other, being the high-post road for Scotland, goes on to Wetherby, over Bramham Moor,[37] famous for a fight between the Royalists and the famed Sir Thomas Fairfax, in which the last was worsted and wounded, but made a retreat, which gained him as great reputation as a victory would have done.

Wetherby is a small town, but being a great thoroughfare to the north, has several good inns, and a very lofty stone bridge over the River Wharfe, which comes down from the hills also, as the rest do.

But I must go back to Pontefract, to take notice, that here again the great Roman highway, which I mentioned at Doncaster, and which is visible from thence in several places on the way to Pontefract, though not in the open road, is apparent again, and from Castleford Bridge, which is another bridge over the united rivers of Aire and Calder, it goes on to Abberforth, a small market town famous for pin-making, and so to Tadcaster and York.

As I made this little excursion to see the town of Pontefract from Leeds, you must suppose me now returned thither, and setting out thence northward. I had no sooner passed out of the district of Leeds about four or five miles, and passed the Wharfe, but it was easy to see we were out of the manufacturing country. Now the black moorish lands, like Black Barnsley, showed dismal again and frightful, the towns were thin, and thin of people too; we saw but little enclosed ground, no tenters with the cloths shining upon them, nor people busied within doors, as before; but, as in the Vicarage, we saw inhabited mountains, here we saw waste and almost uninhabited vales. In a word, the country looked as if all the people were transplanted to Leeds and Hallifax, and that here was only a few just left at home to cultivate the land, manage the plough, and raise corn for the rest.

From the Wharfe we went directly north, over a continued waste of black, ill looking, desolate moors, over which travellers are guided, like race horses, by posts set up for fear of bogs and holes, to a town called Ripley, that stands upon another river called the Nud by some, by others the Nyd, smaller than the Wharfe, but furiously rapid, and very dangerous to pass in many places, especially upon sudden rains. Notwithstanding such lofty, high built bridges as are not to be seen over such small rivers in any other place; and, on this occasion, it may be observed here, once for all, that no part of England, I may say so because I can say I have seen the whole island, a very little excepted, I say, no part can show such noble, large, lofty, and long stone bridges as this part of England, nor so many of them; nor do I remember to have seen any such thing as a timber bridge in all the northern part of England, no not from the Trent to the Tweed; whereas in the south parts of England there are abundance, as particularly over the great river of Thames at Kingston, Chertsey, Staines, Windsor, Maidenhead, Reading, Henley, Marlow, and other places.

A little below Ripley, on the same River Nyd, and with a very fine bridge over it also, we saw Knaresborough; known among foreigners by the name of Knaresborough Spaw; in the south of England I have heard it called the Yorkshire

Spaw. I shall not enter here upon the definition of the word *spa*, 'tis enough to speak familiarly, that here is a well of physical or mineral waters, or, to speak more exactly as one viewing the country, here are at the town, and in the adjacent lands, no less than four spas or mineral waters.

The first thing recommended to me for a wonder, was that four springs, the waters of which are in themselves of so different a quality, should rise in so narrow a compass of ground; but I, who was surfeited with country wonders in my passing the Peak, was not so easily surprised at the wonderful strangeness of this part.

2. The springs themselves, and indeed one of them, is nothing extraordinary, namely, that in a little cave a petrifying water drops from the roof of the cavity, which, as they say, turns wood into stone. This indeed I made light of too, because I had already been at Pole's Hole and Castleton in the Peak.

But now to speak of the other two springs, they are indeed valuable rarities, and not to be equalled in England.

1. The first is the Sweet Spaw,[38] or a vitriolic water; it was discovered by one Mr Slingsby, anno 1630, and all physicians acknowledge it to be a very sovereign medicine in several particular distempers.

2. The Stinking Spaw, or, if you will, according to the learned, the Sulphur Well. This water is clear as crystal, but fetid and nauseous to the smell, so that those who drink it are obliged to hold their noses when they drink; yet it is a valuable medicine also in scorbutic, hypochondriac, and especially in hydropic distempers; as to its curing the gout, I take that, as in other cases, *ad referendum*.

We were surprised to find a great deal of good company here drinking the waters, and indeed, more than we found afterwards at Scarborough; though this seems to be a most desolate out-of-the-world place, and that men would only retire to it for religious mortifications, and to hate the world, but we found it was quite otherwise.

From the bridges may be observed, that however low these

waters are in summer, they are high and furious enough in the winter; and yet the River Aire, though its beginning is in the same ridge of mountains as the other,[39] and particularly in the hill called Penigent, which overtops all its neighbours; I say this river is gentle and mild in its stream, when the other are all raging and furious; the only reason I can give for it, which however I think is a very just account, is, that it runs in a thousand windings and turnings more than any other river in those parts; and these reaches and meanders of the river greatly help to check the sharpness of the streams.

Rippon is a very neat, pleasant, well built town, and has not only an agreeable situation on a rising ground between two rivers, but the market place is the finest and most beautiful square that is to be seen of its kind in England. In the middle of it stands a curious column of stone, imitating the obelisks of the ancients, though not so high, but rather like the pillar in the middle of Covent-Garden, or that in Lincoln's Inn, with dials also upon it. But I must not omit to tell you also, however other pretended travelling writers were pleased not to see it as they went by, that here is a large collegiate church, and though it is not a bishopric but a deanery only, in the diocese of York, yet it is a very handsome, ancient and venerable pile of building, and shews it self a great way in the country.

That here was a famous monastery built by Wilfrid,[40] Archbishop of York, and that in the first ages of Christianity, at least in this island, is certain; but this pious gift of the bishop was swallowed up some years after, when the Danes over-running Yorkshire, rifled and burnt it to the ground, as likewise the whole town of Rippon. It afterwards flourished again as a monastery. But those being all given up in the reign of King Henry VIII the church only was preserved.

While it was a monastery, here was a famous sanctuary, a thing however useful in some cases, yet so abused in foreign countries, by making the church a refuge of rogues, thieves and murtherers, that 'tis happy for England it is out of use here. This privilege of sanctuary was, it seems, granted to the church of Rippon by King Athelstan,[41] and with this extraordinary sanction, that whosoever broke the rights of sanctuary of the church of Rippon, and which he extended to a mile on either side the church, should forfeit life and estate; so that, in short, not the church only, but the whole town, and a circle of two miles diameter, was like the Rules of the King's Bench here in Southwark, a refuge for all that fled to it, where they lived safe from all manner of molestation, even from the king, or his laws, or any person whatsoever.

Annexed to this monastery was an hospital, the intent and purposes of which are very remarkable, and would be worthy imitation in our days of Protestant charity, when indeed I see nothing come up to it. Also 'tis recorded, that one branch of this hospital was founded and endowed, and given to a society of religious sisters by a certain Archbishop of York, but the inquisition taken does not find his name, to the intent that they should maintain one chaplain to perform divine service, and to the farther intent that they should maintain all the lepers born and bred in Hipschire, that should come to it for maintenance; and that they should allow to each of them a garment called rak, and two pair of shoes yearly, with every day a loaf fit for a poor man's sustenance, half a pitcher of beer, a sufficient portion of flesh on flesh days, and three herrings on fish days.

After this, other gifts were added to this foundation; and the maintenance of lepers finding no clients, the country proving healthy, that part was turned into a charity, to be dealt out to the poor on St Mary Magdalen's Day. At length all was demolished together, and the house, with the monastery, suppressed, as it now stands, a collegiate church being erected on the room of it.

There were at that time, in this church, nine chantries, besides two out-chantries in the parish, the same which we call now chapels of ease.

There were in the church at that time

	l.	s.	d.	
Three deacons ——	5	10	0	each
Three subdeacons ——	4	10	0	
Six choristers ——	3	10	0	And 1l. 4s. each for their livery
Six tribblers ——	2	12	6	
The organist ——	0	14	4	
The grammar school-master ——	2	0	0	

These were noble stipends in those days. How our clergy would serve at this time under such great encouragement, is left to enquiry, especially the organist's salary was notable; from whence I may, I hope without offence, suppose, that he being a layman, might get business in the town, (perhaps he was a dancing-master, or a music-master, or both) to teach the young ladies of Rippon; and his wife might keep a boarding-school too; and so the grammar school-master might be a writing-master in the town, and the like.

Be that as it will, the church is still standing, though the monastery and hospital are suppressed, and the canons and choir are maintained at a much better rate than as above, for they now eat as good beef, and drink as good Yorkshire ale, as their neighbours.

But I must not leave Rippon without giving the famed tale of St Wilfrid's Needle. St Wilfrid was the saint to whom the monastery was dedicated, and this needle was, it seems, for the trial of chastity. There was a dark vault under the ground in one part of the monastery, into which there was an easy passage one way, but a narrow long entry, also dark and uneven to come out of it. If any person's chastity was suspected, it does not say whether it was not for men as well as women, but to be sure it was for the latter, they were put into this vault, and the first entrance being closed, they were at liberty to come out by the other, which was called the needle, or the eye of the needle; if they were chaste and untainted, they came out boldly, and without any difficulty; but if faulty, they were stopped, and could not get along in the narrow eye or passage, and, as I think the story says, were left there, unable to get out till they had confessed their fault. Whether the priests had no craft in this case, to put some secret barrier cross the narrow passage in the dark, so to impose upon the poor girls that were put to the trial, that I am not to enquire too far into. However it was, the priests made a miracle of it; and the poor Yorkshire lasses have, no doubt, good reason to be satisfied that St Wilfrid has left off showing those miraculous things at this time.[42]

As you now begin to come into the North Riding, for the Eure parts the West Riding from it, so you are come into the place noted in the north of England for the best and largest oxen, and the finest galloping horses, I mean swift horses, horses bred, as we call it, for the light saddle, that is to say, for the race, the chase, for running or hunting.

From this town of Rippon, the north road and the Roman highway also, leads away to a town called Bedal, and, in a straight line (leaving Richmond about two miles on the west) called Leeming Lane, goes on to Piersbridge on the River Tees, which is the farthest boundary of the county of York.

But before I go forward I should mention Burrow Bridge, which is but three miles below Rippon, upon the same River Eure, and which I must take in my way, that I may not be obliged to go farther out of the way, on the next journey. There is something very singular at this town, and which is not to be found in any other part of England or Scotland, namely, two borough towns in one parish, and each sending two members to Parliament, that is, Borough Brigg and Aldborough. Borough Brigg, or Bridge, seems to be the modern town risen up out of Aldborough, the very names importing as much, (viz.) that Burrough at the Bridge, and the Old Borough that was before; and this construction I pretend to justify from all the antiquaries of our age, or the last, who place on the side of Aldborough or Old Borough, an ancient city and Roman colony, called *Isurium Brigantum*; the arguments brought to prove the city stood here, where yet at present nothing of a city is to be seen, no not so much as the ruins, especially not above ground, are out of my way for the present; only the digging up coins, urns, vaults, pavements, and the like, may be mentioned, because some of them are very eminent and remarkable ones. That this Old Burrough is the remain of that city, is then out of doubt, and that the Burrough at the Bridge, is since grown up, and perhaps principally by the confluence of travellers, to pass the great bridge over the Eure there; this seems too out of question by the import of the word. How either of them came to the privilege of sending members to Parliament, whether by charter and incorporation, or mere prescription, that is to say, a claim of age, which we call time out of mind, that remains for the Parliament to be satisfied in. Certain it is, that the youngest of the two, that is, Burrow Bridge, is very old; for here, in the Barons'. Wars, was a battle, and on this bridge the great Bohun,[43] Earl of Hereford, was killed by a soldier, who lay concealed under the bridge, and wounded him, by thrusting a spear or pike into his body, as he passed the bridge.

I met with nothing at or about Bedall, that comes within the compass of my enquiry but this, that not this town only, but even all this country, is full of jockeys, that is to say, dealers in horses, and breeders of horses, and the breeds of their horses in this and the next country are so well known, that though they do not preserve the pedigree of their horses for a succession of ages, as they say they do in Arabia and in Barbary, yet they christen their stallions here, and know them, and will advance the price of a horse according to the reputation of the horse he came of.

They do indeed breed very fine horses here, and perhaps some of the best in the world, for let foreigners boast what they will of barbs and Turkish horses, and, as we know five hundred pounds has been given for a horse brought out of Turkey, and of the Spanish jennets from Cordova, for which also an extravagant price has been given, I do believe that some of the gallopers of this country, and of the bishopric of Durham, which joins to it, will outdo for speed and strength the swiftest horse that was ever bred in Turkey, or Barbary, taken them all together.

My reason for this opinion is founded upon those words all together; that is to say, take their strength and their speed together; for example; match the two horses, and bring them to the race post, the barb may beat Yorkshire for a mile course, but Yorkshire shall distance him at the end of four miles; the barb shall beat Yorkshire upon a dry, soft carpet ground, but Yorkshire for a deep country; the reason is plain, the English horses have both the speed and the strength; the barb perhaps shall beat Yorkshire, and carry seven stone and a half; but Yorkshire for a twelve to fourteen stone weight; in a word, Yorkshire shall carry the man, and the barb a feather. I believe, I do not boast in their behalf, without good vouchers, when I say, that English horses, take them one with another, will beat all the world.

Besides their breeding of horses, they are also good graziers over this whole country, and have a large, noble breed of oxen, as may be seen at North Allerton fairs, where there are an incredible quantity of them bought eight times every year, and brought southward as far as the fens in Lincolnshire, and the Isle of Ely, where, being but, as it were, half before, they are fed up to the grossness of fat which we see in London markets.

Richmond is a large market town, and gives name to this part of the country, which is called after it Richmondshire, as another part of it east of this is called North Allertonshire. Here you begin to find a manufacture on foot again, and, as before, all was clothing, and all the people clothiers, here you see all the people, great and small, a knitting; and at Richmond you have a market for woollen or yarn stockings, which they make very coarse and ordinary, and they are sold accordingly; for the smallest sized stockings for children are here sold for eighteen pence per dozen, or three half pence a pair, sometimes less.

This trade extends itself also into Westmoreland, or rather comes from Westmoreland, extending itself hither, for at Kendal, Kirkby Stephen, and such other places in this county as border upon Yorkshire; the chief manufacture of yarn stockings is carried on; it is indeed a very considerable manufacture in it self, and of late mightily increased too, as all the manufactures of England indeed are.

This town of Richmond is walled, and had a strong castle; but as those things are now all slighted, so really the account of them is of small consequence, and needless; old fortifications being, if fortification was wanted, of very little signification; the River Swale runs under the wall of this castle, and has some unevenness at its bottom, by reason of rocks which intercept its passage, so that it falls like a cataract, but not with so great a noise.

The Swale is a noted river, though not extraordinary large, for giving name to the lands which it runs through for some length, which are called Swale Dale, and to an ancient family of that name, one of whom had the vanity, as I have heard, to boast, that his family was so ancient as not to receive that name from, but to give name to the river it self. One of the worthless successors of this line, who had brought himself to the dignity of what they call in London, a Fleeter, used to write himself, in his abundant vanity, Sir Solomon Swale,[44] of Swale Hall, in Swale Dale, in the county of Swale in the North Riding of York.

Leaving Richmond, we continue through this long Leeming Lane, which holds for about the length of six mile to the bank of Tees, where we passed over the River Tees at Piersbridge; the Tees is a most terrible river, so rapid, that they tell us a story of a man who coming to the ferry place in the road to Darlington, and finding the water low began to pull off his hose and shoes to wade through, the water not being deep enough to reach to his knees, but that while he was going over, the stream swelled so fast as to carry him away and drown him.

This bridge leads into the bishopric of Durham, and the road soon after turns into the great post road leading to the city of Durham. I shall dwell no longer upon the particulars found on this side; as all the country round here are grooms, as is noted before; so here and hereabouts they have an excellent knack at dressing horses' hides into leather, and thinking or making us think it is invulnerable, that is to say, that it will never wear out; in a word, they make the best bridle reins, belts broad or narrow, and all accoutrements for a complete horse-master, as they do at Rippon for spurs and stirrups.

Barnard's Castle stands on the north side of the Tees, and so is in the bishopric of Durham. 'Tis an ancient town, and pretty well built, but not large; the manufacture of yarn stockings continues thus far, but not much farther; but the jockeys multiply that way; and here we saw some very fine horses indeed; but as they wanted no goodness, so they wanted no price, being valued for the stallion they came of, and the merit of the breed.

The length of the late war,[45] it seems, caused the breeders here to run into a race or kind of horses, differing much from what they were used to raise, that is to say, from fine fleet horses for galloping and hunting, to a larger breed of charging horses, for the use of the general officers, and colonels of horse, aides du camp, and the like, whose service required strong charging horses, and yet if they were fleet horses too, they had a vast advantage of the enemy; for that if the rider was conquered and forced to fly, there was no overtaking him; and if his enemies fled they could never get away from him. I saw some of this breed, and very noble creatures they were, fit for any business whatever; strong enough for charging, fleet enough for hunting, tempered enough for travelling.

I was come now to the extent of the country of York northward. But as I have all the East Riding and the eastern part of the North and West Riding to go over, I shall break off here, and conclude my first circuit; and am, with due respect,

SIR,

Your most humble servant.

Letter 9

SIR, – I am now come back, as the French say, *sur mes pas*, to the same bank of the Trent, though lower down, towards the east, and shall gather up some fragments of Nottinghamshire and the West Riding of Yorkshire, as I go, and then hasten to the sea side, where we have not cast our eye yet.

Passing Newark Bridge, we went through the lower side of Nottinghamshire, keeping within the River Idle. Here we saw Tuxford in the Clays, that is to say, Tuxford in the Dirt, and a little dirty market town it is, suitable to its name. Then we saw Rhetford, a pretty little borough town of good trade, situate on the River Idle; the mayor treated us like gentlemen, though himself but a tradesman; he gave us a dish of fish from the River Idle, and another from the Trent, which I only note, to intimate that the salmon of the Trent is very valuable in this country.

From Rhetford, the country on the right or east lies low and marshy, till, by the confluence of the Rivers Trent, Idle, and Don, they are formed into large islands, of which the first is called the Isle of Axholm, where the lands are very rich, and feed great store of cattle. But travelling into those parts being difficult, and sometimes dangerous, especially for strangers, we contented our selves with having the country described to us, as above, and with being assured that there were no towns of note, or any thing to be called curious, except that they dig old fir trees out of the ground in the Isle of Axholm, which they tell us have lain there ever since the Deluge; but, as I shall meet with the like more eminently in many other places, I shall content my self with speaking of it once for all, when we come into Lancashire.

There are some few market towns in these low parts between this place and the Humber, though none of great consideration, such as Thorne upon the Don, Snathe upon the

Aire, Selby upon the Ouse, and Howdon near the same river; the two last are towns of good trade, the first being seated where the Ouse is navigable for large vessels, has a good share in the shipping of the river, and some merchants live and thrive here; the latter is one of the towns in England, where their annual fairs preserve the name of a mart, the other Lyn, Boston, Ganesborough, Beverley, though of late they begin to lose the word. The fair or mart held here is very considerable for inland trade, and several wholesale tradesmen come to it from London.

Having found nothing in this low part of the country but a wonderful conflux of great rivers, all pouring down into the Humber, which receiving the Aire, the Ouse, the Don and the Trent, becomes rather a sea than a river, we left it on the right; and we turned up into the post road, where, as I said, I left it before near Brotherton, and went on for Tadcaster.

On this road we passed over Towton,[1] that famous field where the most cruel and bloody battle was fought between the two houses of Lancaster and York, in the reign of Edward IV. I call it most cruel and bloody, because the animosity of the parties was so great, that though they were countrymen and Englishmen, neighbours, nay, as history says, relations; for here fathers killed their sons, and sons their fathers; yet for some time they fought with such obstinacy and such rancour, that, void of all pity and compassion, they gave no quarter, and I call it the most bloody, because 'tis certain no such numbers were ever slain in one battle in England, since the great battle between King Harold and William of Normandy, called the Conqueror, at Battle in Sussex; for here, at Towton, fell six and thirty thousand men on both sides, besides the wounded and prisoners (if they took any).

Tradition guided the country people, and they us, to the very spot; but we had only the story in speculation; for there remains no marks, no monument, no resemblance of the action, only that the ploughmen say, that sometimes they plough up arrow-heads and spear-heads, and broken javelins, and helmets, and the like; for we could only give a short sigh to the memory of the dead, and move forward.

Tadcaster has nothing that we could see to testify the antiquity it boasts of, but some old Roman coins, which our landlord the post master showed us. Here is the hospital and school, still remaining, founded by Dr Oglethorp,[2] Bishop of Carlisle, who, for want of a Protestant archbishop, set the crown on the head of Queen Elizabeth. Here also we saw plainly the Roman highway, as seen at Aberforth; and, as ancient writers tell us, of a stately stone bridge here, I may tell you, here was no bridge at all; but perhaps no writer after me will ever be able to say the like; for the case was this, the ancient famous bridge, which, I suppose, had stood several hundred years, being defective, was just pulled down, and the foundation of a new bridge, was laid, or rather begun to be laid, or was laying; and we were obliged to go over the river in a ferry boat; but coming that way since, I saw the new bridge finished, and very magnificent indeed it is.

From Tadcaster it is but twelve miles to York; the country is rich, fruitful and populous; it bears good corn, and the city of York being so near, and having the navigation of so many rivers also to carry it to Hull, they never want a good market for it.

The antiquity of York, though it was not the particular enquiry I proposed to make, yet showed it self so visibly at a distance, that we could not but observe it before we came quite up to the city, I mean the mount and high hills, where the ancient castle stood, which, when you come to the city, you scarcely see, at least not so as to judge of its antiquity.

The cathedral, or the minster, as they call it is a fine building, but not so ancient as some of the other churches in the city seem to be. The mount I mentioned above, and which, at a distance, I saw was a mark of antiquity, is called the old Bale,[3] which was some ages ago fortified and made very strong; but time has eaten through not the timber and plank only, which they say it was first built with, but even the stones and mortar; for not the least footstep of it remains but the hill.

York is indeed a pleasant and beautiful city, and not at all the less beautiful for the works and lines about it being demolished, and the city, as it may be said, being laid open, for the beauty of peace is seen in the rubbish; the lines and bastions and demolished fortifications, have a reserved secret pleasantness in them from the contemplation of the public tranquillity, that outshines all the beauty of advanced bastions, batteries, cavaliers, and all the hard named works of the engineers about a city.

It boasts of being the seat of some of the Roman emperors, and the station of their forces for the north of Britain, being it self a Roman colony, and the like, all which I leave as I find it; it may be examined critically in Mr Cambden,[4] and his continuator, where it is learnedly debated.

But now things infinitely modern, compared to those, are become marks of antiquity; for even the castle of York, built by William the Conqueror, anno 1069, is not only become ancient and decayed, but even sunk into time, and almost lost and forgotten; fires, sieges, plunderings and devastations, have often been the fate of York; so that one should wonder there should be any thing of a city left. But 'tis risen again,[5] and all we see now is modern; the bridge is vastly strong, and has one arch which, they tell me, was near 70 foot in diameter; it is, without exception, the greatest in England, some say it's as large as the Rialto at Venice, though I think not.

The cathedral too is modern; it was begun to be built but in the time of Edward the First, anno 1313 or thereabouts, by one John Roman, who was treasurer for the undertaking; the foundation being laid, and the whole building designed by the charitable benevolence of the gentry. It was building during the lives of three archbishops,[6] all of the Christian name of John, whereof the last, (viz.) John Thoresby, lived to see it finished, and himself consecrated it.

It is a Gothic building, but with all the most modern addenda that order of building can admit; and with much more ornament of a singular kind, than we see any thing of that way of building graced with. The royal chapel at Windsor, and King's College Chapel, at Cambridge, are indeed very gay things, but neither of them can come up to the minster of York on many accounts. The only deficiency I find at York Minster, is the lowness of the great tower, or its want of a fine spire upon it, which, doubtless, was designed by the builders; he that lately writing a description of this church, and that at Doncaster, placed high fine spires upon them both, took a great deal of pains to tell us he was describing a place where he had never been, and that he took his intelligence grossly upon trust.

As then this church was so completely finished, and that so lately that it is not yet four hundred years old, it is the less to be wondered that the work continues so firm and fine, that it is now the beautifullest church of the old building that is in Britain. In a word, the west end is a picture, and so is the building, the outsides of the choir especially, are not to be equalled.

The choir of the church, and the proper spaces round and behind it, are full of noble and magnificent monuments, too many to enter upon the description of them here, some in marble, and others in the old manner in brass, and the windows are finely painted; but I could find no body learned enough in the designs that could read the histories to us that were delineated there.

But to return to the city it self; there is abundance of good company here, and abundance of good families live here, for the sake of the good company and cheap living; a man converses here with all the world as effectually as at London; the keeping up assemblies among the younger gentry was first set up here, a thing other writers recommend mightily as the character of a good country, and of a pleasant place; but which I look upon with a different view, and esteem it as a plan laid for the ruin of the nation's morals, and which, in time, threatens us with too much success that way.

However, to do the ladies of Yorkshire justice, I found they did not gain any great share of the just reproach which in some other places has been due to their sex; nor has there been so many young fortunes carried off here by half-pay men, as has been said to be in other towns, of merry fame, westward and southward.

The government of the city is that of a regular corporation, by mayor, aldermen and common-council; the mayor has the honour here, by ancient prescription, of being called My Lord. The city is old but well built; and the clergy, I mean such as serve in, and depend upon the cathedral, have very good houses, or little palaces rather here, adjoining the cemetery, or churchyard of the minster; the bishop's is indeed called a palace, and is really so; the deanery is a large, convenient and spacious house; and among these dwellings of the clergy is the assembly house. Whence I would infer, the conduct of it is under the better government, or should be so.

No city in England is better furnished with provisions of every kind, nor any so cheap, in proportion to the goodness of things; the river being so navigable, and so near the sea, the merchants here trade directly to what part of the world they will; for ships of any burthen come up within thirty mile of the city, and small craft from sixty to eighty ton, and under, come up to the very city.

With these they carry on a considerable trade; they import their own wines from France and Portugal, and likewise their own deals and timber from Norway; and indeed what they please almost from where they please; they did also bring their own coals from Newcastle and Sunderland, but now have them down the Aire and Calder from Wakefield, and from Leeds, as I have said already.

The old walls are standing, and the gates and posterns; but the old additional works which were cast up in the late rebellion, are slighted; so that York is not now defensible as it was then. But things lie so too, that a little time, and many hands, would put those works into their former condition, and make the city able to stand out a small siege. But as the ground seems capable by situation, so an ingenious head, in our company, taking a stricter view of it, told us, he would undertake to make it as strong as Tourney in Flanders, or as Namure, allowing him to add a citadel at that end next the river. But this is a speculation; and 'tis much better that we should have no need of fortified towns than that we should seek out good situations to make them.

While we were at York, we took one day's time to see the fatal field called Marston Moor,[7] where Prince Rupert, a third time, by his excess of valour, and defect of conduct, lost the royal army, and had a victory wrung out of his hands, after he had all the advantage in his own hands that he could desire. Certain it is, that charging at the head of the right wing of horse with that intrepid courage that he always showed, he bore down all before him in the very beginning of the battle, and not only put the enemies' cavalry into confusion, but drove them quite out of the field.

Could he have bridled his temper, and, like an old soldier, or rather an experienced general, have contented himself with the glory of that part, sending but one brigade of his troops on in the pursuit, which had been sufficient to have finished the work, and have kept the enemies from rallying, and then with the rest of his cavalry, wheeled to the left, and fallen in upon the croup of the right wing of the enemies' cavalry, he had made a day of it, and gained the most glorious victory of that age: for he had a gallant army. But he followed the chase clear off, and out of the field of battle; and when he began to return, he had the misfortune to see that his left wing of horse was defeated by Fairfax [8] and Cromwell, and to meet his friends flying for their lives; so that he had nothing to do but to fly with them, and leave his infantry, and the Duke, then Marquis of Newcastle's, old veteran soldiers to be cut in pieces by the enemy.

I came back extremely well pleased with the view of Marston Moor, and the account my friend had given of the battle; 'twas none of our business to concern our passions in the cause, or regret the misfortunes of that day; the thing was over beyond our ken; time had levelled the victors with the vanquished, and the royal family being restored, there was no room to say one thing or other to what was passed; so we returned to York the same night.

York, as I have said, is a spacious city, it stands upon a great deal of ground, perhaps more than any city in England out of Middlesex, except Norwich; but then the buildings are not close and thronged as at Bristol, or as at Durham, nor is York so populous as either Bristol or Norwich. But as York is full of gentry and persons of distinction, so they live at large, and have houses proportioned to their quality; and this makes the city lie so far extended on both sides the river. It is also very magnificent, and, as we say, makes a good figure every way in its appearance, even at a distance; for the cathedral is so noble and so august a pile, that 'tis a glory to all the rest.

There are also two fine market-houses, with the town-hall upon the bridge, and abundance of other public edifices, all which together makes this city, as I said, more stately and magnificent, though not more populous and wealthy, than any other city in the king's dominions, London and Dublin excepted. The reason of the difference is evidently for the want of trade. Here is no trade indeed, except such as depends upon the confluence of the gentry. But the city, as to lodgings, good houses, and plenty of provisions, is able to receive the King, Lords and Commons, with the whole Court, if there was occasion; and once they did entertain King Charles I with his whole Court.

We went out in a double excursion from this city, first to see the Duke of Leeds's[9] house, and then the Earl of Carlisle's, and the Earl of Burlington's in the East Riding; Carlisle House is by far the finest design, but it is not finished, and may not, perhaps, [be] in our time; they say his lordship sometimes observes noblemen should only design, and begin great palaces, and leave posterity to finish them gradually, as their estates will allow them; it is called Castle Howard. The Earl of Burlington's is an old built house, but stands deliciously, and has a noble prospect towards the Humber, as also towards the Woulds.

At Hambledon Down, near this city, are once a year very great races, appointed for the entertainment of the gentry, and they are the more frequented, because the king's plate of a hundred guineas is always run for there once a year;. a gift designed to encourage the gentlemen to breed good horses.

From York we did not jump at once over the whole country, and, like a late author, without taking notice on any thing, come out again sixty or seventy miles off, like an apparition, without being seen by the way. The first thing we did, we took a view of the suburb of York over the river, opposite to the city, and then entering the East Riding, took our audience *de conge* in form, and so stood over that division towards Hull.

The River Derwent, contrary to the course of all the rivers in Yorkshire, (as I have observed) runs north and south, rising in that part of the country called Cleveland, and running through, or hard by, several market towns, as Pickering, Pocklington, North Malton, and others, and is, by the course, a good guide to those who would take a view of the whole country.

I observed the middle of this riding or division of Yorkshire is very thin of towns, and consequently of people, being overspread with wolds, that is to say, plains and downs, like those of Salisbury; on which they feed great numbers of sheep, and breed also a great many black cattle and horses; especially in the northern part, which runs more mountainous, and makes part of the North Riding of York. But the east and west part is populous and rich, and full of towns, the one lying on the sea coast, and the other upon the River Derwent, as above; the sea coast or east side, is called Holderness.

After passing the Derwent we saw little of moment, but keeping under the wolds or hills mentioned above, we came to your old acquaintance John a Beverley, I mean the famous monastery at that town.

It is a large and populous town, though I find no considerable manufacture carried on there. The great collegiate church is the main thing which ever did, and still does, make the town known in the world. The famous story of John of Beverley,[10] is, in short, this: that one John, Archbishop of York, a learned and devout man, out of mere pious zeal for religion, and contempt of the world, quitted or renounced his honours and superiority in the Church, and, laying aside the pall, and the mitre, retired to Beverley, and lived here all the rest of his time a recluse. This story will prompt you to enquire how long ago 'twas, for you know as well as I, and will naturally observe, that very few such bishops are to be found now; it was indeed a long time ago, for it is this very year just five year above a thousand year ago that this happened; for the good man died Anno Dom. 721, you may soon cast up the rest to 1726.

The memory of this extraordinary man has been much honoured; and had they gone no farther, I should have joined with them most heartily. But as to sainting him, and praying to him, and offering at his shrine, and such things, that we Protestants must ask their leave to have nothing to say to. However, King Athelstan, after making a vow to him if he got the victory over the Danes, made him his tutelar saint, and gave great gifts and immunities to this place on his account; among the rest, the king granted his peace to it, as was the word in those days; that is to say, made it a sanctuary, as he did much about the same time to the church at Rippon.

The minster here is a very fair and neat structure; the roof is an arch of stone, in it there are several monuments of the Piercy's, Earls of Northumberland, who have added a little chapel to the choir, in the windows of which are the pictures of several of that family drawn in the glass at the upper end of the choir. On the right side of the altar-place stands the freed stool, made of one entire stone, and said to have been removed from Dunbar in Scotland, with a well of water behind it. At the upper end of the body of the church, next the choir, hangs an ancient table with the picture of St John (from whom the church is named) and of King Athelstan the founder of it, and between them this distich:

Als free make I thee,
As heart can wish, or egh can see.

Hence the inhabitants of Beverley pay no toll or custom in any port or town in England; to which immunity (I suppose) they owe, in great measure, their riches and flourishing condition; for indeed, one is surprised to find so large and handsome a town within six miles of Hull. In the body of the church stands an ancient monument, which they call the Virgins' Tomb, because two virgin sisters lay buried there who gave the town a piece of land, into which any freeman may put three milch kine from Ladyday to Michaelmas.

Near the minster, on the south side of it, is a place named Hall Garth, wherein they keep a court of record, called the Provost's Court. In this may be tried causes for any sum arising within its liberties; (which are very large, having about a hundred towns and parts of towns in Holderness, and other places of the East Riding belonging to it). It is said to have also a power in criminal matters, though at present that is not used.

But to come to the present condition of the town, it is above a mile in length, being of late much improved in its buildings, and has pleasant springs running quite through its streets. It is more especially beautified with two stately churches, and has a free-school that is improved by two fellowships, six scholarships, and three exhibitions in St John's College, in Cambridge, belonging to it; besides six alms-houses, the largest whereof was built lately by the executors of Michael Warton, Esq;[11] who, by his last will, left one thousand pounds for that use.

The principal trade of the town is making malt, oatmeal, and tanned leather; but the poor people mostly support themselves by working bone-lace, which of late has met with particular encouragement, the children being maintained at school to learn to read, and to work this sort of lace. The clothing trade was formerly followed in this town, but Leland[12] tells us, that even in his time it was very much decayed.

They have several fairs, but one more especially remarkable, called the Mart, beginning about nine days before Ascension Day, and kept in a street leading to the Minster Garth, called Londoners Street, for then the Londoners bring down their wares, and furnish the country tradesmen by wholesale.

About a mile from Beverley to the east, in a pasture belonging to the town, is a kind of spa, though they say it cannot be judged by the taste whether or no it comes from any mineral; yet taken inwardly it is a great drier, and washed in, dries scorbutic [13] scurf, and all sorts of scabs, and also very much helps the king's evil.

It is easy to conceive how Beverley became a town from this very article, namely, that all the thieves, murtherers, housebreakers and bankrupts, fled hither for protection; and here they obtained safety from the law whatever their crimes might be.

After some time, the town growing bigger and bigger, the church was also enlarged; and though it fell into the king's hands, King Henry VIII having done by this as he did by others; and the monks of Beverley were suppressed, yet the town continues a large, populous town; and the River Hull is made navigable to it for the convenience of trade.

I remember, soon after the Revolution,[14] when the late King William hired six thousand Danish auxiliaries to assist him in his wars in Ireland, they landed at Hull, and, marching from thence for West-Chester, in order to embark for Carrickfergus, they came through this town, and halted here a few days for refreshment. Here two of their foot soldiers quarrelled and fought a duel, in which one of them was killed. The other being taken, was immediately tried and sentenced to a court marshal of their own officers, and by the rules of war, such as were in force among them, was sentenced and put to death, and was then buried in the same grave with the man he had killed; and upon their grave is set up a stone with an English inscription thus:

Under this stone two Danish soldiers lie.

There are other lines mentioning the story, as above, but I do not remember them, it being some years since I made this observation.

From Beverley I came to Hull, distance six miles. If you would expect me to give an account of the city of Hamburgh or Dantzick, or Rotterdam, or any of the second rate cities abroad, which are famed for their commerce, the town of Hull may be a specimen. The place is indeed not so large as those; but, in proportion to the dimensions of it, I believe there is more business done in Hull than in any town of its bigness in Europe; Leverpool indeed of late comes after it apace; but then Leverpool has not the London trade to add to it.

In the late war, the fleets from Hull to London were frequently a hundred sail, sometimes including the other creeks in the Humber, a hundred and fifty to a hundred and sixty sail at a time; and to Holland their trade is so considerable, that the Dutch always employed two men of war to fetch and carry, that is, to convoy the trade, as they called it, to and from Hull, which was as many as they did to London.

In a word, all the trade at Leeds, Wakefield and Hallifax, of which I have spoken so justly and so largely, is transacted here, and the goods are shipped here by the merchants of Hull; all the lead trade of Derbyshire and Nottinghamshire, from Bautry Wharf, the butter of the East and North Riding, brought down the Ouse to York. The cheese brought down the Trent from Stafford, Warwick and Cheshire, and the corn from all the counties adjacent, are brought down and shipped off here.

Again, they supply all these countries in return with foreign goods of all kinds, for which they trade to all parts of the known world; nor have the merchants of any port in Britain a fairer credit, or fairer character, than the merchants of Hull, as well for the justice of their dealings as the greatness of their substance or funds for trade. They drive a great trade here to Norway, and to the Baltick, and an important trade to Dantzick, Riga, Narva and Petersburgh; from whence they make large returns in iron, copper, hemp, flax, canvas, pot-ashes, Muscovy linen and yarn, and other things; all which they get vent for in the country to an exceeding quantity. They have also a great importation of wine, linen, oil, fruit, &c. trading to Holland, France and Spain; the trade of tobacco and sugars from the West-Indies, they chiefly manage by the way of London. But besides all this, their export of corn, as well to London as to Holland and France, exceeds all of the kind, that is or can be done at any port in England, London excepted.

The town is situated at the mouth of the River Hull, where it falls into the Humber, and where the Humber opens into the German Ocean,[15] so that one side of their town lies upon the sea, the other upon the land. This makes the situation naturally very strong; and, were there any occasion, it is capable of being made impregnable, by reason of the low situation of the grounds round it.

The greatest imperfection, as to the strength of Hull in case of a war, is, that, lying open to the sea, it is liable to a bombardment; which can only be prevented by being masters at sea, and while we are so, there's no need of fortifications at all; and so there's an end of argument upon that subject.

The town is exceeding close built, and should a fire ever be its fate, it might suffer deeply on that account; 'tis extraordinary populous, even to an inconvenience, having really no room to extend it self by buildings. There are but two churches, but one of them is very large, and there are two or three very large meeting-houses, and a market stored with an infinite plenty of all sorts of provision.

They show us still in their town-hall the figure of a northern fisherman, supposed to be of Greenland, that is to say, the real Greenland, being the continent of America to the north of those we call the north west passage; not of Spiltbergen, where our ships go a whale fishing, and which is, by mistake, called Greenland. He was taken up at sea in a leather boat, which he sate in, and was covered with skins, which drew together about his waist, so that the boat could not fill, and he could not sink; the creature would never feed nor speak, and so died.

They have a very handsome exchange here, where the merchants meet as at London, and, I assure you, it is wonderfully filled, and that with a confluence of real merchants, and many foreigners, and several from the country; for the navigation of all the great rivers which fall into the Humber centres here.

There is also a fine free-school, over which is the merchant's hall. But the Trinity-House here is the glory of the town. It is a corporation of itself, made up of a society of merchants. It was begun by voluntary contribution for relief of distressed and aged seamen, and their wives and widows; but was afterwards approved by the government, and incorporated. They have a very good revenue, which increases every day by charities, and bounties of pious minded people.

They maintain thirty sisters now actually in the house, widows of seamen; they have a government by twelve elder brethren and six assistants; out of the twelve they choose annually two wardens, but the whole eighteen vote in electing them, and two stewards. These have a power to decide disputes between masters of ships and their crews, in matters relating to the sea affairs only; and with this limitation, that their judgement be not contrary to the laws of the land; and, even in trials at law, in such affairs they are often called to give their opinions.

The old hospital, called GOD's House, stands near it, with a chapel rebuilt since the late war, and the arms of Michael de la Pole,[16] the first founder, set up again; so that the foundation is restored, the building is nobly enlarged, and an entire new hospital built as an addition to the old one. Sir Michael de la Pole was a merchant of Hull, but first at a place called Raven's Rood in Brabant, where, growing rich, he advanced to King Richard II several thousand pounds in gold for his urgent occasions in his wars; upon which the king invited him to come and live in England, where he did; here the king knighted him, made his son, Michael de la Pole, Earl of Suffolk, and gave him several lordships in Holderness.

Farther east from Hull there is a little pleasant town called Headon, handsome, well built, and having a little haven from the sea, which threatens Hull, that it will in time grow up to be a great place, for it indeed increases daily; but I fear for them, that their haven will do nothing considerable for them, unless they can do something very considerable for that.

They tell us at Headon, that the sea encroaches upon the land on all that shore, and that there are many large fields quite eaten up; that several towns were formerly known to be there, which are now lost; from whence they may suppose, that as the sea by encroachment had damnified their harbour, so if it grows upon them a little more they shall stand open to the sea, and so need no harbour at all, or make a mole, as 'tis called abroad, and have a good road without it. But this is a view something remote.

The Spurn Head, a long promontory thrusting out into the sea, and making the north point of Humber, is a remarkable thing. But I leave that to the description of the sea coasts, which is none of my work; the most that I find remarkable here, is, that there is nothing remarkable upon this side for above thirty miles together; not a port, not a gentleman's seat, not a town of note; Bridlington or Burlington is the only place, and that is of no note, only for a bay or road for shipping, which is of use to the colliers on this coast to defend them, in case of extremity of weather.

The country people told us a long story here of gipsies which visit them often in a surprising manner. We were strangely amused with their discourses at first, forming our ideas from the word, which, in ordinary import with us, signifies a sort of strolling, fortune-telling, hen-roost-robbing, pocket-picking vagabonds, called by that name. But we were soon made to understand the people, as they understood themselves here, namely, that at some certain seasons, for none knows when it will happen, several streams of water gush out of the earth with great violence, spouting up a huge height, being really natural *jette d'eaus* or fountains; that they make a great noise, and, joining together, form little rivers, and so hasten to the sea. I had not time to examine into the particulars; and as the irruption was not just then to be seen, we could say little to it. That which was most observable to us, was, that the country people have a notion that whenever those *gipsies*, or, as some call 'em, *vipseys*, break out, there will certainly ensue either famine or plague.

Scarborough next presents it self, a place formerly famous for the strong castle, situate on a rock, as it were hanging over the sea, but now demolished, being ruined in the last wars. The town is well built, populous and pleasant, and we found a great deal of good company here drinking the waters, who came not only from all the north of England, but even from Scotland. It is hard to describe the taste of the waters; they are apparently tinged with a collection of mineral salts, as of vitriol, alum, iron, and perhaps sulphur, and taste evidently of the alum. Here is such a plenty of all sorts of fish, that I have hardly seen the like, and, in particular, here we saw turbets of three quarters of a hundred weight, and yet their flesh eat exceeding fine when taken new.

At the entrance of a little nameless river, scarce indeed worth a name, stands Whitby, which, however, is an excellent harbour, and where they build very good ships for the coal trade, and many of them too, which makes the town rich. From hence the North Riding holds on to the bank of Tees, the northern bounds of Yorkshire, and where there are two good towns, (viz.) Stockton and Yarum, towns of no great note.

I began now to consider the long journey I had to go, and that I must not stop at small matters. We went from Stockton to Durham. North Allerton, a town on the post road, is remarkable for the vast quantity of black cattle sold there, there being a fair once every fortnight for some months, where a prodigious quantity are sold.

I have not concerned this work at all in the debate among us in England, as to Whig and Tory. But I must observe of this town, that, except a few Quakers, they boasted that they had not one Dissenter here, and yet at the same time not one Tory, which is what, I believe, cannot be said of any other town in Great Britain.

I must now leave Yorkshire, which indeed I might more fully have described, if I had had time; for there are abundance of rarities in nature spoken in this North Riding, which I had not leisure to enquire into; as the alum mines or pits near Moultgrave or Musgrave. Next here are the snake stones, of which nothing can be said but as one observes of them, to see how nature sports her self to amuse us, as if snakes could grow in those stones. Then the glates or gargates, that is, in short jet, a black smooth stone found in Cleveland; also a piece of ground, which, if the wild geese attempt to fly over, they fall down dead. But I cannot dwell any longer here.

Darlington, a post town, has nothing remarkable but dirt, and a high stone bridge over little or no water, the town is eminent for good bleaching of linen, so that I have known cloth brought from Scotland to be bleached here.

Durham is next, a little compact neatly contrived city, surrounded almost with the River Wear, which with the castle standing on an eminence, encloses the city in the middle of it; as the castle does also the cathedral, the bishop's palace, and the fine houses of the clergy, where they live in all the magnificence and splendour imaginable.

I need not tell you, that the Bishop of Durham is a temporal prince, that he keeps a court of equity, and also courts of justice in ordinary causes within himself. The church of Durham is eminent for its wealth; the bishopric is esteemed the best in England; and the prebends and other church livings, in the gift of the bishop, are the richest in England. They told me there, that the bishop had thirteen livings in his gift, from five hundred pounds a year to thirteen hundred pounds a year; and the living of the little town of Sedgfield, a few miles south of the city, is said to be worth twelve hundred pounds a year, beside the small tithes, which maintain a curate, or might do so. Going to see the church of Durham, they showed us the old Popish vestments of the clergy before the Reformation, and which, on high days, some of the residents put on still. They are so rich with embroidery and embossed work of silver, that indeed it was a kind of a load to stand under them.

The town is well built but old, full of Roman Catholics, who live peaceably and disturb no body, and no body them; for we being there on a holiday, saw them going as publicly to mass as the Dissenters did on other days to their meeting-house.

From hence we kept the common road to Chester in the Street, an old, dirty, thoroughfare town, empty of all remains of the greatness which antiquaries say it once had, when it was a Roman colony. Here we had an account of a melancholy accident, and in it self strange also, which happened in or near Lumley Park, not long before we passed through the town. A new coal pit being dug or digging, the workmen worked on in the vein of coals till they came to a cavity, which, as was supposed, had formerly been dug from some other pit; but be it what it will, as soon as upon the breaking into the hollow part, the pent up air got vent, it blew up like a mine of a thousand barrels of powder, and, getting vent at the shaft of the pit, burst out with such a terrible noise, as made the very earth tremble for some miles round and terrified the whole country. There were near three-score poor people lost their lives in the pit, and one or two, as we were told, who were at the bottom of the shaft, were blown quite out, though sixty fathom deep, and were found dead upon the ground.

Lumley Castle is just on the side of the road as you pass between Durham and Chester, pleasantly seated in a fine park, and on the bank of the River Were. The park, besides the pleasantness of it, has this much better thing to recommend it, namely, that it is full of excellent veins of the best coal in the country, (for the Lumley coal are known for their goodness at London, as well as there).

From hence the road to Newcastle gives a view of the inexhausted store of coals and coal pits, from whence not London only, but all the south part of England is continually supplied; and whereas when we are at London, and see the prodigious fleets of ships which come constantly in with coals for this increasing city, we are apt to wonder whence they come, and that they do not bring the whole country away; so, on the contrary, when in this country we see the prodigious heaps, I might say mountains, of coals, which are dug up at every pit, and how many of those pits there are; we are filled with equal wonder to consider where the people should live that can consume them.

Newcastle is a spacious, extended, infinitely populous place; 'tis seated upon the River Tyne, which is here a noble, large and deep river, and ships of any reasonable burthen may come safely up to the very town. As the town lies on both sides the river, the parts are joined by a very strong and stately stone bridge of seven very great arches, rather larger than the arches of London Bridge; and the bridge is built into a street of houses also, as London Bridge is.

Here is a large hospital built by contribution of the keel men, by way of friendly society, for the maintenance of the poor of their fraternity, and which, had it not met with discouragements from those who ought rather to have assisted so good a work, might have been a noble provision for that numerous and laborious people. The keel men are those who manage the lighters, which they call keels, by which the coals are taken from the staithes or wharfs, and carried on board the ships, to load them for London.

Here are several large public buildings also, as particularly a house of state for the mayor of the town (for the time being) to remove to, and dwell in during his year. Also here is a hall for the surgeons, where they meet, where they have two skeletons of human bodies, one a man and the other a woman, and some other rarities.

The situation of the town to the landward is exceeding

unpleasant, and the buildings very close and old, standing on the declivity of two exceeding high hills, which, together with the smoke of the coals, makes it not the pleasantest place in the world to live in; but it is made amends abundantly by the goodness of the river, which runs between the two hills, and which, as I said, bringing ships up to the very quays, and fetching the coals down from the country, makes it a place of very great business. Here are also two articles of trade which are particularly occasioned by the coals, and these are glass-houses and salt pans; the first are at the town it self, the last are at Shields, seven miles below the town; but their coals are brought chiefly from the town. It is a prodigious quantity of coals which those salt works consume; and the fires make such a smoke, that we saw it ascend in clouds over the hills, four miles before we came to Durham, which is at least sixteen miles from the place.

Here I met with a remark which was quite new to me, and will be so, I suppose, to those that hear it. You well know, we receive at London every year a great quantity of salmon pickled or cured, and sent up in the pickle in kits or tubs, which we call Newcastle salmon; now when I came to Newcastle, I expected to see a mighty plenty of salmon there, but was surprised to find, on the contrary, that there was no great quantity, and that a good large fresh salmon was not to be had under five or six shillings. Upon enquiry I found, that really this salmon, that we call Newcastle salmon, is taken as far off as the Tweed, which is three-score miles, and is brought by land on horses to Shields, where it is cured, pickled, and sent to London, as above; so that it ought to be called Berwick salmon, not Newcastle.

They build ships here to perfection, I mean as to strength, and firmness, and to bear the sea; and as the coal trade occasions a demand for such strong ships, a great many are built here. This gives an addition to the merchants' business, in requiring a supply of all sorts of naval stores to fit out those ships. Here is also a considerable manufacture of hard ware, or wrought iron, lately erected after the manner of Sheffield, which is very helpful for employing the poor, of which this town has always a prodigious number.

West of this town lies the town of Hexham, a pass upon the Tine, famous, or indeed infamous, for having the first blood drawn at it, in the war against their prince by the Scots in King Charles the First's time, and where a strong detachment of English, though advantageously posted, were scandalously defeated by the Scots.[17] The country round this town is vulgarly called Hexamshire.

I was tempted greatly here to trace the famous Picts Wall, built by the Romans, or rather rebuilt by them, from hence to Carlisle; of the particulars of which, and the remains of antiquity seen upon it, all our histories are so full; and I did go to several places in the fields through which it passed, where I saw the remains of it, some almost lost, some plain to be seen. But antiquity not being my business in this work, I omitted the journey, and went on for the north.

Northumberland is a long coasting county, lying chiefly on the sea to the east, and bounded by the mountains of Stainmore and Cheviot on the west, which are in some places inaccessible, in many unpassable. Here is abundant business for an antiquary; every place shows you ruined castles, Roman altars, inscriptions, monuments of battles, of heroes killed, and armies routed, and the like. The towns of Morpeth, Alnwick, Warkworth, Tickill, and many others, show their old castles, and some of them still in tolerable repair, as Alnwick in particular, and Warkworth; others, as Bambrough, Norham, Chillingham, Horton, Dunstar, Wark, and innumerable more, are sunk in their own ruins, by the mere length of time.

We had Cheviot Hills so plain in view, that we could not but enquire of the good old women every where, whether they had heard of the fight at Chevy Chace [18]. They not only told us they had heard of it, but had all the account of it at their fingers' end; and, taking a guide at Woller to show us the road, he pointed out distinctly to us the very spot where the engagement was, here, he said Earl Piercy was killed, and there Earl Douglas, here Sir William Withington fought upon his stumps, here the Englishmen that were slain were buried, and there the Scots.

A little way off of this, north, he showed us the field of battle, called Flodden Field, where James IV, King of Scotland, desperately fighting, was killed, and his whole army overthrown by the English, under the noble and gallant Earl of Surrey, in the reign of King Henry VIII upon their perfidiously invading England, while the king was absent on his wars in France.

I must not quit Northumberland without taking notice, that the natives of this county, of the ancient original race or families, are distinguished by a shibboleth upon their tongues, namely, a difficulty in pronouncing the letter *r*, which they cannot deliver from their tongues without a hollow jarring in the throat, by which they are plainly known, as a foreigner is, in pronouncing the *th*. This they call the Northumbrian *r*, and the natives value themselves upon that imperfection, because, forsooth, it shows the antiquity of their blood.

From hence lay a road into Scotland, but at present not willing to omit seeing Berwick upon Tweed, we turned to the east, and visited that old frontier, where indeed there is one thing very fine, and that is, the bridge over the Tweed, built by Queen Elizabeth, a noble, stately work, consisting of sixteen arches, and joining, as may be said, the two kingdoms. As for the town it self, it is old, decayed, and neither populous nor rich; the chief trade I found here was in corn and salmon.

I am now on the borders of Scotland, and must take in my way, the three north west counties of Lancaster, Westmoreland and Cumberland.

I cannot but say, that since I entered upon the view of these northern counties, I have many times repented that I so early resolved to decline the delightful view of antiquity, here being so great and so surprising a variety, and every day more and more discovered; and abundance since the tour which the learned Mr Cambden made this way, for as the trophies, the buildings, the religious, as well as military remains, as well of the Britains, as of the Romans, Saxons, and Normans, are but, as we may say, like wounds hastily healed up, the callous spread over them being removed, they appear presently; and though the earth, which naturally eats into the strongest stones, metals, or whatever substance, simple or compound, is or can be by art or nature prepared to endure it, has defaced the surface, the figures and inscriptions upon most of these things, yet they are beautiful, even in their decay, and the venerable face of antiquity has some thing so pleasing, so surprising, so satisfactory in it, especially to those who have with any attention read the histories of passed ages, that I know nothing renders travelling more pleasant and more agreeable.

But I have condemned my self (unhappily) to silence upon this head, and therefore, resolving however to pay this homage to the dust of gallant men and glorious nations, I say therefore, I must submit and go on; and as I resolve once more to travel through all these northern countries upon this very errand, and to please, nay, satiate my self with a strict search into every thing that is curious in nature and antiquity, I mortify my self now with the more ease, in hopes of letting the world see, some time or other, that I have not spent those hours in a vain and barren search, or come back without a sufficient reward to all the labours of a diligent enquirer; but of this by the way, I must, for the present, make this circuit shorter than usual, and leave the description of the other three counties to my next.

I am, &c.

Letter 10

SIR, – Having thus finished my account of the east side of the north division of England, I put a stop here, that I may observe the exact course of my travels; for as I do not write you these letters from the observations of one single journey, so I describe things as my journeys lead me, having no less than five times travelled through the north of England, and almost every time by a different route; purposely that I might see every thing that was to be seen, and, if possible, know every thing that is to be known, though not (at least till the last general journey) knowing or resolving upon writing these accounts to you.

I entered Lancashire at the remotest western point of that county, having been at West-Chester upon a particular occasion, and from thence ferried over from the Cestrian Chersonesus, as I have already called it, to Liverpoole. This narrow slip of land, rich, fertile and full of inhabitants, though formerly, as authors say, a mere waste and desolate forest, is called Wirall or by some Wirehall. Here is a ferry over the Mersee, which, at full sea, is more than two miles over. We land on the flat shore on the other side, and are contented to ride through the water for some length, not on horseback but on the shoulders of some honest Lancashire clown, who comes knee deep to the best side, to truss you up, and then runs away with you, as nimbly as you desire to ride, unless his trot were easier; for I was shaken by him that I had the luck to be carried by more than I cared for, and much worse than a hard trotting horse would have shaken me.

Liverpoole is one of the wonders of Britain, and that more, in my opinion, than any of the wonders of the Peak; the town was, at my first visiting it, about the year 1680, a large, handsome, well built and increasing or thriving town,[1] at my second visit, anno 1690, it was much bigger than at my first seeing it, and, by the report of the inhabitants, more than twice as big as it was twenty years before that; but, I think, I may safely say at this my third seeing it, for I was suprised at the view, it was more than double what it was at the second; and, I am told, that it still visibly increases both in wealth, people, business and buildings. What it may grow to in time, I know not.

There are no fortifications either to landward or seaward, the inhabitants resting secure under the protection of the general peace; though when the late northern insurrection[2] spread down their way, and came to Preston, they could have been glad of walls and gates; and indeed, had the rebel party had time to have advanced to Warrington, seized the pass there, and taken Manchester, as they would certainly have done in three days more, it would have fared but very ill with Liverpoole; who could have made but little resistance against an armed and desperate body of men, such as they appeared to be, and by that time would have been. But heaven had Liverpoole in its particular protection, as well as the whole kingdom; the rebels were met with, fought and defeated, before they gat leave to get so far, or to make any offer that way.

The town has now an opulent, flourishing and increasing trade, not rivalling Bristol, in the trade to Virginia, and the English island colonies in America only, but is in a fair way to exceed and eclipse it, by increasing every way in wealth and shipping. They trade round the whole island, send ships to Norway, to Hamburgh, and to the Baltick, as also to Holland and Flanders; so that, in a word, they are almost become like the Londoners, universal merchants.

Bristol lies open to the Irish Sea, so does Liverpoole: Bristol trades chiefly to the south and west parts of Ireland; from Dublin in the east, to Galloway west; Liverpoole has all the trade of the east shore and the north from the harbour of Dublin to London Derry. Bristol has the trade of South Wales; Liverpoole great part of the trade of North Wales; Bristol has the south west counties of England. It is some advantage to the growing commerce of this town, that the freemen of it are, in consequence of that freedom, free also of Bristol; and they are free also of the corporations of Waterford and Wexford in the kingdom of Ireland.

The people of Liverpoole seem to have a different scene of commerce to act on from the city of Bristol, which to me is a particular advantage to both, namely, that though they may rival one another in their appearances, in their number of shipping, and in several particulars, yet they need not interfere with one another's business, but either of them seem to have room enough to extend their trade, even at home and abroad, without clashing with one another. One has all the north, and the other all the south of Britain to correspond in. As for Wales, 'tis, as it were, divided between them by nature it self.

Ireland is, as it were, all their own, and shared between them, as above; and for the northern coast of it, if the Liverpoole men have not the whole fishery, or, at least, in company with the merchants of London Derry, the fault is their own. The situation of Liverpoole gives it a very great advantage to improve their commerce, and extend it in the northern inland counties of England, particularly into Cheshire and Staffordshire, by the new navigation of the Rivers Mersee, the Weaver, and the Dane, by the last of which they come so near the Trent with their goods, that they make no difficulty to carry them by land to Burton, and from thence correspond quite through the kingdom, even to Hull; and they begin to be very sensible of the advantage of such a commerce.

I return therefore to the description of it as a town; the situation being on the north bank of the river, and with the particular disadvantage of a flat shore. This exposed the merchants to great difficulties in their business; for though the harbour was good, and the ships rode well in the offing, yet they were obliged to ride there as in a road rather than a harbour. Here was no mole or haven to bring in their ships and lay them up, (as the seamen call it) for the winter; nor any key for the delivering their goods. Upon this, the inhabitants and merchants have, of late years, and since the visible increase of their trade, made a large basin or wet dock,[3] at the east end of the town, where, at an immense charge, the place considered, they have brought the tide from the Mersee to flow up by an opening that looks to the south, and the ships go in north; so that the town entirely shelters it from the westerly and northerly winds, the hills from the easterly, and the ships lie, as in a mill-pond, with the utmost safety and convenience.

The new church [4] built on the north side of the town is worth observation. 'Tis a noble, large building, all of stone, well finished; has in it a fine font of marble placed in the body of the church, surrounded with a beautiful iron pallisado. There is a beautiful tower to this church, and a new ring of eight very good bells.

In a word, there is no town in England, London excepted, that can equal Liverpoole for the fineness of the streets, and beauty of the buildings; many of the houses are all of free stone, and completely finished; and all the rest (of the new part I mean) of brick, as handsomely built as London it self.

Mr Cambden says, it was a neat and populous town in his time; his reverend continuator confirms what I have said thus, that it was more than doubly increased in buildings and people in twenty-eight years, and that the customs were augmented tenfold in the same time; to which I am to add, that they are now much greater, that being written about two and thirty years ago, before the new church, or the wet dock, mentioned above, were made, and we know they have gone on increasing in trade, buildings and people, to this day. I refer the reader therefore to judge of the probable greatness of it now.

The sea coast affords little remarkable on the west side of this port, till we come farther north; so we left that part of the county, and going east we came to Warrington. This is a large market town upon the River Mersee, over which there is a stately stone bridge, which is the only bridge of communication for the whole county with the county of Chester;

it is on the great road from London leading to Carlisle and Scotland, and, in case of war, has always been esteemed a pass of the utmost importance. Had the rebels advanced thus far in the late Preston affair, so as to have made themselves masters of it, it would have been so again; and, on that account, the king's forces took special care, by a speedy advance to secure it.

Warrington is a large, populous old built town, but rich and full of good country tradesmen. Here is particularly a weekly market for linen, as I saw at Wrexham in Wales, a market for flannel. The linen sold at this market, is, generally speaking, a sort of table linen, called huk-a-back or huk-a-buk; 'tis well known among the good housewives, so I need not describe it. I was told there are generally as many pieces of this linen sold here every market day as amounts to five hundred pounds value, sometimes much more, and all made in the neighbourhood of the place.

From hence, on the road to Manchester, we passed the great bog or waste called Chatmos, the first of that kind that we see in England, from any of the south parts hither. It extends on the left-hand of the road for five or six miles east and west, and they told us it was, in some places, seven or eight miles from north to south. The nature of these mosses, for we found there are many of them in this country, is this, and you will take this for a description of all the rest. The surface, at a distance, looks black and dirty, and is indeed frightful to think of, for it will bear neither horse or man, unless in an exceeding dry season, and then not so as to be passable, or that any one should travel over them. What nature meant by such a useless production, 'tis hard to imagine; but the land is entirely waste, except for the poor cottager's fuel, and the quantity used for that is very small.

From hence we came on to Manchester, one of the greatest, if not really the greatest mere village in England. It is neither a walled town, city, or corporation; they send no members to Parliament; and the highest magistrate they have is a constable or headborough; and yet it has a collegiate church, several parishes, takes up a large space of ground, and, including the suburb, or that part of the town called —[5] over the bridge; it is said to contain above fifty thousand people.

The Manchester trade we all know; and all that are concerned in it know that it is, as all our other manufactures are, very much increased within these thirty or forty years especially beyond what it was before; and as the manufacture is increased, the people must be increased of course. It is true, that the increase of the manufacture may be by its extending itself farther in the country, and so more hands may be employed in the county without any increase in the town. But I answer that though this is possible, yet as the town and parish of Manchester is the centre of the manufacture, the increase of that manufacture would certainly increase there first, and then the people there not being sufficient, it might spread itself further.

But the increase of buildings at Manchester within these few years, is a confirmation of the increase of people; for that within very few years past, here, as at Liverpoole, and as at Froom in Somersetshire, the town is extended in a surprising manner; abundance, not of new houses only, but of new streets of houses, are added, a new church also, and they talk of another, and a fine new square is at this time building; so that the town is almost double to what it was a few years ago. I think my computation of fifty thousand people to be not reasonable only, but much within compass; and some of the ancient inhabitants are of the opinion there are above sixty thousand.

If then this calculation is just, as I believe it really is, you have here then an open village, which is greater and more populous than many, nay, than most cities in England, not York, Lincoln, Chester, Salisbury, Winchester, Worcester, Gloucester, no not Norwich it self, can come up to it; and for lesser cities, two or three put together, would not equal it, such as Peterborough, Ely, and Carlisle, or such as Bath, Wells and Litchfield, and the like of some others.

The town of Manchester boasts of four extraordinary foundations, viz. a college, an hospital, a free-school, and a library, all very well supported. The college was the charity of Thomas, Lord Delaware,[6] who being but the cadet of the family, was bred a scholar, and was in orders. He founded the college anno 1421, after he was come to the honour and estate of his brother. The foundation escaped the general ruin in the time of Henry VIII but was dissolved in the reign of his successor Edward VI and the revenues fell to the Crown; but they were restored by Queen Mary, and the house re-established upon the first foundation, though with several additions. Queen Elizabeth enquiring into the nature of the gift, and having a favourable representation of it as a seminary not of Popery but of learning and true religion, founded it anew. This was anno 1578 and as, I say, she refounded it, so she new christened it, gave it the name it still enjoys, of Christ's College in Manchester, and settled its ancient revenues as far as they could be recovered; but there had been great dilapidations in the time of the former unsettled governors of it by several former foundations.

As for the antiquity of the place, the antiquity of the manufacture indeed is what is of most consideration; and this, though we cannot trace it by history, yet we have reason to believe it began something earlier than the great woollen manufactures in other parts of England, of which I have spoken so often, because the cotton might it self come from the Mediterranean, and be known by correspondents in those countries, when that of wool was not pushed at, because our neighbours wrought the goods, and though they bought the wool from England, yet we did not want the goods; whereas, without making the cotton goods at home, our people could not have them at all; and that necessity, which is the mother of invention, might put them upon one; whereas having not the same necessity, ignorance and indolence prevented the other.

I cannot doubt but this increasing town will, some time or other, obtain some better face of government, and be incorporated, as it very well deserves to be.

About eight mile from Manchester, north west, lies Bolton, the town which gives title to the noble family of Powlet, Dukes of Bolton. We saw nothing remarkable in this town, but that the cotton manufacture reached hither; but the place did not, like Manchester, seem so flourishing and increasing.

On the left hand of this town, west, even to the sea-shore, there are not many towns of note, except Wiggan, on the high post road, and Ormskirk, near which we saw Latham House, famous for its being not only gallantly defended in the times of the late fatal wars, but that it was so by a woman; for the Lady Charlotte, Countess of Derby,[7] defended the house to the last extremity against the Parliament forces; nor could she ever be brought to capitulate, but kept the hold till Prince Rupert, with a strong body of the King's army, came to her relief, and obliged the enemy to raise their siege, anno 1644. It was indeed ruined in a second siege, and is not yet fully recovered from the calamity of it.

In the neighbourhood of this town, that is to say, between Wiggan and Bolton, is found that kind of coal they call Canell or Candle Coal, which, though they are found here in great plenty, and are very cheap, are yet very singular; for there are none such to be seen in Britain, or perhaps in the world besides. They so soon take fire, that, by putting a lighted candle to them, they are presently in a flame, and yet hold fire as long as any coals whatever, and more or less, as they are placed in the grate or hearth, whether flat or edged, whether right up and down, and polar, or level and horizontal.

They are smooth and slick when the pieces part from one another, and will polish like alabaster; then a lady may take them up in a cambric handkerchief and they will not soil it, though they are as black as the deepest jet. They are the most pleasant agreeable fuel that can be found, but they are remote; and though some of them have been brought to London, yet they are so dear, by reason of the carriage, that few care to buy them; we saw some of them at Warrington too, but all from the same pits.

It is not to be forgot that Warrington is near Winnick, a

small town, but a large parish, and great benefice; but though it might be the greatest in England in those days, 'tis very far from being now so; for we never heard that it was worth above 800*l.* per annum, whereas Sedgfield, near Durham, is valued at this time at 1200*l.* per annum at least.

I must not pass over here the Burning Well, as 'tis called, near Wiggan, though I must acknowledge, that being turned from Bolton towards Rochdale, before I heard any thing of it that I gave any credit to, I did not go back to see it; not that I had not curiosity enough, if I had been satisfied it was valuable, but the country people, who usually enlarge upon such things rather than lessen them, make light of this; and so I cooled in my curiosity.

We turned east here, and came to Bury, a small market town on the River Roch, where we observed the manufacture of cotton, which are so great at Manchester, Bolton, &c. was ended, and woollen manufacture of coarse sorts, called half-thicks and kerseys, began, on which the whole town seemed busy and hard at work; and so in all the villages about it.

From thence we went on to Rochdale, a larger and more populous town than Bury, and under the hills, called Black-stone Edge. But I must now look northward. This great county, as we advance, grows narrow, and not only so, but mountainous, and not so full of towns or inhabitants as the south part; Preston and Lancaster are the only towns of note remaining.

Preston is a fine town, and tolerably full of people, but not like Liverpoole or Manchester; besides, we come now beyond the trading part of the county. Here's no manufacture; the town is full of attorneys, proctors, and notaries, the process of law here being of a different nature than they are in other places, it being a duchy and county palatine, and having particular privileges of its own. The people are gay here, though not perhaps the richer for that; but it has by that obtained the name of Proud Preston. Here is a great deal of good company, but not so much, they say, as was before the late bloody action [8] with the northern rebels; not that the battle hurt many of the immediate inhabitants, but so many families there and thereabout, have been touched by the consequences of it, that it will not be recovered in a few years, and they seem to have a kind of remembrance of things upon them still.

Lancaster is the next, the county town, and situate near the mouth of the River Lone or Lune. The town is ancient; it lies, as it were, in its own ruins, and has little to recommend it but a decayed castle, and a more decayed port (for no ships of any considerable burthen); the bridge is handsome and strong, but, as before, here is little or no trade, and few people.

This part of the country seemed very strange to us, after coming out of so rich, populous and fruitful a place, as I have just now described; for here we were, as it were, locked in between the hills on one side high as the clouds, and prodigiously higher, and the sea on the other, and the sea it self seemed desolate and wild, for it was a sea without ships, here being no sea port or place of trade, especially for merchants; so that, except colliers passing between Ireland and Whitehaven with coals, the people told us they should not see a ship under sail for many weeks together.

Here, among the mountains, our curiosity was frequently moved to enquire what high hill this was, or that. Indeed, they were, in my thoughts, monstrous high; but in a country all mountainous and full of innumerable high hills, it was not easy for a traveller to judge which was highest.

Nor were these hills high and formidable only, but they had a kind of an unhospitable terror in them. Here were no rich pleasant valleys between them, as among the Alps; no lead mines and veins of rich ore, as in the Peak; no coal pits, as in the hills about Hallifax, much less gold, as in the Andes, but all barren and wild, of no use or advantage either to man or beast. Indeed here was formerly, as far back as Queen Elizabeth, some copper mines, and they wrought them to good advantage; they are all given over long since, and this part of the country yields little or nothing at all.

But I must not forget Winander Meer, which makes the utmost northern bounds of this shire, which is famous for the char fish found here and hereabout, and no where else in England; it is found indeed in some of the rivers or lakes in Swisserland among the Alps, and some say in North Wales; but I question the last. It is a curious fish, and, as a dainty, is potted, and sent far and near, as presents to the best friends.

Here we entered Westmoreland, a country eminent only for being the wildest, most barren and frightful of any that I have passed over in England, or even in Wales it self; the west side, which borders on Cumberland, is indeed bounded by a chain of almost unpassable mountains, which, in the language of the country, are called Fells, and these are called Fourness Fells, from the famous promontory bearing that name, and an abbey built also in ancient times, and called Fourness.

But 'tis of no advantage to represent horror, as the character of a country, in the middle of all the frightful appearances to the right and left; yet here are some very pleasant, populous and manufacturing towns. Such as Kirby Launsdale, or Lunedale, because it stands on the River Lune, which is the boundary of the county, and leaves the hills of Mallerstang Forest, which are, in many places, unpassable. The manufacture which the people are employed in here, are chiefly woollen cloths, at Kirkby Launsdale, and Kendal, and farther northward, a security for the continuance of the people in the place; for here is a vast concourse of people. In a word, I find no room to doubt the hills above mentioned go on to Scotland, for from some of the heights hereabouts, they can see even into Scotland it self.

The upper, or northern part of the county, has two manufacturing towns, called Kirkby Stephen, and Appleby; the last is the capital of the county, yet neither of them offer any thing considerable to our observation, except a great manufacture of yarn stockings at the former.

When we entered at the south part of this county, I began

indeed to think of Merionethshire, and the mountains of Snowden in North Wales, seeing nothing round me, in many places, but unpassable hills, whose tops, covered with snow, seemed to tell us all the pleasant part of England was at an end. The great Winander Meer, like the Mediterranean Sea, extends it self on the west side for twelve miles and more, reckoning from North Bridge on the south, where it contracts it self again into a river up to Grasmere north, and is the boundary of the county, as I have said, on that side; and the English Appenine, that is, the mountains of Yorkshire North Riding, lie like a wall of brass on the other; and in deed, in one sense, they are a wall of brass; for it is the opinion of the most skilful and knowing people in the country, that those mountains are full of inexhaustible mines of copper, and so rich, as not only to be called brass, copper being convertible into brass, but also to have a quantity of gold in them also.

But notwithstanding this terrible aspect of the hills, when having passed by Kendal, and descending the frightful mountains, we began to find the flat country show it self; we soon saw that the north and north east part of the county was pleasant, rich, fruitful, and, compared to the other part, populous. The River Eden, the last river of England on this side, as the Tyne is on the other, rises in this part out of the side of a monstrous high mountain, called Mowill Hill, or Wildbore Fell, which you please; after which, it runs through the middle of this vale, which is, as above, a very agreeable and pleasant country, or perhaps seems to be so the more, by the horror of the eastern and southern part.

In this vale, and on the bank of this river, stands Appleby, once a flourishing city, now a scattering, decayed, and half-demolished town, the fatal effects of the ancient inroads of the Scots, when this being a frontier county, those invasions were frequent, and who several times were masters of this town, and at length burnt it to the ground, which blow it has not yet recovered.

The Roman highway, which I have so often mentioned,

and which, in my last letter, I left at Leeming Lane, enters this county from Rear Cross upon Stanmore, and crossing it almost due east and west, goes through Appleby, passing the Eden a little north from Perith, at an ancient Roman station called Brovoniacam, where there was a large and stately stone bridge; but now the great road leads to the left-hand to Perith.

Perith, or Penrith, is a handsome market town, populous, well built, and for an inland town, has a very good share of trade. It was unhappily possessed by the late party of Scots Highland rebels, when they made that desperate push into England, and which ended at Preston; in the moor or heath, on the north part of this town, the militia of the county making a brave appearance, and infinitely out-numbering the Highlanders, were drawn up; yet, with all their bravery, they ran away, as soon as the Scots began to advance to charge them, and never fired a gun at them, leaving the town at their mercy. However, to do justice even to the rebels, they offered no injury to the town, only quartered in it one night, took what arms and ammunition they could find, and advanced towards Kendal.

From hence, in one stage, through a country full of castles, for almost every gentleman's house is a castle, we came to Carlisle, a small, but well fortified city, the frontier place and key of England on the west sea, as Berwick upon Tweed is on the east; and in both which there have, for many years, I might say ages, been strong garrisons kept to check the invading Scots; from below this town the famous Picts Wall began, which crossed the whole island to Newcastle upon Tyne, where I have mentioned it already. Here also the great Roman highway, just before named, has its end, this being the utmost station of the Roman soldiers on this side.

But before I go on to speak of this town, I must go back, as we did for our particular satisfaction, to the sea coast, which, in this northern county, is more remarkable than that of Lancashire, though the other is extended much farther in length; for here are some towns of good trade.

I enquired much for the pearl fishery here, which Mr Cambden speaks of, as a thing well known about Ravenglass and the River Ire, which was made a kind of bubble[9] lately. But the country people, nor even the fishermen, could give us no account of any such thing; nor indeed is there any great quantity of the shell-fish to be found here (now) in which the pearl are found, I mean the large oyster or mussel. What might be in former times, I know not.

Under this shire, the navigation being secured by this cape of St Bees, is the town of Whitehaven, grown up from a small place to be very considerable by the coal trade, which is increased so considerably of late, that it is now the most eminent port in England for shipping off coals, except Newcastle and Sunderland, and even beyond the last. They have of late fallen into some merchandising also, occasioned by the great number of their shipping, and there are now some considerable merchants; but the town is yet but young in trade.

About ten miles from Whitehaven north east, lies Cockermouth, upon the little River Cocker, just where it falls into the Derwent. This Derwent is famous for its springing out of those hills, called Derwent Falls, where the ancient copper mines were found in Queen Elizabeth's time, and in which, it was said, there was a large quantity of gold. But they are discontinued since that time, for what reason, I know not; for there are several copper mines now working in this county, and which, as they told me, turn to very good account.

Some tell us, the copper mines on Derwent Falls were discontinued, because there being gold found among the ore, the queen claimed the royalty, and so no body would work them; which seems to be a reason why they should have been applied to the search with more vigour; but be that how it will, they are left off, and the more probable account is, what a gentleman of Penrith gave us, namely, that the charge of working them was too great for the profits.

Here we saw Skiddaw, one of those high hills of which, wherever you come, the people always say, they are the highest in England. Skiddaw indeed is a very high hill, but seems the higher, because not surrounded with other mountains, as is the case in most places where the other hills are, as at Cheviot, at Penigent, and at other places. From the top of Skiddaw they see plainly into Scotland, and quite into Dumfries-shire, and farther.

Cockermouth stands upon the River Derwent, about twelve miles from the sea, but more by the windings of the river, yet vessels of good burthen may come up to it. This River Derwent is noted for very good salmon, and for a very great quantity, and trout. Hence, that is, from Workington at the mouth of this river, and from Carlisle, notwithstanding the great distance, they at this time carry salmon (fresh as they take it) quite to London. This is performed with horses, which, changing often, go night and day without intermission, and, as they say, very much out-go the post; so that the fish come very sweet and good to London, where the extraordinary price they yield, being often sold at two shillings and sixpence to four shillings per pound, pay very well for the carriage.

They have innumerable marks of antiquity in this county, as well as in that of Westmoreland, mentioned before; yet, passing these, I could not but take notice of two or three more modern things, and which relate to our own nation. Such as,

1. That of Hart-Horn Tree, where they showed us the head of a stag nailed up against a tree, or rather showed us the tree where they said it was nailed up, in memory of a famous chase of a stag by one single dog. It seems the dog chased a stag from this place, (Whi[n]field Park) as far as the Red Kirk in Scotland, which, they say, is sixty miles at least, and back again to the same place, where, being both spent, and at the last gasp, the stag strained all its force remaining to leap the park pales, did it, and died on the inside; the hound, attempting to leap after him, had not strength to go over, but fell back, and died on the outside just opposite; after which the heads of both were nailed up upon the tree.

2. Another thing they told us was in the same park, viz. three oak trees which were called the Three Brether, the least of which was thirteen yards about; but they owned there was but one of them left, and only the stump of that; so we did not think it worth going to see, because it would no more confirm the wonder, than the people's affirming it by tradition only. The tree or stump left, is called the Three Brether Tree, that is to say, one of the three brothers, or brethren.

3. West of this Hart-horn Tree, and upon the old Roman way, is the famous column, called the Countess Pillar, the best and most beautiful piece of its kind in Britain. It is a fine column of free-stone, finely wrought, enchased, and in some places painted. There is an obelisk on the top, several coats of arms, and other ornaments in proper places all over it, with dials also on every side.

[The] Countess of Pembroke [10] had a noble and great estate in this county, and a great many fine old seats or palaces, all which she repaired and beautified, and dwelt sometimes at one, and sometimes at another, for the benefits of her tenants, and of the poor, who she always made desirous of her presence, being bettered constantly by her bounty, and her noble house-keeping. But those estates are all since that time gone into other families.

4. At Penrith also we saw several remarkable things, viz. (1.) Two remarkable pillars fourteen or fifteen foot asunder, and twelve foot high the lowest of them, though they seem equal. The people told us, they were the monument of Sir Owen Caesar.[11] This Sir Owen, they tell us, was a champion of mighty strength, and of gigantic stature, and so he was, to be sure, if, as they say, he was as tall as one of the columns, and could touch both pillars with his hand at the same time. They relate nothing but good of him, and that he exerted his mighty strength to kill robbers, such as infested the borders much in those days, others related wild boars; but the former is most probable. (2.) On the north side of the vestry of this church is erected in the wall an ancient square stone, with a

memorial, intimating, that in the year 1598 there was a dreadful plague in those parts, in which there died:

	Persons
In Kendal,	2500
In Penrith,	2266
In Richmond,	2200
In Carlisle,	1196
	8162

But though I am backward to dip into antiquity, yet no English man, that has any honour for the glorious memory of the greatest and truest hero of all our kings of the English or Saxon race, can go to Carlisle, and not step aside to see the monument of King Edward I at Burgh upon the Sands, a little way out of the city Carlisle, where that victorious prince died.

Near this town, and, as the inhabitants affirm, just on the spot where the king's tent stood in which he expired, for he died in the camp, is erected a pillar of stone near thirty foot high, besides the foundation. This monument was erected by a private gentleman, for the eternal memory of a prince, who, when he lived, was the darling of the world, both for virtue and true fame.

But I return to Carlisle: the city is strong, but small, the buildings old, but the streets fair; the great church is a venerable old pile, it seems to have been built at twice, or, as it were, rebuilt, the upper part being much more modern than the lower. King Henry VIII fortified this city against the Scots, and built an additional castle to it on the east side; there is indeed another castle on the west, part of the town rounds the sea, as the wall rounds the whole, is very firm and strong. But Carlisle is strong by situation, being almost surrounded with rivers.

Here is a bridge over the Eden, which soon lets you into Scotland; for the limits are not above eight miles off, or thereabout. The south part of Scotland on this side, coming at least fifty miles farther into England, than at Berwick. There is not a great deal of trade here either by sea or land, it being a mere frontier. On the other side the Eden we saw the Picts Wall, of which I have spoken already, and some remains of it are to be seen farther west. But being now at the utmost extent of England on this side, I conclude also my letter, and am,

SIR, &c.

INTRODUCTION TO THE ACCOUNT AND DESCRIPTION OF SCOTLAND

HITHERTO all the descriptions of Scotland, which have been published in our day, have been written by natives of that country, and that with such an air of the most scandalous partiality, that it has been far from pleasing the gentry or nobility of Scotland themselves, and much farther has it been from doing any honour to the nation or to the country.

One known author has taken pains to describe their commerce as an immense thing for magnitude, has set off their manufactures in such a figure, and as such extraordinary things, that the English are trifles to them, and their merchandising, according to his account, must be inferior to very few, if any nation in Europe; nay, he is not ashamed to give us an account of the particulars of their exportations to China and the East Indies, to Turkey, and the Levant, where, I believe, never Scots ship yet sailed, unless it was in the service of English merchants, or some other foreign nation.

A more modern, and I must acknowledge, more modest writer than this, knowing he could not, with a front that, perhaps, he had not yet arrived to, set forth his country to her advantage, by giving a real description of that part which would necessarily show her deficiences, as well as her beauties; and retaining still that piece of northern vanity peculiar to the climate, to think mighty well of his own country, takes up with describing the seats of the nobility and gentry; a subject, which, it must be confessed, give him a greater scope, and in which he has good materials to work on. But, even in this, it must be added he would have done better, if he would have given the noblemen and gentlemen of Scotland leave to have known their own houses again, when they saw his description of them.

I have so much honour for the noblemen and gentlemen of

Scotland, that I am persuaded they will be as well pleased to see justice done them and their country, as to see themselves flattered, and the world imposed upon about them. Their country is not so void of beauty, or their persons of merit, as to want it; and (I believe) they will not seek to be flattered, or be obliged by it, when 'tis attempted.

But be that as it will, the world shall, for once, hear what account an Englishman shall give of Scotland, who has had occasion to see most of it, and to make critical enquiries into what he has not seen; and, if describing it, as it really is, and as in time it may be, with probable reasons for the variation, will give satisfaction to the Scots, they will be obliged; on the contrary I shall neither flatter them or deceive them. Scotland is here described with brevity, but with justice; and the present state of things there, placed in as clear a light as the sheets, I am confined to, will admit; if this pleases, more particulars may be adventured on hereafter; if it should not, it would make me suspect the other authors I have mentioned, knew what would please their countrymen better than I. But I must run the venture of that, rather than trespass upon my own truth and their modesty.

I hope it is no reflection upon Scotland to say they are where we were, I mean as to the improvement of their country and commerce; and they may be where we are.

Here are but a few things needful to bring Scotland to be (in many parts of it at least) as rich in soil, as fruitful, as populous, as full of trade, shipping, and wealth, as most, if not as the best counties of England. These few things, indeed, are such as are absolutely necessary, and, perhaps, as things stand, may be difficult: such as

1. Time, public changes cannot be brought about in a day.

2. A change in the disposition of the common people, from a desire of travelling abroad, and wandering from home, to an industrious and diligent application to labour at home.

3. Stock and substance, to encourage that application: sloth is not a mere disease of the nation. The Scots are as diligent, as industrious, as apt for labour and business, and as

capable of it, when they are abroad, as any people in the world; and why should they not be so at home? and, if they had encouragement, no doubt they would.

4. Some little alteration in their methods of husbandry, by which their lands would be improved, and the produce thereof turn better to account; of all which something may be said in our progress through the country, as occasion presents.

In the meantime, as I shall not make a paradise of Scotland, so I assure you I shall not make a wilderness of it. I shall endeavour to show you what it really is, what it might be, and what, perhaps, it would much sooner have been, if some people's engagements were made good to them, which were lustily promised a little before the late Union: such as erecting manufactures there under English direction, embarking stocks from England to carry on trade, employing hands to cut down their northern woods, and make navigations to bring the fir-timber, and deals to England, of which Scotland is able to furnish an exceeding quantity; encouraging their fishery, and abundance of fine things more which were much talked of I say, but little done; and of which I could say more, but it is not the business of this work, nor, perhaps, will the age care to hear it.

I must, therefore, be contented to give an account of Scotland in the present state of it, and as it really is; leaving its misfortunes, and want of being improved as it might be, and, perhaps, ought to have been, for those to consider of, in whose power it is to mend it.

Letter 11

Sir, – I am now just entered Scotland, and that by the ordinary way from Berwick. We tread upon Scots ground, after about three miles riding beyond Berwick; the little district between, they say, is neither in England or Scotland, and is called Berwickshire, as being formerly a dependant upon the town of Berwick; but we find no towns in it, only straggling farm-houses; and one sees the Tweed on one side, which fetches a reach northward, the sea on the other, and the land between lies so high, that in stormy weather 'tis very bleak and unpleasant; however, the land is good, and compared to our next view, we ought to think very well of it.

The first town in Scotland is called Mordintown, where the minister, at that time, was a man of learning, particularly in matters of religious antiquity; his name is Lauder.[1] Mordintown lying to the west, the great road does not lie through it, but carries us to the brow of a very high hill, where we had a large view into Scotland. But we were welcomed into it with such a Scots gale of wind, that, besides the steepness of the hill, it obliged us to quit our horses, for real apprehensions of being blown off, the wind blowing full north, and the road turning towards the north, it blew directly in our faces. And I can truly say, I never was sensible of so fierce a wind, so exceeding keen and cold, for it pierced our very eyes, that we could scarcely bear to hold them open.

When we came down the hill, the strength of the wind was not felt so much, and, consequently, not the cold. The first town we come to is as perfectly Scots, as if you were 100 miles north of Edinburgh; nor is there the least appearance of any thing English, either in customs, habits, usages of the people, or in their way of living, eating, dress, or behaviour; any more than if they had never heard of an English nation; nor was there an Englishman to be seen, or an English family to be found among them.

On the contrary, you have in England abundance of Scotsmen, Scots customs, words, habits, and usages, even more than becomes them; nay, even the buildings in the towns, and in the villages, imitate the Scots almost all over Northumberland; witness their building the houses with the stairs (to the second floor) going up on the outside of the house, so that one family may live below, and another above, without going in at the same door; which is the Scots way of living, and which we see in Alnwick and Warkworth, and several other towns; witness also their setting their corn up in great numbers of small stacks without doors, not making use of any barns, only a particular building, which they call a barn, but, which is itself no more than a threshing-floor, into which they take one of those small stacks at a time, and thresh it out, and then take in another; which we have great reason to believe was the usage of the ancients, seeing we read of threshing-floors often; but very seldom, of a barn, except that of the rich glutton.

Being down this hill, we passed a bridge over the little River Eye, at the mouth of which there is a small harbour, with a town called Eyemouth, or, as some call it, Heymouth, which has of late been more spoken of than formerly, by giving the title of Baron to the late Duke of Marlborough, who was Duke of Marlborough, Marquis of Blandford, and Baron Eyemouth in Scotland; and, by virtue of this title, had a right of peerage in the Parliament of Scotland. But notwithstanding all this, I never heard that he did any thing for the town, which is, at present, just what it always was, a good fishing town, and some fishing vessels belong to it; for such it is a good harbour, and for little else; in Queen Elizabeth's time, indeed, the French held it and fortified it for their particular occasion; because, being the first port in Scotland, they might safely land their supplies for the Queen-Mother, who stood in great need of their assistance against the reformers. But they were obliged to quit both that and all the kingdom some time after, by a treaty; Queen Elizabeth supporting the reformers against her.

From this bridge we enter upon a most desolate, and, in winter, a most frightful moor for travellers, especially strangers, called Coudingham, or, to speak properly, Coldingham Moor; upon which, for about eight miles, you see hardly a hedge, or a tree, except in one part, and that at a good distance; nor do you meet with but one house in all the way, and that no house of entertainment; which, we thought, was but poor reception for Scotland to give her neighbours, who were strangers, at their very first entrance into her bounds.

The place called Coudingham, from whence this moor derives, is an old monastery, famous before the Reformation; the monks of Coldingham being eminent for their number and wealth; as for any thing else, this deponent saith not.

Having passed this desert, which indeed, makes a stranger think Scotland a terrible place, you come down a very steep hill into the Lothains, so the counties are divided, and they are spoken of in plural. From the top of this hill you begin to see that Scotland is not all desert; and the Low Lands, which then show themselves, give you a prospect of a fruitful and pleasant country. As soon as we come down the hill, there is a village called Cockburnspeth, vulgarly Cobberspeth, where nature forms a very steep and difficult pass, and where, indeed, a thousand men well furnished, and boldly doing their duty, would keep out an army, if there was occasion.

The first gentleman's house we met with in Scotland was that of Douglass, the seat of Sir James Hall;[2] a gentleman so hospitable, so courteous to strangers, so addicted to improve and cultivate his estate, and understood it so well, that we began to see here a true representation of the gentry of Scotland; than whom, I must say, without compliment, none in Europe, understand themselves better, or better deserve the name of gentlemen. We began also to see that Scotland was not so naturally barren, as some people represent it, but, with application and judgment, in the proper methods of improving lands, might be made to equal, not England only, but even the richest, most fruitful, most pleasant, and best improved part of England.

The first town of note, from hence, is Dunbar, a royal burgh, so they are called in Scotland, which is (much what) we call a corporation in England, and which sent members to parliament, as our corporations in England do, only that in Scotland, as is generally to be understood, they had some particular privileges separate to themselves; as that, for example, of holding a parliament, or convention of burghs by themselves, a method taken from the union of the Hans-Towns in the north, and not much unlike it, in which they meet and concert measures for the public good of the town, and of their trade, and make by-laws, or acts and declarations, which bind the whole body.

Nor have they lost this privilege by the Union with England; but it is preserved entire, and, perhaps, is now many ways more advantageous to them than it was before, as their trade is like to be, in time, more considerable than before.

This town of Dunbar is a handsome well-built town, upon the sea-shore where they have a kind of a natural harbour, though in the middle of dangerous rocks. They have here a great herring-fishery, and particularly they hang herrings here, as they do at Yarmouth in Norfolk, for the smoking them; or, to speak the ordinary dialect, they make red herrings here. I cannot say they are cured so well as at Yarmouth, that is to say, not for keeping and sending on long voyages, as to Venice and Leghorn, though with a quick passage, they might hold it thither too. However, they do it very well.

On the south-west side of this town, under the mountains, near a place called Dun-Hill, is the fatal field where the battle, called the battle of Dunbar,[3] was fought, between Oliver Cromwell and General Lesly, who then commanded the royal army; where the desperate few, for Cromwell's army was not above 8,000 men, defeated and totally overthrew the great army of the other side, killed 6,000, and took 10,000 prisoners, to the surprise of the world; but that is matter of history, and none of my business at present.

Here we turned out of the way to see the Marquess of Tweedal's[4] fine park, and which is, indeed, the main thing, his fine planting at Yester, or, as antiquity calls it, Zester; I say the park, because, though there is the design of a noble house or palace, and great part of it built; yet, as it is not yet, and perhaps, will not soon be finished, there is no giving a complete description of it.

The old Earl of Tweedale, who was a great favourite of King Charles II though not much concerned in politic affairs at least, not in England, yet took in from the king the love of managing what we call forest trees, and making fine vistas and avenues. As the success of this planting is a great encouragement to the nobility of Scotland to improve their estates by the same method, so we find abundance of gentlemen of estates do fall into it, and follow the example. And you hardly see a gentleman's house, as you pass the Louthains, towards Edinburgh, but they are distinguished by groves and walks of fir-trees about them; which, though in most places they are but young, yet they show us, that in a few years, Scotland will not need to send to Norway for timber and deal, but will have sufficient of her own, and perhaps, be able to furnish England too with considerable quantities.

From this town of Dunbar to Edinburgh, the country may be reckoned not only as fruitful and rich in soil, but also as pleasant and agreeable a country as any in Scotland, and, indeed, as most in England; the sea on the right hand, at a moderate distance, and the hills on the left, at a farther distance; and even those hills not extremely high, not barren, not desolate mountains. But these hills are passable and habitable, and have large flocks of sheep, in many places, feeding on them, and many open roads lie over them, as from Edinburgh, and other parts towards England; as particular to Yester, and to Duns and Coldstream on the Tweed; another way to Kelsoe, where also there is a ford and a ferry over the

Tweed, and likewise by another way to Tiviotdale, to Peebles and Jedburgh, of which hereafter.

The greatest thing this country wants is more enclosed pastures, by which the farmers would keep stocks of cattle well foddered in the winter, and, which again, would not only furnish good store of butter, cheese, and beef to the market, but would, by their quantity of dung, enrich their soil, according to the unanswerable maxim in grazing, that stock upon land improves land.

Two other articles would increase and enrich them, but which they never practise.

1. Folding their sheep.
2. Fallowing their ploughed land.

The first would fatten the land, and the latter destroy the weeds: but this is going out of my way. They have, indeed, near the sea, an equivalent which assists them exceedingly, namely, the sea weed, they call it the sea ware, which the sea casts up from November to January in great quantities, and which extremely fattens and enriches the lands, so that they are ploughed from age to age without lying fallow. But farther from the sea, and where they cannot fetch it, there they are forced to lay the lands down to rest; when, as we say in England, they have ploughed them out of heart, and so they get no advantage by them; whereas could they, by a stock of cattle, raise a stock of muck, or by folding sheep upon them, mend them that way, and lay them down one year in three or four, as we do in England, the lands would hold from one generation to another.

But at present, for want of enclosures, they have no winter provision for black cattle; and, for want of that winter provision, the farmers have no dairies, no butter or cheese; that is to say, no quantity, and no heaps of dung in their yards to return upon the land for its improvement. And thus a good soil is impoverished for want of husbandry.

From Dunbar we pass another River Tyne, which, to distinguish it from the two Tynes in Northumberland, I call

Scots Tyne, though not forgetting to let you know it is not so distinguished there, the inhabitants thereabouts scarce knowing any other. It rises in the hills near Yester, and watering part of the fine and pleasant vale I mentioned before, runs by Haddington, an old half ruined, yet remaining town; which shows the marks of decayed beauty, for it was formerly a large, handsome, and well built town, or city rather; for, besides the walls of stone, which were in those times esteemed strong, the English fortified it with lines and bastions, four of which bastions were very large, as may be seen, by the remains of them, to this day; also they had a large ditch; as for counterscarps, they were scarce known in those times.

However, Haddington is still a good town, has some handsome streets, and well built; and they have a good stone bridge over the Tyne, though the river is but small. The church was large, but has suffered in the ruin of the rest, and is but in part repaired, though 'tis still large enough for the number of inhabitants; for, though the town is still what may be called populous, 'tis easy to see that it is not like what it has been. There are some monuments of the Maitlands, ancient lords of this part of the country, remaining; but as the choir of the church is open and defaced, the monuments of the dead have suffered with the rest.

I saw here something of a manufacture, and a face of industry; and it was the first that I had seen the least appearance of in Scotland; particularly here, as a woollen manufacture, erected by a company, or corporation, for making broad cloths, such as they called English cloth. And as they had English workmen employed, and, which was more than all, English wool, they really made very good cloth, well mixed, and good colours. But I cannot say they made it as cheap, or could bring it so cheap to market as the English; and this was the reason, that, though before the late Union, the English cloth being prohibited upon severe penalties, their own cloth supplied them very well; yet, as soon as the Union was made, and by that means the English trade opened, the clothiers from Worcester, and the counties adjoining such as

Gloucester and Wilts, brought in their goods, and under selling the Scots, those manufactories were not able to hold it.

At the mouth of this river stands the remains of Tantallon Castle, mostly buried in its own ruins; it was famous, in the Scots history, for being the seat of rebellion, in the reign of King James V.[5] And hence came the old, and odd fancy among the soldiers, that the drums beating the Scots March, say, 'Ding down tan-tallon.' That beat or march being invented by King James the Vth's soldiers (or, perhaps, drummers). But this by the way: Tantallon is now no more a fortress, or able to shelter a rebel army.

Neither is the Bass worth naming any more, which being a mere rock, standing high out of the sea, and in its situation inaccessible, was formerly made a small fortification, rather to prevent its being made a retreat for pirates and thieves, than for any use it could be of to command the sea; for the entrance of the Forth, or Firth, is so wide, that ships would go in and out, and laugh at any thing that could be offered from the Bass. The most of its modern fame is contained in two articles, and neither of them recommend it to posterity.

1. That in the times of tyranny and cruelty, under the late King Charles II and King James II it was made a state-prison, where the poor persecuted western people, called, in those times, Cameronians, were made close prisoners, and lived miserably enough, without hope or expectation of deliverance but by death.

2. That after the Revolution a little desperate crew of people got possession of it; and, having a large boat, which they hoisted up into the rock, or let down at pleasure, committed several piracies, took a great many vessels, and held out the last of any place in Great Britain, for King James; but their boat being at last seized, or otherwise lost, they were obliged to surrender.

The Soland geese are the principal inhabitants of this island, a fowl rare as to the kind; for they are not found in any part of Britain, that I can learn, except here, and at some of the lesser islands in the Orcades, and in the island of

Ailzye, in the mouth of the Clyde. They come as certainly at their season, as the swallows or woodcocks, with this difference, if what the people there tell us may be depended on; that they come exactly, to the very same day of the month, or, if they change it for reasons best known to themselves, then they keep exactly to the new fixed day; and so, upon any alteration of their time, which also is very seldom.

They feed on the herrings, and therefore 'tis observed they come just before, or with them, and go away with them also; though, 'tis evident, they do not follow them, but go all away to the north, whither, as to that, none knows but themselves, and he that guides them. As they live on fish, so they eat like fish, which, together with their being so exceeding fat, makes them, in my opinion, a very coarse dish, rank, and ill relished, and soon gorging the stomach. But as they are looked upon there as a dainty, I have no more to say; all countries have their several gusts and particular palates. Onions and garlic were dainties it seems, in Egypt, and horse-flesh is so to this day in Tartary, and much more may a Soland goose be so in other places.

From hence, keeping the shore of the Firth, or Forth, due west, we find a range of large and populous villages all along the coast, almost to Leith, interspersed with abundance of the houses of the nobility and gentry, at a small distance from them, farther into the country.

But I must enter a caution for your notice, and please to take it here once for all. I am writing a description of places, not of persons, giving the present state of things, not their history: and therefore, though in some cases I may step back into history, yet, it shall be very seldom, and on extraordinary occasions. The nobility of Scotland are ancient, illustrious, and personally great, and, if spoken of at all, require and ought to have a full and authentic description of their families and glorious ancestors performed by itself; and, I must confess, 'tis great pity such a thing is not undertaken by some hands equal to so great a work, both here and in England also; for want of which, many, if not most of the great actions of the nobility and gentry of these two kingdoms, are either quite lost and dropped out of knowledge, or are dwindled into fable and romance, and, like the battle of Chevy-Chase, preserved only in ballad and song.

And I must add here, the ancient and noble house of Seaton and Winton: both the palaces, for so they deserve to be called, of the late Earl of Winton,[6] who did so many weak and rash things, to say no worse of him, in the affair of the late rebellion; and the kindest thing can be said of him now is, to leave it upon record, that he seemed to be turned in his head. The houses are now in a state of ruin, and as fine an estate, for its value, as any in Scotland, all lying contiguous with itself, and valued at almost 5,000 *l.* sterling per annum besides; but all now under forfeiture, and sold to the York-Buildings Company. The fine gates and stone-wall were demolished by the government, after it had been made a garrison by the Highlanders; who, from hence began their harebrained march to England, which expedition ended at Preston.

The towns upon this coast, as I said, stand very thick, and here are two or three articles of trade which render them more populous, and more considerable than they would otherwise be.

1. There are great quantities of white fish taken and cured upon this coast, even within, as well as at the mouth of the Firth; and, as I had occasion to inspect this part, I took notice the fish was very well cured, merchantable, and fit for exportation; and there was a large ship at that time come from London, on purpose to take in a loading of that fish for Bilboa in Spain.

2. There is great plenty of coal in the hills, and so near the sea as to make the carriage not difficult; and much of that coal is carried to Edinburgh, and other towns, for sale.

3. The coal being thus at hand, they make very good salt at almost all the towns upon the shore of the Firth; as at Seaton, Cockenny, Preston, and several others, too many to name. They have a very great trade for this salt to Norway, Ham-

burgh, Bremen, and the Baltick; and the number of ships loaded here yearly with salt is very considerable; nay, the Dutch and Bremers in particular, come hither on purpose to load salt, as they do on the opposite side of the Firth also, (viz.) the shore of Fife, of which I shall speak in its place.

4. They take great quantities of oysters upon this shore also, with which they not only supply the city of Edinburgh, but they carry abundance of them in large, open boats, called cobles, as far as Newcastle upon Tyne, from whence they generally bring back glass bottles. But there has, within a few years, a bottle-house been set up at Leith, which, for a while, worked with success; also some furnaces were erected at Preston-Pans, one of those villages, for making flint-glass, and other glass ware. But I hear they are discontinued for want of skilful hands.

We come now to Musclebro, a large borough-town and populous, and may, indeed, be said to be a cluster of towns, all built together into one, namely, Musclebro, Innerask, or Inneresk, and Fisheraw; all which amount to no more than this. Musclebro, or the main or chief town of Musclebro; Inneresk, or that part of Musclebro which stands within, or on the inner side of the River Esk, and Fisheraw, or the row of houses where the fishermen usually dwell; for here is still many fishermen, and was formerly many more, when the mussel fishing was counted a valuable thing; but now 'tis given over, though the mussels lie on the shore, and on the shoals of sand in the mouth of this river, in vast quantities.

These three towns together make one large borough, very populous for here are thought to be more people than at Haddington. Here also we saw the people busy on the woollen manufacture; and as the goods they made here were an ordinary kind of stuff for poor people's wearing, we do not find they are out-done at all from England, so that the manufacture is carried on here still with success.

They call this a sea-port town; but as their river, though sometimes full enough of water, is not navigable; for, at low water, people ride over the mouth of it upon the sands, and even walk over it; so they do not meddle much with trading by sea. At that part of the town called Inner-Esk are some handsome country houses with gardens, and the citizens of Edinburgh come out in the summer and take lodgings here for the air, as they do from London at Kensington Gravel-Pits, or at Hampstead and Highgate.

From hence we have but four miles to Edinburgh. But, before I go thither, I must dip so far into story, as to observe that here it was the famous Battle of Musclebro [7] was fought between the English, under the Duke of Somerset, in the time of King Edward VI of England, and the Scots royal army under the Regent, which was afterwards called, the English way of wooing. The quarrel was to obtain the young Queen of Scots for a wife to King Edward, which the Scots Popish Party, backed by the French, were obstinately against and that so much, that though the English won the battle, yet they lost the prize, for the young queen was privately embarked, carried away into France, and there married to the dauphin.

I say this battle was fought here, though we call it the Battle of Musclebro: and some Scots gentlemen, who rode out with us afterwards to show us the place, particularly marked out every step to us, where the action was both begun and ended, as well the fight as the pursuit; and we agreed that the Scots are in the right, who call it the Battle of Pinkie, not of Musclebro. 'Tis none of my business to give an account of battles and sieges; besides, the English being victors, I shall not mingle any of our trophies and triumphs with my account of Scotland; that would not be using the Scots fairly. I shall speak freely of those where they were victors, but not throw the English, as it were, in their faces; that would be to act the very part which I blame the Scots writers for, namely to be always crying up my own country, and my own people. Certain it is, the Scots' great error at this battle, as it was afterwards at the Battle of Dunbar, was want of unanimity among themselves; for we must always blush when we pretend to say the Scots ever wanted courage in the field, let the cause, or the time, or the government be what, when, and how they will.

I am now at the gates of Edinburgh; but before I come to describe the particulars of that city, give me leave to take it in perspective, and speak something of its situation, which will be very necessary with respect to some disadvantage which the city lies under on that account.

When you stand at a small distance, and take a view of it from the east, you have really but a confused idea of the city, because the situation being in length from east to west, and the breadth but ill proportioned to its length, you view under the greatest disadvantage possible; whereas if you turn a little to the right hand towards Leith, and so come towards the city, from the north you see a very handsome prospect of the whole city, and from the south you have yet a better view of one part, because the city is increased on that side with new streets, which, on the north side, cannot be.

The particular situation then of the whole is thus. At the extremity of the east end of the city stands the palace or court, called Haly-Rood House; and you must fetch a little sweep to the right hand to leave the palace on the left, and come at the entrance, which is called the Water Port, and which you come at through a short suburb, then bearing to the left again, south, you come to the gate of the palace which faces the great street.

From the palace, west, the street goes on in almost a straight line, and for near a mile and a half in length, some say full two measured miles, through the whole city to the castle, including the going up the castle in the inside; this is, perhaps, the largest, longest, and finest street for buildings and number of inhabitants, not in Britain only, but in the world.

From the very palace door, which stands on a flat, and level with the lowest of the plain country, the street begins to ascend; and though it ascends very gradually at first, and is no where steep, yet 'tis easy to understand that continuing the ascent for so long a way, the further part must necessarily be very high; and so it is; for the castle which stands at the extremity west, as the palace does east, makes on all the three sides, that only excepted, which joins it to the city, a frightful and impassable precipice.

Together with this continued ascent, which, I think, 'tis easy to form an idea of in the mind, you are to suppose the edge or top of the ascent so narrow, that the street, and the row of houses on each side of it, take up the whole breadth; so that which way soever you turn, either to the right, or to the left, you go down hill immediately, and that so steep, as is very troublesome to those who walk in those side lanes which they call Wynds, especially if their lungs are not very good. So that, in a word, the city stands upon the narrow ridge of a long ascending mountain.

On the right side, or north side of the city, and from the very west end of it, where the castle stands, is a lough, or lake of standing water; there is, indeed, a small brook runs through it, so that it cannot be said to be quite standing water. And we were told, that in former days there was another lough on the south side of it, which, being now filled up, is built into a street, though so much lower than the high street, or ridge, that, as I said before, the lanes or wynds between them are very steep.

It is easy to conclude, that such a situation as this could never be picked out for a city or town, upon any other consideration than that of strength to defend themselves from the sudden surprises and assaults of enemies. And, though the building is so ancient, that no history has recorded the foundation, either when, or by who, or on what occasion it was built; yet, I say, it seems most natural to conclude, that it was built for a retreat from the outrages and attempts of the Picts or Irish, or whatever other enemies they had to fear.

On the top of the ridge of a hill, an impregnable castle and precipice at one end, a lough, or lake of water on either side; so that the inhabitants had nothing to defend but the entrance at the east end, which it was easy to fortify.

If this was not the reason, what should have hindered them from building the city in a pleasant, delightful valley, with the sea flowing up to one side, and a fresh water river running through the middle of it; such as is all that space of ground between the city, as it now stands, and the sea, or Firth, and on the south shore, whereof the town of Leith now stands?

These things they did not foresee, or understand in those days; but, regarding immediate safety, fixed on the place as above as a sure strength, formed by Nature, and ready at their hand. By this means the city suffers infinite disadvantages, and lies under such scandalous inconveniences as are, by its enemies, made a subject of scorn and reproach; as if the people were not as willing to live sweet and clean as other nations, but delighted in stench and nastiness; whereas, were any other people to live under the same unhappiness, I mean as well of a rocky and mountainous situation, thronged buildings, from seven to ten or twelve story high, a scarcity of water, and that little they have difficult to be had, and to the uppermost lodgings, far to fetch; we should find a London or a Bristol as dirty as Edinburgh, and, perhaps, less able to make their dwelling tolerable, at least in so narrow a compass; for, though many cities have more people in them, yet, I believe, this may be said with truth; that in no city in the world so many people live in so little room as at Edinburgh.

On the north side of the city, as is said above, is a spacious, rich, and pleasant plain, extending from the lough, which as above joins the city, to the river of Leith, at the mouth of which is the town of Leith, at the distance of a long Scots mile from the city. And even here, were not the north side of the hill, which the city stands on, so exceeding steep, as hardly, (at least to the westward of their flesh-market) to be clambered up on foot, much less to be made passable for carriages. But, I say, were it not so steep, and were the lough filled up, as it might easily be, the city might have been extended upon the plain below, and fine beautiful streets would, no doubt, have been built there; nay, I question much whether, in time, the high streets would not have been forsaken, and the city, as we might say, run all out of its gates to the north.

This might have been expected, if the city had been in a state of increase, for the trade having flourished, as was reasonably expected upon the Union, the inhabitants had likewise increased; whereas, there being reason to doubt that this is not the case, but rather the contrary, we cannot talk of this as prospect in hope.

Having thus considered the city in its appearance, and in its present situation, I must look next into its inside, where we shall find it under all its discouragements and disadvantages, (and labouring with whatever inconveniences) a large, populous, noble, rich, and even still a royal city. The main street, as above, is the most spacious, the longest, and best inhabited street in Europe; its length I have described; the buildings are surprising both for strength, for beauty, and for height; all, or the greatest part of free-stone, and so firm is every thing made, that though in so high a situation, and in a country where storms and violent winds are so frequent, 'tis very rare that any damage is done here. No blowing of tiles about the streets, to knock people on the head as they pass: no stacks of chimneys and gable-ends of houses falling in to bury the inhabitants in their ruins, as we often find it in London, and other of our paper built cities in England; but all is fixed, and strong to the top, though you have, in that part of the city called the Parliament-close, houses, which, on the south side, appear to be eleven or twelve story high, and inhabited to the very top.

From the palace gate, westward, this street is called the Cannon-Gate, vulgarly the Canni-gate, which part, though a suburb, is a kind of corporation by itself, as Westminster to London; and has a toll-booth, a prison, and a town-guard by itself, though under the government of the provost and bailiffs of Edinburgh as Leith itself also is. In this part of the street, though otherwise not so well inhabited as the city itself, are several very magnificent houses of the nobility, built for their residence when the court was in town, and on their other occasions, just as was the case in the Strand between London and Whitehall, before the increase of the city prompted the building those fine houses into streets.

At the upper, or west end of this street, and where it joins to the city, is a gate which, just as Ludgate, or Temple-Bar, stands parting the city itself from the suburb, but not at all discontinuing the street, which rather widens, and is more spacious when you are through the gate than before. This gate, or Bow, is called the Nether-Bow, or, by some, the Nether-Bow port.

We now enter the city, properly so called; in almost the first buildings of note on the north side of the street, the Marquess of Tweedale has a good city house, with a plantation of lime-trees behind it, instead of a garden, the place not allowing room for a large garden; adjoining to which are very good buildings, though in the narrow wynds and alleys, such as if set out in handsome streets, would have adorned a very noble city, but are here crowded together, as may be said, without notice.

Here the physicians have a hall, and adjoining to it a very good garden; but I saw no simples in it of value, there being a physic garden at the palace which furnishes them sufficiently. But they have a fine museum, or chamber of rarities, which are worth seeing, and which, in some things, is not to be matched in Europe. Dr Balfour, afterwards knighted, began the collection. Sir Robert Sibbald has printed a catalogue of what was then deposited in his time. The physicians of Edinburgh have preserved the character of able, learned, and experienced, and have not been outdone by any of their neighbours. And the late Dr Pitcairn,[8] who was the Ratcliff of Scotland, has left large testimonies of his skill in nature and medicine to the world.

It must not be expected I can go on to describe all the buildings of the city; I shall therefore only touch at such things, and go on. From the Nether-Bow, you have an open view up the high street. On the south side is the Trone kirk, and a little farther, in the middle of the street the guard house, where the town guard does duty every night. These are in the stead of our watchmen; and the town maintains two full companies of them, clothed and armed as grenadiers.

Those are as a guard to keep the public peace of the city; but I cannot but acknowledge that they are not near so good a safe-guard to the citizens, against private robberies, as our watchmen in London are; and Edinburgh is not without such fellows as shop-lifters, house-robbers, and pick-pockets, in proportion to the number of people, as much as London itself.

About midway, between the Nether-Bow and the Castle-Hill, is the great church, formerly it was called the cathedral, and was all one church, dedicated to St Giles. But since the abolishing episcopacy, and that the Presbyterian church is now established by the Union, so as never legally to suffer another change; I say never legally, because it cannot be done without dissolving the Union, which I take to be indissolvable. Since this establishment, the cathedral church is divided into four parochial churches.

In one of those churches, which they call the new church, were seats for the Parliament, high commissioners, and the nobility, when the Parliament was assembled, though that occasion is now over. In a room, formerly a kind of consistory room, on the south side of the church, the General Assembly hold their meetings once a year, as also does the Commission of the Assembly in the intervals of the General Meeting, as occasion requires. In the great tower of this church they have a set of bells, which are not rung out as in England, for that way of ringing is not known here but they are played upon with keys, and by a man's hand, like a harpsichord; the person playing has great strong wooden cases to his fingers, by which he is able to strike with the more force, and he plays several tunes very musically, though they are heard much better at a distance than near at hand; the man plays every day, Sunday and the fast days excepted, at twelve a clock, and has a yearly salary for doing it, and very well he earns the money.

On the south side of this church is a square of very fine buildings, which is called by the name of the Parliament Close; the west side of the square, and part of the south, is taken up with the Parliament House, and the several courts of justice, the Council-Chamber, the Treasury, the public offices, registers, the public library, &c. the court for the meeting of the royal boroughs, and several offices needful, when the independency of Scotland was in being, but now not so much in use. But as the Session, or College of Justice, the Exchequer, and the Justiciary, or courts for criminal causes still exist, the usual places for their assembling are still preserved. These buildings are very fine, all of free-stone, well finished, and very magnificent. The great church makes up the north side of the square, and the east remaining part of the south side is built into private dwellings very stately, lofty, and strong, being seven story high to the front of the square, and the hill they stand on giving so sudden a descent, they are eleven or twelve story high backward.

The great opening in to the High Street, being the only passage into it for coaches, is at the north east corner, between the south east corner of the High Kirk, and the opposite high buildings, and a little from the opening is the market-cross, where all their proclamations and public acts are read and published by sound of trumpet. Here is the great parade, where, every day, the gentlemen meet for business or news, as at an Exchange; the usual time of meeting is from eleven to one. Here is also another passage at the north west corner, which goes into the Land-market, and another passage down innumerable stone stairs, on the south side, leading into the Cowgate.

On the west end of the great Church, but in a different building, is the Tolbooth, or common prison, as well for criminals as debtors, and a miserable hole it is, to say no worse of it; though for those that can pay for it, there are some apartments tolerable enough, and persons of quality are sometimes confined here. The great church and this prison also standing in the middle of the street, the breadth and beauty of it is for some time interrupted, and the way is contracted for so far as those buildings reach on the north side. But those buildings past, the street opens again to a breadth rather wider than before, and this is called the Land-market.

Here the High Street ends, and parting into two streets, one goes away south west, and descending gradually, leads by the West Bow, as 'tis called, to the Grass-market. This street, which is called the Bow, is generally full of wholesale traders, and those very considerable dealers in iron, pitch, tar, oil, hemp, flax, linseed, painters' colours, dyers, drugs and woods, and such like heavy goods, and supplies country shopkeepers, as our wholesale dealers in England do. And here I may say, is a visible face of trade; most of them have also warehouses in Leith, where they lay up the heavier goods, and bring them hither, or sell them by patterns and samples, as they have occasion.

The markets in Edinburgh are not in the open street, except that in the High Street, where there is every morning a herb and fruit market, which yet abates before noon, and what remains then is no grievance. Besides this, there are several distinct market places walled in, and reserved for the particular things they are appointed for, and very well regulated by the magistrates, and well supplied also; as

1. The Meal-market.
2. The Flesh-market.
3. The Poultry-market.
4. The Butter-market.
5. The Grass-market. } Kept open, and in the same street
6. The Horse-market. } just within the west port, with

several others. There is also, in the street called the Land-market, a weekly market for all sorts of woollen manufactures, and some mercery and drapery goods, and also for linen cloth.

But I must not omit the seminaries of learning, and the attendants upon them, nor the surgeons and apothecaries, with the great hospital, all which stand on the south side of the city; the first of them is the surgeons hall, or surgeon-apothecaries, for here they make but one profession. They have set up a large building all at their own charge, in which is their great hall, hung round with the pictures of all the surgeons of the city, that are, or have been since the building was erected.

They have also a Chamber of Rarities, a theatre for dissections, and the finest bagnio in Britain; 'tis perfectly well contrived, and exactly well finished, no expense being spared to make it both convenient and effectually useful. In their Chamber of Rarities they have several skeletons of strange creatures, a mummy, and other curious things, too many to be particular in them here. The Humanity school is kept in the same part, which is reckoned as a part of the university, as being employed in the finishing youth for the college. West of these is the college itself, they call it the university. But as it consists of but one college, I call it no more. However, here are all the usual methods of academic learning in their full perfection.

The college has a very handsome public library; and, though not famous for number of books, is yet so for its being a valuable collection of antiquity, and has some very good manuscripts. The late Act of Parliament [of 1709] for settling the right of copies, has made provision for a constant supply of modern books, especially such as are printed in England; so the library is like to increase, in time, to a great one.

Here was formerly a mint, but that is now laid aside, the Union having made one and the same coinage common to the whole island.

The churches in this populous city are but ten.

There are also many meeting-houses of the Episcopal party who call themselves Church of England, though they do not all use the English Common-Prayer. These are the dissenters in Scotland, as the Presbyterians are dissenters in England.

There are also two churches at Leith, and very large and

very full they are, and so indeed are all the churches in the city, for the people of Scotland do not wander about on the sabbath-days, as in England; and even those who may have no more religion than enough, yet custom has made it almost natural to them, they all go to the kirk.

They have also one very good custom as to their behaviour in the church, which I wish were practised here, namely, that after the sermon is over, and the blessing given, they all look round upon their friends, and especially to persons of distinction, and make their civilities and bows as we do here, for, by the way, the Scots do not want manners. But if any person come in when the worship is begun, he takes notice of no body, nor any body of him; whereas here we make our bows and our cringes in the middle of our very prayers.

I have now done with the city; the palace only, and the castle remain to be mentioned; the last is strong by situation, not much bettered by art, and far from being impregnable, as has been proved more than once. It is now of little use, unless for salutes, and firing guns upon festivals, and in some cases to lay up a magazine of arms and ammunition, and to receive prisoners of state.

The palace is a handsome building, rather convenient than large. The entrance is majestic, and over the gate a large apartment, which the Duke of Hamilton [9] claims as house-keeper, or rather gate-keeper of the palace; within this is a large, irregular court, where, I must needs say, are very improperly placed the coach-houses and stables, which should much rather have been farther off, either in the park, or without the outgate. And, if here had been a barrack, or guard-house, like the Horse-Guards at Whitehall, it would have looked much more like a royal palace for the king. On either side of this court are gardens, yards the Scots call them, whereof one is like our apothecaries' garden at Chelsea, called a physic garden, and is tolerably well stored with simples, and some exotics of value; and, particularly I was told, there was a rhubarb-tree, or plant, and which throve very well. In this garden stands Queen Mary's Dial, which is a very curious one, but neglected.

Antiquity claims the fee simple here, and tells us that the church is still ground landlord for, before the Reformation, this was a monastery; and, though it was converted into a palace before the suppression of religious houses, yet, that till then the monks had a fair apartment, and was therefore called Haly-Rood House, and they did but entertain the kings and queens in the other as a kind of guest mates, or, as we call them, lodgers.

I have not room to describe the particular apartments, nor is it of moment. The great staircase is at the south-west corner of the house, and the guard-chamber and rooms of state take up the south side of the house, as the king's lodgings do the east side, which the Lord Commissioner makes use of in time of parliament; and the west side would be supposed to be the queen's lodgings, if such a thing was to be seen again in Scotland, but at present are out of use. The north side is taken up with one large gallery, reaching the whole length of the house, famous for having the pictures of all the kings of Scotland.

The old Chapel Royal, or church of the convent, stands in its *disshabile*, ruined and decayed, and must fall down. In King James IId's time, the old council-chamber was consecrated for a chapel, instead of the ancient fabric; and there the Roman priests officiated for some time, promising themselves not only to restore the great ancient chapel, but even to seize upon the palace itself in the right of the Church, and make a noble monastery of it which it must be confessed might have been done with very little charge. But their reign was too short for the undertaking.

I must now visit Leith, the sea-port of Edinburgh, as it is properly called. It is a large and populous town, or rather two towns, for the river or harbour parts them, and they are joined by a good stone bridge, about half a mile, or more, from the mouth of the river. Up to this bridge ships of burthen may come, and, at high water, lay their sides close to the shore; but at low water people pass over on foot, even without the pier; but the water flows in the Firth near three fathom right up and down.

Here is a very fine quay well wharfed up with stone, and fenced with piles, able to discharge much more business than the place can supply, though the trade is far from being inconsiderable too. At the mouth of the harbour is a very long and well built pier, or head, which runs out beyond the land a great way, and which defends the entrance into the harbour from filling up with sand, as, upon hard gales of wind at north east, would be very likely. There are also ranges of piles, or break-waters, as the seamen call them, on the other side the harbour, all which are kept in good repair; and by this means the harbour is preserved, and kept open in spite of a flat shore, and a large swell of the sea.

On the other side the bridge is the remains of a strong castle, built by Oliver Cromwell to command the port, but demolished; yet not so much, but that a little expense and a few hands would soon restore it. Here the late rebel Highlanders [10] made a bold stop, and took possession of it for one night but not finding their friends in the city in any condition to join them; and the troops preparing to attack them, they quitted it in the night, and marched off to the Earl of Winton's house, as has been said.

Leith, though it has a particular bailiff, is yet under the jurisdiction of the magistrates of Edinburgh, and is governed by them. The town had a great disaster a few years before the Union, by a store-house of gunpowder taking fire, which demolished almost a whole street of houses; the loss is not fully repaired to this day. Many lives also were lost, and many people miserably hurt and bruised, which, I think, should serve as a hint to all governments, not to suffer quantities of powder to be kept in populous towns.

There is a ferry at Leith, the boats going from Leith to Burnt-Island, or, as the Scots call it, Bruntillian; but as 'tis no less than seven miles, and that sometimes they meet with bad weather, the passengers are so often frighted, that I knew several gentlemen that would always choose to go round to the Queens-Ferry, rather than venture over at Leith.

Queens-Ferry is not a passage over the water only, but a very good town also, and a corporation. And here I must take notice of a thing which was to me surprising, I mean as to the quantity of herrings taken, and that might be taken in those seas. There was, at that time, a fleet of between seven and eight hundred sail of Dutch Busses come into the Firth, loaden with herrings, and their convoy with them, for it was in the time of the late wars.

All the country between Edinburgh and this place, is thronged with gentlemen's houses, also as it was observed to be on the other side. But the beauty of all this part is Hopton House, built upon a delightful plain, and yet upon the edge, as we may say, of a high precipice; from whence you, as it were, look down upon the ships as they sail by, for you stand above the top-mast heads of them.

From hence the Firth widens again, and soon after is three or four miles wide, and makes a safe and deep road, with good anchor ground; and if there was a trade to answer it, here might ride a thousand sail of ships of any burthen. On the south-shore, upon a narrow slip or point of land, running far into the water, lies Blackness Castle, in former times infamous for the cruel confining state-prisoners, and especially such as were taken up for religious differences, where many perished, either by the unhealthiness of the place, or want of conveniences, or something worse. It might be of use, if the harbour, as I have said, was frequented; but as it is, there seems to be no occasion at all for it.

Farther west is Boristown Ness, a long town, of one street, and no more, extended along the shore, close to the water. It has been, and still is, a town of the greatest trade to Holland and France, before the Union, of any in Scotland, except Edinburgh; and, for shipping, it has more ships belong to it than to Edinburgh and Leith put together; yet their trade is declined of late by the Dutch trade, being carried on so much by way of England.

Letter 11

As I resolve to go through my account of the south part of Scotland first, I shall not pass the Firth at all, till giving you an account of the western part, I come back to Sterling Bridge; mean time

I am, &c.

Letter 12

Containing a Description of the South-Western part of Scotland, including the City of Glasgow

SIR, – As I entered the east side of Scotland from Berwick upon Tweed, and have carried on my accounts through the Louthians, which are deservedly called the best and most pleasant, as well as most fruitful part of Scotland; so the west part having been travelled over by me at another particular journey from England and that I went from England by another road, I shall give you my account of it also by itself.

Passing the River Eden, or (as it is ordinarily called) the Solway Firth at Carlisle, we entered upon Scotland, on the side of Dumfries-shire, the southmost shire of the west of Scotland. The Esk is a tolerable large river, and gives name to the south-east part of this county; but we saw little worth notice but Kirsop, a small market town on a river of the same name, which afterwards falls into Esk, and is famous for being the place where, by a treaty, after the battle of Pinkey, the limits or borders of the two kingdoms were settled; though the borderers observed it no longer than served for their purpose, robbing and plundering one another upon all occasions, as opportunity offered.

The first place of note we came to in Scotland was Annand, or as some call it, Annandale, as they do the county, though, I think, improperly. It was a town of note, and a sea-port, and having a good river and harbour, was esteemed a town of good trade; but it was not situated for strength and the English took it so often, and specially the last time burnt it to the ground, in that war so fatal to the Scots, in the reign of Edward VI that it never recovered. Here was a good salmon fishery, and a trade to the Isle of Man, and by that to Ireland. But as the face of trade is altered since that time, and by the ruins of the place the merchants, and men of substance, removed to Dumfries, the town continues, to all appearance, in a state of irrevocable decay.

It was but a dull welcome into Scotland to see, not only by this town, that the remains of the old devastations, committed in the time of the hostilities between the two nations, were so visible, so unrepaired, and, as we might say, so likely to continue unrepaired; whereas, though there are remains also on the English side, yet, not so plain, and in many places things much restored, and in a way to be more so. But the poverty of the common people, and the indolence of the gentry, will fully account for the difference.

From hence, keeping the sea as close as we could on our left, we went on due west to Dumfries, a sea-port town at the mouth of the River Nid, or Nith. Here, indeed, as in some other ports on this side the island, the benefits of commerce, obtained to Scotland by the Union, appear visible; and that much more than on the east side, where they seem to be little, if any thing mended, I mean in their trade.

Dumfries was always a good town, and full of merchants. By merchants, here I mean, in the sense that word is taken and understood in England (viz.) not mercers and drapers, shopkeepers, &c. but merchant-adventurers, who trade to foreign parts, and employ a considerable number of ships. But if this was so before, it is much more so now; and as they have (with success) embarked in trade, as well to England as to the English plantations, they apparently increase both in shipping and people; for as it almost every where appears, where trade increases, people must and will increase; that is, they flock to the place by the necessary consequences of the trade, and, in return, where the people increase, the trade will increase, because the necessary consumption of provisions, cloths, furniture, &c. necessarily increases, and with them the trade.

There is a very fine stone bridge here over the River Nid; as also a castle, though of old work, yet still good and strong enough; also an exchange for the merchants, and a Tolbooth, or town-hall for the use of the magistrates. They had formerly a woollen manufacture here. But as the Union has, in some manner, suppressed those things in Scotland, the English supplying them fully, both better and cheaper; so they have more than an equivalent by an open trade to all the English plantations, and to England itself.

The castle in this town, as well as that at Carlavrock, near the mouth of the river, and opening to the Firth of Solway, was formerly belonging to the ancient family of Nithsdale. That last mentioned castle has been a very magnificent structure, though now, like its owner, in a state of ruin and decay.

We could not pass Dumfries without going out of the way upwards of a day, to see the castle of Drumlanrig, the fine palace of the Duke of Queensberry, which stands at twelve miles distance, upon the same river; the vale on either side the river is pleasant, and tolerably good. But when these rapid rivers overflow their banks, they do not, like Nile, or even like the Thames, and other southern streams, fatten and enrich the soil; on the contrary, they lodge so much sand and splinters of stone upon the surface of the earth, and among the roots of the grass, that spoils and beggars the soil; and the water is hurried on with such force also, as that in a good light soil it washes the best part of the earth away with it, leaving the sand and stones behind it.

Drumlanrig, like Chatsworth in Darbyshire, is like a fine picture in a dirty grotto, or like an equestrian statue set up in a barn; 'tis environed with mountains, and that of the wildest and most hideous aspect in all the south of Scotland; as particularly that of Enterkin, the frightfullest pass, and most dangerous that I met with, between that and Penmenmuir in North Wales; but of that in its place.

We were not so surprised with the height of the mountains, and the barrenness of the country beyond them, as we were with the humour of the people, who are not in this part, by many degrees, so populous, or so polished, as in the other parts of Scotland. But that which was more surprising than all the rest, was to see a palace so glorious, gardens so fine, and every thing so truly magnificent, and all in a wild, mountainous country, the like we had not seen before. This was certainly a foil to the buildings, and sets them off with all possible advantage; upon which the same hand [1] which before gave us the lines upon the waters of Buxton-Bath, being in the company, bestowed the following upon Drumlanrig Castle.

Just thus, with horrid desart hills embrac'd,
Was Paradise on *Euphra's* border plac'd.
The God of Harmony to grace the view,
And make the illustrations just and true,
Strong contraries presented to the eye,
And circled beauty in deformity.
The happy discord entertains the sight,
And as these shew more black, that shews more bright.

The house stands on the top of a rising ground, which, at its first building, lay with a steep and uncouth descent to the river, and which made the lookers-on wonder what the duke meant to build in such a disproportioned place. But he best understood his own design; for the house once laid out, all that unequal descent is so beautifully levelled and laid out in slopes and terraces, that nothing can be better designed, or, indeed, better performed than the gardens are, which take up the whole south and west sides of the house; and, when the whole design will be done, the rest will be more easy, the ground being a plain the other way, and the park and avenues completely planted with trees.

The inside is answerable to the outside, the apartments finely placed and richly furnished. And the gallery may well be called a gallery of beauties, itself's a beauty. And being filled from end to end, the whole length of one side of the building, with the family-pieces of the Duke's ancestors, most of them at full length, and in their robes of state, or of office, as their history directed. They were first ennobled for the real merit of their services, in the person of the first Lord of Drumlanrig, *Ann.* 1640. And King Charles I made the then Lord of Drumlanrig Earl of Queensberry; after the Restoration, the grandson [2] of the Earl was created Marquess and Duke by King Charles II. This was the person who built the noble palace I am speaking of, who, every way, merited the honours which the prince rather loaded him with, than bestowed on him. He lies buried in the parish church of Disdier or Didier, with a fine monument over him; but not like that lately erected for his son the late Duke.

This last mentioned Duke would require a history rather than a bare mention, in a work of this kind. But I have forbid myself entering far into the characters of persons and families; and therefore, though I think myself bound to honour the merit of so great a person, I shall sum it up all in this; that as I had the honour to be known to his Grace, so I had the opportunity to see and read by his permission, several letters written to him by the late King William, with his own hand, and several more by Queen Anne, written also by her Majesty's own hand; with such expressions of their satisfaction in his fidelity and affection to their Majesties' service, his ability and extraordinary judgment in the affairs entrusted to him; his knowledge of, and zeal for the true interest of his country, and their dependence upon his councils and conduct, that no minister of state in Europe could desire greater testimonies of his services, or a better character from his sovereign, and this from differing princes, and at the distance of several years from one another, and, to be sure, without any manner of corresponding one with the other.

That this noble person was Lord Commissioner at the time of the Union, sat in the throne at the last parliament of Scotland, and touched with the sceptre the Act of Parliament, which put an end to parliaments for ever in that part of Great Britain, will always be matter of history to the end of time; whether the Scots will remember it to the advantage of the Duke's character, in their opinion, that must be as their several opinions guide them.

But I dwell too long here. While I was at Drumlanrig, being desired by the late Duke to make some observations on his Grace's estate there, which is very great, in order to some

English improvement, I, in particular, viewed some of the hills to the north of the castle, and having a Darbyshire gentleman with us, who was thoroughly acquainted with those things, we discovered in several places evident tokens of lead-mines, such as in Darbyshire, and in Somersetshire, are said never to fail; and to confirm our opinions in it, we took up several small pieces of ore in the gulls and holes, which the rains had made in the sides of the mountains, and also of a plain spar, such as is not found any where without the ore. But the Duke's death put an end to these enquiries, as also to several other improvements then in view.

Here we were surprised with a sight, which is not now so frequent in Scotland as it has been formerly, I mean one of their field meetings, where one Mr John Hepburn,[3] an old Cameronian, preached to an auditory of near 7,000 people, all sitting in rows on the steep side of a green hill, and the preacher in a little pulpit made under a tent at the foot of the hill; he held his auditory, with not above an intermission of half an hour, almost seven hours and many of the poor people had come fifteen or sixteen miles to hear him, and had all the way to go home again on foot. I shall say nothing to it, for my business is not to make remarks on such things; only this I may add, that if there was an equal zeal to this in our part of the world, and for that worship which we acknowledge to be true, and of a sacred institution, our churches would be more thronged, and our ale-houses and fields less thronged on the sabbath-day than they are now. But that also by the way.

From Drumlanrig I took a turn to see the famous pass of Enterkin, or Introkin Hill. It is, indeed, not easy to describe, but by telling you that it ascends through a winding bottom for near half a mile, and a stranger sees nothing terrible, but vast high mountains on either hand, though all green, and with sheep feeding on them to the very top; when, on a sudden, turning short to the left, and crossing a rill of water in the bottom, you mount the side of one of those hills, while, as you go on, the bottom in which that water runs down from between the hills, keeping its level on your right, begins to look very deep, till at length it is a precipice horrible and terrifying; on the left the hill rises almost perpendicular, like a wall; till being come about half way, you have a steep, unpassable height on the left, and a monstrous calm or ditch on your right; deep, almost as the monument is high, and the path, or way, just broad enough for you to lead your horse on it, and, if his foot slips, you have nothing to do but let go the bridle, lest he pulls you with him, and then you will have the satisfaction of seeing him dashed to pieces, and lie at the bottom with four shoes uppermost. I passed twice this hill after this, but the weather was good, and the way dry, which made it safe; but one of our company was so frighted with it, that in a kind of an ecstasy, when he got to the bottom, he looked back, and swore heartily that he would never come that way again.

Indeed, there were several things this last time we passed it, which rendered it more frightful to a stranger. One was, that there had been, a few days before, a sudden frost, with a great deal of snow; and though, a little before the snow, I passed it, and there was nothing to be seen; yet then I looked down the frightful precipice, and saw no less than five horses in several places, lying at the bottom with their skins off, which had, by the slipperiness of the snow, lost their feet, and fallen irrecoverably to the bottom, where the mountaineers who make light of the place, had found means to come at them, and get their hides off.

But I must go back to Dumfries again, for this was but an excursion from thence, as I observed there: I resolved, before I quitted the west coast, to see all that was worth seeing on that side, and the next trip we made was into Galloway. And here, I must confess, I could not but look with grief and concern upon the country, and indeed upon the people.

The first town on the coast, of any note, is Kirkubright, or as vulgarly called Kirkubry. It must be acknowledged this very place is a surprise to a stranger, and especially one whose business is observation, as mine was.

Here is a pleasant situation, and yet nothing pleasant to be seen. Here is a harbour without ships, a port without trade, a fishery without nets, a people without business; and, that which is worse than all, they do not seem to desire business, much less do they understand it. I believe they are very good Christians at Kirkubry, for they are in the very letter of it, they obey the text, and are contented with such things as they have. They have all the materials for trade, but no genius to it; all the opportunities for trade, but no inclination to it. In a word, they have no notion of being rich and populous, and thriving by commerce. They have a fine river, navigable for the greatest ships to the town quay; a haven, deep as a well, safe as a mill-pond; 'tis a mere wet dock, for the little island of Ross lies in the very entrance, and keeps off the west and north west winds, and breaks the surge of the sea; so that when it is rough without, 'tis always smooth within. But, alas! there is not a vessel, that deserves the name of a ship, belongs to it; and, though here is an extraordinary salmon fishing, the salmon come and offer themselves, and go again, and cannot obtain the privilege of being made useful to mankind for they take very few of them. They have also white fish, but cure none; and herrings, but pickle none. In a word, it is to me the wonder of all the towns of North-Britain; especially, being so near England, that it has all the invitations to trade that Nature can give them, but they take no notice of it. A man might say of them, that they have the Indies at their door, and will not dip into the wealth of them; a gold mine at their door, and will not dig it.

It is true, the reason is in part evident, namely, poverty; no money to build vessels, hire seamen, buy nets and materials for fishing, to cure the fish when it is catched, or to carry it to market when it is cured; and this discourages the mind, checks industry, and prevents all manner of application. People tell us, that slothfulness begets poverty, and it is true; but I must add too, that poverty makes slothfulness, and I doubt not, were two or three brisk merchants to settle at Kirkubry, who had stocks to furnish out ships and boats for these things, they would soon find the people as industrious, and as laborious as in other places; or, if they did not find them so, they would soon make them so, when they felt the benefit of it, tasted the sweet of it, had boats to fish, and merchants to buy it when brought in; when they found the money coming, they would soon work. But to bid men trade without money, labour without wages, catch fish to have them stink, when they had done, is all one as to bid them work without hands, or walk without feet; 'tis the poverty of the people makes them indolent.

Again, as the people have no hands (that is, no stock) to work, so the gentry have no genius to trade; 'tis a mechanism which they scorn; though their estates are not able to feed them, they will not turn their hands to business or improvement; they had rather see their sons made foot soldiers, (than which, as officers treat them now, there is not a more abject thing on earth), than see them apply to trade, nay, to merchandise, or to the sea, because those things are not (forsooth) fit for gentlemen.

In a word, the common people all over this country, not only are poor, but look poor; they appear dejected and discouraged, as if they had given over all hopes of ever being otherwise than what they are. They are, indeed, a sober, grave, religious people, and that more, ordinarily speaking, than in any other part of Scotland, far from what it is in England; I assure you, they have no assemblies here, or balls; and far from what it is in England, you hear no oaths, or profane words in the streets; and, if a mean boy, such as we call shoe-blackers, or black-guard boys, should be heard to swear, the next gentleman in the street, if any happened to be near him, would cane him, and correct him; whereas, in England, nothing is more frequent, or less regarded now, than the most horrid oaths and blasphemies in the open streets, and that by the little children that hardly know what an oath means.

It must be acknowledged, and there my opinion concurs, they might be as religious and as serious as they are; and the more so, the better, and yet, they might at the same time be industrious, and apply themselves to trade, and to reap the advantages that nature offers them; might build ships, catch and cure fish, and carry them to all the markets in Europe, as the Glasgow merchants show them the example. But the hindrance is in the nature of the thing; the poverty of the commons, and the indolence of the gentry forbid it; and so Kirkubry, and all the shores of Galloway must remain unnavigated; the fine harbours be unfrequented, the fish be secure and safe from nets till time and better opportunities alter the case, or a people better able, and more inclined to business, comes among them, and leads them into it.

But I must speak no more in generals. I left Kirkubright with a sort of concern; it is so noble a prospect, of what business, and commerce might, and I am persuaded, some time or other will do for it; the river, that enters the sea here, and makes the fine harbour I mentioned, is called the Dee, or the Dea, and is of a considerable long course, coming out of the mountains, in the remotest north-angle of this shire towards Carrick.

The wester Galloway, which is also called the shire of Wigtoun, from the town of Wigtoun, its capital, runs out with a peninsula, so far into the sea, that from the utmost shores, you see the coast of Ireland very plain, as you see Calais from Dover; and here is the town of Port Patrick, which is the ordinary place for the ferry or passage to Belfast or other ports in Ireland. It has a tolerable good harbour, and a safe road; but there is very little use for it, for the packet boat, and a few fishing vessels are the sum of the navigation; it is true, the passage or ferry is wide, and the boats very indifferent, without the least convenience or accommodation; and yet, which is strange, they very rarely, if every miscarry. Nay, they told us there, they had never lost one in the memory of the oldest man in the town, except one full of cattle; which, heeling to one side more than ordinary, all the cattle run to that side, and as it were, slid out into the sea; but the loading being out, the boat came to rights again, and was brought safe into the port, and none but the four-footed passengers were drowned.

Port Patrick has nothing on it to invite our stay, 'tis a mean dirty homely place; and as we had no business here, but to see the coast, we came away very ill satisfied with our accommodations.

But now having said thus much of the stupidity of the people of Galloway, and especially on the sea coast, for not falling into merchandising, fishing, &c. which would doubtless turn to great account: I must premise two things, that I may not lead the reader into an error.

1. It is not so with all the people on this western coast of Scotland, as we shall soon see in the other countries, upon the coast of Clyde, farther north, up to, and inclusive of Glasgow itself.

2. The people of Galloway itself are not perfectly idle, and neither the country, or the people capable of any thing; if it were so, the place would be uninhabited, and, indeed, uninhabitable; whereas, on the contrary, it is very populous, and full of inhabitants, as well of noblemen and gentlemen, as of common people; all, which, I shall explain in few words.

1. It is not so with all the people, they are not all stupid, and without any notions of commerce, navigation, shipping, fishing, &c. that is to say, though in Galloway they are generally so, from the coast, a little west of Dumfries, that is, from the mouth of the River Fleet, yet to the northward, and upon the coast of Air, Kyle, and Cunningham; it is quite another thing, as you shall hear presently.

2. The people of Galloway do not starve; though they do not fish, build ships, trade abroad, &c. yet they have other business, that is to say, they are mere cultivators of the earth, and in particular, breeders of cattle, such as sheep, the number of which I may say is infinite, that is to say, innumerable; and black cattle, of which they send to England, if fame lies not, 50 to 60,000 every year, the very toll of which before the Union, was a little estate to some gentlemen upon

the borders; and particularly the Earl of Carlisle had a very good income by it.

Besides the great number of sheep and runts, as we call them in England, which they breed here; they have the best breed of strong low horses in Britain, if not in Europe, which we call pads, and from whence we call all small truss-strong riding horses Galloways. These horses are remarkable for being good pacers, strong, easy goers, hardy, gentle, well broke, and above all, that they never tire, and they are very much bought up in England on that account.

By these three articles, the country of Galloway is far from being esteemed a poor country; for the wool, as well as the sheep, is a very great fund of yearly wealth to them, and the black cattle and horses are hardly to be valued.

But I was sick of Galloway, through which the travelling is very rough, as well for the road, as for the entertainment; except, that sometimes we were received by the gentlemen, who are particularly very courteous to strangers, merely as such, and we received many extraordinary civilities on that only account.

We now entered the shire of Air, full north from the Mull of Galloway, and as before, we coasted the south Bay or Firth of Solway, parting England from Scotland. The shire of Air is divided into three parts, Carrick, Kyle, and Cunningham. Carrick is a more fruitful and better cultivated country than Galloway, and not so mountainous; but it is not quite so rich in cattle, and especially, not in sheep, or horses. There is no considerable port in this part of the country, yet, the people begin to trade here, and they are (particularly on the coast) great fishermen, and take abundance of fish, but not merchants to carry it abroad; sometimes they are employed by the merchants at Glasgow, and other places, to catch herrings for them. Balgony is the chief town, but though it stands on the coast, it has no harbour, and is a poor decayed town; the market is good, because there are many gentlemen in the neighbourhood, and the coast near it is full of people, the houses are mean, and low, and very coarse.

Coming to the north bounds of Carrick, we passed the River Dun, upon a bridge of one arch, the largest I ever saw, much larger than the Rialto at Venice, or the middle arch of the great bridge at York. This bridge led us into the county of Kyle, the second division of the shire of Air and here I observed, that, contrary to what is usual, the farther north we travelled, the better, finer, and richer the country was, whereas, ordinarily the farther north we expect it to be the worse.

Kyle is much better inhabited than Carrick, as Carrick is better than Galloway; and as the soil here is better, and the country plainer and leveller, so on the banks of the river, here are abundance of gentlemen's seats, some of them well planted, though most of the houses are old built, that is, castle-wise, because of enemies. But now that fear is over they begin to plant, and enclose after the manner of England; and the soil is also encouraging, for the land is fruitful.

The capital of this country is Air, a sea-port, and as they tell us, was formerly a large city, had a good harbour, and a great trade: I must acknowledge to you, that though I believe it never was a city, yet it has certainly been a good town, and much bigger than it is now. At present like an old beauty, it shows the ruins of a good face; but is also apparently not only decayed and declined, but decaying and declining every day, and from being the fifth town in Scotland, as the townsmen say, is now like a place forsaken; the reason of its decay, is, the decay of its trade, so true is it, that commerce is the life of nations, of cities, towns, harbours, and of the whole prosperity of a country. What the reason of the decay of trade here was, or when it first began to decay, is hard to determine; nor are the people free to tell, and, perhaps, do not know themselves. There is a good river here, and a handsome stone bridge of four arches.

The town is well situated, has a very large ancient church, and has still a very good market for all sorts of provision. But nothing will save it from death, if trade does not revive, which the townsmen say it begins to do since the Union.

From Air, keeping still north, we come to Irwin; here is more trade by a great deal than at Air; particularly here is a considerable trade for Scots coal, which they carry by sea to Ireland. They have also of late, as I was told, launched into a considerable trade abroad to other countries, and have some share in the fishery: but this I cannot come into the particulars of here. The town is the capital of that division of the shire of Ayre, which they call Cunningham, and is really within the Firth of Clyde, though not actually within the river itself; they cannot but go beyond their neighbours of Greenock, who sometimes cannot come out as the wind may blow, when the fishing-boats of Irwin can both go out and return.

As the town is better employed in trade than the other parts I have been speaking of, so it is better built. Here are two handsome streets, a good quay, and not only room in the harbour for a great many ships, but a great many ships in it also; and, in a word, a face of thriving appears every where among them.

As is the town, so is the country in which it is situated; for when we came hither, we thought ourselves in England again. Here we saw no more a Galloway, where you have neither hedge or tree, but about the gentlemen's houses; whereas here you have beautiful enclosures, pleasant pastures, and grass grounds, and consequently store of cattle well fed and provided.

With the division of Cunningham I quitted the shire of Ayre, and the pleasantest country in Scotland, without exception. Joining to it north, and bordering on the Clyde itself, I mean the river, lies the little shire of Renfrew, or rather a barony, or a sheriffdom, call it as you will. It is a pleasant, rich, and populous, though small country, lying on the south bank of the Clyde; the soil is not thought to be so good as in Cunningham. But that is abundantly supplied by the many good towns, the neighbourhood of Glasgow, and of the Clyde, and great commerce of both. We kept our route as near along the coast as we could, from Irwin; so that we saw all the coast of the Firth of Clyde, and the very opening of the Clyde itself. The first town of note is called Greenock; 'tis not an ancient place, but seems to be grown up in later years, only by being a good road for ships, and where the ships ride that come into, and go out from Glasgow, just as the ships for London do in the downs. It has a castle to command the road and the town is well built, and has many rich trading families in it. It is the chief town on the west of Scotland for the herring fishing; and the merchants of Glasgow, who are concerned in the fishery, employ the Greenock vessels for the catching and curing the fish, and for several parts of their other trades, as well as carrying them afterwards abroad to market.

Their being ready on all hands to go to sea, makes the Glasgow merchants often leave their ships to the care of those Greenock men; and why not? for they are sensible they are their best seamen; they are also excellent pilots for those difficult seas.

The country between Pasely and Glasgow, on the bank of Clyde, I take to be one of the most agreeable places in Scotland, take its situation, its fertility, healthiness, the nearness of Glasgow, the neighbourhood of the sea, and altogether, at least, I may say, I saw none like it.

I am now come to the bank of Clyde: the Clyde and the Tweed may be said to cross Scotland in the south, their sources being not many miles asunder; and the two firths, from the Firth of Clyde to the Firth of Forth, have not an interval of above twelve or fourteen miles, which, if they were joined, as might easily be done, they might cross Scotland, as I might say, in the very centre.

Nor can I refrain mentioning how easy a work it would be to form a navigation, I mean a navigation of art from the Forth to the Clyde, and so join the two seas, as the King of France has done [4] in a place five times as far, and five hundred times as difficult, namely from Thouloze to Narbonne. What an advantage in commerce would this be, opening the Irish trade to the merchants of Glasgow, making a communication between the west coast of Scotland, and the east coast of England, and even to London itself; nay, several ports of England, on the Irish Sea, from Liverpool northward, would all trade with London by such a canal, it would take up a volume by itself, to lay down the several advantages of Scotland, that would immediately occur by such a navigation, and then to give a true survey of the ground, the easiness of its being performed, and the probable charge of it, all which might be done. But it is too much to undertake here, it must lie till posterity, by the rising greatness of their commerce, shall not only feel the want of it, but find themselves able for the performance.

I am now crossed the Clyde to Glasgow, and I went over dry-footed without the bridge on which occasion I cannot but observe how differing a face the river presented itself in, at those two several times when only I was there; at the first, being in the month of June, the river was so low, that not the horses and carts only passed it just above the bridge, but the children and boys playing about, went every where, as if there was no river, only some little spreading brook, or wash, like such as we have at Enfield-Wash, or Chelston-Wash in Middlesex; and, as I told you, we crossed it dry-foot, that is, the water was scarce over the horses' hoofs.

But my next journey satisfied me, when coming into Glasgow from the east side, I found the river not only had filled up all the arches of the bridge, but, running about the end of it, had filled the streets of all that part of the city next the bridge, to the infinite damage of the inhabitants, besides putting them in to the greatest consternation imaginable, for fear of their houses being driven away by the violence of the water, and the whole city was not without apprehensions that their bridge would have given way too, which would have been a terrible loss to them, for 'tis as fine a bridge as most in Scotland.

Glasgow is, indeed, a very fine city; the four principal streets are the fairest for breadth, and the finest built that I have ever seen in one city together. The houses are all of stone, and generally equal and uniform in height, as well as in front; the lower story generally stands on vast square Doric columns, not round pillars, and arches between give passage into the shops, adding to the strength as well as beauty of the building; in a word, 'tis the cleanest and beautifullest, and best built city in Britain, London excepted.

It stands on the side of a hill, sloping to the river, with this exception, that the part next the river is flat, as is said above, for near one third part of the city, and that exposed it to the water, upon the extraordinary flood mentioned just now. Where the streets meet, the crossing makes a spacious market-place by the nature of the thing, because the streets are so large of themselves. As you come down the hill, from the north gate to the said cross, the Tolbooth, with the Stadhouse, or Guild-Hall, make the north east angle, or, in English, the right-hand corner of the street, the building very noble and very strong, ascending by large stone steps, with an iron balustrade. Here the town-council sit, and the magistrates try causes, such as come within their cognizance, and do all their public business.

On the left-hand of the same street is the university, the building is the best of any in Scotland of the kind; it was founded by Bishop Turnbull,[5] *Ann.* 1454, but has been much enlarged since, and the fabric almost all new built. It is a very spacious building, contains two large squares, or courts, and the lodgings for the scholars, and for the professors, are very handsome; the whole building is of freestone, very high and very august.

The cathedral is an ancient building, and has a square tower in the middle of the cross, with a very handsome spire upon it, the highest that I saw in Scotland, and, indeed, the only one that is to be called high. This, like St Giles's at Edinburgh, is divided now, and makes three churches, and, I suppose, there is four or five more in the city, besides a meeting or two. But there are very few of the episcopal dissenters here; and the mob fell upon one of their meetings so often, that they were obliged to lay it down, or, if they do meet, 'tis very privately.

Glasgow is a city of business; here is the face of trade, as well foreign as home trade; and, I may say, 'tis the only city in Scotland, at this time, that apparently increases and improves in both. The Union has answered its end to them more than to any other part of Scotland, for their trade is new formed by it; and, as the Union opened the door to the Scots in our American colonies, the Glasgow merchants presently fell in with the opportunity; and though, when the Union was making, the rabble of Glasgow made the most formidable attempt to prevent it, yet, now they know better, for they have the greatest addition to their trade by it imaginable; and I am assured that they send near fifty sail of ships every year to Virginia, New England, and other English colonies in America, and are every year increasing.

The share they have in the herring-fishery is very considerable, and they cure their herrings so well, and so much better than is done in any other part of Great Britain; that a Glasgow herring is esteemed as good as a Dutch herring, which in England they cannot come up to.

As Scotland never enjoyed a trade to the English plantations till since the Union, so no town in Scotland has yet done any thing considerable in it but Glasgow: the merchants of Edinburgh have attempted it; but they lie so out of the way, and the voyage is not only so much the longer, but so much more hazardous, that the Glasgow men are always sure to outdo them, and must consequently carry away that part of trade from them, as likewise the trade to the south, and to the Mediterranean, whither the ships from Glasgow go and come again with great advantage in the risk, so that even in the insuring there is one per cent difference, which is a great article in the business of a merchant.

The Glasgow merchants have of late suffered some scandal in this branch of trade, as if they were addicted to the sin of smuggling; as to that, if others, for want of opportunity, are not in capacity to do the same, let those who are not guilty, or would not, if they had room for it, throw the first stone at them; for my part I accuse none of them.

I have not time here to enlarge upon the home trade of this city, which is very considerable in many things, I shall only touch at some parts of them (viz.)

1. Here is one or two very handsome sugar-baking houses, carried on by skilful persons, with large stocks, and to a very great degree. I had the curiosity to view one of the houses, and I think it equal to, if not exceeding most in London. Also there is a large distillery for distilling spirits from the molasses drawn from the sugars, and which they called Glasgow brandy, and in which they enjoyed a vast advantage for a time, by a reserved article in the Union, freeing them from the English duties, I say for a time.

2. Here is a manufacture of plaiding, a stuff cross-striped with yellow and red, and other mixtures for the plaids or veils, which the ladies in Scotland wear, and which is a habit peculiar to the country.

3. Here is a manufacture of muslins, and, perhaps the only manufacture of its kind in Britain, if not in Europe; and they make them so good and so fine, that great quantities of them are sent into England, and sold there at a good price; they are generally striped, and are very much used for aprons by the ladies, and sometimes in head-clothes by the English women of a meaner sort, and many of them are sent to the British plantations.

4. Here is also a linen manufacture; but as that is in common with all parts of Scotland, I do not insist so much upon it here, though they make a very great quantity of it, and send it to the plantations also as a principal merchandise.

Nor are the Scots without a supply of goods for sorting their cargoes to the English colonies, even without sending to England for them, or at least not for many of them; and 'tis needful to mention it here, because it has been objected by some that understood trade too, that the Scots could not send a sortable cargo to America without buying from England; which goods, so bought from, must come through many hands, and by long carriage, and consequently be dear bought, and so the English merchants might undersell them.

But to answer this in the language of merchants, as it is a merchant-like objection. It may be true, that some things cannot be had here so well as from England, so as to make out a sortable cargo, such as the Virginia merchants in London ship off, whose entries at the Custom-house consist sometimes of 200 particulars; and they are at last fain to sum them up thus: certain tin, turnery, millinery, upholstery, cutlery, and Crooked-Lane [6] wares; that is to say, that they buy something of every thing, either for wearing, or kitchen, or house-furniture, building houses or ships (with every thing else in short) that can be thought of, except eating.

But though the Scots cannot do this, we may reckon up what they can furnish, and what is sufficient, and some of which they can go beyond England in.

1. They have several woollen manufactures which they send of their own making; such as the Sterling serges, Musclebrow stuffs, Aberdeen stockings, Edinburgh shalloons, blankets, &c. So that they are not quite destitute in the woollen manufacture, though that is the principal thing in which England can outdo them.

2. The trade with England being open, they have now, all the Manchester wares, Sheffield wares, and Newcastle hard wares; as also the cloths, kerseys, half-thicks, duffels, stockings, and coarse manufactures of the north of England, as cheap brought to them by horse-packs as they can be carried to London; nor is the carriage farther, and, in some articles, not so far by much.

3. They have linens of most kinds, especially diapers and table-linen, damasks, and many other sorts not known in England, cheaper than England, because made at their own doors.

4. What linens they want from Holland, or Hamburgh, they import from thence as cheap as can be done in England; and for muslins, their own are very acceptable, and cheaper than in England.

5. Gloves they make better and cheaper than in England, for they send great quantities thither.

6. Another article, which is very considerable here, is servants, and these they have in greater plenty, and upon better terms than the English; without the scandalous art of kidnapping, making drunk, wheedling, betraying, and the like; the poor people offering themselves fast enough, and thinking it their advantage to go; as indeed it is, to those who go with sober resolutions, namely, to serve out their times, and then become diligent planters for themselves; and this would be a much wiser course in England than to turn thieves, and worse, and then be sent over by force, and as a pretence of mercy to save them from the gallows.

This may be given as a reason, and, I believe, is the only reason why so many more of the Scots servants, which go over to Virginia, settle and thrive there, than of the English, which is so certainly true, that if it goes on for many years more, Virginia may be rather called a Scots than an English plantation.

I might go on to many other particulars, but this is sufficient to show that the Scots merchants are at no loss how to make up sortable cargoes to send with their ships to the plantations, and that if we can outdo them in some things, they are able to outdo us in others; if they are under any disadvantages in the trade I am speaking of, it is that they may perhaps, not have so easy a vent and consumption for the goods they bring back, as the English have, at London, or Bristol, or Liverpool; and that is the reason why they are now, as they say, setting up a wharf and conveniences at Alloway in the Forth, in order to send their tobaccos and sugars thither by land-carriage, and ship them off there for Holland, or Hamburgh, or London, as the market presents.

Now, though this may be some advantage (viz.) carrying the tobacco from fourteen to fifteen miles over land; yet, if on the other hand it be calculated how much sooner the voyage is made from Glasgow to the capes of Virginia, than from London, take it one time with another, the difference will be found in the freight, and in the expense of the ships, and especially in time of war, when the channel is thronged with privateers, and when the ships wait to go in fleets for fear of enemies; whereas the Glasgow men are no sooner out of the Firth of Clyde, but they stretch away to the north west, are out of the wake of the privateers immediately, and are oftentimes at the capes of Virginia before the London ships get clear of the channel. Nay, even in times of peace, and take the weather to happen in its usual manner, there must always be allowed, one time with another, at least fourteen to twenty days difference in the voyage, either out or home; which, take it together, is a month to six weeks in the whole voyage, and for wear and tear, victuals and wages, is very considerable in the whole trade.

I went from Glasgow to the palace of Hamilton, or as we should call it in England, to Hamilton-house. It is the palace of Hamilton, and the palace at Hamilton, for the family is according to the Scots dialect, Hamilton of that ilk, that is of a place or town of the same name, for the town of Hamilton joins to the outhouses, or offices of the house of Hamilton. The house is large as it is, though part of the design is yet unfinished; it is now a fair front, with two wings, two wings more there are laid out in the ichnography of the building, but are not attempted; the successor if he thinks fit, may build them.

I was here in some doubt, whether I should take the south or the north in the next part of my progress; that is to say, whether to follow up the Clyde, and so into, and through Clydesdale, and then crossing east, view the shire of Peebles, the country on the banks of Tweed and Tivyot, or keeping to the north, go on for the Forth; and after a short debate we concluded on the latter. So we turned to the left for Sterlingshire, and passing the Clyde we came to Kilsyth, a good plain country burgh, tolerably well built, but not large; here we rested, and upon a particular occasion went to see the ancient seat of Calendar, which seems, as well as that of Kilsyth, to be in its widow's weeds, those two families, collateral branches both of the name of Livingston, having had their several decays, though on different occasions.

From Kilsyth we mounted the hills black and frightful as they were, to find the road over the moors and mountains to Sterling, and being directed by our guides, came to the river Carron. The channel of a river appeared, indeed, and running between horrid precipices of rocks, as if cut by hand, on purpose for the river to make its way; but not a drop of water was to be seen. Great stones, square and formed, as if cut out by hand, of a prodigious size, some of them at least a ton, or ton and a half in weight, lay scattered, and confusedly, as it were, jumbled together in the very course of the river, which the fury of the water, at other times, I doubt not, had hurried down from the mountains, and tumbled them thus over one another. Some of them might, I suppose, have been some ages upon their journey down the stream; for it may not be once in some years that a flood comes with a force sufficient to move such stones as those; and, 'tis probable, 'tis never done, but when a weight of ice, as well as water, may come down upon them together.

From hence, descending on the north side, we had a view of Firth, or Forth, on our right, the castle of Sterling on the left; and in going to the latter we passed the famous water, for river it is not, of Bannock Bourn,[7] famous in the Scots history for the great battle fought here between King Robert de Bruce and the English Army, commanded by King Edward II in person, in which the English were utterly overthrown; and that with so terrible a slaughter, that of the greatest army that ever marched from England into Scotland, very few escaped; and King Edward II with much ado, saved himself by flight. How, indeed, he should save himself by a little boat, (as Mr Cambden says) that, indeed, I cannot understand, there being no river near that had any boats in it but the Forth, and that had been to make the king fly north; whereas, to be sure, he fled for England with all the speed he could; he might, perhaps, make use of a boat to pass the Tweed; but that was at least thirty or forty miles off.

Sterling was our next stage, an ancient city, or town rather, and an important pass, which, with Dumbarton, is indeed the defence of the Lowlands against the Highlands; and, as one very knowingly said, Dunbarton is the lock of the Highlands, and Sterling-Castle keeps the key. The town is situated as like Edinburgh as almost can be described, being on the ridge of a hill, sloping down on both sides, and the street ascending from the east gradually to the castle, which is at the west end; the street is large and well built, but ancient, and the buildings not unlike Edinburgh, either for beauty or sight.

The church is also a very spacious building, but not collegiate; there was formerly a church, or rather chapel, in the castle, but it is now out of use; also a private chapel, or oratory in the palace, for the royal family. But all that is now laid aside too.

The castle is not so very difficult of access as Edinburgh; but it is esteemed equally strong, and particularly the works are capable to mount more cannon, and these cannon are better pointed; particularly there is a battery which commands, or may command the bridge; the command of which is of the utmost importance; nay, it is the main end and purpose for which, as we are told, the castle was built.

They who built the castle, without doubt built it, as the Scots express it, to continue aye, and till somebody else should build another there, which, in our language, would be for ever and a day after. The walls, and all the outer works are firm, and if no force is used to demolish them, may continue inconceivably long, at least we have reason to believe they will; for though the other buildings grow old, the castle seems as firm and fair, as if it had been but lately built.

The park here is large and walled about, as all the parks in Scotland are, but little or no wood in it. The Earl of Mar,[8] who claims to be hereditary keeper of the king's children, as also hereditary keeper of the castle, has a house at the upper end of the town, and very finely situated for prospect, but I cannot say it is so for any thing else, for it is too near the castle; and was the castle ever to suffer a close siege, and be vigorously defended, that house would run great risks of being demolished on one side or other; it stands too near the castle also for the site of it to be agreeable.

As this little, but very pleasant spot, was on the north side of the castle, we had from thence a most agreeable prospect indeed over the valley and the river; as it is truly beautiful, so it is what the people of Sterling justly boast of, and, indeed seldom forget it, I mean the meanders, or reaches of the River Forth. They are so spacious, and return so near themselves, with so regular and exactly a sweep, that, I think, the like is not to be seen in Britain, if it is in Europe, especially where the river is so large also. It is an admirable sight indeed, and continues from a little below the great bridge at Sterling to Alloway, the seat of the present, or rather late Earl of Marr, the present Earl being attainted for treason, and so dead, as a peer or earl, though alive in exile. The form of this winding may be conceived of a little by the length of the way, for it is near twenty miles from Sterling to Alloway by water, and hardly four miles by land. One would think these large sweeps, or windings of the stream, should check the tide very much. But, on the contrary, we found the tide of flood made up very strong under Sterling-bridge, even as strong almost as at London-bridge, but does not flow above seven or eight miles farther: the stream of the river growing narrow apace, and the rapid current of all rivers in that country checking the tide, when it comes into narrow limits.

I was, indeed, curious to enquire into the course of this river, as I had been before into that of the Clyde as to the possibility of their waters being united for an inland navigation; because I had observed that the charts and plans of the country brought them almost to meet; but when I came more critically to survey the ground, I found the map-makers greatly mistaken, and that they had not only given the situation and courses of the rivers wrong, but the distances also. However, upon the whole, I brought it to this; that notwithstanding several circumstances which might obstruct it, and cause the workmen to fetch some winding turns out of the way, yet, that in the whole, a canal of about eight miles in length would fairly join the rivers, and make a clear navigation from the Irish to the German Sea; and that this would be done without any considerable obstruction; so that there would not need above four sluices in the whole way, and those only to head a basin, or receptacle, to contain a flash, or flush of water to push on the vessels this way or that, as occasion required, not to stop them to raise or let fall, as in the case of locks in other rivers.

How easy then such a work would be, and how advantageous, not to Scotland only, but even to Ireland and England also, I need not explain, the nature of the thing will explain itself. I could enter upon particular descriptions of the work, and answer the objections raised from the great excess of waters in these streams in the winter, and the force and fury of their streams. But 'tis needless, nor have we room for such a work here; besides, all those who are acquainted with such undertakings, know that artificial canals are carefully secured from any communication with other waters, except just as their own occasion for the navigating part demands; and that they are so ordered, as to be always in a condition to take in what water they want, and cast off what would be troublesome to them, by proper channels and sluices made for that purpose.

Those gentlemen who have seen the royal canal in Languedoc from Narbon to Thoulouse, as many in Scotland have, will be able to support what I say in this case, and to understand how easily the same thing is to be practised here; but I leave it to time, and the fate of Scotland, which, I am persuaded, will one time or other bring it to pass.

There is a very considerable manufacture at Sterling, for what they call Sterling serges, which are in English, shalloons; and they both make them and dye them there very well; nor has the English manufacture of shalloons broke in so much upon them by the late Union, as it was feared they would. This manufacture employs the poor very comfortably here, and is a great part of the support of the town as to trade, showing what Scotland might soon be brought to by the help of trade and manufactures; for the people are as willing to work here as in England, if they had the same encouragement, that is, if they could be constantly employed and paid for it too, as they are there. The family of Ereskin is very considerable here; and besides the Earl of Marr and the Earl of Buchan,[9] who are both of that name, there are several gentlemen of quality of the same name.

We had here a very fine prospect both east and west; eastward we could plainly see the castle of Edinburgh, and the hill called Arthur's Seat, in the Royal Park at Haly-Rood House, also the opening firth presents all the way from Alloway to the Queens-Ferry, mentioned above. North we could see Dumfermling, and the field of battle, called Sherriff-muir, between it and Sterling; and some told as we might see Dumbarton castle west; but it was hazy that way, so that we could not see it, the prospect south is confined by the hills.

But our business was not to the north yet; still having a part of the border to view, that we might leave nothing behind us to oblige us to come this way again. So we went from Sterling, first east and then south-east, over some of the same hills, which we passed at our coming hither, though not by the same road.

From Sterling, as I said, we came away [east], and went directly to Lithgow, or Linlithgow, and from thence to Clydsdale, that is to say, the country upon the banks of the Clyde. Lithgow is a large town, well built, and anciently famous for the noble palace of the kings of Scotland, where King James VI and his queen kept their Court in great magnificence. This Court, though decaying with the rest, is yet less decayed, because much later repaired than others; for King James repaired, or rather rebuilt some of it. Here it was that the good Lord Murray,[10] the Regent, who they called good, because he was really so, as he was riding through the town into the palace, was shot most villainously from a window, and the murtherer was discovered. He died of the wound with the utmost tranquillity and resignation, after having had the satisfaction of being the principal man in settling the Reformation in Scotland in such a manner, as it was not possible for the Popish party to recover themselves again; and after seeing the common people over the whole kingdom embrace the Reformation, almost universally, to his great joy, for he was the most zealous of all the nobility in the cause of the Reformation, and unalterably resolved never to give way to the least allowance to the Popish Court, who then began to crave only a toleration for themselves, but could never obtain it; for this reason the Papists mortally hated him, and, at length, murthered him. But they got little by his death, for the reformers went on with the same zeal, and never left, till they had entirely driven Queen Mary, and all her Popish adherents out of the kingdom, yet we do not find the true murtherer was ever discovered. But this is matter of history.

At Lithgow there is a very great linen manufacture, as there is at Glasgow; and the water of the lough, or lake here, is esteemed with the best in Scotland for bleaching or whitening of linen cloth : so that a great deal of linen made in other parts of the country, is brought either to be bleached or whitened.

Here the kings of Scotland, for some ages, kept their Courts on occasion of any extraordinary ceremony. And here King James V reinstituted, or rather restored the Order of the Knights of St Andrew, as the Order of Knights of the Bath were lately restored in England. Here he erected stalls, and a throne for them in St Michael's Church, and made it the Chapel of the Order, according to the usage at Windsor. Also he first ordered the Thistle to be added to the badge of the Order; and the motto, which since is worn about it in the royal arms, was of his invention (viz.) *Nemo me impune lacessit*. The Cordon Verd, or Green Ribband, was then worn by the Knights Companions: but the late King James II or (as I should say, being in Scotland) the VIIth, changed it to the Blue Ribband, as the Knights of the Garter wear it in England.

Lithgow is a pleasant, handsome, well built town; the Tolbooth is a good building, and not old, kept in good repair, and the streets clean. The people look here as if they were busy, and had something to do, whereas in many towns we passed through they seemed as if they looked disconsolate for want of employment. The whole green, fronting the lough or lake, was covered with linen-cloth, it being the bleaching season, and, I believe, a thousand women and children, and not less, tending and managing the bleaching business; the town is served with water by one very large basin, or fountain, to which the water is brought from the same spring which served the Royal Palace.

From Lithgow we turned to the right, as I said above, into the shire of Clydesdale. Some business also calling us this way, and following the Clyde upwards, from a little above Hamilton, where we were before, we came to Lanerk, which is about eight miles from it due south.

From Lithgow, by this way to Lanerk, is thirty long miles; and some of the road over the wildest country we had yet seen. Lanerk is the capital indeed of the country, otherwise it is but a very indifferent place; it is eminent for the assembling of the Bothwell-Bridge Rebellion,[11] and several other little disturbances of the Whigs in those days; for Whigs then were all Presbyterians, and Cameronian Presbyterians too, which, at that time, was as much as to say rebels.

A little below Lanerk the River Douglass falls into the Clyde, giving the same kind of usual surname to the lands about it, as I have observed other rivers do, namely Douglassdale. In this dull vale stands the ancient, paternal estate and castle, which gives name (and title too) to the great family of Douglass. The castle is very ill adapted to the glory of the family; but as it is the ancient inheritance, the heads or chief of the name have always endeavoured to keep up the old mansion, and have consequently, made frequent additions to the building, which have made it a wild, irregular mass; yet there are noble apartments in it, and the house seems, at a distance, rather a little town than one whole fabric. The park is very large; the garden, or yards, as they call them, not set out with fine plants or greens, or divided into flower-gardens, parters, wildernesses, kitchen-gardens, &c. as is the modern usage. In short 'tis an ancient, magnificent pile, great, but not gay; its grandeur, in most parts, consists in its antiquity, and being the mansion of one of the greatest families in Scotland above 1,000 years.

From Lanerk we left the wild place called Crawford Muir on the right, the business that brought us round this way being finished, and went away west into the shire of Peebles, and so into Tweedale; the first town we came to of any note upon the Tweed, is the town of Peebles, capital of the country. The town is small, and but indifferently built or inhabited, yet the High Street has some good houses on it. There is a handsome stone-bridge over the Tweed, which is not a great river here, though the current is sometimes indeed very violent.

The country is hilly, as in the rest of Tweedale, and those hills covered with sheep, which is, indeed, a principal part of the estates of the gentlemen; and the overplus quantity of the sheep, as also their wool, is mostly sent to England, to the irreparable damage of the poor; who, were they employed to manufacture their own wool, would live much better than they do, and find the benefit of the Union in a different manner, from what they have yet done.

Before the Union this wool, and more with it, brought by stealth out of England, went all away to France, still (as I say) to the great loss of the poor, who, had they but spun it into yarn, and sent the yarn into France, would have had some benefit by it; but the Union bringing with it a prohibition of the exportation, upon the severest penalties, the gentlemen of the southern countries complained of the loss, at the time that affair was transacted in parliament; to make them amends for which, a large sum of money was appointed to them as an equivalent, and to encourage them to set the poor to work, as appears by the Act of Union; this money, I say, was appropriated by the Act to be employed in setting hands to work in Scotland, to manufacture their own wool by their own people. How much of the money has been so employed, I desire not to examine. I leave it to them whose proper business it is.

Here we saw the ruins of the once famous Abbey of Mailross, the greatness of which may be a little judged of by its vastly extended remains, which are of a very great circuit. The building is not so entirely demolished but that we may distinguish many places and parts of it one from another; as particularly the great church or chapel of the monastery, which is as large as some cathedrals, the choir of which is visible, and measures 140 foot in length, besides what may have been pulled down at the east end; by the thickness of the foundations there must have been a large and strong tower or steeple in the centre of the church, but of what form or height, that no guess can be made at. There are several fragments of the house itself, and of the particular offices belonging to it; the court, the cloister, and other buildings are so visible, as that 'tis easy to know it was a most magnificent place in those days. But the Reformation has triumphed over all these things, and the pomp and glory of Popery is sunk now into the primitive simplicity of the true Christian profession; nor can any Protestant mourn the loss of these seminaries of superstition, upon any principles that agree, either with his own profession, or with the Christian pattern prescribed in the scriptures. So I leave Mailross with a singular satisfaction, at seeing what it now is, much more than that of remembering what it once was.

Following the course of the Tweed, we passed by abundance of gentlemen's seats and ancient mansions, whose possessions are large in this country. The country next this, south east, is called Tiviotdale, or otherwise the shire of Roxburgh; and the Duke of Roxburgh [12] has several fine seats in it, as well as a very great estate; indeed most of the country belongs to the family. His house called Floors is an ancient seat, but begins to wear a new face; and those who viewed it fifteen or sixteen years ago, will scarce know it again, if they should come a few years hence, when the present Duke may have finished the additions and embellishments, which he is now making, and has been a considerable time upon. Nor will the very face of the country appear the same, except it be that the River Tweed may, perhaps, run in the same channel. But the land before, lying open and wild, he will find enclosed, cultivated and improved, rows, and even woods of trees covering the champaign country, and the house surrounded with large grown vistas, and well planted avenues, such as were never seen there before.

From hence we came to Kelsoe, a handsome market-town upon the bank of the Tweed. Here is a very large ancient church, being built in the place of an old monastery of friars, the ruins of which are yet to be seen. Kelsoe, as it stands on the Tweed, and so near the English border, is a considerable thorough-fare to England, one of the great roads from Edinburgh to Newcastle lying through this town, and a nearer way by far than the road through Berwick. They only want a good bridge over the Tweed: at present they have a ferry just at the town, and a good ford through the river, a little below it; but, though I call it a good ford, and so it is when the water is low, yet that is too uncertain; and the Tweed is so dangerous a river, and rises sometimes so suddenly, that a man scarce knows, when he goes into the water, how it shall be ere he gets out at the other side; and it is not very strange to them at Kelso, to hear of frequent disasters, in the passage, both to men and cattle.

Here we made a little excursion into England, and it was to satisfy a curiosity of no extraordinary kind neither. By the sight of Cheviot Hills, which we had seen for many miles riding, we thought at Kelso we were very near them, and had a great mind to take as near a view of them as we could; and taking with us an English man, who had been very curious in the same enquiry, and who offered to be our guide, we set out for Wooller, a little town lying, as it were, under the hill.

Cheviot Hill or Hills are justly esteemed the highest in this part of England, and of Scotland also; if I may judge I think 'tis higher a great deal than the mountain of Mairock in Galloway, which they say is two miles high.

When we came to Wooller we got another guide to lead us to the top of the hill; for, by the way, though there are many hills and reachings for many miles, which are all called Cheviot Hills, yet there is one Pico or Master-Hill, higher than all the rest by a great deal, which, at a distance, looks like the Pico-Teneriffe at the Canaries, and is so high, that I remember it is seen plainly from the Rosemary-Top in the East Riding of Yorkshire, which is nearly sixty miles. We prepared to clamber up this hill on foot, but our guide laughed at us, and told us, we should make a long journey of it that way. But getting a horse himself, told us he would find a way for us to get up on horse-back; so we set out, having five or six country boys and young fellows, who ran on foot, volunteer to go with us; we thought they had only gone for their diversion, as is frequent for boys; but they knew well enough that we should find some occasion to employ them, and so we did, as you shall hear.

Our guide led us very artfully round to a part of the hill, where it was evident in the winter season, not streams of water, but great rivers came pouring down from the hill in several channels, and those (at least some of them) very broad; they were overgrown on either bank with alder-trees, so close and thick, that we rode under them, as in an arbour. In one of these channels we mounted the hill, as the besiegers approach a fortified town by trenches, and were gotten a great way up, before we were well aware of it.

But, as we mounted, these channels lessened gradually, till at length we had the shelter of the trees no longer; and now we ascended till we began to see some of the high hills, which before we thought very lofty, lying under us, low and humble, as if they were part of the plain below, and yet the main hill seemed still to be but beginning, or, as if we were but entering upon it.

As we mounted higher we found the hill steeper than at

first, also our horses began to complain, and draw their haunches up heavily, so we went very softly. However, we moved still, and went on, till the height began to look really frightful, for, I must own, I wished myself down again; and now we found use for the young fellows that ran before us; for we began to fear, if our horses should stumble or start, we might roll down the hill together; and we began to talk of alighting, but our guide called out and said, No, not yet, by and by you shall; and with that he bid the young fellows take our horses by the head-stalls of the bridles, and lead them. They did so, and we rode up higher still, till at length our hearts failed us all together, and we resolved to alight; and though our guide mocked us, yet he could not prevail or persuade us; so we worked it upon our feet, and with labour enough, and sometimes began to talk of going no farther.

We were the more uneasy about mounting higher, because we all had a notion, that when we came to the top, we should be just as upon a pinnacle, that the hill narrowed to a point, and we should have only room enough to stand, with a precipice every way round us; and with these apprehensions, we all sat down upon the ground, and said we would go no farther. Our guide did not at first understand what we were apprehensive of; but at last by our discourse he perceived the mistake, and then not mocking our fears, he told us, that indeed if it had been so, we had been in the right, but he assured us, there was room enough on the top of the hill to run a race, if we thought fit, and we need not fear any thing of being blown off the precipice, as we had suggested; so he encouraging us we went on, and reached the top of the hill in about half an hour more.

I must acknowledge I was agreeably surprised, when coming to the top of the hill, I saw before me a smooth, and with respect to what we expected a most pleasant plain, of at least half a mile in diameter; and in the middle of it a large pond, or little lake of water, and the ground seeming to descend every way from the edges of the summit to the pond, took off the little terror of the first prospect; for when we walked towards the pond, we could but just see over the edge of the hill; and this little descent inwards, no doubt made the pond, the rain-water all running thither.

The day happened to be very clear, and to our great satisfaction very calm, otherwise the height we were upon, would not have been without its dangers. We saw plainly here the smoke of the salt-pans at Shields, at the mouth of the Tyne, seven miles below New Castle; and which was south about forty miles. The sea, that is the German ocean, was as if but just at the foot of the hill, and our guide pointed to show us the Irish sea. But if he could see it, knowing it in particular, and where exactly to look for it, it was so distant, that I could not say, I was assured I saw it. We saw likewise several hills, which he told us were in England, and others in the west of Scotland, but their names were too many for us to remember, and we had no materials there to take minutes. We saw Berwick east, and the hills called Soutra Hills north, which are in sight of Edinburgh. In a word there was a surprising view of both the united kingdoms, and we were far from repenting the pains we had taken.

Nor were we so afraid now as when we first mounted the sides of the hill, and especially we were made ashamed of those fears, when to our amazement, we saw a clergy-man, and another gentleman, and two ladies, all on horse-back, come up to the top of the hill, with a guide also as we had, and without alighting at all, and only to satisfy their curiosity, which they did it seems. This indeed made us look upon one another with a smile, to think how we were frighted, at our first coming up the hill. And thus it is in most things in nature; fear magnifies the object, and represents things frightful at first sight, which are presently made easy when they grow familiar.

Satisfied with this view, and not at all thinking our time or pains ill bestowed, we came down the hill by the same route that we went up; with this remark by the way, that whether on horseback or on foot we found it much more troublesome, and also tiresome to come down than to go up.

When we were down, our guide carried us not to the town of Wooller, where we were before, but to a single house, which they call Wooller Haugh-head, and is a very good inn, better indeed than we expected. Here we enquired after the famous story of Cheviot-Chase,[13] which we found the people there have a true notion of, not like what is represented in the ballad of Chevy Chase, which has turned the whole story into a fable. But here they told us, what all solid histories confirm, namely that it was an in-road of the Earl of Douglass into England, with a body of an army, to ravage, burn, and plunder the country, as was usual in those days; and that the Earl of Northumberland, who was then a Piercy, gathering his forces, marched with a like army, and a great many of the gentry and nobility with him, to meet the Scots; and that both the bodies meeting at the foot of Cheviot Hills, fought a bloody battle, wherein both the earls were slain, fighting desperately at the head of their troops; and so many killed on both sides, that they that out-lived it, went off respectively, neither being able to say which had victory.

They showed us the place of the fight, which was on the side of the hill, if their traditions do not mislead them, on the left hand of the road, the ground uneven and ill enough for the cavalry; 'tis supposed most of the Scots were horse, and therefore 'tis said, the English archers placed themselves on the side of a steep ascent, that they might not be broken in upon by the horse. They show also two stones which, if *as I say* they are not mistaken, are on the ground where the two earls were slain.

But they showed us the same day, a much more famous field of battle than this, and that within about six or seven miles of the same place, namely Floden-field,[14] where James IV King of Scotland with a great army invading England, in the year 1538, when the King of England was absent in his wars abroad, at the Siege of Tournay, was met with, and fought by the Earl of Surrey, of the ancient family of Howard, and the English army; in which the Scots, though after a very obstinate fight, were totally routed and overthrown, and their king valiantly fighting at the head of his nobility was slain.

Having viewed these things, which we had not time for in our passing through Northumberland, we came back to Kelso, and spent the piece of a day that remained there, viewing the country, which is very pleasant and very fruitful on both sides the Tweed, for the Tweed there does not part England from Scotland, but you are upon Scots ground for four miles, or thereabouts, on the south side of the Tweed, and the farther west the more the Tweed lies within the limits of the country.

From Kelso we went north, where we passed through Lauderdale. The country is good here, though fenced with hills on both sides; the River Lauder runs in the middle of it, keeping its course north, and the family-seat of Lauder, stands about the middle of the valley. From hence we kept the great road over a high ridge of mountains, from whence we had a plain view of that part of the country called Mid-Lothian, and where we also saw the city of Edinburgh at the distance of about twelve or fourteen miles. We passed these mountains at a place which they call Soutra-Hill, and which gives the title of Laird of Soutra to a branch of the family of Maitland.

I could not pass this way to Edinburgh without going off a little to the right, to see two very fine seats, one belonging to the Marquess of Louthian,[15] at Newbattle or Newbottle. 'Tis an old building, but finely situated among the most agreeable walks and rows of trees, all full grown, and is particularly to be mentioned for the nicest, and best chosen collection of pictures of any house I have seen in Scotland. Not two miles from hence is the Duchess of Bucclugh's [16] house at Dalkeith, the finest and largest new built house in Scotland; the Duchess, relict of the late Duke of Monmouth, has built it, as I may say, from the foundation, or as some say, upon the foundation of the old castle of Dalkeith, which was the estate of the great Earl of Morton,[17] Regent of Scotland, who was beheaded by King James VI that is, of England, James I, the same that brought the engine to behead human bodies from

Hallifax in Yorkshire, and set it up in Scotland, and had his own head cut off with it, the first it was tried upon. The palace of Dalkeith is, indeed, a magnificent building, and the inside answerable to the grandeur of the family. The park is very large, and there are fine avenues, some already made and planted, others designed, but not yet finished; also there are to be water-works, *Jette D'eaus*, and a canal, but these are not yet laid out; nor are the gardens finished, or the terraces, which will be very spacious, if done according to the design.

The town of Dalkeith is just without the park, and is a pretty large market-town, and the better market for being so near Edinburgh; for there comes great quantities of provisions hither from the southern countries, which are bought up here to be carried to Edinburgh market again, and sold there. The town is spacious, and well built, and is the better, no doubt, for the neighbourhood of so many noblemen's and gentlemen's houses of such eminence in its neighbourhood.

This brought us to the very sight of the city of Edinburgh, where we rested a few days, having thus finished our circuit over the whole south of Scotland, on this side of the River Forth, and on the south side of the Firth of Clyde. So I shall conclude this letter,

And am, &c.

Letter 13

Containing a description of the North of Scotland

SIR, – I am now to enter the true and real Caledonia, for the country on the north of the firth is alone called by that name, and was anciently known by no other. I went over the firth at the Queens-Ferry, a place mentioned before, seven miles west of Edinburgh; and, as he that gives an account of the country of Fife, must necessarily go round the coast, the most considerable places being to be seen on the sea-side, or near it; so I took that method, and began at the Queens-Ferry. A mile from hence, or something more, is the borough of Innerkeithin, an ancient walled town, with a spacious harbour, opening from the east part of the town into the Firth of Forth; the mouth of the harbour has a good depth of water, and ships of burthen may ride there with safety; but as there is not any great trade here, and consequently no use for shipping of burthen, the harbour has been much neglected. However, small vessels may come up to the quay, such as are sufficient for their business.

The town is large, and is still populous, but decayed, as to what it has formerly been; yet the market for linen not only remains, but is rather more considerable than formerly, by reason of the increase of that manufacture since the Union. The market for provisions is also very considerable here, the country round being very fruitful, and the families of gentlemen being also numerous in the neighbourhood.

Near Innerkeithin, a little within the land, stands the ancient town of Dumfermling, as I may say, in my Lord Rochester's words, in its full perfection of decay;[1] nay, the decay is threefold.

1. There is a decayed monastery, for before the Reformation here was a very large and famous abbey, but demolished at the Revolution; and saving, that part of the church was

turned into a parochial church, the rest, and greatest part of that also lies in ruins, and with it the monuments of several kings and queens of Scotland.

2. Here is a decayed court or royal palace of the kings of Scotland. They do not tell us who built this palace, but we may tell them who suffers it to fall down; for it is now (as it was observed before all the royal houses are) sinking into its own ruins; the windows are gone, the roof fallen in, and part of the very walls mouldered away by the injury of time, and of the times. In this palace almost all King James the VIth's [2] children were born; as particularly King Charles I, and the Princess Elizabeth, afterwards Queen of Bohemia; and their mother, which was Queen Ann daughter of the Queen of Denmark, made this place her particular residence. The figure of the house remains, but as for the lodgings they are all, as I have said, in their decay, and we may now call it the monument of a court.

3. Here is a decayed town, and we need go no further for that part than the decay of the palace, which is irrecoverable; there might be something said here of what was done at this town, upon receiving the crowning King Charles II, by the Covenanters, &c. But this is matter of history, and besides, it seems to have something in it that is not, perhaps so well to be remembered as to be forgot.

The church has still a venerable face, and at a distance seems a mighty pile; the building being once vastly large, what is left appears too gross for the present dimensions.

The people hereabout are poor, but would be much poorer, if they had not the manufacture of linen for their support, which is here, and in most of the towns about, carried on with more hands than ordinary, especially for diaper, and the better sort of linen.

From hence, turning east, we see many seats of private gentlemen, and some of noblemen, as particularly one belonging to the said Marquess of Tweedale [3] at Aberdour. The house is old, but magnificent, and the lands about it, as all must do, that come into the managing hands of the family of

Tweedale, have been infinitely improved by planting and enclosing.

This house of Aberdour fronts the firth to the south, and the grounds belonging to it reach down to the shores of it. From this part of the firth, to the mouth of Innerkeithen harbour, is a very good road for ships, the water being deep and the ground good; but the western part, which they call St Margaret's Bay, is a steep shore, and rocky, there being twenty fathom water within a ship's length of the rocks. So that in case of a south east wind, and if it blow hard, it may be dangerous riding too near. But a south east wind blows so seldom, that the ships often venture it; and I have seen large ships ride there.

He that will view the country of Fife must, as I said before, go round the coast; and yet there are four or five places of note in the middle of the country which are superior to all the rest. And here, since I am upon generals, it may not be improper to mention, as a remark only, that however mean our thoughts in England have been of the Scots Court in those times, the kings of Scotland had more fine palaces than most princes in Europe, and, in particular, many more than the Crown of England has now; for example, we see nothing in England now of any notice but Hampton-Court, Windsor, Kensington, and St James's.

Whereas the kings of Scotland had in King James the VIth's time all in good repair, and in use, the several royal palaces of

Haly-Rood House,
The castle, } at Edinburgh.
The royal palace in the castle at Sterling.
Linlithgow.
Dumfermling.
Falkland.
Scoon.

Having seen Aberdour, I took a turn, at a friend's invitation, to Lessly; but by the way stopped at Kinross, where we had a view of two things worth noting. The famous lake or lough, called Lough Leven, where, in an island, stands the old castle where Queen Mary, commonly known in England by the name of Queen of Scots, was confined by the first reformers, after she had quitted, or been forced to quit her favourite Bothwel, and put herself into the hands of her subjects. One would have thought this castle, standing as it were in the middle of the sea, for so it is in its kind, should have been sufficient to have held her, but she made shift to get out of their hands, whether by a silver key, or without a key, I believe is not fully known to this day.

At the west end of the lake, and the gardens reaching down to the very water's edge, stands the most beautiful and regular piece of architecture, (for a private gentleman's seat) in all Scotland, perhaps, in all Britain, I mean the house of Kinross. The town lies at a little distance from it, so as not to annoy the house, and yet so as to make it the more sociable; and at the town is a very good market, and the street tolerably well built.

The house is a picture, 'tis all beauty; the stone is white and fine, the order regular, the contrivance elegant, the workmanship exquisite. Sir William Bruce,[4] the skilful builder, was the Surveyor-General of the Works, as we call it in England, or the Royal Architect, as in Scotland. In a word, he was the Kit Wren of North Britain; and his skill in the perfect decoration of building, has many testimonials left upon record for it. Sir William, according to the new and laudable method of all Scots gentlemen, has planted innumerable numbers of fir-trees upon the estate round his house, and the present possessor Mr Bruce, is as careful to improve as his predecessor. Posterity will find the sweet of this passion for planting, which is so happily spread among the people of the south-parts of Scotland, and which, if it goes on, will in time make Scotland a second Norway for fir; for the Lowlands, as well as the Highlands, will be overspread with timber.

From Kinross, I came to Lessley, where I had a full view of the palace of Rothess, both inside and outside, as I had before of that of Bruce. The magnificence of the inside at Lessly is unusually great; but what is very particular, is the long gallery, which is the full length of one side of the building, and is filled with paintings, but especially (as at Drumlanrig) of the great ancestors of the house of Rothes or Lessly at full lengths, and in their robes of office or habits of ceremony; particularly the late Duke of Rothess,[5] who built the house, and who was Lord High Chancellor of Scotland. The town of Lessly is at a small distance west from the house or a little north-west. There is a good market, but otherwise it is not considerable. The house is the glory of the place, and indeed of the whole province of Fife.

From Lessly, we turned away south to the coast, and came to Bruntisland; this is a port upon the Firth of Forth, and lies opposite to Leith, so that there is a fair prospect as well of the road of Leith, and the ships riding there, as of the city and castle of Edinburgh. There is a very good harbour which enters as if it has been made by hand into the centre of the town; for the town is as it were built round it, and the ships lay their broad sides to the very houses. There is water enough at spring-tides, for ships of good burthen to come into the basin; but at low-water some of the ships lie a-ground. But want of trade renders all this useless; for what is the best harbour in the world without ships? And whence should ships be expected without a commerce to employ them; it is true, the ships of several other towns on the coast frequently put into this harbour, to lay up, as we call it, and to lie by in the winter. But this does not so much better the town as to make it be called a trading town; so that, indeed, the place is unhappy, and must decay yet farther, unless the trade revive, which, I confess, I do not yet foresee.

Here is, however, a manufacture of linen, as there is upon all the coast of Fife, and especially for that they call green-cloth, which is now in great demand in England for the printing-trade, in the room of calicoes, which were lately prohibited.

Next to this is Kinghorn upon the same coast, where, not the sea, but the manufacture upon land may be said to maintain the place; for here is a thread manufacture, which they make very good, and bleach or whiten it themselves. The women, indeed, chiefly carry on this trade, and the men are generally seamen upon all this coast, as high as the Queens-Ferry. Where I observed the men carried on an odd kind of trade, or sport rather (viz.) of shooting of porpoises, of which very great numbers are seen almost constantly in the firth; when they catch them thus, they bring them on shore, and boil the fat of them as they do of whales, into train-oil, and the like they do with several other great fish, which sometimes they find in the sea there; and sometimes they have grampusses, finn fish, and several species of the small whale kind which come up there, and which they always make the best of, if they can take them. One year in particular there came several such fish on shore, which they could find no name for; there was eight or nine of them, which I saw lying on the shore of Fife, from Kinghorn to the Easter Weems, some of which were twenty foot long and upward.

But this sort of fishing is but by accident, and the profit's not certain; the firth affords a much more certain and profitable fishery lower down, of which in its place. The ferry, from Leith to the shore of Fife, is fixed in this town, though sometimes the boats in distress, and by force of wind and weather, are driven to run into Borunt Island. This constant going and coming of the ferry-boat, and passengers, is also a considerable benefit to the town of Kinghorn, and is a very great article in its commerce.

East of this town is Kirkcaldy, a larger, more populous, and better built town than the other, and indeed than any on this coast. Its situation is in length, in one street running along the shore, from east to west, for a long mile, and very well built, the streets clean and well paved; there are some small by streets or lanes, and it has some considerable merchants in it, I mean in the true sense of the word merchant. There are also several good ships belonging to the town. Also as Fife is a good corn country, here are some that deal very largely in corn, and export great quantities both to England and Holland. Here are great quantities of linen shipped off for

England; and as these ships return freighted either from England or Holland, they bring all needful supplies of foreign goods; so that the traders in Kirkcaldy have really a very considerable traffic, both at home and abroad.

There are several coal-pits here, not only in the neighbourhood, but even close to the very sea, at the west end of the town, and where, one would think, the tide should make it impossible to work them. At the east end of the town is a convenient yard for building and repairing of ships, and farther east than that several salt-pans for the boiling and making of salt.

Dysert is next, a town in the full perfection of decay, and is, indeed, a most lamentable object of a miserable, dying corporation; the only support which, I think, preserves the name of a town to it, is, that here is, in the lands adjoining, an excellent vein of Scots coal, and the Lord Dysert,[6] the landlord, has a good salt-work in the town; close to the sea there is a small pier or wharf for ships, to come and load both the salt and the coal. And this, I think, may be said to be the whole trade of the town, except some nailers and hardware workers, and they are but few.

I take the decay of all these sea-port towns, which 'tis evident have made a much better figure in former times, to be owing to the removing of the court and nobility of Scotland to England; for it is most certain, when the court was at home, they had a confluence of strangers, residence of foreign ministers, being of armies, &c. and consequently the nobility dwelt at home, spent the income of their estates, and the product of their country among their neighbours. The return of their coal and salt, and corn and fish, brought them in goods from abroad and, perhaps, money; they sent their linen and other goods to England, and received the returns in money; they made their own manufactures, and though not so good and cheap as from England, yet they were cheaper to the public stock, because their own poor were employed. Their wool, which they had over and above, went to France, and returned ready money. Their lead went to Holland, and their cattle and sheep to England, and brought back in that one article above 100,000*l.* sterling *per ann.*

Then it was the sea-port towns had a trade, their Court was magnificent, their nobility built fine houses and palaces which were richly furnished, and nobly finished within and without. They had infinitely more value went out than came back in goods, and therefore the balance was evidently on their side; whereas, now their Court is gone, their nobility and gentry spend their time, and consequently their estates in England; the Union opens the door to all English manufactures, and suppresses their own, prohibits their wool going abroad, and yet scarcely takes it off at home; if the cattle goes to England, the money is spent there too. The troops raised there are in English service, and Scotland receives no *premio* for the levies, as she might have done abroad, and as the Swiss and other nations do at this time.

It is true, Scotland would have an advantageous trade with England, and not the worst for the Union, were not the Court removed, and did not their nobility dwell abroad, and spend their estates abroad. Scotland has a plentiful product for exportation, and were the issue of that product returned and consumed at home, Scotland would flourish and grow rich, but as it is, I may venture to say, it is not to be expected.

All the product of Scotland which is sent abroad, and exported to foreign countries, and consumed there, is so much clear gain to the public stock, excepting only the cost of its manufacturing at home, or curing and sending out; and except so much as is brought back in goods of the growth, and manufacture of foreign countries, and is consumed in Scotland, which is not reckoned as gain, because consumed; if it is exported again, the article goes to the account of public gain again. Now to state the case briefly between the exportation and importation of goods in Scotland, that the difference, which is the balance of the trade, may appear.

The product of Scotland, which it exports into foreign countries, England included, for I am now considering Scotland as if not united, is as follows.

Corn Black Cattle Sheep Wool, Linen of several sorts Some woollen manufactures, stockings in particular.	All these carried to England, and that in great quantities.
Corn Lead Salt Coal Barrelled pork Salmon.	To Holland, Bremen, and Hambrough.
Salt Oatmeal Salmon Lead Stockings Linen.	To Norway.
Salt Woollen manufactures of Sterling and Aberdeen.	To Sweden, Dantzick, and to Riga, &c.
Herrings pickled. Barrelled and dried salmon. Herring and white fish.	To Spain and the Straits.
Coal Salt Lead Herrings White fish Wool.	To France.

For all these exportations the returns are, or at least were before the Union:

Pewter Block-tin Wrought iron Glass ware Sugars Tobacco Drugs and dyers' stuffs.	From England.

N.B. All the English woollen and silk manufactures were prohibited upon the several penalties; so that the returns from England, in goods, were very small; the grand return from thence was in specie. And 'tis known, that above an hundred thousand pounds a year was paid into Scotland every year, for cattle only.

Fine linens, not much, because of their own Lace and fine threads, gimp, incle, &c. East-India goods Linseed, and lint or flax Linseed-oil, train-oil, and whalebone.	From Holland.
Pitch and tar Deals and fir-timber	From Norway.
Iron in bars and copper Deals and timber.	From Sweden
Plank, called east country Clap-board, or wainscot Oak timber, and in quarters. Hemp Pitch Tar Turpentine Sturgeon Flax.	From Dantzick, Koningsberg, Riga, Narva, and Petersburg.

Wine Brandy Apples (rennets) Rosin Cork Paper Wrought silks Raw silk Toys Perfumes, &c.	From France.
Oil and Italian pickles from Leghorn, by way of	The Royal Canal through France.
Staves for casks Clap-board Rhenish wine Old hock.	From Hamburgh.

And all these put together, if I am rightly informed, do not balance the lead, coal, and salt, which they export every year. So that the balance of trade must stand greatly to the credit of the account in the Scots commerce. And what then, would not such an annual wealth in specie do for Scotland in a year, if there was not a gulf, into which it all runs as into a sink?

I know this is abundantly answered, by saying that Scotland is now established in a lasting tranquillity; the wars between the nations are at an end, the wastings and plunderings, the ravages and blood are all over; the lands in Scotland will now be improved, their estates doubled, the charges of defending her abroad and at home lies upon England; the taxes are easy and ascertained, and the West-India trade abundantly pours in wealth upon her; and this is all true; and, in the end, I am still of opinion Scotland will be gainer. But I must add, that her own nobility, would they be true patriots, should then put their helping hand to the rising advantages of their own country, and spend some of the large sums they get in England in applying to the improvement of their country, erecting manufactures, employing the poor, and propagating the trade at home, which they may see plainly has made their united neighbours of England so rich.

Why might not wool, which they send to England, be manufactured in Scotland? If they say they know not how to make the goods, or how to dispose of them when made, my answer is short; I know 'tis not the work of gentlemen to turn manufacturers and merchants: and I know also a number of projectors, that is to say, thieves and cheats, have teased and hanged about them, to draw them into manufacturing, only to bubble them of their wool and money.

But here is a plain scheme, let the Scots gentlemen set but their stewards to work to employ the poor people to spin the wool into yarn, and send the yarn into England; 'tis an easy manufacture, and what the Scots are very handy at, and this could never be difficult. They may have patterns of the yarn given them here, a price agreed on, and good security for payment. This can have no difficulty; the Irish are fallen into this way, to such a degree, that 40,000 packs of wool and worsted yarn are brought into England now every year, and sold here, where, about thirty years ago, not a pound of it was imported ready spun.

This, and many such advantages in trade, Scotland might find in her own bounds, her gentlemen assisting the poor only with their stocks of wool; by which means the poverty and sloth of the meaner people would be removed, and Scotland enriched. But I have done my part, and have not room to enlarge.

The decayed burghs being passed, we came to a village called the Weems, or by way of distinction, the Wester Weems, or Wemys. This is a small town, and no borough, belonging to the Earl of Weemys,[7] whose house stands a little farther east, on the top of a high cliff, looking upon the sea.

From hence you pass through the East Weemys to another village, called Buckhaven, inhabited chiefly, if not only, by fishermen, whose business is wholly to catch fresh fish every day in the firth, and carry them to Leith and Edinburgh markets. And though this town be a miserable row of cottage-like buildings, and people altogether mere fishermen, as I have said, yet there is scarce a poor man in the town, and in general the town is rich.

Here we saw the shore of the sea covered with shrimps, like the ground covered with a thin snow; and as you rode among them they would rise like kind of dust, being scared by the footing of the horse, and hopping like grasshoppers.

Beyond this is the Methuel, a little town, but a very safe and good harbour, firmly built of stone, almost like the Cobb at Lime, though not wholly projecting into the sea, but standing within the land, and built out with two heads, and walls of thick strong stone. It stands a little on the west side of the mouth of the River Leven; the salmon of this river are esteemed the best in this part of Scotland.

Here my Lord Weemys brings his coal, which he digs above two miles off, on the banks of the River Leven, and here it is sold or shipped off; as also what salt he can make, which is not a great deal. Nor is the estate his lordship makes from the said coal-works equal to what it has been, the water having, after an immense charge to throw it off, broken in upon the works, and hindered their going on, at least to any considerable advantage.

The people who work in the coal mines in this country, what with the dejected countenances of the men, occasioned by their poverty and hard labour, and what with the colour or discolouring, which comes from the coal, both to their clothes and complexions, are indeed, frightful fellows at first sight. But I return to my progress from the Methuel; we have several small towns on the coast, as Criel or Crail, Pitten-Ween, Anstruther, or Anster, as 'tis usually called. These are all royal burghs, and send members to parliament, even still upon the new establishment, in consequence only that now they join three or four towns together to choose one or two members, whereas they chose every town for itself.

Over against this shore, and in the mouth of the Forth, opposite to the Isle of the Bass, lies the Isle of May, known to mariners by having a light-house upon it; the only constant inhabitant, is said to be the man maintained there by the Government, to take care of the fire in the light-house.

Here (you may observe) the French fleet lay with some assurance, when the Pretender was on board. And here the English four-a-clock-gun, on board their approaching squadron, unhappily gave them the alarm; so that they immediately weighed, got under sail, and made the best of their way, the English pursuing them in vain, except only that they took the *Salisbury*, which was a considerable way behind the fleet, and could not come up with the rest; the story is well known, so I need not repeat it.

The shore of the firth or frith ends here, and the aestuarium or mouth opening, the land of Fife falls off to the north, making a promontory of land, which the seamen call Fife-Ness, looking east to the German Ocean, after which the coast trends away north, and the first town we saw there was St Andrew's, an ancient city, the seat of an archbishop, and an university.

As you must expect a great deal of antiquity in this country of Fife, so you must expect to find all those ancient pieces mourning their own decay, and drooping and sinking in ashes. Here it was, that old limb of St Lucifer, Cardinal Beaton,[8] massacred and murthered that famous sufferer and martyr of the Scots Church, Mr William Wishart, whom he caused to be burnt in the parade of the castle, he himself sitting in his balcony to feed and glut his eyes with the sight of it. The old church here was a noble structure; it was longer than St Paul's in London, by a considerable deal, I think, by six yards, or by twenty-five foot. This building is now sunk into a simple parish church, though there are many plain discoveries of what it has been, and a great deal of project and fancy may be employed to find out the ancient shape of it.

The city is not large, nor is it contemptibly small; there are some very good buildings in it, and the remains of many more. The colleges are handsome buildings, and well supplied with men of learning in all sciences, and who govern the youth they instruct with reputation; the students wear gowns here of a scarlet-like colour, but not in grain, and are very numerous. The university is very ancient as well as the city; the foundation was settled, and the public buildings appointed in the beginning of the fifteenth century by King James I.

There are three colleges in all; the most ancient, and which, they say, was the public school so long before, is called St Salvadore. How it was made to speak Portuguese, I know not, unless it might be that some Portuguese clergymen came over hither as the first professors or teachers. The building is ancient, but appears to have been very magnificent considering the times it was erected in, which was 1456. The gate is large, and has a handsome spire over it all of stone. Were this college supported by additional bounties and donations, as has been the case in England; and were sufficient funds appointed to repair and keep up the buildings, there would few colleges in England go beyond it for magnificence. But want of this, and other encouragements, causes the whole building to seem as if it was in its declining state, and looking into its grave. The truth is, the college wants nothing but a good fund to be honestly applied for the repair of the building, finishing the first design, and encouraging the scholars.

The story of St Andrew and of his bones being buried here; of the first stone of the cathedral church being laid upon one of St Andrew's legs or thigh-bone, and of those bones being brought from Patras in the Morea, near the Gulph of Lepanto; these things are too ancient, and sound too much of the legend for me to meddle with.

In the second college, which is called St Leonard's, is a principal, who must be a Doctor of Divinity by the foundation; but the present Church Government insisting upon the parity of the clergy, are pleased to dispense with that part.

The revenue of this college is larger than that of the old college; it has also more students. It was founded and endowed by the Earl of Lenox,[9] being before that a religious house, of the Order of St Benedict. It is not so large and magnificent as St Salvador originally was; but 'tis kept in much better repair. It has but one court or square, but it is very large. The old building of the monastery remains entire, and makes the south side, and the old cells of the monks make now the chambers for the students. The chapel takes up the north side, and a large side of more modern apartments on the west, which are nevertheless old enough to be falling down; but they are now repairing them, and adding a great pile of building to complete the square, and join that side to the north where the chapel stands.

The new college, called St Mary's, was founded by Cardinal Beaton Archbishop of St Andrew's, and is very singular in its reserved and limited laws. Here are no scholars at all; but all those scholars who have passed their first studies, and gone through a course of philosophy in any of the other colleges, may enter themselves here to study Hebrew and the mathematics, history, or other parts of science.

It was in this college King Charles I held a parliament; the place is called the Parliament Room to this day, and is a very large, spacious room, able to receive 400 people, placed on seats to sit down; the form is reserved very plain, and the place, where the tables for the clerks and other officers were set, is to be seen.

In the new church in this city lies the body of the late Archbishop Sharp,[10] who was assassinated upon a moor or heath, as he was coming in his coach home to this city from the Court. There is a fine monument of marble over his grave, with his statue kneeling on the upper part, and the manner of his murther is cut in brass relief below. This murther is matter of history, but is so foolishly, or so partially, or so imperfectly related by all that have yet written of it, that posterity will lose both the fact and the cause of it in a few years more. I shall only say here, that the archbishop had been a furious and merciless persecutor, and, indeed, murtherer of many of the innocent people, merely for their keeping up their field-meetings, and was charged in particular with two actions; which, if true will, though not justify, yet take off much of the black part, which the very murther itself leaves on the memory of the actors.

Now 'tis as certain that these men knew nothing of meeting with the archbishop at that time; but being themselves outlawed men, whom any man that met might kill, and who (if taken) would have been put to death. They always went armed, and were, at that time, looking for another man, when unexpectedly they saw the bishop coming towards them in his coach, when one of them says to the other, we have not found the person we looked for; but lo, God has delivered our enemy, and the murtherer of our brethren into our hands, against whom we cannot obtain justice by the law, which is perverted. But remember the words of the text, If ye let him go, thy life shall be required for his life.

In a word, they immediately resolved to fall upon him, and cut him in pieces; I say they resolved, all but one (viz.) Hackston of Rathellet, who was not willing to have his hand in the blood, though he acknowledged he deserved to die. So that when they attacked the bishop, Hackston went off, and stood at a distance. Nor did he hold their horses, as one has ignorantly published; for they attacked him all mounted; nor could they well have stopped a coach and six horses, if they had been on foot. I mention this part, because, however providence ordered it, so it was, that none of the murtherers ever fell into the hands of justice, but this Hackston of Rathelett, who was most cruelly tortured, and afterwards had his hands cut off, and was then executed at Edinburgh.

I have not time to give the rest of this story, though the particulars are very well worth relating, but it is remote from my purpose, and I must proceed. The city of St Andrew's is, notwithstanding its many disasters; such as the ruin of the great church, the demolishing its castle, and the archbishop's palace, and Oliver Cromwell's citadel; yet, I say, it is still a handsome city, and well built, the streets straight and large, being three streets parallel to one another, all opening to the sea.

From St Andrew's we came to Cowper, the shire town, (as

it would be called in England) where the public business of the country is all done, where the sheriff keeps his Court. The Earl of Rothess is hereditary sheriff of the shire of Fife, and the Duke of Athol was chancellor of the university of St Andrew's, in the times of the Episcopal Government; but that dignity seems now to be laid aside.

We now went away to the north east part of the county, to see the ruins of the famous monastery of Balmerinoch, of which Mr Cambden takes notice; but we saw nothing worth our trouble, the very ruins being almost eaten up by time.

Hence we came to the bank of another firth or frith, called the Firth of Tay, which, opening to a large breadth at its entrance, as the Firth of Edinburgh does, draws in afterwards as that does at the Queens-Ferry, and makes a ferry over at the breadth of two miles to the town of Dundee; and then the firth widening again just as that of the Forth does also, continues its breadth as four to six miles, till it comes almost to Perth, as the other does to Sterling.

This River Tay is, without exception, the greatest river in Scotland, and of the longest course, for its rises out of the mountains, on the edge of the Argyle Shire; and running first north into the shire of Bradalbin, there receiving other rivers, it spreads itself into a large lake, which is called Lough Tay, extending for forty miles in length, and traversing the very heart of Scotland, comes into the sea near this place. Now, as I design to keep in this part of my work to the east coast of the country, I must for the present quit the Tay itself, keeping a little on the hither side of it, and go back to that part of the country which lies to the south, and yet east of Dunbarton and Lenox shires; so drawing an imaginary line from Sterling Bridge, due north, through the heart of the country to Inverness, which I take to lie almost due north and south.

In this course then I moved from the ferry, mentioned above, to Perth, lying upon the same River Tay, but on the hither bank. It was formerly called St Johnston, or St John's Town, from an old church, dedicated to the Evangelist, St

John, part of which is still remaining, and is yet big enough to make two parochial churches, and serve the whole town for their public worship.

The chief business of this town is the linen manufacture; and it is so considerable here, all the neighbouring country being employed in it, that it is a wealth to the whole place. The Tay is navigable up to the town for ships of good burthen; and they ship off here so great a quantity of linen, (all for England) that all the rest of Scotland is said not to ship off so much more.

This town was unhappily for some time, the seat of the late rebellion; but I cannot say it was unhappy for the town. For the townsmen got so much money by both parties, that they are evidently enriched by it and it appears not only by the particular families and persons in the town, but by their public and private buildings which they have raised since that; as particularly a new Tolbooth or Town-hall. The salmon taken here, and all over the Tay, is extremely good, and the quantity prodigious. They carry it to Edinburgh, and to all the towns where they have no salmon, and they barrel up a great quantity for exportation. The merchants of this town have also a considerable trade to the Baltic, to Norway, and especially, since as above, they were enriched by the late rebellion. It seems a little enigmatic to us in the south, how a rebellion should enrich any place; but a few words will explain it. First, I must premise, that the Pretender and his troops lay near, or in this place a considerable time; now the bare consumption of victuals and drink, is a very considerable advantage in Scotland, and therefore 'tis frequent in Scotland for towns to petition the government to have regiments of soldiers quartered upon them, which in England would look monstrous, nothing being more terrible and uneasy to our towns in England.

The town was well built before, but now has almost a new face; (for as I said) here are abundance of new houses, and more of old houses new fitted and repaired, which look like new. The linen trade too, which is their main business, has mightily increased since the late Act of Parliament in England, for the suppressing the use and wearing of printed calicoes; so that the manufacture is greatly increased here, especially of that kind of cloth which they buy here and send to England to be printed, and which is so much used in England in the room of the calicoes, that the worsted and silk weavers in London seem to have very little benefit by the bill, but that the linen of Scotland and Ireland are, as it were, constituted in the room of the calicoes.

From Perth I went south to that part of the province of Fife, which they call Clackmanan, lying west from Dumfermling, and extending itself towards Sterling and Dumblain. From Perth to Sterling there lies a vale which they call Strathmore, and which is a fine level country, though surrounded with hills, and is esteemed the most fruitful in corn of all that part of the country. It lies extended on both sides the Tay, and is said to reach to Brechin north east, and almost to Sterling south west. Here are, as in all such pleasant soils you will find, a great many gentlemen's seats; though on the north side of the Tay, and here in particular is the noble palace of Glames, the hereditary seat of the family of Lyon, Earls of Strathmore.

When the Pretender lodged here, for the Earl of Strathmore entertained him in his first passage to Perth with great magnificence, there were told three and forty furnished rooms on the first floor of the house; some beds, perhaps, were put up for the occasion, for they made eighty beds for them, and the whole retinue of the Pretender was received, the house being able to receive the court of a real reigning prince.

It would be endless to go about to describe the magnificent furniture, the family pictures, the gallery, the fine collection of original paintings, and the nobly painted ceilings of the chapel, where is an organ for the service after the manner of the Church of England. In a word, the house is as nobly furnished as most palaces in Scotland; but it was at the brink of destruction; for had the Earl not been killed, 'tis odds but it had been gutted by the army, which presently spread all the country; but it was enough, the Earl lost his life, and the present Earl enjoys it peaceably.

From hence I came away south west, and crossing the Tay below Perth, but above Dundee, came to Dumblain, a name made famous by the late battle [11] fought between the army of King George, under the command of the Duke of Argyle, and the Pretender's forces under the Earl of Marr, which was fought on Sheriff-Moor, between Sterling and Dumblain. The town is pleasantly situated, and tolerably well built, but out of all manner of trade; so that there is neither present prosperity upon it, or prospect of future.

Going from hence we took a full view of the field of battle, called Sheriff-Muir, and had time to contemplate how it was possible, that a rabble of Highlanders armed in haste, appearing in rebellion, and headed by a person never in arms before, nor of the least experience, should come so near to the overthrowing an army of regular, disciplined troops, and led on by experienced officers, and so great a general. But when the mistake appeared also, we blessed the good Protector of Great Britain, who, under a piece of the most mistaken conduct in the world, to say no worse of it, gave that important victory to King George's troops, and prevented the ruin of Scotland from an army of Highlanders.

From this place of reflection I came forward in sight of Sterling bridge, but leaving it on the right hand, turned away east to Alloway, where the Earl of Marr has a noble seat, I should have said had a noble seat, and where the navigation of the Firth of Forth begins. The town is pleasant, well built, and full of trade; for the whole country has some business or other with them, and they have a better navigation than most of the towns on the Firth, for a ship of 300 ton may lie also at the very wharf; so that at Alloway a merchant may trade to all parts of the world, as well as at Leith or at Glasgow.

From Alloway, east, the country is called the shire of Clackmannan, and is known for yielding the best of coal, and the greatest quantity of it of any country in Scotland; so that it is carried, not to Edinburgh only, but to England, to Holland, and to France; and they tell us of new pits, or mines of coal now discovered, which will yield such quantities, and so easy to come at, as are never to be exhausted; though such great quantities should be sent to England, as the York-Buildings company[12] boast of, namely, twenty thousand ton a year; which, however, I take it as it is, for a boast, or rather a pretence to persuade the world they have a demand for such a quantity; whereas, while the freight from Scotland is, as we know, so dear, and the tax in England continues so heavy, the price of these coals will always be so high at London, as will not fail to restrain the consumption; nor is it the interest of Scotland to send away so great a quantity of coal as shall either make a scarcity, or raise the price of them at home.

On this shore of the firth, farther down, stands the town of Culross, a neat and agreeable town, lying in length by the water side, like Kirkcaldy, and being likewise a trading town, as trade must be understood in Scotland. Here is a pretty market, a plentiful country behind it, and the navigable firth before it; the coal and the linen manufacture, and plenty of corn, such exportations will always keep something of trade alive upon this whole coast.

Having made this little excursion to the south from Perth, you may suppose me now returned northward again; and having given you my account of Perth, and its present circumstances, I now proceed that way, taking things as well in their ordinary situation as I can; we could not be at Perth and not have a desire to see that ancient seat of royal ceremony, for the Scots kings, I mean of Scone, where all the kings of Scotland were crowned.

Scone lies on the other side of the Tay, about a mile north west from Perth; it was famous for the old chair in which the kings of Scotland were crowned, and which Edward I, King of England, having pierced through the whole kingdom, and nothing being able to withstand him, brought away with him. It is now deposited in Westminster, and the kings of Scotland are still crowned in it, according to an old Scots prophecy, which they say, (mark it, I do but tell you they say so) was cut in the stone, which is enclosed in the lower part of the wooden chair in which the kings are crowned.

> Ni fallat fatum, Scoti quocunque locatum
> Inveniunt Lapidem, regnare tenentur ibidem.

Englished thus;

> Or Fates deceived, and Heaven decrees in vain,
> Or where this Stone is found, the Scots shall reign.

This palace was in those days a great monastery, and famous on occasion of this stone in the chair; the monks appropriating to themselves not the custom only, but the right of having all the kings crowned on it, as if it had been a sacred right, and instituted in heaven; and that the kings would not prosper if they were crowned any where else.

But enough of fable, for this, I suppose, to be no other; yet, be it how it will, this is no fable, that here all the kings of Scotland were crowned, and all the kings of Great Britain have been since crowned on it, or in the chair, or near it ever since.

The palace of Scoon, though ancient, is not so much decayed as those I have already spoken of; and the Pretender found it very well in repair for his use. Here he lived and kept his court, a fatal court to the nobility and gentry of Scotland, who were deluded to appear for him; here I say, he kept his court in all the state and appearance of a sovereign, and received honours as such; so that he might say he reigned in Scotland, though not over Scotland, for a few days. But it was but a few (about twenty) till he and all his adherents were obliged to quit, not the place only, but the island, and that without fighting, though the royal army was not above ten thousand men.

From Scoon to Dunkel is so little a way we desired to see it, being the place where the first skirmish was fought between the forces of King William, after the Revolution, and the Laird of Claverhouse,[13] after called Viscount Dundee, but

Dundee's men, though 5,000, were gallantly repulsed by a handful, even of new raised men.

Dundee being killed by an accidental shot after the fight, the resistance ended soon after; whereas, indeed, had that accident not happened, Dundee, who was a bold enterprising man, had certainly marched southward, and bid fair to have given King William a journey into the north, instead of a voyage to Ireland; but providence had better things in store for Great Britain.

But our determined route lay up the eastern shore, and through the shires, adjacent on that side, as particularly Angus, Mearns, Marr, Aberdeen, Buchan or Bucquhan, &c. so as I laid it out before to Inverness.

Mr Cambden tells us, that the Firth of Tay was the utmost bounds of the Roman Empire in Britain. That Julius Agricola, the best of generals under the worst of emperors, Domitian, though he pierced farther, and traversed by land into the heart of the Highlands, yet seeing no end of the barbarous country, and no advantage by the conquest of a few Barbarian mountaineers, withdrew and fixed the Roman eagles here. But our English Caesars have outgone the Romans; for Edward I as is said, passed the Tay, for he rifled the Abbey at Scoon; and, if we may believe history, penetrated into the remotest parts, which, however, I take to be only the remotest parts of what was then known to the English; for as to the Highlands, the mountains of Loquhaber, Ross, Murray, Sutherland, and Caithness, we read nothing of them. And from these retreats the Scots always returned, Antæus like, with double strength after every defeat.

Oliver Cromwell, indeed, rode through;[14] he penetrated to the remotest part of the island, and that he might rule them with a rod of iron in the very letter of it, he built citadels and forts in all the angles and extremes, where he found it needful to place his stationary legions, just as the Romans did; as at Leith, at St Andrew's, at Inverness, Irwin, Innerlochy, and several other places: and just now we find King George's forces marching to the remotest corners, nay, ferrying over into the western, and north-western islands; but then this is not as a foreigner and conqueror, but as a sovereign, a lawful governor and father of the country, to deliver from, not entangle her in the chains of tyranny and usurpation.

We left Strathern therefore, with the little country of Mentieth, for our return, and went down into Angus, on the northern banks of Tay to Dundee, a pleasant, large, populous city, and well deserves the title of Bonny Dundee, so often given it in discourse, as well as in song (bonny, in Scots, signifying beautiful).

As it stands well for trade, so it is one of the best trading towns in Scotland, and that as well in foreign business as in manufacture and home trade. It has but an indifferent harbour, but the Tay is a large, safe, and good road, and there is deep water and very good anchor-hold almost all over it. It is exceedingly populous, full of stately houses, and large handsome streets; particularly it has four very good streets, with a large market-place in the middle, the largest and fairest in Scotland, except only that of Aberdeen. The inhabitants here appear like gentlemen, as well as men of business, and yet are real merchants too, and make good what we see so eminently in England, that true bred merchants are the best of gentlemen. They have a very good and large correspondence here with England, and ship off a great deal of linen thither, also a great quantity of corn is sent from hence, as well to England as to Holland. They have likewise a good share of the Norway trade; and as they are concerned in the herring-fishery, they consequently have some east country trade, viz. to Dantzick, Koningsberg, Riga, and the neighbouring parts. They send ships also to Sweden, and import iron, copper, tar, pitch, deals, &c. from the several trading ports of that kingdom.

The great church was formerly collegiate, being the cathedral of the place, and was a very large building; but part of it was demolished in the Civil War; the remainder is divided, like as others are at Edinburgh, Glasgow, &c. into three churches for the present use of the citizens. They have also a meeting-house or two for the episcopal worship; for you are to take it once for all, that north by Tay, there are far more of the episcopal persuasion than are to be found in the south; and the farther north, the more so, as we shall see in its order.

It is twenty Scots miles from Dundee to Montrose, the way pleasant, the country fruitful and bespangled, as the sky in a clear night with stars of the biggest magnitude, with gentlemen's houses, thick as they can be supposed to stand with pleasure and conveniency. We did not find so kind a reception among the common people of Angus, and the other shires on this side the country, as the Scots usually give to strangers. But we found it was because we were English men; and we found that their aversion did not lie so much against us on account of the late successes at, and after the rebellion, and the forfeiture of the many noblemen's and gentlemen's estates among them as fell on that occasion, though that might add to the disgust. But it was on account of the Union, which they almost universally exclaimed against though sometimes against all manner of just reasoning.

This town of Montrose is a sea-port, and, in proportion to its number of inhabitants, has a considerable trade, and is tolerably well built, and capable of being made strong, only that it extends too far in length.

The French fleet made land at this port, when they had the Pretender on board, in the reign of Queen Ann,[15] having overshot the mouth of the firth so far, whither they had first designed. But this mistake, which some thought a misfortune, was certainly a deliverance to them; for as this mistake gave time to the English fleet to come up with them, before they could enter the firth, so it left them time and room also to make their escape, which, if they had been gone up the firth, they could never have done, but must inevitably have been all burnt and destroyed, or taken by the British fleet under Sir George Bing, which was superior to them in force.

From Montrose the shore lies due north to Aberdeen: by the way is the castle of Dunnoter, a strong fortification, upon a high precipice of a rock, looking down on the sea, as on a thing infinitely below it. The castle is walled about with invincible walls, said the honest Scots man that showed us the road to it, having towers at proper distances, after the old way of fortifying towns. This was chiefly made use of as a prison for state-prisoners; and I have seen a black account of the cruel usage the unhappy prisoners have met with there; but those times are over with Scotland.

From hence there is nothing remarkable till we come to Aberdeen, a place so eminent, that it commands some stay upon it. Aberdeen is divided into two towns or cities, and stands at the mouth of two rivers; the towns are the new and the old Aberdeen, about a mile distant from one another, one situate on the River Don or Dune, the other on the River Dee, from whence it is supposed to take its name; for Aber, in the old British language, signifies a mouth, or opening of a river, the same which in Scotland is understood by a frith or firth. So that both these towns are described in the name, (viz.) Aberdee, the mouth of the River Dee, and Aberdeen, the mouth of the River Don.

Old Aberdeen is also on one side the county, and new Aberdeen on another, though both in that which is called in general the county of Marr. The extraordinaries of Aberdeen, take both cities together, are

1. The cathedral dedicated to St Machar, though none knows who that Saint was, is a large and ancient building; the building majestic, rather than curious, and yet not without its beauty in architecture; it appears to have been built at several times, and, perhaps, at the distance of many years, one part from another. The columns on which the great steeple stands are very artful, and the contrivance shows great judgement in the builder or director of the work. This church has been divided into several parts since the abolishing of episcopacy, as a government in the Church; (for it is not abolished in Aberdeen, as a principle, to this day) abundance of the people are still episcopal in their opinion; and they have, by the gentle government they live under, so much liberty still, as that they have a chapel for the public exercise of their worship, after the manner of the Church of England,

besides several meetings for the episcopal dissenters, which are not so public.

2. The two colleges; one of these are in the old city, and the other in the new. (1) That in the old city is also the oldest college, being founded *Anno* 1500 by the famous Bishop Elphingstone,[16] who lies buried in the chapel or college church, under a very magnificent and curious monument. The steeple of this church was the most artificial that I have seen in Scotland, and very beautiful, according to the draught of its building. But it is much more so now, having been injured, it not quite broken down by a furious tempest *anno* 1361; but rebuilt after the first model.

(2.) The new college, which is in the new city of Aberdeen, and is called the Marshallian or Marshal's College, because founded by Keith Earl Marshal, in the year 1593. And though it was a magnificent building at first, and well endowed, yet the citizens have much beautified and enlarged it, and adjoined to it a noble library well stocked with books, as well by the citizens as by the benefactions of gentlemen, and lovers of learning; as also with the finest and best mathematical instruments.

Those two colleges form the university, and are so called, but they are independent on one another; they are famed for having bred many men of learning; but that is not to my purpose here.

3. The third article is the great market-place, which, indeed, is very beautiful and spacious; and the streets adjoining are very handsome and well built, the houses lofty and high; but not so as to be inconvenient, as in Edinburgh; or low, to be contemptible as in most other places. But the generality of the citizens' houses are built of stone four story high, handsome sash-windows, and are very well furnished within, the citizens here being as gay, as genteel, and, perhaps, as rich, as in any city in Scotland.

4. The bridges; particularly that at Old Aberdeen, over the Don. It consists of one immense arch of stone, sprung from two rocks, one on each side, which serve as a buttment to the

arch, so that it may be said to have no foundation, nor to need any. The workmanship is artful, and so firm, that it may possibly end with the conflagration only. The other bridge is upon the River Dee, about a mile west above New Aberdeen, and has seven very stately fine arches.

5. and 6. The commerce and the fishery.

The fishery is very particular; the salmon is a surprising thing, the quantity that is taken in both rivers, but especially in the Dee, is a kind of prodigy; the fishing, or property, is erected into a company, and divided into shares, and no person can enjoy above one share at a time; the profits are very considerable, for the quantity of fish taken is exceeding great, and they are sent abroad into several parts of the world, particularly into France, England, the Baltick, and several other parts. The herring-fishing is a common blessing too all this shore of Scotland, and is like the Indies at their door; the merchants of Aberdeen cannot omit the benefit.

They have a very good manufacture of linen, and also of worsted stockings, which they send to England in great quantities, and of which they make some so fine, that I have seen them sold for fourteen, and twenty shillings a pair. They also send them over to Holland, and into the north and east seas in large quantities.

They have also a particular export here of pork, pickled and packed up in barrels, which they chiefly sell to the Dutch for the victualling their East-India ships and their men of war, the Aberdeen pork having the reputation of being the best cured, for keeping on very long voyages, of any in Europe.

In a word, the people of Aberdeen are universal merchants, so far as trade of the northern part of the world will extend. They drive a very great trade to Holland, to France, to Hambrough, to Norway, to Gottenburgh, and to the Baltick; and it may, in a word, be esteemed as the third city in Scotland, that is to say, next after Edinburgh and Glasgow.

From Aberdeen the coast goes on to a point of land, which is the farthest north-east part of Britain, and is called by the sailors Buchanness, being in the shire or county of Buchan. It was to this point the French squadron, with the Pretender on board, in the reign of Queen Ann, kept their flight in sight of the shore, being thus far pursued by Sir George Bing with the English fleet; but from hence steering away north-east, as if for the Norway coast, and the English admiral seeing no probability of coming up with them, gave over the chase, when they, altering their course in the night, stood away south, and came back to Dunkirk where they set out.

Upon this part are several good towns; as particularly Peter-Head; a good market-town, and a port with a small harbour for fishing vessels, but no considerable trade, Aberdeen being so near. This country, however remote, is full of nobility and gentry, and their seats are seen even to the extremest shores. Nor does the remote situation hinder, but these gentlemen have the politest and brightest education and genius of any people so far north, perhaps, in the world, being always bred in travel abroad, and in the universities at home. The Lord Pitsligo,[17] though unhappily drawn into the snare of the late insurrection, and forfeiting his estate with the rest, yet carries abroad with him, where-ever he goes, a bright genius, a head so full of learning and sound judgment, and a behaviour as polite, courtly, and full of all the good qualities that adorn a noble birth, as most persons of quality I ever saw.

From hence, the east shore of Scotland being at an end, the land trends away due west; and the shire of Bamf beginning, you see the towns of Bamf, Elgin, and the famous monastery of Kinloss, where the murthered body of King Duff [18] was, after many years, dug up, and discovered to be the same by some tokens, which, it seems, were undoubted.

From Fifeness, which is the northermost point, or head land on the mouth of Edinburgh Firth, being the southermost land of Fife, to this point of Buchan-Ness, the land lies due north and south, and the shore is the eastermost land of Scotland; the distance between them is thirty-three leagues one mile, that is just 100 miles; though the mariners say that measuring by the sea it is but twenty-eight; and from Winterton-Ness, near Yarmouth, to this point called Buchan-Ness, is just 300 miles.

The river, or Firth of Tay, opens into the sea, about four leagues north from Fife-Ness; and as there is a light-house on the Isle of May, in the mouth of the Firth of Forth of Edinburgh, a little south of this point called Fife-Ness; so there are two light-houses at the entrance of the Firth of Tay, being for the directions of the sailors, when they are bound into that river; and particularly for their avoiding and sailing between two sands or shoals, which lie off from the south side of the entrance.

This point of land, called Buchan-Ness, is generally the first land of Great Britain, which the ships make in their voyages home from Arch-Angel in Russia, or from their whale-fishing-voyages to Greenland and Spits-Berghen in the north seas; and near this point, namely, at Pitsligo, a great ship was cast away in Queen Elizabeth's time, bound home from Arch-Angel, in which was the first ambassador, which the great Duke of Muscovy sent to any of the Christian princes of Europe, and who was commissioned to treat with Queen Elizabeth for a league of peace and commerce; and on board which was a most valuable present to the queen of rich and costly furs; such as sables, ermine, black fox skins, and such like, being in those days esteemed inestimable. The ambassadors, it seems, were saved and brought on shore by the help of the people of Pitsligo; but the ship and all the goods, and among them the rich furs, intended for the queen, were all lost, to her Majesty's great disappointment; for the queen valued such fine things exceedingly.

From this point of easterly land all that great bay, or inlet of the sea, reaching quite to the north of Scotland, is called Murray Firth; and the northermost point is Dungsby Head, which is the east point of Caithness, and opens to Pentland Firth. By Pentland Firth you are to understand the passage of the sea beyond Caithness, that is to say between Scotland and the Isles of Orkney. This bay, called Murray-Firth, is not in the nature of a firth, as that of Edinburgh or Tay, being the mouths of rivers; as the Humber, or the mouth of Thames in England: but it is an open gulf or bay in the sea; as the Bay of Biscay, or the Gulph of Mexico are, and such-like: and though it may receive several rivers into it, as indeed it does, and as those bays do; yet itself is an open sea, and reaches from, as I have said, Peter-Head to Dungsby Head, opposite to the Orkneys; the distance upon the sea twenty-six leagues one mile, or seventy-nine miles.

This country of Buchan, is, indeed, more to be taken notice of from what is to be seen on the sea-shore than in the land; for the country is mountainous, poor, and more barren than its neighbours; but as we coasted along west, we came into a much better country, particularly the shires of Bamff, Elgin, and the country of Murray, from whence the bay, I just now mentioned, is called Murray Firth.

Murray is, indeed, a pleasant country, the soil fruitful, watered with fine rivers, and full of good towns, but especially of gentlemen's seats, more and more remarkable than could, indeed, be expected by a stranger in so remote a part of the country.

The River Spey, passes through the middle of the country. All the country, on the west side of the Spey, is surprisingly agreeable, being a flat, level country, the land rich and fruitful, well peopled, and full of gentlemen's seats. This country is a testimony how much the situation of the land is concerned in the goodness of the climate; for here the land being level and plain, for between twenty and thirty miles together, the soil is not only fruitful and rich, but the temperature of the air is softened, and made mild and suitable to the fruitfulness of the earth; for the harvest in this country, and in the vale of Strath-Bogy, and all the country to Inverness, is not only forward and early, as well as rich and strong; but 'tis more early than in Northumberland, nay, than it is in Darbyshire, and even than in some parts of the most southerly counties in England; as particularly in the east of Kent. Nor is the forwardness of the season the only testimony of the goodness of the soil here; but the crops are large, the straw strong and tall, and the ear full; and that which is still more the grain, and that particularly of the wheat, is as full, and the kind as fine, as any I have seen in England.

In this rich country is the city, or town rather, of Elgin; I say city, because in ancient time the monks claimed it for a city; and the cathedral shows, by its ruins, that it was a place of great magnificence. Nor must it be wondered at, if in so pleasant, so rich, and so agreeable a part of the country, all the rest being so differing from it, the clergy should seat themselves in a proportioned number, seeing we must do them the justice to say, that if there is any place richer and more fruitful, and pleasant than another, they seldom fail to find it out.

As the country is rich and pleasant, so here are a great many rich inhabitants, and in the town of Elgin in particular; for the gentlemen, as if this was the Edinburgh, or the court, for this part of the island, leave their Highland habitations in the winter and come and live here for the diversion of the place and plenty of provisions; and there is, on this account, a great variety of gentlemen for society, and that of all parties and of all opinions. This makes Elgin a very agreeable place to live in, notwithstanding its distance, being above 450 measured miles from London, and more, if we must go by Edinburgh.

This rich country continues with very little intermission, till we come to Strath-Nairn, that is the valley of Nairn, where it extends a little farther in breadth towards the mountains. Nor is Strath-Nairn behind any of the other in fruitfulness. From the western part of this country you may observe that the land goes away again to the north; and, as if you were to enter into another island beyond Britain, you find a large lake or inlet from the Sea of Murray, mentioned above, going on west, as if it were to cut through the island, for we could see no end of it; nor could some of the country people tell us how far it went, but that it reached to Loquabre: so that we thought, till our maps and farther inquiries informed us, it had joined to the western ocean.

After we had travelled about twelve miles, and descended from a rising ground, which we were then upon, we perceived the lake contracted in one particular place to the ordinary size of a river, as if designed by nature to give passage to the inhabitants to converse with the northern part; and then, as if that part had been sufficiently performed, it opened again to its former breadth, and continued in the form of a large lake, as before, for many more miles than we could see; both sides the pass, 'tis above thirty-five miles in length.

In the narrow pass (mentioned above over the lake) stands the town and fortress of Inner-Ness, that is a town on the inner bank of the River Ness. The situation of it, as I have said before, intimates that it is a place of strength; and accordingly it has a castle, founded in ancient times to command the pass. And some authors write that it was anciently a royal house for the kings of Scotland. Be that as it will, Oliver Cromwell thought it a place of such importance, that he built a strong citadel here, and kept a stated garrison always in it, and sometimes more than a garrison, finding it needful to have a large body of his old veteran troops posted here to preserve the peace of the country, and keep the Highlands in awe, which they did effectually all his time.

Here it is observed, that at the end of those troublesome days, when the troops on all sides came to be disbanded, and the men dispersed, abundance of the English soldiers settled in this fruitful and cheap part of the country, and two things are observed from it as the consequence.

1. That the English falling to husbandry, and cultivation of the earth after their own manner, were instrumental, with the help of a rich and fruitful soil, to bring all that part of the country into so good a method and management, as is observed to outdo all the rest of Scotland to this day; for as they reap early, so they sow early, and manure and help the soil by all the regular arts of husbandry, as is practised in England.

2. As Cromwell's soldiers initiated them thus into the arts and industry of the husbandman, so they left them the English accent upon their tongues, and they preserve it also to

this day; for they speak perfect English, even much better than in the most southerly provinces of Scotland; nay, some will say that they speak it as well as at London; though I do not grant that neither. It is certain they keep the southern accent very well, and speak very good English.

The fort, which was then built, and since demolished, has been restored since the revolution; and a garrison was always kept here by King William, for the better regulating the Highlands; and this post was of singular importance in the time of the late insurrection of the Lord Marr for the Pretender; when, though his party took it, they were driven out again by the country, with the assistance of the Earl of Sutherland, and several other of the nobility and gentry, who stood fast to the king's interest.

Here is a stately stone bridge of seven large arches over the River Ness, where, as I said above, it grows narrow between the sea and the lake; small vessels may come up to the town, but larger ships, when such come thither, as they often do for corn, lie at some distance east from the town.

When you are over this bridge you enter that which we truly call the north of Scotland, and others the north Highlands; in which are several distinct shires, but cannot call for a distinct description, because it is all one undistinguished range of mountains and woods, overspread with vast, and almost uninhabited rocks and steeps filled with deer innumerable, and of a great many kinds; among which are some of those the ancients called harts and roebucks, with vast overgrown stags and hinds of the red deer kind, and with fallow-deer also.

And here, before I describe this frightful country, it is needful to observe that Scotland may be thus divided into four districts, or distinct quarters, which, however, I have not seen any of our geographers do before me, yet, I believe, may not be an improper measurement for such as would form a due idea of the whole in their minds, as follows:

1. The South Land, or that part of Scotland south of the River Tay, drawing a line from the Tay, about Perth, to Loch-

Lomond, and down again to Dumbarton, and the bank of Clyde.

2. The Middle, or Midland, being all the country from the Tay and the Lough-Lomon, north to the Lake of Ness and the Aber, including a long slope to the south, taking in the western Highlands of Argyle and Lorn, and the isles of Isla and Jura.

3. The North Land, being all the country beyond Innerness and the Lough, or River Ness, north, drawing the line over the narrow space of Glangary, between the Ness and the Aber, and bounded by them both from the eastern to the western sea.

4. The islands, being all the western and northern islands (viz.) the Hebrides, the Skye, the Orkneys, and the Isles of Shetland.

Upon the foot of this division I am now, having passed the bridge over the Ness, entered upon the third division of Scotland, called the North Land; and it is of this country that, as I am saying, the mountains are so full of deer, harts, roebucks, &c. Here are also a great number of eagles which breed in the woods, and which prey upon the young fawns when they first fall. Some of these eagles are of a mighty large kind, such as are not to be seen again in those parts of the world. Here are also the best hawks of all the kinds for sport which are in the kingdom, and which the nobility and gentry of Scotland make great use of; for not this part of Scotland only, but all the rest of the country abounds with wild-fowl.

The rivers and lakes also in all this country are prodigiously full of salmon; it is hardly credible what the people relate of the quantity of salmon taken in these rivers, especially in the Spey, the Nairn, the Ness, and other rivers thereabout.

Innerness is a pleasant, clean, and well built town. There are some merchants in it, and some good share of trade. It consists of two parishes, and two large, handsome streets, but no public buildings of any note, except as above, the old castle and the bridge.

North of the mouth of this river is the famous Cromarty

Bay, or Cromarty Firth, noted for being the finest harbour, with the least business, of, perhaps, any in Britain; 'tis, doubtless, a harbour or port, able to receive the Royal Navy of Great Britain, and, like Milford-Haven in Wales, both the going in and out safe and secure. But as there is very little shipping employed in these parts, and little or no trade, except for corn, and in the season of it some fishing, so this noble harbour is left entirely useless in the world.

Our geographers seem to be almost as much at a loss in the description of this north part of Scotland, as the Romans were to conquer it; and they are obliged to fill it up with hills and mountains, as they do the inner parts of Africa, with lions and elephants, for want of knowing what else to place there. Yet this country is not of such difficult access, as to be passed undescribed, as if it were impenetrable.

All the country beyond this river, and the Loch flowing into it, is called Cathness, and extends to the northermost land in Scotland. Some people tell us they have both lead, copper, and iron in this part of Scotland, and I am very much inclined to believe it: but it seems reserved for a future, and more industrious age to search into; which, if it should happen to appear, especially the iron, they would no more have occasion to say, that nature furnished them with so much timber, and woods of such vast extent to no purpose, seeing it may be all little enough to supply the forges for working up the iron stone, and improving that useful product. And should a time come when these hidden treasures of the earth should be discovered and improved, this part of Scotland may no longer be called poor, for such a production would soon change the face of things, bring wealth and people, and commerce to it; fill their harbours full of ships, their towns full of people; and, by consuming the provisions, bring the soil to be cultivated, its fish cured, and its cattle consumed at home, and so a visible prosperity would show itself among them.

Nor are the inhabitants so wild and barbarous as, perhaps, they were in those times, or as our writers have pretended. We see every day the gentlemen born here; such as the

Mackenzies, McLeans, Dundonalds, Gordons, McKays, and others, who are named among the clans as if they were barbarians, appear at court, and in our camps and armies, as polite, and as finished gentlemen as any from other countries, or even among our own; and, if I should say, outdoing our own in many things, especially in arms and gallantry, as well abroad as at home. But I am not writing panegyrics or satires here, my business is with the country.

Here are few towns, but the people live dispersed, the gentry leading the commons or vassals, as they are called, to dwell within the respective bounds of their several clans, where they are, as we may say, little monarchs, reigning in their own dominions; nor do the people know any other sovereign, at least many of them do not.

This occasions the people to live dispersed among the hills without any settled towns. Their employment is chiefly hunting, which is, as we may say, for their food; though they do also breed large quantities of black cattle, with which they pay their lairds or leaders the rent of the lands. And these are the cattle which, even from the remotest parts, as well as from other in the west and south, are driven annually to England to be sold, and are brought up even to London, especially into the countries of Norfolk, Suffolk, and Essex.

Having thus, as I say, few or no towns to describe north of Innerness, it must suffice that I thus give a just description of the country in general. For example, it is surrounded with the sea, and those two great inlets of water, mentioned above, called the Ness and the Abre. In a word, the great Northern Ocean surrounds this whole part of Scotland; that part of it to the east, mentioned just now, lies open to the sea without any cover; the west and north parts are, as it were, surrounded with out-works as defences, to break off the raging ocean from the north; for the western islands on one side, and the Orkneys on the other, lie as so many advanced fortifications or redoubts, to combat that enemy at a distance. I shall view them in their course.

From Dunrobin Castle, you have nothing of note offers

itself, either by sea or land; but an extended shore lying north and south without towns and without harbours, and indeed, as there are none of the first, so there are wanting none of the last; for, as I said of Cromarty Bay, there is a noble harbour without ships or trade; so here nature, as if providentially foreseeing there was no room for trade, forbore giving herself the trouble to form harbours and creeks where they should be useless, and without people.

The land thus extended as above, lies north and south to Dungsby-Head, which is the utmost extent of the land on the east side of Britain, north, and is distant from Cromarty eighteen leagues north. Here the land bears away west, leaving a large strait or sea, which they call Pentland Firth, and which divides, between the island of Great Britain, and the isles of the Orkneys; a passage broad and fair, for 'tis not less than five leagues over, and with a great depth of water; so that any ships, or fleets of ships may go through it. But the tides are so fierce, so uncertain, and the gusts and sudden squalls of wind so frequent, that very few merchants-ships care to venture through it; and the Dutch East-India ships, which come north about, (as 'tis called) in their return from India, keep all farther off, and choose to come by Fair Isle, that is to say, in the passage between the islands of Orkney and Shetland. And here the Dutch send their squadron of men of war generally to meet them, because, as if it were in a narrow lane, they are sure to meet with them there.

In the passage, between the land's end of Britain and the Orkneys, is a small island, which our mariners call Stroma, Mr Cambden and others Sowna; 'tis spoken much of as dangerous for ships. But I see no room to record any thing of that kind any more than that there are witches and spirits haunting it, which draw ships on shore to their misfortunes. Such things I leave to the people who are of the opinion the Devil has such retreats for doing mischief; for my own part I believe him employed in business of more moment.

As Dingsby-Head is the most northerly land of Great Britain, 'tis worth observing to you that here, in the month of June, we had so clear an uninterrupted day, that, though indeed the sun does set, that is to say, the horizon covers its whole body for some hours, yet you might see to read the smallest print, and to write distinctly, without the help of a candle, or any other light, and that all night long.

No wonder the ancient mariners, be they Phoenician or Carthaginian, or what else you please, who in those days knew nothing of the motion of the heavenly bodies, when they were driven thus far, were surprised at finding they had lost the steady rotation of day and night, which they thought had spread over the whole globe. No wonder they talked much of their Ultima Thule, and that the Elysian fields must lie this way; when they found that they were already come to everlasting day, they could no longer doubt but heaven lay that way, or at least that this was the high way to it; and accordingly, when they came home, and were to give an account of these things among their neighbours, they filled them with astonishment; and 'twas wonderful they did not really fit out ships for the discovery; for who would ever have gone so near heaven, and not ventured a little farther to see whether they could find it or no?

From hence west we go along the shore of the firth or passage, which they call Pentland; and here is the house so famous, called John a Grot's house, where we set our horses' feet into the sea, on the most northerly land, as the people say, of Britain, though, I think, Dungsby-Head is as far north. 'Tis certain, however, the difference is but very small, being either of them in the latitude of 59⅙ north, and Shetland reaching above two degrees farther.

Here we found, however mountainous and wild the country appeared, the people were extremely well furnished with provisions; and especially they had four sorts of provisions in great plenty; and with a supply of which 'tis reasonable to say they could suffer no dangerous want.

1. Very good bread, as well oat bread as wheat, though the last not so cheap as the first.

2. Venison exceeding plentiful, and at all seasons, young or

old, which they kill with their guns wherever they find it; for there is no restraint, but 'tis every man's own that can kill it. By which means the Highlanders not only have all of them fire-arms, but they are all excellent marksmen.

3. Salmon in such plenty as is scarce credible, and so cheap, that to those who have any substance to buy with, it is not worth their while to catch it themselves. This they eat fresh in the season, and for other times they cure it by drying it in the sun, by which they preserve it all the year.

They have no want of cows and sheep, but the latter are so wild, that sometimes were they not, by their own disposition, used to flock together, they would be much harder to kill than the deer.

From hence to the west point of the passage to Orkney is near twenty miles, being what may be called the end of the island of Britain; and this part faces directly to the North Pole; the land, as it were, looking forward just against the Pole Star, and the Pole so elevated, that the tail of the Ursa Major, or the Great Bear, is seen just in the zenith, or over your head; and the day is said to be eighteen hours long, that is to say, the sun is so long above the horizon. But the rest of the light is so far beyond a twilight, by reason of the smallness of the arch of that circle, which the sun makes beneath the horizon, that it is clear and perfect day almost all the time; not forgetting withal, that the dark nights take their turn with them in their season, and it is just as long night in the winter.

Yet it is observable here, that they have more temperate winters here generally speaking, than we have to the most southerly part of the island, and particularly the water in some of the rivers as in the Ness, for example, never freezes, nor are their frosts ordinarily so lasting as they are in the most southerly climates, which is accounted for from the nearness of the sea, which filling the air with moist vapours, thickens the fluids and causes that they are not so easily penetrated by the severity of the cold.

On the most inland parts of this country, especially in the

shire of Ross, they have vast woods of fir trees, not planted and set by men's hands, as I have described in the southern part of Scotland, but growing wild and undirected, otherwise than as nature planted and nourished them up, by the additional help of time, nay of ages. Here are woods reaching from ten, to fifteen and twenty miles in length, and proportioned in breadth, in which there are firs, if we may believe the inhabitants, large enough to make masts for the biggest ships in the Navy Royal, and which are rendered of no use, merely for want of convenience of water carriage to bring them away; also they assure us there are a sufficient quantity of other timber for a supply to all Britain.

How far this may be true, that is to say, as to the quantity, that I do not undertake to determine. But I must add a needful memorandum to the Scots noblemen, &c. in whose estates these woods grow, that if they can not be made useful one way, they may be made so another, and if they cannot fell the timber, and cut it into masts and deals, and other useful things for bringing away, having no navigation; they may yet burn it, and draw from it vast quantities of pitch, tar, resin, turpentine, &c. which is of easier carriage, and may be carried on horses to the water's edge, and then shipped for the use of the merchant, and this way their woods may be made profitable, whatever they might be before.

We were now in the particular county called Strathnaver, or the Vale on the Naver, the remotest part of all the island, though not the most barren or unfruitful; for here as well as on the eastern shore is good corn produced, and sufficient of it at least for the inhabitants; perhaps they do not send much abroad, though sometimes also they send it over to the Orkneys, and also to Shetland. This county belongs to the Earl of Sutherland whose eldest son bears the title of Lord Strathnaver.

And now leaving the northern prospect we pass the opposite point west from Dingsby-head, and which the people call Farrohead. From hence the vast western ocean appears, what name to give it the geographers themselves do not seem to agree, but it certainly makes a part of the great Atlantick Sea, and is to be called by no other name, for it has no land or country to derive from.

And now we were to turn our faces S. for the islands of this sea, which make the fourth division of Scotland as mentioned before. I may if I have room give as just a description of them as I can from authentic relations; for being on horseback and no convenience of shipping presenting itself here, I am to own that we did not go over to those islands personally, neither was it likely any person whose business was mere curiosity and diversion, should either be at the expense, or run the risk of such a hazardous passage where there was so little worth observation to be found.

We therefore turned our faces to the south, and with great satisfaction after so long and fatiguing a journey; and unless we had been assisted by the gentlemen of the country, and with very good guides, it had been next to an impossibility to have passed over this part of the country. I do confess if I was to recommend to any men whose curiosity tempted them to travel over this country, the best method for their journeying, it should be neither to seek towns, for it would be impossible to find such in proper stages for their journey; nor to make themselves always burthensome to the Highland chiefs, though there I can assure them they would always meet with good treatment, and great hospitality. But I would propose travelling with some company, and carrying tents with them, and so encamping every night as if they were an army.

It is true they would do well to have the countenance of the gentlemen, and chiefs as above, and to be recommended to them from their friends from one to another, as well for guides as for safety, otherwise I would not answer for what might happen. But if they are first well recommended as strangers, and have letters from one gentleman to another, they would want neither guides nor guards, nor indeed would any man touch them; but rather protect them if there was occasion in all places; and by this method they might in the summer time lodge, when, and wherever they pleased, with safety and pleasure; travelling no farther at a time, than they thought fit; and as for their provisions, they might supply themselves by their guns, with very great plenty of wild fowl, and their attendants and guides would find convenient places to furnish other things sufficient to carry with them.

Indeed in our attempt to come down to the southward by the coast of Tain, and the shire of Ross, we should have been extremely disappointed, and perhaps have been obliged to get a ship or bark, to have carried us round the Isle of Skye into Loquhaber, had it not been for the extraordinary courtesy of some of the gentlemen of the country. On the other hand we unexpectedly met here some English men, who were employed by merchants in the S. (whether at London or Edinburgh I do not now remember) to take and cure a large quantity of white fish, and afterwards herrings, on account of trade. Here we had not only the civility of their assistance and accommodation in our journey, but we had the pleasure of seeing what progress they made in their undertaking.

As for herrings indeed the quantity was prodigious, and we had the pleasure of seeing something of the prodigy, for I can call it no other; the shoal was as I might say beginning to come, or had sent their vant-couriers before them, when we first came to the head of Pentland Firth, and in a fortnight's time more, the body of their numberless armies began to appear; but before we left the coast you would have ventured to say of the sea, as they do of the River Tibiscus, or Theisse in Hungary, that it was one third water, and two thirds fish; the operation of taking them, could hardly be called fishing, for they did little more than dip for them into the water and take them up.

Here we found the town of Tain, and some other villages tolerably well inhabited, and some trade also, occasioned principally by the communication with the western islands, and also by the herring fishing, the fishing boats from other parts often putting into these ports; for all their coast is full of loughs and rivers, and other openings which make very good harbours of shipping.

We could understand nothing on this side of what the people said, any more than if we had been in Morocco; and all the remedy we had was, that we found most of the gentlemen spoke French, and some few spoke broad Scots; we found it also much for our convenience to make the common people believe we were French.

Should we go about here to give you an account of the religion of the people in this country, it would be an unpleasant work, and perhaps scarce seem to deserve credit; you would hardly believe that in a Christian island, as this is said to be, there should be people found who know so little of religion, or of the custom of Christians, as not to know a Sunday, or Sabbath, from a working day, or the worship of God from an ordinary meeting, for conversation. I do not affirm that it is so, and I shall say no more of it here, because I would not publish what it is to be hoped may in time find redress; but I cannot but say that his Majesty's gift of 1,000*l.* annually to the Assembly of Scotland, for sending ministers and missionaries for the propagating Christian knowledge in the Highlands, is certainly one of the most needful charities that could have been thought of, worthy of a king, and well suited to that occasion; and if prudently applied, as there is reason to believe it will be, may in time break in upon this horrible ignorance, that has so far spread over this unhappy part of the country.

On the other hand, what shall we say to the neglect, which for so many years past has been the occasion of this surprising darkness among the people, when the poor abandoned creatures have not so much as had the common instruction of Christianity, so much as to know whether there was any such thing as a God or no, much less how to worship him; and if at any time any glimpse of light had been infused into them, and they had been taught any knowledge of superior things, it has been by the diligence of the Popish clergy, who to do them justice, have shown more charity, and taken more pains that way, than some whose work it has been, and who it might much more have been expected from?

On this coast is the Isle of Skye, lying from the west north west, to the east south east, and bearing upon the main island, only separated by a narrow strait of water; something like as the Isle of Wight is separated from the county of Southampton. We left this on our right, and crossing the mountains, came with as little stay as we could to the lough of Abre, that is, the water which assists with Lough Ness, to separate the north land of Scotland from the middle part.

From this river or water of Abre, all that mountainous barren and frightful country, which lies south is called Loquabre. It is indeed a frightful country full of hideous desert mountains and unpassable, except to the Highlanders who possess the precipices. Here in spite of the most vigorous pursuit, the Highland robbers, such as the famous Rob Roy in the late disturbances, find such retreats as none can pretend to follow them into, nor could he be ever taken.

On this water of Abre, just at the entrance of the loch, was anciently a fort built, to curb the Highlanders, on either side. It was so situated, that though it might indeed be blocked up by land and be distressed by a siege, yet as it was open to the sea, it might always receive supplies by shipping, the government being supposed to be always masters of the sea. This fort the late King William caused to be rebuilt, or rather a new fort to be erected; where there was always a good garrison kept for curbing the Highlanders, which fort was for several years commanded by Lieutenant General Maitland,[19] an old experienced general. This wise commander did more to gain the Highlanders, and keep them in peace, and in a due subjection to the British Government, by his winning and obliging behaviour, and yet by strict observance of his orders, and the duty of a governor, than any other before him had been able to do by force, and the sword.

At this place we take our leave of the third division, which I call the north land of Scotland, for this fort being on the south side of the Loch Abre is therefore called inner Lochy. To traverse the remaining part of this country, I must begin upon the upper Tay, where I left off when I turned away east; and here we have in especial manner the country of Brechin, the Blair as 'tis called of Athol, and the country of Bradalbin. This is a hilly country indeed, but as it is watered by the Tay, and many other pleasant rivers which fall into it, there are also several fruitful valleys, interspersed among the hills; nor are even the Highlands themselves, or the Highlanders the inhabitants any thing so wild, untaught, or untractable, as those whom I have been a describing in the north-land division, that is to say, in Strath-Naver, Ross, Tain, &c.

The Duke of Athol [20] is lord, I was almost going to say king of this country, and has the greatest interest, or if you please, the greatest share of vassalage of any nobleman in this part of Scotland. His Grace was always an opposer of the Union in the Parliament holden at Edinburgh, for passing it into an Act; but he did not carry his opposition to the height of tumult and rebellion; if he had, as some were forward to have had done, he would have possibly bid fair, to have prevented the conclusion of it, at least at that time. But the hour was come, when the calamities of war, which had for so many hundred years vexed the two nations, were to have an end; and though the government was never weaker in power than at that time, I mean in Scotland, yet the affair was carried through with a high hand, all the little tumults and disorders of the rabble as well at Edinburgh as at Glasgow, and other places, being timely suppressed, and others by prudent management prevented.

The Grampian mountains, which are here said to cut through Scotland, as the Muscovites say of their Riphaean hills, that they are the girdle of the world. As is the country, so are the inhabitants, a fierce fighting and furious kind of men; but I must add that they are much changed, and civilized from what they were formerly. And though the country is the same, and the mountains as wild and desolate as ever, yet the people, by the good conduct of their chiefs and heads of clans, are much more civilized than they were in former times.

As the men have the same vigour and spirit; but are under a better regulation of their manners, and more under government; so they make excellent soldiers, when they come abroad, or are listed in regular and disciplined troops.

The Duke of Athol, though he has not an estate equal to some of the nobility, yet he is master of more of these superiorities, as they are called there, than many of those who have twice his estate; and I have been told, that he can bring a body of above 6,000 men together in arms at very little warning. The pomp and state in which this noble person lives, is not to be imitated in Great Britain; for he is served like a prince, and maintains a greater equipage and retinue than five times his estate would support in another country.

This castle of Duplin, is a very beautiful seat, and the heads of the families having been pretty much used to live at home, the house has been adorned at several times, according to the genius and particular inclination of the persons, who then lived there; the present earl [21] is not much in Scotland; being created a peer of Great Britain, in the reign of the late Queen Anne, and married into the family of Oxford.

From this place we went to Brechin, an ancient town with a castle finely situate; but the ancient grandeur of it not supported; the family of Penmure, to whom it belonged, having been in no extraordinary circumstances for some time past, and now their misfortunes being finished, it is under forfeiture, and sold among the spoils of the late rebellion.

We were now as it were landed again, being after a long mountain-ramble, come down to the low lands, and into a pleasant and agreeable country; but as we had yet another journey to take west, we had a like prospect of a rude and wild part of Scotland to go through.

The Highlands of Scotland are divided into two parts, and known so as two separate countries, (viz.) the West Highlands, and the North Highlands; the last, of which I have spoken at large, contain the countries or provinces of:

Bradalbin,	Sutherland,	together with the Isle of Skye.
Athol,	Ross,	
Lochaber,	Strathnaver,	
Buchan,	Caithness,	
Mar,		

The West Highlands contain the shires or counties of:

Dunbritton or	Dunbarton,
Lenox,	Argyle,
Bute,	Lorn and Cantyre.

The Western Highlands are the only remaining part of Scotland, which as yet I have not touched upon. This is that particular country, which a late great man in King James the Second's time, called the kingdom of Argyle; and upon which occasion it was a compliment upon King James, that he had conquered two kings, when he suppressed the rebellion of the Whigs; namely, the Duke of Monmouth, whom in derision they called the little king of Lime, and the Earl of Argyle[22] whom they called with much more propriety, the great king of the Highlands.

It is true that the greatest part of these Western Highlands, may be said to be subject, or in some respect to belong to the House of Argyle, or to speak more properly, to the family or clan of the Campbells, of whom the Duke of Argyle is the chief; but then it should be noted too, that those western gentlemen are not so blindly to be led, or guided by their chiefs as those in the north; nor when led on, are they so apt for mischief and violence. But as many of them are touched with the Cameronian Whig, or at least the English Whig principles, they would venture to enquire what they were to do, and whom to fight against, at least before they dipped far in any hazardous undertaking.

Though the people of these countries are something more civilised than those of their brethren mountaineers in the north, yet the countries seem to be so near a kin that no strangers could know them asunder, nor is there any breach in the similitude that I could observe, except it be that in the north Highlands, there are such great woods of fir-trees, which I have taken notice of there, and which we do not see the like of here. Nor did we see so many or so large eagles in these western mountains as in the north, though the people assure us there are such too.

The quantity of deer are much the same, and the kinds too, and the black cattle are of the same kind, and rather more numerous; the people also dress after the same manner, in the plaid and the trews, go naked from below the knee to the mid thighs, wear the dirk and the pistol at their girdle, and the targe or target at their shoulder.

Some reckon the shire of Braidalbin to belong to these Western Highlands, all the reason that I could find they give for reckoning this country among the Western Highlands, is because they say one part of it is inhabited by the Campbells, whose clan, as I have observed, generally possesses all the West Highlands.

But if they will claim the country, they must claim the people too, who are, if I may give my opinion, some of the worst, most barbarous, and ill governed of all the Highlands of Scotland; they are desperate in fight, cruel in victory, fierce even in conversation, apt to quarrel, mischievous, and even murderers in their passion.

At the fight which happened at Gillekranky,[23] in this part of Scotland, they tell us a story of a combat between an English soldier pressed hard by a Highlander, the regiment being in disorder, for the English had the worst of it; the English soldier was singled out in the pursuit by one particular Highlander, and found himself in great danger, he defended himself with the club of his musket as long as he was able, his shot being spent before, after which they came to their swords, the English man understood the backsword very well, but the Scots man received all the blows upon his targe; so that the English man could not come in with him, and at the same time he laid hard at the English man with his broadsword, and had cut him in two or three places, at which the

English man enraged, rather than discouraged, cried out to him, *you dog* says he, *come out from behind the door and fight like a man*, meaning from behind his great target; but the Scots man though as brave as the other, knew better things than that, and laying hard at him had cut him down, and was just going to kill him, when some of the regiment that saw him distressed, came up to him and rescued him, and took the Highlander prisoner.

It is hard to distinguish too among those Highland men, who are the best soldiers. Foreigners give it to the northern men as the more hardy and the larger bodies; but I will not undertake to decide this controversy, either of them make very good soldiers, and all the world are fond of them; nor are they equalled in any part of the world that I have met with, if they are regimented by themselves, unmixed with other nations.

I am now to return to our progress. Leaving the country of Brechin, and the low lands of Strathearn, we went away west; but were presently interrupted by a vast inland sea, rather than a lake called Loch Lomond. It is indeed a sea, and looked like it from the hills from whence we first descried it; and its being a tempestuous day, I assure you it appeared all in a breach, rough and raging, like the sea in a storm. There are several islands in it, which from the hills we could plainly perceive were islands, but that they are a-drift, and float about the lake, that I take as I find it, for a story, namely, a story called a F—— as I do also that of the water of this loch, turning wood into stone.

This lake or loch is, without comparison, the greatest in Scotland, no other can be called half so big; for it is more than twenty miles long, and generally eight miles in breadth, though at the north end of it, 'tis not so broad by far. It receives many rivers into it, but empties itself into the Firth of Clyde, at one mouth; near the entrance of it into Clyde, stands the famous Dunbarton Castle, the most ancient, as well as the most important castle in Scotland; and the gate, as 'tis called, of the Highlands. It is now not much regarded, the whole country being, as it were, buried in peace, yet there is a garrison maintained in it; and the pass would be still of great import, were there any occasion of arms in time to come; 'tis exceeding strong by situation, being secured by the river on one side, the Firth of Clyde on the other, by an unpassable morass on the third side, and the fourth is a precipice.

Passing from Dunbarton castle, we enter the territory of Argyle. The west side of this country lies extended along the Irish Sea for a very great length, at least eighty miles (viz.) from the Mull of Cantyre to Dunstaffnage, and the Isle of Stackar and Listnoc, in the water of Loquhaber. On all this shore there is no town eminent for trade, no port or harbour, at least none made use of for shipping; nor are there any ships to require them, except fishing-barks and boats, which are in the season employed for catching herrings, of which the shoals that are found upon this coast in the season are incredible, especially in the Clyde, in Loch-Finn, and about the Isle of Arran, which lies in the mouth of Clyde.

From the Mull of Cantyre they see Ireland very plain, it being not above fifteen or sixteen miles from the point of land, which they call the Mull to the Fair Foreland, on the coast of Colrain, on the north of Ireland. In the mouth of this sea of Clyde lies a rock, somewhat like the Bass in the Firth of Forth, or of Edinburgh, not for shape, but for this particular, that here, as at the Bass, the Soland geese are pleased to come in the season of the fishery, and to breed and inhabit as they do at the Bass, and to go away and come again just at the same seasons, as at the Bass; this island is called the Ailze. Here are also the islands of Arran and of Bute; the first giving title of earl to the family of Hamilton, and the other the title of Duke of Rothsay to the eldest son of the crown of Scotland, who is called Duke of Rothsay, from the castle of Rothsay in this island; nor is there any thing else considerable to be said of either of the islands; for as for their present condition, which is what is my particular business in this book, they have nothing considerable in or about them, except it be a tumultuous and dangerous sea for sailors, especially when a south-west wind blows hard, which brings the sea rolling in upon them in a frightful manner.

Off of the western shore of Argyle and Lorn there are abundance of islands, which all belong to the family of Argyle, or at least to its jurisdiction; as Isla, Jura, Tyrry, Mull, Lysmore, Coll, and several others of less note.

NOTES

In general I have confined the notes to a limited range of topics. Individuals mentioned in the text are identified where possible, relevant dates supplied where Defoe omits them, and facts corrected in a few places. I have not, however, attempted to provide a commentary on Defoe as social and economic historian. It would be possible to analyse his reports in the light of present-day knowledge, and to indicate errors of balance or emphasis. In these notes I have restricted myself to outright errors, such as the considerable over-estimate in the population of London (p. 294).

My annotation relies heavily on standard works of reference such as the *Dictionary of National Biography*, G. E. Cokayne's *Complete Peerage* and Haydn's *Book of Dignities*. I have not indicated the source in such cases, and have specified only the less obvious or accessible materials used. For the London sections, there is helpful topographical information – but not much aid otherwise – in Sir Mayson M. Beaton and E. B. Chancellor, eds., *A Tour thro' London about the Year 1725*. This is a splendid piece of baroque book-making, a de luxe version of Letter 5 and the start of Letter 6 which was issued in an edition of 350 copies with mock eighteenth-century binding. I use the cue title 'B/C'. Defoe's principal sources are identified as follows; Edmund Gibson's edition of *Britannia* (1695 edn) as 'Camden' (there are no page numbers: reference is by column); John Macky, *A Journey through England in Familiar Letters* (1714–23) as 'Macky'. *The Journeys of Celia Fiennes* are quoted from the edition of Christopher Morris (1947). For parliamentary constituencies, I have used – besides older authorities such as Beatson and Oldfield – W. A. Speck, *Tory and Whig* (1970), referred to here as 'Speck'. This relates principally to Anne's reign, but most facts regarding the electorate apply to the reign of her successor, too.

Information on buildings is chiefly derived from the Victoria County Histories, the *Survey of London* and volumes published by the Royal Commission on Historical Monuments. Ordinarily the source is not specified. Finally, information on Defoe himself is taken from the books listed on p. 40. Healey's edition of the *Letters* is indicated by that short form.

Letter 1

1. p. 47 *I set out, the 3d of April, 1722*: Whether Defoe actually made special journeys for the purpose of his book, or relied on earlier memories, is not certain. However, there seems to be evidence that he did have business in East Anglia in 1722 (some of it private, some perhaps connected with the general election held in that year). Letter 1, therefore, in all probability does rest on up-to-date information and recent first-hand experience.

2. p. 49 *Mr Camden, and his learned continuator, Bishop Gibson*: William Camden (1551–1623), Master of Westminster School, Clarenceux King of Arms, whose *Britannia* (1586) was Defoe's principal source. He used the edition by Edmund Gibson (1669–1748), Bishop of London and the most important ecclesiastical figure in the age of Walpole. This appeared in 1695 and again in two volumes in 1722. Defoe used the 1695 text.

3. p. 49 *the great road*: Iter V, from London to Caistor via Ilford, Romford, Kelvedon and Colchester.

4. p. 50 *fish-pools*: Several projects along these lines were promoted around 1720; Richard Steele was the instigator of one such scheme. See Calhoun Winton, *Sir Richard Steele, M.P.* (1970).

5. p. 50 *Calais, St Maloes*: Bombarded by the British fleet under Admiral Benbow, Lord Berkeley and others, around 1693–5.

6. p. 50 *the Gunpowder Treason Plot ...*: A story that is now generally discounted. The conspiracy was largely mounted in Northamptonshire.

7. p. 51 *Captain Perry*: John Perry (1670–1732), engineer, worked on the Volga–Don canal 1698–1712. Tenders had been invited in 1714 for stopping Dagenham breach; Perry was underbid, and the work allotted elsewhere, but finally he had to be called in to carry out the job. He published an account of the undertaking in 1721.

8. p. 53 *Lord Newbrugh*: George, Baron Newburgh, who became second Earl of Cholmondley in 1725 (*c.* 1666–1733). He was governor of the fort from 1702 until he inherited the earldom.

9. p. 55 *the fogs and damps*: It is a fact that some virulent forms of fever were still common among labourers in the marshy districts of Kent and Essex after they had effectively disappeared in London itself. See Dorothy George, *London Life in the Eighteenth Century*, p. 67.

10. p. 56 *Queen Boadicia*: Boadicea, Queen of the Iceni (d. A.D. 62); led a revolt against the Romans, and after defeating the invaders was herself overcome by Suetonius.

11. p. 56 *Mr Camden*: See Camden, cols. li–liv.

12. p. 56 *Lord Viscount Barrington*: John Shute (1678–1734), first Viscount; a Whig M.P., expelled from the House for complicity in a fraudulent lottery, a fact Defoe discreetly glosses over.

13. p. 57 *Mr Western*: Like most of the others named here, Western can only be identified as a prominent local gentleman. Perhaps William Weston of Rivenhall (d. 1729); George Cressener (d. 1722), J.P. and Deputy Lieutenant for Essex; and Nicholas Wescombe of Wickham Bishops (d. 1744). *Olemus* may be Herman Olmius (d. 1718), a Dutch merchant, or more likely his son John Olmius of Braintree (d. 1731), Deputy Governor of the Bank. *Sir Thomas Webster* (d. 1751), created a baronet in 1703, M.P. for Colchester and Verderer of Waltham Forest. He was the son of a citizen of London.

14. p. 57 *eat*: Obsolete variant for 'ate'.

15. p. 57 *Sir Josiah Child*: See note 62 to p. 110.

16. p. 57 *Sir Charles Lucas*: Royalist (d. 1648), knighted 1638; taken prisoner at Marston Moor and condemned to death by court martial in 1648. *Sir George Lisle* was another royalist commander; fought at Newbury and Naseby; knighted 1645, shot as rebel 1648.

17. p. 58 *adjacent towns*: Here Defoe inserts a long account of the siege of Colchester in 1648, in the form of a diary kept by a witness. It has been suspected that Defoe himself wrote this account, but though the period was a favourite one from the point of view of imaginative reconstruction, it is most unlikely that Defoe can have been responsible for this particular narrative. (The matter is discussed by Professor Godfrey Davies in *Modern Philology*, Vol. 48, 1950.) It is therefore omitted here. *Bays*: An old form of baize, coarse woollens.

18. p. 59 *Sir Isaac Rebow*: M.P. for Colchester in ten parliaments, but lost his seat in 1722. A member of a prominent local family which had come to England from the Low Countries in the reign of Elizabeth I. They were rich industrialists with an interest in Harwich lighthouse. Rebow founded a political dynasty which was durable but of little parliamentary consequence.

19. p. 59 *Earl Cowper*: William, Baron (1706) and Earl (1718) Cowper; Lord Keeper 1705, Lord Chancellor 1707–10, 1714–18; an eminent jurist and a Whig politician of high standing. He died in October 1723, which indicates that Defoe was writing prior to that date. His deputy was a barrister named Price.

20. p. 60 *Constantine the Great*: Emperor of Rome from 306 (*c.* A.D. 272–337). The eldest son of Constantius, called Chlorus ('the pale'), d. 306, by his first wife Helena, whom he subsequently renounced.

21. p. 60 *Mr Camden*: Camden, col. 351.

22. p. 63 *two members*: Defoe names those elected in 1722, i.e. Sir Philip (*sic*) Parker, third Baronet (1682–1741), M.P. from 1715 to 1734;

and Humphrey Parsons, M.P. 1722–7. For Parsons see note 45 to p. 165. Parker, incidentally, later took the surname Parker-a-Morley-Long, which would have taxed Defoe's precarious hold on nomenclature to the utmost.

23. p. 63 *Sir John Eyles*: Sub-governor of the company 1721–33; M.P. for Chippenham; d. 1745.

24. p. 63 *Robert Fitz-Walter*: Led the barons' army against King John; crusader; Lord of Dunmow; d. 1235.

25. p. 64 *Ralph Peverell*: A leading land-holder named in the Domesday Book, especially in East Anglia. Defoe subscribes to a rather dubious genealogy linking William the Conqueror with the Peverel line. The great medieval historian E. A. Freeman is highly sceptical of the alleged connection.

26. p. 64 *the ancient records*: Defoe probably found the verses in Camden, col. 344, and then perhaps looked out an earlier source. But often he attempts to disguise borrowings from Camden by a formula of this kind.

27. p. 67 *Sir Samuel Barnardiston*: Whig politician (1620–1707); baronet 1663; M.P. for Suffolk 1678–1702; deputy governor of the East India Company. The baronetcy rapidly became extinct with the death of its fourth holder in 1712.

28. p. 68 *his wild observations*: Defoe, predictably, is referring to Macky (I, 6). By the fifth edition of 1732, Macky had changed his figure of 'above Two Hundred' tons to five hundred.

29. p. 69 *Greenland fishery*: The Greenland whaling company had been set up early in the seventeenth century. After a lapse in operations an attempt was made to revive the trade in 1692. But before its fourteen-year franchise had run out, the company had run through its capital of £80,000, and the undertaking once more fell into abeyance. The South Sea Company attempted to restore the trade yet again in the 1720s, as a recovery operation following the bubble: but it was no more successful that its predecessors.

30. p. 72 *The large spire steeple ...*: I have not been able to trace this event.

31. p. 72 *Dr Beeston*: Possibly John Beeston (born c. 1675), of New College, Oxford, made Doctor of Medicine 1708.

32. p. 72 *Dr Rowland Taylor*: Ll.D. 1534, incumbent of Hadleigh from 1544, burnt at the stake 1555. *The detestable conspiracy*: a Jacobite intrigue involving Bishop Atterbury and others, discovered in the summer of 1723. *Lenham*: Lavenham.

33. p. 73 *a royal village*: See Camden, col. 368. Edmund, King of the East Angles, martyr and saint (841–70), defeated by the Danes at Hoxne. Siegebert (d. 637), King of the East Angles.

34. p. 74 *King Sweno*: (Svein (d. 1014), King of England and

Denmark, invaded England successively in 994, 1003 and 1013; according to legend, pierced by the spear of St Edmund, whom he had derided. Canute or Cnut, King of England 1016–35.

35. p. 75 *a tragical ... act of barbarity*: A *cause célèbre* of the moment when Defoe was writing. Arundel Coke hired John Woodward to murder Crisp on 1 January 1722. The assassins were arrested on 16 January and convicted on 13 March. Following their execution at the end of the month a number of accounts were published; it is quite likely that Defoe was responsible for one or other of these.

36. p. 75 *The Duke of Grafton*: Charles Fitzroy, second Duke (1683–1757); grandson of Charles II; courtier and soldier. Recalled as Lord Lieutenant in the spring of 1724. His mother died in February 1723. *Cabal*: Often derived from the initials of the five ministers Clifford, Arlington, Buckingham, Ashley (better known as Shaftesbury) and Lauderdale. But the word seems already to have been in use before it was thus popularized. *Andrew Marvell* (1621–78): then perhaps better known for his satires and political writing than the lyric poetry for which he is famous today.

37. p. 76 *a late writer*: Inevitably, Macky (I, 4).

38. p. 77 *Duke of Glocester*: Humphrey, brother of Henry V, patron of learning (1391–1447); Protector rather than Regent. He died in custody on 23 February 1447, having been arrested five days previously, but was probably not murdered. The Parliament had met on 10 February.

39. p. 80 *Montague*: Edward Montagu, first Earl of Sandwich (1625–72), admiral, killed 28 May 1672; his ship, actually the *Royal James*, was set on fire by a Dutch fireship and blew up. Sandwich, 'who had fought magnificently, got away from his sinking ship in an overcrowded rowing boat, but it capsized, and he was drowned. Several days later his body was recovered and given burial in Westminster Abbey' (David Ogg).

40. p. 82 *Queen Mary*: Mary I (1516–58); retired during the ten days' reign of Lady Jane Grey (1537–54) in July 1553. The latter's faction was led by John Dudley, Duke of Northumberland (*c.* 1502–53), who had married his son, Lord Guildford Dudley, to the claimant, who was daughter of the Earl of Suffolk. Northumberland was executed 22 August 1553. Lady Jane Grey followed him to the scaffold 12 February 1554.

41. p. 82 *Gospellers*: Often applied derisively in the sixteenth and seventeenth centuries to extreme or 'enthusiastic' puritans; sectaries. The phrase 'hot gospeller' for a zealous Protestant goes back as far as 1562.

42. p. 82 *Hoxon*: See note 33 to p. 73.

43. p. 84 *Sir John Holt*: Judge; Chief Justice of the King's Bench

1689–1710, and one of the most influential figures on the bench in his age. By virtue of his office he could have presided at the Old Bailey in July 1703, when Defoe stood trial for uttering a seditious libel in the shape of *The Shortest Way with the Dissenters*. However, contemporary accounts omit any reference to his name, which suggests he was not present.

44. p. 85 *an Act of Parliament*: 7 Geo. I, c. 7 (1721).

45. p. 87 *The Duke of Norfolk*: Thomas Howard, thirteenth Duke (1683–1732); arrested in 1722 on suspicion of complicity in a Jacobite plot, but finally released without further action. On the city of Norwich, a contemporary account speaks of a 'strange compound body [among the Whigs] of false churchmen, Presbyterians, Independents, Anabaptists, Antinomians and Quakers'. Quoted by Speck, p. 77.

46. p. 87 *Sir Tho. Brown*: the famous writer Sir Thomas Browne, a doctor in Norwich and author of *Religio Medici* (1605–82). The book to which Defoe alludes is *Reportorium: or some Account of the Monuments in the Cathedral Church of Norwich* (1680).

47. p. 88 *a long fabulous story*: It is a matter of record that Yarmouth and Lowestoft were long at odds over the rights in the herring fishery, and that the affair came to the Lords for settlement as late as 1662.

48. p. 92 *a murther committed in the street*: Not traced.

49. p. 96 *Lord Viscount Townsend*: Charles, second Viscount Townshend (1674–1736), Secretary of State, whose seat was at Raynham. Brother-in-law of Robert Walpole (1676–1745), the famous statesman, later first Earl of Orford, owner of Houghton Hall.

50. p. 98 *Earl of Orford*: Edward Russell (1653–1727), First Lord of the Admiralty, Lord Justice, and member of the Whig 'Junto'. The battle of La Hogue (inaccurately so called) took place on 19 May 1692.

51. p. 98 *Mr Frampton*: Tregonwell Frampton (1641–1727), known as the Father of the Turf, keeper of the King's Horses; his most famous horse was Dragon, winner of many races in the age of Anne.

52. p. 98 *Sir R—— Fagg*: For Sir Robert Fagg, see note 30 to p. 146.

53. p. 99 *Sir Robert Davers*: Defoe evidently means the second Baronet (1653–1722), who married Mary, daughter of the second Baron Jermyn; M.P. for Bury St Edmunds and Suffolk, and a High Tory Tacker (Speck, p. 102). He died 1 October and was buried 7 October 1722. Curiously Defoe does not mention the death of Sir Robert's widow a few days later. To complete an unhappy succession of events, his son and namesake, the third Baronet (*c.* 1684–1723), died in the following May. Apparently Defoe had not heard of this latter death when he sent the *Tour* to the press.

54. p. 99 *the Earl of Dysert*: Lionel Tollemache, third Earl of Dysart (1649–1727).

55. p. 107 *Pie-Powder Courts*: Courts of summary jurisdiction held at fairs, to settle disputes between buyers and sellers. Derived from French *pied-poudreux*, vagabond or wayfarer.

56. p. 108 *Dr Snape*: Andrew Snape, D.D. (1675–1742), Master of Eton, 1711, Provost of King's, 1719. A leading participant in the so-called Bangorian controversy, started by the sermons and writings of Benjamin Hoadly (1676–1761), then Bishop of Bangor. Hoadly subsequently held the sees of Hereford, Salisbury and Winchester, and was regarded as a pillar of the Whig establishment for many years. *Dr Bently*: Richard Bentley (1662–1742), the notoriously contentious Master of Trinity, deprived of his degrees by the University but restored after a long legal battle in March 1724.

57. p. 108 *the late Earl of Radnor*: The second Earl died on 3 August 1723. Wimpole was acquired by Pope's friend Edward Harley, later second Earl of Oxford (1689–1741), through his marriage in 1713 to Lady Henrietta (*sic*) Cavendish-Holles, only daughter of John Holles, first Duke of Newcastle by the second creation (1662–1711). The Duke, who had bought Wimpole in 1710, died from a fall off his horse in May 1711. For Lord Harley's father, the first Earl of Oxford, see note 36 to p. 372.

58. p. 109 *Olmeus*: See note 13 to p. 57.

59. p. 109 *Mr Lydiat*: Simon Lydiatt, of Christ Church, Oxford; master of Felsted from *c.* 1707 to his death in November 1712. His successor, Hugh Hutchin, held office till his own death in March 1725.

60. p. 109 *the present duke*: The second Duke of Manchester (1700–1739), succeeded 1722. Katherine Darnley (1682–1743), widow of John Sheffield, Duke of Buckinghamshire (1648–1721), and illegitimate daughter of James II. She was allegedly the original of Pope's 'Atossa'.

61. p. 110 *King Harold:* Killed at Hastings, 14 October 1066; buried near the site of the battle; William was offered the weight of his body in gold to return his corpse to the family, but refused. However, at some subsequent date the remains were transferred to Waltham Abbey. They were again moved in the twelfth century. A legend grew up that Harold had survived the battle and become a monk at Chester, but there is no reason to give the story any credence.

62. p. 110 *Lord Castlemain*: Wanstead House, built c. 1715–20, by Richard Child, created Viscount Castlemain 1718. His father, Sir Josiah Child (1630–99), London merchant and economic pamphleteer; chairman of the East India Company, baronet 1678. He bought Wanstead Abbey in 1673. It may be noted that Defoe spends a fair amount of space describing this seat, as he does with other residences. Contrary to the general impression, Defoe allots much of his *Tour* to stately homes, those belonging to the older gentry as well as those

of the new men of mercantile England like the Child family. It is true that the proportion of such material was even higher in later editions of the *Tour*. But it should be remembered that the first edition itself covers scores of these seats, many of which have had to be left out of this text for reasons of space.

63. p. 112 *I conclude my first letter*: Defoe added an Appendix, bringing up to date one or two small points, including the new work at Walpole's seat, Houghton Hall (cf. p. 96).

Letter 2

1. p. 113 *Flamstead House*: The Royal Observatory at Greenwich, built 1675–6, named after the first Astronomer Royal, John Flamsteed, F.R.S. (1646–1719), friend of Newton.

2. p. 113 *the park*: Designed by the famous French landscape gardener, Lenôtre.

3. p. 114 *Sir John Vanburg*: Vanbrugh (1664–1726), architect and dramatist, leased a property in Greenwich in 1717, and built a number of houses including Maze Hill.

4. p. 114 *an hospital*: Morden College, founded in 1695, by the first Baronet (1623–1708), M.P. for Colchester, Levant merchant. Lady Morden died in 1721.

5. p. 116 *Royal-Sovereign*: Originally the *Sovereign of the Seas*, launched in 1637; a three-deck man of war, carrying 104 guns and displacing some 1,500 tons; 127 feet long. Accidentally destroyed by fire off Chatham in 1696.

6. p. 117 *the Dutch*: The Dutch navy under Van Ghent raided Chatham on 12/13 June 1667. The English defences had been weakened by mismanagement and pilfering, and hasty measures were taken to remedy the situation in a mood of acute embarrassment after this humiliating reverse.

7. p. 118 *Queen Elizabeth, who was born at Greenwich*: On 7 September 1533, to Anne Boleyn.

8. p. 121 *Mr Nicks*: The story is also told of John or William Nevison (1630–85), hanged at York; of a certain Harris; and, of course, of Dick Turpin. But since Turpin was active only in the years after Defoe wrote, his connection is obviously a posthumous legend.

9. p. 125 *the Royal Sovereign*: See note 5 to p. 116. For Shovell, see note 1 to p. 235.

10. p. 126 *that dreadful tempest*: The Great Storm of 26–7 November 1703.

11. p. 126 *that memorable attempt*: See note 6 to p. 117. The *Royal Charles*, a flagship, and the *Unity* were carried off, and the ships destroyed included the *Loyal London (sic)*, the *Royal Oak* and the

Royal James. Upnore Castle had become chiefly a place of entertainment and most of the gunpowder was unusable. Not surprisingly, the attack induced a fit of self-criticism and inquiry, with the improvement in defensive arrangements which Defoe speaks of.

12. p. 128 *Queenborough*: There were fewer than seventy electors for the borough (Speck, pp. 61–2). The Mayor of Queenborough seems to have been a sort of proverbial instance, something like the legal use of John Doe. See Locke's *Essay Concerning Human Understanding*, 2, xxvii, 19.

13. p. 128 *his escape into France*: In December 1688. See note 25 to p. 275.

14. p. 131 *the Three Cranes*: Near present-day Cannon Street station.

15. p. 133 *St Augustin*: Augustine (d. A.D. 604) was sent by Gregory the Great (540–604), Pope from 590, and reached Britain in 597. For Joseph of Arimathea, see note 14 to p. 256.

16. p. 133 *King Stephen*: King of England from 1135 (*c*. 1105–54); died at Dover, and buried at Feversham Abbey, which he had founded.

17. p. 134 *Erasmus Roterdamus*: Desiderius Erasmus (1466–1536), Dutch humanist, author of *Praise of Folly* and other works; spent many years in England. His comments on the opulence of Canterbury, with which he contrasts the state of the poor, appear in his *Colloquies*. Thomas à Becket (1118–70), assassinated 29 December 1170, canonized 1172.

18. p. 134 *the Walloons*: Protestants from the Low Countries, who left their homes after the savage repressions of the Spanish commander sent by Philip II in 1567, Fernando Alvarez de Toledo, third Duke of Alba (1507–82). The Duke issued harsh ordinances and introduced severe taxes, 1569–71.

19. p. 134 *the first Act*: 11 Wm. III, c. 10 (1699); the English clothing industry had lobbied Parliament to ensure that the East India Company should be able only to re-export Eastern silks. The second measure Defoe alludes to is 7 Geo. I, c. 7 (1721), by which the import of printed calicoes was forbidden. 'These Indian novelties had attracted women who, in the opinion of Parliament and the manufacturers, ought to have dressed in the lighter fabrics made all of wool, or at least in fabrics with a warp of wool and a weft of cotton or silk spun honestly from the raw materials in England [raw silk was imported by Levant Company]. Pamphlets were written; agitations were raised; "calico chaces" were organised – or perhaps started as rowdy larks – to slit or foul the calico frocks' (Sir John Clapham).

20. p. 135 *an Act of Parliament*: 6 Henry VIII, c. 17 (1515).

21. p. 135 *Sir Tho. Hales*: of Beakesbourne, Kent (*c.* 1662–1748); M.P. in eight parliaments, succeeded as second Baronet in 1695. Others named are Endymion Smythe, third Viscount Strangford, who owned an estate at Ashford; bred as a Catholic, but conformed and took his seat in the Lords, 1715; died on 8 September 1724, just after Defoe wrote. Sir George (*sic*) Oxenden, the fifth Baronet (1694–1775), a Lord of the Admiralty, M.P. for Sandwich, a noted profligate (Defoe is often confused over Christian names). *Roman*: i.e. Catholic. Sir George Rooke (1650–1709), Admiral, successfully attacked Vigo, 12 October 1702, and took Gibraltar, 24 July 1704; removed from command largely for political reasons, early in 1705, when Sir Cloudesley Shovell supplanted him. 'The High Tories were tempted by Gibraltar and Malaga to set up the deeds of Rooke and the Navy in rivalry to those of Marlborough and the Army' (G. M. Trevelyan). Defoe cordially disliked Rooke (*Letters*, pp. 18–25). The battle in the Straits is that of Malaga on 24 August 1704; the French commander was the Comte de Toulouse. Rooke and Tourville were in opposition only at Lagos Bay (16 June 1692), a decisive French victory.

22. p. 137 *about —— miles*: Six, approximately.

23. p. 137 *the Great Storm*: A topic of inexhaustible fascination for Defoe, who wrote a book called *The Storm; or a Collection of the most Remarkable Casualties and Disasters which happen'd in the late dreadful Tempest, both by Sea and Land* (1704). He made a special trip to view the damage in Kent, and never ceased in later years to recall the event. For Shovell, see note 1 to p. 235.

24. p. 139 *Between this point of land and Beachy*: Defoe describes the defeat of the Anglo-Dutch navy by the French under Tourville, 10 July 1690. Defoe is in error when he supposes that Admiral Herbert was restored to favour. He had already been granted his earldom in the previous year: and though he was cleared of the grosser forms of dereliction, he was never reinstated in his command. See also note 6 to p. 248.

25. p. 141 *one inexhaustible store-house of timber*: A decidedly over-optimistic judgement, repeated elsewhere by Defoe. 'Only the introduction of coal as a fuel for use in all processes of the iron trades saved the woods of England from complete destruction through the development of the metal industries' (G. D. H. Cole). There had in fact been a shortage of wood ever since the time of Henry VIII; the Tudors and Stuarts had been notably wasteful in their use of timber. Iron-working consumed 300,000 loads of timber annually by the end of the seventeenth century, usually in the form of grown oaks. Wood was also in heavy demand for house-building right through the eighteenth century. Even the measures which were taken in the reign of Charles II, to preserve the timber of the Forest of Dean, and

during the reign of William III, to plant fresh trees in the New Forest, fell into neglect. The warnings of John Evelyn in his *Sylva* (1664), against an undue concentration on tillage, received too little attention; and by the time of the Napoleonic wars England might have been severely embarrassed for timber, had it not been for the fresh planting that was carried out, often by private individuals. (This note is based chiefly on R. G. Albion, *Forests and Sea Power*.)

26. p. 141 *the Prince of Wales*: See note 2 to p. 182. The occasion Defoe describes may perhaps be placed in the summer of 1720. Lionel Sackville, first Duke of Dorset (1687–1765), created 1720, held various offices including the Lord Lieutenancy of Ireland and the Lord Presidency of the Council. He was perhaps rather a courtier than a politician.

27. p. 145 *Bright Helmston*: Perhaps not immediately recognizable as Brighton, then a small and far from elegant fishing village. Its renown as a watering-place did not begin for another fifty years.

28. p. 145 *three borough towns*: Shoreham had some seventy electors, Steyning eighty, and Bramber about thirty burgage-holders. See Speck, p. 130.

29. p. 146 *nothing of a town*: Celia Fiennes had written, with unaccustomed poetry, 'Grass grows now where Winchelsea was, as was once said of Troy [by Ovid]; there are but a very few houses now but the Corporation still continues and the mayor and aldermen which 13 makes most of the inhabitants' (*Journeys*, p. 138). The corrupt election of which Defoe speaks was held as far back as 1678. Defoe's recollection, not surprisingly, is a little vague. Several details are wrong; but briefly it may be said that Banks, created a baronet in 1661 and Lord Mayor of London, lost despite spending two or three thousand pounds himself. The result was six votes to Banks and six to his opponent, Chesheld Draper. Banks then received the Mayor's casting vote, but Draper petitioned Parliament to reverse the result because of bribery on the part of Colonel Austin, a supporter of Banks. His appeal was sustained. Heneage Finch, first Earl of Aylesford (1627–99), married Banks's daughter. For fuller details see D. C. Coleman, *Sir John Banks* (1963).

30. p. 146 *Sir John Fagg*: The first Baronet, created 1660; M.P. for Sussex and Steyning; died 1701. Sir Robert Fagg, third Baronet (1673–1736), succeeded in 1715.

31. p. 147 *the present Duke of Somerset*: Charles Seymour, sixth Duke (1662–1748), politician; the 'proud Duke'. His wife, Elizabeth, Baroness Percy, daughter of the eleventh Earl of Northumberland (1667–1722). Thrice married, she was a favourite of Queen Anne, despite her Whiggish sentiments, and a strong antagonist of Swift. She died 23 November 1722.

32. p. 148 *the death of her grace the duchess*: This sentence is useful in dating the composition of Volume I. The Duchess died on 9 December and her husband on 27 May following. In the same paragraph Defoe lists five dukes (not including Richmond), two duchesses and three earls who had died in the year 1722. In fact some of those concerned had died in 1721, but the necrology is still an impressive roll-call of the Augustan ruling class. It includes Marlborough and his son-in-law, the statesman Sunderland (see note 28 to p. 407).

33. p. 149 *when Dr —— Williams was bishop*: About 1709; John Williams (*c.* 1636–1709), Bishop since 1696, died on 24 April of that year in London.

34. p. 153 *Mr Cardonell*: Adam Cardonell (d. 1719). *Mr Cromwell*: Oliver Cromwell (1656–1705), eldest son of Richard Cromwell.

35. p. 154 *Bevis of Southampton*: Sir Bevis of Hamtown (wrongly identified with Southampton), hero of a chivalric romance allied to the Charlemagne cycle, retold in Drayton's *Poly-Olbion.*

36. p. 155 *a castle*: Farnham Castle, built by Henry de Blois, Bishop of Winchester, brother of King Stephen.

37. p. 157 *Sir John Denham*: Poet and royalist (1615–69). His *Cooper's Hill*, first written *c.* 1642, and extensively revised by 1668, was among the most celebrated works of English literature for many generations. The couplet Defoe prints was constantly quoted, parodied, imitated and analysed; it served as a kind of microcosm of Augustan poetry.

38. p. 157 *the incomparable Cowley*: Abraham Cowley (1618–67), another immensely popular and influential poet. Henry VI was deposed by Edward IV in 1461; died in 1471, allegedly murdered by the Duke of Gloucester, later Richard III.

39. p. 157 *the old Countess of Richmond*: Lady Margaret Beaufort (1344–1409), married Edmund Tudor, Earl of Richmond; founded St John's College, Cambridge, and refounded Christ's College.

40. p. 159 *Sir Tho. Bludworth*: Lord Mayor in 1665–6. Narcissus Luttrell records his death on 12 May 1682. Pepys calls him a 'silly man, I think'.

41. p. 160 *The bishop*: Edmund Gibson. See Camden, col. 163.

42. p. 162 *all the country round*: Here Defoe tells a story concerning the exploits of certain young men in this district (including, no doubt, Defoe, then at Fisher's academy) in the year 1676. The anecdote supplies further proof that the Mole does not pass underground.

43. p. 162 *Mr Howard*: Defoe seems to mean Charles Howard (d. 1720), whose son became the fifteenth Duke of Norfolk. The house was called Deepden.

44. p. 163 *Sir Adam Brown*: or Browne (d. 1690), the leading landowner in this district when Defoe was living there.

45. p. 165 *Sir John Parsons*: Member of an important brewing family and Lord Mayor in 1703–4; d. 1717. His son Humphrey (1676–1741) was to be Lord Mayor in 1730–31. He was elected an alderman in 1721 and sheriff on 25 June 1722, holding office between November 1722 and November 1723. This supplies another clue regarding the composition of the *Tour*.

46. p. 165 *Sir Robert Clayton*: A scrivener, Lord Mayor 1679–80, M.P. from 1689 to his death; a benefactor of St Thomas's and Christ's Hospital. Evidently known to Defoe, who introduces Clayton into *Roxana*.

47. p. 166 *Dr Warner*: John Warner (1581–1666), Bishop of Rochester 1637, benefactor of Bromley College.

48. p. 167 *the Lady Dowager Onslow*: She drowned herself on 25 November 1718. Defoe is vague about such intervals of time. She was the wife of the first Baron (1654–1717), a Lord of the Treasury. *The present lord*: Thomas, second Baron (*c.* 1679–1740).

49. p. 168 *Mr Scawen*: William Scawen, knighted 1692, died 1722. *Sir John Fellows* (*c.* 1671–1724), created a baronet 1719, died 26 July 1724 just after Volume I was published. He bought Dr Ratcliff's house at Carshalton.

50. p. 168 *one unhappy stock jobbing year*: 1720.

51. p. 172 *Cassibellanus*: Cassivellaunus, ruler of the Catrivellauni, who lived in the northern Home Counties; defeated by Caesar's army in the summer of 54 B.C. (the exact place is not known).

52. p. 172 *the late Duke of Lauderdale*: John Maitland, first Duke (1616–82), statesman. Laurence Hyde, first Earl of Rochester (1641–1711), Tory leader; son of the Earl of Clarendon mentioned by Defoe in the next paragraph, i.e. Edward Hyde (1609–74), chief minister of Charles II, historian and autobiographer.

53. p. 173 *a most unhappy disaster*: The fire at Ham House took place on 1 October 1721; a number of servants were burnt or injured, apart from the destruction of property mentioned by Defoe.

54. p. 174 *Mr Temple*: Henry Temple, later first Viscount Palmerston (1673–1762), appointed 12 March 1723 – another dating clue. He was not in fact a son of the famous Sir William, the statesman and author (1628–99), to whom Swift was secretary at Moor Park.

55. p. 177 *Sir Josiah Child*: See note 62 to p. 110. *Sir John Lethulier*: A Levant merchant, and member of the Barber-Surgeons' Company, Alderman from 1676, d. 1719. *Sir James Bateman*: Lord Mayor 1716–17, director of the East India Company, governor of the Bank of England; d. 1718.

56. p. 178 *Sir Joseph Hodges*: The second Baronet, who dissipated a large fortune in his early youth; d. 1722, aged only about eighteen. *Sir Justus Beck*: Created a baronet in 1714 (the first baronetcy of the

Hanoverian dynasty); d. 1722. The widow Cock has not been positively identified.

57. p. 178 *the Mint*: The old refuge for debtors, notorious for its cheap lodging-houses and narrow alleys, and the scene of many irregular marriages. It lay near to the site of the Borough underground station.

Letter 3

1. p. 181 *Hampton-Court*: Built on the site of the manor of the Knight Hospitallers, and ceded to Henry VIII in 1525. Thomas Wolsey (1471–1550), Archbishop of York, Cardinal and Lord Chancellor; fell rapidly from power and died in disgrace.

2. p. 182 *The Prince and Princess*: George Augustus, Prince of Wales (1683–1760), from 1727 King George II: and Wilhelmina Caroline of Anspach, later Queen Caroline (1683–1737). The Princess, who already had a son and three daughters, was delivered of a still-born son in November 1716, and a son who died young in the following November. Her second surviving son, William, Duke of Cumberland (the future victor of Culloden), was born in 1721, and two further daughters in 1722 and 1724. A good deal of the typical Hanoverian friction attended these various *accouchements*. The likelihood is that Defoe refers to the occasion at the end of October 1716 when the Court returned to St James's by water 'in a gilded state barge, accompanied at a distance by boatloads of musicians. It was an exceptionally fine day' (Peter Quennell, *Caroline of England*). The still-birth occurred within a fortnight.

3. p. 184 *especially two of them*: Cartoons by Raphael, bought by Charles I in 1625, now in the Victoria and Albert Museum.

4. p. 186 *her spouse*: Prince George died on 28 October 1708. See also note 11 to p. 345.

5. p. 187 *a sudden and surprising fire*: The town was almost destroyed in 1689; there had been another bad fire in 1644.

6. p. 188 *the bishop's palace*: George Morley (1597–1684), Bishop of Winchester 1660, rebuilt Wolvesey Palace, supposedly to a design by Wren. It was largely demolished in 1781. For Waller, see note 19 to p. 266.

7. p. 188 *Bishop Fox*: Richard Foxe (*c.* 1448–1528), Bishop from 1501, founder of Corpus Christi College, Oxford.

8. p. 189 *Bishop Mew*: Peter Mew (1619–1706), Bishop of Bath and Wells 1672, translated to Winchester 1684; Vice-Chancellor of Oxford University 1669–73.

9. p. 189 *William of Wickham*: Churchman (1324–1404); Bishop

from 1366, Lord Chancellor 1367–71, founded New College, Oxford, in 1379 and Winchester College in 1387.

10. p. 191 *a very noble design*: The so-called King's House, designed by Wren, begun in 1683 but discontinued by James II: cf. *The Journeys of Celia Fiennes*, p. 47.

11. p. 192 *The hospital*: St Cross, founded *c.* 1136; a second benefaction by Cardinal Henry Beaufort (d. 1447), Bishop of Winchester, son of John of Gaunt, made about 1446. The original founder was not William II but Henry de Blois, half-brother of King Stephen.

12. p. 194 410 *foot*: 404 feet is the modern reckoning.

13. p. 195 *the painting in the choir*: Washed out in 1789. Celia Fiennes was more favourably impressed (*Journeys*, p. 6).

14. p. 195 *Lord Sturton*: Charles, eighth Baron, murdered William Harthill and his son, hanged at Salisbury 6 March 1557.

15. p. 197 *the Earl of Pembroke*: Thomas Herbert, eighth Earl (*c.* 1656–1733).

16. p. 197 *pieces of antiquity*: The Earl was well known as a collector. 'He bought the Arundel marbles and Mazarin busts, with pedestals, many of which remain at Wilton. He added a large number of rare books to the library. His great speciality was gems and intaglios, of which he amassed an important selection' (James Lees-Milne, *Earls of Creation*). Pope sneered at his taste in the *Epistle to Burlington*: 'He buys for Topham, Drawings and Designs,|For Pembroke Statues, dirty Gods, and Coins'. He also had some pretensions as a literary patron, whilst his son became an architect of minor distinction.

17. p. 199 *Mr Jones*: The story is that James I, after a visit to Wilton, commanded Inigo Jones to investigate the origins of Stonehenge. The result was *The most notable Antiquity of Great Britain, vulgarly called Stoneheng, restored by Inigo Jones esq....*, published by his disciple Webb in 1655. John Aubrey (1626–97) made extensive collections for his *Natural History of Wiltshire*, but this was known only in manuscript when Defoe wrote. So was *Monumenta Britannica*, part one of which contains a review of the subject. Jones believed the site to be of Roman origin; the Danish school included Walter Charleton, whose arguments impressed Dryden amongst others. Aubrey offered the 'probability' that the remains were Druidic. See Anthony Powell, *John Aubrey and his Friends* (1948).

18. p. 202 *a proposal*: Made by Defoe in 1709 to Sidney, first Earl Godolphin (1645–1712). The scheme was originally outlined in the *Review* in the summer of 1709, when more than ten thousand refugees from the Rhenish Palatinate arrived in England. Two thousand of them turned out to be Papists and were sent home at once. The most part remained, a charge on English charity, and competitors for

English employment in a bad year [for corn]' (G. M. Trevelyan, *England under Queen Anne*).

19. p. 204 *according to the design*: Defoe specifies his ideas at some length, outlining the complete economic organization of the community, an estimate of growth prospects, a projection of the likely occupational spread, and allied matters.

20. p. 206 *King Ethelred*: Ethelred I, king from 866 to 871; defeated at Merton 871.

21. p. 209 *Dorchester*: Defoe had formed his opinion of the moderate behaviour found in this town during his fact-finding mission for Harley in 1705; see *Letters*, p. 105.

22. p. 211 *two light-houses*: The Trinity House patent licensing their erection was granted in May 1716.

23. p. 212 *the landing of the Duke of Monmouth*: On 11 June 1685.

24. p. 213 *Lord Howard of Effingham*: Also took part in the capture of Cadiz in 1596 (1536–1624).

25. p. 219 *Sir William Petre*: Statesman (1505–72). Others named, as well as those too familiar to require any note, are: Richard Hooker (*c.* 1554–1600), theologian, author of *The Laws of Ecclestiastical Polity* (1593–7); Sir John Glanville the elder (1542–1600) and the younger (1558–1661); and Peter King, first Baron King, Lord Chancellor 1725–33 (1669–1734), a strong Whig who rose from comparatively humble origins to eminence both as an advocate and as a judge. Several other more obscure figures mentioned by Defoe have been left out. The list derives from Camden, cols. 38–42.

26. p. 223 *the famous Mr Winstanley*: Henry Winstanley (1644–1703); first designs for Eddystone lighthouse, 1696. He contrived a number of unusual inventions, often on a clockwork principle. Defoe's visit was actually made in August 1705, not 1704.

27. p. 226 *a considerable town*: Devonport.

28. p. 227 *Mr Carew*: Richard Carew (1555–1620), antiquarian, author of *The Survey of Cornwall* (1602).

29. p. 228 *another way*: To the crown. A system of heavy duties survived into the nineteenth century.

30. p. 230 *a mock cavalcade*: Defoe quotes a description of this custom from Carew's *Survey*.

31. p. 232 *a new commerce*: Following the Methuen Treaty in 1703, when four weekly packets went into service.

Appendix to Letter 3

1. p. 235 *Sir Cloudesly Shovel*: Or Shovell, the celebrated admiral (1655–1707), lost when the *Association* and other ships were wrecked

off the Bishop Rock, when returning from an expedition to Toulon, 22 October 1707.

2. p. 236 *during the war with France*: In the early 1690s: perhaps the summer of 1690.

3. p. 238 *Cherosonese*: See note 2 to p. 391. A brief set of Addenda to Volume I are omitted here; they concern new buildings in the course of erection when the book was going through the press, around March 1724.

Letter 4

1. p. 241 *Agricola*: Gnaeus Julius Agricola (A.D. 40–93), governor of Britain, over-ran the country in seven campaigns, conquered Anglesey, reformed the government (78–84).

2. p. 243 *Arthur*: Legendary king of Britain, perhaps a late-fifth-century chieftain. Many of the stories concerning him derive from Nennius in the eighth century. Arthur's supposed father, Uther Pendragon, was certainly mythical.

3. p. 243 *whirle-bats*: Whirlbat or whorlbat, the word used in the fifteenth and sixteenth centuries to translate *caestus*, a game played by the ancients involving lead plummets.

4. p. 244 *Richard, Earl of Cornwall*: Defoe presumably refers to Richard, second son of King John, Count of Poitou (1209–72), crowned King of the Roman Empire at Aachen 1257; joint Guardian of England. Defoe's text hereabouts is heavily dependent on Camden and Bishop Gibson.

5. p. 247 *Bartlet*: Depending on when Defoe made his visit, this could be any one of the following: (1) William Bartlet (d. 1682), ejected minister; (2) his son John (d. 1679); (3) his grandson William (1678–1720). Each in turn served in Bideford. The third is the likeliest candidate but the first is quite possible.

6. p. 248 *General Monk*: George Monck, first duke of Albemarle (1608–70); instrumental in bringing about the Restoration of Charles II; earlier adviser of Cromwell. *Admiral Herbert*: Arthur Herbert (1647–1716), Admiral of the Fleet, created Earl of Torrington 1689. *Bing*: George Byng (1663–1733), created Earl 9 September 1721; Admiral of the Fleet, 1718; seized twenty-one Spanish ships off Cape Passaro, 31 July 1718.

7. p. 249 *Blundel*: Peter Blundell (1520–1601), merchant and philanthropist.

8. p. 252 *Warren*: Matthew Warren (1642/3–1706), master of the dissenters' academy and minister of St Paul's meeting. For Jeffreys, see note 13 to p. 397.

9. p. 253 *Lord Mohun*: Charles, fifth Baron Mohun (*c.* 1675–1712), the 'noble rake', killed in a famous duel by the Duke of Hamilton, 15 November 1712; the episode is used in Thackeray's *Henry Esmond*.

10. p. 254 *Blake*: Robert Blake (1599–1657), admiral and general at sea.

11. p. 254 *Monmouth*: See note 15 to p. 348. The battle of Sedgemoor, described in this paragraph, took place on 6 July 1685. It is probable, though not certain, that Defoe himself took part.

12. p. 254 *Lord Feversham*: Louis Duras, general (1640–1709), led James II's victorious army at Sedgemoor.

13. p. 255 *Mr Moor*: Probably John Moore (1642/3–1717), minister of Christ Church chapel from 1676, founder of Bridgwater Academy, *c.* 1690; was succeeded by his son, also John Moore (d. 1747). Either man is possible but the father more likely.

14. p. 256 *Joseph of Arimathea*: The rich Jew of Scripture (see Matt. xxvii, 57–60), who according to fable brought the Grail to Britain and founded the abbey of Glastonbury; the story taken up by Malory amongst others.

15. p. 257 *universally attested ...*: Here Defoe inserts an account of the abbey, taken from Dugdale's *Monasticon*.

16. p. 257 *Mr Cambden*: See Camden, cols. 64–5, where the drawing of the inscription is also to be found. Giraldus de Barri, called Cambrensis (*c.* 1146–1220), topographer, author of *Iteranium Cambriae* as well as lives of the saints.

17. p. 263 *the late severe Acts*: By a measure of 1698, 9 Wm. III, c. 40, restrictions were placed on the sale of wool within fifteen miles of the coast of Kent and Sussex. Owners of wool stored within ten miles of the coast had to obtain a special certificate from the nearest port officer before they could move a consignment. The preamble to the Act mentions the prevalence of smuggling in the Romney Marsh district (cf. p. 139). The threat, of course, was illegal *export*, rather than import.

18. p. 266 *made navigable by Act of Parliament*: Most recently 7 Geo. I, c. 8 (1721). The Reading–Newbury stretch had been covered in 1715.

19. p. 266 *Roundway Down*: Fought on 13 July 1743. *Waller*: William Waller (*c.* 1597–1668), parliamentary commander. *Wilmot*: Henry, Baron Wilmot; helped Charles II in his escape after Worcester; created Earl of Rochester 1652; died in 1658. Father of the poet John Wilmot, second Earl of Rochester.

20. p. 266 *a double scene of blood*: The two battles of Newbury: 20 September 1643 and 27 October 1644.

21. p. 268 *Jack of Newbery*: John Winchcombe, died c. 1519, hero

of popular tales, many brought together in Thomas Deloney's *Story of Jack of Newbury* (1597).

22. p. 268 *Mr Kenrick*: A London draper, Sheriff in 1645, left a fortune of over £30,000. His will is found in Strype's edition of Stow (1720); see note 8 to p. 295.

23. p. 270 *Sir Owen Buckingham*: A salter, knighted in 1695, Lord Mayor of London 1704–5, died 1713.

24. p. 271 *Sir John Lanier*: Military commander, killed at Steenkirk 1692. *Sir John Fenwick*: Conspirator (*c.* 1645–97). Executed 28 January 1697 for his part in a plot to assassinate William III.

25. p. 275 *King James's flight*: The King, having retreated from Salisbury on 24 November 1688, fled from Whitehall on 10 December (by which time William of Orange had reached Hungerford). The next day he was recognized at Faversham and brought back to London. He set out again on 18 December and reached France on Christmas Day.

26. p. 277 *Lord Lovelace*: John, third Earl (1640–93); his daughter Martha (*c.* 1667–1745) married Sir Henry Johnson (d. 1719) in 1693. Johnson, knighted in 1685, built up his yard until it surpassed the nearby royal dockyards in size. The Lovelace barony survived until 1736.

27. p. 281 *painting it all over again*: The work was done by Varrio (see note 43 to p. 422).

28. p. 282 *other men's performances*: Despite what he says, Defoe quotes at this point a number of facts regarding the Garter, derived from Elias Ashmole's *History* of the Order (1672; reprinted with additional matter 1715).

29. p. 284 *Admiral Churchill*: George Churchill (1654–1710), Admiral of the Blue; effectively First Sea Lord in Anne's reign. Brother of the great Duke of Marlborough, and thus brother-in-law of the famous Sarah Churchill (1660–1744).

Letter 5

1. p. 286 *two large volumes in folio*: i.e. John Strype's edition (1720) of Stow's *Survey of London*.

2. p. 286 *Tot-Hill Fields*: An open space, somewhat marshy, in Westminster, lying in the vicinity of present-day Victoria Street.

3. p. 288 *St Gyles's*: A crowded and unsalubrious area which then covered what is now upper Shaftesbury Avenue, St Giles High Street, Cambridge Circus, etc.

4. p. 288 *Montague House*: The site of the British Museum.

5. p. 288 *my Lord Godolphin*: Francis, second Earl (1678–1766),

Congreve's executor, married Henrietta Churchill who was daughter of the first Duke of Marlborough and became Duchess on her father's death.

6. p. 294 *Sir William Petty*. Political economist (1623–87).

7. p. 294 *fifteen hundred thousand*: This is certainly an over-estimation, even allowing for the fact that Defoe is thinking of greater London. The City together with Westminster and Southwark perhaps contained 800,000 people at this period; the out-parishes and adjoining villages (such as Deptford and Islington) cannot have brought the total higher than a million and a quarter at the most.

8. p. 295 *Stow and his continuators*: John Stow (1525–1605), antiquarian, author of the *Survey of London* (1598), to which Anthony Munday added further material in 1618 and Strype in 1720.

9. p. 299 *the D—— of Powis*: William Herbert, titular Duke of Powis (d. 1745), restored to his marquisate and estates after the Jacobite troubles in 1722. The house was burnt on 26 January 1713. *A very convenient church*: St George's, Bloomsbury, made parochial 1723, a fact with which Defoe had not caught up.

10. p. 301 *Fleet ditch*: A notoriously filthy channel which ran southwards along the line of Farringdon Street into the Thames. After generations of trouble, in 1666 plans were drawn up for a canal, forty feet wide, and navigable up to Holborn Bridge. Work eventually started to a design by the scientist Robert Hooke and under the general supervision of Wren. The work was completed in 1674. Unfortunately this costly and imaginative scheme proved a failure. Ultimately, in 1733, the canal was partially arched over and a covered market built; the remainder disappeared in 1766. Before then the ditch was a byword for squalor, and a favourite *motif* of Augustan satire, as in the mud-diving games of Pope's *Dunciad*.

11. p. 302 *The Royal Exchange*: Rebuilt in 1669, by Edward Jerman, City Surveyor.

12. p. 303 *fifty churches*: The new churches to be built from the proceeds of a coal-tax, as proposed by 9 Anne, c. 22 (1711). In the event only twelve completely new churches were built, plus a few renovations.

13. p. 304 *lines of Mr Dryden*: From Dryden's poem 'To my honoured Friend Mr [William] Congreve, on his Comedy called *The Double Dealer*' (1694), lines 17–19.

14. p. 308 *The shutting up the Exchequer*: The stop of the Exchequer by Charles II in January 1672. *A quo warranto*: Brought by the King in January 1682. A legal dispute followed in 1683, which led to the surrender of the charter of the City corporation and the issue of a more restricted one.

15. p. 310 *The Bank*: From shortly after its inception in 1694 until

1734 the Bank of England was housed in the Grocers' Company hall.

16. p. 311 *Mr William Dockraw*: Or Dockwra or Dockwray (d. 1716), merchant and projector; controller of the penny post 1697–1700, dismissed for alleged maladministration.

17. p. 312 *the opportunity in rebuilding*: Thomas Ripley rebuilt the Custom House between 1718 and the early 1720s.

18. p. 319 *the New-River*: A canal, 38 miles in length, from Ware to Islington, constructed in 1613; water-pipes connected at Islington supplied a large part of London.

19. p. 320 *Sir Robert Viner*: First Baronet (1631–88), Lord Mayor in 1674. The statue Defoe mentions was erected in 1672 and taken down in 1736.

20. p. 321 *Public Gaols*: The King's Bench, Marshalsea and Clink were all in Southwark. The Dutchy was in the Savoy; Bale-Dock in the Old Bailey; and Little Ease was a dungeon in the Tower.

21. p. 323 *rebuilding the ancient palace*: Whitehall was severely damaged by fires in 1691 and 1698. Proposals for its rebuilding were made by Colen Campbell and William Kent amongst others. Defoe prints an extensive 'scheme' for this purpose, possibly devised by 'Mr Weedon', mentioned by Strype (?Cavendish Weedon of Lincoln's Inn). See B/C, p. 93.

22. p. 324 *Mr Benson*: William Benson (1682–1754), patron, littérateur, amateur architect, and strong Whig; succeeded Wren as royal surveyor, but satirized by Pope and others as an incompetent muddler.

23. p. 326 *The Cottonian Library*: Formed by Sir Robert Cotton (1571–1631), antiquarian; the library was presented to the nation in 1702, transferred to Essex House in 1712, to Ashburnham House in 1730 – where it suffered heavily in a fire of 1731 – thence to Westminster School and finally to the British Museum. The Library therefore was actually at Essex House in the Strand when Defoe wrote, despite what he says. The new church described by Defoe is that of St John's, Smith Square, built 1714–28 by Thomas Archer: since reconstructed.

24. p. 328 *the great new theatre*: Apparently not the most recent arrival, the Little Theatre in the Haymarket (opened in December 1721), but Vanbrugh's Opera House, built in 1704. See B/C, p. 67.

25. p. 329 *Bethlem*: The hospital had been rebuilt by Hooke after the Fire and stood in Moorfields. Bridewell was in Whitefriars, near the Fleet Ditch. Swift had been a governor of the hospitals a few years earlier.

26. p. 330 *Dr Ridley*: Nicholas Ridley (*c.* 1500–1555), Bishop of Rochester and London, martyred 16 October 1555.

27. p. 332 *Mr Thomas Guy*: Bookseller (born *c.* 1645), died 27

December 1724; will proved 4 January 1725; sixty patients admitted to the hospital on 24 January 1725. Guy was an astute investor and among the few people to come out of the Bubble period with his fortune not merely intact but augmented.

28. p. 334 *Lady Ann Dacres*: Anne Fiennes, Lady Dacre (d. 1595). *The French refugees*: Huguenots who had left France after the revocation of the Edict of Nantes in 1685.

29. p. 335 *St Martin's in the Fields*: Foundation stone laid on 19 March 1721; building going on until 1726, in spite of Defoe's apparent suggestion that the work was complete in 1725.

30. p. 335 *Several very fine new churches*: Those named (mainly the work of Nicholas Hawksmoor) are Christ Church, Spitalfields (approximate date 1723–9); St George in the East (*c.* 1715–23); St Luke's, Old Street (consecrated 1733); St Anne's, Limehouse (1712–24); and St George's, Bloomsbury (completed *c.* 1730). The five not finished may indicate St Luke's, Shoreditch; St Giles in the Fields; St Olave's, Southwark; St Mary Woolnoth; St John, Horsleydown; St Alfege, Greenwich; or possibly other churches.

31. p. 336 *Figg's Theatre*: James Figg (d. 1734) set up his boxing booth around 1721, and it remained a leading attraction for visitors to London for the next few years.

Letter 6

1. p. 337 *bills of mortality*: Records of burials and baptisms kept by the Company of Parish Clerks, issued weekly and annually: hence, by transference, the area covered by these figures – the City of London and Westminster, together with the 'out-parishes' or inner suburbs.

2. p. 337 *a certain satirical author*: B/C, p. 81, suggests this may be Tom Brown, but the reference has not been located. Brown (1663–1764) was a miscellaneous writer, best known for his *Amusements Serious and Comical* (1700).

3. p. 338 *Sir William Ashurst*: Lord Mayor of London in 1694, knighted by James II in 1687, M.P. for the City of London; d. 1720. The property which Defoe mentions was erected on the site of Arundel House at the end of the seventeenth century. It was sold by Ashurst's grandson in 1725, and in the nineteenth century a church was built on the site.

4. p. 338 *the chase, at Enfield*: Parliament first proposed to enclose the chase around 1652, and in the following years there were popular riots against the measure, notably in 1659. The park was not finally

dischased until 1779. *The Earl of Denbigh*: Basil Fielding, fourth Earl of Denbigh (1668–1717). *General Pepper*: John Pepper, Major-General 1710, fought at Almanza and in William III's Irish campaign; sold his commission in 1719. Died 22 December 1725, a few months after Defoe wrote these words.

5. p. 340 *a true house of pleasure*: Belsize House was acquired by a certain Howell and opened as a pleasure resort about 1720. In 1722 the High Constable of Holborn was ordered to take steps to end unlawful gaming, rioting and the like. On 7 July 1722 the *London Journal* reported that 'the Gaming-house at Bellsize is put under a remarkable Alteration for the better'; but the improvement was apparently short-lived. The next summer Howell was hiring twenty 'stout labouring men' to protect visitors on their way to the establishment.

6. p. 341 *Chandos*: James Brydges, first Duke of Chandos (1673–1744). The famous 'princely Chandos', Handel's patron and a byword first for acquisitiveness (as Paymaster to the Forces, when he was thought to have grown rich through graft) and later for profligacy. His house at Cannons lasted only a generation before it was demolished. The North London Collegiate School for Girls now stands on the site.

7. p. 341 *Pargotti ... Paolucci*: Errors by Defoe for Artari and Bellucci, Italian stuccadors employed by Chandos. They have been called 'a mysterious pair' and 'among the famous obscure'. Singly or together they worked at great houses such as Houghton, Meresworth and Ditchley; they embellished St Martin's in the Fields and Marylebone Chapel. Antonio Bellucci (1654–1726) is perhaps the more eminent.

8. p. 341 *Cavendish Square*: Edward Shepherd began building two houses, long planned, for Chandos around March 1724. The Duke had moved during 1720 to the other town-house mentioned by Defoe, Chandos House in St James's Square. Its former owner, James Butler, second Duke of Ormonde (1665–1745), had been impeached for his part in the Jacobite rebellion of 1715, and his property sequestrated.

9. p. 344 *Earl of Essex*: William Capel, twenty-third Earl (1697–1743). *Duke of Bridgewater*: Scroop Egerton, first Duke (1681–1745). Cassiobury was near Watford; Ashridge, at Little Gaddesden.

10. p. 344 *the king's palace*: William III bought Kensington palace soon after his accession. The fire to which Defoe alludes took place on 10 November 1691.

11. p. 345 *Prince George of Denmark*: Consort of Queen Anne; died in October 1708.

12. p. 346 *the late Earl of Ranelagh*: Defoe means the first Earl, Richard Jones (1641–1712), courtier and placeman, who built the house in 1691. Around 1733 his daughter sold it to a speculative builder who divided the estate into lots. It was not until 1742 that the famous pleasure gardens were opened.

13. p. 347 *Secretary Johnson*: James Johnston(e) (1643–1737), formerly Secretary of State for Scotland. A neighbour of Alexander Pope, who held him in little regard; cultivated by Queen Caroline. He bought his Twickenham residence, later known as Orleans House, in 1702 and devoted many years to improving it.

14. p. 348 *blessed St Paul*: I Thess. ii, 18. The abortive treaty to which Defoe refers was the meeting between commissioners in January 1645. *Story*: history.

15. p. 348 *Duke of Monmouth*: James Scott (1649–85), natural son of Charles II by Lucy Walter, led rebellion of 1685.

16. p. 348 *Earl of Orkney*: George Hamilton, general (1666–1737).

17. p. 349 *Mr Guy*: Henry Guy (1631–1710). *Mr Lowndes*: William Lowndes (1652–1744). Important early civil servants who sat in Parliament but acted in effect as permanent officials.

18. p. 350 *Magdalen College*: James II attempted to impose his own choice of Master on the College in 1687, and deprived non-complying Fellows. Omitted here is a list of the Oxford colleges with a résumé of the history of each.

19. p. 352 *Archbishop Sheldon*: Gilbert Sheldon (1598–1677), Archbishop of Canterbury from 1663.

20. p. 353 *Sir Thomas Bodley*: Benefactor of the library which bears his name (1545–1613).

21. p. 353 *Dr Radcliff*: John Radcliffe (1650–1714), physician, is commemorated by the Radcliffe Camera, built by James Gibbs between 1737 and 1749.

22. p. 354 *Rosamond*: Rosamond Clifford (d. 1176).

23. p. 354 *Duke of Marlborough*: John Churchill (1650–1722), the famous general, rewarded by the nation with the gift of Blenheim Palace.

24. p. 356 *Croprady Bridge*: The battle of Cropredy (*sic*) Bridge, fought on 29 June 1644. For Waller see note 19 to p. 266.

25. p. 356 *Edge-Hill*: Fought on 23 October 1642; described by Defoe in *Memoirs of a Cavalier*.

26. p. 357 *a statute law*: The Statute of Artificers, 5 Eliz. c. 4 (1563).

27. p. 359 *King Bladud*: Legendary British king, said to be the father of King Lear; his reign is usually ascribed to an earlier period, around the ninth century B.C.

28. p. 363 *The Tolsey*: The ancient exchange of Bristol was called the Tolzey. It was replaced by a new building by John Wood, 1740–44.

29. p. 365 *Edward II*: Believed to have been murdered by the contrivance of Queen Isabella and her lover Mortimer, 21 September 1327.

30. p. 366 *the last battle*: Fought at Tewkesbury, 4 May 1471.

31. p. 368 *Cromwel's forces*: At the battle of Worcester, 3 September 1651.

32. p. 369 *St Oswald, and St Woolstan*: Oswald (d. 992), Archbishop of York, Wulfstan (*c.* 1012–95), Bishop of Worcester, canonized 1203.

33. p. 369 *new order of knighthood*: Generally dated 23 April 1344.

34. p. 370 Potosi: Silver mines in Peru, discovered in 1545.

35. p. 371 *in our days*: By an act of 1689. The Lugg navigation, mentioned in the next paragraph, dates from 1696 (7 & 8 Wm. III, c. 14, s. 2).

36. p. 372 *the late Earl of Oxford*: Robert Harley (1661–1724), Tory statesman; Sir Edward Harley (1624–1700), Colonel in the Parliamentary army.

37. p. 375 *Jeoffry of Monmouth*: Geoffrey (1100–1154), chronicler and Bishop of St Asaph.

38. p. 377 *the famous Glendower*: Owen Glendower (1359–1415).

39. p. 377 *Vortigern, and Roger of Mortimer*: The former, a British leader of the fifth century A.D.; the latter, Earl of March (1287–1330).

40. p. 378 *St Dobricius*: Dubricius (*c.* 475–560), Bishop of Llandaff from 505.

41. p. 380 *the landing of King Henry VII*: In August 1485, when Richmond landed and wrested the throne from Richard III at Bosworth.

42. p. 381 *St David*: His death is now placed around 601; canonized 1120. Others named are Owen Tudor (d. 1461); Edmund Tudor (*c.* 1430–56), Earl of Richmond, father of Henry VII.

43. p. 382 *Sir Carbery Price*: Baronet, d. 1694; mines discovered in 1690.

44. p. 384 *Philosophical Transactions*: An account of this phenomenon was published in the *Philosophical Transactions of the Royal Society*, Vol. 18, pp. 49. 223 (1694). It is described as a 'fiery damp or exhalation', witnessed by an 'intelligent' person at Harlech. According to Gibson in Camden, col. 659, the author was 'Mr Jones', but in the reprint of the *Transactions* the account seems to be attributed to Edward Lhwyd, archaeologist and philologist.

45. p. 385 *Edward of Caernarvon*: Born in 1284.

46. p. 387 *Bulkeley*: Arthur Bulkeley, Bishop of Bangor 1541–55.

Letter 7

1. p. 390 *Caractacus*: British prince of the first century A.D., who resisted the Roman invasion until his betrayal. *Owen ap Tudor*: See note 42 to p. 381. *Llewellin*: Llywelyn ap Gruffydd. Recognized by Henry III as Prince of Wales, 1267; effectively deposed, 1276, by Edward I; led rebellion, 1281–2, and met his death after battle of Aber Edw.

2. p. 391 *Cestria Chersonesus*: The Wirral; from *cherronesus* or *chersonesus*, Latin form of a Greek word for peninsula.

3. p. 391 *Leverpool*: The population of the town increased by ten times between 1680 and 1760, from 4,000 to about 40,000. For the new church, see note 4 to p. 543.

4. p. 391 *a great wet dock ... Sir Henry Johnson's*: See note 3 to p. 543, and note 26 to p. 277.

5. p. 393 *Roodee*: The Roodeye, a meadow lying close to the Dee.

6. p. 393 *Preston*: Following the battle fought on 12–13 November 1715, during the rising of the Old Pretender.

7. p. 393 *Hugh Lupus*: Hugh of Avranches, Earl of Chester (d. 1101), called 'the Wolf' from his savage conquest of North Wales. Endowed the monastery dedicated to St Werbugh (d. 700?), Abbess of Ely and patron saint of women and children. *Edgar*: (944–975), King of England from 959 to his death.

8. p. 394 *King William*: The army of William III was led by the Duke of Schomberg against the forces of James II, who had besieged Londonderry in April 1689.

9. p. 395 *Lord Delamere*: George Booth, third Baron Delamer and later second Earl of Warrington (1675–1758).

10. p. 396 *Talbot*: John Talbot, created Earl 1442, soldier (*c.* 1384–1453).

11. p. 396 *from Nottingham to Shrewsbury*: In September 1642, at the start of the Civil War.

12. p. 396 *Pelagius*: A British monk of the fourth century, who instituted the so-called Pelagian heresy denying the existence of original sin. His followers appeared in Rome around A.D. 400.

13. p. 397 *Jefferies*: George Jeffreys, first Baron (1648–89), judge, Lord Chancellor 1685, notorious for his severe treatment of Monmouth's adherents in the Bloody Assizes; after James II's flight, captured and sent to the Tower, where he died.

14. p. 398 *battle*: Shrewsbury, fought on 23 July 1403.

15. p. 398 *at Nottingham*: On 22 August 1642.

16. p. 399 *sweating sickness*: Sudor Anglicus, of which there were numerous outbreaks in the fifteenth and sixteenth centuries. There were at least four epidemics in England prior to the onset of the fever in 1551. The mortality rate was very heavy, and death exceptionally rapid – sometimes within three hours from the appearance of the symptoms.

17. p. 399 *ancient free-school*: Shrewsbury School, founded by Edward VI in 1551, further endowed by Elizabeth; opened in 1562.

18. p. 399 *Charles II*: The King arrived at White Ladies House on 4 September 1651, the day after his defeat at Worcester, and spent the next two days in hiding there. On 7 September he moved about three quarters of a mile to Boscobel House, in whose grounds stood the famous oak tree that was to form so conspicuous a part of Stuart legend in time to come.

19. p. 402 *St Chad*: St Ceadda (d. 672), Bishop of York and later Bishop of the Mercians, *c.* 670.

20. p. 403 *Lord Digby*: William Digby, fifth Baron (1661/2–1752). Digby later made his peace with the Hanoverian regime.

21. p. 403 *The late incumbent*: John Kettlewell (1653–95), non-juror and devotional writer, became vicar of Coleshill in 1682 and was deprived in 1690 for refusing the oaths to William III. *His successor*: Evidently Defoe means Thomas Carte (1686–1754), who had concealed himself with the curate of Coleshill after the Jacobite rebellion in 1715. Carte was a friend of Bishop Atterbury, and after the exposure of Atterbury's plot a proclamation was issued in November 1722 offering the reward mentioned by Defoe. Carte escaped to France and later became well known as a historian.

22. p. 403 *when I first came*: Probably during the election of 1705, although Coventry was notorious for regularly producing an ill-conducted and riotous poll. See Speck, pp. 27, 53, and 130, and *Letters*, pp. 105–8.

23. p. 405 *Guy Earl of Warwick*: A hero of legend and romance, whose exploits were recorded by Anglo-Norman writers of the twelfth century and later accepted as historically authentic.

24. p. 405 *a terrible fire*: Actually in 1694, more like thirty years before Defoe was writing.

25. p. 406 *suddenly burnt down*: In 1675; the church of All Saints was rebuilt by the first decade of the eighteenth century.

26. p. 406 *he took very little notice of Northampton*: Macky mentions a chapter-house (*A Journey through England*, II, 173), and may be intended here. *Magna Britannia* supplies an accurate entry and I have not traced any source which lists all the features named by Defoe.

27. p. 407 *imprisonment of King Charles the First*: In the spring and early summer of 1647, in the custody of Parliament, prior to his committal to the army.

28. p. 407 *The Earl of Sunderland*: Charles Spencer, third Earl (1674–1722), statesman and bibliophile, son-in-law of the Duke of Marlborough; died suddenly on 19 April 1722, leaving the way open for Robert Walpole to assume unchallenged power.

29. p. 407 *Duke of Mountague*: John Montagu, second Duke (1690–1749). *The late Duke*: Ralph Montagu (1638–1709).

30. p. 407 *John Wickliff*: Religious reformer, d. 1384.

31. p. 407 *Bosworth-Field*: Fought on 22 August 1485; the victor, the Earl of Richmond, established on the throne as Henry VII.

32. p. 409 *assaulted by the Royalists*: In May 1645, just prior to Naseby.

33. p. 410 *commanded the governor to deliver it up*: In May 1646.

34. p. 412 *Lincoln was ...*: Quoted by an earlier traveller, John Taylor, in A *Very Merry-Wherry-Ferry Voyage* (1622), where Defoe very likely came on it.

35. p. 416 *The Adventurers*: Thirteen co-adventurers combined with the fourth Duke of Bedford in 1631 in order to execute the drainage of the Fens. In 1634 they were granted a charter. The Dutch engineer Cornelius Vermuyden was employed as chief engineer. Before a lull caused by the Civil War, the Old Bedford River was cut; and afterwards the New River, half a mile to the east.

36. p. 416 *500l. a year rent*: At this point Defoe incorporates a long account of the breeding and use of decoy-ducks.

37. p. 418 *beheaded not far off*: On 8 February 1587.

38. p. 418 *Lady Katherine of Spain*: Catherine of Aragon (1485–1536), first wife of Henry VIII, divorced in 1526. The last part of this sentence refers not to her but to Mary I (1516–58).

39. p. 419 *that excellent poet*: Almost certainly John Taylor, the so-called Water Poet (1580–1653), Thames waterman and hack writer. These are Taylor's usual accents; he wrote a great deal of topographical poetry; and he was the habitual recipient of ironical commendations such as Defoe's. However, I have not traced the line in his works.

40. p. 419 *Earls of Gainsborough and Nottingham*: Baptist Noel, fourth Earl of Gainsborough (1708–51), at the time Defoe wrote a student at Cambridge. Daniel Finch, second Earl of Nottingham and later sixth Earl of Winchilsea (1647–1730), a famous Tory politician called 'Dismal' by Swift. It was he who had caused Defoe to be arrested after the publication of *The Shortest Way with the Dissenters* (1702), which argues either tolerance or prudence on Defoe's part in referring so generously to Nottingham here.

Appendix to Volume II

41. p. 421 *Sir William Cecil*: William Cecil, Baron Burghley (1520–98), statesman, Lord High Treasurer from 1572.

42. p. 421 *the late Earl of Excester*: Defoe seems to have got the generations mixed up, unless he was writing earlier than December 1721, when the sixth Earl of Exeter died. His reference undoubtedly points to the fifth Earl (1648–1700). Yet by 1724 two grandsons had succeeded in turn to the title, the seventh Earl (1700–1722) having been followed by his brother (1701–54).

43. p. 422 *Varrio*: Antonio Verrio (1639–1707), famous for his work at Hampton Court, Windsor and elsewhere; introduced from France the style of baroque decorative painting developed by Thornhill, Hawksmoor and others.

44. p. 424 *Sir Francis St John*: Apparently an error; no knight or baronet so named can be traced. Defoe perhaps means the first Baron St John (d. 1757). *Lord FitzWilliams*: John, second Earl Fitzwilliam (1685–1728).

45. p. 427 *a terrible fire*: In June 1724.

46. p. 427 *the present Duke*: Wriothesley Russell, sixth Duke of Bedford (1708–32), married in April 1725 before these words were in print; had succeeded at the age of three.

Appendix to Volume II

1. p. 429 *Appendix . . .*: Here Defoe inserted some corrections and additions to Letters 4–7, most of them relating to Bristol and specifically St Mary Redcliffe church. These were evidently contributed by a third person and have been omitted from this text.

2. p. 430 *turnpikes or toll-bars*: Originally a turnpike was a barrier of pikes stretched across the road, swivelling open on a pivot when the toll had been paid. Later by extension the word was applied to the system of roads managed by turnpike trusts under Act of Parliament. The first Act was that of 15 Charles II, c. 1 (1663), permitting the Justices of the Peace for Hertfordshire, Cambridgeshire and Huntingdonshire to raise funds for the maintenance of the Great North Road and to construct toll-bars. The first gates were erected in that year at Wadesmill, near Ware. By the start of the nineteenth century there were over a thousand such trusts.

3. p. 433 *set up by Act of Parliament*: 7 & 8 Wm. III, c. 9. (1696).

4. p. 437 *beyond Dunstable down into Hockley Lane*: This was one of the most notorious stretches of English road, prior to a series of repairs first instituted by 9 Anne, c. 14 (1709). Celia Fiennes (*Journeys*, p. 120) calls it 'a sad road', and adds that 'in the winter it must be impasable'. Other black spots included the Baldock/Royston area,

sections of the Bath road, and much of Sussex – particularly around Horsham.

Introduction to Volume III

1 p. 445 *Introduction . . .*: A preface which is little more than a puff has been omitted.

2. p. 446 *The Union*: With Scotland in the year 1707.

Letter 8

1. p. 450 *it . . . is navigable*: A section dealing with the tributaries of the Trent is omitted here.

2. p. 450 *the navigation lately*: The Trent was made navigable from Wilne Ferry to Burton by 10 Wm III, c. 26 (1699), and the Derwent, from Derby to the Trent, by 6 George I, c. 27 (1719).

3. p. 452 *King Humber*: Legendary king of the Huns, who according to the fable invaded Britain *c.* 1000 B.C., and on his defeat was cast into the River Abus, thenceforth called by his name. The story is told by Geoffrey of Monmouth.

4. p. 452 *a tower here*: The Danes under Hubba occupied Nottingham in A.D. 868. Eventually they managed to subdue Mercia without a major battle.

5. p. 453 *Robert Earl Ferrers*: Robert Ferrers, sixth Earl of Derby (c. 1239–79), rebelled against Henry III during the Barons' Wars in 1266.

6. p. 453 *Roger Mortimore*: Roger de Mortimer, first Earl of March (1287–1330); executed at Nottingham Castle.

7. p. 453 *his bastard son*: E. A. Freeman, still perhaps the leading authority, disputes this alleged relationship in *The Norman Conquest*. See note 25 to p. 64.

8. p. 453 *Marquis of Newcastle*: William Cavendish, first Duke of Newcastle (1593–1676), royalist general. Thomas Pelham-Holles, fourth Duke (1693–1768), for forty years Secretary of State and subsequently First Lord of the Treasury; created Duke 1715. George Villiers, second Duke of Buckingham (1628–87), politician, rake and dramatist.

9. p. 453 *Count Tallard*: Camille, Duc d'Hostun (1652–1728), exiled in Nottingham until 1711.

10. p. 454 *a handsome town-house*: Repairs were in hand by 1723 or 1724, according to the Corporation minutes; but I have not located the exact date of the event Defoe mentions.

11. p. 454 *the increase of tea-drinking*: This was very much a Restoration habit; the fashion started among the wealthy in the 1660s, and spread when the East India Company began to trade in tea.

12. p. 457 *the good bishop*: Paulinus, Bishop of York and of Rochester (d. 644). Here Defoe inserts a long 'account of the town and county of Southwell' supplied by a friend of his who was a prebendary of Southwell. It is omitted in this edition.

13. p. 457 *the Duke of Kingston*: Evelyn Pierrepont, first Duke (1665–1726), minor politician, socialite and father of the letter-writer Lady Mary Wortley Montagu. He died just before Volume III of the *Tour* came out. By Halifax Defoe presumably intends William Savile, second Marquis (1665–1700), though the title had long been extinct.

14. p. 458 *one Soracule*: George Sorocold, an engineer, played a relatively minor part in the introduction of silk-throwing machinery to England. The mill was owned by the Lombe family. John Lombe had gone to Leghorn in 1716 and smuggled back the secret of the process inside pieces of silk – an early piece of industrial espionage. In 1718, on his return, he patented the machinery. He died in 1727 but his half-brother, Sir Thomas Lombe (1685–1739), built up the business and acquired both fame and wealth. Sorocold's part seems to have been purely technological.

15. p. 459 *the Countess of Shrewsbury*: Elizabeth Talbot, married the sixth Earl of Shrewsbury; known as Bess of Hardwick; built Chatsworth, Worksop and Hardwick; gaoler of Mary Queen of Scots (1518–1608). See further Celia Fiennes's *Journeys*, pp. 74, 169.

16. p. 459 *Cotton's Wonders of the Peak*: *The Wonders of the Peake* (1681) by Charles Cotton (1630–87), poet and translator, follower of Isaak Walton. There were several reprints of the poem, including one published at Nottingham in 1725.

17. p. 461 *Mr Hobbes*: Thomas Hobbes, the celebrated author of *Leviathan* (1588–1679), had produced among his diverse minor works *De Mirabibus Pecci: being the wonders of the Peak in Darby-shire*, in English and Latin verse (1678). Hobbes wrote only the Latin. Defoe speaks slightingly of Cotton and Hobbes, but he had obviously read them with some care.

18. p. 469 *The Duke of Devonshire*: William Cavendish, second Duke (1673–1729), at one time a soldier; a representative Whig dynast of the early Hanoverian period, and member of the Kit-Cat Club.

19. p. 470 *Mr Burnet's theory*: Thomas Burnet (*c.* 1635–1715), master of the Charterhouse, famous in his day for *Telluris Theoria Sacra* (1682–9), a blend of cosmology, imaginative geology and theology.

20. p. 470 *Dr Leigh*: Charles Leigh, M.D. (1662–1701), physician and

naturalist, author of *The Natural History of Lancashire, Cheshire and the Peak in Derbyshire* (1700).

21. p. 472 *The Devil's A——e*: The word of course is 'arse'. Typically, Celia Fiennes, with sub-aristocratic directness, names this wonder far more openly: see her *Journeys*, pp. 107–8.

22. p. 473 *the cave of Adullam*: See I Sam. xxii, 1–2. *The cave of Mackpelah*: The tomb of the patriarchs: see Gen. xxiii, 17–19; the burial place of Abraham (Gen. xxv, 9), Isaac and Rebecca (xlix, 30–31) and Joseph (l. 13). *Hebrews*: The reference is rather xi, 38.

23. p. 475 *Sir William Cavendish*: Statesman (*c.* 1505–52). For his wife see note 15 to p. 459.

24. p. 477 *a mile perpendicular*: Celia Fiennes had heard similar stories, but in 1730 an F.R.S. found the depth to be no more than 76 feet: *Journeys*, p. 106.

25. p. 481 *two several authors*: Macky (II, 209) speaks of the view from the spire of York minster, whilst *Magna Britannia*, VI, 429, says that 'the steeple [of Doncaster church] is an admirable Work'. This volume was not published until 1731 but had previously been issued in periodical parts.

26. p. 482 *Geoffry Chaucer*: The opening lines of the 'Reeve's Tale' from the *Canterbury Tales*, slightly misquoted.

27. p. 482 *Mr Serocoal*: See note 14 to p. 458.

28. p. 483 *Bishop Rotherham*: Thomas Rotherham (1423–1500), Archbishop of York from 1480, benefactor of Lincoln College, Oxford. He was the son of Sir John Rotherham, and was educated at Eton (probably) and King's College, Cambridge, so that the suggestion of his being a foundling can be discounted.

29. p. 485 *Pendle-Hill and Pennigent ...*: Not true: even if we disregard a large number of the Lakeland fells, within the Pennine chain itself Cross Fell (2,930 feet) is one of several hills much higher than Pen y ghent (2,231 feet) or Pendle Hill (1,831 feet).

30. p. 486 *a cross-post*: This was a postal route running from one major route to another; as opposed to bye-posts, which followed major roads which did not run to or from London. The famous Ralph Allen, philanthropist and friend of literary men, offered to farm the cross- and bye-posts in 1720, after which there was a steady growth in these services. The cross-post from Bristol to Exeter was set up in 1696, that from Bristol to Chester via Worcester and Shrewsbury in 1700. At the end of the seventeenth century a number of important new roads had been built, including the Liverpool–Manchester route.

31. p. 492 *St Giles's*: See note 3 to p. 288.

32. p. 495 *the late Revolution*: In 1688. The 'reverend clergyman' was probably Nathaniel Priestley – see *Letters*, p. 117.

33. p. 500 *the cloth market*: The conditions in Briggate as described by Defoe seem to antedate the erection of the White Cloth Hall in 1711.

34. p. 503 *an Act of Parliament*: 10 Wm. III, c. 25 (1699).

35. p. 504 *Henry, the great Earl of Lancaster*: A mistake; Henry (1281–1345) survived to consolidate the position of Edward III on the throne and to destroy the power of Queen Isabella and Mortimer. *Richard II* (1367–1400), died at Pontefract 14 February 1400, probably murdered. *Anthony, Earl Rivers*: Second Earl, executed 1483. *Sir Richard Gray*: Rather Lord Richard Grey, also beheaded in 1483. The two latter were respectively brother and son of Elizabeth Grey, née Wydeville, who took as her second husband King Edward IV. They were put to death by Richard III as part of his design to crush the Lancastrians after he had sent the boy king Edward V to the Tower.

36. p. 505 *Queen Margaret*: Second wife of Edward I, whom she married in 1299; died 1317.

37. p. 505 *Bramham Moor*: Fought on 29 March 1643. *Sir Thomas Fairfax*: Parliamentary general; third baronet (1612–71).

38. p. 507 *Sweet Spaw*: Also known as the Chalybeate spring. Celia Fiennes visited all four springs and made extensive comments – *Journeys*, pp. 79–81. But Defoe's informant is Bishop Gibson, in Camden, col. 732.

39. p. 508 *the other*: Either the Wharfe or the Nidd, both of which Defoe had recently mentioned. In fact the Aire rises near Malham Tarn, some miles south of Pen y ghent.

40. p. 508 *Wilfrid*: St Wilfrid (634–709), Bishop of York *c.* 665.

41. p. 509 *Athelstan*: King of the West Saxons, later of all England (895–940).

42. p. 511 *at this time*: Here Defoe quotes a versified form of the charter granted to Ripon by King Athelstan.

43. p. 512 *the great Bohun*: Humphrey de Bohun, fourth Earl of Hereford (1276–1322), Constable of England, defeated by Edward II at Boroughbridge.

44. p. 514 *Sir Solomon Swale*: The first Baronet (*c.* 1609–78) might be intended; more likely is the third (*c.* 1665–1733), who frittered away most of the estate, although he was still alive when Defoe wrote. *Fleeter*: a shifty person or deserter; a fugitive (here no doubt from creditors).

45. p. 515 *the late war*: The War of the Spanish Succession, 1702–13; following quickly upon the prolonged international conflict ended by the Peace of Ryswick in 1697.

Letter 9

1. p. 517 *Towton*: Fought on 29 March 1461.

2. p. 518 *Dr Oglethorp*: Owen Oglethorp, Bishop of Carlisle, President of Magdalen College, Oxford, deprived of his bishopric in 1569; native of Tadcaster.

3. p. 518 *old Bale*: The ancient (probably Roman) fortifications on the mount known as the Old Baile were already ruinous by the time of Edward I. They were surrounded by the Foss and stood opposite Clifford's Tower.

4. p. 519 *in Mr Cambden*: See Camden, cols. 718–20. Defoe makes silent use of Camden to an increasing extent as the book proceeds.

5. p. 519 *'tis risen again*: The bridge had been rebuilt in 1701.

6. p. 519 *three archbishops*: Presumably John de Romayn, who laid the foundations of the nave (his father, the treasurer, began the transept around 1260); John Thoresby (d. 1373), Archbishop from 1351; and John de Bingham, who added the west towers c. 1402. In fact other archbishops, such as William de Melton, were concerned in the growth of the structure during the fourteenth century.

7. p. 522 *Marston Moor*: Scene of the battle on 2 July 1644, described in Defoe's *Memoirs of a Cavalier*.

8. p. 522 *Fairfax*: See note 37 to p. 505. *Newcastle*: See note 8 to p. 453.

9. p. 523 *the Duke of Leeds*: Peregrine Osborne, second Duke (1659–1729), admiral. *Earl of Carlisle*: Charles Howard, sixth Earl (1669–1738), First Lord of the Treasury, employed Vanbrugh to build Castle Howard. *Earl of Burlington*: Richard Boyle, third Earl (1695–1753), architect, connoisseur and patron; friend of the Pope circle. The high priest of English Palladianism. His house was at Londesborough, but none of it survives.

10. p. 525 *John of Beverley*: Bishop of York 705–18; died 721; canonized 1037. For Athelstan see note 41 to p. 509.

11. p. 526 *Michael Warton*: Warton's almshouses in Minster Moorgate received a further benefaction from the founder's relative, Sir Michael Warton, M.P. (d. 1725). Defoe takes these facts from Gibson's edition of Camden.

12. p. 526 *Leland*: John Leland (*c.* 1506–52), antiquarian writer whose works were published by Thomas Hearne: see Introduction, p. 18.

13. p. 527 *scorbutic*: Another word for scurvy. *The king's evil*: Scrofula, supposed to be cured by the touch of the monarch.

14. p. 527 *soon after the Revolution*: The duel was actually fought in December 1689, as the King's troops made their way to the Irish campaign. The gravestone can still be seen at St Mary's church in Beverley. Defoe had probably not been in the region since 1712. At this point, incidentally, he quotes a versified form of the charter granted to Beverley by King Athelstan; like the Ripon charter, this is unfortunately too long to include here.

15. p. 529 *the German Ocean:* The North Sea or Mare Germanicum.

16. p. 530 *Michael de la Pole*: In this paragraph (here considerably reduced in length) Defoe confused Michael, the first Earl of Suffolk and Lord Chancellor (*c.* 1330–89) with his father Sir William de la Pole (d. 1366), the Hull merchant who advanced large sums to Edward II and became a Baron of the Exchequer. It was the father who founded the *maison de dieu* about 1350, although his son augmented the gift.

17. p. 537 *scandalously defeated*: Hexham yielded to the Scots on 23 February 1744, and the town was compelled to support them for the following months.

18. p. 537 *Chevy Chace ... Flodden Field*: See notes 13 and 14 to p. 624. Defoe had made his way north to Scotland via Wooler in the autumn of 1709, and the text here may well derive from his recollection of that year.

Letter 10

1. p. 540 *a large, handsome ... town*: In 1680 the population of Liverpool was probably only some 4,000. See also note 3 to p. 391.

2. p. 541 *the late northern insurrection*: The Jacobite Rebellion in 1715.

3. p. 543 *a large basin or wet dock*: Proposed in 1708, made possible by the act 8 Anne, c. 25 (1709), in operation by 1715.

4. p. 543 *The new church*: St Peter's was made a separate parish from St Nicholas, Walton, in 1699, and the church itself was consecrated in 1703. The principal benefactor, as Defoe notes in a section which has had to be omitted here, was Robert Heysham (d. 1723), merchant and M.P. for the City of London. See also p. 391.

5. p. 545 *part of the town called* —— : Salford. Defoe's estimate of the population of Manchester and Salford is certainly a considerable overstatement; see Introduction, p. 11.

6. p. 546 *Lord Delaware*: Thomas, fifth Baron (d. 1427), became Rector of Manchester 1382, succeeded to the barony 1398.

7. p. 547 *Countess of Derby*: Charlotte de la Trémaille (d. 1664), married the sixteenth Earl of Derby; the siege of Latham House finally raised 27 May 1644.

8. p. 548 *the late bloody action*: On 12–13 November 1715, when the southward march of the Pretender's forces was halted.

9. p. 553 *a bubble*: A fraudulent speculation or confidence trick; a (deceptively) promising offer to investors.

10. p. 555 *The Countess of Pembroke*: Anne, Baroness Clifford (*c.* 1590–1676), married the fourth Earl of Pembroke; she was daughter of the third Earl of Cumberland; Defoe quotes the inscription (omitted here) to the memory of her mother, placed on the pillar when it was erected in 1656.

11. p. 555 *Sir Owen Caesar*: Or Ewen Caesarius, a legendary giant who is said to have killed wild boars in the nearby Forest of Inglewood. In fact the pillars probably mark the site of a family tomb. See also Camden, col. 842.

Letter 11

1. p. 563 *Lauder*: Probably Alexander Lauder, author of *The Ancient Bishops Considered* (1707) and *The Divine Visitation of Bishops* (1711).

2. p. 565 *Sir James Hall*: Second Baronet, died 1742.

3. p. 566 *the battle of Dunbar*: Fought on 3 September 1650. The Scottish forces were commanded by David Leslie (d. 1682).

4. p. 567 *Marquess of Tweedal*: John Hay, fourth Marquis of Tweedale (*c.* 1695–1762). *The old Earl*: The second Earl and first Marquis (1625–97).

5. p. 570 *James V*: King of Scotland (1512–42, succeeded to the throne 1513); grandson of Henry VII and father of Mary Queen of Scots.

6. p. 572 *Earl of Winton*: George Seton, fifth Earl; condemned to death for his part in the Jacobite rebellion after a show trial in 1716; escaped from the Tower and joined the Pretender; d. 1749. *The York-Buildings Company*: See note 12 to p. 648.

7. p. 574 *Battle of Musclebro*: Fought on 10 September 1547, generally known as the battle of Pinkey, as on p. 589.

8. p. 579 *Dr Pitcairn*: Archibald Pitcairne (1652–1713), poet and physician; professor of physic at Leiden. Sir Andrew Balfour (1630–94), M.D., started a public botanical garden *c.* 1680: his life written by Robert Sibbald (1699). *Ratcliff*: See note 21 to p. 353.

9. p. 584 *Duke of Hamilton*: James Hamilton, fifth Duke (1703–43), a somewhat half-hearted Jacobite.

10. p. 586 *the late rebel Highlanders*: A force under the command of Mackintosh of Borlum crossed the Forth in fishing boats, and spent the night of 15–16 October 1715 at Leith.

Letter 12

1. p. 592 *the same hand*: Almost certainly Defoe himself.

2. p. 593 *the grandson*: William Douglas, third Earl, first Marquis and first Duke (1637–95). *His son*: James Douglas, second Duke (1622–1711). For Defoe's contact with the latter during the negotiations for the Union in 1707, see *Letters*, pp. 205 ff.

3. p. 594 *Mr John Hepburn*: For a fuller account of Hepburn (d. 1723), a Cameronian clergyman, and a second-hand report by Defoe of a similar meeting conducted by Hepburn in December 1706, see *Letters*, pp. 150, 180–81.

4. p. 603 *as the King of France has done*: The Canal du Midi, or Languedoc canal, built between 1666 and 1681; 150 miles in length.

5. p. 605 *Bishop Turnbull*: William Turnbull (d. 1454), Bishop of Glasgow 1447, founded the University 1451.

6. p. 608 *Crooked-Lane*: A street near London Bridge, noted for smallware; hence used here apparently in the sense of 'general household goods or haberdashery'. The term is not recorded in O.E.D.

7. p. 611 *Bannock Bourn*: Fought on 24 June 1314.

8. p. 612 *The Earl of Mar*: John Erskine, sixth Earl (1675–1732), attainted as leader of the Jacobite rebellion, fled to France with the Pretender and forfeited his estates.

9. p. 615 *the Earl of Buchan*: David Erskine, twenty-second Earl (1672–1745), a Hanoverian but opposed to the Union.

10. p. 615 *Lord Murray*: James Stewart, sixteenth Earl of Moray (*c.* 1531–70), Regent of Scotland from 1567; assassinated by James Hamilton, 21 January 1570. There is an apparent ambiguity in what Defoe says: but his meaning is that the true instigator of the crime was never caught, although Hamilton was.

11. p. 617 *Bothwell-Bridge Rebellion*: The Scottish Covenanters rose against the government but were defeated at Bothwell Bridge or Brig by Monmouth, 22 June 1679 (a Sunday). The Cameronians were members of the Reformed Presbyterian church under the leadership of Richard Cameron (d. 1680). The episode forms the background for Scott's novel *Old Mortality*.

12. p. 619 *the Duke of Roxburgh*: John Ker, first Duke of Rox-

burghe (*c.* 1680–1741), statesman and member of the 'Squadrone Volante' group of politicians.

13. p. 624 *Cheviot-Chase*: The battle of Otterburn, fought on 14 August 1388, celebrated by the folk ballad to which Joseph Addison had recently given renewed currency. James Douglas, second Earl (*c.* 1358–88), emerged victorious but was himself killed; Henry Percy, known as Hotspur (1364–1403), taken prisoner.

14. p. 624 *Floden-field*: The battle of Flodden, fought on 9 September 1513; the victor, Thomas Howard, fourteenth Earl of Surrey and later eighth Duke of Norfolk (1473–1554).

15. p. 625 *Marquess of Louthian*: William Ker, third Marquis (*c.* 1690–1767).

16. p. 625 *the Duchess of Bucclugh*: Anne Scott (1651–1732), Countess of Buccleugh in her own right, married the Earl (later Duke) of Monmouth.

17. p. 625 *the great Earl of Morton*: James Douglas, fourth Earl of Morton (*c.* 1516–81), Regent of Scotland 1572–8, accused of high treason 1580, executed with 'the Maiden' in the Grassmarket, Edinburgh, on 2 June 1581.

Letter 13

1. p. 627 *full perfection of decay*: The phrase is not found in modern editions of Rochester's works. It perhaps comes from his extensive apocrypha: a very large number of poems were attributed to Rochester in Defoe's time, generally without any warrant. The nearest to this expression I have located in the genuine works is 'The last perfection of misery' (*The Discovery*).

2. p. 628 *James the VIth*: Son of Mary Stuart, King of England as James I from 1603 (1566–1625). His daughter by Anne of Denmark, the Princess Elizabeth (1596–1662) married in 1613 Frederick (1596–1632), Elector Palatine and titular King of Bohemia from 1618.

3. p. 628 *Marquess of Tweedale*: See note 4 to p. 567.

4. p. 630 *Sir William Bruce*: Architect (d. 1710); worked at Holyrood House 1671–9.

5. p. 631 *the late Duke of Rothess*: John Leslie, first Duke of Rothes (1630–81), Lord High Treasurer 1663–7.

6. p. 633 *Lord Dysert*: See note 54 to p. 99.

7. p. 638 *the Earl of Weemys*: James Wemyss, fifth Earl (1699–1756).

8. p. 640 *Cardinal Beaton*: David Beaton (1494–1546), murdered by John Leslie. Actually it was George Wishart who was condemned for heresy and burnt on 2 March 1546.

9. p. 641 *the Earl of Lenox*: Perhaps the second Duke and eighteenth Earl (1574–1624).

10. p. 642 *Archbishop Sharp*: James Sharp, Archbishop of St Andrews (1613–79), murdered by a group of men led by David Hackston on 3 May 1679.

11. p. 647 *the late battle*: Sheriffmuir, fought on 13 November 1715. The commander-in-chief of the royal forces was John Campbell, second Duke of Argyll (1678–1743), soldier and politician, for long a supporter of Walpole, and finally an opponent; a friend of Alexander Pope. At this battle John Lyon, third Earl of Strathmore (1696?–1715) was killed. His successor Charles, fourth Earl (1699–1728), entertained the Chevalier at Glamis, 4–6 January 1716. But his 'peaceable' enjoyment of the house was not to last long; he died as a result of a brawl in Forfar two years after Defoe wrote these words.

12. p. 648 *York-Buildings company*: Set up in 1675 to manage a waterworks near Villiers Street off the Strand. From the beginning the company was flirting with financial disaster. A fire in 1690 destroyed the works, but they were re-erected in the following year and an Act of Parliament obtained to license the company. At the time of the South-Sea Bubble the company opened a subscription of more than a million pounds in order to buy up forfeited estates. This served only to increase its difficulties. Defoe probably regarded the company as the epitome of the speculative enterprise which had occasioned the downfall of many prudent businessmen. See also p. 572.

13. p. 649 *the Laird of Claverhouse*: James Graham of Claverhouse, first Viscount Dundee (*c.* 1649–89); known as Bonnie Dundee; killed at Killiecrankie.

14. p. 650 *Oliver Cromwell ... rode through*: Cromwell defeated the Scots in 1650 and thereafter set about fixing his hold on the country.

15. p. 652 *in the reign of Queen Ann*: Actually on 12–14 March 1708. For Byng see note 6 to p. 248.

16. p. 654 *Bishop Elphingstone*: William Elphinstone (1431–1514), Bishop of Aberdeen from 1488. King's College received its charter from James IV in 1598. *Artificial*: Artistic, skilfully wrought.

17. p. 656 *Lord Pitsligo*: William Forbes, fourteenth Baron Forbes of Pitsligo (d. 1730), suffered heavy losses in the South-Sea Bubble.

18. p. 656 *King Duff*: King of Scotland (d. 967), killed fighting against the usurper Colin.

19. p. 672 *Lieutenant General Maitland*: Probably James Maitland, brigadier in 1696, lieutenant-general in 1709. In a passage omitted here, Defoe describes how Maitland lost a hand at the battle of Trèves in late 1704.

20. p. 673 *The Duke of Athol*: Defoe evidently means John Murray, the first Duke (1660–1724), rather than the second Duke (1690–1764). The former had died on 26 November 1724, almost two years before these words went into print. He had been attainted and fled to Brittany in 1716.

21. p. 674 *the present earl*: George Hay, eighth Earl of Kinnoul, succeeded 1719; married Abigail Harley, daughter of Robert (later Earl of Oxford) 1709; d. 1758.

22. p. 675 *the Earl of Argyle*: Archibald Campbell, ninth Earl of Argyll (1629–85), leader of Monmouth's Scottish forces, executed for high treason after failing to rouse the clans.

23. p. 676 *Gillekranky*: The battle of Killiecrankie, 27 July 1689. Dundee led the Highlanders to victory against the army of William III, under General Hugh Mackay, but was himself killed.

INDEX

Names are entered according to their modern spelling, since Defoe often uses more than one form for a given town. Main entries are shown in bold type.